COMPANION
TO
CHINESE
HISTORY

Hugh B. O'Neill

Facts On File Publications
New York, New York ● Oxford, England

COMPANION TO CHINESE HISTORY

Library of Congress Cataloging in Publication Data
O'Neill, Hugh (Hugh B.)
      Companion to Chinese History

      Includes bibliographical references and index.
      1. China—Handbooks, manuals, etc. I. Title.
DS705.063 1984 951 83-11685
ISBN 0-87196-841-X (hc)
ISBN 0-8160-1825-1 (pb)

Printed in United States of America
10 9 8 7 6 5 4 3 2 1

To my parents, and all my teachers, formal and otherwise

CONTENTS

INTRODUCTION

Literally thousands of books have been written in Western languages about some aspect of China in the last 200 years, and a few even before that. Much is known about China's history and civilization, but much of the information is not easily accessible. This book is an attempt to provide basic information on several hundred topics and a number of individuals. Bibliographic references have been provided at the end of as many entries as possible to help the reader pursue the topic if so inclined. The criteria used in selecting the books have included accuracy, availability and readability. Some references listed do not meet the last two criteria, but frequently there is little choice. Naturally, there are many other books that have not been mentioned. Many of those cited contain bibliographies of their own, and the reader is urged to consult them.

THE SCHOLARLY APPARATUS.

1.   The late Henri Cordier (1849-1925), in the years 1900-1920, produced a five-volume work entitled *Bibliotheca Sinica* that listed all known works on China in Western languages. It is out of print, and so are most of the works listed, but it provides a baseline. The late YUAN T'ung-li (1895-1965) compiled *China in Western Literature: A Continuation of Cordier's Bibliotheca Sinica*, New Haven: Yale University Press, 1958, which brings the bibliography through 1956. This reference work should be accessible in major public and university libraries, and should be consulted by those in search of references on some special topic. For later published works, the reader should consult the annual bibliography published by the *Journal of Asian Studies*.

2.   While scholarly biographies of important figures in Chinese history are more common now than they were a generation ago, the fact remains that few individuals have received such attention in a Western language. The reader should be aware that four important biographic dictionaries are now in existence. If the person in whom you are interested was born within the last 650 years (since 1335 A.D.) he or she may be listed in one of the following:

Goodrich, L.C. and Chaoying Fang, eds. *Dictionary of Ming Biography: 1368-1644*. New York: Columbia University Press, 1976.
Hummel, Arthur W., ed. *Eminent Chinese of the Ch'ing Period*. Washington: Government Printing Office, 1943.
Boorman, Howard L., ed. *Biographical Dictionary of Republican China*. New York: Columbia University Press, 1967-1971.

Klein, Donald W., and Anne B. Clark. *Biographic Dictionary of Chinese Communism, 1921-1965*. Cambridge: Harvard University Press, 1971.

There is some overlap between the last two, but both have been organized to dovetail with Hummel's work, which preceded them in publication. No serious library should be without any of these reference works.

3. Because of the nature of the Chinese written language, it has been necessary for Westerners to use some form of romanization (q.v.) in transcribing Chinese words. While the desirability of uniformity was recognized at least as early as the 16th century, it has never been achieved. For technical reasons, systems that approach accuracy in recording Chinese sounds tend to flounder in complexity. The two systems currently in widest use in English-language publications are the Wade-Giles and the *pinyin* (see under **Romanization**). The first was developed in the 19th century by the two Englishmen whose names are attached to it, and the second was developed in the People's Republic of China (q.v.) in the 1950s by Chinese linguists working with Soviet advisers. It has been used within continental China since that time for such things as railway-station signs, and has now been adopted by the U.S. government and many American publications. It is used in this book only rarely, and is usually given within parentheses. The reason is that the English-language scholarly apparatus is keyed to the Wade-Giles system, and if you are looking for a reference in a library, the chances of your finding it under the *pinyin* spelling are minimal. However, a conversion table is included, so that conversions may be made in either system.

4. Traditional Chinese names give the surname first and the given name last, the opposite of English-language usage. Some Westernized Chinese have reversed the order of their names to conform to non-Chinese usage. For this reason, all Chinese surnames in this book are printed in upper case, e.g., WANG Yang-ming. In this way the reader can be sure which is the surname. Most surnames consist of a single syllable, and most given names of two syllables. There are exceptions: SSU-MA Ch'ien. The use of the upper case should clarify which is which. Japanese names are given in the customary Japanese order, that is, surname first, given name second, e.g., TOYOTOMI Hideyoshi.

Most Chinese names are given in the Wade-Giles romanization of their pronunciation in standard Mandarin, even if the individual pronounced his own name in some other dialect, such as Cantonese. Exceptions have been made for those who used a non-standard romanization, and whose names are familiar to the English-speaking public, e.g., SUN Yat-sen, T.V. SOONG.

5. An attempt has been made to cover Chinese history from the earliest times to 1985. Much of what purports to be accounts of mythical emperors, etc., is now generally accepted as being forgeries created during the Han dynasty (206 B.C.-221 A.D., q.v.). The Burning of the Books (q.v.) in 213 B.C. provided an opportunity for such forgery, and the scholarly imperative of an ancient authority from which to quote provided the motivation. The result was a wide range of texts purporting to date from much earlier times.

COMPANION
TO
CHINESE
HISTORY

A

Abacus. A mechanical device used for arithmetical calculations. It consists of a series of parallel rods on which beads of wood or other material are strung. The rods are mounted in a rectangular frame, divided into two fields, separated by a bar through which the rods, but not the counters, pass. The upper field has two counters on each rod; the lower has five. The counters in the lower field have the value of one digit, those in the upper field, five. The number eight, for example, would be shown by bringing one of the counters in the upper field down to the bar (representing five) and three of the counters in the lower field up to the bar.

An abacus is not a computer, but rather a device on which the operator performs certain arithmetic functions mechanically, and which will retain the final result until moved. Chinese learning to use an abacus are usually taught rhymes which help them to remember the moves to be made in addition, subtraction, multiplication and division. A skillful operator can thus use it at great speed, while a beginner will do so more slowly.

The abacus was used in the Mediterranean world in the early centuries of the Christian era, and also in medieval Europe. It was introduced in China during the Yuan dynasty (1279-1368, q.v.), replacing an earlier system of calculation (see under **Mathematics**). It is still widely used in East Asia today. The Japanese version usually has only one counter in the upper field, instead of two.

Lau, Chung Him. *The Chinese Abacus*. Hong Kong: Lau Chung Him & Co., 1958.

Abahai. 1592-1643. Second ruler of the Later Chin dynasty (q.v.) which name he changed to Ch'ing (q.v.) in 1636. He was the eighth son of Nurhaci (q.v.). At the death of the latter in 1626, Abahai was one of four princes designated to rule jointly, though he alone was named as khan. By 1633 he had concentrated imperial power in his own hands, and in 1636 he declared himself emperor and changed the name of the dynasty. He also changed his reign title (q.v.) from T'ien T'sung to Ch'ung Te. Since he never ruled or reigned in Peking (q.v.), traditional Chinese histories usually count his son and successor, Shun Chih (r. 1644-1661, q.v.), as the first Ch'ing emperor.

Abahai's successful wars against the Chinese, Koreans and the tribes of Inner Mongolia greatly strengthened the foundations of empire laid down by Nurhaci, and were the basis of the successful conquest of China after his death. Many of the Chinese officers who surrendered were enlisted in the government of the new dynasty. Both Chinese and Mongols who were subjects of the Later Chin became members of one of the eight banners (see under **Banners**) as the Manchu (q.v.) already were. The tribes of Inner Mongolia maintained their allegiance to the Ch'ing until the end of the dynasty. The Koreans, forced to transfer their allegiance from Ming (q.v.) to Ch'ing emperors in 1639, acknowledged Ch'ing suzerainty until nearly the end of the dynasty.

In 1635 Abahai established the use of the word Manchu to refer to his people and banned the use of the words Juchen (q.v.) and Chienchou in this context. The purpose was to conceal the fact that his people had been under Chinese rule at various times, and had offered tribute to the Ming until the recent past.

Abahai died of illness in 1643, having successfully spread Manchu rule through Inner Mongolia and having sent armies to invade North China (q.v.) several times. He was succeeded by his ninth son, reign title Shun Chih, who was proclaimed emperor of China in Peking on October 30, 1644.

Hummel, Arthur W. (ed.) *Eminent Chinese of the Ch'ing Period*. Washington, Government Printing Office, 1943.

Academia Sinica. The Chinese name is *Chung-yang yen-chiu yüan*, which may be translated "central research institute." It was founded in 1928 as China's most advanced research organization, with TS'AI Yüan-p'ei (q.v.) as its first president. One of the early accomplishments of its Archaeology Section was the excavation of the Shang capital at Anyang (q.v.). This work was suspended in 1937 as a result of the war with Japan.

The war years caused serious disruptions, and the establishment of the People's Republic of China (q.v.) in 1949 saw some of the members of the Academia in Taiwan, while others remained in mainland China. As a result there are now two institutions calling themselves the Academia Sinica: one in Peking and the other in Taipei.

Acupuncture. This is one of the nine branches of practice in Chinese traditional medicine (q.v.). The procedure calls for the insertion of sharp needles into one or more of several hundred spots on the body (the number varies between 350 and 450) to cure or alleviate any of a long list of ailments. The practice apparently originated about the fifth century B.C.

The point at which the needle is injected may seem to the observer to have no connection with the malady to be treated. In the belief of the practitioner the body is laced with a network of channels or "meridians" which connect various organs with other points in the body. At certain places these are close enough to the surface to be reached by the needle, thus affecting the organ to be treated.

While not completely understood by medical scientists, the method seems to work for a number of illnesses where the relief of pain is important, such as sciatica and rheumatism. It is also claimed to be effective in treating diseases such as typhoid fever. The supposition in that case is that it may stimulate the production of antibodies in some way.

Manaka, Yoshio, M.D., and Ian A. Urquhart, Ph.D. *The Layman's Guide to Acupuncture*. New York: Weatherhill, 1972.

Mann, Felix. *Acupuncture: The Ancient Chinese Art of Healing and How It Works Scientifically*. New York: Vintage Books, 1973.

Aigun, Treaty of. Signed May 16, 1858, by I-shan (q.v.) for China, and Nikolai Muraviev for Russia. It superseded the Treaty of Nerchinsk

(1689, q.v.), and ceded to Russia the land on the left bank of the Amur river as far as its junction with the Ussuri, giving Russia the river mouth of the Amur. The area between the Ussuri and the sea was to be held under joint jurisdiction for later demarcation. Muraviev lost no time in founding Vladivostok (meaning "rule of the east") at the southern tip of this territory in 1860.

The treaty was not well received in Peking, where officials accused I-shan of handing over vast and valuable territory. However, the Treaty of Peking (q.v.), signed in 1860, forced the Ch'ing authorities to grant Russia sole control of the area between the Ussuri and the sea, now the Soviet Maritime Province, thus going even further than the Treaty of Aigun.

Clubb, O. Edmund. *China and Russia*. New York: Columbia University Press, 1971.

American Volunteer Group. Also known informally as the Flying Tigers and by its initials, AVG, it was formed August 1, 1941, under the leadership of Col. Claire Chennault of the Chinese air force. He had retired from the U.S. Army Air Corps in 1937 for reasons of disability, and had then gone to China, where he made a careful study of the strengths and weaknesses of the Japanese air force in action. He concluded that a skilled air force using appropriate strategy and tactics could either defeat the Japanese or seriously hinder their success in China.

A contract was signed in February 1941 to create the AVG, and pilots and crew were recruited from the U.S. Army Air Corps and the Navy, with the consent of both services. The first contingent of flyers arrived in Burma in July 28, 1941, and began training on P-40s. Problems included the fact that the P-40s were old and the manufacturer had ceased making spare parts. The airfield, near Toungoo, belonged to the British Royal Air Force, which made it available on condition that it not be used as a base to attack the Japanese.

The Japanese attack on Pearl Harbor and British possessions in the Far East in December 1941 brought both Britain and the United States into the war in the Pacific, and ended British neutrality. For a period of several months the Japanese seemed to be sweeping all before them, and the reports of AVG victories over the Japanese air force were the only pieces of good news for the Allies from Asia. The AVG made a significant contribution to delaying the Japanese capture of Rangoon until March 6, 1942.

Chennault agreed to the transfer of the AVG to American military auspices and to serve under Gen. Joseph W. Stilwell (q.v.) in March 1942, and on July 4 the AVG ceased to exist. It was succeeded by the China Air Task Force. The latter, in turn, was supplanted by the 14th Air Force, activated on March 11, 1943, commanded by Chennault, who was also promoted to major general.

Amoy (Xiamen). A major port in Fukien province (q.v.), and one of the five treaty ports (q.v.) opened to foreign commerce by the Treaty of Nanking (1842, q.v.). Population: 240,000 (1980). Amoy has a long tradition of ocean trade, and many of the Overseas Chinese (q.v.) in Southeast Asia originally came from the area. Amoy dialect (distinct from that of Foochow, q.v.) is the main dialect spoken by Overseas Chinese in Singapore and Jakarta. It is also the native language of the majority of the natives of Taiwan (q.v.), where it is called Taiwanese.

Amoy was occupied briefly by British troops in the Opium War (1839-1842, q.v.). The island of Quemoy (Jinmen) lies in Amoy harbor.

Amur river. Known in Chinese as Hei Lung Kiang (Heilongjiang), meaning Black Dragon River, it is the ninth longest river in the world. Some 4,700 km. (2,900 mi.), it drains an area of 1,620,000 sq. km. (625,000 sq. mi.) and has a runoff averaging 11,000 cubic meters per second. For about half its length it is the boundary between China and the Soviet Union, as it was the boundary between the Russian and Ch'ing (q.v.) empires, according to the terms of the Treaty of Aigun (1858, q.v.).

AN Lu-shan (703-757 A.D.). General and rebel of the T'ang dynasty (618-906, q.v.). Born in what is now Manchuria (q.v.) of a father whose military forebears may have originated in Iran and a Turkic mother, AN spent part of his childhood in Turkic territory. He returned to China to join the army, and by the age of 33 had achieved the rank of general. Less than a decade later, in 744, he held absolute power in North China (q.v.) with his base near present-day Peking.

Since the T'ang imperial family and many of the military leaders were of mixed ethnic stock, AN's exotic background would hardly have seemed strange to them.

AN's rebellion against the T'ang ruler in 755 followed a series of natural disasters: drought, floods, storms and fires. Since in traditional Chinese belief the emperor was considered a mediator between heaven and earth, such a series of catastrophes was regarded as proof of imperial misbehavior. Contemporary accounts, such as the poems of LI Po and TU Fu (qq.v.), indicate widespread suffering on the part of the general population while the court led a life of extravagant luxury.

AN captured Loyang (q.v.), the second T'ang capital, at the end of 755 and proclaimed a new dynasty in early 756. He took Changan (see **Sian**), the main T'ang capital, later that year. The emporor T'ang Ming Huang (r. 713-755) escaped with his favorite consort, YANG Kuei Fei (qq.v.), only a few days before the fall of the city. AN was assassinated in January 757 by his second son, AN Ch'ing-hsü.

While the rebellion was eventually suppressed, it marked a watershed in the history of the T'ang. The dynasty lasted until 906, but it was disturbed by invasions and internal military uprisings. The northeast, AN's base, was never again under close Chinese control until the establishment of the Ming dynasty (1368-1643, q.v.). After the fall of the T'ang in 906, the northeast was ruled by the Liao (907-1125, q.v.).

Levy, Howard S. trans. *Biography of An Lu-shan*. Berkeley: University of California Press, 1960.

Pulleyblank, E.G. *The Background of the Rebellion of An Lu-shan*. London: Oxford University Press, 1955.

Ancestor Worship. The term is a misnomer, since the Chinese did not worship their ancestors. In Confucianism (q.v.) filial piety is a virtue of the highest importance. It requires respect be paid to one's antecedents both alive and dead. In a traditional Chinese home, over the last millennium or so, wooden tablets bearing the names of one's deceased parents and grandparents held a special place. Expressions of reverence and respect toward these plaques were punctuated periodically by offerings of food, which were then consumed by the family.

To the Christian missionaries, such rites had all the earmarks of religious observances. Linguistic problems added further complications, since explanations were likely to be incomplete or misunderstood. The earliest Jesuits (q.v.) believed that the practices involved were indeed religious, and therefore impermissible to Christians. However, Father Matteo Ricci (q.v.), the first European missionary to achieve fluency in both written and spoken Chinese, decided after some years' study that Confucianism per se was not a religion. That is, while it had ethical content, it had no theological content. The rites were merely expressions of respect. A later Jesuit expressly distinguished the respect due to dead ancestors from the Catholic practice of veneration of the saints.

The Jesuit position on what became known as the "rites controversy" (q.v.) was not accepted by other Catholic missionaries, such as the Dominican and Franciscan orders, and the disagreement was carried to Rome. The issue arose again in the 19th century, with the resumption of missionary activity (see under **Christianity**).

Baker, Hugh D.R. *Chinese Family and Kinship*. New York: Columbia University Press, 1979.

Gernet, Jacques, and Janet Lloyd, trans. *China and the Christian Impact: A Conflict of Cultures*. Cambridge: Cambridge University Press, 1986.

Anhui. See **Anhwei**.

Anhwei Clique. The term refers to one of two opposing factions, the other being the Chihli Clique (q.v.), whose rivalry dominated Chinese politics 1916-1920. Both were composed of military officers of the Peiyang Group (q.v.), protégés and supporters of YUAN Shih-k'ai (1859-1916, q.v.). Their earlier support had enabled YUAN to become president and ruler of the Republic of China (q.v.) in 1912, and his death in June 1916 led to a struggle for dominance.

The leader of the Anhwei Clique, TUAN Ch'i-jui (1865-1936, q.v.), was minister of war and the most important official after YUAN himself. He opposed YUAN's plan to become emperor, and after YUAN's death became the de facto ruler, with the vice president, LI Yuan-hung (1864-1928, q.v.), succeeding YUAN as a figurehead president. TUAN forced LI from office in July 1917, and in August, under TUAN's influence, China entered World War I by declaring war on Germany.

Succeeding LI as the new president of the republic was FENG Kuo-chang (1859-1919, q.v.), leader of the opposition Chihli Clique, but since he commanded no troops in North China (q.v.), TUAN remained the dominant figure in government. His pro-Japanese policies drew much public opposition, but what eventually brought him down was the Chihli Clique, then headed by TS'AO K'un (1862-1938, q.v.), who made an alliance with CHANG Tso-lin (1873-1928, q.v.), warlord ruler of Manchuria (q.v.). War between the two factions broke out in July 1920, and resulted in the defeat of TUAN and the Anhwei Clique.

Anhwei (Anhui) **province**. Area 130,000 sq. km. (50,000 sq. mi.). Population: 48,030,000 (1980). Capital: Hofei (Hefei). Anhwei is bounded on the northeast by Kiangsu, on the southeast by Chekiang, on the south by Kiangsi, on the west by Hupei and

Honan, and on the north, for a short distance, by Shantung (qq.v.).

The Huai and Yangtze rivers flow through it. Rice is the main crop in the central area, with winter wheat and cotton in the north, and tea in the hilly southern region.

Anyang. Located in the northern part of Honan province (q.v.), Anyang is the site of the capital of the Shang dynasty (1766-1122 B.C., q.v.). Archaeological excavations undertaken by the Academia Sinica (q.v.) between 1928 and 1937 turned up a wealth of bronze and stone artifacts, until further work was stopped by the war with Japan.

The significance of the Anyang excavations was to provide archaeological confirmation to much of Shang history, which had been considered to be mythological.

Li, Chi. *Anyang*. Seattle: University of Washington Press, 1977.

Li, Chi. *The Beginnings of Chinese Civilization*. Seattle: University of Washington Press, 1957.

Chang, Kwang-chih. *The Archaeology of Ancient China*. New Haven: Yale University Press, 1968.

Arabs. Sometime close to the beginning of the Christian era, the Arabs solved the problem of sailing to India and back during the northeast monsoon (October-April), and not long after that they appeared as traders on the China coast. The history of the T'ang dynasty (618-906 A.D., q.v.) reports a resident community in Canton, and Arabs may have lived in other places in China as well. Arab and Persian traders were prominent in the China trade until the arrival of the Europeans in the 16th century.

The conversion of the Arab traders to Islam (q.v.), which dates from 622 A.D., had little impact in China. But the new religion inspired military conquests in the Middle East, Iran and Central Asia. By the eighth century Arab armies were in conflict with Chinese troops and defeated them in the battle of Talas (q.v.) in 751 A.D. In later centuries Chinese armies fought a number of battles in Central Asia with Muslim adversaries. While there may well have been Arabs in these armies, the majority of the troops were not.

Hourani. G.F. *Arab Seafaring in the Indian Ocean in Ancient and Medieval Times*. Princeton: Princeton University Press, 1951.

Architecture. Most Chinese buildings were made of wood. The traditional method of construction was post-and-lintel, that is, a timber frame constructed of vertical posts or pillars joined by horizontal members at top and bottom to provide stability. The roof rests on this structure, and the walls are filled in between the posts. The walls are not load-bearing.

Formal structures, such as palaces and temples, were usually constructed on a rectangular plan with the major axis in a north-south direction. The entrance was ordinarily at the south and the main building at the extreme north. East and west sides may have been occupied by other buildings or, occasionally, just by walls. Even private houses of the well-to-do tended to be built in this fashion. Surviving examples of traditional houses dating from the Ming (1368-1644) and Ch'ing (1644-1811) dynasties (qq.v.) usually follow this plan.

While actual buildings from early periods do not exist, we have both paintings and sculptures in relief to show us what they looked like. In addition, a number of tombs dating from the Han dynasty (206 B.C.-221

A.D., q.v.) have been found to contain pottery models of farm houses, some of which are several stories high.

The oldest wooden structure in China presently known is at Mt. Wu T'ai in Shansi province (q.v.). It is dated in accordance with 857 A.D. However, there are a number of surviving buildings in Japan which were built even earlier, under the inspiration of similar buildings of the T'ang dynasty (618-906, q.v.).

A book written in the Sung dynasty (960-1279, q.v.), the *Ying Tsao Fa Shih*, on the proper construction of buildings, has come down to the present day and was reprinted in the 1920s. It is a very technical guide to the proper design and construction of palace halls and the like.

Chinese architecture had immense influence on the cultures of Japan, Korea, Vietnam and Tibet, and echoes of it may be seen even farther afield.

Boyd, Andrew. *Chinese Architecture.* Chicago: University of Chicago Press, 1962.

Liang, Ssu-ch'eng, and Wilma Fairbank, eds. *A Pictorial History of Chinese Architecture.* Cambridge: MIT Press, 1984.

Sickman, Laurence, and Alexander Soper. *The Art and Architecture of China.* Baltimore: Penguin Books, 1956.

Steinhardt, Nancy S. *Chinese Traditional Architecture.* New York: China Institute in America, 1984.

Arrow War (1857-1860). Also known as the Second Opium War, it started with Chinese seizure of a small sailing vessel and ended with the presence of European troops in Peking, the flight of the emperor Hsien Feng to Jehol (qq.v.), and the burning of the Summer Palace (q.v.).

The end of the Opium War (1839-1842, q.v.), was marked by the signing of the Treaty of Nanking on August 29, 1842 (q.v.), which provided for diplomatic equality between high Chinese and British officials. In practice, however, the British found they could never make direct contact with the governor of Canton, the official in charge of dealing with Western countries. This position was held 1848-1858 by YEH Ming-ch'en (q.v.), who never received any foreign envoy.

In 1854 the British requested revision of the Treaty of Nanking, joined by the Americans seeking revision of the Treaty of Wanghia and the French of the Treaty of Whampoa (qq.v.). Collectively, the terms of these treaties provided for such revision, but YEH responded that his government saw no need for it. The foreign envoys went to Shanghai and Tientsin (qq.v.) to press their claims, but without success. They reported to their governments that force would be necessary. In 1856 the powers again sought revision, and YEH again refused.

On October 8, 1856, the lorcha *Arrow* was boarded at Canton by Chinese officials who arrested the Chinese crew on suspicion of piracy, and lowered the flag. Since the vessel was registered in Hong Kong (q.v.) and its captain was a British subject, the flag was also British, and the British protested. When that proved ineffectual, they bombarded Canton, aiming at YEH's residence.

In December, a British sailor was killed and the village involved was burned as a warning. In retaliation, the Chinese burned the "factories" outside Canton where the foreigners lived.

In July 1857 the earl of Elgin and Baron Gros, representing Great Britain and France, arrived as high commissioners authorized by their governments to present final demands to YEH. On December 12 they presented simultaneous notes demanding direct negotiations, occupation of some nearby territory and an indemnity. YEH refused. On December 24 they sent an ultimatum. The reply was unsatisfactory and bombardment of the city began December 28. It fell the next day and remained under Western occupation until the signing of the Conventions of Peking (q.v.) on October 24, 1860.

In March 1858 the British and French fleets sailed north and on May 20 arrived in Tientsin accompanied by the American and Russian envoys. Four Treaties of Tientsin (q.v.) were signed in June with the four powers. Salient features were the right of residence in Peking for foreign envoys and the opening of the Yangtze river to trade.

In June, 1859, the British and French envoys returned to exchange ratifications and take up residence in Peking. They found the fortifications strengthened and their way barred. They returned with stronger forces in August 1860, and outflanked the defender, Seng-ko-lin-ch'in (q.v.). The allies proceeded toward Tungchow, outside Peking, and defeated the Chinese forces on September 21. On the following day the emperor fled the Summer Palace for Jehol. Allied troops entered Peking October 13, and the Summer Palace was sacked October 18-19 in retaliation for Chinese executions of several allied prisoners.

The war was concluded on October 24 with the exchange of ratifications of the Treaties of Tientsin and the signing of the Conventions of Peking. In these negotiations China was represented by I-hsin (q.v.), half brother of the emperor. The Conventions of Peking conceded the right of foreign envoys to reside at Peking, as well as the cession of Kowloon to the British, and the opening of Tientsin as a treaty port (q.v.).

The *Arrow* War brought great changes in China's relations with foreign powers, though it was fought with relatively little loss of life, particularly when compared with the Taiping Rebellion (1850-1864, q.v.).

Hurd, Douglas. *The Arrow War*. New York: Macmillan, 1967.

Art of War, The. See under **Sun Tzu**.

Astronomy, Board of. See under **Jesuits, Christianity**.

B

Banners. A system of military organization established in 1601 by Nurhaci (q.v.), founder of the Later Chin dynasty, which became the Ch'ing dynasty (1644-1911) under his son and successor Abahai (qq.v.). Nurhaci divided his fighting men into four companies of 300 men each, and assigned a banner of a different color to each company. With continuing military success, Nurhaci attracted other fighting men, who were then attached to one or another banner. In 1615 each banner was divided in two, half remaining under the original color and the other half being assigned a banner with the original color and an added border. At this time each subject of what became the Later Chin—whether Manchu, Chinese or Mongol—was assigned to a banner, and since each banner included the fighting men and their families as well, and was hereditary, the entire population was harnessed as a military machine.

The system worked for well over half a century, and even in the declining years of the dynasty (in the 19th century) descendants of those who had belonged to the original banners retained their original identification with the banner of their ancestors.

Beijing. See **Peking**.

Big Wild Goose Pagoda. See under **Sian**.

Board of Rites. The Book of Rites, *Li Ching*, is one of the Five Classics (q.v.), and rites have always been important in traditional Chinese government. The Board of Rites' main concern was the proper performance of formal imperial activities, such as enthronements, annual sacrifices, audiences, funerals, etc. At least since the T'ang dynasty (618-906, A.D.), it was also charged with arranging protocol for missions bringing tribute (q.v.) from vassal states, and in this sense it was responsible for foreign affairs. This was the system under the Ming dynasty (1368-1644, q.v.).

During the Ch'ing dynasty (1644-1911, q.v.), the Board of Rites was one of six major government departments. In addition to its more important activities, it dealt with such tributary states as Annam (Vietnam), Burma, Korea and the Liu Ch'iu Islands (qq.v.). A separate office, the Li Fan Yuan (q.v.), was used for relations between the Manchu court and the Mongol princes, and later expanded its responsibilities to include Russia, Sinkiang and Tibet (qq.v.).

Western traders, whose ships started arriving on the China coast early in the 16th century, dealt with local authorities on trading matters. Embassies to the imperial court found themselves dealing with a Board of Rites whose members had little or no idea of the countries they represented, and who were more concerned with getting the envoys to perform the kotow (q.v.) than with substantive matters.

Western dissatisfaction with this arrangement was a contributary factor in the Opium War (1839-1842) and the *Arrow* War (1857-1860, qq.v.). In 1861, the Tsungli Yamen (q.v.), the forerunner of the Ministry of Foreign Affairs, was created and relieved the Board of Rites of its responsibilities in most foreign matters, though it still controlled protocol for tribute missions.

Bodhisattva. A concept restricted to Mahayana Buddhism (q.v.), a Bodhisattva is a being who has reached the point at which enlightenment, Nirvana or Buddhahood can be achieved. This is accomplished through successive incarnations, each typically in higher form than the preceding life. The Bodhisattva, however, out of love for all forms of suffering life, postpones his own enlightenment until all sentient beings will have attained the same advanced level.

In Hinayana Buddhism (q.v.), by contrast, the belief is that each person must achieve his own liberation from the wheel of existence, and that there is little that one person can do to help another to achieve the ultimate enlightenment. For this reason, bodhisattvas do not exist in this school.

Bodhisattvas, according to some Mahayana theogonies, may number in the thousands. Only a few are familiar to most Buddhists. These include Avalokitesvara, representing mercy, Manjusri, bodhisattva of wisdom, and Maitreya, whose incarnation as a Buddha some 5 billion years in the future was said to have been predicted by the historical Buddha. In China, Avalokitesvara was transformed into a woman and became the Goddess of Mercy.

Bogue, Treaty of the. Signed October 8, 1843, by Ch'i-ying (q.v.) for the Chinese and Sir Henry Pottinger for the British, it was a supplementary treaty to the Treaty of Nanking, August 29, 1842 (q.v.). The importance of this second treaty was that it granted consular jurisdiction and other extraterritorial rights to the British, and it contained the "most-favored nation" clause, which provided that if China granted privileges to any other nation, the British could claim treatment equal to that given the "most-favored nation." This clause was included in many later treaties leading to what many Chinese perceived as progressive erosion of China's sovereignty.

Books. The earliest Chinese books were inscribed on slips of wood or bamboo which were joined with thongs. These were bulky, and since the thongs broke or disintegrated over time, the earliest books had to be reconstructed. Some of the texts we have today may not be in the proper order.

With the development of the writing brush, silk and then paper were used in long scrolls. The invention of block printing (q.v.) in the eighth century led to a vast expansion in the number of books available.

The new books were printed on long sheets of paper pasted end to end. These were given an accordion fold and covers of wood were attached. The printing was done on one side only, and the book could be placed on a table and read by turning one fold at a time.

A new development produced the more familiar book bound in limp paper and sewn together. For this kind the text was written on broad sheets of thin paper which was ruled in vertical columns, with a distinctive center column designed for the title of the work, plus chapter and page numbers. Each sheet was then pasted face down on a smooth block of wood (pear wood was a favorite), and the background carved away. The characters then stood out in relief, and in reverse.

The printer would then brush ink over the block, put down a fresh sheet of paper and brush it carefully to make sure of a good impression, and peel it off. Printing was on one side only, and the sheet would be folded in half, through the center column, so that the title is partly visible from either side. The cut edges of the page were then sewed together with another hundred or so, forming the book.

Books of this type were very common in the early part of the 20th century and are still produced occasionally. Today they appear as art books, and collectors' items. However, most Chinese books still are published with paper covers.

Since printing was not introduced in Europe until about 1450, the Chinese had about a 400-year head start on publishing books. It is estimated that until about 1750, more books had been published in Chinese than in all the other languages of the world put together.

Borodin, Mikhail (1884-1952). Alias of a professional Communist revolutionary whose family name was Grusenberg. Born into a Jewish family in Belorussia, he grew up in Latvia and, after the revolution of 1905 in Russia, emigrated to the United States. He returned to Russia in 1917 and was sent the following year by Lenin as an emissary to the Comintern, the Third Communist International. In 1923 he was sent to Canton to work with SUN Yat-sen (1866-1925, q.v.), and was instrumental in the reorganization of the party structure of the Kuomintang (KMT, q.v.). This was the period of close cooperation between the KMT and the Chinese Communist party (CCP, q.v.), and between the KMT and the USSR. Russian advisers had great influence in Canton, and Borodin became a close confidant of SUN. SUN died in early 1925, and CHIANG Kai-shek (1887-1975, q.v.), launched the Northern Expedition (q.v.) the following year, in an effort to reunite China by military force. Borodin advised against a premature march north, as this might interfere with his mission, which was to assist in strengthening the KMT, place CCP members in strategic positions within the KMT and prepare China for Communist revolution.

KMT forces succeeded in taking the main cities of the Yangtze river valley, and early in 1927 there were two KMT seats of government: the left wing was based at Wuhan (q.v.), with Borodin as adviser, and the right wing at Nanking (q.v.), under CHIANG. CHIANG broke with the Communists in March, and executed many in Shanghai and Nanking. The Wuhan government broke with the CCP in July (see under **WANG Ching-wei**) and Borodin returned to the USSR. He was arrested in the Great Purge of the 1930s and died in a Siberian labor camp.

Jacobs, Dan N. *Borodin: Stalin's Man in China*. Cambridge: Harvard University Press, 1981.

Boxer Indemnity. The treaty which brought the Boxer Rebellion (1900, q.v.) to an end provided for an indemnity of £67,500,000 (about $335,000,000 at that time) to be paid by China to the allies. An American attempt to reduce this sum by one third was unsuccessful. Ninety-one percent of this was to be divided among eight powers, with the largest share, 29 percent, going to Russia, and lesser shares going to Germany, France, Great Britain, the United States and Italy, in that order. The sum was to be paid in annual installments, with interest computed at four percent, starting in 1902 and ending in 1940.

The indemnity was never paid in full. The Unites States remitted half its share in 1908, to be used for the establishment of Tsing Hua University in Peking, and for the support of Chinese students there and in the United States. Germany lost its claim as a result of World War I. All the other nations arranged to remit their indemnities in the 1920s, mostly for educational and cultural purposes.

Boxer Rebellion (1900). This grassroots, anti-foreign movement started in Shantung province (q.v.) in 1898, and spread through much of North China (q.v.). Its Chinese name, *I Ho Ch'uan*, may be translated "Fists of Righteous Harmony," and its motto "Preserve the dynasty; destroy the foreigners." Adherents practiced martial arts, performed rituals designed to make them invulnerable to weapons and swore to destroy Christian converts.

Its origins lie in the decline of the Ch'ing dynasty (1644-1911, q.v.), and the series of humiliations and defeats it received at the hands of foreign powers. The first of these was the Treaty of Nanking (1842, q.v.), by which Hong Kong was ceded to Great Britain. More recent was the Treaty of Shimonoseki (1895, q.v.), by which Taiwan was ceded to Japan. In 1898

China was forced to grant territorial leases to Germany (Shantung), Russia (Manchuria), France (Kwangtung) and Britain (Kwangtung and Shantung) (qq.v.). The powers were also active in carving out spheres of influence in which their own interests would be paramount.

As a result, 1899 saw rebellion and unrest, anti-Manchu or anti-foreign or both, in nearly all Chinese provinces. Conditions in North China were particularly bad, since two years of drought and famine had been followed by the bursting of dikes along the Huang Ho (Yellow river, q.v.), and the flooding of hundreds of miles of farmland. According to traditional belief, such disasters might be construed as reflections of evils in the national life and portents of a change in dynasty. In Shantung feeling against the Germans was strong and was reflected in antipathy to all foreigners, especially missionaries and their Christian converts.

Boxer activity in Shantung, encouraged by the Manchu governor in 1899, was suppressed by his Chinese successor, YUAN Shih-k'ai (q.v.) in 1900. Boxer adherents moved into Honan and Chihli (Hopeh) provinces (qq.v.) and rebel activity was widespread in North China, with arson and the murder of thousands of Christians widely reported. It soon became apparent that the Boxers had the support of many at court, including that of the empress dowager Tz'u Hsi (q.v.). Several imperial edicts of 1900 give evidence of this.

Those missionaries within reach of Peking sought asylum there with their congregations. Others fled north to Manchuria and Russian protection, or south to the treaty ports (q.v.) on the Yangtze river. Nevertheless, the diplomatic corps at Peking seemed oblivious to the danger until late May, when it became obvious that Boxer irregulars were being assisted and supported by imperial troops. On June 10 an international military force of slightly more than 2,000 men sent to protect the foreigners in the capital started from Tientsin by train. They were turned back by military opposition and a destroyed rail line.

On June 19 the Chinese government delivered an ultimatum to the diplomatic corps to leave Peking within 24 hours, and opened fire on the legations the following day. Telegraph lines were cut, and the isolation of Peking was nearly complete. The siege became front-page news throughout the world. It was broken August 14 by the arrival of a second military force which fought its way in from the coast. The following day the empress dowager fled from Peking, taking the emperor with her. They stayed in Sian (q.v.) for more than a year, and returned after the terms of peace had been settled.

The terms, signed September 7, 1901, caused considerable squabbling among the victorious allies, but were accepted by a defeated China. They included the Boxer Indemnity (q.v.), about $335,000,000; the transformation of the Tsungli Yamen (q.v.) into a full fledged foreign ministry; punishment for officials responsible for attacks on foreigners; and other conditions.

Fleming, Peter. *The Siege at Peking*. New York: Harper & Brothers, 1959.

Tan, Chester C. *The Boxer Catastrophe*. New York: Octagon, 1967 (reprint).

Bronze age. China's bronze age covers the period from the middle of the second to the middle of the first millenium B.C., or the Shang and most of the Chou dynasties (q.v.).

Buddhism. Buddhism originated in India about the sixth century B.C. and probably reached China by way of Central Asia sometime in the Later Han dynasty (25-220 A.D., q.v.). The two branches of Buddhism are Mahayana and Hinayana, meaning the "greater vehicle" and the "lesser vehicle," respectively (qq.v.). Followers of the second branch find the term Hinayana somewhat pejorative, and prefer to refer to their branch as Theravada. It is the Mahayana school of Buddhism which reached China, and through China traveled to Korea, Japan and Vietnam. In a somewhat different form—Lamaism—it is also the religion of Tibet and Mongolia. The Theravadin version is prevalent in Ceylon, Burma, Thailand, Cambodia and Laos.

Once a major religion in India, Buddhism has all but disappeared there, though a revival is under way. It was also dominant in what is now Afghanistan and parts of Central Asia, but has been replaced by Islam. Much of our knowledge of that area in the first millennium after Christ is derived from reports of travelers on Buddhist pilgrimages, such as Fa-hsien and Hsüan-tsang (qq.v.).

Unlike Confucianism (q.v.), the Buddhist message is other-worldly. Confucianism purposely avoids discussion of heaven and the spirits and concentrates on the relationships between men. (Women tend to get short shrift in both religions.) Buddhists believe that we live in a world of illusion and that the ultimate purpose of existence is to achieve rebirth on a higher plane and eventually to attain enlightenment, or nirvana. Since each soul is faced with this problem individually, it is necessary to cut family ties and devote one's life to the religious pursuit.

Not surprisingly, this view of life

was repugnant to Confucians, for whom the veneration and respect due to ancestors required marriage and children, particularly sons who would be able to perform the ritual ceremonies. Anyone who accepted the Buddhist call to abandon all ties and spend his life in a personal search for enlightenment was regarded by Confucians as abandoning the very aspects which made him a civilized man.

Yet, such a concept was not wholly unknown to the Confucian Chinese. Followers of Taoism (q.v.) had been abandoning the world in search of something unknowable, or at least indescribable, for several centuries. The parallels between Taoism and Buddhism caused confusion in China from the beginning, which frequently resulted in borrowing back and forth on several philosophical and religious levels.

The perception of the decline in prosperity and security in the Later Han dynasty, and the Period of Disunity (q.v.) which followed it, enhanced the appeal of an otherworldly religion, like Buddhism, particularly in comparison to Confucianism. Also, because of the universality of its message, Buddhism was more acceptable to the non-Chinese populations of the north than Confucianism with its emphasis on the actions of earlier Chinese rulers.

Some of the finest examples of Chinese Buddhist art are ascribed to the period of the Northern Wei, 386-532 A.D. (See under **Wei**.) By the time of the restoration of unity by the Sui (q.v.) in 589, Buddhism had become an essential part of Chinese culture and had transformed that culture in several ways. At the same time, the Chinese had also placed their imprint on the new religion, developing the Ch'an (Zen), Pure Land and Tien T'ai sects (qq.v.), all of which, though unknown in India and Central Asia, became the most popular sects in China, Japan and Korea.

Many of the rulers of the Period of Disunity, as well as those of the Sui dynasty, 589-618, and the T'ang 618-906, were ardent Buddhists. Buddhism reached its peak during the T'ang, with the imperial court subsidizing offices for the translation of scriptures and providing patronage for temples and monasteries. It also saw the expansion of the religious community, and an increase in the amount of land owned by religious institutions. Both resulted in a loss of revenue to the state. A backlash was probably inevitable.

The first well-known T'ang critic of Buddhism was the Confucian scholar HAN Yü, 768-824 (q.v.). HAN memorialized the throne, objecting to the reception of Buddhist relics in the capital. While his anti-Buddhist campaign was not successful in his lifetime, a massive suppression of Buddhism occurred in the middle of the century, reaching its peak in 845. It resulted in expropriation of clerical property and the return to lay life of hundreds of thousands of religious. It also involved the destruction of many ritual objects. First-hand reporting on some aspects of this persecution is to be found in the diary of the Japanese monk Ennin (q.v.), although the dynastic history of the T'ang tends to pass over the whole affair.

Although Buddhism would never again reach the level of influence it reached in the early T'ang dynasty, it had irrevocably altered the intellectual climate of Chinese civilization. HAN Yü had called for a restoration of Confucianism to a place of intellectual respect, and one response in later years was the Neo-Confucianism (q.v.) of CHU Hsi (1130-1200, q.v.), of the Sung dynasty (q.v.). But Neo-Confucianism was a synthesis of Buddhist and Confucian concepts and would have been surprising if not incomprehensible to Confucianists a millennium earlier.

At the same time, Buddhism was transformed into a religion or philosophy with a distinct Chinese imprint. The Ch'an school (q.v.), known in Japan as Zen, in which sudden enlightenment may take the place of years of arduous intellectual exercise, is a Chinese contribution, quite unknown in the Buddhist kingdoms of India or Central Asia.

While few present-day Chinese concern themselves with serious Buddhist philosophy, religious Buddhism survives in various forms. Buddhist temples can be found in Taiwan, Hong Kong and many countries of Southeast Asia. Sometimes the temple may present an eclectic combination of Buddhist, Taoist and local tutelary divinities. Devotees burn incense and seek guidance through divination. Buddhist practices also survive in traditional Chinese society. A Chinese with no religious affiliation may be given a Buddhist funeral or memorial service.

Such practices were banned after the establishment of the People's Republic of China (q.v.) on October 1, 1949. Buddhist monks and nuns were returned to lay life, and thousands of religious edifices were destroyed or turned to other uses. According to press reports in the mid-1980s, some temples have been maintained as museums and some religious observances are permitted.

Chen, Kenneth. *The Chinese Transformation of Buddhism*. Princeton: Princeton University Press, 1973.

Fung, Yu-lan, and Derk Bodde, trans. *History of Chinese Philosophy, Vol. II*. Princeton: Princeton University Press, 1953.

Chen, Kenneth. *Buddhism in China: A Historical Survey*. Princeton: Princeton University Press, 1964.

Wright, Arthur F. *Buddhism in Chinese History*. New York: Atheneum, 1965. (paper, reprint)

Burlingame, Anson (1820-1870). American legislator and diplomat, born in New Berlin, N.Y., and educated at the University of Michigan and Harvard Law School. A congressman from Massachusetts from 1855, he was appointed in 1860 by President Lincoln as minister to Vienna. The appointment was unacceptable to the Austrian court, and he was sent instead to China. The first American minister to reside in Peking, from 1861 to 1867, the Tsungli Yamen (q.v.) found him very sympathetic. When Burlingame resigned as minister, he was offered an appointment as ambassador from the emperor of China to all the courts of the world. Sir Robert Hart, inspector general of the Chinese Maritime Customs Service (qq.v.) supported the idea, on the principle that the Chinese should have channels of communication other than the ministers resident in Peking. Burlingame accepted and traveled first to the United States with two Chinese officials, a representative of the Customs and the Chinese Secretary of the British mission, as well as a staff of 30 Chinese. An excellent orator, Burlingame made eloquent speeches in San Francisco and New York. He was received by President Andrew Johnson, who noted that no American diplomat had ever been received by the emperor of China, and negotiated a treaty with Secretary of State William H. Seward (see under **United States**) in 1868. He died in St. Petersburg in 1870.

Burma. The first reference to Burma in Chinese records occurs in the account of the traveler CHANG Ch'ien (q.v.), who reported finding cloth and bamboo from Szechwan province (q.v.) in Bactria (Afghanistan) about 128 B.C. Told that they came via India, he deduced a trading route through southwest China and Burma.

Early contact was minimal, though a Pyu king sent an embassy from Burma to the T'ang court in 801 A.D. The Mongols destroyed the kingdom of Pagan in 1287, and invaded again in 1301. The rise of the Ming dynasty (1368-1644, q.v.), brought the Chinese and the Burmese into direct conflict. The Ming wanted a trade route to the West via the Irrawaddy river, to replace the Silk Road (q.v.), which had been closed by the Mongols in Central Asia. In 1451 the ruler of the Burmese kingdom of Ava accepted investiture from the Chinese, indicating Chinese suzerainty.

In 1659 the last Ming pretender fled to Burma seeking sanctuary from the forces of the Ch'ing dynasty (1644-1912, q.v.) but the Ch'ing troops invaded and forced the Burmese to surrender him. Ch'ing forces invaded Burma again in 1767 and 1769, but were defeated. The Burmese promised tribute, but failed to send it. In 1788 the Burmese acknowledged Chinese suzerainty and sent tribute, a practice which continued until the disruption of the Boxer Rebellion (q.v.) in 1900.

Burma lost its independence in the 19th century. The first British invasion took Rangoon in 1824, and the final step, the annexation of Upper Burma, was taken in 1886. Britain's conquest of Burma was based partially on the idea of opening China's southwest to international trade. One result was the Margary Affair, 1875 (q.v.), in which a member of the British Consular Service was murdered. The Burma-Tibet Convention signed on July 24, 1886, by Britain and China surrendered Chinese suzerainty and recognized Britain's claim to the area. On March 1, 1894, another convention was signed defining the border between Burma and China.

Burma remained a British possession until after World War II. It was the scene of fierce fighting in which American, British and Chinese troops opposed the Japanese. The Allied purpose was to protect India and the Burma Road (q.v.) lifeline to China. By taking Rangoon in March 1942, the Japanese were able to close the Burma Road, but failed in their attempt to invade India. In any event, the final outcome of the war was decided by actions in other areas.

Burma achieved independence from Britain on January 4, 1948, and recognized the People's Republic of China (q.v.) immediately after its establishment on October 1, 1949. A new problem arose with the arrival of Chinese Nationalist troops in northern Burma, fleeing their victorious Communist adversaries. To avert pursuit, the Burmese attacked the Nationalists and succeeded in reducing their effectiveness, though without eliminating them completely. In 1953, more than 2,000 Nationalist troops and their dependents were evacuated to Taiwan, though others stayed on in Burma.

Boundary problems between China and Burma were discussed in 1956 and settled in 1960, with the cession of three villages to China and two minor parcels of land to Burma. Relations between the two governments in 1985 are friendly and correct.

Aung, Maung Htin. *A History of Burma*. New York: Columbia University Press, 1967.

Hall, D.G.E. *A History of South-East Asia*. New York: St. Martin's Press, 1981. (Fourth edition).

Watson, Francis. *The Frontiers of China*. New York: Praeger, 1966.

Burma Road, The term refers to the 715 mi. (1,150 km.) highway from Kunming, capital of Yunnan province (q.v.), to Lashio, northern railhead of the Burma Railway. The road follows a trading route believed to have existed in the second century B.C. or even earlier. Such a route was suspected by the Han dynasty traveler CHANG Ch'ien (q.v.) in 128 B.C., when he identified Chinese products in Bactria (Afghanistan), which were said to arrive by a southern route, i.e., through Burma and India.

While locally important, trade on the Burma Road was never as large or significant as that on the Silk Road (q.v.). The Mongols used it in their invasions of Burma in 1287 and 1301. Officials of the Ming dynasty (1368-1644, q.v.), pressed the Burmese to permit use of the route to replace the Silk Road, which had been closed by the Mongols. While the Chinese succeeded in forcing the Burmese to accept Chinese suzerainty, the use of the trade route did not live up to expectations.

The British annexed Burma in stages in the 19th century, and one of their aims was to open southwest China to international trade via the Irrawaddy river and the Burma Road. While they succeeded in controlling Burma, and the Chinese were forced to open Yunnan province to trade, the trade itself was insignificant.

The Burma Road achieved international fame during World War II (q.v.). In the wake of the Japanese attack in the Marco Polo Bridge Incident, July 7, 1937 (q.v.), Yunnan provincial authorities took steps to pave and modernize the road, and to construct bridges over such major rivers as the Salween and the Mekong. By 1938 the road was a major lifeline to the besieged Chinese, as the Japanese captured the major Chinese seaports.

Acting under Japanese pressure, the British closed the railhead at Lashio for three months in the summer of 1940, leaving the French-built railway from Haiphong in Vietnam (q.v.) to Kunming as the only entry route for imports. The Japanese closed the railway in September, and the British reopened Lashio on October 10.

The Japanese invaded Burma in January 1942, and captured Rangoon, the southern terminus of the railway, on March 6, closing the Burma Road. The effort to reopen the road called for the construction of another road from the railhead at Ledo, Assam, to a point just south of the Chinese border. The necessity to clear Japanese troops from the area delayed construction, but the new road, known as the Stilwell Road, in honor of General Joseph W. Stilwell (q.v.), was opened in January, 1945. The Burma Road was of military importance during the war, but its economic importance today is slight.

Franck, Irene M., and David M. Brownstone. *To the Ends of the Earth*. New York: Facts On File, 1984.

Burma-Tibet Convention. See under **Burma**.

Burning of the Books (213 B.C.). Emperor Ch'in Shih Huang Ti (q.v.), a follower of the Legalist school of philosophy (see **Legalism**), regarded all other philosophical speculation a waste of time, and its practitioners parasites. Consequently he ordered all books burned with the exception of those in the imperial library. The *I Ching*, which was used in divination, was excepted.

The effect of the decree was to destroy much of the literature of the period, particularly that of the Confucians, the official ideologists of the succeeding Han dynasty (206 B.C.-221 A.D., q.v.), and of most later dynasties down to the beginning of the 20th century. The Ch'in emperor has remained a target of disparagement in the eyes of most Chinese throughout the centuries.

C

Cairo Conference (November, 1943). Also known by the code name Sextant, this was the only occasion when Generalissimo CHIANG Kai-shek (q.v.) met British Prime Minister Winston Churchill and U.S. President Franklin Delano Roosevelt in person. The purpose of the meeting was to formulate long-range objectives and to plan a counterattack against the Japanese in Burma. The participants agreed that Japan was to be stripped of all overseas possessions; that Manchuria and Taiwan were to be returned to China; and that Korea was to regain its independence.

Concluded with a joint statement reflecting unity between China and the Western Allies, the conference itself was characterized by differing views of strategy, and the apprehension on the part of the Western participants that Chinese commitments were not firm. From Cairo, Churchill and Roosevelt flew on to meet with Soviet Marshal Joseph Stalin at the Tehran Conference (q.v.). It was not possible to combine the two, since the USSR was not at war with Japan at the time.

Romanus, Charles F., and Riley Sunderland. *Stilwell's Command Problems*. Washington: Department of the Army, 1956.

Calendar. Traditional China observed both a solar and a lunar year. The two calendars run concurrently and coincide about every 20 years. The solar calendar divides the year into 24 periods, each having a name indicating the probable weather to be expected in the North China plain, or an astronomical event such as a solstice or equinox. Only one popular holiday is fixed according to the solar calendar, Ch'ing Ming (q.v.), which occurs on April 5 (April 4 in leap years). The chart showing the traditional dates and names of these periods is shown below.

SOLAR CALENDAR CHART

February	5	Li ch'un	Spring begins
February	19	Yü shui	The rains
March	5	Ching chih	Insects awaken
March	20	Ch'un fen	Vernal equinox
April	5	Ch'ing ming	Clear and bright
April	20	Ku yü	Grain rains
May	5	Li hsia	Summer begins
May	21	Hsiao man	Grain fills

June	6	Mang chung	Grain in ear
June	21	Hsia chih	Summer solstice
July	7	Hsiao shu	Moderate heat
July	23	Ta shu	Great heat
August	7	Li ch'iu	Autumn begins
August	23	Ch'u shu	Limit of heat
September	8	Pai lu	White dew
September	23	Ch'iu fen	Autumnal equinox
October	8	Han lu	Cold dew
October	23	Shuang chiang	Hoar frost
November	7	Li tung	Winter begins
November	22	Hsiao hsueh	Light snow
December	7	Ta hsueh	Heavy snow
December	21	Tung chih	Winter solstice
January	6	Hsiao han	Moderate cold
January	21	Ta han	Severe cold

The lunar calendar is more widely known, if less well understood. The lunar year ordinarily consists of 12 lunar months, which add up to 354 or 355 days. Consequently, about every three years, or, more accurately, 22 times in every 60 year cycle, an extra month is added, making a 13-month year. The Chinese months use numbers, not names, and the intercalary month becomes the second fourth month, or wherever it may occur.

It cannot be inserted after the first, eleventh or twelfth month, and its location is determined by the rule that the vernal equinox must occur in the second month, the summer solstice in the fifth, the autumnal equinox in the eighth, and the winter solstice in the eleventh. There is a further provision that the intercalary month shall be one in which the sun enters no sign of the zodiac.

The Lunar New Year occurs on the second new moon after the winter solstice, that is, between January 21 and February 20. The months may have either 29 or 30 days and are computed by astronomical means. Because of the Chinese belief in a correspondence between the course of nature and the affairs of men (see under **Mandate of Heaven**), determination of the calendar was of great political importance. Each new dynasty published a revised calendar, in many cases changing the date of the observance of the new year. The private publishing of an unofficial calendar could be viewed as lèse majesté. The accurate prediction of such phenomena as eclipses acquired political overtones of great moment.

The lunar calendar is the one by which events were recorded, whether private events, such as the birth of a child, or public events, such as the death of a monarch. The years were organized in a cycle of 60 years, each of which is characterized by two Chinese characters. The first character is one of a series of 10, traditionally described as the Ten Celestial Stems, and the second is one of a series of 12, described as the Twelve Hourly Branches. (They are also used to identify the 12 two-hour periods of the Chinese day.) Each series is repeated, the Stems six times, and the Branches five times to make a 60-year cycle.

This cycle has been in use for at least 2,000 years and has been extrapolated back to 2697 B.C. It is extremely unlikely that it was in use at that time. The Han dynasty historian SSU-MA Ch'ien, 145-90 B.C., author of the *Shih Chi* (qq.v.), made a serious effort to collate the various histories which had survived to his own time, and found some problems insoluble: the histories had not been dated uniformly.

Dating of Chinese historical records since the beginning of our era is a different matter. The cyclical year is used, along with the emperor's reign title (q.v.). Using the emperor's personal name was taboo as long as the dynasty lasted, and after his death he was known by his temple name (q.v.), but while he lived, events were dated by the title he adopted for his reign. Unfortunately, from one point of view, an emperor might adopt a whole series of such reign titles, as a result of good or bad occurrences, such as military victories or catastrophic famines. The first reign titles were introduced by the emperor known by his temple name of Han Wen Ti (r. 179-157 B.C.). His grandson, Han Wu Ti, (r. 140-87, B.C., q.v.), used 11 titles in his long reign. In the Ming dynasty (1368-1644 A.D., q.v.), each emperor, with one exception, used only one reign title. The Ch'ing dynasty emperors (1644-1911, q.v.) followed the same practice.

Each of the Ten Celestial Stems is identified with one of the five elements which the Chinese believed made up the universe: wood, fire, earth, metal and water. The Twelve Branches are identified with animals.

The table given below shows the correspondence between the lunar year of three 60-year cycles and its counterpart. To find any other year simply add or subtract in multiples of 60. Bear in mind that in historic times the Chinese year has started in the period January 21-February 20. A date which occurs in the early part of the Christian year may be assignable to the preceding Chinese year. The same cycle of 60 is also applied to days, and many historical texts refer to the cyclical day when dating an event. This permits great accuracy in dating by reference, since such events as eclipses can be calculated by modern methods.

YEAR	CYCLICAL NAME	ELEMENT	ANIMAL
1864 1924 1984	Chia tzu	Wood	Rat
1865 1925 1985	Yi ch'ou	Wood	Ox
1866 1926 1986	Ping yin	Fire	Tiger
1867 1927 1987	Ting mao	Fire	Hare

YEAR	CYCLICAL NAME	ELEMENT	ANIMAL
1868 1928 1988	Wu ch'en	Earth	Dragon
1869 1929 1989	Chi szu	Earth	Snake
1870 1930 1990	Keng wu	Metal	Horse
1871 1931 1991	Hsin wei	Metal	Sheep
1872 1932 1992	Jen shen	Water	Monkey
1873 1933 1993	Kuei yu	Water	Chicken
1874 1934 1994	Chia hsü	Wood	Dog
1875 1935 1995	Yi hai	Wood	Pig
1876 1936 1996	Ping tzu	Fire	Rat
1877 1937 1997	Ting ch'ou	Fire	Ox
1878 1938 1998	Wu yin	Earth	Tiger
1879 1939 1999	Chi mao	Earth	Hare

YEAR	CYCLICAL NAME	ELEMENT	ANIMAL
1880 1940 2000	Keng ch'en	Metal	Dragon
1881 1941 2001	Hsin szu	Metal	Snake
1882 1942 2002	Jen wu	Water	Horse
1883 1943 2003	Kuei wei	Water	Sheep
1884 1944 2004	Chia shen	Wood	Monkey
1885 1945 2005	Yi yu	Wood	Chicken
1886 1946 2006	Ping hsü	Fire	Dog
1887 1947 2007	Ting hai	Fire	Pig
1888 1948 2008	Wu tzu	Earth	Rat
1889 1949 2009	Chi ch'ou	Earth	Ox
1890 1950 2010	Keng yin	Metal	Tiger
1891 1951 2011	Hsin mao	Metal	Hare

YEAR	CYCLICAL NAME	ELEMENT	ANIMAL
1892 1952 2012	Jen ch'en	Water	Dragon
1893 1953 2013	Kuei szu	Water	Snake
1894 1954 2014	Chia wu	Wood	Horse
1895 1955 2015	Yi wei	Wood	Sheep
1896 1956 2016	Ping shen	Fire	Monkey
1897 1957 2017	Ting yu	Fire	Chicken
1898 1958 2018	Wu hsü	Earth	Dog
1899 1959 2019	Chi hai	Earth	Pig
1900 1960 2020	Keng tzu	Metal	Rat
1901 1961 2021	Hsin ch'ou	Metal	Ox
1902 1962 2022	Jen yin	Water	Tiger
1903 1963 2023	Kuei mao	Water	Hare

YEAR	CYCLICAL NAME	ELEMENT	ANIMAL
1904 1964 2024	Chia ch'en	Wood	Dragon
1905 1965 2025	Yi szu	Wood	Snake
1906 1966 2026	Ping wu	Fire	Horse
1907 1967 2027	Ting wei	Fire	Sheep
1908 1968 2028	Wu shen	Earth	Monkey
1909 1969 2029	Chi yu	Earth	Chicken
1910 1970 2030	Keng hsü	Metal	Dog
1911 1971 2031	Hsin hai	Metal	Pig
1912 1972 2032	Jen tzu	Water	Rat
1913 1973 2033	Kuei ch'ou	Water	Ox
1914 1974 2034	Chia yin	Wood	Tiger
1915 1975 2035	Yi mao	Wood	Hare

YEAR	CYCLICAL NAME	ELEMENT	ANIMAL
1916 1976 2036	Ping ch'en	Fire	Dragon
1917 1977 2037	Ting szu	Fire	Snake
1918 1978 2038	Wu wu	Earth	Horse
1919 1979 2039	Chi wei	Earth	Sheep
1920 1980 2040	Keng shen	Metal	Monkey
1921 1981 2041	Hsin yu	Metal	Chicken
1922 1982 2042	Jen hsü	Water	Dog
1923 1983 2043	Kuei hai	Water	Pig

Calendrical Bureau. See under **Jesuits**.

Canton (Guangzhou). Canton is the name by which the capital city of Kwangtung province (q.v.) has been known to the West for several centuries. The city and surrounding counties have a population of 5.3 million (1980). The city and its province were incorporated into the Chinese empire under the T'ang dynasty (618-906 A.D., q.v.) and for this reason the Cantonese call themselves "men of T'ang" rather than "men of Han" which is the term used by Chinese of more northern areas.

Canton has been a trading port for well over 1,500 years, and its populace has been exposed to a wide variety of foreign influences. Trade was conducted with India, Southeast Asia, Persia and the Arab world. There was a resident Muslim community during the T'ang dynasty (618-906 A.D.). Early in the 16th century the Portuguese arrived, followed by the Spanish, Dutch and English.

Because of trouble with European

traders, the Ming dynasty (q.v.) in 1550 restricted all Europeans to trade only at Canton, though none were permitted to reside in the city. The Portuguese established themselves at Macao (q.v.), nearby. The Treaty of Nanking (1842, q.v.) ceded the island of Hong Kong to the British, and also granted the right of residence in Canton to British traders. That clause was resented by the Cantonese and was never implemented. Canton was captured by British troops in the *Arrow* War (q.v.).

The Cantonese formed a sizable proportion of emigrants, who are called Overseas Chinese (q.v.), in Southeast Asia and other areas. Most of the early Chinese immigrants to the United States were Cantonese. The largest Cantonese centers outside of China in the first three-quarters of the 20th century were Hong Kong, Saigon and San Francisco, and the Cantonese dialect was widely used in all three places, as well as, to a lesser extent, in other centers.

The Cantonese have a reputation for innovation and distrust of authority. HUNG Hsiu-ch'üan, leader of the Taiping Rebellion (qq.v.) was a Cantonese of the Hakka (q.v.) community. SUN Yat-sen, considered the father of the revolution of 1911, was a Cantonese. Canton was a base for the Republican government in its early struggles with the warlords in Peking and North China. (See **Republic of China**.)

Canton is also the home of one of China's regional cuisines, the first, in many cases, to be sampled by non-Chinese, at the many Cantonese restaurants to be found throughout the world.

Cathay. From 907 to 1125 A.D., North China was ruled by the non-Chinese Liao dynasty (q.v.), an ethnic group known to the Chinese as Ch'itan or Khitan, and to their Central Asian neighbors as Khitai, from which the word Cathay is derived. The Liao were succeeded by the Chin dynasty (1115-1234, q.v.), but the empire over which they ruled continued to be called Khitai or some cognate equivalent by their neighbors. Peking (q.v.) was the capital for most of this period. At the same time, Central and South China were ruled by the Five Dynasties (906-960) and the Sung dynasty (960-1278, qq.v.), whose capitals were at Kaifeng and Hangchow (Hangzhou, qq.v.). The Mongols conquered Peking in 1215, and in 1234 extinguished the Chin. After the conquest of the Sung, they established the Yuan dynasty (1279-1368, q.v.), and reunited China for the first time since the fall of the T'ang dynasty (618-906, q.v.). Marco Polo (1254-1324, q.v.), who spent several years in China, makes a distinction between the two areas.

Since the Arabs (q.v.) who traded at Canton had never used the term Cathay, European geographers were confused by the existence of two entities, China and Cathay. Confirmation that the two were one came in 1607, when the Jesuit Bento Goes reached Cathay by the overland route and sent word to Father Matteo Ricci (1552-1610, q.v.), who had reached Peking by way of Canton and Macao (qq.v.).

Cathay is still the name used in the USSR, and in Western and Central Asia. Its use in English is considered literary.

CC Clique. The term refers to the brothers CH'EN Kuo-fu (1892-1951) and CH'EN Li-fu (1900-) and their group of supporters who dominated the Kuomintang (q.v.) from 1928 until 1950. The brothers were committed anti-Communists and by skillful control of the party organization managed to make CHIANG Kai-shek (q.v.) the dominant man. Although they were anti-Communist, the party structure which they perfected and set in place was clearly fashioned after a Leninist model.

Boorman, Howard L., ed. *Biographical Dictionary of Republican China.* New York: Columbia University Press, 1968.

————.*United States Relations With China.* Washington: Department of State, 1949.

Chahar. Name of a province during the Republican period (1911-1949); it is now a part of Inner Mongolia.

Ch'an Buddhism. This form is a unique Chinese contribution to Buddhism (q.v.). Ch'an (known in Japanese as Zen) is short for *ch'an-na*, the Chinese form of the Sanskrit *dhyana*, meaning meditation. According to tradition, this is a set of esoteric teachings passed on by the historical Buddha to one of his disciples without being transcribed. They were transmitted without texts since their proper apprehension requires an intuitive grasp, rather than a chain of logical steps, such as is traditional in other Mahayana (see under **Buddhism**) schools.

In this way, a Ch'an follower who achieves instantaneous enlightenment suddenly finds that all his problems have disappeared, not that they have necessarily been solved in a worldly way, but that they are no longer of any concern to him.

The more traditional view is that enlightenment is achieved by the acquisition of merit over a long series of reincarnations, capped at the end by rebirth as a being who will become a religious and devote his life to a study of Buddhist texts and good deeds. The concept of instantaneous illumination is difficult to harmonize with that set of beliefs.

Ch'an Buddhism has a connection with Taoism (q.v.), which also stresses meditation and sudden enlightenment. It attracted many followers through the T'ang (618-906) and Sung (960-1279) dynasties (qq.v.) and the period of unrest in between. Despite, or perhaps because of, its Chinese origin, it attracted great interest and support in its Japanese form. The interested reader should consult sources on the Japanese version.

Ch'en, Kenneth K.S. *The Chinese Transformation of Buddhism*. Princeton: Princeton University Press, 1973.

Fung, Yu-lan, and Derk Bodde, trans. *History of Chinese Philosophy, Vol. II.* Princeton: Princeton University Press, 1953.

Barrett, William, ed. *Zen Buddhism: Selected Writings of D.T. Suzuki.* Garden City, N.Y.: Doubleday & Co., Inc., 1956 (paper).

CHANG Ch'ien. Official and traveler of the Han dynasty (206 B.C.-221 A.D., q.v.). He was a minister in the government of Emperor Han Wu Ti (r. 140-87 B.C., q.v.). Chinese border areas in Central Asia were coming under attack by the Hsiung-nu (q.v.), a nomadic people identified with the Huns who later invaded Europe. Using a classic Chinese strategy, the emperor sent CHANG to another and more distant people, the Yueh-chih (q.v.) or Tocharians, who had also suffered at the hands of the Hsiung-nu. CHANG's mission was to persuade the Yueh-chih to attack the Hsiung-nu while the Chinese pressed them on the other side.

CHANG set out in 138 B.C., but spent 10 years as a captive of the Hsiung-nu. He escaped and traveled on to find the Yueh-chih settled in

Bactria (Afghanistan). They refused to accede to the Chinese request, and CHANG returned to China in 126 B.C.

While he did not achieve his primary goal, he did not return empty-handed. He had reached Alexandria (present-day Kandahar), then ruled by descendants of the Greeks led by Alexander the Great, and was thus in touch with the eastern-most reaches of the Mediterranean world. He brought back plant specimens, including alfalfa and grapevines, as well as word that Chinese products from Szechwan (q.v.), such as silk cloth and bamboo, were reaching Bactria via a southern route, i.e., Burma and India (qq.v.).

The emperor followed up on CHANG's Central Asian discoveries and succeeded in reducing several of the peoples of the area to submission. CHANG himself was sent on another diplomatic mission, but did not go as far as on his first trip.

Franck, Irene M., and David M. Brownstone. *The Silk Road*. New York: Facts On File, 1986.

CHANG Ch'un-ch'iao. See under **Gang of Four**.

CHANG Fei (d. 220 A.D.). An official of one of the Three Kingdoms (q.v.), the kingdom of Shu (q.v.), who together with KUAN Yü and LIU Pei, founder of the kingdom (qq.v.), is depicted in the *Romance of the Three Kingdoms* (q.v.) as one of the sworn brothers of the "Peach Garden Oath," and is so known to millions of Chinese and other Asians.

CHANG Hsueh-liang (1898-). Warlord known as the "Young Marshal." The son of CHANG Tso-lin (1873-1928, q.v.), he inherited control of Manchuria (q.v.) at the latter's death in 1928. He prepared for a military career and joined his father's army in 1917. In 1919 he was made a colonel and participated in some of the fighting and maneuvering characteristic of the warlord period of the 1920s (see under **Warlords**). In late 1925, CHANG was involved in an attempt by FENG Yü-hsiang (1882-1948, q.v.), to overthrow CHANG Tso-lin. This so angered his father that he contemplated having his son executed. In 1926 father and son cooperated in opposing the Northern Expedition (q.v.), as they did in 1928.

CHANG Tso-lin was assassinated by the Japanese on June 4, 1928, and CHANG Hsueh-liang inherited control of Manchuria. The elder CHANG's death was kept secret for several weeks, but the younger CHANG took less than a year to assert his power. Faced with the same problem his father had, namely, safeguarding his relative independence from the USSR and Japan, in December he joined the Republic of China and raised the Nationalist flag in Mukden, his capital.

In 1929 CHANG cooperated with the Nanking government in an unsuccessful attempt to reduce Soviet influence in Manchuria. His police raided the Soviet Consulate General in Harbin (q.v.), and seized the Chinese Eastern Railway (q.v.), ousting the Soviet railway officials. Soviet protests were followed by military action, resulting in a restoration of the status quo.

On September 18, 1931, Japan's Kwantung Army occupied Mukden as the first step in a takeover of all Manchuria. On Nanking's advice, CHANG did not offer direct opposition, and as a result his troops were defeated and demoralized. Some surrendered, some withdrew into

Soviet territory, and the rest retreated into North China. Weakened by the Japanese victory and the establishment of the puppet state of Manchukuo (q.v.) in March, 1932, CHANG then proved unable to impede Japanese movements toward Inner Mongolia. In 1935 his troops were withdrawn from North China and sent to oppose the Communists in Northwest China. As the troops had little stomach for fighting other Chinese while Japanese occupied their Manchurian homeland, a de facto truce was arranged.

CHANG was a key figure in the Sian Incident (q.v.) of December 1936, in which CHIANG Kai-shek (1887-1975, q.v.) was kidnapped and forced to agree to a united front with the Chinese Communists against the Japanese. CHANG accompanied CHIANG back to Nanking (q.v.), where he was tried by a military court and subsequently held under house arrest. He spent the war years mostly in Kweichow (q.v.), and was taken to Taiwan (q.v.) probably in 1948. In January, 1949, LI Tsung-jen (1890-1969, q.v.), became acting president of the Republic of China (q.v.), and ordered CHANG's release, but the order was ignored. As of 1986 CHANG remained under surveillance in Taiwan.

Boorman, Howard L., ed. *Biographical Dictionary of Republican China*. New York: Columbia University Press, 1967-1973.

CHANG Kuo-t'ao (Zhang Guotao, 1897-1979). One of the founders of Chinese communism and an important leader until 1938, when he defected to the Nationalists. Born in Kiangsi province (q.v.) of a prosperous family, he attended middle school in Nanchang, the provincial capital, was active in the movement to overthrow the Ch'ing dynasty (q.v.) before 1911 and led activities against YUAN Shih-k'ai (q.v.) in 1915.

CHANG entered Peking University in the fall of 1916 and achieved prominence as a radical student leader, particularly during the May 4th Incident (q.v.) in 1919, for which he was jailed. He met SUN Yat-sen (q.v.) in Shanghai in 1919 and participated in the founding of the Chinese Communist party (CCP, q.v.) in July, 1921. He was appointed head of the China Trade Union Secretariat and later that year made his first trip to the Soviet Union.

In July, 1922, at the CCP's Second National Congress in Shanghai, he opposed the Soviet decision to work with SUN Yat-sen and the Kuomintang (KMT, q.v.), but accepted Moscow's ruling. In February, 1923, he organized a railroad strike which was suppressed with the loss of 80 lives, both workers and Communist organizers. In January, 1924, he was elected in absentia an alternate member of the KMT Central Executive Committee, resulting in his arrest and imprisonment in Peking, then under warlord control. He was released in October and in 1925 was in Shanghai (q.v.) organizing trade unions. In 1926 the KMT left wing moved to Wuhan (q.v.) in the wake of the Northern Expedition (q.v.) and CHANG joined them there.

In April, 1927, the KMT right wing, based in Nanking (q.v.), purged Shanghai and other cities under its control of Communists, and the left wing, based in Wuhan, was obviously about to do so. In spite of this, the Comintern insisted on the preservation of the CCP-KMT alliance. On orders from the CCP, CHANG made a trip to Nanchang to avert a planned coup, but discovered on his arrival that it was too late. In consequence, he found himself the ranking party member at the Nanchang Uprising (q.v.) of August 1, 1927. When the rebels were forced out after a few days, CHANG accompanied them, planning to take Canton. They were soundly defeated, and while CHU Teh (q.v.) led the troops back north to an eventual rendezvous with MAO Tse-tung, CHANG, CHOU En-lai and others escaped to Hong Kong.

CHANG spent the next three years in the Soviet Union and returned to Shanghai in 1931. It was becoming difficult for the Communists to remain there, and while others fled to join MAO Tse-tung at Juichin, Kiangsi (q.v.), CHANG was sent to another soviet on the borders of Hupeh, Honan and Anhwei (qq.v.) to establish a border region administration and to serve as a political commissar to the Fourth Front Army. In 1932 CHIANG Kai-shek (q.v.) launched a campaign against this group and they were forced to retreat into northern Szechwan (q.v.). In 1933 they established the Szechwan-Shensi border area with CHANG as chairman. By early 1935 they had been forced to retreat again to the border between Szechwan and Sikang (q.v.).

In June, 1935, the remnant forces of the Long March (q.v.) arrived in the area, and a conflict between CHANG and MAO Tse-tung became apparent. The two had not met since 1927 in Wuhan and their policies and strategies were at variance. Both were elected to membership on the Executive Committee of the Comintern, but that could not conceal their competition for the control of the CCP.

CHANG proposed moving west into Sikang, while MAO wanted to move north into Shensi. CHU Teh, who had accompanied MAO from Kiangsi, went with CHANG to Sikang, while MAO and the First Front Army went north. By June,

1936, CHANG's forces had been joined by the Third Front Army from Hunan-Hupeh but both were forced to retreat by KMT forces. They reached Shensi (q.v.) in October, and CHANG pushed on to Sinkiang province (q.v.) in the hopes of establishing a Chinese soviet government contiguous to the Soviet Union. They were rebuffed with losses by Sinkiang troops and were forced back to Shensi.

CHANG's military failure undermined his position. In 1938 he left Yenan and defected to the Nationalist government. He spent the war years in Chungking, and moved to Hong Kong before the establishment of the People's Republic of China (q.v.) on October 1, 1949.

Chang, Kuo-tao. *The Rise of the Chinese Communist Party*. Lawrence: Kansas University Press, 1972.

Klein, Donald W., and Anne B. Clark. *Biographic Dictionary of Chinese Communism, 1921-1965*. Cambridge: Harvard University Press, 1971.

Boorman, Howard L., ed. *Biographical Dictionary of Republican China*. New York: Columbia University Press, 1968.

Schwartz, Benjamin I. *Chinese Communism and the Rise of Mao*. Cambridge: Harvard University Press, 1951.

CHANG Tso-lin (1873-1928). Warlord of Manchuria (q.v.), which he ruled as a nearly autonomous area from 1919 to 1928. He was also known as the "Old Marshal" to distinguish him from his son and successor CHANG Hsueh-liang (1898- , q.v.). CHANG Tso-lin was born in Fengtien (now Liaoning province, q.v.) in Manchuria. After fighting in the Sino-Japanese War (1894-1895, q.v.), he returned to Fengtien and built up a military force of his own. In the Russo-Japanese War (1904-1905, q.v.), CHANG's troops acted as irregulars on the Japanese side. He emerged from the war with enhanced power and prestige, and his irregular forces were incorporated in the Ch'ing imperial armies. After the outbreak of revolution at Wuchang on October 10, 1911, CHANG put down a military rebellion and maintained order in Manchuria.

With the establishment of the Republic of China in 1912 (q.v.), and the accession of YUAN Shih-k'ai (1859-1916, q.v.) as president, Manchuria was under the nominal control of the Peking government, but CHANG continued to increase his power, and by 1919 he was for all practical purposes sole ruler of an autonomous Manchuria.

In the early 1920s, CHANG's posture embarrassed the Peking government (q.v.). The Sino-Soviet Treaty of May 31, 1924, defined the rights of the USSR and China in the operation of the Chinese Eastern Railway (q.v.). CHANG refused to recognize the validity of the treaty in Manchuria, where the railway was located, and finally signed a separate agreement with the USSR in September. Peking's protests, both to CHANG and to Moscow, went unanswered.

CHANG was an active participant in the civil wars which wracked China during the warlord period, and succeeded in pushing into the area of the lower Yangtze valley in 1925. Unstable alliances soon forced him to withdraw his forces to the north. In July, 1926, CHIANG Kai-shek (1887-1975, q.v.), launched the Northern Expedition (q.v.), whose purpose was to unify China through military conquest. In early 1927, CHANG Tso-lin was in possession of Peking, as the last president of the Republic to head a government there, TUAN Ch'i-jui (1865-1936, q.v.), had resigned in April, 1926, and sought refuge in Tientsin (q.v.).

Although CHANG adopted a title indicating he was a successor to YUAN Shih-k'ai, he was not regarded as a legitimate successor. For a period of more than two years, China had no legitimate head of state, though CHANG dealt with the diplomats in Peking.

The final phase of the Northern Expedition began in April, 1928, and CHANG left Peking for Mukden, his Manchurian capital, on June 3. His private railway car was wrecked by a Japanese bomb outside Mukden early the following morning. CHANG died a few days later, and was succeeded by his son, CHANG Hsueh-liang.

Boorman, Howard L., ed. *Biographical Dictionary of Republican China.* New York: Columbia University Press, 1967-1973.

Lattimore, Owen. *Manchuria: Cradle of Conflict.* New York: Macmillan, 1935.

Changan. Alternative name for Sian (q.v.).

Changchun. Capital of Kirin province (q.v.).

Chao. 1. One of the principal warring states (see under **Warring States Period**) located mainly in present-day Shansi province (q.v.). It was conquered by the state of Ch'in (q.v.) in 222 B.C. Chao is associated with two important philosophers, HSUN Tzu (q.v.) and KUNG-SUN Lung, a Confucianist and a dialectician respectively.

2. The name of two brief and minor dynasties of the fourth century A.D.

Chefoo Convention. Signed September 13, 1876, by Sir Thomas Wade for Great Britain and LI Hung-chang (q.v.) for China. Wade, the British Minister at Peking, took advantage of the Margary Affair (q.v.) to press not only for redress for Margary's murder and the forcible exclusion of the authorized expedition for which he was official interpreter, but also for several unrelated issues. Wade learned of the incident on March 11, 1875, by cable from the India Office in London. He then presented six demands: (1) a commission of inquiry to be conducted with British officers present; (2) permission for a second expedition to be sent; (3) compensation to the sum of 150,000 taels of silver; (4) a new interpretation of the treaty stipulations regulating diplomatic audiences with the emperor; (5) enforcement of treaty stipulations that British trade be free of all imposts except tariff duty; and (6) all claims to be satisfied at once.

The Chinese made no objection to the first three, since they were directly connected with the incident, but they declined to reopen the question of audience procedure. They also insisted on the need for a full report from TS'EN Yü-ying (1829-1889), the governor of Yunnan province (q.v.), where the incident occurred. Because of difficulties in communications, that report did not reach Peking until July.

Negotiations were complicated by Minister Wade's threats to break off diplomatic relations, and by his demand that Governor TS'EN be tried for the crime, which the Chinese flatly refused. He also absented himself from Peking to be near the cable office in Shanghai.

The Convention was negotiated at Chefoo, a seaside resort in Shantung province (q.v.), during the summer of 1876, and contained three sections. The first concluded the Margary Affair by providing for trade between Yunnan and Burma, authorizing a second exploratory expedition, providing for an indemnity and a diplomatic mission of apology to be sent to London. The second section concerned diplomatic procedure and the administration of justice at the treaty ports (q.v.). The third section concerned details of trade, including the opening of four treaty ports and special arrangements for other ports of call on the Yangtze river. China ratified the convention on September 17, 1876.

Since the "most-favored-nation" clause (q.v.) occurred in treaties with other Western nations, all the foreign envoys were concerned with the terms of the Chefoo Convention, and none were entirely pleased with it. While sympathetic with Wade's desire for redress, they disapproved of his raising other issues and felt that in certain details the Convention was a step backward, particularly in spelling out the clause concerning application of *likin* (q.v.), internal trade duties, on imported goods. The second and third sections of the convention required the assent of all the other powers, and in identical notes the envoys informed the Chinese that without individual negotiations they would not consent to "abridgement of existing treaty stipulations."

Criticism of the Convention was not restricted to the other foreign powers. It was also vocally expressed by British residents in China who made it clear that they would prefer meticulous enforcement of the provisions of the Treaty of Tientsin of 1858. In view of this opposition, British ratification was postponed until 1885, at which time another article was added concerning taxation of imported opium.

Chekiang (Zhejiang) **province.** Area: 100,000 sq. km. (38,600 sq. mi.). Population: 37,900,000 (1980). Capital: Hangchow (q.v.). Chekiang is bounded on the northeast by Shanghai municipality, on the east by the East China Sea, on the south by Fukien province, on the west by

Kiangsi and Anhwei, and on the north by Kiangsu (qq.v.).

The northern region is part of the lower Yangtze valley, and rice is planted twice yearly in the alluvial plain. Tea is grown in the hilly south, and is a main export crop. Chekiang's long, indented coast supports considerable fishing. Other crops include jute, silk and cotton.

Ch'en. 1. One of the warring states. (See **Warring States Period**.) It was conquered by Ch'u in 479 B.C.

2. The name of a minor dynasty in South China of the sixth century A.D. It was the last of the kingdoms to be conquered by YANG Chien, who then founded the Sui dynasty (589-618, q.v.), thus reuniting a divided China.

CH'EN Tu-hsiu (1879-1942). Intellectual and founder of the Chinese Communist Party (CCP, q.v.). Born in a wealthy family in Anhwei province (q.v.), he spent the years 1900-1903 studying in Japan. He also spent some time in France prior to 1910, and became an admirer of Western civilization. After the revolution of 1911, he headed the Provincial Education Department in Anhwei, a position he held until driven from it by the efforts of YUAN Shih-k'ai (1859-1916, q.v.), to suppress the Second Revolution in 1913. In September 1915 he started a publication, the *Youth Magazine*, which soon established his reputation as an intellectual revolutionary. In 1917 he was invited to become dean of the College of Letters of the National University of Peking, a position in which he encouraged the pai-hua (vernacular) system of written Chinese, and the May 4th Movement (qq.v.) of 1919.

CH'EN moved to Shanghai in the fall of 1919 and became interested in Marxist doctrines. In August 1920 he founded the Socialist Youth League, which soon established branches in other cities. In December, CH'EN accepted an invitation to head the Provincial Education Department in Kwangtung province (q.v.), and for this reason was not present at the founding of the CCP in Shanghai in July, 1921. However, he did send in his organizational recommendations and was elected secretary of the Central Committee.

At the Third Congress of the CCP, held in June, 1923, he was elected general secretary of the party, a post in which he was expected to implement the Comintern's policy of cooperation with the Kuomintang (KMT, q.v.). He disagreed with this policy and denounced it several times. Nevertheless, when CHIANG Kai-shek (1887-1975, q.v.), started his purge of Communists in Shanghai in April, 1927, CH'EN was made the scapegoat and replaced in his party position. At the Sixth National Congress of the CCP held in Moscow in 1928, he was censured.

In 1929, CHANG Hsueh-liang (1898- , q.v.), the Manchurian warlord, seized the Chinese Eastern Railway from Russian control. The CCP denounced the action as an imperialist attack on the USSR. CH'EN protested because, he said, the CCP put Soviet interests above those of China. In November, he was expelled from the CCP.

He then became a Trotskyist and worked with several splinter groups. With advice and funds from Trotsky and his supporters in Europe, he founded the Chinese Communist Party Left Opposition Faction in May, 1931, with himself as general secretary of the central committee. Its life was brief.

In October 1932, CH'EN was arrested, tried and sentenced to 15 years in prison as a danger to the republic. He was released in August 1937 in connection with a general amnesty issued on the outbreak of the war with Japan. CH'EN lived successively in Wuhan (q.v.), Changsha and Chungking (q.v.), and died in a small town near the latter city.

Boorman, Howard L., ed. *Biographical Dictionary of Republican China*. New York: Columbia University Press, 1967-1973.

CH'EN Yi (CHEN Yi, 1901-1972). Born in Szechwan province (q.v.), where his father was a local magistrate under the Ch'ing dynasty (1644-1911, q.v.), CH'EN attended local schools and qualified for a government scholarship to go to France under a work-study program. He arrived in Paris in October 1919, and worked at several jobs, including a Michelin plant, and attended several schools. In 1921 he joined the Chinese Socialist Youth Corps, and in September 1921 was a member of a group which staged a demonstration at the Institut Franco-Chinois at Lyon, for which all participants were deported.

In 1923 CH'EN was in Peking, where he joined both the Chinese Communist party (CCP) and the Kuomintang (KMT, qq.v.). In 1925 he went to Canton where he became an instructor in the political department of the Whampoa Military Academy (q.v.) under CHOU En-lai (q.v.). He accompanied the Northern Expedition, 1926 (q.v.), and participated in the Nanchang Uprising (August 1, 1927, q.v.), frequently termed the origin of the CCP's armed forces.

In 1928 the Fourth Red Army was formed in the Ching-Kang mountains, with CHU Teh (q.v.) as commander, MAO Tse-tung (q.v.) as political commissar, and CH'EN as chief of the political department. In 1930 CH'EN supported MAO in a disagreement over tactics, and in

December of that year, on MAO's instructions, carried out one of the most extensive purges in CCP history prior to 1949, known as the Fu-t'ien Incident.

When Nationalist pressure forced the Communists under MAO to begin the Long March (q.v.) in 1934, CH'EN stayed behind to cover the retreat. While his troops were savagely attacked, he managed to preserve some of them. At the beginning of the war with Japan in July 1937, CH'EN's troops were to be reorganized and incorporated into the Nationalist forces to fight the Japanese in Central China. Relations between CCP and KMT forces deteriorated in 1940, culminating in the New Fourth Army Incident (q.v.) in January 1941. As a result, CH'EN moved his headquarters to northern Kiangsu province (q.v.), and established a base area which was of great importance in the Civil War, 1945-1949 (q.v.).

CH'EN traveled to the CCP wartime capital at Yenan in 1944, and was elected to membership on the Central Committee in June 1945. CH'EN was commander of the New Fourth Army in the Civil War (q.v.), later redesignated the East China People's Liberation Army.

After the Communist victory in 1949, CH'EN held several positions simultaneously, one of which was mayor of Shanghai. After the reorganization of the government in 1954, he became a vice premier of the State Council and a vice chairman of the National Defense Council. In 1958 he replaced CHOU En-Lai (q.v.) as foreign minister, and in that capacity made several trips abroad. However, he continued to be overshadowed by CHOU, whose international recognition was much greater.

The start of the Cultural Revolution (q.v.) in 1966 brought trouble for CH'EN, as he became one of its most conspicuous targets. In 1967 he was harassed by Red Guards (q.v.) at the ministry, and was periodically attacked, in spite of the efforts of CHOU to protect him, until his death in January 1972.

Boorman, Howard L., ed. *Biographical Dictionary of Republican China*. New York: Columbia University Press, 1971.

Klein, Donald W., and Anne B. Clark. *Biographic Dictionary of Chinese Communism, 1921-1965*. Cambridge: Harvard University Press, 1971.

CHENG Ch'eng-kung (1624-1662). Better known in the West as Koxinga, he was the most famous member of a Fukienese family which successfully combined piracy and support for the fallen Ming dynasty (1368-1644, q.v.), over four generations. His father, CHENG Chih-lung (1604-1661), worked for the Portuguese in Macao (and was baptized a Catholic), for the Spanish in Manila and possibly for the Dutch in Taiwan. CHENG Chih-lung went to Japan in 1623 and married a Japanese woman. CHENG Ch'eng-kung was his oldest son.

At first the older CHENG was a pirate, but the Ming court offered him preferments to abandon piracy and police the coast, an offer he accepted in 1628. This enabled him to offer military support to the Ming pretenders after the establishment of the Ch'ing emperor in Peking in 1644. He presented his son to the Ming pretender in 1645, and the latter was so taken with the young man that he bestowed the imperial surname on him. As a result he was called "Kuo-hsing-yeh," meaning "Lord of the Imperial Surname" which the Dutch transcribed as Koxinga.

In 1646 CHENG Chih-lung despaired of a Ming victory and surrendered to the Ch'ing forces. He was taken to Peking and given great honors, but his failure to obtain the surrender of his son led to his eventual execution in 1661.

CHENG Ch'eng-kung never abandoned the Ming cause and fought, usually successfully, in Fukien, Kuangtung and along the coast as far north as Shantung (qq.v.), although many of his allies and relatives came to perceive the Ming as a lost cause and shifted allegiance to the Ch'ing forces. Faced with this problem, CHENG did not hesitate to execute even his close relatives. He even ordered the execution of his oldest son, CHENG Ching but subordinate officials refused to carry out the order. In 1659 he was defeated in a major battle near Nanking (q.v.).

In 1661 CHENG invaded Taiwan, then tenuously held by the Dutch. After several clashes, the Dutch agreed in 1662 to surrender the island and withdraw to Batavia. In 1662 the Ch'ing authorities ordered the entire population of the coast from Kuangtung to Shantung moved inland to deprive CHENG of supplies. Later that year, CHENG committed suicide, apparently enraged by reversals in his fortunes, probably including the execution of his father and brothers in Peking.

CHENG Ch'eng-kung's death resulted in a power struggle among his close relatives. CHENG Ching was the eventual victor, but not until several other relatives had been executed or had surrendered to the Ch'ing. Forced to abandon his base at Amoy under Ch'ing pressure, CHENG Ching moved his base of operations to Taiwan in 1664 and proceeded to harass the Fukien coast, now protected by Ch'ing fleets and Dutch ships and men.

CHENG Ching died in 1681 and was succeeded by his second son, CHENG K'o-shuang. However, the Ch'ing forces forced the surrender of

Taiwan in 1683. CHENG K'o-shuang was taken to Peking, where he was made a duke.

Hummel, Arthur W., ed. *Eminent Chinese of the Ch'ing Period*. Washington: Government Printing Office, 1943.

CHENG Ho (1371-1433). Eunuch commander of the Ming fleet established by Emperor Ming Yung Lo (r. 1403-1424, q.v.) which made seven voyages between 1405 and 1433, he is the most famous Chinese navigator in history, and sailed the greatest distance of any ship captain up to his time.

CHENG Ho was born in Yunnan province (q.v.) of a Muslim family named MA, which may have been of Mongol or Arab origin. His grandfather was a Hajji—a Muslim who had made the pilgrimage to Mecca. He was castrated at age 10 to enable him to serve in the imperial household and, as was customary, was given a new name. He fought in the campaigns against the Mongols in the 1390s and became a trusted aide of Ming Yung Lo (q.v.) while the latter was still prince of Yen.

Ming Yung Lo reversed the policy of his father, Ming Hung Wu (r. 1368-1398, q.v.), who wished to preserve Chinese society by banning foreign intercourse and foreign trade. Ming Yung Lo, determined to expand China's contacts, sent CHENG on a first expedition to Southeast Asia, Ceylon and India with a fleet of 62 ships and nearly 28,000 men. Later expeditions visited several ports on the Persian Gulf, and, finally, the African coast from Somaliland to Zanzibar.

Many of the countries and principalities visited were heavily dependent on the China trade for their prosperity, and had been trading with China since the T'ang dynasty (618-906 A.D., q.v.). While some of the trade had been carried in Chinese ships, never before had imperial fleets appeared in this way, and CHENG's fleets were welcomed as an indication of a reversal of Ming Hung Wu's commercial policies that had affected them so adversely. Paying tribute to the emperor of China seemed a small price to pay for the privilege of trading. In consequence, many tributary missions were carried back to Nanking.

CHENG's fifth and sixth expeditions (1417-1419 and 1421-1422) stressed exploration of the Arab and African coasts, and much of Chinese geographic knowledge prior to the arrival of the Jesuits (q.v.) in the late 16th century was based on CHENG's reports.

CHENG's expeditions, while endorsed by the emperor, came under strong criticism from a segment of the scholar bureaucracy. Their opposition was based on the Confucian concept that China produced all that was necessary for its needs, and that foreign expeditions introduced exotic luxuries which were unnecessary if not harmful.

After Ming Yung Lo's death in 1424, further voyages were banned by his successor, Ming Hung Hsi (r. 1425), who was determined to reverse those of his father's policies which did not conform to Confucian ideas. He reigned for less than one year, and his son, Ming Hsuan Te (r. 1426-1435), permitted CHENG to lead one last expedition (1431-1433) before he retired as military commandant of Nanking. However, the Confucian opposition was finally victorious, and even the plans for CHENG's ships were later destroyed.

CHENG Ho was widely revered by the Overseas Chinese (q.v.) of Southeast Asia for centuries, and images of him may still occasionally be found in temples there.

Goodrich, L.C., and Chaoying Fang,

eds. *Dictionary of Ming Biography: 1368-1644*. New York: Columbia University Press, 1976.

Chengde. See under **Jehol**.

Chengteh. See under **Jehol**.

Chengtu (Chengdu). Population: 3.85 million (1980). Capital of Szechwan province (q.v.). It was the capital of Shu, one of the Three Kingdoms (qq.v.) 221-263, and has been a provincial capital for centuries.

Ch'i. 1. One of the warring states (see **Warring States Period**), located on the Shantung peninsula. Ch'i was one of the three major states in the last years of the period, the others being Ch'u and Ch'in (qq.v.). Ch'in's conquest of Ch'i in 221 B.C. marked the end of the period and the beginning of the Ch'in dynasty. Confucianism (q.v.) was a major ideology in Ch'i.
2. Minor dynasty (479-502) in the Period of Disunity (q.v.) in South China.
3. Northern Ch'i (550-577) successor state to the Northern Wei (q.v.) in North China.

Ch'i-shan (1780[?]-1854). Manchu (q.v.) official and key figure in the Opium War (1839-1842, q.v.). Known as Kishen in comtemporary Western accounts. Ch'i-shan was in charge of the defense of Tientsin when a British naval squadron arrived in August, 1840. He dealt with the British diplomatically and persuaded them to return to Canton to negotiate their demands. These included reimbursement for opium destroyed by orders of LIN Tse-hsü (q.v.), High Commissioner at Canton, and cession of the island of Hong Kong.
Because of his success with the British, Ch'i-shan was appointed to replace LIN, with instructions to soften LIN's hard-line policy, and otherwise to act as he saw fit, provided he kept local officials informed.

The British, dissatisfied with the slow pace of negotiations, on January 7, 1841, attacked and took the forts at Chuenpi, near Canton. Recognizing the inadequacy of Canton's defense, Ch'i-shan on January 20 signed an agreement which ceded Hong Kong. The British occupied it immediately and declared it a part of the British Empire. The governor of Kwangtung, I-liang, reported this to Peking, professing ignorance of the negotiations. In February the emperor dismissed Ch'i-shan from all his posts, and stripped him of honors, titles and wealth. In March he was led from Canton in chains, and sent to Peking where he was tried and sentenced to death. The sentence was commuted to banishment, and after the war ended he was reinstated in official life. He served in a variety of posts, including that of Imperial Commissioner to Tibet, and was actively engaged in fighting against the Taiping Rebellion (1851-1864, q.v.), at the time of his death.

Hummel, Arthur W., ed. *Eminent Chinese of the Ch'ing Period*. Washington: Government Printing Office, 1943.

Ch'i-ying (d. 1858). Known as Kiying in contemporary Western accounts. Manchu (q.v.) official and key figure in the Opium War (1839-1842, q.v.). In March 1842, he was transferred from his post of military governor of southern Manchuria to that of Tartar General of Canton. However, he was stopped en route and given a similar appointment at Hangchow. The British had already taken several cities in Chekiang province (q.v.), and by July the emperor recognized the hopelessness of the military situation. Ch'i-ying was instructed to accept

British terms. He signed the Treaty of Nanking (q.v.) on August 29, 1842, and on October 8, 1843, he signed the supplementary Treaty of the Bogue (q.v.).

The Treaty of Nanking ceded Hong Kong to the British and opened five treaty ports (q.v.) to foreign trade. The Treaty of the Bogue granted consular jurisdiction and other extraterritorial rights to the British, and included the "most-favored nation" clause (q.v.), which granted the British any benefits which the Chinese might in future grant to any other nation. Many historians doubt that Ch'i-ying had any concept of the far-reaching consequences of these concessions.

Ch'i-ying also signed the Treaties of Wanghia and Whampoa (qq.v.) with the Americans and French respectively. The American representative, Caleb Cushing, introduced a provision for renegotiating the treaty after 12 years. Because of the "most-favored nation" clause in the Treaty of the Bogue, that meant that all treaties could be reopened in 1854.

During the *Arrow* War (1857-1858, q.v.), the French and British forced their way to Tientsin and demanded that officials with full powers, such as Ch'i-ying had had in 1842, be sent to negotiate. Ch'i-ying himself was sent, and was intimidated by the British interpreters. He disobeyed orders to remain in Tientsin and was arrested outside Peking. He was ordered to commit suicide and did so.

Hummel, Arthur W., ed. *Eminent Chinese of the Ch'ing Period*. Washington, Goverment Printing Office, 1943.

Chia Ch'ing (1760-1820). Reign name of the fifth emperor of the Ch'ing dynasty (r. 1796-1820). The fifth son of emperor Ch'ien Lung (r. 1736-1796, q.v.), he acceded to the throne in 1796, when his father abdicated, but his position was not assured until the death of Ch'ien Lung in 1799.

The empire which he inherited was very different from that inherited by his father. China's population had nearly doubled, from about 150 million to 300 million, leading to food shortages in times of war or floods, which were frequent. The Huang Ho (Yellow river, q.v.) flooded some 17 times during his reign, and the first few years Chia Ch'ing held power were spent in suppressing rebellions in the south and west.

Many of the emperor's problems were traceable to the injurious effects of the influence of Ch'ien Lung's corrupt favorite Ho-shen (q.v.) on public affairs and over other officials. Chia Ch'ing removed him from power immediately after Ch'ien Lung's death.

The position of the English in China's foreign trade increased during the reign to the point at which it exceeded all the other Western powers' combined. The English, still dissatisfied with their terms of trade, sent William Pitt, Earl Amherst, on an embassy in 1816. A major stumbling block in diplomatic contact was British reluctance to perform the series of prostrations known as the *kotow* (q.v.), which Chinese ritual required of envoys bearing tribute from vassal states. Perhaps in the belief that in the grip of fatigue Amherst could be persuaded to perform the kotow, the Chinese officials hurried him along in the last stage of his journey so that he arrived at the Summer Palace at 5 A.M., August 29. The court officials were assembled in full dress and insisted on taking him in to an immediate audience. Amherst was exhausted, and without uniform or ceremonial presents. He refused and the embassy was ordered back to Canton.

Chia Ch'ing died September 2,

1820, in Jehol, probably of apoplexy brought on by a hot and tiring journey from Peking. He was succeeded by his second son, who reigned as Tao Kuang (r. 1821-1850, q.v.).

Hummel, Arthur W., ed. *Eminent Chinese of the Ch'ing Period*. Washington: Government Printing Office, 1943.

CHIANG Ching-kuo (1909-). General and president of the Republic of China. Elder son of CHIANG Kai-shek (q.v.). Born in Chekiang province of CHIANG's first wife, he was educated in Chekiang, Shanghai and Peking. CHIANG Ching-Kuo was arrested in Peking in 1925 for participation in student demonstrations against the government. He went to study in the USSR and was permitted to enter SUN Yat-sen University, from which he graduated in April 1927. However, because of the break between the Kuomintang (KMT) and the Chinese Communist party (CCP, qq.v.) which occurred in that year, CHIANG was held until 1937. After the Sian Incident of December 1936 (q.v.), which brought a truce in the CCP-KMT war, he was permitted to return to China with his Russian wife and two children. (Two more children were born in China.)

In 1939 he was made administrator of the Kiangsi area which had been occupied by the Communists prior to the Long March, 1934-1935 (q.v.), and proved rigorous in his suppression of gambling, opium and prostitution. In July 1945, he accompanied T.V. SOONG (q.v.) to negotiate the Sino-Soviet Treaty of 1945 (q.v.). He was then appointed special foreign affairs commissioner for Manchuria (q.v.), in which position he attempted to deal with the forces of the USSR. In December 1945, he again flew to Moscow as his father's personal representative, and negotiated with Marshal Joseph Stalin and Foreign Minister Vyacheslav Molotov. He returned to China in January 1946, and held a series of posts.

In August 1948, he was named deputy economic control advisor in the Shanghai area. A new gold-yuan scrip, designed to check the runaway inflation, was issued, and CHIANG reaped much publicity by announcing draconian measures and executing several black marketers. New economic measures were introduced in late October and CHIANG resigned, issuing a public apology for his failures.

For the next year he was involved in the holding operation as the Nationalists tried to stem the Communist advance, negotiate a truce, and finally evacuate to Taiwan. In August 1950, CHIANG was named head of the general political department of the Ministry of National Defense, in control of political indoctrination programs and political officers in all branches of the military. He was also chief of military intelligence and security agencies in Taiwan. In October 1952, he was elected to the Central Committee of the KMT, and in 1957 became the top-ranking member.

CHIANG Kai-shek died in April 1975, and was succeeded as president by YEN Chia-kan (C.K. YEN, b. 1905-),a former finance minister, governor of Taiwan and premier, who had been elected vice president in 1966 and again in 1972. It was clear, however, that CHIANG Ching-kuo was still powerful, and in 1978 he was elected president of the Republic of China (q.v.), a position still held in 1986.

Boorman, Howard L., ed. *Biographical Dictionary of Republican China*. New York: Columbia University Press, 1967-1971.

CHIANG Ch'ing (Jiang Qing, b. 1914-). Last wife and widow of MAO Tse-tung (q.v.). Born in Shantung province (q.v.), she studied modern drama at the Shantung Provincial Experimental Art Theater, and in 1930 joined an itinerant troupe which performed anti-Japanese propaganda plays in North China (q.v.). In 1933 she joined the Chinese Communist party (CCP, q.v.) and went to Shanghai (q.v.), where she acted in proletarian dramas and propaganda films. In 1936-1937 she played in similar films under the name Lan P'ing.

She left Shanghai in 1937 and made her way to Yenan, where she brought herself to MAO's attention, and often visited his cave apartment to seek instruction on ideological matters. She then moved in to serve as personal secretary and archivist. After she became pregnant, MAO sought agreement from CCP leaders to his proposed marriage. They reluctantly consented on the condition that she stay out of politics. This she did for some 20 years.

By the early 1960s, CHIANG was determined to reform the classical Peking opera, moving away from its traditional concern with kings, generals, officials and beautiful women to more realistic "socialist themes." The launching of the Cultural Revolution (q.v.) in 1966 brought CHIANG enormous power over all aspects of culture and propaganda—books, magazines, newspapers, films, opera and painting.

The vanguard of the Cultural Revolution was composed of millions of young people, collectively called the Red Guards (q.v.), and CHIANG showed great skill in exciting the young rebels to fury against those she perceived as her own and MAO's enemies. Senior officials of the party and the government, as well as their families, were subjected to insult and disgrace at the hands of the Red Guards and at the instigation of CHIANG.

The death of MAO on September 9, 1976, marked the end of the Cultural Revolution, and a month later CHIANG and her three colleagues, known collectively as the Gang of Four (q.v.), together with many of their followers, were purged from the CCP, arrested and tried. As of 1985 many of them, including CHIANG herself, were still imprisoned.

Witke, Roxane. *Comrade Chiang Ch'ing*. Boston: Little, Brown, 1977.

CHIANG Kai-shek (1887-1975). Generalissimo and president of the Republic of China (q.v.). He is known to the Chinese as CHIANG Chung-cheng (his official name), or as CHIANG Chieh-shih, of which CHIANG Kai-shek is the Cantonese pronunciation. CHIANG was born in Chekiang province (q.v.), the son of a middle-class salt merchant. His interest in a military career was stimulated by study of the texts of the ancient Chinese writer SUN Tzu (q.v.) and by his concern, widely shared by others, at the weakness of the Ch'ing dynasty (1644-1912, q.v.). This weakness was made evident by the first Sino-Japanese War (1894-1895), which China lost, and by the Russo-Japanese War (1904-1905, qq.v.), in which China did not officially participate but which was fought on Chinese soil, for essentially Chinese spoils.

CHIANG attended military school in Japan from 1908 to 1910. Already a revolutionary (he had cut off his queue in 1906, a popular act of defiance against the Manchu regime, which had imposed the hairstyle as a symbol of its authority), he easily fell in with the anti-Ch'ing ferment widespread among the thousands of Chinese students there, joined the T'ung-meng-hui, predecessor of the Kuomintang (KMT, qq.v.), and made friends with many of its leaders. He met Sun Yat-sen (1866-1925, q.v.), who visited Japan in 1910. On hearing news of the outbreak of revolution at Wuhan (q.v.) on October 10, 1911, CHIANG left immediately for Shanghai (q.v.) with a number of like-minded Chinese. He contributed to the success of the revolution and soon found himself a supporter of SUN and an opponent of YUAN Shih-k'ai (1859-1916, q.v.), the second president of the new Republic of China. YUAN's efforts to suppress the military supporters of the KMT forced CHIANG to spend some time in Japan until after YUAN's death in June 1916. Since SUN was also in temporary exile there, acquaintance developed into friendship.

The years following YUAN's death saw many Chinese leaders jockeying for power, of whom SUN Yat-sen was only one. CHIANG supported SUN but served only briefly in Canton (q.v.), SUN's usual base. He was in Chekiang observing mourning rites on the anniversary of his mother's death in June 1922, when he learned of an attempt to oust SUN. He hastened to Canton and accompanied SUN to Hong Kong and Shanghai, an action which solidified his position in the KMT.

In January 1923, SUN signed an agreement with a Soviet official, Adolf Joffe, officially announcing cooperation between the KMT and Russian and Chinese communists. In August, CHIANG was sent to the USSR as head of a military mission to obtain arms and to study military organization. On his return he sub-mitted a report and was named to the KMT Military Council. He was appointed commandant of the newly-established Whampoa Military Academy (q.v.) in May 1924. He supervised the military training of some 2,000 men in the first three classes of cadets, and many of his close associates in later years came from this group. Since this was the period of cooperation between the KMT and the Chinese Communist party (CCP, q.v.), CHIANG worked closely with Russian advisers, such as Mikhail Borodin (1884-1952, q.v.), and with CCP members such as CHOU En-lai (1898-1976, q.v.).

SUN's death in Peking in March 1925 left a succession problem, and CHIANG's position as a potential leader of the KMT was enhanced by infighting among other contenders, including WANG Ching-wei (1883-1944, q.v.) and HU Han-min (1879-1936), both of whom were senior to CHIANG within the KMT hierarchy. He was elected to the KMT Central Executive Committee at the Second National Congress in January 1926. In March he moved against the Communists and detained many Soviet advisers, an action which made him the dominant figure in the Canton power structure. In May his proposals to the Central Executive Committee to curtail Communist influence in the KMT were accepted, and in June he was named commander in chief of the National Revolutionary Army. In July he launched the Northern Expedition (q.v.) aimed at unifying China through military conquest.

By August most of Hunan province (q.v.) had been taken, and by October the Wuhan cities of the central Yangtze river valley. Kiangsi, Fukien and Chekiang provinces (qq.v.) were next, and by March 1927, both

Shanghai and Nanking had fallen. By this time it had become clear that there were two centers of KMT power. The left wing had set up a government in Wuhan (q.v.), while the right wing, led by CHIANG, had established a new national capital in Nanking. In April CHIANG launched a purge of Communists in Shanghai. In July, WANG Ching-wei, the leader of the Wuhan government, followed suit. In August CHIANG, having suffered a military defeat, and faced with internal opposition which included both WANG and HU Han-min, resigned. In December he married SOONG Mei-ling (q.v.). Because his first wife, the mother of CHIANG Ching-kuo (q.v.), was still living, and in the traditional Chinese view no grounds for divorce existed, the marriage drew much unfavorable comment.

CHIANG resumed his position as commander in chief early in 1928 and set in motion the second stage of the Northern Expedition, whose aim was to break the power of the northern warlords and conquer North China (q.v.). This went well, except for the May Third Incident (q.v.), in which Nationalist forces clashed with Japanese troops at Tsinan, Shantung province. In June the Nationalists took Peking, thus, in theory, completing the unification of China south of the Great Wall (q.v.).

In Nanking on October 10, 1928, CHIANG became chairman of a new national government, based on SUN Yat-sen's five-yuan concept (see under **Republic of China**). By the end of December the Manchurian warlord, CHANG Hsueh-liang (1898- , q.v.), had accepted Nationalist rule and raised the flag in Manchuria (q.v.). Unity, however, was more seeming than real, and there were many areas where no more

than lip service was paid to the new government. Opposition came both from the CCP and from dissident generals and political leaders within the KMT coalition. The most serious external threat was Japanese aggression.

While recognizing the Japanese threat, CHIANG's major objective was to achieve national unity. Perceiving the CCP as his major opponent, he launched five successive annual campaigns against the Communist forces in south Central China, starting in 1930 and ending in 1934-1935, when he forced them to evacuate their base in Kiangsi (q.v.) and begin the Long March (q.v.) to the northwest.

CHIANG's policies and leadership provoked opposition and a break-away government was formed in May 1931. The Japanese invasion of Manchuria in September precipitated a national emergency, and reconciliation was achieved with CHIANG's resignation as chairman of the national government, replaced by LIN Sen (1868-1943, q.v.). Nevertheless, although CHIANG was not chief of state, he controlled the government through his position in the KMT and his military power. The Japanese attack on Shanghai in January 1932, and the establishment of Manchukuo (q.v.) in March, caused further Chinese anger and increased sentiment for a suspension of KMT-CCP hostilities.

In 1935 CHIANG ordered the displaced warlord of Manchuria, CHANG Hsueh-liang to deploy his troops against the CCP, now centered at Yenan, Shensi province (q.v.). The Manchurians were displeased to find themselves fighting their fellow countrymen while the Japanese occupied their homeland, and, in consequence, there was a tacit cease-fire. In December 1936, CHIANG flew to

Sian, CHANG Hsueh-liang's headquarters, on an inspection trip and was taken prisoner. The Sian Incident (q.v.), as it was known, resulted in a KMT-CCP truce and an agreement to fight against Japanese aggression in North China (q.v.). Joint meetings were held to work out cooperative agreements, but these took months and were eventually ineffective.

The second Sino-Janapese war started on July 7, 1937, with a Japanese attack on the Marco Polo Bridge (q.v.) near Peking. The Japanese occupied Peking and Tientsin, and in August attacked Shanghai, which resisted until November. The Rape of Nanking (q.v.), in which several hundred thousand Chinese were killed by Japanese troops, followed the city's fall on December 13, and generated international criticism. By this time the national government had moved to Wuhan. The Japanese moved up the Yangtze river valley in 1938, and by the end of the year the government was in Chungking (q.v.). By early 1939, when their air raids on Chungking started, the Japanese controlled over half of China's area and population, from Manchuria in the far north to the borders of Indochina.

The Japanese attack on Pearl Harbor, December 7, 1941, brought the United States into the war and effectively transformed the war against Japan into World War II (q.v.). The Western powers recognized the national government in Chungking as the government of China. The American ambassador had moved to Chungking with most of his staff, leaving behind in Nanking a three-man housekeeping unit which dealt with the Japanese-puppet government of WANG Ching-wei (q.v.). The Western allies established a China Theater of Operations with CHIANG as supreme commander in 1942. The American general Joseph W. Stilwell (q.v.) was appointed as his deputy. In November 1943, CHIANG and Stilwell participated in the Cairo Conference (q.v.) at which the decision was made to counterattack Japanese forces in Burma.

CHIANG's conduct of the war against Japan drew much criticism both from Chinese and their allies. His best troops, trained between 1928 and 1938 by a military mission from Germany (q.v.), were successful in delaying the Japanese conquest of Shanghai and Nanking from August to November-December 1937, but were ultimately pushed back by superior Japanese strength. Many of the armed forces theoretically under CHIANG's control were only partially responsive to directives from Chungking.

In the view of many Western observers, China's main contribution to the war effort was in keeping much of the Japanese army occupied. Certainly, the primary causes of Japan's defeat were the American Navy and Air Force. Victory in 1945 brought the Nationalist government back to Nanking, and renewed the civil war with the Communists, with Manchuria as a major prize. The USSR had declared war on Japan on August 8, 1945, the day the second atomic bomb was dropped, on Nagasaki. They invaded Manchuria the following day, where they removed as much of the Japanese-built industrial base as they were able, and destroyed much of the rest, a loss estimated in the billions of dollars. Whey they had finished that task, they turned the area and all surrendered Japanese weapons over to Chinese Communist troops.

CHIANG had reassumed the position of head of state in October 1943, on the death of LIN Sen, and held it until January 1949. The period after 1945 was one of civil war, marked by American efforts to bring the two parties together, notably through the Marshall Mission (q.v.). The final result was the Communist victory and the establishment of the People's Republic of China (q.v.) in October 1949.

CHIANG retired from the presidency in January 1949 to be succeeded by LI Tsung-jen (q.v.) as acting president. CHIANG traveled back to his home in Chekiang, then visited the Philippines in July, where he issued a joint anti-Communist statement with President Elpidio Quirino, and to Korea in August, where he did the same with President Syngman Rhee. On his return to China he visited Kwangtung, Szechwan and Yunnan provinces (qq.v.), and finally on December 10, 1949, flew from Chengtu (q.v.) to Taiwan, the day Chengtu fell to Communist forces.

On March 1, 1950, CHIANG resumed the presidency, which he retained until his death in 1975. This period was in great contrast to his earlier years since he faced no effective opposition. American support had been cut off as a result of the failure of the Marshall Mission, but this policy was reversed by U.S. President Harry Truman on June 27, 1950, two days after the start of the Korean War. This military and economic aid effectively prevented any attempt by the Communists to oust CHIANG, and laid the groundwork for the economic development of the island.

Boorman, Howard, ed. *Biographical Dictionary of Republican China*. New York: Columbia University Press, 1967.

Tsou, Tang. *America's Failure in China: 1941-50*. Chicago: Chicago University Press, 1963.

Ch'ien Lung (1711-1799). Reign title of the fourth emperor of the Ch'ing dynasty (q.v.). He was the fourth son of the emperor Yung-cheng, and reigned from 1736 to 1796. In that year he abdicated in favor of his son, who became the emperor Chia-ch'ing (q.v.), though he continued to rule until his death. He was thus the longest-ruling emperor in recorded Chinese history.

Ch'ien Lung's reign marked the high point of Ch'ing power and wealth. Militarily there were successful invasions of Burma (q.v.) and Nepal (q.v.) (in defense of Tibet, q.v., which was tributary to the Ch'ing), and intervention in Vietnam (q.v.), then convulsed with civil war during the change of dynasty from the Ly to the Nguyen. More important were the conquests of Ili and Turkestan (q.v.), which added some six million square miles to the empire and effectively neutralized the possibility of Mongol or Turkish invasion—an objective which previous Chinese rulers had sought for over two millenia.

The 18th century saw a tremendous increase in Chinese population and in the area of tilled land. This resulted in a great increase in imperial revenues, but that led to high-level corruption and improvident increases in expenditure, both military and civilian.

Ch'ien Lung saw himself as a patron of the arts and literature. A collector of paintings on an enormous scale, he dabbled in painting himself. Many of the pieces which found their way to his collection received an imperial poem and one or more imperial seals to confirm their authenticity. He supported painters at court and encouraged the production of decorative porcelain, cloisonné and jade and ivory carvings. He expanded and enriched the Summer Palace (q.v.), using Jesuit missionaries to design and supervise several buildings in the European baroque style.

He was also interested in literature and supported large numbers of scholars engaged in compiling and editing official works, the most ambitious of which contained more than 36,000 volumes. The emperor's motivation was not entirely historical. He had many works revised to eliminate all pejorative references to the Manchus (the ethnic group to which the Ch'ing rulers belonged). Others were banned or burned. He was also very harsh with writers who made comments, however inadvertent, which might be considered prejudicial to the Manchus or the reigning dynasty. One result was that many serious scholars refrained from writing on political and economic subjects.

European trade increased dramatically during this reign. The earliest trade dated from the 16th century, with the Portuguese and the Dutch the earliest arrivals. By the middle of the 18th century the British had achieved the dominant place at Canton (q.v.), but were unhappy with the restrictions put on their nationals and by the restriction of all trade to Canton, which was decreed in 1757. In 1793 a British embassy led by Lord George Macartney (q.v.) was received at the Summer Palace in Jehol by Ch'ien Lung. The British petitions regarding trade were not successful, however.

Ch'ien Lung had Jesuits at his court in various capacities such as astronomers and artists. One of these, Guiseppe Castiglione, painted a picture of the emperor which is still extant. When the Jesuit order was dissolved in 1773, its position at the Ch'ing court was taken over by the French Society of Foreign Missions.

The last two decades of Ch'ien Lung's life were marred by the emperor's infatuation with his Manchu adviser, Ho-shen (q.v.), a young man of good family who came to the emperor's attention while a guard at the palace. Contemporaries agree that Ho-shen was good-looking, agreeable and well-spoken. He soon rose to be the most powerful man in the empire. He was also corrupt and, eventually, fabulously wealthy.

Ch'ien Lung abdicated in 1796, citing filial piety as one reason, since his grandfather had ruled for 61 years, and he did not wish to exceed that span. He lived for another three years, but his successor, Chia-ch'ing, was not permitted to exercise any of the power which was supposedly his. Instead, Ho-shen continued his career until the death of his patron.

Most historians agree that the last years of Ch'ien Lung's long reign, marked as they were by excessive court luxury and widespread corruption, marked the beginning of the decline of the dynasty. None of his successors were able to reverse the decline more than temporarily.

Kahn, Harold L. *Monarchy in the Emperor's Eyes.* Cambridge: Harvard University Press, 1971.

Hummel, Arthur W., ed. *Eminent Chinese of the Ch'ing Period.* Washington: Government Printing Office, 1943.

Goodrich, L. Carrington. *The Literary Inquisition of Ch'ien Lung.* Baltimore: Waverly Press, 1935.

Chihli Clique. The term refers to one of two opposing factions, the other being the Anhwei Clique (q.v.), whose rivalry dominated Chinese politics from 1916 to 1920. Both were composed of military officers of the Peiyang Group (q.v.), protégés and supporters of YUAN Shih-k'ai (1859-1916, q.v.). Their earlier support had enabled YUAN to become president and ruler of the Republic of China in 1912, and his death in June 1916 led to the struggle for dominance.

With the death of YUAN, FENG Kuo-chang (1859-1919, q.v.), leader of the Chihli Clique, hoped to become president, but was outmaneuvered by TUAN Ch'i-jui (1865-1936, q.v.), leader of the Anhwei Clique, who arranged for the vice president, LI Yuan-hung (1864-1928, q.v.), to become a figurehead president. In October 1916, the National Assembly elected FENG vice president, and in July 1917, when TUAN forced LI out of the presidency, FENG succeeded to the position. However, since he did not bring his military forces north, TUAN still dominated the government. FENG's term of office expired in October 1918, and he lived in retirement until his death the following year.

The new leader of the Chihli Clique was TS'AO K'un (1862-1938, q.v.), whose dissatisfaction with TUAN's policies led him to an alliance with CHANG Tso-lin (1873-1928, q.v.), warlord ruler of Manchuria. Together they defeated TUAN's troops in July 1920, bringing the rule of the Anhwei Clique to an end. The alliance did not last, however, and by 1922 fighting between CHANG's Manchurian forces and the Chihli troops forced CHANG back into Manchuria. TS'AO attempted the unification of China, and served as president of the republic from October 1923 to November 1924. At that point he was forced to resign by the combined forces of CHANG and the warlord FENG Yü-hsiang (1882-1948, q.v.). This ended the dominance of the Chihli Clique.

Chihli province. Former name of what is now Hopeh (Hebei), Chihli is the area around Tientsin and Peking.

The province also gave its name to the Chihli military clique (q.v.) which dominated North China (q.v.) from 1920-1924.

Chihli means an area directly controlled by the central government. When the nationalists moved the government to Nanking in 1928, Chihli was obviously no longer to be administered by the central government, hence the change of name.

Chin (Jin). The name of an ancient state and several later dynasties. The first three of those noted below are written with a Chinese character having several meanings, one of which is "to flourish." The last two are written with the character meaning "gold." Some earlier English-language histories romanize the first character *Tsin* to distinguish the two.

1. Name of one of the warring states (see **Warring States Period**) At the end of the 5th century B.C., it was divided into Chao, Han and Wei.

2. Western and Eastern Chin—successive dynasties from 266-316 and 317-420 A.D., respectively. Western Chin was the successor to the state of Wei of the Three Kingdoms (q.v.) period. Just as the TS'AO family of Wei had deposed the last emperor of the Han dynasty in 221 A.D., so SSU-MA Yen deposed the TS'AO ruler and changed the name from Wei to Chin. He then conquered the state of Wu and reunited China.

The unification did not last. By 316 the Chin had been driven from North China and had reestablished their capital at Nanking as the Eastern Chin. North China was ruled by a series of non-Chinese states known collectively as the Sixteen Kingdoms (q.v.). The Eastern Chin fell in 420 and was succeeded by the Earlier Sung (see under **Sung**).

3. Later Chin—name of a short-

lived dynasty (936-947) of the Five Dynasties period (q.v.).

4. Chin ("gold") dynasty (1115-1234)—second of the Tartar dynasties and successor to the Liao dynasty (qq.v.). The fall of the T'ang dynasty (q.v.) in 906 A.D. brought Chinese unity, such as it was, to an end. A non-Chinese dynasty, the Liao, ruled in the north from 907 to 1125. In the south, the Sung dynasty (q.v.) continued T'ang civilization. In the north, competition among the ethnic elements which made up the Liao empire led to the establishment of a rival Chin empire in 1115. The Chin were ethnically and linguistically related to the Liao, and many of those who had served the Liao rulers continued service under the Chin. At first the Sung welcomed Chin pressure on the Liao, but after the Liao had been eliminated in 1125, the Chin seized the Sung emperor in his capital at Kaifeng (q.v.) in 1126, forcing the Sung to remove their capital to Hangchow (q.v.).

At its peak, the Chin empire stretched from Korea to Central Asia, with the capital in present-day Peking or nearby. Its southern boundary was the Huai river, though efforts were made from time to time to extend it further south. The Chin were threatened by the Mongols under Chingis Khan (q.v.) early in the 13th century. In 1215 the Mongols took Peking, and completed their conquest of the Chin in 1234.

The Chin rulers, like the Liao before them, spoke an Altaic language and used a writing system based on Chinese characters. The ethnic group which the Chin represented was referred to in Chinese as Juchen (q.v.).

5. Later Chin dynasty (1616-1636). Important because it was the forerunner of the Ch'ing dynasty (q.v.), which ruled China 1644-1911, the Later Chin was founded by Nurhaci (1559-1626, q.v.), who intended the use of the name to imply a restoration of the Chin dynasty (1115-1234, see above). Nurhaci, a Juchen himself, at first acknowledged the suzerainty of the Ming dynasty (1368-1643, q.v.), by paying tribute. By 1616 he felt himself strong enough to renounce his fealty to the Ming, and he founded the new dynasty. In 1626 he was succeeded by his son Abahai (q.v.), who changed the name of the dynasty to Ch'ing (q.v.) in 1636.

Chin P'ing Mei. Also known under the title *The Golden Lotus*. This is the famous erotic novel of the Ming dynasty (1368-1644, q.v.). Its author is unknown. The novel was not held in high regard as a literary form, and an erotic novel was even less likely to be acknowledged by its author.

The subject of the novel is a Sung dynasty (960-1279, q.v.) merchant and official named HSI-MEN Ch'ing and his six wives. HSI-MEN is depicted as lascivious, and his sexual activities with his wives, as well as with prostitutes and casual conquests, are described in detail. His fifth wife is Golden Lotus, depicted as a murderess of her first husband, who then tries to seduce her brother-in-law, but finally marries HSI-MEN. The latter eventually dies after an overdose of aphrodisiac pills and sexual activity.

The novel borrows from a number of sources, notably the *Shui Hu Chuan* (q.v.). While there are a great many internal inconsistencies, it does provide an interesting picture of life during the Sung dynasty.

Egerton, Clement, trans. *The Golden Lotus*. New York: Paragon Book Gallery, 1962 (reprint).

Miall, Bernard, trans. *Chin P'ing Mei*. New York: Capricorn Books, 1962 (reprint).

Ch'in (Qin).

1. Name of one of the warring states (see under **Warring States Period**) and of the Ch'in dynasty which followed. The name is also the source of the word "China." The state of Ch'in was founded in 821 B.C., according to the records, and its people were always regarded by other Chinese as being semi-barbarian. The state was located in the northwest and its farther neighbors were Tibetans and Central Asians. Their capital was near the present city of Sian, after the rulers of the Chou dynasty (1122-255 B.C., q.v.) moved their capital to Loyang (q.v.).

The Ch'in rulers were followers of the philosophy known as Legalism (q.v.), two of whose most prominent exponents were Shang Yang and HAN Fei Tzu (qq.v.). The Ch'in state was the most successful of the warring states and in 255 B.C. effectively brought the remnant of the Chou dynasty to an end. After conquering the states of Chao in 222 and Ch'i in 221 B.C., Ch'in Shih Huang Ti (q.v.), the 32nd ruler of the state, declared himself *huang ti*, usually translated as "emperor." The dynasty lasted until 206 B.C., when it was succeeded by the Han dynasty (206 B.C.-221 A.D., q.v.).

The Ch'in dynasty represented a drastic break with the past. The emperor and his minister LI Ssu to a great extent destroyed the feudal families which had dominated the preceding two millennia and replaced them with an imperial bureaucracy. The new rulers standardized the length of axles to insure uniformity and improve transport, they standardized the writing system, and rebuilt and consolidated the Great Wall, utilizing many of their former enemies, such as Confucian scholars, for the purpose. They also made an effort to ensure orthodoxy in the Burning of the Books (q.v.), which took place in 213 B.C. Many thousands of people were executed, and thousands more died in a variety of imperial activities.

The emperor died in 210 B.C., but his death was concealed by LI Ssu until he could send a forged instruction to the heir apparent to commit suicide, leaving the empire in the hands of a younger and more compliant emperor. Unrest became widespread, fed by the dissatisfaction of the dispossessed feudal families, the suppressed Confucianists and the disgruntled participants in forced labor. Civil war ensued, with the most prominent commanders being the aristocratic HSIANG Yü and the plebeian LIU Pang (qq.v.), the latter of whom went on to found the Han dynasty.

The Ch'in dynasty succeeded in uniting China to a greater degree than had existed before, and set the stage for the Han. The Han was dominated by Confucians, who sought revenge upon the first emperor by impugning his ancestry and by ensuring that his name would be infamous in their histories. But a number of Han institutions were based on Ch'in foundations, and while there was an official policy of Confucianism, many Legalist institutions survived. For example, the system of pao chia (q.v.), a method of social control through mutual responsibility, has survived into the present day.

2. The name of three different states of the Sixteen Kingdoms (q.v.) period (302-439). They are the Earlier and Later Ch'in, established by Tibetans, and the Western Ch'in established by a nomadic group.

Ch'in Shih Huang Ti (Qin Shi Huang Di, 259-210 B.C.). Thirty-second ruler of the feudal state of Ch'in of the Warring States Period (484-255 B.C., qq.v.) and founder of the Ch'in dynasty (221-206 B.C., q.v.). Official records show him as the son of the 31st ruler, but he may have been the son of a rich merchant, LÜ Pu-wei. He acceded to the throne in 246 B.C. and brought the feudal period to an end by conquering the remaining feudal states. The last to fall were Chao in 222 and Ch'i in 221 B.C. He then declared himself universal ruler, giving himself the title *huang ti*, usually translated as "emperor."

Rulers of the Ch'in state were adherents of the school of Legalism (q.v.), a philosophy in which all the activities of the population were tightly controlled and directed toward subsistence and warfare. The emperor's success in imposing this draconian theory on feudal China was dramatic. He eliminated feudalism (though it crept back occasionally over the centuries), replacing it with a centralized imperial bureaucracy. He standardized axle lengths to permit uniform road widths, thus improving transport. He standardized the written language, and in 213 B.C. ordered the "Burning of the Books" (q.v.) to eliminate all the records of the feudal families, and to prevent possible restoration of feudal states. An opponent of Confucianism (q.v.), he was a devotee of Taoism (q.v.), and spent much money and effort on the search for immortality.

Ch'in Shih Huang Ti was assisted throughout his reign by his chief minister, LI Ssu, and when the emperor died in 210 B.C., LI concealed the fact and sent a forged instruction to the heir to commit suicide, which he obligingly did, leaving LI with a younger and more compliant emperor. The dynasty fell in 206, being supplanted by the Han dynasty (206 B.C.-221 A.D., q.v.).

Succeeding dynasties were officially Confucian, with few exceptions, and much of the historical commentary on the Ch'in was written by highly critical Confucian scholars. There have been exceptions, however, and in 1972 a more favorable view of the first emperor was promulgated in the People's Republic of China, causing considerable controversy both within and outside China. The book cited below provides English translations of relevant historical texts as well as modern essays by Chinese scholars.

Li, Yu-ning, ed. *The First Emperor of China: The Politics of Historiography.* White Plains: International Arts and Sciences Press, 1975.

China Proper. The term was used in the 19th and early 20th centuries in referring to the 18 provinces into which China was divided in the Ch'ing dynasty (1644-1911, q.v.). This was the area taken over from the Ming dynasty (1368-1644, q.v.), and did not include the following dependencies: Manchuria, Mongolia, Sinkiang and Tibet (qq.v.).

Chinese Communist party (CCP). Founded officially in July 1921, at the First National Congress in Shanghai, as successor to the Socialist Youth League (q.v.), by twelve Chinese and two representatives from the Comintern (Communist International) in Moscow. It was agreed from the first that the CCP would follow policy decisions made by the Comintern, and that the latter would provide funds for the party's support.

The Second Comintern Congress, held in Moscow in July 1920, had accepted Lenin's recommendation to cooperate with nationalist and anti-imperialist forces in Asian countries. Consequently, the CCP's Second National Congress, held in Shanghai in July 1922, accepted the Comintern's decision to work with the

Kuomintang (KMT) and its leader, SUN Yat-sen (qq.v.), and also with Soviet instructions that CCP members join the KMT as individuals. On January 26, 1923, a joint resolution was signed by SUN and Adolf Joffe, a Soviet official, announcing the alliance of the Soviet Union and the KMT in the task of unifying China.

The CCP's Third National Congress, held in Canton in June 1923, voted that the KMT "must be the central force . . . and assume the leadership of the revolution." The Fourth National Congress, held in Shanghai in January 1925, was probably the high point of cooperation between the two parties. Several CCP members had achieved high positions in the KMT, of which they were concurrent members. The rift between the two parties came after SUN's death in March 1925, and the subsequent split of the KMT into left- and right-wing factions.

In spite of the action taken by CHIANG Kai-shek (q.v.), leader of the right-wing faction of the KMT, in arresting several CCP members and Soviet advisers in Canton in March 1926 on suspicion of a plot, many Communists participated in the Northern Expedition (q.v.), launched from Canton in August 1926 for the purpose of uniting China. The Northern Expedition achieved its first goals quickly, and by December right-wing KMT officials had established temporary government headquarters in Nanchang, capital of Kiangsi province (q.v.), before moving to Nanking (q.v.). In January 1927, left-wing KMT officials, together with their Communist allies, set up a rival government in Wuhan (q.v.).

The CCP's Fifth National Congress was held in Wuhan in April-May 1927 at the same time that CHIANG was purging Communists in Shanghai. At this congress, CCP founding member CHANG Kuo-t'ao (q.v.) proposed an end to the KMT alliance, but Comintern representatives insisted on continuing it. When it became clear that the CCP had no intention of abandoning its radical policies, such as land reform, the Wuhan government concluded that the CCP was violating the SUN-Joffe agreement of 1923. When the KMT leader in Wuhan, WANG Ching-wei (q.v.), learned from a Comintern agent of the revolutionary plans for China, a purge began in July. This marked the end of the alliance and served as a signal for the Nanchang Uprising (q.v.) of August 1, 1927, usually considered the birth of the Red Army.

From the founding of the CCP in 1921, Comintern policy assumed the primacy of the urban proletariat in achieving the revolution. In defiance of this policy, MAO Tse-tung (q.v.), another CCP founding member, led a peasant uprising in Hunan province (q.v.) in the autumn. It failed, and in consequence he was removed from the Central Committee and other posts. Yet the survival of the party may be credited to his refusal to accept the party line. He retreated from Hunan to the Ching-Kang mountains on the Hunan-Kiangsi border, where he was joined in April 1928 by CHU Teh (q.v.) and the survivors of the Nanchang Uprising.

With the Communists largely underground or on the run, the CCP's Sixth National Congress was held in Moscow in the summer of 1928. LI Li-san (q.v.), the dominant figure, though not the general secretary, was highly critical of MAO's guerrilla tactics and urged a return to dependence on urban workers. On his return to China he called for attacks on industrial centers. MAO and CHU responded with an attack on Nanchang in the summer of 1930. It failed and they returned to Kiangsi, disobeying orders from LI. LI was summoned to Moscow and spent the next 15 years in exile.

The winter of 1930 saw the Nationalist government in a strong position and determined to crush the Communists by military force. CHIANG continued the military pressure even after Japan invaded Manchuria in 1931. The Nationlists encircled MAO's base at Juichin in 1934, and in October he began the Long March (q.v.).

The marchers captured the city of Tsunyi, Kweichow province (q.v.), in January 1935, and immediately convened an enlarged conference of the CCP Political Bureau. The conference accepted MAO as the leader of the CCP, and adopted his policy based on mobile and guerrilla warfare, instead of the revolt of the urban proletariat. MAO's leadership was challenged somewhat later when the marchers joined CHANG Kuo-t'ao's (q.v.) Fourth Front Army in Szechwan (q.v.). CHANG proposed moving west into Sikang province (q.v.), while MAO insisted on going north to Shensi (q.v.), where another Communist base already existed. He eventually settled in Yenan, which became the CCP's wartime capital.

The history of the CCP from its founding in 1921 until 1935 was not identified with any one leader. From 1935 until his death in 1976, it was closely identified with MAO. From 1935 until 1949 MAO consolidated his hold on the party structure and rebuilt the military strength of his guerrilla forces. He also projected an image as a most effective spokesman against Japanese imperialism and the necessity for united Chinese resistance to it.

The CCP's forces in 1936 were not militarily impressive; only 7000 or so had survived the Long March, out of some 100,000 who had started. They were faced with Nationalist troops from Manchuria (q.v.) who had been defeated by the Japanese and ejected from their homeland. Ordered by CHIANG Kai-shek to continue the extermination campaign against the Communists, they balked at the idea of fighting fellow Chinese when they had a more hated enemy. As a result, a tacit cease-fire came into existence, and in December 1936, as a result of the Sian Incident (q.v.) CHIANG was forced to agree to cooperation with the Communists in a united front against Japan. While CHIANG was being held prisoner in Sian, a delegation from the CCP, headed by CHOU En-lai (q.v.), flew in with the message that the USSR wanted CHIANG's life preserved and favored him as the leader of China.

The Japanese opened the war against China on July 7, 1937, with the Marco Polo Bridge Incident (q.v.). Before the end of the year they had captured most of the coastal cities and the communications network. In 1938 they moved upriver to Wuhan and captured Canton as well. Resistance to the Japanese advance was borne mostly by Nationalist troops, since they were charged with the defense of the major cities and communications. In accordance with MAO's guerrilla doctrines, the CCP's forces attacked the Japanese when circumstances were favorable, and retreated when they were not, thus not losing men or weapons in defending strong points. Both Communists and Nationalists maintained administration of sorts in the countryside, which the Japanese made varying efforts to control. The Communists were far more successful in spreading their own control, particularly in North China. It is estimated that by the end of the war in 1945 the Communists controlled an area containing 90 million people, nearly 20 percent of the population.

Efforts to coordinate military actions between the two groups finally broke down in January 1941 in the New Fourth Army Incident (q.v.), in which the Communist forces in Anhwei province (q.v.) were decisively defeated by the Nationalists and retreated north of the Yangtze river. For the rest of the war there was little or no cooperation between the two forces.

The growth of the CCP was also reflected in figures released in April 1945. The party held its Seventh National Congress in Yenan at that time and reported CCP membership at 1.2 million, with another 900,000 in the military. MAO was chairman of the Central Committee, the Political Bureau, and the Secretariat of the Central Committee, making him the dominant figure of the CCP.

Contact with Westerners did not start with World War II. Several sympathetic journalists had written of various aspects of the CCP. Probably the best-known book is Edgar Snow's *Red Star Over China*, written after a visit to Yenan in 1936. The CCP maintained an office in Wuhan in 1937-1938, the period of the united front. After Wuhan fell to the Japanese they had a liaison group in Chungking (q.v.), where CHOU En-lai spent considerable time on friendly terms with foreign journalists, diplomats and military officials. This channel of information about conditions in Communist-held areas became of pressing interest to the United States after the Japanese attack on Pearl Harbor, December 7, 1941, brought the Americans into World War II.

The American interest was in using Chinese forces to fight the Japanese. Nationalist troops, for several reasons, were not doing this effectively. Consequently, the opportunity to employ existing troops for the purpose had to be explored, at the least. In the face of opposition from the Nationalist government, it was not until July 1944 that a U.S. Army observer group went to Yenan. The mission's objectives were to assess Communist military capabilities, acquire military intelligence through use of the extensive network of guerrilla bases, and rescue downed American airmen. The observers were favorably impressed by the spartan quality of life in Yenan, in contrast to the perceived corruption of Chungking. However, the group's performance was a disappointment to the American military, because of its preoccupation with political matters.

The Americans also tried to arrange a coalition government in China. The concept was given lip service by both sides, but each set conditions which the other refused to meet. The Americans feared an outbreak of civil war, which might embroil the United States and which would certainly be harmful to the war effort.

While negotiations continued, the war was drawing to a close. On August 6 the first atomic bomb was dropped on Hiroshima. On August 8 the second was dropped on Nagasaki, and the USSR declared war on Japan. On August 9, Soviet troops entered Manchuria, in conformity with the terms of the Yalta Conference (q.v.). In spite of CHIANG Kai-shek's orders that all Japanese troops surrender to the Nationalists, many surrendered to the Communists. In Manchuria the Communists also had the support of the Soviets who turned over captured Japanese weapons to CCP troops in the area.

From 1946 to 1949 CCP efforts were devoted almost entirely to military affairs, yet while the area and population under CCP control increased vastly, MAO was able to reinforce his tight control over the party structure.

The establishment of the People's Republic of China (PRC, q.v.) on October 1, 1949, reflected the near-total control of mainland China which the CCP had achieved by that time.

The history of the CCP after 1949 is hardly distinguishable from that of the PRC. MAO was chairman of both. Implementation of CCP programs was immediate. The first move was to suppress opposition and confiscate landholdings. An estimated 1 to 3 million people lost their lives as a result of this program. In January 1952, the Three Anti Movement (q.v.) against corruption, decay and bureaucracy was launched against officials who had served under the Nationalist government. In March, the Five Anti Movement (q.v.) against bribery, tax evasion, theft of state assets, theft of state economic secrets and fraud, was launched against private businessmen. In 1957 the Hundred Flowers Campaign (q.v.) invited intellectuals to criticize government and party policies, and those critics deemed to have gone too far were subjected to an anti-rightist backlash.

In 1958 MAO proposed the Great Leap Forward (q.v.), an attempt to "achieve communism" within his lifetime. Unreachable production targets were set, and within a year the disruption of the economy was clearly visible. An estimate 20 million people died of starvation because of the damage done in the agricultural sector. In 1959 MAO stepped down as chairman of the PRC in favor of LIU Shao-ch'i (q.v.), though he retained the chairmanship of the CCP until his death. In 1966 MAO launched the Cultural Revolution (GPCR, q.v.), an effort to establish continuing revolution. Part of the process was continuing attacks on government organs and officials by the Red Guards (q.v.). Their most prominent target was LIU Shao-ch'i, chairman of the PRC and the second-ranking member of the CCP. LIU was toppled, along with other well-known figures, such as TENG Hsiao-p'ing (q.v.). CHOU En-lai was a target, but managed to ride out the storm of criticism. Control of the CCP was in MAO's hands but it became clear that he firmly backed his wife CHIANG Ch'ing and the Gang of Four (qq.v.). Their efforts to conduct continuing revolution led to the closing of all schools and colleges and the suspension of education. The recall of nearly all Chinese diplomats and the maltreatment of foreign diplomats in Peking led to near-paralysis in China's foreign relations.

MAO's death on September 9, 1976, brought the GPCR to a halt, and also left a vacancy at the head of the CCP. It was filled by HUA Kuo-feng, a relatively unknown figure. At the same time a purge of CHIANG Ch'ing and the Gang of Four was undertaken. TENG Hsiao-p'ing returned to power in July 1977, as deputy premier. HUA fell from power in August 1980, and was replaced as chairman of the CCP in July 1981 by HU Yao-pang. The office of chairman of the CCP was abolished in September 1982, and HU became general secretary, a position still held at the end of 1985. However, the dominant figure in both the CCP and the PRC is TENG Hsiao-p'ing.

Schwartz, Benjamin I. *Chinese Communism and the Rise of Mao*. Cambridge: Harvard University Press, 1951.

Service, John S. *Lost Chance in China*. New York: Random House, 1974.

Snow, Edgar. *Red Star Over China*. New York: Random House, 1938.

Chinese Eastern Railway. This 950-mi. line crosses Manchuria (q.v.) from Manchouli, on the border with Siberia, southeast to Suifenho, on the border with the USSR's Maritime Province, not far from Vladivostok. Permission to build the railroad was extracted by the Russians from LI Hung-chang (q.v.) in 1896 in a secret treaty. The railroad was built with French capital, and Harbin (q.v.) was built as its administrative center. It was much more than a railroad, since the administration established agricultural experiment stations, mines, industrial works, shipping and schools—all the paraphernalia of a colonial administration.

In 1898 the Russians forced the Chinese to agree to the construction of the South Manchurian Railway, connecting Harbin with Dairen and Port Arthur (qq.v.). The Japanese took this line over in the aftermath of the Russo-Japanese war (q.v.).

In 1929, the Chinese attempted to oust the Russians from their control of the Chinese Eastern Railway, but were unsuccessful. The Japanese finally took control of all of Manchuria with the establishment of Manchukuo (q.v.) in 1932, and in 1933 the Soviet Union sold its interests in the Railway for about one eighth of its investment. It finally came under Chinese control after World War II.

Chinese Turkestan. The name used in the 19th century to refer to that part of Central Asia which is now known as Sinkiang province (q.v.).

Clubb, O. Edmund. *China and Russia*. New York: Columbia University Press, 1971.

Ch'ing (Qing) **dynasty.** 1644-1911. The traditional dates cover the period when 10 consecutive emperors reigned in Peking. (See under **Ch'ing Dynasty Emperors** and individual entries.) The dynasty was actually founded in 1616 by Nurhaci (1559-1626, q.v.), a talented Juchen (q.v.) military leader. He called his dynasty

the Later Chin (q.v.), a reference to the Chin dynasty (1115-1235 A.D., q.v.), also ruled by the Juchen. Although they probably did not number more than 400,000 in 1600, Nurhaci had the example of the Chin, the Liao (907-1125) and the Yuan (1279-1368, qq.v.) dynasties, all of which ruled a much larger Chinese population through military dominance. Nurhaci was succeeded by his son Abahai (1592-1643, q.v.), who reigned 1626-1643. In 1635 he banned the use of the word Juchen as pejorative and mandated the use of Manchu (q.v.) to refer to his people. In 1636 he changed the name of the dynasty to Ch'ing.

The final decades of the Ming dynasty (1368-1644, q.v.) were chaotic, with the Manchus making incursions in the northeast, and freebooters ravaging the countryside in other parts of the empire. One of these, LI Tzu-ch'eng (1605-1645, q.v.), took Peking in 1644 and an orgy of death and destruction followed. The emperor, Ming Ch'ung Chen (1611-1644, q.v.), hanged himself on April 25. The Chinese general WU San-kuei (1612-1678, q.v.), commander of the Ming troops opposing the Manchus at Shanhaikuan, northeast of Peking, joined the Manchus in expelling LI's forces. The Ch'ing emperor, Shun Chih (r. 1644-1661, q.v.), was proclaimed emperor of China on October 30, 1644.

The Ch'ing rulers continued Ming administrative practices with certain adaptations. While Manchus, and to some extent Mongols (q.v.), were favored for government positions, Chinese manned the majority of posts, particularly the lower ranks. Princes of the tribes of Inner Mongolia had become vassals of the Ch'ing in 1636, at its founding by Abahai. Princes of Outer Mongolia swore allegiance in 1691. The Manchu rulers encouraged intermarriage between Manchus and Mongols, particularly among the nobility, and both groups were heavily represented in the military.

The first four Ch'ing emperors, who reigned from 1644 to 1796, were able rulers and China was both prosperous and strong. While most of China fell to the successful Manchus in the first two decades of the dynasty, the elimination of the last Ming supporters did not occur until the conquest of Taiwan (q.v.) in 1683. The 18th century saw the following neighboring countries acknowledge Ch'ing suzerainty when invading armies proved victorious: Tibet, 1720; Turkestan (Sinkiang), 1759; Burma, 1770; Vietnam, 1789; and Nepal, 1792 (qq.v.).

The first major external challenge to the Ch'ing was the appearance of traders from Russia (q.v.) along the Amur river, which the Manchus regarded as their territory. The matter was settled at the Treaty of Nerchinsk (1689, q.v.), which defined the boundary between the Russian and Manchu empires as following the watershed between the valleys of the Lena and Amur rivers to the Sea of Okhotsk. It was the first treaty signed with a Western nation and departed from Chinese custom in treating the two signatories as putative equals.

In 1793 Britain's ambassador, Lord George Macartney, was received informally by the emperor Ch'ien Lung (q.v.), but British refusal to perform the kotow (q.v.) precluded a treaty, or even a formal audience. The second British embassy, led by Lord Amherst in 1816, was not received by the emperor Chia ch'ing (q.v.), and the Ch'ing reluctance to conduct diplomatic relations in accordance with European patterns was a major factor in the Opium War (1839-1842, q.v.). By this time a declining dynasty

faced the threat of growing industrial power in the West.

British defeat of Ch'ing forces in that war forced the opening of five "treaty ports" (q.v.); the cession of Hong Kong to Great Britain; and made clear the dynastic weakness. This was a contributing factor to the Taiping Rebellion (1851-1864, q.v.). At the same time the dynasty faced this internal challenge, it was fighting the *Arrow* War (1857-1860, q.v.). That brought British and French troops into Peking, the destruction of the Summer Palace (q.v.) and the flight of Emperor Hsien Feng (q.v.) to Jehol (q.v.), where he died. In the settlement, the Ch'ing were forced to agree to permanent residence for foreign diplomats in Peking, to the opening of more ports to foreign trade and to the establishment of the Tsungli Yamen (q.v.), the forerunner of the Ministry of Foreign Affairs. (Previously, diplomatic matters had been handled by the Board of Rites.) An additional result was the loss to Russia of the area north of the Amur and east of the Ussuri rivers. At the same time the Western powers saw that it was not in their own interests to topple the dynasty and assisted the Ch'ing in suppressing the Taiping Rebellion (q.v.).

The latter half of the 19th century saw the beginnings of modernization in China, and also the loss of vassal states, as well as Chinese territory. Japan absorbed the Liu Ch'iu Islands (q.v.) in 1875. France detached Vietnam in 1885. China recognized British paramountcy in Burma in 1886. As a result of the first Sino-Japanese War (1894-1895, q.v.), China was forced to cede Taiwan (q.v.) to Japan and to concede the independence of Korea (q.v.). In 1898 China was forced to grant territorial leases to Britain, France, Germany and Russia.

Chinese resentment at these developments took several forms. One was the growth of a revolutionary/republican movement. (See under **SUN Yat-sen**.) Another was the Hundred Days' Reform (q.v.) of 1898, in which the emperor Kuang Hsu, r. 1875-1908, tried to reorganize the government, but this was cut short by the empress dowager (1835-1908, q.v.), who kept the emperor prisoner until his death, one day before her own. Still another was the Boxer Rebellion (q.v.) of 1900, which was an attempt to exterminate all the foreigners in North China. The Legation Quarter in Peking endured a siege by Boxers supported by Ch'ing troops at the order of the empress dowager. The siege was lifted by an international force, and the Ch'ing court was required to make still further concessions to the foreign powers.

While China did not participate in the Russo-Japanese War (1904-1905, q.v.), it was fought on Chinese soil and its objectives were territory and privileges in China. The end of the dynasty was signaled by the revolutionary uprising in Wuchang on October 10, 1911, and the Republic of China (q.v.) was proclaimed in Nanking on January 1, 1912. The last act of the dynasty was the abdication of the infant emperor P'u-yi (q.v.) on February 12, 1912. The articles of abdication, drafted by YUAN Shih-k'ai (q.v.), transferred title to all remaining Ch'ing territory to the Republic of China. This is the basis for 20th-century Chinese claims to Mongolia, Sinkiang and Tibet.

Hummel, Arthur W., ed. *Eminent Chinese of the Ch'ing Period*. Washington: Government Printing Office, 1943.

Morse, Hosea Ballou. *The International Relations of the Chinese Empire*. London and New York: Longmans, 1910-1918.

Spence, Jonathan D., and John E. Wills, Jr., eds. *From Ming to Ch'ing*. New Haven: Yale University Press, 1979.

Teng, Ssu-yü, and John K. Fairbank. *China's Response to the West*. Cambridge: Harvard University Press, 1954.

CH'ING (QING) DYNASTY EMPERORS.

Reign title		Temple Name	Personal name	Dates of reign
LATER CHIN DYNASTY				
1 T'ien Ming		T'ai Tsu	Nurhaci **	1616-1626
(Tian Ming		Tai Zu)		
2 T'ien T'sung		T'ai Tsung	Abahai ** "	1627-1636
(Tian Cong		Tai Zong)		
CH'ING DYNASTY (NAME CHANGED IN 1636)				
Ch'ung Te		T'ai Tsung	Abahai	
(Chong De		Tai Zong)		1636-1643
1* Shun Chih	(q.v.)	Shih Tsu	Fu-lin **	
(Shun Zhi		Shi Zu	Fu-lin)	1644-1661
2 K'ang Hsi	"	Sheng Tsu	Hsuan-yeh **	
(Kang Xi		Sheng Zu	Xuan-ye)	1662-1722
3 Yung Cheng	"	Shih Tsung	Yin-chen **	
(Yong Zheng		Shi Zong	Yin-zhen)	1723-1735

Reign title		Temple Name	Personal name	Dates of reign
4 Ch'ien Lung (Qian Long	„	Kao Tsung Gao Zong	Hung-li ** Hong Li)	1736-1795
5 Chia Ch'ing (Jia Qing	„	Jen Tsung Ren Zong	Yung-yen ** Yong-yan)	1796-1820
6 Tao Kuang (Dao Guang	„	Hsuan Tsung Xuan Zong	Min-ning ** Min-ning)	1821-1850
7 Hsien Feng (Xian Feng	„	Wen Tsung Wen Zong	I-chu ** Yi-zhu)	1851-1861
8 T'ung Chih (Tong Zhi	„	Mu Tsung Mu Zong	Tsai-ch'un ** Zai-chun)	1862-1874
9 Kuang Hsu (Guang Xu	„	Te Tsung De Zong	Tsai-t'ien ** Zai-tian)	1875-1908
10 Hsuan T'ung (Xuan Tong		none	P'u-yi (q.v.) Pu-yi)	1909-1911

* Shun Chih was the first Ch'ing emperor to rule from Peking, and is usually counted as the first of the dynasty.

** Biographies of these emperors are listed under their personal names in Hummel, Arthur W., ed. *Eminent Chinese of the Ch'ing Period*. Washington: Government Printing Office, 1943.

Note: Ch'ing emperors from Shun Chih to Kuang Hsu are listed in this book under their reign titles, since those are more familiar to most Western readers. Ming emperors are listed under the dynasty + the reign title, e.g. Ming Hung Wu. Emperors of previous dynasties are generally listed under the dynasty + the temple name, e.g. Han Wu Ti.

Chingis Khan (1167-1227). Title, meaning "Emperor Within the Seas," by which the Mongol conqueror Temuchin is known to history. Temuchin's father, a Mongol chief, died while his son was in his teens. The boy rose through effort, character and military genius to the leadership of the fragmented peoples of the steppes. He assumed the title in 1206 when he had achieved the rule of all Mongolia.

He next turned his attention to China, divided at the time among the Chin dynasty (1115-1234), the Hsi Hsia (882-1227) and the Sung (960-1279, qq.v.). In 1209 he invaded the Hsi Hsia territory and forced the ruler to become his vassal. In 1211 he invaded the Chin, and in 1214 the Chin emperor made peace with the gift of a royal princess, a large retinue, horses, gold and silk. He then decamped to Kaifeng (q.v.), further south. The Chin capital fell to the Mongols in 1215.

Chingis Khan died at the end of August 1227, while engaged in the final conquest of the Hsi Hsia. He was succeeded by his son Ogodai, who completed the conquest of the Chin and started the war with the Sung.

Neither ever ruled over all of China. The first to do so was Khubilai Khan (1214-1294, q.v.), who was Chingis's grandson and the fifth ruler of the dynasty.

Martin, H. Desmond. *The Rise of Chingis Khan and His Conquest of North China*. New York: Octagon Books, 1977.

Ch'inghai (Qinghai). See **Tsinghai**.

Ch'ing-ming. *Ch'ing-ming* means "clear and bright" and is the fifth of the 24 periods of the solar calendar (q.v.). It also refers to the festival which is called "sweeping the tombs." It is the only folk festival which is calculated on the solar instead of the lunar calendar. It comes 106 days after the winter solstice, which by Chinese calculations puts it on April 4th or 5th.

The festival is one at which the family gathers and proceeds to the family graves to sweep them clean and tidy up. Food is brought to be offered to the spirits of the departed, and may then be consumed as a sort of picnic.

Eberhard, Wolfram. *Chinese Festivals*. New York: Henry Schuman, 1952.

Chingtechen (Jingdezhen). Population: 500,000 (1982). Major ceramic center located in northern Kiangsi province (q.v.), east of Po Yang lake. Ceramics have been produced in this area since the Han dynasty (206 B.C.-221 A.D., q.v.), but the city is better known for the wares produced under imperial patronage in the Sung, Yuan, Ming and Ch'ing dynasties (qq.v.) over the past 1,000 years. For several generations it was the largest ceramic manufacturing center in the world. The first Westerner to report on it was the French priest Father d'Entrecolles, who visited it in 1712. The city was captured during the Taiping Rebellion (1851-1864, q.v.), and badly damaged.

The kilns were restored in 1864 and are still in use.

Chin-shih. See under **Examination system**.

Ch'itan. See under **Cathay**.

Chongqing. See **Chungking**.

Chou (Zhou) dynasty. 1. 1122-255 B.C. Historians divide the Chou, longest-lived of the Chinese dynasties, into three periods: Western Chou (1122-771 B.C.), discussed below; Spring and Autumn period (771-484 B.C.); and the Warring States Period (484-255 B.C., qq.v.). The Chou dynasty followed the Shang (1766-1122 B.C.) and was eventually overthrown by the Ch'in dynasty (qq.v.).

The Western Chou capital was near present-day Sian (q.v.). At its zenith, Chou power extended as far north as Mongolia and south beyond the Yangtze valley. This was followed by its slow decline, with a concurrent rise in the power of the great vassal states. In 771 the capital was sacked by northern invaders, and a new capital was established father east near Loyang (q.v.).

Historical information about the Chou is derived mainly from the *Shih Chi* of SSU-MA Ch'ien (qq.v.). Archaeological evidence tends to confirm the historical record. Chou social organization comprised three classes: the rulers, including warriors and court attendants; craftsmen; and farmers. The structure was remarkably similar to the feudalism of Europe and Japan in later periods. It was marked by the existence of hereditary lords of great estates, who increased their own power at the expense of the Chou kings. Technologically, Western Chou continued the use of bronze which had marked the preceding Shang dynasty.

One significant aspect of the Chou dynasty is that it was used by later Confucian scholars as a supposed example of a golden age—an ideal towards which later governments might aspire.

2. Northern Chou dynasty (557-581 A.D.). Conqueror of Western Wei (534-557, see under **Wei**) and Northern Ch'i (550-577, see under **Ch'i**), it became the unifier of North China. It was conquered by the Sui dynasty, 589-618.

3. Dynastic style adopted by the Empress WU (q.v.) for the period 685-705 A.D. Since her heirs reinstated the T'ang dynasty (618-906, q.v.), it is not usually included in lists of recongnized dynasties.

4. Later Chou dynasty (951-960). The last of the Five Dynasties (q.v.) period (906-960), it was replaced by the Sung dynasty (960-1279, q.v.).

Chang, Kwang-chih. *The Archaeology of Ancient China*. New Haven: Yale University Press, 1968.

CHOU En-lai (ZHOU Enlai; 1898-1976). The most successful Chinese statesman and diplomat of the 20th century, CHOU was born in Chekiang province (q.v.) of a gentry family. His father died when he was a child, and he was sent to relatives for his education in various places. After graduation from middle school in Tientsin in 1917, he went to Japan where he was introduced to Marxist thought. After the May Fourth Incident (q.v.) of 1919, he returned to Tientsin and enrolled in Nankai University. He also joined a small group in Peking to study Marxism under CH'EN Tu-hsiu (q.v.).

He was arrested in 1920 for participating in an anti-Japanese student demonstration, and was jailed for several months. After his release he sailed for France with the work-study program in October 1920. He was present at the establishment of the European headquarters of the Chinese Communisty party (CCP, q.v.) in Paris. At that time, the CCP was cooperating with the Kuomintang (KMT, q.v.) under instructions from the Comintern, and CHOU was active in promoting the interests of both parties.

In 1924 CHOU went to Canton, where SUN Yat-sen (q.v.) was planning a revolution against the northern generals. CHOU was appointed deputy director of the political department of the Whampoa Military Academy (q.v.). When the Northern Expedition (q.v.) was launched in July 1926 he went to Shanghai to organize labor unions and other groups in support of the revolution. In March 1927, CHOU directed a general strike of Communist-controlled unions in Shanghai which prepared the city for the entrance of the troops of CHIANG Kai-shek (q.v.). In April, CHIANG struck against the Communists and CHOU was imprisoned, but later released.

CHOU then went to Wuhan (q.v.), where the left-KMT government of WANG Ching-wei (q.v.) was in control. The Fifth National Congress of the CCP was held in Wuhan in April-May 1927, and CHOU was elected to the Central Committee. In July WANG ordered a purge of CCP members from the KMT, and CHOU went to Nanchang where he participated in the Nanchang Uprising (q.v.) on August 1. He accompanied forces under CHU Teh (q.v.) south to Kwangtung province (q.v.) and after their defeat by the KMT at Swatow, made his way to Hong Kong.

CHOU went to the Soviet Union in 1928 to the Sixth National Congress of the CCP, at which he was reelected to the Central Committee and given several other posts. He made another trip to Moscow in 1930 to brief the Comintern on the situation in China. On his return he criticized the line taken by LI Li-san (q.v.), which stressed the urban proletariat as the basis of the revolution, thus separating himself from what was the orthodox Communist policy.

CHOU left Shanghai in 1931 to join the rural base in Kiangsi province (q.v.) under the leadership of MAO Tse-tung (q.v.) and CHU Teh. He held several important posts there and when Nationalist pressure made it clear the area could no longer be held, he played an important role in preparing for the Long March (q.v.). CHOU stayed with MAO throughout the Long March and, after their arrival in Shensi province (q.v.), became an important negotiator and spokesman for the CCP. He negotiated with the Manchurian warlord CHANG Hsueh-liang (q.v.) for the tacit cease-fire with CHANG's troops which led to the Sian Incident (q.v.) in December 1936. The result was the emergence of a united front between the CCP and the KMT, and on July 7, 1937, the Marco Polo Bridge Incident (q.v.), generally regarded as the beginning of the war with Japan.

In 1938 CHOU headed the CCP delegation to the united front, and stayed in Hankow as liaison with the Nationalist government until the city fell to the Japanese. He then returned to Yenan, the CCP wartime capital, but soon went to Moscow for medical treatment. Upon his return he again became the principal CCP liaison with the Nationalists.

Based in Chungking, CHOU's activities involved working with various disaffected groups of liberals and intellectuals, and developing a propaganda program through the New China News Agency. This was designed to attract students, but it also appealed to non-Chinese, and CHOU made himself readily accessible to the diplomatic community and the international press corps. He arranged for members of the latter group to visit Yenan occasionally, and the result was usually favorable to the CCP.

CHOU spent the period from July 1943 to November 1944 in Yenan, and then returned to Chungking to discuss establishing a coalition government with CHIANG Kai-shek. These talks continued intermittently after the end of the war in August 1945, but CHOU returned to Yenan in November 1946, and stayed in CCP-held territory until the establishment of the People's Republic of China (PRC, q.v.) on October 1, 1949. At that time he was named premier and, concurrently, foreign minister.

CHOU's dual position and the skill with which he represented the PRC in international affairs soon made his name known worldwide. On February 14, 1950, he signed a 30-year Sino-Soviet mutual assistance treaty. CHOU was also China's spokesman during the Korean War, 1950-1953 (see under **Korea**). On September 30, 1950, he warned that if United Nations troops crossed the 38th parallel, China would intervene. The "Chinese People's Volunteers" went into action along the Yalu river on October 26, and by March 1951 a stalemate had been reached roughly where the conflict had begun. The Russians called for negotiations, which lasted from July 1951 until July 1953. After the death of Stalin in March 1953, CHOU's new proposals formed the basis of the armistice agreement.

CHOU was also a participant in the Geneva Conference of April 1954, convened to discuss both Korea and Vietnam. CHOU's diplomacy won him the respect of most of the other participants, and, with French Premier Pierre Mendes-France, he drew up the framework of a basic agreement. CHOU also emerged from the Afro-Asian Conference, held in Bandung, Indonesia, in April 1955, as an advocate of reason and moderation.

The Hundred Flowers movement (q.v.) was launched by Chairman MAO on May 1, 1957, and CHOU loyally supported the chairman. It lasted only until June, by which time many intellectuals had criticized the government and party policies severely. The backlash was expressed in repression, and CHOU's support of the movement led to criticism of him by more doctrinaire members of the CCP.

One result was pressure on him to resign his post as foreign minister, which he did in February 1958, succeeded by CH'EN Yi (q.v.). The year 1958 also saw the launching of the Great Leap Forward (q.v.) program, which CHOU did not approve of but which he supported out of loyalty to MAO. Its failure was followed by the retirement of MAO from his position of chairman of the PRC in April 1959, in favor of LIU Shao-ch'i (q.v.), but CHOU, continuing as premier, undertook to set the economy back on course.

The early 1960s saw CHOU making several overseas tours, negotiating with India (q.v.) over border questions and the USSR over aid.

On May 1, 1966, MAO Tse-tung launched the Cultural Revolution (q.v.), but CHOU had outlined the new policy in a speech given one day earlier. It was, he said, "a fierce and long-term struggle in the ideological sphere between the proletariat and the bourgeoisie." In spite of MAO's support, CHOU soon became a target of the Red Guards (q.v.), and at one point in August 1967, he was held a prisoner in his office by thousands of them. CHOU's role in the Cultural Revolution was complex, since he not only encouraged the movement but tried to shield many of his old colleagues from its effects.

CHOU's final diplomatic achievement was the normalization of relations with the United States. He communicated his willingness to address the matter by letters through third countries, and in 1971 President Nixon's security adviser, Henry Kissinger, made a secret visit to Peking. Nixon visited China in 1972, and relations were then established.

CHOU continued to be a target of the Gang of Four (q.v.), who had taken command of the Cultural Revolution, but he became seriously ill in early 1974. His last public appearance was at the Fourth National People's Congress in January 1975, and he died January 8, 1976.

Boorman, Howard L., ed. *Biographical Dictionary of Republican China.* New York: Columbia University Press, 1971.

Klein, Donald W., and Anne B. Clark *Biographic Dictionary of Chinese Communism, 1921-1965.* Cambridge: Harvard University Press, 1971.

Wilson, Dick. *Zhou Enlai: A Biography.* New York: Viking, 1985.

Christianity. Archaelogical evidence indicates that Nestorian Christians (q.v.) were present in the capital of the T'ang dynasty, 618-906 A.D. (q.v.), and emissaries from the pope to the emperors of the Yuan dynasty (1279-1368, q.v.) reported their presence in China, as did Marco Polo (q.v.). The Nestorians, however, seem to have been Central Asians, rather than Chinese. The Franciscan John of Monte Corvino (1247-1294, q.v.) was sent on a papal mission to Khubilai Khan (r. 1260-1294, q.v.), and then appointed the first Roman Catholic bishop of Peking (then known as Khanbalick or Cambaluc). In a letter to Rome dated 1305, he claimed some 3,000 converts. However, the decline of the Yuan made communication between China and Europe impossible after the middle of the 14th century, and there is no evidence of the survival of a Christian community in China through the Ming dynasty (1368-1644, q.v.).

The next Christians to arrive in East Asia were Portuguese traders, the first of whom arrived on the coast of Kwangtung province (q.v.) in 1517. Christian missionaries accompanied the traders, but the Ming exclusion policy prevented their entrance to China. The Spanish Jesuit Francis Xavier died on a small island off the coast in 1552. The establishment of Macao (q.v.) in 1557 provided permanent residence for the missionaries, but access to China was still denied. The Jesuits (q.v.) were the first to succeed in getting permission to reside in China, in 1583, and that was granted only after they had undertaken the study of the Chinese language and were able to communicate. The first to do this successfully was Father Matteo Ricci, 1552-1610 (q.v.).

The Jesuit strategy was to gain access to the ruling class of mandarins and thus obtain approval for missionary work. Early Jesuits, frequently trained mathematicians and astronomers, not only wore Chinese dress, they achieved proficiency in spoken and written Chinese. Father Ricci's success in obtaining imperial approval in Peking paved the way for Jesuit participation in the Board of Astronomy and the preparation of the official calendar during the Ch'ing dynasty (1644-1911, q.v.).

The mendicant orders used a more direct approach, but with little success. Preaching in languages other than Chinese and wearing the habits they had worn in Europe, they attracted unfavorable attention and few converts, and were usually deported. Nevertheless, there were some successes in Kwangtung and Fukien provinces (qq.v.), and by the beginning of the Ch'ing dynasty in 1644, some 50,000 converts were claimed.

The Jesuits proved useful to the Ch'ing court for other purposes besides astronomy and calendars. Two members of the order served as interpreters at the negotiations resulting in the Treaty of Nerchinsk (1689, q.v.), the first treaty between an emperor of China and a Western power, Russia. In later years Jesuits also served as architects for a Western-style baroque pavilion built as part of the Summer Palace (q.v.).

At the local level, Christianity clashed with Chinese customs because Christians were forbidden to participate in local festivals which were inextricably combined with worship at local temples, some Buddhist, some Taoist, and some a mixture of the two.

At another level, Christians found themselves in controversy over ancestor worship (q.v.). The Jesuits permitted participation in the rite, on the grounds that Confucianism (q.v.) had no theological content, and therefore its rites were nonreligious. The other orders disagreed and eventually the rites controversy (q.v.) was decided against the Jesuits in 1704 by the Congregation of Rites in Rome.

These issues stirred up periodic persecutions, and in 1724 the emperor Yung Cheng (r. 1723-1735, q.v.), banned all missionary activity and forced all missionaries to leave, with the exception of the handful of Jesuits in Peking.

The first Protestant missionaries to arrive in Chinese territory were

Dutchmen assigned to their settlement in Taiwan (q.v.), which lasted from 1627 to 1662. They were successful in converting many of the aboriginal inhabitants, but there is no report of conversions among the Chinese settlers. The Ming loyalist CHENG Ch'eng-kung (1624-1662, q.v.), ousted the Dutch in 1662 and executed five of the missionaries.

The next Protestant missionary to arrive was an Englishman, Dr. Robert Morrison (1782-1834), who reached Canton in 1807. However, access to the interior was not achieved until the signing of the Treaty of Whampoa (1844, q.v.), between France and China. It rescinded the ban of 1724 and granted religious toleration. At first this affected only Catholics, as the Manchu negotiator, Ch'i-ying (d. 1858, q.v.), was unaware that Christians were not all alike, but regulations were issued to provide for this. The treaty authorized protection to missionaries proceeding to the interior, and this was augmented by the Treaties of Tientsin (1858, q.v.), which guaranteed their freedom of movement. In 1860 the right to own property was conceded. At this point the legal bars to Christian missionary activity may be said to have been eliminated, though very real impediments continued to exist.

While the numbers of missionaries, both Catholic and Protestant, increased dramatically, the rate of conversion disappointed both groups. They soon concluded that the establishment of schools might pave the way for a more effective ministry. The mission boards which provided the financial support were not enthusiastic, but there was no acceptable alternative.

The first schools taught Chinese classics and mathematics. The addition of courses in English drew the sons of the business class in the treaty ports (q.v.), as the value of a command of English became apparent. China's defeat in the Sino-Japanese War (1894-1895, q.v.), which many attributed to the Westernization of Japan, added impetus to the growth of missionary schools and also stimulated their development into colleges. The imperial examination system was abolished in the wake of the Boxer Rebellion (1900, q.v.), and after the republican revolution in 1911, several government universities were opened. To meet what was perceived as a challenge, several of the Christian colleges were consolidated to provide better-funded and better-equipped institutions.

Christian schools were attacked in the anti-foreign and anti-imperialist campaigns which swept China in the 1920s, but suffered less in the 1930s, when Japan was the target of Chinese antipathy. Students at the Christian colleges joined their counterparts at government schools in student movements of the time. The start of the war against Japan, precipitated by the Marco Polo Bridge Incident, July 7, 1937 (q.v.), led many Christian schools to join their government counterparts in moving to areas under Nationalist control, usually in Szechwan or Yunnan provinces (qq.v.). Others stayed in Japanese-occupied areas until the attack on Pearl Harbor, December 7, 1941, rendered any connection with Western nations useless in dealing with Japanese authorities.

Although the Christian impact on China in the first half of the 20th century was significant, Chinese Christians were a very small minority. The first converts were Catholic, and from an estimated 50,000 at the beginning of the Ch'ing dynasty in 1644, their number rose to about 250,000 by 1700. 18th-century persecution and official disapproval reduced the total to about 200,000 when the ban on missionary activity was lifted in 1844. The number rose to an estimated 3.5 million by 1950.

The Protestants arrived later and never achieved such numbers. In 1900, Chinese Protestants were estimated at 90,000, and reached about 500,000 by 1950. The Protestant impact was increased by the visibility and influence of their schools and colleges, and also by the importance of such Christians as the family of Charles Jones SOONG (q.v.) in the republican government.

The establishment of the People's Republic of China (q.v.) on October 1, 1949, was followed by the expropriation of church property, the expulsion of most foreign missionaries and the trial and imprisonment of others. Most Christian churches were closed and during the Cultural Revolution (1966-1976, q.v.), many churches were destroyed. In 1979 only one Catholic church was open in China, the Nantang Cathedral in Peking, though by 1985 others had been permitted to reopen.

Varg, Paul. *Missionaries, Chinese and Diplomats*. Princeton: Princeton University Press, 1958.

Dunne, George H., S.J. *Generation of Giants*. Notre Dame: University of Notre Dame Press, 1962.

Lutz, Jessie Gregory. *China and the Christian Colleges, 1850-1950*. Ithaca: Cornell University Press, 1971.

Lach, Donald F. *The Preface to Leibniz' Novissima Sinica*. Honolulu: University of Hawaii Press, 1957 (paper).

CHU Hsi (1130-1200). Sung dynasty (q.v.) Neo-Confucian philosopher and official. Born of an official family in Fukien province (q.v.), where his father was serving as a magistrate, his ancestral home was in Anhwei (q.v.). In his early years he studied both Buddhism and Taoism (qq.v.), but renounced them in favor of Confucianism (q.v.) at the age of 30. He passed the imperial examinations (see under **Examination system**) at 19 and spent most of his life in official posts. He showed administrative ability in those which required activity, and in several sinecures devoted himself to study and teaching students who were attracted by his reputation. He was the target of court intrigue at the end of his life and suffered undeserved disgrace just before his death.

CHU was the most notable philosopher of his period and was responsible for the codification of Neo-Confucianism (q.v.) in the form in which it persisted to the beginning of the 20th century. It was CHU who established the "Four Books" (q.v.) as the basis for Chinese education. His school of thought is sometimes known as rationalism.

CHU has been called the greatest synthesizer in the history of Chinese thought, since he was able to combine the theories of a number of his predecessors into a coherent whole. In so doing, he was able to blend the Confucianism of Mencius (q.v.) with such non-Confucian concepts as the preexistence of a principle even before the thing itself exists; for example, the principle of a chair has always existed, even before there were any chairs.

One reason for the widespread acceptance of Neo-Confucianism and, accordingly, the philosophy of its foremost proponent, was the recognition that at heart both Taoism and Buddhism are inherently antisocial and therefore unacceptable as the guiding philosophy of the state. Taoism recommends the search for "pure" nature and shows contempt for civilization. Buddhism teaches the "emptiness" of things and the desirability of escape from this world. The syncretic thought of CHU was appealing to the Chinese scholars who were responsible for the governance of the state and who had to act in conformity with some ideology. Neo-Confucianism gave them a theoretical framework for philosophic speculation as well as concrete examples of ethical behavior. As late as 1894, the Ch'ing emperor Kuang Hsü (r. 1875-1908, q.v.), proscribed the sale of a book attacking the doctrines of CHU Hsi on the grounds that it would do "great harm to our literature."

Fung Yu-lan, and Derk Bodde, trans. *A History of Chinese Philosophy*. Princeton: Princeton University Press, 1953.

CHU Teh (Zhu De, 1886-1976). Communist military leader. Born in Szechwan of a family originally from Kwangtung province (qq.v.), CHU attended traditional schools and sat for the provincial examinations (see **Examination system**) in 1905, the last time they were given in China. With the abolition of the traditional system, he switched to a modern school, the Chengtu Higher Normal School. He graduated from the Yunnan Military Academy in 1911 and entered the 37th Brigade as lieutenant.

Shortly after the outbreak of the revolution in October 1911, the military commander led his brigade in revolt against the Manchus (q.v.). CHU was sent with his regiment to overthrow Ch'ing authority in Szechwan. His military career progressed over the next few years of internal strife in southwest China until 1921, when he made his way to Shanghai. There he met CH'EN Tu-hsiu and SUN Yat-sen (qq.v.) and in the autumn of 1922 he went to Europe, studied German in Berlin, and then attended the University of Göttingen. He met CHOU En-lai

(q.v.) and joined the European branch of the Chinese Communist party (CCP, q.v.), which CHOU was organizing. He also assisted CHOU in organizing the German branch of the Kuomintang (KMT, q.v.), since under the Comintern policy of the time, the Communists were cooperating with the KMT.

He was arrested twice in 1925 for participation in student demonstrations and was expelled from Germany in June 1926. He returned to China via the Soviet Union. In October 1926, CHU became the head of the political department of the KMT's 20th Army in the upper Yangtze valley, and proceeded to arrange political organization and indoctrination. When the army commander discovered that his troops were being given Marxist indoctrination, he executed 23 cadres and CHU left to join another KMT army. He reached Nanchang, capital of Kiangsi province (q.v.) in January 1927, and was given a series of responsible posts by his new commander. He kept his membership in the CCP a secret until August 1, when he participated in a Communist attempt to seize the city. This incident, known as the Nanchang Uprising (q.v.), is considered the first military clash between the forces of the CCP and the KMT and the birth of the Red Army. It failed, however, and the troops under CHU were forced out of Nanchang.

CHU and his troops eventually arrived at the Ching-kang mountains, where another Communist group under MAO Tse-tung (q.v.) had retreated after an unsuccessful uprising in Hunan province (q.v.). The two men met in April 1928 and combined their forces as the Fourth Red Army, with CHU as commander and MAO as political commissar. They were forced out of their stronghold in 1930, and moved to Juichin in southeastern Kiangsi.

Using that as a base, CHU conducted a number of campaigns in Fukien (q.v.), Kwangtung and Kiangsi. While these did not result in permanent gains, CHU's forces were recognized as the strongest Communist military force in central China. In November 1931, the Communists in Kiangsi formed a soviet government with MAO as chairman and CHU as commander in chief and military commissar.

In the autumn of 1934, Nationalist forces had surrounded the base at Juichin, forcing the Communists to withdraw. CHU served as commander of the First Front Army during the Long March (q.v.) which followed. In July 1935, they met the Fourth Front Army, the forces under CHANG Kuo-t'ao (q.v.), in northwest Szechwan. After some debate over policy, the two groups separated, with CHU accompanying CHANG into Sikang province (q.v.), while MAO went north to Shensi province (q.v.). Some time later, the Sikang group marched north and CHU rejoined MAO in October 1936.

The Sian incident (q.v.), which forced CHIANG Kai-shek (q.v.) to abandon his anti-Communist campaign and agree to a united front against Japan, occurred in December 1936, and the war with Japan started on July 7, 1937, with the Marco Polo Bridge incident (q.v.). CHU became commander in chief of the Communist Eighth Route Army, and participated in actions in Shansi province (q.v.) in that year. The rest of the war he spent as commander of all Communist military forces.

He also rose to be second only to MAO in the party hierarchy. In 1946, after the failure of the Marshall Mission (q.v.) to mediate between the Communists and the Nationalists,

CHU became commander in chief of the People's Liberation Army, a position he held until 1954. With the establishment of the People's Republic of China (PRC, q.v.) in Peking in October 1949, CHU became the senior vice chairman of the Central People's Govermnent, and in 1954 vice chairman of the PRC. He held this position until denounced during the Cultural Revolution (q.v.) in 1967. He was restored to his posts in 1971 and died in 1976.

Boorman, Howard L., ed. *Biographical Dictionary of Republican China*. New York: Columbia University Press, 1971.

Elegant, Robert S. *China's Red Masters*. New York: Twayne Publishers, 1951.

CHU Yuan-chang. Personal name of the founder of the Ming dynasty (1368-1643). See under **Ming Hung Wu**.

Ch'u, Kingdom of. Largest and southernmost of the warring states (see **Warring States Period**, 484-255 B.C.), at its greatest extent it covered most of the Yangtze valley, including all or part of Anhwei, Chekiang, Honan, Hunan, Hupeh, Kiangsi, Shensi and Szechwan provinces (qq.v.). Ch'u was regarded as semi-barbarous (meaning inadequately Sinicized) by those states which had received more of the culture of the Chou dynasty (1122-255 B.C., q.v.). Ch'u was one of the last states to fall to Ch'in (q.v.) in what led eventually to the establishment of the Ch'in dynasty, 221-206 B.C.

The most famous native of Ch'u was the poet CH'Ü Yüan (q.v.), whose death is commemorated to the present day in the Dragon Boat Festival (q.v.).

CH'Ü Yüan (d. 288 B.C. [?]). Poet of the Kingdom of Ch'u (q.v.) of the Warring States Period (5th-3rd centuries B.C., q.v.). He was a member of the royal house disappointed in his official career. He was particularly upset by the monarch's failure to perceive a diplomatic ruse from the state of Ch'in (q.v.). The long-term result was the fall of Ch'u to Ch'in, one of the last of the steps before Ch'in established hegemony over all of China. CH'Ü did not live to see that, reportedly committing suicide by jumping into a river. That event is commemorated to this day by the Dragon Boat Festival (q.v.).

CH'Ü was the author of Li Sao, "On Encountering Sorrow," a long allegorical poem which is the most famous of a collection called Ch'u Tz'u, "The Songs of the South." Although the entire collection was originally attributed to CH'Ü, later scholarship assigns some of the poems to others. CH'Ü was the first Chinese to become famous primarily as a poet, though others before him had written poetry. His biography is included in the Shih Chi (q.v.) and the collection of poems has for centuries been a part of the curriculum for any aspiring Chinese literary scholar.

Hawkes, David. Ch'u Tz'u: The Songs of the South. Boston: Beacon Press, 1962.

Waters, Geoffrey R. Three Elegies of Ch'u. Madison: University of Wisconsin Press, 1985.

CHUANG Tzu (329 [?]-286 [?] B.C.). Taoist philosopher. His name, meaning Master CHUANG, is also applied to the book he wrote, one of the most entertaining of the Chinese classics. The book is an essential part of the canon of Taoism (q.v.).

Chuang Tzu. Burton Watson, trans. The Complete Works of Chuang Tzu. New York: Columbia University Press, 1969.

Waley, Arthur. Three Ways of Thought in Ancient China. London: Allen & Unwin, 1939.

Chü-jen. See under **Examination system**.

CHU-KO Liang (181-234). He was prime minister of the kingdom of Shu Han, one of the Three Kingdoms (q.v.), and reputedly the greatest military strategist of his era, though he was not a soldier. Because he is a key figure in the Romance of the Three Kingdoms (q.v.), China's first novel, and in many of the dramas which are based on it, his name and many of his strategems are known to all Chinese familiar with the traditional culture, and to millions of other Asians.

Ch'un Ch'iu. See under **Five Classics**.

Ch'ung Te. See under **Abahai**.

Chungking (Chongqing). Population: 6,300,000 (1980). Commercial center and largest city in Szechwan province (q.v.), it lies at the confluence of the Kialing (Jialing) and Yangtze rivers, some 1,400 miles from the sea. Chungking was opened to foreign trade as a treaty port (q.v.) in 1890, and its status was confirmed by the Treaty of Shimonoseki (1895, q.v.). It had an estimated population of 500,000 in the 1920s; but that number increased dramatically after 1937, when Chungking became the wartime capital of the Nationalist government.

Civil War (1946-1949). Full-scale civil war between the forces of the Chinese Communist party (CCP) and those of the Kuomintang (KMT, qq.v.) broke out within months of the surrender of Japan in August 1945, at the end of World War II (q.v.). Disagreement between the two parties was both doctrinal and historical. In 1927, after several years of cooperation, the KMT, on the initiative of CHIANG Kai-shek (q.v.), purged CCP members from its ranks and by 1934 had limited the CCP to the control of a very small area. In October 1934, CCP forces, led by MAO Tse-tung (q.v.), abandoned their base in Kiangsi province (q.v.) and commenced the Long March (q.v.) which ended the following year at Yenan, Shensi province (q.v.). KMT forces harassed them en route, and war between the two parties was only suspended by the truce and the anti-Japanese alliance which resulted from the Sian Incident (q.v.) of December 1936. It was then agreed that CCP forces were to be integrated into the Nationalist army to fight against Japan. That proved to be unworkable, and the forces spent much of World War II in opposition to each other as much as against Japan. During this period, CCP forces showed remarkable growth. Of the 100,000 who left Kiangsi in 1934, fewer than 10,000 arrived in Yenan; however, by the end of the war in 1945, party membership was estimated at 1.2 million, with another .9 million in the armed forces, controlling an area with a population of 90 million, largely in the north and northwest.

In February 1945, leaders of Great Britain, the United States and the USSR met at the Yalta Conference (q.v.) and agreed that the USSR would enter the war against Japan after the defeat of Germany. In return, the Soviets demanded restoration of rights in Manchuria (q.v.) which had been lost in the Russo-Japanese War (1904-1905, q.v.). The Western allies agreed, and the responsibility for conveying these terms to the Chinese was accepted by the United States.

When apprised of the terms, the Chinese pointed out that they conflicted with the Sino-Soviet Treaty of May 31, 1924; however, they proceeded to negotiate a new Sino-Soviet treaty (qq.v.). The terms

agreed upon included a Soviet promise to give moral support and military aid solely to the national government as the central government of China.

The USSR declared war on Japan on August 8, 1945, the day the second atomic bomb was dropped (on Nagasaki, Japan), and Soviet troops entered Manchuria the following day. By the end of the month they had completed the occupation of the area and proceeded to loot and destroy the Japanese industrial establishment there, thus denying to the Chinese a desperately needed industrial base. Chinese Communist troops were permitted to enter from adjacent areas and were armed with surrendered Japanese weapons. Nationalist troops were denied entry through Soviet-held Dairen (q.v.), but did eventually push their way into Manchuria and by mid-1946 held most of the major cities. The Communist troops controlled most of the countryside.

American efforts to mediate between the CCP and the KMT, notably the Marshall Mission (q.v.), failed, and by late 1946 civil war between the two forces was in full swing. At first the Nationalist forces seemed to be successful, but eventual victory went to the Communists, who established the People's Republic of China (q.v.) in Peking on October 1, 1949. The Nationalist defeat has been attributed to military ineptitude, but there were other factors. One was that the communist forces were better skilled at guerrilla warfare, and used their experience fighting the Japanese to good effect against the Nationalists. By cutting railroads which had operated without hindrance for the Japanese, the Communists were able to disrupt Nationalist communications and transport. Nationalist morale was affected not only by military reversals, but also by the economic disruption whose most conspicuous expression was massive inflation.

Botjer, George. *A Short History of Nationalist China: 1919-1949*. New York: G.P. Putnam's Sons, 1979.

Coal. The use of coal may date as far back as the third century A.D. Certainly it was known and used during the Sui dynasty (589-618 A.D., q.v.) and the Japanese monk Ennin (q.v.) noted its presence and use in 838 A.D. Coal was mined and widely used during the Sung dynasty (960-1279 A.D., q.v.), and Marco Polo (q.v.) reports on its use also.

In 1984 China produced 772 million metric tons of coal; the second largest producer, after the United States, in the world. In that year coal accounted for 70 percent of China's energy.

Coeducation. Though rarely, individual Chinese women did learn to read and write, although Chinese tradition disapproved of education for women. The earliest schools for girls were established by Christian missionaries in the 19th century. In the early 20th century, segregated government schools were established in major cities. The May Fourth Movement (q.v.) of 1919 included representatives of all the middle and high schools of Peking, and the resolution to introduce coeducation evolved from that. Women students were permitted to audit courses at Peking University early in 1920, and by summer were admitted as students, setting a national precedent. In fact, Canton Christian College had actually started the practice in 1918, but this did not have the same impact.

Cohong. Properly, kung hang (gong hang). Name applied to the corporation of merchants at Canton who had the exclusive right to conduct foreign trade. While occasionally suspended, it controlled the trade for most of the period from 1760 until it was abolished by the Treaty of Nanking (1842, q.v.). The chief merchant of the monopoly bore the title of Howqua (q.v.), meaning great official, but most Westerners assumed it was his name.

Membership in the Cohong was practically a guarantee of immense wealth during the 80 years it lasted, as the foreign merchants were effectively prevented from dealing with anyone else. Dissatisfaction with the system was a contributory factor in the rise of the opium trade and the outbreak of the Opium War (1839-1842, qq.v.).

College of Foreign Languages. See under **T'ung-wen Kuan**.

Comprador (Compradore). A Portuguese word meaning "buying agent," it was first used to designate the chief servant of a European household in Asia; then applied to the chief native employee of a foreign firm; and eventually came to mean any Chinese whose occupation was broker or middleman between Europeans and other Chinese. By the late 19th and early 20th centuries, it came to have pejorative connotations, particularly among Chinese revolutionaries, who criticized the "compradore mentality."

Confucian classics. See under **Five Classics**.

Confucianism. This is a school of thought based on the teachings of Confucius (551-479 B.C., q.v.). Confucius taught that the early period of the Chou dynasty (Western Chou, 1122-771 B.C.) was a golden age, and that to restore such a golden age it was necessary for the feudal leaders of his time to observe *li*, sometimes translated as "rites," and to practice *jen*, or "benevolence."

In the years following his death, his school of thought was carried on by such philosophers as HSUN Tzu and Mencius (qq.v.) and was one of the dominant influences in the period of the Warring States (484-221 B.C., q.v.). This period was the most philosophically diverse in Chinese history, and the contenders were sometimes referred to as "the hundred schools of thought." The main schools were Confucianism, Legalism, Mohism and Taoism (qq.v.), but there were many others.

The elimination of all the other states by Ch'in and the establishment of the Ch'in dynasty by Ch'in Shih Huang Ti (qq.v.) in 221 B.C. was a victory for the Legalists, since the Ch'in state was organized according to Legalism's totalitarian principles. The Ch'in dynasty was replaced by the Han in 206 B.C. (q.v.) and the Confucianists took their revenge. The Ch'in had burned the Confucian classics (see **Five Classics**), along with all other texts which did not conform to the Ch'in canon, and executed a great many Confucianists. But the Han dynasty officially adopted Confucianism, while retaining many Legalist structures for the control of the population. Confucianism remained the official philosophy, with some lapses, until the beginning of the 20th century.

Confucianism concerned itself specifically with relations between prince and minister, man and wife, father and son, elder brother and younger brother, friend and friend. Confucius refused to discuss the spirit world, advising only to sacrifice to the spirits "as if they were there." Since the Confucian tradition required a man to have a son to sacrifice at his grave, the practice of celibacy was thoroughly disapproved of.

But while Confucian philosophy was technically dominant, and the imperial examinations (see under **Examination system**) continued to be based on study of the Confucian classics, Buddhism (q.v.) attracted the attention of intellectuals, particularly after the fall of the Han dynasty in 221 A.D. In the rapid succession of minor states and dynasties which followed, the message of Buddhism seemed to have more validity than the Confucian tradition of stable relations under a sage-king.

This situation persisted until the middle of the T'ang dynasty, 618-906 A.D. The first scholar to speak out boldly and effectively was HAN Yü (768-824, q.v.), who, in doing so, laid the basis for Neo-Confucianism (q.v.). This was a synthesis which included certain concepts from Buddhism and popular Taoism in the Confucian scheme of beliefs. Its most effective spokesman was CHU Hsi (1130-1200, q.v.), a scholar and philosopher of the Southern Sung (1127-1279, see under **Sung**). He set the syllabus of the "Four Books" (q.v.) which was the standard for Chinese education for the next 800 years.

The decline of Confucianism was a result of a combination of factors. Study of the Confucian classics had for centuries been the key to the examination system and the subsequent attainment of wealth and power by successful aspirants. The arrival of the 19th century and the technical superiority of the Europeans cast doubt on the concept of the Confucian gentleman as the ideal government official. (It might be noted that many millions of Chinese had come to that conclusion quite independent of Western intellectual challenges.)

Another problem was the disappearance of the Confucian state.

The earliest Confucian rites were performed by feudal lords who went through rituals of various kinds. Over the centuries this had become a system in which the emperor made annual sacrifices to Heaven and Earth. With the abolition of the empire, there were no more rites to be performed, and no one to perform them. A Confucianist could not expect to be appointed a minister in a republican government on the basis of his acquaintance with the Confucian canon.

While there is no longer a Confucian state, and civil service examinations on the Confucian canon have not been administered since the beginning of the 20th century, traditional Chinese scholars continue to offer survey courses in the classics. Chinese occasionally quote the sage, and the persistence of this influence caused Confucius to become a target of the Cultural Revolution (q.v.) in the 1960s and 1970s.

Nivison, David S., and Arthur F. Wright, eds. *Confucianism in Action*. Stanford: Stanford University Press, 1959.

Wright, Arthur F. *The Confucian Persuasion*. Stanford: Stanford University Press, 1960.

Confucius (551-479 B.C.). The Latin version of K'UNG Fu Tzu, which means Master K'UNG, Confucius is also known as K'UNG Tzu. His real name was K'UNG Ch'iu, but it would be disrespectful to refer to him in this familiar way. A long chapter in the *Shih Chi* (q.v.) is devoted to his biography. He was born in the state of Lu of an impoverished noble family. His father died when he was an infant, and he was brought up by his mother. He married at 19 and started on an official career. He attained the position of prime minister of the state of Lu but, disappointed at the dissolute ways of his ruler, he resigned in 497 B.C. and later commenced his travels. Accompanied by many of his disciples, he spent 13 years in other states before returning to Lu. He died some three years later; his tomb remains in Shantung province (q.v.), near Chüfu.

Confucius was the first man in Chinese history to support himself by teaching, that is, by charging tuition to his students. He was also the first to make instruction available to commoners. Previously, education was provided to members of the nobility by officials paid by the ruler for other services. Confucius moved from court to court, discussing matters of state with the various rulers and accepting their support without actually having an official position.

Confucius is traditionally credited with composing the *Spring and Autumn Annals*, and editing the *Book of Songs* and the *Book of History*. Our best view of the man himself is in the *Analects of Confucius*, a work compiled by his disciples. The *Analects* is an anecdotal compilation, showing the philosopher in a wide variety of situations and describing his actions and reactions. It bears no resemblance to a systematic treatise of Confucianism, though it is certainly the source from which that philosophy springs.

His instruction was not pragmatic. He declined to teach agriculture, and was critical of pupils with an interest in commerce. What he taught might be called propriety, if it is understood that this means that proper actions by rulers and officials would result in a peaceful and prosperous polity.

Confucius was not an innovator and looked back with favor upon the practices of the early Chou dynasty (q.v.), which by his time held de jure authority only. While his stress on continuing the ancient sacrifices raises the question of his belief in spirits, he seems to have circumscribed the issue by commenting: "When still unable to do your duty to men, how can you do your duty to the spirits?" (*Analects*, XI,11.) If Confucius was not concerned with the spirits, nor with man's relationship to god (or gods), he was concerned with what became known as the five relationships and with terrestrial harmony. (Also see **Mencius** and **Confucianism**.)

Fung, Yu-lan, and Derk Bodde, trans. *A History of Chinese Philosophy*. Princeton: Princeton University Press, 1952.

Conventions of Peking. Signed October 24, 1860, by I-hsin (q.v.) for China and Lord Elgin for Great Britain, and October 25 by I-hsin and Baron Gros for France. The conventions confirmed the terms of the Treaties of Tientsin (q.v.), provided for permanent residence in Peking for foreign envoys; for the opening of Tientsin as a treaty port (q.v.); the lease of Kowloon to Britain; and promised that all property confiscated from Catholic missions would be returned.

Coolie Trade. The word "coolie," probably of Tamil origin, has been translated into Chinese characters meaning bitter labor. It refers to those who earn their livings by physical exertion. The coolie trade was a system under which Chinese laborers were sent abroad under contract. It developed in the 1840s, and demand for Chinese labor increased as anti-slavery sentiment cut off the supply of African slaves. The major destinations of coolies included the West Indies and Peru.

In the early years of the trade, government concern for Chinese resident abroad was limited by the fact that emigration (q.v.) was banned. The British and French included clauses permitting recruitment of Chinese labor in the Treaties of Tientsin (1858, q.v.). The conditions of recruitment (which sometimes included kidnapping) were frequently bad, as were transportation and working conditions. As a result, in 1866 the Ch'ing government established regulations to govern the trade, but the British and French governments refused to ratify them, under pressure from British planters and French shippers. Spain accepted them in 1867, and the Chinese regulations did control conditions of recruitment, except in Macao, which remained a sore spot until the trade was outlawed there in 1873.

Cotton. Cotton is indigenous to tropical Asia, where it appears in a perennial as well as an annual form. It requires a dry season, and only the annual variety can be successfully grown in areas with a cold season. It was introduced from India around the end of the Han dynasty (q.v.), both over the Silk Road (q.v.) of Central Asia and through Indochina to Yunnan (q.v.). It is first noted as clothing of Buddhist priests, and references to it in T'ang poetry are frequent.

Cotton was grown in Central Asia and by non-Chinese in Yunnan considerably before it was grown in China. It was grown in Kwangtung and Fukien in the Sung dynasty (960-1279, qq.v.), and was introduced into North China from Central Asia in the 13th century. While it did not replace silk (q.v.) for luxury fabrics, cotton rapidly replaced most of the other vegetable fibers, such as hemp and ramie, which had been used since prehistoric times.

Schafer, Edward H. *The Golden Peaches of Samarkand: A Study of T'ang Exotics*.

Berkeley: University of California Press, 1963.

Wittfogel, Karl A., and Feng Chia-sheng. *History of Chinese Society: Liao (907-1125)*. Philadelphia: American Philosophical Society, 1949.

Cultural Revolution (1966-1976). Also known as the Great Proletarian Cultural Revolution (GPCR), it was launched in May 1966 by MAO Tse-tung (q.v.) to combat elitism, revisionism and the "bourgeois mentality" of the bureaucracy. It soon came under the control of MAO's wife, CHIANG Ch'ing (q.v.) and the Gang of Four (q.v.). The revolutionaries rejected most of China's traditional culture and brought education and many govern-ment activities to a complete halt.

In August 1966, the Soviet embassy in Peking was the target of demonstrations by students and Red Guards (q.v.). In September all embassies in Peking were requested to repatriate their student nationals. In October the USSR announced the expulsion of all Chinese students in retaliation. In January 1967 all Chinese studying abroad were recalled to participate in the GPCR. Demonstrations around the Soviet embassy increased, and Soviet diplomatic dependents were sent home, suffering ill treatment at the hands of the Red Guards at the airport. The Soviet embassy was attacked in August 1967, and the British legation was burned.

According to Soviet press reports, Red Guard activities in Sinkiang province led to the flight of hundreds of thousands of minority people to the USSR. The Red Guards were active in Tibet destroying hundreds of monasteries and temples there. Within China, they not only attacked and destroyed religious structures, they vandalized private homes and destroyed libraries, furniture and works of art.

The Red Guards attacked most of the leaders of the government and the party, with the exception of MAO and CHIANG Ch'ing. CHOU En-lai (q.v.) played a complex role in that he seemed to be a supporter and a leader at first, but was eventually criticized for his bourgeois background and even held hostage by the Red Guards for a brief period. CHOU also sought to protect some of his colleagues and other members of the Communist elite, though not always successfully.

The Cultural Revolution came to an end only with the death of MAO on September 9, 1976. One month later the Gang of Four and many of their followers were arrested and tried. Several are still in prison.

Robinson, Thomas W., ed. *The Cultural Revolution in China*. Berkeley: University of California Press, 1971.

D

Dalien. See under **Dairen**.

Dairen. Japanese name for the port of Dalien (Lüda), located near Port Arthur (Lüshun) on the Liaotung peninsula (qq.v.). Population: 4,270,000 (1978). Dairen is the major port for the three provinces of the Northeast (Manchuria). The city was occupied by Russia when the latter leased the Liaotung peninsula in 1898, and by Japan in 1905, in the aftermath of the Russo-Japanese War (1904-1905, q.v.). The Japanese laid the foundations for the major port and industrial city it is now. In 1945, at the end of World War II, Dairen was jointly occupied by the USSR and Chinese authorities. The Soviets left after the establishment of the People's Republic of China (q.v.) on October 1, 1949.

Dalai Lama. Title of the spiritual and temporal rulers of Tibet (q.v.) from 1642 to 1959. It means "Ocean of Wisdom" in Mongolian, and was bestowed in 1578 by the Mongol Altan Khan on the Tibetan Sonam Gyatso (1543-1588), abbot of Drepung Monastery and the most eminent lama of the Yellow Sect of Tibetan Buddhism of his time. Since he was third in his line, he became the third Dalai Lama. Each Dalai Lama is considered to be a reincarnation of his predecessor, and all of them successive reincarnations of the boddhisattva (q.v.) Avalokitesvara, known in Tibetan as Chen-re-zi.

Since no reincarnation can occur until after the death of the previous lama, each successor is identified as a very young child, and while his reign is considered to start from birth, he does not begin to rule until he reaches his majority.

The 4th and 5th Dalai Lamas were Mongols, and it was the 5th, Ngawang Lobsang Gyatso (1617-1682), who assumed both spiritual and temporal authority in 1642 with the support of Gushi Khan, leader of the Khoshote tribe of the Western Mongols. His rule over Tibet was recognized in 1652 by Emperor Shun Chih (r. 1644-1661), of the Ch'ing dynasty (1644-1911, qq.v.).

The Depa, or administrator, for the 5th Dalai Lama concealed his death until 1696, when under Ch'ing pressure he announced that the 6th would accede to power in 1697. The young man proved dissolute and was assassinated in 1706. Another lama was named in his place, but was not accepted.

In 1720 a Ch'ing army invaded Tibet, bringing with them the 7th Dalai Lama. His reign was from 1708 to 1757, and his successor's from 1758 to 1804. The next four did not reach majority, and Tibet was ruled by regents from 1804 until 1895, when the 13th Dalai Lama, Thupten Gyatso, 1876-1933, acceded to power. His successor, the 14th Dalai Lama, Tenzin Gyatso, was born in 1935, and acceded to power at the age of 15 in November 1950, after the People's Republic of China announced plans for the liberation of Tibet. The Chinese invaded in 1951, and the Dalai Lama fled in 1959 to Dharamsala, India, where he was living in exile in 1986.

Description of the East. See under **Odoric of Pordenone**.

Disunity, Period of. See under **Period of Disunity**.

Door gods. These are pictures either painted on the doors of Taoist temples or occasionally pasted on other doors to preserve the sleep and serenity of the occupants from ghostly visitations. There are three door gods, of whom the most famous is WEI Cheng (q.v.). All three were real officials of the emperor T'ang Tai Tsung (r. 626-649, q.v.). According to the traditional account of their origin, the emperor was afflicted with dreams of ghosts and dragons. The officials stood outside his doors and guarded his sleep. They were later replaced with painted images.

A more complete account of the origin may be found in Chapter X of Arthur Waley's translation of the *Hsi Yu Chi* (q.v.), *Monkey*, as well as in Wechsler's book on WEI Cheng (q.v.).

Dorgon (1612-1650). Manchu prince and regent for Emperor Shun Chih. He was the son of Nurhaci, half-brother of Abahai and uncle of Shun Chih (qq.v.). Abahai gave him command of the Plain White Banner (see **Banners**) and named him a prince when he proclaimed himself emperor in 1636. Dorgon was a brave and effective soldier, commanding an army that raided 40 cities in northeastern China in 1639, returning with captives and booty. At Abahai's death in 1643, Dorgon was one of those proposed to succeed him, but he refused. Instead he became one of two regents for the young Shun Chih.

By 1643 the Ming dynasty (q.v.) was on the point of collapse. The Chinese general WU San-kuei (q.v.), facing the Manchu troops at Shanhaikuan, was ordered in May 1644 to come to the defense of Peking against the free-booter LI Tzu-ch'eng (q.v.), but Peking fell before he arrived. Unwilling to serve under the usurper, LI, WU surrendered his troops to Dorgon. Their combined forces defeated LI and entered Peking on June 6, 1644.

The Ming officials, demoralized by corruption and misrule at the end of the dynasty, and horrified by the slaughter and rapine inflicted by LI's troops, offered little resistance. Dorgon welcomed Chinese support, sent troops in pursuit of LI and made the transition from one dynasty to the next the least bloody in Chinese history.

Under Dorgon's direction the Ch'ing takeover of all of China made great progress. He centralized power and control in his own hands, punishing those princes who opposed him and generating considerable resentment in the process. Dorgon died suddenly on the last day of 1650, leaving only an adopted nephew as a male heir. Considerable confusion among the imperial clan resulted, with various contenders for the regency and/or its power. The new emperor abolished the regency on February 1, 1651, and Dorgon was denounced posthumously on March 12. This verdict was reversed by the emperor Ch'ien Lung (q.v.) in 1773.

Hummel, Arthur W., ed. *Eminent Chinese of the Ch'ing Period*. Washington: Government Printing Office, 1943.

Dragon Boat Festival. This occurs on the 5th day of the 5th month of the lunar calendar (q.v.). It is marked today in many places by boat races in which the boats, rowed by crews of young men, are decorated to look like dragons. (Chinese dragons inhabit lakes and rivers, or clouds. They are not denizens of the element of fire.) The festival originated in the Yangtze valley, or perhaps even further south, and may have been an annual propitiation of the water spirits. Floods have been a constant in Chinese history, and deaths by drowning not uncommon. For this reason, annual rites to appease the spirits, possibly even including human sacrifice, were customary.

The festival is now connected with the story of the poet CH'Ü Yüan (q.v.), who is said to have committed suicide by jumping into a river in about 288 B.C. CH'Ü was a court official of the Kingdom of Ch'u (q.v.) of the Warring States Period (fifth to third centuries B.C., q.v.). He opposed the monarch's diplomatic policy and drowned himself in protest. The mistaken policy eventually led to the destruction of the kingdom, thus vindicating the poet.

The festival is also celebrated by consuming cakes of rice and sweets with chopped meat, steamed in lotus leaves and tied with colored string. Originally, these cakes were thrown into the water to appease the ghost of the dead poet.

Eberhard, Wolfram. *Chinese Festivals.* New York: Henry Schuman, Inc., 1952.

Drama. Traditional Chinese drama, Peking opera being the most widely known in the West, has its origins in the performances of shamans as early as the Chou dynasty (1122-256 B.C., q.v.). Early classics mention such rituals with the shamans dressed in ceremonial costumes and dancing to musical accompaniment. Court performances of nonreligious singing and dancing are also mentioned.

Public performances of storytelling accompanied by acting are reported in the Han dynasty (206 B.C.-221 A.D., q.v.). The emperor T'ang Ming Huang (r. 713-755, q.v.) established the Li Yuan (Pear Garden, q.v.) as a training institute for singers and dancers. In the Sung dynasty (960-1279, q.v.), there were popular performances in all the major cities. However, the oldest extant dramatic texts date to the late 13th century, the early years of the Yuan dynasty (1279-1368, q.v.). In all, there are 171 Yuan plays extant. The Yuan, unlike the dynasties which preceded it, used many non-Chinese in official capacities. Consequently, many Chinese scholars turned their attention to vernacular literature, of which both novels (q.v.) and drama are examples. As a result, the Yuan is known as the golden age of Chinese drama, and many of its traditions persist to this day.

Traditional drama is accompanied by music, singing, and, usually, dancing. Customarily there are four or five acts, but the Western concept of dramatic unity is not observed. Exposition is straightforward, with each character explaining his role. The stage is bare except for a few props. Specific conventions indicate such things as dismounting from horseback or entering a doorway. The latter, for example, is shown by the actor taking a high step to indicate crossing a raised doorsill. Traditional houses had high doorsills, and it was customary to step over them, not on them, on entering. The audience, acquainted with the custom, accepted the pantomime without question.

There are four categories of roles: male, female, painted face and comic.

The painted faces are the most striking, and the character being portrayed can frequently be recognized by the pattern of his makeup. A number of colors are used, each with its own significance. Red symbolizes courage and loyalty; white symbolizes trickery; and green is used for evil spirits. The color of an actor's costume also has significance, but the symbolism is somewhat different.

The plots of the drama are derived from several sources. Many are historical, drawn from such eras as the Three Kingdoms (221-265 A.D., q.v.). The plays are not usually historically accurate, but they were often the way the largely illiterate population learned their history. Other operas, such as the *Romance of the West Chamber*, are simply fictional. Still others make use of the supernatural and are frequently based on stories written in the T'ang and Sung dynasties.

Convention usually divides these dramas into two categories: literary and military. This dichotomy reflects the two categories of officials who served the empire: the civilians who administered the country, and the military who protected it from outside invasion or internal rebellion. One aspect of the military dramas is the acrobatics which symbolize combat, always popular with the audience.

Hung, Josephine Huang, comp. *Classical Chinese Plays*. London: Vision Press, 1972.

Scott, A.C. *The Classical Theatre of China*. London: George Allen & Unwin, 1957.

Shih, Chung-wen. *The Golden Age of Chinese Drama: Yuan Tsa-chu*. Princeton: Princeton University Press, 1976.

The Dream of the Red Chamber. Known in Chinese as *Hung Lou Meng*, this is generally agreed to be the best novel of premodern China. It was first published in 1792, after having circulated in manuscript form for a generation. The author was TS'AO Hsueh-ch'in (Cao Xueqin), 1716 (?)-1763 (?), though the last 40 of its 120 chapters are sometimes ascribed to another hand. The story concerns the activities of different members of the very rich CHIA family, centering on the young hero, Pao-yu, and his relationships with the young maids and his female cousins. Unlike the *Chin P'ing Mei* (q.v.), this is not an erotic novel, though sexual relationships play a major part in the complex plot.

What makes the novel stand out from many stories written in the Ch'ing dynasty (1644-1911, q.v.), at least in the eyes of most Chinese critics, is the degree of character and personality development of each of the participants in its long and complex plot. The plot itself is concerned with the fall from favor of the CHIA family, and its near restoration to its previous position.

The author belonged to a family that had held imperial favor for several generations, and he was brought up under conditions of extreme wealth, which gave him first-hand knowledge of how a wealthy household was run in the early Ch'ing period. In 1728 the TS'AO family fell afoul of the emperor Yung-cheng (q.v.), and most of its property was confiscated. TS'AO Hsueh-chin spent the rest of his life in straitened circumstances.

Cao Xueqin, and David Hawkes, trans. *The Story of the Stone (Dream of the Red Chamber)*. Vols. 1-4. Bloomington: Indiana University Press, 1979-1983.

Hsia, C.T. *The Classic Chinese Novel*. New York: Columbia University Press, 1968.

Dunhuang. See **Tunhuang**.

Dynastic histories. The term refers to a series of official histories which provide China with the most extensive, continuous and accurate record of its past of any nation on earth. The first of these, the *Shih Chi* (q.v.), is not a dynastic history since it covers the history of China from the age of myth to the early years of the Han dynasty. The format, however, was followed by Pan Ku in his "History of the Former Han Dynasty" (qq.v.), and also by subsequent historians. The later histories were compiled by teams of historians, rather than by a single individual. It was considered the responsibility of a new dynasty to complete the history of its predecessor.

Not all Chinese historians have been happy with either the concept of dynastic histories or with the format set up in the *Shih Chi*. While the original format fits political and military developments to some extent, economic and cultural developments are not adequately provided for. The Sung dynasty (q.v.) historian, SSU-MA Kuang (q.v.), for this reason wrote a very long account of Chinese history covering the period from 403 B.C. to 959 A.D.

Because of the format of the histories, translations are more useful to scholars than to the general public. In 1739, the Ch'ing government started a new recension of the 21 histories then accepted as authorized. The number was increased to 24 later in the century, and, with the completion of the draft history of the Ch'ing and its publication in 1927-28, the accepted canon now stands at 25.

According to an estimate made by Homer H. Dubs, translator of the *History of the Former Han Dynasty* (in three volumes), it would require about 45 million English words to translate the 25 dynastic histories, which are only a portion of the historic records still extant.

Gardner, Charles S. *Chinese Traditional Historiography*. Cambridge: Harvard University Press, 1961.

Hsia (Xia) 2205-1766 B.C. (traditional dates)				
Shang/Yin 1766-1122 B.C. (traditional dates)				
Western Chou (Zhou) 1122-771 B.C. Eastern Chou (Zhou) 700-255 B.C. Spring & Autumn Period 774-484 B.C. Warring States Period 484-221 B.C.				
Ch'in (Qin) 221-206 B.C. Western Han 206 B.C.-8 A.D. Hsin (Xin) 9-23 A.D. Eastern Han 25-221 A.D.				

Period of Disunity

Three Kingdoms: Wei 220-266 A.D., Wu 222-280 A.D., Shu-Han 221-263 A.D.		
Western Chin (Jin) 266-316 A.D.		
Sixteen Kingdoms in the north 302-439 A.D.	Imperial Dynasties in the south: Eastern Chin (Jin) 317-420 A.D. Earlier Sung (Song) 420-479 A.D.	
Northern Wei 386-534 A.D. Western & Eastern Wei 534-557 A.D.	Southern Ch'i (Qi) 479-502 A.D. Southern Liang 502-557 A.D. Southern Ch'en (Chen) 557-589 A.D.	
Northern Ch'i (Qi) 550-577 A.D.	Northern Chou (Zhou) 557-581 A.D.	Later Liang 555-587 A.D.

Sui 589-618 A.D.			
T'ang (Tang) 618-906 A.D.			

Hsi Hsia (Xi Xia) (Tibetans) 882-1227 A.D.	Liao (Khitan) 907-1125 A.D.	The 5 Dynasties: Later Liang 907-923 A.D. Later T'ang (Tang) 923-936 A.D. Later Chin (Jin) 936-947 A.D. Later Han 947-951 A.D. Later Chou (Zhou) 951-960 A.D.	Ten Kingdoms 901-979 A.D.
		Northern Sung (Song) 960-1127 A.D.	
	Chin (Jin) (Juchen) 1115-1234 A.D.	Southern Sung (Song) 1127-1279 A.D.	

Yuan (Mongol) 1206-1368 A.D.
Ming 1368-1643 A.D.
Ch'ing (Qing) (Manchu) 1644-1911 A.D.

E

Eight Immortals. The most popular example of the iconography of Taoism (q.v.), the company in its present form dates from the Sung dynasty (960-1279 A.D., q.v.). They pertain to Taoism as a popular religion, rather than as a school of philosophy. To make the eight figures identifiable to illerate devotees, each carries an emblematic object, such as a flute, a flywhisk, a lotus blossom etc. Each of the eight is identified with some positive attribute, such as longevity, fertility etc., and each is regarded as the patron divinity of some guild, such as barbers, actors, musicians, flowervendors etc. Representations of the eight can usually be found in Taoist temples, where they may be the objects of veneration, but are also frequently found as good-luck symbols in the decoration of everyday articles.

Eight-legged Essay. The term refers to a highly structured essay form used in the civil service examinations (see **Examination system**) during the Ming (1368-1644) and Ch'ing (1644-1911) dynasties (qq.v.). Success in the examinations was the prerequisite to an official career, which made mastery of the essay form an essential. Criticism of the examination system was frequently phrased in terms of criticizing the essay. Toward the end of the 19th century the weakness of the declining Ch'ing dynasty in dealing with the European powers was increasingly clear. Many of the reformers, e.g., K'ang Yu-wei (q.v.), attributed much of China's backwardness to the method of recruiting officials which stressed skills in essay writing on subjects derived from the Confucian classics, rather than expertise in areas of modern knowledge.

Emigration. Chinese emigration dates from the T'ang dynasty (618-906 A.D., q.v.) or even earlier. The earliest emigrants were traders who settled in Southeast Asia (see under **Overseas Chinese**). Emigration was usually illegal, but the ban was not actively enforced. From the imperial point of view, emigrants were criminals, and not of concern to the Chinese government.

The rise of anti-slavery sentiment in the 19th century provided an opportunity for the development of the coolie trade (q.v.), under which Chinese laborers were sent abroad under contract, replacing African slaves. For the first time, Chinese laborers appeared in Hawaii, California, the West Indies (notably Cuba), and Peru. Most of them worked on plantations, but in California they built railroads, among other things. In 1866 the Chinese government established regulations to govern the trade, and by the early 1870s it had been eliminated.

The first Chinese immigrants to the United States (q.v.) arrived in California in response to the gold rush of 1848. They were welcomed because of a perceived need for labor, and by 1853 there were 25,000 in that state. The economic depression which followed made the Chinese unwanted competitors, and in 1855 California passed the first in a series of legislative acts discriminating against them. Yet the treaty negotiated in 1868 by Secretary of State William H. Seward and Anson Burlingame (q.v.), representing China, provided for free immigration. On that basis the restrictive laws were declared unconstitutional.

Anti-Chinese sentiment continued to rise in the United States, and in 1880 the first of several treaties severely restricting Chinese immigration was negotiated. By law, Chinese immigrants could not apply for naturalization, though children born in the United States were accepted as American citizens. The next restrictive step was to ban immigration of those ineligible for naturalization. The problem became a major issue between the two countries and was finally laid to rest only by passage of the Immigration and Naturalization Act of 1952.

Chinese emigrants also found the doors closing in Southeast Asia. The European colonial powers strictly controlled immigration, as did Thailand, the only independent state in the area prior to World War II. The successor states have not encouraged immigration, and some have moved toward enforced assimilation by closing Chinese-operated schools and banning Chinese-language publications and even shop signs. While Chinese emigration continues, it is on a limited basis, restricted mostly by the receiving countries.

Huang, Tsen-ming. *The Legal Status of the Chinese Abroad*. Taipei: China Cultural Service, 1954 (reprint).

Emperors. The Chinese term for emperor is *huang-ti*. The first ruler to use the term was Ch'in Shih Huang Ti, the ruler of the state of Ch'in during the Warring States Period (qq.v.). Since that time, except for periods of disunity and unrest, China has theoretically been under one of a long series of emperors belonging to different dynasties.

The personal name of an emperor was taboo, not only during his reign, but throughout the dynasty until its fall. For this reason each emperor was posthumously given a temple name by which he would be known. With the exception of rulers of the Ming and Ch'ing dynasties, it is this temple name which is familiar to students of Chinese history, preceded by the name of the dynasty, e.g., Han Wu Ti (reigned 140-87 B.C.) and T'ang T'ai Tsung (reigned 627-649 A.D., qq.v.).

The fourth ruler of the Han dynasty, Han Wen Ti (reigned 179-157 B.C.) was the first to adopt a reign title, which could be used to refer to a specific date, i.e., the fourth year of the Hou Yuan reign. His successor used two, and the sixth, Han emperor Han Wu Ti, used eleven in succession. The occasion for changing the reign title might be either good or evil fortune. This pattern continued until the end of the Yuan dynasty (1279-1367, q.v.).

The establishment of the Ming dynasty (1368-1644, q.v.) saw a new development: the adoption of a reign title and its retention throughout the reign. An apparent deviation occurred when the sixth emperor, whose reign title was Cheng T'ung, was captured by the Mongols in 1450 and released after several years. Upon resuming the throne, he adopted a new reign title, T'ien Shun. For this reason the Ming dynasty has 17 reign titles, but only 16 emperors. For the Ch'ing dynasty (1644-1911, q.v.), each emperor had only one reign title.

The fact that individual Ch'ing emperors are known in the West by the reign titles they used rather than the posthumous temple names later bestowed was the deciding factor in listing their entries that way in this book. Since many of the Ming emperors are also known by their reign titles, particularly by students of Chinese porcelains, they are also listed in that way.

Not all of the scores of China's emperors are included in this book. Those that are included are listed by dynasty and temple name (e.g., Han Wu Ti) until 1368. Ming emperors are listed by dynasty and reign title (e.g., Ming Yung Lo, reigned 1403-1424), and Ch'ing emperors by reign title alone (e.g., K'ang Hsi, r. 1662-1722).

Since the beginning of a new reign was supposed to start at the beginning of a new lunar year, there are some anomalies in the dating of traditional Chinese historiography. There is at least one example of an emperor being assigned a year when, in fact, he had reigned for a few weeks or months and died in the preceding year.

The rules of inheritance of the throne varied from one dynasty to the next. Chinese dynasties tended toward inheritance by the oldest son, particularly if his mother was the empress, rather than one of the lesser consorts. The Tartar dynasties, including the Ch'ing, tended toward traditions of inheritance which involved selecting the most fit from a pool of eligible males, usually the sons of the preceding emperor. Both systems led to intense and frequently fatal competition, and experience with naming an heir apparent did not appear to solve the problem. In fact, it was never satisfactorily solved before the fall of the last dynasty in 1911.

There are only two examples of women holding imperial power in their own names: Empress Kao of the Han dynasty, who reigned from 188-181 B.C., and Empress Wu (q.v.) of the T'ang dynasty, who reigned from 690-704 B.C. The latter changed the name of the dynasty from T'ang to Chou, and earned the execration of Confucian scholars by her seizure of power and her executions of members of the T'ang imperial family. Empress Kao, also known as Empress Lü, has no such reputation.

Chinese history has a number of examples of women exercising imperial power "from behind the screen." The best known to Westerners is Empress Dowager Tz'u Hsi (1835-1908, q.v.). She has several Chinese names, but the one most widely used is Tz'u Hsi. She was the consort of one emperor, the mother of another, and the aunt of a third. With the exception of a period of a few months in 1898, she acted as regent for the empire for nearly half a century.

There are other examples and all are deplored by traditional Chinese historians, who cite them as examples of the evil influence of women in general, in accordance with customary Confucian views.

Traditionally the emperors were surrounded by women and eunuchs (q.v.), who tended to be the only companions of their leisure hours, since officials would be present only for more formal purposes. This gave rise to factional infighting between the eunuchs' party and the party of the officials. Occasionally the family of the favorite consort would also seek to achieve wealth and prominence through imperial, though irregular, appointments.

Empress Dowager Tz'u Hsi (Ci Xi). 1835-1908. A Manchu (q.v.), her maiden name was Yehonala. She entered, as a concubine, the court of the seventh Ch'ing emperor, whose reign title was Hsien Feng (r. 1851-1861, q.v.). Though not his senior consort, she became his favorite and bore his only surviving son. Tz'u Hsi is said to have assisted the emperor in dealing with state papers, thereby gaining insight into the workings of the court. As the new emperor, T'ung Chih (r. 1862-1874, q.v.), was only five years old when his father died, the two empresses (Tz'u Hsi and the late emperor's senior consort) ruled as co-regents, with Tz'u Hsi gradually assuming authority and responsibility.

T'ung Chih's marriage in 1872 brought the regency to an end, but Tz'u Hsi's influence did not decline. After T'ung Chih's death in January 1875, she engineered the choice of her nephew, who reigned as Kuang Hsu (q.v.) from 1875 to 1908, as successor. This was a clear violation of the Ch'ing dynastic law of succession, as Kuang Hsu was of the same generation as his predecessor. The motives for Tz'u Hsi's choice, however, were clear. If T'ung Chih's successor were of the next generation, her hated daughter-in-law would become Empress Dowager, with painful results for Tz'u Hsi. Her daughter-in-law, rumored to be pregnant, committed suicide.

Kuang Hsu came of age in 1886, but Tz'u Hsi did not surrender the regency until his marriage in 1889. Even then she continued to read all state documents. As regent for her son, and later for her nephew, Tz'u Hsi became the most important figure at the court for nearly half a century before her death.

Foreign encroachments on the Chinese empire reached their peak during the period of Tz'u Hsi's influence. The vassal states detached included the Liu Ch'iu Islands, Burma, Korea and Vietnam (qq.v.). Rebellion in Central Asia provided Russia with an opportunity to occupy Kuldja and Ili, though most of the area was restored to Chinese control by TSO Tsung-t'ang (q.v.). The Sino-Japanese War (1894-1895, q.v.), resulted in the cession of Taiwan to Japan. In 1898, China was forced to grant leases of territory to Germany, Russia, France and Great Britain.

Tz'u Hsi must bear some responsibility, though China's plight was not of her making. Its defeat by France in 1884 made China's naval weakness painfully clear. Money was appropriated to build a modern naval force, but Tz'u Hsi still resented the destruction of the Summer Palace (q.v.) in 1860, and diverted vast sums for the construction of a new one between 1886 and 1891. As a result, China's navy was unprepared for the Sino-Japanese War.

That defeat, and the pressure of foreign powers for territorial leases, led many Chinese to believe that China was about to be dismembered, and encouraged the emperor to undertake the Hundred Days Reform (q.v.), which lasted from June 11 to September 20, 1898. On that day the Empress Dowager, reportedly learning of a plot to take her prisoner, intervened and resumed the regency. The next day she placed the emperor in confinement and rescinded the reform decrees. She assumed the regency until her death.

In 1900, the Boxer Rebellion (q.v.) ended in the occupation of Peking by an international military force, Tz'u Hsi and the emperor in flight and a punitive settlement dictated by the foreign powers. Tz'u Hsi was known to dislike foreigners, but her support of the Boxers is puzzling. It seems unlikely that she could have believed their claims to supernatural powers, or that the massacre of the diplomatic community in Peking and the missionaries in North China would remove the problems they represented.

On November 14, 1908, Kuang Hsu died. On the following day the empress dowager died, thus giving rise to rumors that the emperor had been murdered. The interval gave her the opportunity to name her grandnephew, P'u Yi (q.v.), to succeed his uncle as the last emperor of the Ch'ing dynasty. She had ruled China directly for 37 years, and indirectly for another 11. After her death it was reported that she had left a private fortune in silver and gold in the palace vaults valued at $100 million.

Hummel, Arthur W., ed. *Eminent Chinese of the Ch'ing Period*. Washington: Government Printing Office, 1943.

Empress Wu (625-705 A.D.). Usually known as WU Tse-t'ien, her original name is WU Chao. She entered the palace as a member of T'ang T'ai Tsung's (q.v.) female entourage in 638. The emperor died in 649, and WU Chao, with all the other court ladies, entered a Buddhist nunnery. Late in 650, she left the convent and returned to the palace, this time as a concubine of the new emperor, T'ang Kao Tsung (q.v.). Palace intrigue was behind this move, but in the Chinese view, both then and later, such an arrangement was incestuous.

WU Chao soon managed to dispose of her two main rivals, and not long after being named empress, had the ex-empress and another rival murdered. She took advantage of the emperor's illness in 660 to take her place beside his, though at first behind a screen. This was later dispensed with, and she ruled openly.

After Kao Tsung's death in December 683, WU Chao ruled as empress dowager until 690, when she established herself as the first empress of the Chou dynasty (q.v.). She was overthrown on February 20, 705, and died in December. All later T'ang emperors were her descendants.

The two books cited below take somewhat different views of the Empress Wu. Fitzgerald makes no excuses for her brutality toward her rivals and towards officials who opposed her, or who simply fell afoul of her plans. But he points out that at the end of her long rule China was "stronger, more united, and richer than ever before . . . ." That suggests that many of her policies were effective, whatever criticism of her personal morals may be made.

Lin's book takes the traditional Confucian view of a woman usurper, and provides lists of 23 members of her household, 50 T'ang princes and 36 high officials who were murdered on her orders, in many cases with members of their families.

Fitzgerald, C.P. *The Empress Wu*. Vancouver: University of British Columbia Press, 1970.

Lin, Yutang. *Lady Wu*. London: Heinemann, 1957.

Ennin (793-864 A.D.). Ennin, a Japanese Buddhist monk of the T'ien T'ai (q.v.) sect (Japanese: *Tendai*), is more commonly known in Japan by his posthumous title, Jikaku Daishi. A member of the last embassy sent by the Japanese imperial court to T'ang China in 838 A.D., he stayed until 847. He kept a diary of his years in China, the oldest extant first-hand report on China by any foreign observer. While not as well-known in

Japan as Marco Polo's (q.v.) later report is to Europeans, it bears comparison with it. Unlike Polo, Ennin was literate in Chinese before he went to China, and probably spoke the language before he returned home. Ennin started his Buddhist studies at the age of nine and became a monk at the age of 23. In 834 he was appointed a Scholar Monk to an embassy to China that finally sailed in 838. He hoped to visit Mt. T'ien T'ai (Chekiang province, q.v.), but permission was denied on the grounds that the time remaining before the return of the embassy to Japan was too short. He did visit Changan (see **Sian**), the T'ang capital, and Mt. Wu T'ai, a major center of the T'ien T'ai sect. The time of his arrival in China coincided with the apogee of Buddhist power and influence, but the flood tide started to recede immediately. Emperor T'ang Wu Tsung (r. 840-845) revealed himself as an ardent follower of Taoism (q.v.), Buddhism's chief rival at the time. In 842 the first edicts returning Buddhist monks and nuns to lay status, and expropriating temple property, appeared. The persecution reached its peak in 845. Early in 846, Wu Tsung died and was succeeded by the second Hsuan Tsung, who eased the anti-Buddhist measures. Ennin was able to return to Japan in 847, taking with him a number of texts and sacred objects, and, most important of all to historians, the diary of his years abroad.

Written in classical Chinese, the diary is filled with detailed descriptions of various aspects of the China he observed. It has been translated (see below), and together with the companion volume, *Ennin's Travels in T'ang China*, is of particular interest to students of Buddhism because of the details of the persecution which Ennin observed.

Reischauer, Edwin O. *Ennin's Diary*. New York: Ronald Press, 1955.

Reischauer, Edwin O. *Ennin's Travels in T'ang China*. New York: Ronald Press, 1955.

Eunuchs. Castrated males, incapable of siring offspring, were used by many imperial dynasties to attend the emperor and run the imperial household, from the Han dynasty (206 B.C.-221 A.D.) down to the end of the Ch'ing dynasty (1644-1911). Their duties ranged from the most menial to positions of great power. Conflict between the eunuchs and scholar-officials who competed for power was recurrent. Eunuchs were frequently accused of corruption and do not fare well in the dynastic histories (q.v.), which were compiled by officials.

Possibly the most widely-condemned eunuch in Chinese history was WEI Chung-hsien (1568-1627, q.v.), whose misrule has been credited by some historians with making a major contribution to the downfall of the Ming dynasty (1368-1644, q.v.). Another Ming period eunuch with a vastly different record was CHENG Ho (1371-1433, q.v.), an accomplished mariner who led several expeditions to India and as far as the African coast.

The example of eunuch power at the end of the Ming period led the early rulers of the Ch'ing dynasty (1644-1911, q.v.), to restrict eunuchs to palace activities, but in the declining years of the dynasty, notably during the period of the ascendancy of the empress dowager, 1835-1908 (q.v.), certain eunuchs held great power. As late as 1985 a few eunuchs of the Ch'ing dynasty still survived.

Examination system. The Chinese examination system dates from the reign of Emperor Han Wu Ti (140-86

B.C., q.v.). Candidates were recommended by high officials and were required to take a written examination. Since books existed only in manuscript form and were not easily available, this restricted the candidates to a small and privileged group. Nevertheless, throughout the Han from that period, China was governed by literate bureaucrats selected systematically.

Preservation of the system during the period of disunity which followed the fall of the Han in 221 A.D. was spotty, but the Sui (581-617, q.v.) set in place the system which the T'ang (618-906, q.v.) carried further. T'ang efforts to broaden the base of the official class hardly brought official appointments within the grasp of the poor, but it is worth noting that only 1 percent of those taking the examinations were successful. The goal of a profitable and successful government career encouraged large numbers to try.

The Sung (960-1279, q.v.) went even further in opening the examinations, by establishing schools in various prefectures. They were also aided by the spread of printing, which brought books within the reach of many more people. Examinations were held spottily under the non-Chinese dynasties which ruled the north (Liao [907-1125] and Chin [1115-1234]) and under the Yüan (1206-1368, qq.v.).

The system was revived and refined by the Ming. There were three levels of examinations. Candidates who passed the prefectural examination were called *hsiu-ts'ai* (or *sheng-yüan*). They were then eligible to take the next provincial examination, and if successful were designated *chü-jen*. These men were eligible for low-level appointments, or they could go on to take the metropolitan examinations. A subsequent palace examination ranked the successful *chin-shih* in order of excellence. The top few were appointed to the Hanlin Academy (q.v.).

The Ming system provided for the *chü-jen* and *chin-shih* examinations to be held triennially, and this lasted into the early 20th century. The proportion of candidates who made it through was less than one in a hundred at each level.

The subject matter of the examinations varied somewhat over the centuries, but the Confucian classics were always the dominant element.

It should be borne in mind that at no time were all Chinese officials successful graduates of the examination system. Few military officials were so qualified, and under the various foreign dynasties officials from the ruling group were appointed on recommendations only. That also happened under Chinese dynasties. Beginning in the Han, many rich men were encouraged to purchase office and status. The practice waxed and waned but never completely disappeared. Still, a remarkable number of China's bureaucrats over the last 2,000 years were selected on the basis of their qualifications as demonstrated by their skill in passing examinations.

The examination system made a great impression on the Jesuits (q.v.) in China, and through their reports made a similar impression on intellectual circles in Europe. The first European attempt to use the system was made in the 1690s in Prussia. It was later widely used in other countries and is now standard practice for certain government offices in many countries.

Extraterritoriality. The term is interchangeable with consular jurisdiction. It provides that a foreigner be subject to the jurisdiction of his own consular authorities rather than to that of the local legal system. Extraterritoriality was introduced to China by the Treaty of Nerchinsk, concluded with imperial Russia in 1689 (q.v.). In this case the privilege was mutual, and any subject of the Russian tsar was to be handed over to Russian authorities by the Chinese, and vice versa.

Extraterritoriality was one of the provisions of the Treaty of Nanking (1842), which ended the Opium War (qq.v.). The treaty provided the right to British subjects, and the later inclusion of the most-favored-nation provision in other treaties extended it to subjects/citizens of other nations which had treaties with China. This right was not reciprocal, however, and Chinese abroad enjoyed no such protection. At first, since emigration was illegal under Ch'ing dynasty (1644-1911) regulations, this was not a matter of great concern to the Chinese. By the end of the 19th century, however, it had come to be a source of deep Chinese resentment.

Starting in 1928, the Nationalist government opened negotiations with the Western powers to eliminate extraterritoriality. It was not successful and decided to abolish the practice by unilateral decree as of January 1, 1932. The Japanese invasion of Manchuria directed the government's attention to other matters and implementation was postponed.

On January 11, 1943, the Nationalist government signed new treaties with Great Britain and the United States abolishing extraterritoriality, and other nations followed suit in the aftermath of World War II.

The principle of extraterritoriality was important to Western traders in the 19th century because of their distrust of the Chinese legal system. (Because of the necessity of an admission of guilt under that system, torture was not unusual.) But as Chinese legal practice became more closely aligned with that of other countries, the need for such protection was seen to diminish. But it was partly this concept which caused the Chinese to label all treaties signed in the 19th and early 20th centuries as "unequal treaties" (q.v.).

Fishel, Wesley R. *The End of Extraterritoriality in China*. Berkeley: University of California Press, 1952.

Vincent, John Carter. *The Extraterritorial System in China*. Cambridge: Harvard University Press, 1970.

Fa-hsien (4th-5th century A.D.). Fa-hsien was a Buddhist monk who traveled from China to India and back between 399-414. This period of Chinese history was one of disunity, war and unrest, a period marked by the rise and fall of several dynasties in many small states after the fall of the Han dynasty in 221 A.D. and before the reunification achieved under the Sui (q.v.) in 589. Buddhism, with its emphasis on the transience of this illusory world, prospered in this period.

Fa-hsien's account of his travels is nearly all that is known of him. The difficulties he describes are impressive. He crossed the Gobi Desert and the Hindu Kush to Gandhara in present-day Afghanistan. From there he traveled to India and visited a number of cities which can be identified—Kapilavastu, Magadha, Benares and Gaya, e.g.—then down to present-day Calcutta and then to Ceylon. From there a ship carried him to Java, and after five months, another ship carried him to China. The sailors were making for Canton but were blown off course and eventually landed on the coast of Shantung. From there Fa-hsien traveled overland to Nanking.

Fa-hsien's purpose in traveling was to bring back religious texts and icons, both of which he accomplished. His account of his long journey is an important documentary of the places he visited. Originally it was primarily of interest to Buddhist clergy and scholars, who may well have regarded it as somewhat mythical.

Fa-hsien's account may be compared with those of Marco Polo (q.v.), well known in the Western world, and of Ennin (q.v.), whose account of T'ang China is a source of much important information. See also **Hsuan-tsang**.

Giles, H.A. *The Travels of Fa-hsien*. London: Routledge & Kegan Paul, 1959.

Family. The traditional Chinese concept of the family is heavily influenced by Confucianism (q.v.). According to that tradition, three of the five fundamental human relationships have to do with the family: father/son, elder brother/younger brother and husband/wife. All three were superior/inferior relationships.

The ideal family was seen as one in which five generations lived under one roof. Such a family would consist of a patriarch and his wife, his male descendants and their wives, if any, and any unmarried female descendants. Such families have existed, but they have always been rare, since they are predicated on the possession of sufficient farmland to support such an establishment.

Under traditional Chinese law, real property must be divided among male heirs. Thus the death of the patriarch would lead to the dissolution of the extended family and division of the farmland. The alternative was the continuation of joint residence by the brothers and their families. Since this also entailed the acceptance of the oldest brother's authority, the younger brothers were more likely to opt for division of the land and separate residences.

Seperation also occurred even before the patriarch's death, and it was not uncommon for the oldest son to remain with his parents while younger sons established nuclear families elsewhere. A family with daughters but no sons would frequently adopt a male who would take the family name and inherit the property.

Within the family it was customary to address relatives by their relationship, as "uncle" or "elder brother," rather than by name, which reinforced the concept of hierarchy. Male first cousins whose fathers were brothers were often considered as brothers and so numbered in the extended family. A male could not marry a female cousin if they were related through their fathers, i.e., bore the family surname. Such a marriage was considered licit if they bore different surnames, i.e., if the relationship was through the mother of one.

The position of women within the family was not equal. The birth of a daughter was not greeted with as much joy as the birth of a son. An incoming bride found herself in a disadvantageous position. She could usually expect difficulty from her mother-in-law, and since she had probably met her husband for the first time at the marriage ceremony, could expect little support from him. Her position improved when she gave birth to a son, and still more when her son married, making her a mother-in-law in her turn.

Baker, Hugh D.R. *Chinese Family and Kinship*. New York: Columbia University Press, 1979.

Chiang, Yee. *A Chinese Childhood*. New York: W.W. Norton & Co., 1963.

FENG Kuo-chang (1859-1919). Military leader and fourth president of the Republic of China (July 1917-October 1918, q.v.). As a protégé of YUAN Shih-k'ai (1859-1916, q.v.), FENG was one of his chief assistants in the modernization of the Chinese military in the wake of the Sino-Japanese War (1894-1895, q.v.), and was known as a leader of the Peiyang Group (q.v.), a term for YUAN's military supporters. At the outbreak of revolution in October 1911, FENG was sent by the imperial court as commander of one of two armies to suppress the revolutionaries. Under YUAN's instructions, FENG delayed his march, enabling the revolution to spread and increasing the pressure on the imperial court to have the emperor abdicate, thus ending the Ch'ing dynasty (1644-1911, q.v.) and paving the way for YUAN to become the president of the new Republic of China in February 1912.

FENG remained loyal to YUAN until the latter proclaimed himself emperor of a new dynasty in January 1916. In May, FENG convened a conference in Nanking calling for YUAN's resignation. YUAN died in June, and the Peiyang Group split into two factions, the Anhwei Clique under TUAN Ch'i-jui (1865-1936, qq.v.), and the Chihli Clique (q.v.) under FENG. TUAN was in military control of Peking, and established himself as de facto ruler, with LI Yuan-hung, 1864-1928 (q.v.) as figurehead president and FENG as vice president.

When LI was forced out of the presidency in July 1917, FENG succeeded him. FENG had retained his position as military governor of Nanking while vice president, but proceeded to Peking to take office as president. Once again he found himself in competition with TUAN. When his term of office was up, in October 1918, both men resigned, but since TUAN still had his troops in Peking, he retained power. FENG turned over the presidency to his successor, HSÜ Shih-ch'ang (1855-1939, q.v.), and lived quietly in Peking until his death the following year.

Boorman, Howard L., ed. *Biographical Dictionary of Republican China*. New York: Columbia University Press, 1967.

Powell, Ralph L. *The Rise of Chinese Military Power, 1895-1912*. Princeton: Princeton University Press, 1955.

FENG Yü-hsiang (1882-1948). Warlord, widely known as the Christian General, who dominated much of North China (q.v.) before 1930. FENG had little formal education but taught himself to read vernacular literature, though he was never completely at home with the literary language. He accompanied his father to the Sino-Japanese War (1894-1895, q.v.), and spent his life as a military man. As an officer in Manchuria (q.v.) in 1911, he became involved with a revolutionary group. They were betrayed after the October 10 outbreak at Wuchang (see under **SUN Yat-sen**). Some of the officers were executed but FENG was spared.

In 1914 FENG became a Christian and joined the Methodist church. The next few years were filled with military activity, as different leaders struggled to dominate China.

FENG was devoted to training his troops in physical fitness as well as moral precepts. Hard military training, forced marches and competitive athletics strengthened the bodies of his troops; the prohibition of such vices as gambling, prostitution and opium smoking were elements of his moral training. FENG would not permit corruption, and his officers lived with their men and underwent the same training.

He was largely successful in the complex infighting which characterized China in the early 1920s, and in 1924 FENG forced TS'AO K'un (q.v.) to surrender the presidency, and removed the last Ch'ing emperor, P'u-yi (q.v.) from the Forbidden City (q.v.). Late in 1925 he engaged in a war against CHANG Tso-lin (1873-1928, q.v.), the Manchurian warlord, but was defeated, and retreated to Outer Mongolia. From there he went to Moscow where he stayed from May to August 1926, returning to China after hearing of the Northern Expedition (q.v.). He accepted membership in the Kuomintang (KMT, q.v.) in a formal statement in September 1926, and soon found himself in a strategic position to negotiate between the two KMT factions: the left wing at Wuhan (see under **WANG Ching-wei**) and the right wing at Nanking (see **CHIANG Kai-shek**). FENG supported CHIANG, thus bringing the era of working with communist Russian advisers to an end.

FENG's troops assisted CHIANG's in taking Peking in June 1928, and in October FENG was named Minister of War in the Nanking government. Relations with CHIANG Kai-shek became strained in 1929 because FENG distrusted CHIANG's effort to centralize control, and in May he declared his independence of the National Government. He still controlled his troops, however, and while he was read out of the party and all offices, managed in the following year to arrange a coalition with YEN Hsi-shan (q.v.) to fight the government. The coalition was scuttled by the intervention of CHANG Hsueh-liang (q.v.) on Nanking's behalf. It was the end of FENG's military power.

FENG served in a number of posts in the government in the years following, and in 1946 was sent to the United States to make a study of irrigation and water conservancy. He abandoned the study about one-third through and devoted much of his time to propaganda activities directed against CHIANG Kai-shek. In July 1948, he and his wife sailed to Odessa on a Russian ship. Shortly before arrival, there was a fire aboard in which FENG died.

Boorman, Howard L., ed. *Biographical Dictionary of Republican China*. New York: Columbia University Press, 1967.

Sheridan, James E. *Chinese Warlord: The Career of Feng Yü-hsiang*. Stanford: Stanford University Press, 1966.

Feng-shui (Geomancy). The words mean "wind/water" and describe a system of determining the auspicious and inauspicious influences on a particular site. Believers in the system engage a geomancer to determine the appropriate siting of a building, a house or a grave.

The geomancer uses a compass centered in a circular wooden plate engraved with several concentric circles of Chinese characters, for signs of the zodiac, stars, etc., the whole representing a Neo-Confucian (see **Neo-Confucianism**) cosmography. Geomancers were at one time government officials with responsibility for the siting of buildings, graves, etc. That no longer holds true, but geomancers are used privately in many areas including Hong Kong, Taiwan and Korea.

Feuchtwang, Stephen D.R. *An Anthropological Analysis of Chinese Geomancy*. Vientiane, Laos: Vithaga, 1974.

Fengtien. Original name of the present-day province of Liaoning (q.v.). In 1903, Manchuria (q.v.) was divided into three provinces: Fengtien, Heilungkiang and Kirin (qq.v.). Fengtien was the power base of CHANG Tso-lin (1873-1928, q.v.), warlord of Manchuria after 1912, and his forces are sometimes referred to as the Fengtien armies. It was sometimes also known as Shengking, but the change to Liaoning was made in 1928.

Feudalism. Certain elements of the social structure in ancient China bore striking resemblances to European and Japanese feudalism of later eras. The existence of a warrior class, fighting between feudal lords for the possession of lands and cities, the transmission of such possessions through the practice of primogeniture—all of these elements existed in the Shang (1766-1122 B.C.) and Chou (1122-255 B.C.) dynasties (qq.v.). In establishing the Ch'in empire, the first emperor made a great effort to centralize authority and destroy all alternate power centers. In so doing he caused the deaths of many thousands and effectively eliminated the feudal order.

The first emperor of the Han (206 B.C.-221 A.D., q.v.) restored the system by enfeoffing a number of his comrades in arms, as well as members of his own family. Suspicion of the ambitions of the first group led to their elimination in the first reign, and an uneasy feeling that the existence of territorial lords of the imperial family threatened the throne led to the conclusion that they, too, should be brought under control. It remained for Han Wu Ti (r. 140-87 B.C., q.v.) to ban primogeniture by edict, thus forcing the feudal lords to divide their estates among several heirs.

Some aspects of feudalism, such as fealty to one's lord, or to the emperor, persisted or were revived from time to time. In the Ch'ing dynasty (1644-1911, q.v.), Mongol princes bore allegiance to the emperors, not to the Chinese state they ruled.

In the 20th century, the term is frequently applied in the People's Republic of China (q.v.) to any previous period, and to many of the customs of earlier ages, from possession of private property to concubinage and foot-binding.

Five Anti Movement. An internal struggle campaign launched by the People's Republic of China (q.v.) on March 1, 1952. The five targets were bribery, fraud, tax evasion, theft of state assets and theft of state economic secrets. The Three Anti Movement (q.v.), which preceded it, had been aimed at government officials. The second movement was aimed at private businessmen.

Five Classics. The Five Classics are the ancient books with which Confucius (q.v.) was familiar and which formed the syllabus for his disciples. They were the *Shu Ching* (Book of History), *Shih Ching* (Book of Songs), *I Ching* (Book of Changes), *Li Ching* (Book of Rites, actually three books), and the *Ch'un Ch'iu* (Spring and Autumn Annals of the state of Lu, qq.v.).

Five Dynasties (906-960 A.D.). The T'ang dynasty (q.v.) fell in 906 and was succeeded in the north by the Liao (907-1125) and in the south by a series of shortlived regimes known as the Five Dynasties, as well as by some independent entities known collectively as the Ten Kingdoms. Later Chinese historians assign legitimacy,

i.e., the Mandate of Heaven (q.v.), to the Five Dynasties, which were as follows: Later Liang, Later T'ang, Later Chin, Later Han and Later Chou (qq.v.). None lasted longer than 16 years. The last named was followed by the Sung dynasty (960-1279, q.v.), which succeeded in uniting all of China except for that portion held by the Liao.

Five Elements school. The five elements are earth, wood, metal, fire and water. Wood can overcome earth; metal can overcome wood; fire can overcome metal; water can overcome fire; and earth can overcome water. According to the Five Elements school, one of the Hundred Schools of philosophy which flourished during the Warring States Period (q.v.), the cosmos is made up of the five elements, and each element has a period of dominance which is succeeded by the next. This theory was applied to the three dynasties Hsia (wood), Shang (metal) and Chou (fire), and Ch'in Shih Huang Ti (q.v.) was persuaded that his Ch'in dynasty's element was water.

The five elements are commonly used in casting horoscopes, and in the 60-year calendrical cycle each of the twelve animals appears with a different element until the cycle is complete. The elements are also attached to the hours of the day, particularly for use in horoscopes.

By the time of the *Shih Chi* (q.v.), the Five Elements school had been indiscriminately combined with the *yin-yang* school (q.v.). Both traditions have been used in divination up to the present day.

Fung, Yu-lan, and Derk Bodde, trans. *A History of Chinese Philosophy*. Princeton: Princeton University Press, 1952.

Flying Tigers. This is the informal name given to the American

Volunteer Group (q.v.) of the Chinese Air Force.

Foochow (Fuzhou). Foochow is the capital of Fukien province, and one of the original treaty ports (q.v.). Population: 1 million (1981). It is situated on the Min river, which gave its name to an independent Fukien, the Empire of Min (q.v.), in the 10th century, A.D.

The standard Fukien dialect is that of Foochow city. (See also **Amoy**.) Foochow has a long history of international trade, and many Overseas Chinese (q.v.) hail from the city and its environs.

Foot-binding. The Chinese euphemism for the bound foot is "golden lotus." In order to keep the female foot at a tiny size the binding had to be done between the ages of five and ten. The process was painful for the first year or two and rendered the woman incapable of walking normally. Unbinding the foot in later years was also painful, so that a woman whose feet were once bound was likely to keep them that way. Judging by poetic references, the bound foot was regarded as an erotic stimulus by some Chinese men. It also had the effect of restricting a woman's movements and advertising the status of her family, since such a woman was incapable of working in the fields. Even when the practice was most widespread, many Chinese peasant women had unbound feet for economic reasons.

Foot-binding seems to have started in court circles and spread to the upper classes. The first reliable reference dates from the Southern Sung dynasty (1127-1278 A.D., q.v.). It wasn't mentioned by Marco Polo (1254-1324, q.v.), who visited China during the Yuan dynasty (1279-1368, q.v.), but it was by Odoric de Pordenone (1286-1331, q.v.). The Mongols of the Yuan dynasty did not permit their own women's feet to be bound, but encouraged it among the Chinese. The Hakka (q.v.), a Chinese minority group which migrated from north to south China during this period, have never bound the feet of their women.

The practice probably reached its peak during the Ming dynasty (1368-1644, q.v.), with imperial encouragement. This attitude was immediately reversed by the Manchu rulers of the Ch'ing dynasty (1644-1911, q.v.), who detested the practice, and whose women's feet were never bound. They issued repeated edicts banning the practice, the last of them in 1902, but with little effect.

Christian missionaries disapproved of the practice, but their influence was slight. The establishment of a handful of Christian schools for girls at the end of the 19th century had some small effect on the elite of Shanghai and other ports, since girls with bound feet could not attend.

The Republic of China again banned the practice soon after its establishment in 1912, though enforcement was not immediately effective. It was banned again by the People's Republic of China after its establishment in 1949, but it is unlikely that such a ban was needed, since the practice had already been abandoned. There are still a very few elderly women with bound feet, though they are rarely seen in public.

Levy, Howard S. *Chinese Footbinding*. New York: Bell Publishing Co., 1967.

Forbidden City. The English term for the imperial palace in Peking, it is a direct translation of one of several terms used in Chinese. More common until the end of the Sung dynasty (960-1279 A.D., q.v.) was the term *Ta Nei*, "Great Within." During most of the Ming (1368-1644) and Ch'ing (1644-1911) dynasties (qq.v.), access to the palace was granted on a very limited basis to high officials, but most of the time it was occupied only by the emperor, an army of eunuchs (q.v.), and ladies of the court, ranging from empresses to menials.

The Forbidden City continued to be the residence of the ex-emperor P'u Yi (1906-1967, q.v.) until late 1924. Access to parts of the palace, though not to P'u Yi's living quarters, was occasionally provided to foreign diplomats and important visitors from abroad.

The National Palace Museum was opened in the Forbidden City on October 10, 1925, and its exhibits have been available to the public intermittently since that time.

Foreign Relations. In 1815 the Congress of Vienna went to great lengths to establish the principle that sovereign states are equal—a fiction, but a useful one. Traditional Chinese diplomacy was based on quite a different principle: that the Chinese emperor was the paramount ruler, and that all nations in diplomatic contact with China were in some way tributary to the Chinese state.

The earliest Chinese culture developed in isolation, and the assumption of Chinese superiority was accepted by the surrounding peoples. The Chinese invention of writing led to its adoption for certain purposes by several neighbors: Japanese, Koreans and Vietnamese. While these and other neighboring national groups had cultures of their own, there was no tradition of states with differing cultures coexisting on a theoretical basis of equality. This is reflected in an early term for the Chinese cultural/political realm, *T'ien Hsia*, which may be translated as "all under heaven." (The term for the

Chinese emperor, *T'ien Tzu*, meaning "son of heaven," is cognate with it and implies that the emperor is the mediator between heaven and the rest of humanity.)

In some cases this acceptance of Chinese superiority was reinforced by military conquest. Some of the areas so conquered were absorbed into China itself. Others, such as Korea and Vietnam (qq.v.), managed to reassert independence, while acknowledging suzerainty through the tribute system (q.v.). The concept of foreign rulers accepting the primacy of the Chinese emperor persisted. In the early 15th century, Admiral CHENG Ho (1371-1433, q.v.) carried the concept as far as the coast of Africa and returned to China with tribute from a number of rulers of South and Southeast Asia.

The Chinese custom was to provide gifts to ambassadors which exceeded the value of those they brought. As a consequence, Chinese history records the arrival of numerous embassies whose bona fides are open to question, such as those purporting to represent the Roman Empire (q.v.). As late as the end of the Ming dynasty, Peking maintained a "palace of foreigners." It is described as a large enclosure with about a thousand rooms, but these were without doors or furniture. Its occupants were Asian merchants who came in the guise of envoys, though the Chinese were aware of the fiction.

One notable characteristic of the Chinese system was the assignment of responsibility for foreign relations to the Board of Rites (q.v.). From the T'ang dynasty (618-906 A.D., q.v.) through the Ming (1368-1644, q.v.), the reception of foreign envoys and the presentation of their tribute to the emperor was one of several responsibilities of this board, though not its most important activity. The

Ch'ing dynasty (1644-1911, q.v.) established the Li Fan Yuan (q.v.) for the specific purpose of regulating relations between Manchus and Mongols. Its responsibilities were later expanded to include relations with Sinkiang, Tibet and Russia (qq.v.).

In 1689 the Treaty of Nerchinsk (q.v.) was signed by representatives of the Ch'ing emperor K'ang Hsi (q.v.) and the Russian emperor Peter the Great. It was occasioned by the arrival of Russian traders in Siberia and their appearance in the northern reaches of the Manchu homeland. It was the first treaty between China and a Western power and is notable for the fact that it was negotiated on the basis of equality between the two rulers.

In the 17th century both the Dutch and the Portuguese sent embassies to the imperial court, and those that were received performed the ceremonial kotow (q.v.), as required by Chinese protocol. Their main purpose was to improve conditions of trade, but the Chinese regarded them merely as bearers of tribute and no discussions of such matters took place. The first British embassy was sent under Earl Macartney in 1793. He was received with far more pomp than any of the Dutch or Portuguese embassies, but the Chinese were firm that it was a mission of tribute, and placards announcing this were attached to the boats and cars transporting the embassy. The Chinese tried to persuade the earl to perform the kotow. His counteroffer was to suggest that a Chinese official of similar rank perform the same obeisance to a portrait of King George III, which was declined. Eventually it was agreed that Macartney would bend one knee as he would in showing respect to his own sovereign. He was granted two audiences with the emperor Ch'ien Lung at the Summer Palace in Jehol province (qq.v.), but nothing satisfactory came of the mission.

The British sent a second mission under William Pitt, earl of Amherst, in 1816, but he was not received by the emperor Chia Ch'ing (r. 1796-1820, q.v.). Both these missions were intended to ease restrictions on British trade, limited at the time to dealings with the merchant cartel known as the Cohong (q.v.) at Canton.

The failure of the missions laid the groundwork for the Opium War (1842) and the *Arrow* War (1857-1860, qq.v.), which followed. The Opium War resulted in the Treaty of Nanking (1842, q.v.), which China regarded as the first of the unequal treaties (q.v.). China's defeat in the *Arrow* War led to the establishment of the Tsungli Yamen (q.v.), China's first agency equivalent to a ministry of foreign affairs, in 1861. It was renamed the Ministry of Foreign Affairs in the wake of the Boxer Rebellion (1900, q.v.).

It should be noted that China has another history of diplomacy which was practiced among Chinese and Sinicized states during periods of disunity, such as during the Warring States Period (484-255 B.C.); the Three Kingdoms (221-265 A.D.) and the Sung dynasty (960-1279 A.D., qq.v.). The states involved treated each other on a more nearly equal basis, characterized by deception and intermittent warfare. Their minimum goal was survival, and the maximum conquest of the empire.

Historically, China rarely sent embassies abroad. Emperor Yung Cheng (r. 1723-1735) sent two embassies to Moscow, the first to be sent to any Western nation. The next such occurrence was under the emperor T'ung Chih (r. 1862-1874). The first Chinese diplomat to reside abroad was KUO Sung-t'ao (q.v.), who was stationed in London and Paris, 1877-1878.

Fairbank, John K., ed. *The Chinese World Order: Traditional China's Foreign Relations.* Cambridge: Harvard University Press, 1968.

Morse, H.B. *The International Relations of the Chinese Empire.* London: Longmans, 1910-1918. 3 Vols.

Formosa. See **Taiwan.**

Four Books. The "Four Books" are *Lun Yü* (Confucian Analects), *Ta Hsüeh* (Great Learning), *Chung Yung* (Doctrine of the Mean) and *Meng Tsu* (Book of Mencius). All the texts date from the period of the Chou dynasty (q.v.) and form part of the Confucian canon. CHU Hsi (q.v.), the Sung dynasty Neo-Confucian philosopher, selected them as the basis for classical elementary education, and for centuries every educated Chinese could quote passages from the Four Books and recognize references to them. (Just as, for many years, any educated English speaker was expected to be acquainted with the Bible and the works of Shakespeare, and to recognize references and quotations.)

The Four Books have been translated many times, notably by the late James Legge, D.D. LL.D.

Four Seas. The traditional Chinese concept of the world is one in which heaven is round and the earth is square. At the center is China, surrounded by inner barbarians, who are, in turn, surrounded by outer barbarians. Beyond them are the Four Seas, named after the cardinal directions. (See also under **yin-yang school.**)

The term "within the four seas" means all the world. A common Chinese adage is: "Within the Four Seas, all men are brothers." In this sense, "Four Seas" is frequently used in the names of commercial establishments.

France. In 1253 A.D. King Louis IX, the crusader, sent William of Rubruck (q.v.) as his envoy to Mengu, the Mongol Khan who ruled North China. It was the first attempt by a French ruler to open relations with East Asia, and while it had no sequel for several centuries, the mixture of religion and diplomacy marked French policy in Asia until the end of the 19th century.

The next Frenchmen known to have reached China were Jesuits (q.v.) whose order became influential at the court in Peking in the 17th century because of their skill in mathematics and astronomy. The 17th century also saw the arrival of the first French trading ship at Canton in 1660, the founding in 1664 of the French East India Company, whose goal was a trade monopoly in Asia, and the establishment of the Society of Foreign Missions in Paris that same year. When the Jesuit order was dissolved in 1773, the Society of Foreign Missions was given their responsibilities in Peking, further strengthening French involvement with Catholic missions in Asia.

In the 18th century France was occupied with her American and Indian colonies, most of which were lost to Great Britain. Trade with China was desultory, though a French factory was established at Canton in 1728, and an effort to effect a French political presence in Vietnam (q.v.) proved abortive, though French missionaries were active there. Early 19th-century efforts were no more successful, but an anti-Catholic policy was established by the Vietnamese emperor Minh Mang (r. 1820-1841), and this roused the missionaries to ask for support from the French government. Their campaign, while not immediately successful, eventually resulted in military action.

Observing the British success in the Opium War (1839-1842, q.v.), and the subsequent cession of Hong Kong, the French immediately pressed to obtain privileges similar to those the British had been granted by the Treaty of Nanking, concluded August 29, 1842 (q.v.). They succeeded with the Treaty of Whampoa (q.v.), concluded October 24, 1844. They also received confirmation of France's position as protector of the Roman Catholic Church, and the rescission of the 1724 ban on Christianity.

France was allied with Great Britain in the *Arrow* War, 1857-1860 (q.v.), and by the treaty of Tientsin, 1858 (q.v.), obtained more rights for Christian missionaries as well as the opening of Tientsin as a treaty port. As soon as the Treaty had been ratified, in 1860, the French appointed a consul and built a cathedral as well as a convent. Friction between the missionaries and the Chinese gentry led to the Tientsin Massacre (q.v.) on June 21, 1870. France was impeded in exerting pressure on China because of the outbreak of the Franco-Prussian War in Europe, but eventually apologies, indemnities and the execution of 16 Chinese brought the incident to a close.

The French had invaded Saigon in February 1859, and a small garrison held out there until reinforcements arrived in 1861. On June 6, 1862, a treaty was signed between France and Annam (Vietnam) ceding Saigon and three provinces of Cochin-China to France. On March 15, 1874, a second treaty was signed, announcing Annam's complete independence of any foreign power and granting it French protection. China protested, pointing out that Annam had been either a part of the Chinese empire or a tributary state for 2,000 years. In spite of this treaty, the Vietnamese emperor, Tu Duc (r. 1847-1883) continued sending tribute to Peking.

French designs on Vietnam included opening China's Yunnan province (q.v.) to trade, banned by Peking. Exploration proved the Mekong river, in the south, to be impractical for this purpose, but the Red river, in Tongking in the north, had better potential. In attempting to block French intrusions into Tongking, the Vietnamese called for assistance from the suzerain power. China sent irregular troops, known as "Black Flags," and they were soon in control of the Red river.

In spite of an agreement reached between China and France at Shanghai on December 20, 1882, France continued preparations for a military expedition. In August 1883, such a force arrived in Tongking, and on August 25 a Treaty of Protectorate was signed. This enlarged the area of Cochin-China under French control, put Tongking directly under a French Resident and put an end to Vietnam's independence.

China and France signed an agreement covering Vietnam on May 11, 1884, in which both sides made concessions. The Chinese agreed to withdraw all troops and to open the provincial borders to trade. Before the troops were withdrawn, fighting broke out in the border area. France then prepared for war on a wider scale. On July 13 a French fleet moved into Foochow (q.v.) harbor, where they were welcomed by the Chinese.

On August 5 another fleet opened fire on Keelung, Taiwan. On August 23 the French opened fire on Chinese ships at Foochow and on August 27 the Chinese announced that a state of war existed. In September the French occupied Keelung, and in October blocked the other Taiwanese ports.

Hostilities then gave way to diplomacy, and on June 9, 1885, another treaty was signed at Tientsin. This confirmed the earlier agreement and surrendered Chinese suzerainty over Vietnam.

In 1895 France joined Germany and Russia in a joint note advising Japan to retrocede the Liaotung peninsula, which Japan had acquired from China as a result of the Sino-Japanese War (1894-1895, q.v.). In 1898, Russia obtained the lease of Port Arthur, Germany was granted concessions in Shantung province and France got a 99-year lease on Kwangchowan, north of Hainan Island, for use as a naval station. The French also played a minor role in the Boxer Rebellion (1900, q.v.).

In July 1937, Japan opened the war with China, and immediately protested the use of the French-built railroad from the port of Haiphong to Kunming, the capital of Yunnan province, for the transport of war materials. The French limited the use of the line to the shipment of trucks, gasoline and textiles. France fell to the Germans in June 1940, and that same month the Japanese demanded the closure of the border with China to all war materials. The French complied, leaving the Burma Road (q.v.) as China's only lifeline.

Japanese troops entered French Indochina in September 1940, and on December 8, 1941 (Pearl Harbor Day), surrounded the French garrisons and threatened to disarm them. The French capitulated, and Vietnam was incorporated into the Japanese Co-Prosperity Sphere. On March 9, 1945, the Japanese disarmed the French forces, and on March 10 declared an independent Vietnam under emperor Bao Dai.

The participants at the Potsdam Conference, held in July 1945, anticipating the conclusion of World War II, agreed that Nationalist Chinese troops would accept the Japanese surrender north of the 16th parallel, and British troops south of it. The British paved the way for the French, but the Chinese would not permit their entry until the signing of a Franco-Chinese treaty, on February 28, 1946. Under its terms, France surrendered its lease on Kwangchowan, and relinquished its Concessions in Shanghai and other treaty ports.

France maintained diplomatic relations with the Republic of China (q.v.) until January 1964. At that time it recognized the People's Republic of China.

Cady, John F. *The Roots of French Imperialism in Eastern Asia*. Ithaca: Cornell University Press, 1954.

Fu Hsi. First of the Three Emperors of the legendary period (q.v.). He is credited with teaching his people to fish with nets, domesticate animals, and to make musical instruments. He is also given credit for creating the pictograms which developed into the Chinese written language, and the eight trigrams which are used in divination (see under **I Ching**).

Fujian. See **Fukien**.

Fukien (Fujian) **province**. Area: 120,000 sq. km. (46,300 sq. mi.). Population: 24,800,000 (1980). Capital: Foochow (Fuzhou). Fukien is bounded on the northeast by Chekiang province, on the southeast by the Taiwan Strait, on the southwest by Kwangtung, and on the northwest by Kiangsi (qq.v.).

Fukien is mountainous and communications have traditionally been difficult. This has resulted in the development of a variety of dialects, a number of which are mutually incomprehensible. The two largest cities are Amoy and Foochow (qq.v.), each of which has its own dialect.

The climate is subtropical, and some areas have heavy rainfall. Rice is the staple grain, and is planted twice yearly in parts of the southern region. Tea is a major export crop.

Fuzhou. See **Foochow**.

G

Gang of Four. The term refers to
CHIANG Ch'ing (q.v.), CHANG
Ch'un-ch'iao, WANG Hung-wen and
YAO Wen-yuan (JIANG Qing,
ZHANG Chunqiao, WANG
Hongwen and YAO Wenyuan),
militant leaders of the Cultural
Revolution, 1966-1976 (q.v.).
CHIANG Ch'ing, wife of MAO Tse-
tung (q.v.), provided access to the
chairman of the Chinese Communist
party and protection for their disrup-
tive activities. They came under attack
a month after MAO's death on
September 9, 1976. All four leaders
and many of their followers were
arrested and tried, and in 1985 some
were still in prison.

Robinson, Thomas W., ed. *The Cultural
Revolution in China.* Berkeley: University
of California Press, 1971.

Gansu. See *Kansu*.

Germany. German commerce with
China started in the 18th century,
with ocean trade to Canton as well as
overland trade from North China via
Siberia. The latter soon halted because of Russian tax policy. At the
conclusion of the Opium War (1839-
1842, q.v.), the Treaty of Nanking
(q.v.) between China and Great
Britain provided for the opening of
five treaty ports (q.v.) to foreign trade.
The French and Americans signed
similar treaties, but the Germans did

not. In consequence, the Germans
traded under the auspices and protection of Great Britain, which they
resented.

In 1860 a naval fleet of four ships
was sent to China on a diplomatic
mission to negotiate a commercial
treaty for all the German states. The
Chinese demurred, on the grounds
that the Treaties of Tientsin (1858,
q.v.) provided for the trade of all
Western nations. The Germans
prevailed and a treaty was signed
September 2, 1861.

At the time the Chinese knew little
of Germany, but Prussian success
after 1871 in unifying the German
states and strengthening the *Reich*
aroused interest and admiration in
China. In the 1870s and 1880s German
military instructors and military
equipment held a preeminent position in the modernization of Chinese
forces.

By 1895, German trade was second
only to Britain's, and the Germans
were looking for a suitable territorial
foothold and sphere of influence.
They found it at Tsingtao and
Chiaochou bay on the south side of
the Shantung peninsula. In April
1895, Germany joined France and
Russia in forcing Japan to retrocede
the Liaotung peninsula (q.v.),
obtained as spoils of the Sino-
Japanese War, 1894-1895 (q.v.). In
October 1897, Germany requested a
naval base from China and received a

flat refusal. In November, using the murder of two German missionaries as a pretext, a German naval force seized Tsingtao. The Germans then demanded indemnities, railway and mineral rights in Shantung province (q.v.), and the use of Chiaochou bay as a naval station. Lacking support from other foreign powers, China capitulated in March 1898, granting the concessions and a 99-year lease of Tsingtao and Chiaochou bay.

The German demands set off a scramble by other foreign powers. In March, Russia was granted the lease of the Liaotung peninsula, including Port Arthur and Dairen (qq.v.). In April, France obtained the lease of Kwangchowan, on the coast of Kwangtung province (q.v.). In July, Britain was granted a 99-year lease at Weihaiwei on the northern tip of the Shantung peninsula, facing Port Arthur, as well as a similar lease on the New Territories in Hong Kong.

This evidence of weakness caused widespread concern in China and was probably a factor in such disparate manifestations as the Hundred Days Reform (1898, q.v.) and the Boxer Rebellion (1900, q.v.). The German Minister at Peking was one of the first casualties of the Boxer siege there. His death led to the despatch of a large contingent of troops from Germany to form part of the allied forces, but they did not arrive in time to participate in the march on Peking.

Changed conditions after the Boxer Rebellion encouraged Chinese authorities to restrict German activities so that Shantung never did become a German sphere of interest, though Tsingtao did develop into a "model colony" at great expense to German taxpayers. The Japanese victory in the Russo-Japanese War (1904-1905, q.v.), persuaded the German government that Tsingtao, far from being a military asset, was a hostage to any locally stronger power, in this case Japan.

World War I started on July 28, 1914, and on August 6 China declared her neutrality. On August 23, Japan declared war on Germany and on August 27 a Japanese fleet laid siege to Tsingtao, which fell November 7. By December Japan had occupied all of Shantung province. China declared war on Germany on August 14, 1917, largely for the purpose of denying the Chiaochou Leased Territory and Shantung province to the Japanese in the postwar settlement. However, the Versailles Treaty (q.v.) awarded the German properties to Japan, and in consequence China refused to sign. Chinese anger over the treaty resulted in the May Fourth Incident of 1919 (q.v.).

Germany's presence in East Asia after World War I was slight, though trade was resumed. In 1928 the Nationalist government requested a military mission to assist in training its armies. By the time of its departure in 1938, it had brought some 30 divisions to a standard of efficiency never previously known in China. These troops fought in the defense of the Yangtze valley in that year, but were ultimately pushed back by the Japanese.

Schrecker, John E. *Imperialism and Chinese Nationalism: Germany in Shantung.* Cambridge: Harvard University Press, 1971.

Genghis Khan. See under **Chingis Khan**.

Giles, Herbert. See under **Wade, Sir Thomas Francis**.

Gordon, Charles George (1833-1885). Better known as "Chinese" Gordon, the hero of Khartoum, in whose siege he died, he came of a British military family and served in the Crimean War

(1853-1856). After serving with an Anglo-Russian commission delimiting frontiers, he traveled to China in 1860 and joined British forces in the *Arrow War (1857-1860, q.v.)*, participating in the burning of the Summer Palace (q.v.) in October 1860.

The Taiping Rebellion (1851-1864, q.v.) was at its height in the Yangtze valley. One of the imperial units involved in fighting the rebels, known as the "Ever-Victorious Army," was commanded by Frederick Townsend Ward (q.v.) and officered by European volunteers. Ward was killed in Septmeber 1862, and after a six-month interval, command was given to Gordon. His troops took Soochow (q.v.) in December 1863, but Gordon refused to permit them to loot the city. He was horrified when his Chinese superior, LI Hung-chang (1823-1901, q.v.) had the Taiping leaders executed. Gordon felt that as a British officer he had guaranteed them their safety. He then declined to accept the imperial gifts which the Chinese offered. Eventually the affair was patched up and LI apologized. The rebellion was suppressed in 1864 and Gordon left China. While he made a trip back in later years, his career was largely elsewhere.

Nutting, Anthony. *Gordon of Khartoum, Martyr and Misfit.* New York: Potter, 1966.

Grand Canal. The Grand Canal is the name given to a series of interconnected waterways which provided central and east China with an interconnected system of communication. The first emperor of the Sui dynasty (589-618 A.D., q.v.) is credited with the completion of the first part, which connected his capital of Changan (see **Sian**) with the east and linked the Huang (Yellow) and Yangtze rivers. His son and successor continued the network up to the vicinity of Peking.

The Grand Canal proved very important in later years in linking the rich areas around the Yangtze delta with the various capitals in the north. Maintenance of the Grand Canal was a matter of great importance to succeeding dynasties, and many officials were assigned to the work of supervising its dredging and repair.

Great Britain. While the British were not early arrivals in the China trade, by the end of the 18th century Britain was China's largest trading partner, a position held until World War II, and in the 19th century, Britain was dominant among Western nations dealing with China. The first English trading ships arrived at Canton in 1637, and in 1715 the East India Company opened a "factory" or trading facility there. By the end of the 18th century, British dissatisfactions had grown with the trade. In an attempt to obtain better treatment, two embassies were sent to Peking. The first was headed by Lord George Macartney in 1793, and the second by William Pitt, earl of Amherst in 1816.

Chinese efforts to persuade Macartney to perform the kotow (q.v.) were unsuccessful. He had two audiences with the emperor Ch'ien Lung (r. 1736-1796, q.v.) and returned empty-handed. Amherst also refused the kotow and was not received by the emperor Chia Ch'ing (r. 1796-1820, q.v.). British frustration in dealing with authorities of the Ch'ing dynasty (1644-1911, q.v.) was certainly a primary factor in the Opium War (1839-1842, q.v.), and in the *Arrow War (1857-1860, q.v.)*. The first was ended by the Treaty of Nanking (q.v.), the first of the "unequal treaties" (q.v.). The second was ended by the Treaty of Tientsin (1858, q.v.), and the Conventions of Peking (1860). The Treaty of Nanking provided for the cession of Hong Kong to Britain, and for the opening of five treaty ports (q.v.) to foreign trade. Later treaties increased the number until a total of 48 was reached.

While the Treaty of Tientsin was signed in 1858, the Chinese refused to ratify it until October 1860, after an Anglo-French force had occupied Peking and burned the Summer Palace (q.v.). The Treaty of Tientsin opened the Yangtze river to foreign shipping and permitted foreign envoys to maintain permanent residence in Peking. The Tsungli Yamen (q.v.), predecessor to the Ministry of Foreign Affairs, was established in 1861. Previously, relations with foreign states formed one of the responsibilities of the Board of Rites (q.v.).

The existence of the Tsungli Yamen and the presence of a British minister in Peking greatly improved diplomatic access. The establishment of the Imperial Maritime Customs (IMC, q.v.) in 1859 promoted order and uniformity in foreign trade. The British not only had a minister resident in Peking, they also had a British subject, Sir Robert Hart (q.v.), as Inspector General of the IMC from 1863 to 1908. He had more and better access to the Tsungli Yamen than any of the diplomats.

Britain's example in annexing Hong Kong was later followed by France, Germany, Japan and Russia (qq.v.). Until 1895 the areas involved were in vassal status to the Ch'ing dynasty (q.v.) and were peopled by non-Chinese. Britain's annexation of the southern part of Burma (q.v.) in 1826 went unnoticed in China, since it did not interfere with the decennial tribute the Burmese kings sent to Peking. Britain's annexation of Upper Burma in 1886 met with Chinese protests, but the issues were settled by the Burma-Tibet Convention,

signed at Peking July 24, 1886, which allowed continuation of the tribute while acknowledging British paramountcy in Burma. Britain also agreed not to press for the opening of Tibet (q.v.).

In 1898 Britain signed 99-year leases for Weihaiwei in Shantung province (q.v.) and the New Territories in Hong Kong. At the same time, London resisted calls from the British mercantile community in China for a British "sphere of influence" in the Yangtze valley. Instead, Britain encouraged the American announcement of the Open Door Policy (q.v.) in 1899.

The British mission at Peking played a leading role in the resistance of the foreign legations to the Boxer Rebellion (1900, q.v.), and British (largely Indian) troops were the first to reach the besieged. However, the largest contingents of the allied troops were Japanese and Russian.

In spite of the Burma-Tibet Convention, Britain continued to press for the opening of Tibet to trade. In 1894 an IMC customs house was opened at Yatung, on the border between Tibet and Sikkim, though trade did not flourish. Sino-British disputes over Tibet were not resolved by Col. Younghusband's expedition to Lhasa in 1904, nor by the Sino-British agreement of April 1906, nor by the Simla Convention of 1914.

The Republic of China (q.v.) was established on January 1, 1912, but was not granted immediate diplomatic recognition by any of the major powers. Britain, France, Japan and Russia jointly recognized it on October 10, 1913, the second anniversary of the outbreak of revolution at Wuchang. China entered a period of division and civil war, and Britain was soon engulfed in World War I (1914-1918). Seriously weakened as a result, Britain still maintained its primacy in the China trade, but British political influence declined. In 1928 the Chinese Nationalist government opened negotiations aimed at eliminating extraterritoriality (q.v.). They were abandoned soon, but Britain signed a treaty abolishing the practice on January 11, 1943.

The People's Republic of China (PRC, q.v.) was established October 1, 1949, and Britain extended diplomatic recognition soon after. Relations were not smooth, however, as British residents in China, with few exceptions, were required to leave. Britain sent contingents to the United Nations forces in the Korean War (1950-1953, see under **Korea**), while thousands of Chinese troops, known as Chinese People's Volunteers, fought on the opposite side. In August 1967, the British Legation in Peking was burned during the Cultural Revolution (q.v.). Relations have improved since the death of MAO Tse-tung (1893-1976, q.v.).

In the early 1980s, the major issue between Britain and China was the future of Hong Kong. The lease on the New Territories, which comprises most of the area of the British Crown Colony, is scheduled to expire in 1997. Without that area, which contains the airport and most of the population, Hong Kong is not viable. In December 1984, Britain and the PRC agreed that in 1997 Hong Kong would become an autonomous area under the PRC, with the retention of its economic system for another 50 years.

Morse, H.B. *The International Relations of the Chinese Empire*. London and New York: Longmans, 1910-1918.

Great Leap Forward. This program was launched by MAO Tse-tung (q.v.) in 1958 with the aim of achieving communism through extremely rapid economic development. Very high production targets were set for steel, hydroelectric power and agricultural production. Communes were established in the countryside, and "backyard furnaces" for producing pig iron appeared in many rural areas. In early 1959 the USSR's Nikita Khrushchev asked CHOU En-lai (q.v.), China's premier, where the Russian-trained steel engineers were. CHOU replied that they were in the countryside "forging their proletarian consciousness." Within a short time all Soviet personnel were withdrawn from China and aid was cut off.

The Great Leap Forward caused such disorder that it was abandoned in 1960. However, the man-made famine which resulted from the disruption of agriculture is estimated to have caused the loss of some 20 million lives between 1958 and 1962.

Great Proletarian Cultural Revolution. See under **Cultural Revolution**.

Great Wall. The Great Wall extends about 3,750 miles (6,000 km.) from Shan Hai Kuan, on the seacoast northeast of Peking to a point in the Gobi desert. Although it is the largest man-made structure, it is a myth that it is visible from the moon—it is long enough, but too narrow. The Wall was consolidated by the first emperor, Ch'in Shih Huang Ti (r. 221-206 B.C., q.v.) from earlier segments. It was conceived as a protection from barbarian invasions, and when properly manned and defended served that purpose reasonably well. Even when it was less than effective as a military barrier it was a psychological dividing line, keeping the nomads out and the Chinese in. It did not deter the Mongols and other conquerors, though capturing and crossing it was considered a noteworthy feat.

Guangdong. See **Kwangtung**.

Guangzhou. See **Canton**.

Guilin. See **Kweilin**.

Guizhou. See **Kweichow**.

H

Hai Jui (1513-1587). Ming dynasty (q.v.) official famous for his extreme devotion to honesty and austerity. In a time when official pay was grossly inadequate, he refused to accept any of the unofficial perquisites which other officials took for granted. He lived in extreme poverty, and of his seven children, only one lived to maturity. Two of the others died of malnutrition.

In November 1565, HAI, then an official of the Board of Revenue, sent a memorial to the emperor Ming Chia Ching (r. 1522-1566, q.v.), in which he accused the emperor of responsibility for all the ills of the empire, including extravagance at court, banditry in the countryside and governmental corruption. The emperor was outraged, but did not order HAI's arrest until February 1566. HAI was held in prison until the emperor died in late 1566. In the next reign, that of Ming Lung Ch'ing (r. 1567-1572), he was given a series of posts, the last one being governor of Soochow. Unfortunately, the problems of Soochow did not lend themselves to the solutions favored by HAI, and within a year he was impeached and dismissed. He was recalled to service in 1585 under emperor Ming Wan Li (r. 1573-1619, q.v.), as assistant head of the censorate at Nanking. He was promoted to chief censor in 1586 and submitted another memorial calling for the death penalty for corruption.

In turn he was censured. He was retained in office, however, and died the following year.

In 1962, WU Han, the deputy mayor of Peking, published a play based on HAI Jui's career, which was, in fact, a concealed attack on the ideological policies of MAO Tse-tung (q.v.), and by implication a defense of the pragmatic policies of his critics, such as LIU Shao-ch'i (q.v.). The play was bitterly denounced at the beginning of the Cultural Revolution (q.v.) in 1966. As a result, HAI Jui's name is familiar to millions of Chinese who might otherwise be unaware of his career.

Goodrich, L.C. and Chaoying Fang, eds. *Dictionary of Ming Biography.* New York: Columbia University Press, 1976.

Huang, Ray. *1587, A Year of No Importance.* New Haven: Yale University Press, 1981.

Hainan Island. Located opposite the Luichow (Leizhou) peninsula on the southern coast of Kwangtung province (q.v.), of which it forms a part. With an area of 13,000 sq. mi. (21,000 sq. km.), it is slightly smaller than Taiwan. In 1981 it had a population of 5.5 million.

Hainan came under Chinese control during the T'ang dynasty (618-906 A.D., q.v.) but has never been developed. Mountains in the central area rise over 6,000 feet. The Sung poet SU Tung-p'o (1036-1101) was exiled there, the first government official to receive such a sentence, though other locations had been used previously. The Japanese used it for training their troops in jungle warfare prior to the occupation of Southeast Asia in World War II.

The southern part of the island is the Li-Miao Autonomous Prefecture, inhabited by members of these two minority groups.

The climate is subtropical, and the island produces coconuts, rubber, pepper and palm oil.

Hakka. This is the Cantonese pronunciation of *k'o chia* (*kejia*) meaning "guest people." The Hakka are a Chinese minority group found in Fukien, Kwangtung and Kwangsi (qq.v.), as well as in Hong Kong and Taiwan. They have their own dialect as well as certain cultural traits which set them apart from their neighbors, e.g. they have never practiced foot-binding. They are believed to have moved southward from the Honan and Shansi (qq.v.) area starting about the 9th century A.D., perhaps to avoid warfare, or the increasing influence of non-Chinese groups, such as the Tartars and Mongols, in those areas.

The Hakka in some places have developed communal dwellings which in some respects resemble modern apartment houses. One theory is that hostile receptions from the indigenous inhabitants made defensible residences for the "guest people" more desirable than not. (See Boyd, Andrew. *Chinese Architecture*. Chicago: University of Chicago Press, 1962, for examples.)

HUNG Hsiu-ch'uan (1813-1864), leader of the Taiping Rebellion (1851-1864, qq.v.), was a Hakka, as were many of his followers. The Taiping policy opposing foot-binding may have derived from Hakka practice.

Han.1. The name of a feudal state (408-230 B.C.) of the Warring States Period (q.v.). The Chinese character used to designate this state is also used for present-day Korea. *Han* in the following entries is represented by a different character.

2. Han dynasty (206 B.C.-221 A.D.). The Han dynasty was roughly contemporary with the Roman Empire and has been compared with it. In the Chinese view, the Han was the classic period. Although the T'ang (618-906 A.D.) and the Sung (960-1279, qq.v.), were more brilliant, both dynasties built on foundations laid in the Han period.

The Han dynasty is divided into two periods, the Western or Earlier Han (206 B.C.-9 A.D.) and the Eastern or Later Han (25-221 A.D.), separated by an interregnum under the usurper WANG Mang (q.v.). The Western Han capital was located near present-day Sian (Xi'an, q.v.), while the Eastern Han ruled from Loyang (Luoyang, q.v.). The dynasty was founded by LIU Pang, by whose temple name, Han Kao Tsu (qq.v.), he is usually known to historians. He was the first non-aristocrat to become a monarch in China. A brilliant strategist, he established a firm foundation on the ruins of the hated Ch'in dynasty (221-206 B.C., q.v.), and managed to leave his heirs in undisputed control of China. The philosophy of Legalism (q.v.), adopted by the Ch'in rulers, left a legacy of hatred on the part of the Confucians, and they formed the dominant group in the new dynasty. Han Kao Tsu retained a number of Ch'in policies, though they were usually enforced in the name of Confucianism. For example, pao chia (q.v.), a system of social control through mutual responsibility, was retained and has persisted to the present day.

Han Kao Tsu continued the Ch'in practice of appointing officials to posts where they were not known and had no local power base. However, he did give principalities to some of his relatives and old comrades-in-arms. This resulted in a reemergence of feudalism which had to be checked some decades later. Han Kao Tsu was succeeded by his son, Hui Ti (temple name), but rule was exercised by his mother, the empress Lü, who had been Han Kao Tsu's wife since well before the establishment of the dynasty. She later ruled in her own right, and was succeeded by the two able rulers who were overshadowed by the fifth emperor (and sixth ruler) of the dynasty.

This was Han Wu Ti (r. 140-86 B.C., q.v.), the greatest of the Han rulers, and one of the greatest rulers in Chinese history. The Han empire reached its greatest extent during his reign. At its peak, the Han empire extended into Korea, Vietnam and much of Central Asia. Neither of the first two represented a threat to China, but much of Mongolia was controlled by nomadic people known as Hsiung-nu (q.v.), who are identified with the Huns. The emperor sent his minister CHANG Ch'ien (q.v.) on a diplomatic mission to Western Asia, and the latter brought back the first reports of the area. CHANG Ch'ien's travels in Central Asia were motivated by the need for allies against the Hsiung-nu.

Domestically, Han Wu Ti's reign was notable for his decree banning primogeniture, thus leading to the fragmentation of the great estates and the gradual elimination of feudal power. The emperor supplanted the nobility with appointed officials, selected on merit, in what eventually developed into the examination system (q.v.). It was also in his reign that the historian SSU-MA Ch'ien completed the *Shih Chi* (qq.v.).

Han Wu Ti's successors were weak, and power slipped into the hands of the relatives of empresses and eunuchs (q.v.). This led to the usurpation by WANG Mang in 9 A.D. WANG's sweeping reforms led to dissatisfaction and eventually to rebellion within China and in the outlying areas.

In 25 A.D. a member of the LIU family, whose relationship to the previous emperors is unclear, placed himself on the throne and ruled for the next 32 years. He restored order in China, reasserted control in the outlying areas, maintained most of the administrative structure of the Western Han and bequeathed a revitalized empire to his successor. Unfortunately, none of his successors was his equal. A line of emperors, most of whom acceded to the throne at an early age, did little for the dynasty. Court intrigues, struggles for power among the families of various empresses, the influence of eunuchs and the rise of regional powers eroded the authority of the Eastern Han. Rebellion by the Yellow Turbans (q.v.) in 184 A.D. marked the beginning of the dynasty's end. The emperors became puppets in the hands of military men seeking control of the empire.

The last of the Eastern Han emperors remained the ward of the military leader TS'AO Ts'ao (q.v.) throughout his reign (189-220 A.D.). On TS'AO Ts'ao's death in 220 A.D. he abdicated, thus bringing a formal end to a dynasty whose real power had dissipated half a century earlier.

The Han contribution to Chinese culture was significant. Paper was invented about 100 A.D. and contributed to the spread of literacy. Because of the improvement in writing materials, calligraphy developed into a fine art. The examination system was put in place, though not all Han officials were selected on that basis. The pattern of imperial rule established in the Han became the model for governance for some 2,000 years.

The Han dynasty was succeeded by a period of disunity which lasted until the Sui dynasty (589-618, q.v.) succeeded, where many others had failed, in reuniting the empire. The first successor states to the Han were the Three Kingdoms (q.v.), followed by the Western and Eastern Chin and then a period of division between north and south. The most significant of the states of this period were the Northern and Western Wei (q.v.).

3. Shu-Han (221-263 A.D.). One of the Three Kingdoms which ruled a divided China after the fall of the Han dynasty. It was founded by LIU Pei (q.v.), a member of the imperial family, and was located in Szechwan.

4. Name of four minor and short-lived dynasties, one in the 4th century and three in the 10th century A.D. One of these, the Later Han (947-951), was one of the Five Dynasties (q.v.) that ruled successively between the downfall of the T'ang (618-906) and the rise of the Sung (960-1279) and is accepted by traditional Chinese historians as a legitimate imperial dynasty.

Loewe, Michael. *Everyday Life in Early Imperial China.* New York: Putnam, 1968.

HAN Fei Tzu (280 [?]-233 B.C.). HAN Fei (*Tzu* means "master") was a member of the ruling family of the feudal state of Han. He was the most highly regarded theoretician of the Legalist school of philosophy (q.v.). He studied under the Confucian scholar HSUN Tzu (q.v.) and absorbed some Confucian concepts.

Perhaps HAN's most important philosophical contribution was his belief that historical developments change circumstances, and that what was appropriate for earlier rulers might not be at all useful to their successors. Thus, while the kings of antiquity might have ruled through benevolence, the rulers of the period of the Warring States (q.v.), in which latter years he lived, would be better served by a system of Draconian laws and severe punishments.

Some of HAN's writings reached the ruler of the state of Ch'in, who is known to history as Ch'in Shih Huang Ti (q.v.), the unifier of China and its first emperor. The ruler was already putting Legalist principles to practice. This involved forcing the common people to become soldiers and farmers and the suppression of "idle" scholars. He invited HAN to the court of Ch'in, but HAN declined.

When Ch'in threated the Han state, HAN Fei did go to the former as an ambassador. The chief officer of Ch'in, LI Ssu (see under **Ch'in**), had been a fellow student of HSUN Tzu. Afraid of having a competitor, LI arranged to have HAN Fei imprisoned and poisoned. HAN's theories, however, lived on in the Ch'in state.

Fung, Yülan, and Derk Bodde, trans. *A History of Chinese Philosophy.* Princeton: Princeton University Press, 1953.

Han Kao Tsu (d. 195 B.C.). Temple name (q.v.) of the founder and first emperor of the Han dynasty (206 B.C.-221 A.D., q.v.). He reigned from 206 to 196 B.C. His original name was LIU Pang. LIU came from a peasant family in what is now Kiangsu province (q.v.). He was a military officer of the state of Ch'u (q.v.), which had been conquered by the newly established Ch'in dynasty (255-

206 B.C., q.v.). After the death of Ch'in Shih Huang Ti (q.v.), the first Ch'in emperor, in 210 B.C., rising dissatisfaction with the oppressive rule he had introduced led to civil war. For a short period the incessant warfare of the Warring States period (484-255 B.C., q.v.) seemed to have returned.

The final contest was between two generals of Ch'u—LIU Pang and the aristocrat HSIANG Yü (q.v.). The two were well matched in military skill, but LIU proved to be a better judge of men and selected able counselors to advise him. Further, while he was quite capable of taking life, he was not identified with the policy of massacre that mars HSIANG's reputation.

After HSIANG's defeat and death, LIU initially refused to become ruler; however, he succumbed to the repeated requests of his advisers, and reluctantly accepted the luxury with which the Ch'in emperors had lived. LIU, the first Chinese ruler not to come from an aristocratic family, was criticized by his more noble observers. (The second non-aristocratic Chinese ruler was CHU Yuan-chang who established the Ming dynasty in 1368, qq.v.).

Han Kao Tsu did not reestablish the feudal system which Ch'in Shih Huang Ti had destroyed, though he did give titles and estates to relatives and former comrades-in-arms. This imposed on his great-grandson, Han Wu Ti (q.v.), the necessity of eliminating the system again a half-century later.

Han Kao Tsu retained the Ch'in system of appointing officials to rule on the authority of the emperor. While most of his officials were Confucian scholars, not Legalists (qq.v.), many Confucian precepts were enforced with a thoroughly Legalist severity.

The Han dynasty is regarded as a classical age, and for this reason, Han Kao Tsu is revered as a major figure in Chinese history.

HAN Lin-erh. See under **Red Turbans**.

Han Wu Ti (154-87 B.C.). Temple name (q.v.) of the fifth emperor (and sixth ruler, r. 140-87 B.C.) of the Han dynasty (206 B.C.-221 A.D.), generally regarded as the most capable and powerful ruler of the dynasty, and one of the greatest rulers in Chinese history. During his half-century rule China achieved control of most of what is now Sinkiang (q.v.), parts of southern Manchuria and northern Korea, and integrated parts of Chekiang, Fukien, Kwangtung, Kwangsi and northern Vietnam (qq.v.) into China. He sent the explorer-diplomat CHANG Ch'ien (q.v.) west as far as Afghanistan, where he was the first Chinese known to have encountered men from the Mediterranean world—Greeks descended from those who accompanied Alexander the Great on his conquest of Central Asia.

Internally, the emperor laid the foundation for the examination system (q.v.) by selecting officials with regard to ability, rather than with regard to birth and rank. At the same time, Han Wu Ti took steps to reduce the power of the nobility by requiring each feudal lord to divide his estate equally among his sons, rather than leaving it all to one. This ensured a gradual reduction in the concentration of wealth in the hands of the great houses. The most important literary accomplishment of the reign was the *Shih Chi* of SSU-MA Ch'ien (qq.v.), a comprehensive history of China up until its author's lifetime.

HAN Yü (786-824). T'ang dynasty (q.v.) scholar and official. Four of HAN's poems appear in the compilation *300 Poems of the T'ang Dynasty*, but he is remembered as a philosopher and the greatest writer of prose of his period.

HAN was a staunch Confucianist in an era when most of his intellectual peers were concerned with Buddhism or Taoism (qq.v.). In 819 he wrote a memorial to the throne protesting against the reception given a Buddhist relic (said to be a finger bone of the historical Buddha) by the emperor T'ang Hsien-tsung. In it he referred to Buddhism as a barbarian practice brought in from foreign countries, and described the relic as Buddha's "decayed and rotten bone, his ill-omened and filthy remains." This so enraged the emperor that he banished the writer to Kwangtung province (q.v.).

HAN Yü's lasting contribution to Chinese intellectual history was in laying the groundwork for the Neo-Confucianism developed by CHU Hsi (q.v.) in the Sung dynasty (960-1279, q.v.). He did this by giving new importance to the *Book of Mencius* and to the *Great Learning*, both of which became part of the classic syllabus—the Four Books (q.v.).

HAN's philosophic outlook was deeply influenced by the Taoism and Buddhism he rejected, and as a consequence the Neo-Confucian philosophy which developed later had characteristics which would have seemed very unfamiliar to Confucians of an earlier age.

Fung, Yu-lan, and Derk Bodde, trans. *A History of Chinese Philosophy*. Princeton: Princeton University Press, 1953.

Hangchow (Hangzhou). Capital of Chekiang province (q.v.). Population: 1,000,000 (1980). Hangchow's importance dates from the period of the Sui dynasty (589-618 A.D., q.v.) when it became the terminus of the Grand Canal (q.v.), permitting the shipment of agricultural products to the northern provincial capitals. It was the seat of the Southern Sung dunasty from 1127 to 1276 (see under **Sung**), when it was occupied by the Mongols who established the Yuan dynasty (1279-1368, q.v.).

At its peak, just before the Mongol conquest, Hangchow was probably the largest and richest city in the world, with a population equal to that of the present day. It was visited a few years after the Mongol conquest by the Venetian Marco Polo (q.v.). Polo refers to it as Quinsai, which is a transcription of *hsing-tsai* meaning "temporary capital." Polo's description of the city has been largely confirmed from Chinese sources, and it apparently had changed very little in the period between the end of the Sung and his arrival there.

There is a saying in Chinese "Heaven above, Soochow and Hangchow below" which refers to the beauty of the two cities. Hangchow is justly famous, situated at the side of the West lake (which is artificial and only about 10 feet deep) and nearly surrounded by hills. Because of social and economic conditions the population of Hangchow swelled in the Sung period, and because there was little room for outside expansion, the city grew up. Many houses were three and four stories in height, which was unusual for the China of the period.

Hangchow was badly damaged during the Taiping Rebellion (q.v.) of the mid-19th century, but the setting remains beautiful.

Gernet, Jacques. *Daily Life in China on the Eve of the Mongol Invasion*. Stanford: Stanford University Press, 1962.

Hangzhou. See **Hangchow**.

Hanlin Academy. The name means "forest of writing brushes." Founded by the emperor T'ang Ming-huang (r. 712-755 A.D., q.v.), it was restricted to those scholars who had done extremely well in the imperial examinations. It was a great honor to be a Hanlin scholar and this was always mentioned in the biographies of those who had qualified. The Academy lasted until the end of the Ch'ing dynasty (1644-1911, q.v.), though there were periods when there were no examinations (as during many years of the Yüan dynasty, as well as times of disunion and internal warfare). See **Examination system**.

Harbin. Capital of Heilungkiang province (q.v.). Population: 2 million (1980). Harbin is an important rail center and also a major producer of steam turbines, boilers, electric motors, bearings, machine tools and cement.

Harbin was built to be the administrative center for the Chinese Eastern Railway (q.v.). In spite of its name, the latter was built in the 1890s by the Russians with French capital. The purpose was to cut off several thousand miles of travel between Vladivostok and the rest of Russia. Harbin was built from about 1900. At one point prior to World War II, it was the largest European settlement in Asia, with a population of 100,000 Russians. Only a handful of elderly Russians remain there.

Hart, Sir Robert (1835-1911). Born in Ulster, Northern Ireland, Robert Hart attended the Wesleyan Connexional School in Dublin and matriculated at Queen's College, Belfast, at the age of 15. He graduated with highest honors at the age of 18 and was given an appointment as student interpreter in the British Consular Service. He reached Hong Kong in July 1854, and was sent to Ningpo (q.v.). Hart resigned from the Consular Service in 1859 to accept the post of assistant commissioner in the newly established Imperial Maritime Customs (IMC) at Canton, under Horatio Nelson Lay (qq.v.). When Lay went on leave in 1861, Hart became acting inspector general (I.G.), and in 1863 he succeeded Lay to become the second I.G., a post he held until 1908.

Hart's position as the director of an agency of the Chinese government staffed with Western and Chinese officials was unique. He dealt directly with the Tsungli Yamen (q.v.), predecessor of the Ministry of Foreign Affairs. The director of the Yamen was I-hsin (q.v.), a member of the imperial family. Because Hart could communicate in Chinese, both spoken and written, and because he had access to I-hsin, he was in closer touch with the ruling circles of the Manchu court than any other foreigner.

The British government recognized Hart's capabilities and his special position by knighting him in 1882, offering him the position of minister to China in 1885 (which he declined) and making him a baronet in 1893. Had he accepted the diplomatic appointment in 1885, he probably would have stayed in China no longer than another five years, but by remaining as I.G. in the IMC, he was able to extend that to 1908.

Hart's activities in the IMC were not restricted to customs matters. He established the Chinese Lighthouse Service, the National Post Office and the T'ung Wen Kuan (q.v.), or school for foreign languages. At one point it seemed likely he would be put in charge of the naval department. The Tsungli Yamen also used Hart and his London representative, James Duncan Campbell, in a secret capacity to settle the war with France (q.v.) in 1885.

The Boxer Rebellion (q.v.) in 1900 came as a surprise to the usually well-informed Hart. His house and its contents were destroyed. The only thing saved was his complete set of journals, now held by the Queen's University, Belfast. Nevertheless, Hart was deeply concerned at the extreme anti-Chinese attitudes developing in Europe as a result of the rebellion, and wrote a book, *These from the Land of Sinim*, (London, 1901) to provide a more balanced view.

In May 1906, the Chinese government established a new Board of Customs Affairs to oversee the IMC. This was done without advance notice to Hart, and he saw it as a step toward phasing out the foreign presence and control of the IMC. Typically, he reacted mildly, keeping in mind the interests of all concerned.

Hart retired to England in 1908, but retained the title of I.G. until his death in 1911, a few months before the revolution of October 10 led to the overthrow of the Ch'ing dynasty (q.v.) he had served so well for half a century. His long career coincided with the period when British influence in China was at its peak, and he himself was widely regarded as the most influential Briton in China. He created and administered an agency of the Chinese government staffed by Chinese and foreigners. Free from corruption, it provided the Ch'ing dynasty in its declining years with a steady and increasing source of income. He also worked closely and sympathetically with the Ch'ing government in modernizing its concepts and methods.

Fairbank, J.K., ed. *The I.G. in Peking*. Cambridge: Harvard University Press, 1975.

Wright, Stanley F. *Hart and the Chinese*

Customs. Belfast: Wm. Mullen & Son, 1950.

Hay, John. See under **Open Door Policy**.

Hebei. See **Hopeh**.

Heilongjiang. See **Heilungkiang**.

Heilungkiang (Heilongjiang) **province**. Area: 460,000 sq. km. (180,000 sq. mi.). Population: 31,690,000 (1979). Capital: Harbin (q.v.). Heilungkiang means "Black Dragon River," which is the Chinese name for the Amur river. It is the northernmost of China's provinces, bounded on the north and east by the USSR, on the south by Kirin (Jilin) province (q.v.), and on the west by the Inner Mongolia Autonomous Region (q.v.).

Heilungkiang was part of Manchuria (q.v.), which was divided in 1903 into three provinces. It has a severe continental climate, with cold, dry winters and short, hot and wet summers. Agricultural products include spring wheat, soybeans, sugar beets, sunflowers (used for oil seed), corn, millet and kaoliang (sorghum). The province has both coal and oil, including the famous Ta Ch'ing oilfields, the largest in China.

Henan. See **Honan**.

Hinayana Buddhism. *Hinayana* means "lesser vehicle" in Sanskrit, and is the term used by followers of Mahayana Buddhism (q.v.) to designate the other major tradition. It is considered somewhat pejorative by those so designated, and they prefer the term Theravada Buddhism, and call themselves Theravadins. Theravada Buddhism is considered by many to be closer to the teachings of the historical Buddha. It holds that salvation is an individual matter and that there is little one person can do for another. This contrasts with the bodhisattva (q.v.) concept so important to the Mahayanists.

A number of the texts indentified as Hinayana have been translated into Chinese, but the success of the Mahayanists was evident by the T'ang dynasty (618-906, q.v.). Theravadins are in the majority in Burma, Cambodia, Ceylon and Laos, but not in Vietnam, which derives its Buddhist traditions from China. Most of the Theravadin texts have been preserved in Pali, a form of Prakrit, which is related to Sanskrit. Most of the Buddhist texts which have been translated into English are from the Theravadin canon and have been translated from Pali.

Honan (Henan) **province**. Area: 160,000 sq. km. (61,800 sq. mi.). Population: 71,890,000 (1979). Capital: Chengchou (Zhengzhou), formerly Chenghsien. Honan is bounded on the east by Shantung and Anhwei provinces, on the southwest by Hupei and Shensi, and on the northwest by Shansi and Hopei (qq.v.).

The western part of Honan is mountainous, the central part rises to loess highlands, and the eastern is flat alluvial plain. Wheat is the most important crop, but cotton, sesame and tobacco are also important.

Chengchou is located at the intersection of the only north-south rail line, the Peking-Canton line, and the main east-west line. It is also an important center for textiles and textile machinery.

Because it was the site of the Shang dynasty (1766-1122 B.C., q.v.), Honan may be considered the cradle of Chinese civilization, and agriculture has been practiced there for several thousand years. It contains many historic sites, including the cities of Anyang, Kaifeng and Loyang (qq.v.).

Hong Kong (Xiang Gang). British Crown Colony on the coast of Kwangtung province (q.v.). Hong Kong Island—area 29 sq. mi.—was ceded to Great Britain in perpetuity by the Treaty of Nanking (1842, q.v.). Kowloon and Stonecutters Island were ceded in the Conventions of Peking, 1860 (q.v.). The New Territories were leased for 99 years in 1898. The combined area is about 400 sq. mi.

At the time Hong Kong Island was ceded to Britain it was almost unpopulated. The land is unsuitable for agriculture, and there are no known mineral deposits, but it has one of the finest deep-water harbors in the world.

Hong Kong has always been a trading center, with much of its early prosperity based on the opium trade (q.v.). The population reached .5 million in 1916, and 1.6 million in 1941. Japanese oppression during the occupation of World War II (q.v.) induced many residents to return to their original homes in nearby Kwangtung or to go elsewhere. In 1945 the population was .6 million, but civil war and the establishment of the People's Republic of China (PRC) in 1949 led to a flood of refugees. In 1984 the population was estimated at 5.5 million, 99% of whom are ethnic Chinese. The majority are from Kwangtung, and the most commonly heard dialects are forms of Cantonese.

Most Chinese regard the Treaty of Nanking as "unequal," and therefore invalid. This is the basis for the Chinese position which led to the agreement between Britain and the PRC in December 1984, which provides for the incorporation of

Hong Kong as part of the PRC in 1997. While Britain does not accept the invalidity of the Treaty of Nanking, the lease on the New Territories will expire in 1997, and without them, Hong Kong is not viable. Hence Britain saw no alternative to retrocession.

Hopeh (Hebei) **province**. Area: 180,000 sq. km. (69,500 sq. mi.). Population: 51,050,000 (1980). Capital: Shihkiachwang (Shijiazhuang). Hopeh is bordered on the east by Liaoning province (q.v.), on the southeast by the Pohai (Bohai) Gulf and Shantung (q.v.), on the south by Honan, on the west by Shansi, and on the north by the Inner Mongolia Autonomous Region (qq.v.). The municipalities of Peking and Tientsin are nearly surrounded by Hopeh.

Most of the province is a flat alluvial plain only slightly above sea level. The primary crop is wheat, but corn, kaoliang (sorghum), soybeans and sweet potatoes are also important. Hopeh produces one-quarter of China's cotton. Hopeh has significant coal resources near Tangshan, the site of the massive earthquake in 1976 (measuring 8.2 on the Richter scale), which may have resulted in as many as 700,000 deaths and a like number of injured.

Ho-shen (1750-1799). Manchu Bannerman (see **Banners**) who managed to achieve and hold the complete confidence of the emperor Ch'ien Lung from 1775 until the latter's death in 1799. Ho-shen was physically attractive, pleasant in manner and well-spoken. He was made an imperial bodyguard in 1772 and his meteoric rise generated many rumors, not the least of which was a discreditable relationship with the emperor.

Ho-shen was one of the most con-spicuously corrupt men of a period of imperial luxury and official corruption. His position enabled him to affect the careers of nearly all officials, whether for good or for ill. Attempts by honest officials to curb his power were unsuccessful, though they did occasionally bring ruin to his henchmen.

Ho-shen's dominance of the emperor increased in the latter's old age, and the period between 1796, when Ch'ien Lung abdicated, and 1799, when he died, was practically a Ho-shen regency. The emperor's death, however, brought de facto power to his successor, Chia-ch'ing, who was emperor in name only for the first three years of his reign. Chia-ch'ing moved immediately. While Ho-shen was permitted to take his own life, out of respect for his recently deceased patron, his massive wealth was confiscated.

Hummel, Arthur W., ed. *Eminent Chinese of the Ch'ing Period*. Washington: Government Printing Office, 1943.

Howqua. Properly, *hao kuan* (*hao guan*), meaning "great official." Although Western writers of the 18th and 19th centuries assumed it was a name, it was actually the title of the chief merchant of the monopoly at Canton called the Cohong (q.v.). The title was held by four members of the WU family, one of whom, WU Ping-chien (1769-1843) was reported to have amassed a fortune of $26 million in Spanish currency in 1834, possibly the largest mercantile fortune in the world at the time.

Hsi Hsia (Xi Xia). Name of a semi-independent state located in what is now the Ningxia Hui Autonomous Area, formerly the Ningsia province (q.v.). Its history covers the period from 882 when the T'ang dynasty (618-906, q.v.) recognized it as a dukedom until 1227, when it was subjugated by the Mongols under Chingis Khan (q.v.), who died during the campaign.

Hsi Hsia acknowledged T'ang suzerainty, but never that of the Sung dynasty (960-1279, q.v.), with which it warred from time to time. Its relations with the Liao dynasty (907-1125) and with the Chin (1115-1234, q.v.) were mixed, though it acknowledged the suzerainty of each at different times.

The Hsi Hsia were a Tangut (Tibetan) people who did not speak Chinese. They developed their own form of written language, based on Chinese characters, an example of which may be seen in Chiang Yee, *Chinese Calligraphy*, London: Methuen & Co., 1955. The author, writing in the 1930s, implies that the script was still in use at that time.

HSI Shih (5th century B.C.). HSI Shih was a famous beauty and femme fatale, perhaps the Chinese equivalent of Helen of Troy. She came of a poor family, but her looks were so striking that she was trained in the arts and graces and then sent to be the consort of the ruler of the state of Wu (q.v.), a feudal state of the Warring States period (q.v.). She succeeded in so distracting and debauching the ruler that Wu was destroyed in 473 B.C. Ever since that time HSI Shih's name has been cited as an example of a woman so beautiful that a king might give up everything for her favors.

Hsi Yü Chi. The title means "Journey to the West" and is a novel written by WU Ch'eng-en (c. 1500-1580) of the Ming dynasty (1368-1644, q.v.). It is based on a series of popular stories about the travels of the T'ang dynasty (618-906) monk Hsüan Tsang (qq.v.) who spent 17 years traveling abroad

in search of Buddhist texts. Hsüan Tsang left an account of his travels, but the novel bears only a slight resemblance to it.

The novel is concerned with the monk's journey and the trials he undergoes. It provides him with three animal companions who appear in translations as Monkey, Pigsy and Sandy, and who personify certain qualities. Pigsy, e.g., is depicted as a glutton. The travelers encounter ogres, demons, pirates, storms and other misfortunes, but eventually achieve their objective.

The real hero of the book is Monkey, and this is suggested in the opening chapters, which portray his birth as a stone monkey from a stone egg with a variety of detail drawn from Taoist mythology. All of the details were comprehensible to Chinese of the period, but are confusing to those unfamiliar with this aspect of traditional Chinese lore. In Arthur Waley's translation (see below) the first eight of thirty chapters are devoted to this aspect of the novel. Hsüan Tsang doesn't appear until chapter nine.

Many of the incidents in the novel are comic, or are intended to be so. The general impression is one of boisterous adventure, in spite of the presence of the austere monk. The novel is extremely long, but most Chinese readers are familiar with abridged versions.

Waley, Arthur, trans. *Monkey.* New York: Grove Press, 1958 (reprint).

Waley, Arthur. *The Real Tripitaka, and Other Pieces.* New York: Macmillan, 1952.

Hsia (Xia) **dynasty** (2205-1766 B.C.) 1. The Hsia were a preliterate, Neolithic people centered in Shansi province (q.v.). They are now identified with producers of painted pottery, but had no metal implements. They were overcome and superseded by the Shang dynasty (1766-1122 B.C., q.v.), which was technologically more advanced. The traditional history of the Hsia was transmitted in the *Shih Chi* of SSU-MA Ch'ien (qq.v.). It includes a list of 17 kings, of whom the first, Yü the Great, the last of the Three Sages (see under **Legendary Period)**, is described in very favorable terms, and the last as a brutal tyrant, a pattern which is repeated in several later dynasties. (See under **Mandate of Heaven.**)

2. One of the Sixteen Kingdoms (q.v.). Based in Shensi province (q.v.), it fell in 431 A.D. to the Northern Wei (386-532 A.D., q.v.).

3. Western Hsia. See under **Hsi Hsia**.

HSIANG Yü (d. 205 B.C.). Born of an aristocratic family of the state of Ch'u (q.v.), he was of huge size and strong enough to lift a bronze cauldron by himself. An enthusiastic warrior, he was ready to participate in the wars which arose in the declining years of the Ch'in dynasty (218-206 B.C., q.v.). His announced purpose was to replace the Ch'in ruler with the ruler of Ch'u, in a restoration of the tradition of hegemon of the Warring States period (484-255 B.C., q.v.).

HSIANG was a master strategist, though he had the assistance of some excellent advisers; however, he was a bloodthirsty warrior and his record is one of massacre of surrendered armies and of civilian populations of captured cities. He succeeded in eliminating his competiton, with the exception of LIU Pang, a peasant who had become his comrade-in-arms and sworn brother.

The king of Ch'u directed both of these generals to capture the Ch'in capital, and LIU reached it first. Following the advice of an astute couselor, LIU accepted the surrender of the Ch'in emperor and spared the lives of those in the city. HSIANG arrived later, and as LIU's commander, massacred the emperor and the population, and banished LIU. He then named the king of Ch'u as ruler.

That did not last, however, and after executing the king, HSIANG declared himself the ruler, thus opening the way for LIU to appear as a punisher of rebellion, rather than a rebel himself. Many battles and narrow escapes followed, but ultimately HSIANG was defeated, still puzzled by his ability to win battles but his inability to win the war.

LIU Pang went on to found the Han dynasty (206 B.C.-221 A.D., q.v.). His temple name, by which he is generally known, is Han Kao Tsu (q.v.).

Bloodworth, Dennis and Ching Ping Bloodworth. *The Chinese Machiavelli*. New York: Farrar, Straus & Giroux, 1976.

Hsien Feng (1831-1861). Reign title of the seventh emperor (r. 1851-1862) of the Ch'ing dynasty (1644-1911, q.v.). He was the fourth son of his predecessor, Tao Kuang (r. 1821-1850, q.v.). Hsien Feng inherited an empire which had been in serious decline for more than half a century. China's defeat in the Opium War (1839-1842), and the Treaty of Nanking (1842, qq.v.) which resulted, had revealed to the Chinese the weakness of their Manchu rulers. The major internal challenge to the empire during this reign was the Taiping Rebellion (1851-1864, q.v.), which originated in Kwangtung and Kwangsi (qq.v.), and moved on to the Yangtze basin. The rebels held Nanking as their capital from 1853 to 1864, and in their thrust to the north came within a few miles of Tientsin. At the same time (1851-1868), the Nien rebels (q.v.) kept much of North China in turmoil, and Muslim rebellions broke out in Yunnan and parts of the northwest.

The court's response was to send Manchu troops into action, but it soon became clear that 19th-century Manchus were incapable of repeating their ancestors' exploits. Volunteer forces were then recruited and put under the leadership of such able Chinese as LI Hung-chang, TSENG Kuo-fan and TSO Tsung-t'ang (qq.v.).

The major external challenge arose from pressure by the Western powers, led by Great Britain, to obtain fuller compliance with the terms of the early treaties and also their revision. The court's policy was to hold the foreigners at arm's length and to insist that all transactions be handled by the Imperial Commissioner for Foreign Affairs, YEH Ming-ch'en (1807-1859, q.v.), concurrently the governor of Kwangtung and Kwangsi. YEH was occupied with suppressing rebellion and piracy, and refused to consider treaty revision. He also refused to receive the foreign envoys. The envoys reported to their governments that the use of force would be necessary to achieve their objectives.

These circumstances led to the *Arrow* War (1857-1860, q.v.) and the Treaties of Tientsin (1858, q.v.). British and French attempts to exchange ratifications in 1859 were repulsed militarily. They returned in force in 1860, and proceeded to move toward Peking. Manchu success in defeating the foreign aims in 1859 had led the emperor to believe that they could not reach his capital, but the Western forces were stronger than in the previous year. Negotiations were undertaken and continued until September 18, when imperial forces made prisoners of 39 British and French operating under a flag of truce. Several of these were killed and the others mistreated, though evidence of this did not appear until the release of the survivors on October 8.

On October 6 the allies captured the Summer Palace (q.v.) from which the emperor had decamped and fled to Jehol (q.v.). On October 13 the allies entered Peking, and on October 18 the Summer Palace was destroyed, in retaliation for the deaths of the allied prisoners. The Conventions of Peking (see under **Arrow War**) were signed later that month.

Hsien Feng was ashamed to return to Peking, not wishing to face either his own people or the foreign ambassadors, who had obtained the right of audience as well as residence in the capital. He died in Jehol on August 22, 1861, and was succeeded by his only surviving son, who reigned as T'ung Chih (q.v.). Hsien Feng left two empresses who became regents for the child emperor. One, the empress dowager (q.v.) T'zu Hsi, became the dominant figure in the failing dynasty over the next half century.

Hummel, Arthur W., ed. *Eminent Chinese of the Ch'ing Period*. Washington: Government Printing Office, 1943.

Hsing Chung Hui. This is the name of the first revolutionary party organized by SUN Yat-sen (q.v.). It was founded in Honolulu on November 24, 1894, with the stated purpose of founding schools, newpapers and other progressive institutions for China's benefit, but it was also a secret organization working for the destruction of the Ch'ing dynasty (q.v.). The Hsing Chung Hui made one abortive effort at revolution in Canton in 1895, but that led to SUN's being forced to leave Hong Kong for Japan and other places. The Hsing Chung Hui soon had branches in many overseas Chinese communities. In July 1905 it was merged with several other revolutionary organizations in Japan into the successor T'ung Meng Hui (q.v.).

Hsiung-nu. The term refers to a nomadic group sometimes identified with the Huns of European history. We first hear of them in the Han dynasty (206 B.C.-221 A.D.) when they occupied what is now Mongolia and harried the Chinese to the south. Han Wu Ti (r. 140-87 B.C., q.v.) was able to subdue them, but sent his minister CHANG Ch'ien (q.v.) to Central Asia to persuade another nomadic group, the Yueh-chih (q.v.), to return and counterbalance the Hsiung-nu. They declined.

Weakening of Chinese power at the fall of the Han caused a resurgence of Hsiung-nu activity, and at various times in the Period of Disunity (221-589 A.D., q.v.) they controlled much of North China (q.v.).

HSÜ Shih-ch'ang (1855-1939). Ch'ing dynasty (1644-1911, q.v.) official and fifth president of the Republic of China (October 1918-June 1922). He was the only nonmilitary man to hold that position in the Peking Government (q.v.). HSÜ made friends with YUAN Shih-k'ai (q.v.) about 1880 and was his aide and protégé for many years. His rise in the government accompanied YUAN's and in 1905 he was made acting president of the Board of War.

In 1906 he was sent on a mission to Manchuria (q.v.). The presence there of Russian troops, which had been in residence since the Boxer Rebellion (1900, q.v.), and of Japanese troops as a result of the Russo-Japanese War (1904-05, q.v.), was a source of concern to Peking. HSÜ recommended a reorganization of government, the opening of areas which had previously been reserved to Manchus for

Chinese settlement, construction of Chinese railways to compete with Russia and Japan, and the opening of Manchuria to foreign investment to dilute the influence of the latter two powers. An imperial edict of April 1907 ordered a reorganization and HSÜ was made governor general.

After the death of the empress dowager (q.v.) in 1908, YUAN was forced out of government, but HSÜ remained and was in a position to persuade the court to recall YUAN after the outbreak of the revolution in Wuchang on October 10, 1911, and to negotiate the terms on which YUAN accepted. After the abdication of the last emperor, P'u-yi (q.v.), in 1912, HSÜ retired, out of loyalty to the dynasty he had served.

YUAN persuaded HSÜ out of retirement in 1914, and HSÜ spent the next few years trying to reconcile various military leaders, with limited success. He opposed YUAN's attempt to establish a new dynasty. His reputation for neutrality and for mediation led to his being considered an elder statesman and he was elected to the presidency in 1918, though his legitimacy was not accepted by the southern leaders of the republic.

In early 1919 a Chinese delegation attended the Paris Peace Conference to determine disposition of German possessions around the world. When the terms of the Versailles Treaty allocating German concessions in Shantung province (qq.v.) to Japan became known they led to unrest in China. The most serious example was the May Fourth Incident (q.v.). HSÜ had the riotous students jailed, and feeling that China should sign the treaty, delayed in canceling instructions to that effect. These actions aroused greaty antipathy in the oppostion government in Canton, and among Chinese students and intellectuals.

HSÜ stepped down in 1922 and retired to Tientsin, where he devoted himself to scholarly pursuits. When the Japanese occupied Manchuria in 1931 and established the state of Manchukuo (q.v.), they pressed HSÜ to accept a position in the puppet state. He refused, though they invited him to do so more than once before his death in 1939.

Boorman, Howard L., ed. *Biographical Dictionary of Republican China*. New York: Columbia University Press, 1967.

Hsüan-tsang (602-664 A.D.). Hsüan-tsang was a Chinese Buddhist monk who embarked on a pilgrimage to India in 629 and returned to the T'ang capital of Changan in 645. He left an account of his travels which is historically important because of his descriptions of Buddhist kingdoms which disappeared not long afterwards in the Moslem conquests of the next few centuries. They are, in some cases, the only literary evidence we have, though there is also archaeological and numismatic evidence as well. The story he left was as much a guidebook as a diary, similar in this way to the account of Marco Polo, and differing from that of Ennin (qq.v.). It is called the *Hsi Yü Chi*, "An Account of Western Regions," and was the basis on which the popular Ming-dynasty novel of the same name was written. (See **Hsi Yu Chi**.)

Hsüan-tsang's route led him across the Gobi Desert and down to Afghanistan before he entered India. The area is forbidding to travelers even when political conditions make it accessible. His account of the sandstorms and other natural phemonema was embellished in the novel by additional spiritual problems, i.e., devils, evil spirits, ghosts, etc.

Hsüan-tsang returned to China in triumph and spent the last 20 years of his life translating Sanskrit texts into Chinese. His translations have been admired for centuries as some of the most polished examples of their kind, possibly exceeding those of Kumarajiva (q.v.).

Hsüan-tsang was not only a translator. He became the leader of the Mere Ideation school of Buddhism, based on the writings of the Indian Buddhists Vasubandhu and Dharmapala. (For a discussion of his philosophy, see Fung Yu-lan, op. cit.)

Of the 657 texts brought back from India, about 70 were translated under Hsüan-tsang's supervision. He was also involved, by the command of the emperor, in the curious task of translating the *Tao Te Ching* (q.v.) into Sanskrit for transmission to an Indian king. The Taoists were anxious to demonstrate that Buddhism derived from Taoism, a proposition which Hsüan-tsang was not anxious to promote.

He is also called *Tripitaka* (q.v.), a Sanskrit word denoting the three baskets in which the Buddhist texts were kept in ancient times, in both Waley's biography and in the novel.

Waley, Arthur. *The Real Tripitaka*. London: George Allen & Unwin Ltd., 1952.

Fung, Yu-lan and Derk Bodde, trans. *A History of Chinese Philosophy, Vol. II*. Princeton: Princeton University Press, 1953.

HSUN Tzu (298 [?]-238 [?] B.C.). HSUN Tzu means Master HSUN. He was also known as HSUN Ch'ing or HSUN K'uang. HSUN Tzu was the most prominent Confucian scholar and teacher of his time, which was the end of the Warring States Period, just prior to the establishment of the Ch'in dynasty, 255-206 B.C. (qq.v.). He deplored the corruption and warfare of his time and was extremely critical of superstition as exemplified in the Yin-Yang School (q.v.). HSUN Tzu's concept of Heaven is naturalistic, in contrast to that of Confucius, which is a ruling ethical or personal Heaven.

HSUN Tzu was a synthesizer and combined elements of Taoism and Legalism with Confucianism (qq.v.). Two of his students were the famous Legalists LI Ssu and HAN Fei Tzu (qq.v.), leading some later Confucians to criticize him for being a Legalist. He was also a devotee of logic, and his criticisms of other philosophic schools are regarded as among the most effective of the period.

Note: Do not confuse with SUN Tzu (q.v.).

Fung, Yu-lan, and Derk Bodde, trans. *A History of Chinese Philosophy*. Princeton: Princeton University Press, 1953.

Watson, Burton, trans. *Basic Writings of Mo Tzu, Hsun Tzu and Han Fei Tzu*. New York: Columbia University Press, 1967.

Hu Han Min. See under **Kuomintang**.

HU Shih (1891-1962). Educator, scholar and diplomat. HU's father, a minor official, died in 1895, and the child was brought up by his mother and paternal uncles. A precocious student, he had learned 1,000 characters by the age of four. In 1910 he won a scholarship under the Boxer Indemnity (q.v.) and attended Cornell University, from which he graduated in 1914. He became a disciple of John Dewey and obtained his Ph.D. under Dewey at Columbia University, returning to Shanghai in 1917. He was appointed professor of philosophy at Peking University, and soon became a well-known intellectual.

HU espoused the cause of pai hua (q.v.), the use of the spoken language for literary purposes, and was identified with the May Fourth movement (q.v.) of 1919, which endorsed this idea. HU's years of influence were the 1920s, when he wrote essays which appeared in a variety of magazines. He opposed revolution and supported evolution. He criticized the Communists and the Kuomintang (q.v.), and was criticized in turn. He was opposed to war against Japan because he felt it would destroy all the reforms that had been accomplished over the preceding generation.

HU served as ambassador to the United States from 1938 to 1942, and remained there until 1946, when he returned to China to take up the chancellorship of Peking University. He remained there until mid-1948 when the forces of the Chinese Communist party (CCP, q.v.) surrounded the city. HU flew to Nanking and then went to the United States, where he lived most of the rest of his life in semiretirement.

HU went to Taiwan in 1958 where he became president of the Academia Sinica (q.v.), a post he held until his death.

Boorman, Howard L., ed. *Biographical Dictionary of Republican China*. New York: Columbia University Press, 1967-1973.

Grieder, Jerome B. *Hu Shih and the Chinese Renaissance: Liberalism in the Chinese Revolution*. Cambridge: Harvard University Press, 1970.

Huang Ho (Huang He). Also known as the Hwang Ho, or the Yellow river, and nicknamed "China's Sorrow" for its record of disastrous floods, it is China's second longest river, nearly 5,000 km. (3,000 mi.), with a runoff of about 1,630 cubic meters per second. It drains a basin of about 685,000 sq. km. (265,000 sq. mi.).

The river rises in Tsinghai province (q.v.), flows east to Kansu (q.v.), turns north to form an inverted "U" through part of the Ordos Desert in the Inner Mongolia Autonomous Region (q.v.), then south again where it becomes the border between Shansi and Shensi provinces (qq.v.); then it turns east at Tungkwan through Honan and Shantung provinces (qq.v.) on its way to the sea.

At one twentieth the volume of the Yangtze river, it carries nearly three times as much silt, which has always been a major problem. Successive governments have repeatedly tried to control the river by erecting dikes along its banks. Since much of the sand and silt is deposited on the river bottom, the dikes must frequently be raised. At some points the river bottom is several feet above the surrounding countryside, and the sails of boats on the river can been seen high above ground level. The disparity between the level of the river and that of the land has resulted in calamitous floods when the river breaks through its dikes. The river has changed its course many times, sometimes by hundreds of miles. The mouth of the river is sometimes north of Shantung (q.v.) peninsula, and sometimes south of it. Such changes have been accompanied by great loss of life. One such change occurred in 1852, and another in 1938, in the course of fighting between Chinese and Japanese forces. The mouth is now located north of the Shantung peninsula.

The lower valley of the Huang Ho is the location of many of the earliest Chinese historical sites. Anyang (q.v.), capital of the Shang dynasty (1766-1122 B.C., q.v.), is here, as is Loyang (q.v.), which served as capital of the Later Han (25-221 A.D.) and of the T'ang (618-906 A.D.) dynasties (qq.v.).

Huang Ti. The name means "Yellow Emperor." A ruler (r. 2697-2597 B.C.) of the legendary Period (q.v.), he is the third in line after Fu Hsi and Shen Nung (qq.v.), and is believed to have been invented by Taoists (see **Taoism**) about the third century B.C. While his name appears in Taoist texts after that time, it does not appear in more traditional sources.

Hubei. See **Hupeh**.

Hui-yuan (334-416 A.D.). Hui-yuan was a Buddhist monk who laid the foundation for the Pure Land sect (q.v.). His original name was CHIA, and he was a native of Shansi province (q.v.). He was a Confucian scholar and became interested in Taoism (q.v.) and expert in expounding the works of LAO Tzu and CHUANG Tzu (qq.v.). He retired to a Buddhist monastery at the age of 21, and reportedly became a convert as a result of hearing an exposition of the Prajnaparamita Sutra (Wisdom Sutra). After a few years he began to lecture on the subject, but found that some of his students objected to his explanations. He then couched them in Taoist terms, satisfying his audience but laying the groundwork for a problem which was to confuse his successors.

Hui-yuan himself was conscious of the potential problem and spent much time and effort in the search for a sounder command of Buddhist ideas in Chinese translations. He sent followers to Central Asia in search of texts and discussed translation problems with other translators.

Hui-Yuan's teaching that salvation could be achieved through belief in the Amida Buddha, or Amitabha, was later developed into the popular belief that the mere pronouncing of the name would earn the believer admission into the Western Paradise. The Pure Land sect in consequence became the most popular of all Buddhist sects.

Hukuang. The name of a Ming dynasty (1368-1644, q.v.) province. The name means "of the lakes and the two Kuang provinces." It actually contained the provinces of Hunan and Hupeh (qq.v.), into which it was divided by the Ch'ing dynasty (1644-1912, q.v.).

Hunan province. Area: 210,000 sq. km. (81,000 sq. mi.). Population: 52,230,000 (1980). Capital: Changsha. *Hunan* means "south of the [T'ung-t'ing] lake." It is bordered on the east by Kiangsi province, on the south by Kwangtung and Kwangsi, on the west by Kweichow and Szechwan, and on the north by Hupeh (qq.v.).

Hunan is an agricultural province whose main products are rice and tea. It is reputed to possess considerable wealth and its inhabitants have a reputation for a martial spirit which goes back to the state of Ch'u of the Warring States Period (qq.v.).

Hunan has a distinctive dialect and an individual cuisine, somewhat similar to that of Szechwan in that hot peppers are freely used.

Hunan's most famous son is Mao Tse-tung (1893-1976, q.v.). An earlier native was the poet CH'Ü Yüan (d. 288 B.C. [?], q.v.), author of "On Encountering Sorrow."

Hundred Days Reform. On June 11, 1898, the emperor Kuang Hsü (q.v.) issued an edict which announced a program of reform. Its origins lay in the humiliating defeat which China had suffered in the Sino-Japanese War (1894-1895, q.v.), and the suggestions received from reform-minded officials. The emperor appointed several men with modern ideas to draft reform edicts. These included K'ANG Yu-wei and LIANG Ch'i-ch'ao (qq.v.), among others.

Opposition to the reforms by conservative officials was widespread and finally resulted in intervention from the empress dowager (q.v.) on September 20. The next day she placed the emperor in confinement and had all the reform decrees rescinded. A week later six of the reform officials were executed. K'ANG escaped becaused he had been sent to Shanghai by the emperor the day before, and LIANG was given sanctuary in the Japanese legation and later spirited away to Tokyo.

The empress dowager resumed the regency from which she had retired in 1889 (though she had never given up the practice of reading all state papers) and held it until the day of her death in 1908. The emperor's death preceded hers by one day, giving rise to rumors that he had been murdered.

The failure of the reform led many Chinese to the conclusion that progress under the imperial system was impossible, and contributed greatly to the growth of revolutionary activity. (See under **SUN Yat-sen**.)

Hundred Flowers Campaign (May-June 1957). The term is derived from two lines of a classical poem generally translated: "Let a hundred flowers bloom, let a hundred schools of thought contend." It was launched on May 1, 1957, by MAO Tse-tung (q.v.), with an invitation to intellectuals to criticize the Chinese Communist party (q.v.) as well as the government. After initial hesitation, the intellectuals responded with increasingly harsh critiques of policies and accomplishments. By mid-June the authorities cracked down and severely punished those they felt had gone too far. Six months later the Great Leap Forward program (q.v.) was launched, and this involved sending intellectuals and trained personnel, such as doctors and engineers, to the countryside. The campaign against the intellectuals finally culminated in the Cultural Revolution, 1966-1976 (q.v.).

MacFarquhar, Roderick. *The Hundred Flowers Campaign and the Chinese Intellectuals.* New York: Praeger, 1960.

HUNG Hsiu-ch'uan (1813-1864). Leader of the Taiping Rebellion (1850-1864, q.v.). Born in Kwangtung province of a poor Hakka (qq.v.) family, HUNG competed in the provincial examinations (see **Examination system**) without success. In 1837, after another failure, he took to his bed and professed to have a series of visions. These visions, and a rather unorthodox interpretation of some tracts written by the first Chinese Protestant convert, were the basis for the Taiping ideology.

In these visions, an old man was identified as God the father, and a middle-aged man, called Heavenly Elder Brother, was identified as Jesus Christ. In 1843 HUNG announced that he himself was the younger brother of Jesus and thus formed a new trinity. He was instructed in his visions to cast out demons, destroy pagan idols and restore worship of the true God.

Unwelcome in Kwangtung because of his destruction of religious images in local temples, HUNG and his followers removed to Kwangsi (q.v.), where thousands of converts flocked to his movement, largely Hakkas and members of the Miao tribal minotiry. The Taiping rebellion broke out in July 1850, and was soon joined by thousands of poor people and bandits. In spite of military conflict with the provincial government, the Taiping expanded the area under their control, and in September 1851, HUNG was named "Celestial King of the Celestial Kingdom of Peace."

The Taiping forces moved northward through Hunan and the Yangtze valley in 1852, and captured Nanking in March 1853. From then until its fall to Ch'ing forces in July 1864, HUNG lived in imperial state in his palace, leading a carefree existence surrounded by his concubines.

This circumstance contributed to the failure of the rebellion, since one of the capable generals of the Taiping plotted to supplant HUNG and was assassinated as a result. This led to further dissension and eventual defeat by Ch'ing forces. HUNG was advised to lay in supplies for a long siege, but preferred to believe that God would deliver him. The Siege of Nanking lasted from May 31, 1862, until July 19, 1864. HUNG committed suicide in June 1864, and his body, wrapped in yellow satin embroidered with imperial dragons, was found in a sewer beneath his palace.

Hummel, Arthur W., ed. *Eminent Chinese of the Ch'ing Period.* Washington: Government Printing Office, 1943.

Hupeh (Hubei) **province**. Area: 180,000 sq. km. (69,500 sq. mi.). Population: 46,320,000 (1980). Capital: Wuhan. Hupeh is bordered on the east by Anhwei province, on the southeast by Kiangsi, on the south by Hunan, on the west by Szechwan and Shensi, and on the north by Honan (qq.v.). The western third of the province is mountainous, the rest alluvial plain of the Yangtze and Han rivers.

Rice is Hupeh's main crop. Soybeans, corn, wheat, tea and cotton are also grown.

The capital, Wuhan (q.v.), lies at the junction of the Han and Yangtze rivers, and is one of China's major industrial complexes. It produces steel and heavy engineering. Hankow was opened as a treaty port (q.v.) in 1861.

Hupeh means "north of the [Tung-t'ing] lake."

Hurley, Patrick J. (1883-1963). U.S. Ambassador to the Republic of China (q.v.), 1945. Ambassador Hurley, a successful lawyer and businessman, had achieved the rank of colonel in World War I, and acted as Secretary of War in the Hoover administration (1928-1932). He offered his services to the U.S. government immediately after the United States entry into World War II (q.v.) in December 1941, and succeeded in a series of delicate missions for President Franklin D. Roosevelt. In the fall of 1943 he was sent to China to arrange for the participation of Generalissimo CHIANG Kai-shek (1887-1975, q.v.), at the Cairo Conference (q.v.).

A year later he was sent again to China, this time as Roosevelt's "personal representative" to CHIANG. The U.S. government was concerned that the Chinese government might be in danger of collapse, with unforeseeable impact on the war effort. Disagreements over priorities and strategy had strained relations between CHIANG and Gen. Joseph W. Stilwell (q.v.), commander of the U.S./China-Burma-India Theater. A larger proportion of the armies of the Chinese government and the Chinese Communist party (CCP, q.v.) were apparently facing each other than were fighting the Japanese. Hurley's mission was to smooth CHIANG-Stilwell relations, and to try to unify all the military forces in China in the war against Japan.

Relations between CHIANG and Stilwell proved beyond repair, and the latter was replaced by Lt. Gen. Albert C. Wedemeyer (see under **United States**). U.S. Ambassador Clarence E. Gauss resigned in November 1944, and Hurley replaced him, serving from January to November 1945. Much of his time and effort were expended in an unsuccessful attempt to unify the armed forces of the two Chinese factions. After his resignation, his efforts were continued by the Marshall Mission (1946, q.v.), but the outbreak of the Civil War (1946-1949, q.v.) marked them as failures.

Buhite, Russell D. *Patrick J. Hurley and American Foreign Policy*. Ithaca: Cornell University Press, 1973.

Romanus, Charles F., and Riley Sunderland. *Stilwell's Command Problems* and *Time Runs Out in CBI*. Washington: Department of the Army, 1956 and 1959.

United States Relations with China. Washington: Department of State, 1949.

Hwang Ho. See under **Huang Ho**.

I Ching. Chinese name for the "Book of Changes." This book is one of the Five Classics (q.v.) which formed part of the syllabus of the pupils taught by Confucius, who has been described as much interested in the book, and who is said to have contributed to the commentaries, which is unlikely. The *I Ching* is a book of divination, based on the eight trigrams. Each consists of three lines, either broken or unbroken. The eight trigrams are then combined to make 64 hexagrams. Each hexagram has a name, and an explanatory text to show the meaning.

In common with most other divination systems, the explanations may best be described as Delphic in their obscurity. In addition, they are written in ancient Chinese, which presents particular problems to the translator. (The best explanation of these problems can be found in Holmes Welch's *Taoism: The Parting of the Way*. See under **Taoism**.)

The text and commentaries of the *I Ching* are often assigned great antiquity. The legendary emperor Fu Hsi (c. 3000 B.C., q.v.) is credited with the invention of the eight trigrams. However, there is no indication that the Shang dynasty (1766-1122 B.C., q.v.) was even acquainted with the concept. There is little question that the book and commentaries date to the Chou dynasty (1122-256 B.C., q.v.), since the work was specifically excluded from the Burning of the Books in 213 B.C. by emperor Ch'in Shih Huang Ti (qq.v.).

Fung, Yu-lan, and Derk Bodde, trans. *A History of Chinese Philosophy*. Princeton: Princeton University Press, 1953.

Ibn Batuta (1304-1377). The most famous Arab traveler of his day, he has been compared with Marco Polo (1254-1324, q.v.). Born in Tangier, Morocco, he left in 1325 for extensive travel in the Middle East, the east coast of Africa and India. In 1342 he was appointed by the Sultan of Delhi to accompany an embassy to the last emperor of the Yuan dynasty (1279-1368, q.v.). Instead, he traveled from Bengal to Sumatra and then to Zayton (q.v.). He visited Canton and claims to have visited Hangchow and Peking. He was back in Syria by 1348. He spent his later years as a *qadi* (local judge) in Morocco, compiling the story of his travels, which reportedly covered 75,000 miles.

Lee, Samuel. *Ibn Batuta*. New York: B. Franklin, 1971.

I-hsin (1833-1898). Also known as Prince Kung, he was the son of Emperor Tao Kuang (r. 1821-1850) and the half-brother of Emperor Hsien Feng (r. 1851-1861, qq.v.) to whom he was very close. He was for many years the most important Ch'ing official in the field of foreign affairs.

I-hsin's father-in-law, Kuei-liang, signed the Treaties of Tientsin (q.v.) in

1858, which were supposed to mark the conclusion of the *Arrow* War (q.v.). One of the clauses of the British treaty provided for residence of foreign envoys in Peking, but foreign efforts to proceed to Peking were frustrated. As a result, the British and French sent forces in 1860 which were successful in defeating the Ch'ing forces. In September Emperor Hsien Feng gave I-hsin the responsibility of making peace with the allies. He was able to do this in October, after the destruction of the Summer Palace (q.v.). He exchanged texts of the Treaty of Tientsin with the British representative, Lord Elgin, and signed the Conventions of Peking (q.v.). He also signed treaties with the French and the Russians (see **Treaty of Peking**).

I-hsin's experience in dealing with foreigners led him to propose the establishment of an office whose responsibility would be foreign affairs. This was the Tsungli Yamen (q.v.) and I-hsin headed it from its inception until 1884, though his last years there were overshadowed by the influence of other officials.

I-hsin was blamed for the war with France (q.v.) which erupted in 1884, and was called back at the time of the Sino-Japanese War (1894-95, q.v.), but too late to be of any use. He was highly regarded by Sir Robert Hart (q.v.), long-time inspector general of the Imperial Maritime Customs (q.v.).

Hummel, Arthur W., ed. *Eminent Chinese of the Ch'ing Period*. Washington, Government Printing Office, 1943.

Imperial examinations. See under **Examination system**.

Imperial Maritime Customs. The Treaty of Nanking (1842, q.v.) between China and Great Britain specified five "treaty ports" (q.v.) to be opened to international maritime trade: Canton (Guangzhou), which had previously had a monopoly, Amoy (Xiamen), Foochow (Fuzhou), Ningpo (Ningbuo) and Shanghai (qq.v.). Collection of Chinese customs duties was the responsibility of local officials. During the Taiping Rebellion (1850-1864, q.v.), the customs house in Shanghai was destroyed, and in 1853 the Chinese official in charge transferred his activities to the British-controlled section of the city, which was officially neutral. The British and American consuls required their respective nationals to pay the duty owed, but merchants of other nationalities paid nothing. After nearly a year in which little or no income from customs fees had been collected, the Chinese magistrate reached an agreement in 1854 with the American, British and French consuls under which Chinese customs duties would be collected by Chinese working under foreign supervision. The system was extended to other treaty ports in 1858, and was the basis for the Imperial Maritime Customs (IMC).

The foreigners so recruited were employees of the Chinese government, and were so regarded by the foreign governments. Horatio Nelson Lay (q.v.) was the first inspector general of the IMC, from 1858 until he was replaced in 1863 by Robert Hart (q.v.), who held the position until his departure for England in 1908, and the title until his death in 1911.

Under Hart's leadership, the IMC sponsored the organization of the Chinese Lighthouse service, the National Post Office, and the T'ung Wen Kuan (q.v.), or school of foreign languages, whose purpose was to train Chinese officials in Western languages, mainly English.

In 1906, the Chinese government established a new Board of Customs Affairs, whose head was superior to Hart. However, the IMC continued to be run by non-Chinese inspectors general until 1950. The international nature of the IMC may be seen from the figures: in 1875 there were 400 foreigners and 1,400 Chinese; in 1929, when the Republic of China (q.v.) hired foreigners as technical experts only, the numbers were 1,400 and 6,000 respectively. Over the years some 23 nations were represented, though the British represented more than half the total at any given time. By 1949, only 250 foreigners were left in the service.

The IMC not only had a British accent, in 1898 Britain and China agreed that the Inspector General would be British as long as British trade with China was larger than that of any other nation. Britons held the position for nearly 90 years. The last foreign inspector general was an American, Mr. L.K. Little, 1943-1950. In 1950 he transferred the headquarters to Taiwan and then resigned. He was the last foreigner in the IMC.

Perhaps the IMC's greatest significance was in providing the Ch'ing government with a dependable and increasing source of revenue. Unfortunately, there was no way to control its expenditure. In the 1880s large sums were turned over to the admiralty for the construction of a modern navy, but most of this was appropriated by the empress dowager (q.v.) for the construction of the second Summer Palace (q.v.), leaving China nearly defenseless in the Sino-Japanese War (1894-1895, q.v.).

Fairbank, J.K., ed. *The I.G. in Peking*. Cambridge: Harvard University Press, 1975.

Imperial Sacrifices. Under traditional Confucian belief, the emperor of China was styled Son of Heaven, and was the mediator between heaven and mankind. In this capacity he alone performed certain sacrifices. While these varied from one dynasty to another, in the Ch'ing dynasty (1644-1911, q.v.), the most important were performed twice a year by the emperor at the Altar of Heaven (also known as the Temple of Heaven) in Peking.

The last time the rites were performed was the occasion of the winter solstice in December 1914, with YUAN Shih-k'ai (q.v.) officiating. YUAN was the president of the Republic of China (q.v.), but his actions were a clear indication of his intention to become emperor of a new dynasty, and were so understood by the Chinese.

India. The earliest extant accounts of India come from Western classical sources, but the most important descriptions of Indian civilization in the first eight centuries A.D. can be found in the writings of such early Chinese Buddhist travelers as Fa-hsien and Hsüan-tsang (qq.v.). The Arab conquest of Persia, Afghanistan and parts of Central Asia starting in the seventh century A.D., and the conversion of their peoples to Islam (q.v.), permanently cut off the Chinese Buddhists from their Indian places of pilgrimage, and after the T'ang dynasty (618-906 A.D., q.v.), India became nearly unreachable overland. However, ocean trade through Canton continued to flourish.

During the Yuan dynasty (1279-1368, q.v.), China was under Mongol domination. Trade was encouraged, but overland trade was largely in the hands of Central Asians, while sea-borne trade was in the hands of Arab and Southeast Asian traders. In the Ming dynasty (1368-1644, q.v.), the eunuch admiral CHENG Ho (1371-1433, q.v.) made seven voyages to

Southeast Asia, India and as far as the east coast of Africa. A number of the Indian rulers he visited sent tribute to China. Even later than that, occasional Indian Buddhist monks reached China. However, official Ming policy was to discourage international trade and contact.

European ships arrived in Asian waters soon after 1500 A.D. and soon dominated the seas. Direct contact between Indian and Chinese traders continued intermittently, but there were no official missions from either side. Toward the end of the 19th century, Britain was pressing China to open Tibet (q.v.) to trade with India. A convention signed in December 1893 opened Yatung, on the border between Tibet and Sikkim, for trade with India. An agent of the Imperial Maritime Customs (q.v.) arrived in 1894, but trade never reached a significant level. India achieved independence from Britain in 1947 and was recognized by the Republic of China (q.v.). Soon after the establishment of the People's Republic of China (PRC, q.v.), India transferred recognition to the PRC. Perhaps the high point of Sino-Indian amity was reached in 1955 when Indian Premier Jawaharlal Nehru and Chinese Premier CHOU En-lai (q.v.) represented their nations at the Afro-Asian Conference in Bandung, Indonesia.

The main issue between India and the PRC is Tibet's undefined southern border. In August 1959, India accused China of sending troops into its territory in the North East Frontier Area (NEFA). In October 1962 Chinese troops invaded in force, and India called for British and U.S. military support. The Chinese troops withdrew in November, but the border problem remains.

Giles, H.A., trans. *The Travels of Fa-*

hsien. London: Routledge & Kegan Paul, 1959 (reprint).

Lamb, Alastair. *Asian Frontiers: Studies in a Continuing Problem*. New York: Praeger, 1968.

Majumdar, R.C. *The Classical Accounts of India*. Calcutta: Firma K.L. Mukhopadhyay, 1960.

Waley, Arthur. *The Real Tripitaka*. London: George Allen & Unwin, 1952.

Inner Mongolia Autonomous Region (Nei Menggu). Area: 1,200,000 sq. km. (463,000 sq. mi.). Population: 18,510,000 (1980). Capital: Huhehot (Hohhot). Inner Mongolia is bounded on the east by Heilungkiang, Kirin and Liaoning provinces, on the south by Hopeh, Shansi, Shensi, Ningsia and Kansu provinces (qq.v.), and on the north by the Mongolian People's Republic.

Inner Mongolia consists mostly of the Mongolian plateau, with an average elevation of about 1,000 meters. It is grassland and is used for pasture. Only about 3 percent of the province is cultivated. Its major crops are wheat, kaoliang (sorghum), millet and oats.

Like other autonomous regions, a minority of its population is Han Chinese. The largest ethnic group is Mongol, with Manchus and other minorities also represented.

Interpreters School. See under **T'ung-wen Kuan**.

Islam. Participation in the China trade by Arabs (q.v.) is known before the T'ang dynasty (618-906 A.D., q.v.). Islam dates from 622 A.D. and converts to the new religion probably reached China not long after that. The presence of Muslims in the coastal ports as well as in the T'ang capital at Changan (see under **Sian**) is also confirmed.

Inspired with religious fervor, the Arabs made military conquests which brought them control of the Middle East, Iran and much of Central Asia, finally bringing them face to face with Chinese armies. The first battle which the Chinese lost to the Arabs was the battle of Talas (q.v.) in 751 A.D. The spread of Islam through what is now Afghanistan, Pakistan and northern India caused the destruction of Buddhist states in that area, many of which had had contact with China. It also stopped the travels of Chinese Buddhist monks in the area. While the Mongols and Tibetans preserved Buddhism, most of the other Asian nationalities accepted Islam.

In 755 A.D. the rebellion of AN Lu-shan (q.v.) caused the emperor T'ang Ming Huang (r. 713-755, q.v.) to call for outside assistance to quell the uprising. Several thousand Central Asian mercenaries responded, many of them Muslims who remained in China and married Chinese women, thus establishing the first Chinese Muslim community.

This pattern was repeated over the years, leading eventually to sizable Muslim communities, particularly in western China. Chinese Muslims are mainly to be found in Kansu, Ningsia and Yunnan provinces (qq.v.), though Muslims are also present in the major cities and in parts of other provinces. The province of Sinkiang has many Muslims, but many of these are members of the Uighur (q.v.) minority, rather than Han Chinese. They speak a Turkic language and are closely related to the various Muslim groups across the border in the USSR.

Muslims in China are set apart from their Han brethren by their religious and dietary observances. The majority of Chinese in traditional times regarded religious observances at the village temple or its equivalent as a badge of good citizenship. Muslims would not participate in such functions on religious grounds. In spite of this, Muslims are accepted as Chinese, and in the manifesto announcing the Revolution of 1911, Muslims are specified as one of the five races making up the republic: Han, Manchu, Mongol, Tibetan and Muslim.

Many estimates of the number of Muslims in China have been made over the years, but none has been widely accepted. As of 1981, the People's Republic estimated the number of Hui (Chinese Muslims) at 6.4 million and the number of Uighur at 5.4 million. A total of about 12 million Muslims for the nation as a whole would seem acceptable.

Israeli, Raphael. *Muslims in China: A Study in Cultural Confrontation.* Copenhagen: Scandinavian Institute of Asian Studies, 1980.

Japan. Chinese cultural influence on Japan, at first transmitted through Korea (q.v.), goes back to the first millennium B.C. It persists in many forms today, as evidenced by traditional art, music and religion. Japan's first permanent capital, begun at Nara in the early eighth century, was modeled after Changan (see under **Sian**), capital of the T'ang dynasty (618-906 A.D., q.v.). The Chinese script was the first form of writing the Japanese encountered, and several thousand Chinese characters are still in use in Japan. Both Buddhism and Confucianism were introduced from China.

The first record of direct contact dates from the Later Han dynasty (25-221 A.D., q.v.). Embassies representing Japanese local rulers reached the Han court in 47 and 107 A.D. An embassy representing a unified Japanese state reached the Sui dynasty (589-618, q.v.) in 607. Several embassies were sent during the T'ang dynasty, ending with that of 838. The Japanese Buddhist monk Ennin (q.v.) accompanied the embassy, and left the only known surviving extensive report on T'ang China written by a non-Chinese. While no further embassies were sent, contact was not broken. Merchants continued to trade, and Buddhist monks traveled in both directions. Chinese developments were known in Japan and, to a lesser extent, vice versa.

In 1274, and again in 1281, the emperor Khubilai Khan (r. 1279-1294) of the Yuan dynasty (1279-1368, qq.v.), sent Mongol troops to invade Japan, forcing the Koreans to assist in the venture. Both attempts failed, partly because many of the invaders' ships sank in heavy storms believed to be caused by *kamikaze*, or "divine winds."

The Ming dynasty (1368-1644, q.v.), succeeded the Yuan, and the third Ashikaga shogun (Japanese hereditary military ruler) opened diplomatic relations with the emperor Ming Hung Wu (r. 1368-1398, q.v.) to obtain permission for wider trade. Later Ming emperors were opposed to trade, which then gave way to Japanese piracy. The first Japanese attempt to conquer China was made by the Japanese military regent TOYOTOMI Hideyoshi (1537-1598, q.v.), who invaded Korea in 1592 and again in 1597. Hideyoshi had unified Japan and may have thought his victorious forces could be used to destroy the decaying Ming dynasty. His death ended the threat, and by 1601 Japan was under the control of the first Tokugawa shogun, Ieyasu (1543-1616), who cut nearly all Japan's contacts with the outside world.

The fall of the Tokugawa and the Meiji Restoration in 1868 marked a new phase in Japanese history. On September 13, 1871, Japan and China signed a treaty, more or less as equals.

While commercial provisions were the same as in China's treaties with the Western powers, Japan was not given status as a "most-favored nation" (q.v.). In 1874 Japan annexed the Ryukyu Islands (Liu Ch'iu Islands, q.v.).

In 1876, Japan forced Korea to sign a treaty of peace and amity, thus challenging China's suzerainty over Korea. The Chinese then stepped up their presence in Korea. (See under **YUAN Shih-k'ai**.) By 1894 Japanese and Western influence in Korea had created economic disruption and political turmoil. Japan was prepared to challenge China for dominance there, and the Sino-Japanese War (1894-1895) and the Treaty of Shimonoseki, 1895 (qq.v.) resulted. In the treaty, China acknowledged the independence of Korea, which lasted only until 1910, and ceded the Liaotung peninsula and Taiwan (qq.v.) to Japan. France, Germany and Russia forced Japan to retrocede Liaotung, which Russia leased in 1898. Both Japanese and Russian troops were prominent in the suppression of the Boxer Rebellion (1900, q.v.), and Russia took advantage of the opportunity to strengthen its position in Manchuria (q.v.).

While China did not participate in the Russo-Japanese War (1904-1905, q.v.), all the land engagements were fought on Chinese soil. Japan attacked Port Arthur (q.v.) on February 9, 1904. The port fell on January 1, 1905. On May 27-28 the Japanese fleet defeated the Russian fleet in the Straits of Tsushima, ending a series of European military victories over Asian powers which stretched back to the Battle of Lepanto in 1571. The Treaty of Portsmouth (1905), which brought the war to an end, required the Russians to surrender to the Japanese the Liaotung peninsula and the southern half of Sakhalin, and to evacuate Manchuria. It also recognized Japan's special position in Korea, and agreed that the sovereignty of Korea should not be mentioned in any international treaty. Japan annexed Korea in 1910.

Defeat by Japan in the Sino-Japanese War caused deep resentment in China, but it also stimulated many Chinese to consider the causes of Japanese superiority, and in this way was partially responsible for the Hundred Days Reform (q.v.) of 1898. Japan's victory over Russia was even more convincing, and led to thousands of young Chinese traveling to Japan for education, both civil and military. For this reason, many Chinese leaders of the early 20th century had personal experience in Japan. Their attitudes toward the country ranged from fond nostalgia to bitter resentment.

Shortly after the outbreak of World War I, Japan moved to take over the concessions held by Germany in Shantung province (qq.v.), and on January 18, 1915, presented the Twenty-One Demands (q.v.) to the Chinese government. A toned-down version was accepted in May, after intervention by the Western powers. Two key aspects were Japanese freedom of action in Shantung, Manchuria and parts of Mongolia. The Treaty of Versailles (1919, q.v.) confirmed Japanese control of the German Concessions in Shantung, and because of Chinese disunity after World War I, the Japanese were able to consolidate their hold there and in Manchuria.

On September 18, 1931, Japan occupied Mukden (q.v.), at the start of its complete occupation of Manchuria. In retaliation the Chinese boycotted Japanese goods, particularly in Shanghai, where the Japanese proceeded to land troops. The

Chinese forces resisted; Nanking was bombarded by gunboats on February 1, 1932, and peace was not restored until May. Later that year, Japan established the puppet state of Manchukuo in Manchuria with P'u-yi, the last Ch'ing dynasty emperor (qq.v.), as its puppet ruler. China responded with more boycotts.

With Manchuria secure, Japan moved southward, and in May 1933, in agreement with local Chinese authorities, the area around Peking and Tientsin became a demilitarized zone. Railway traffic and postal service between Manchukuo and China were agreed upon, but China did not officially recognize Manchukuo.

On July 7, 1937, the Marco Polo Bridge Incident (q.v.) brought open warfare to North China (q.v.). The Japanese took Peking on July 27, and Chinese mobs attacked Japanese in the cities of the Yangtze valley. Japanese consulates were closed, civilians were evacuated, and troops poured in, supported by warships. The Chinese faced an enemy superior in equipment, air power and trained officers, and, with total command of the sea, the capability to reinforce at will. In November 1937, the Chinese began the retreat from Shanghai. The Japanese entered Nanking, the national capital, in December, and slaughtered several hundred thousand people in the "Rape of Nanking" (q.v.). The Chinese high command moved upriver to Hankow, and after several months to Chungking. By November 1938, the Japanese controlled most of the seaports and railways, as well as the Yangtze well beyond Hankow.

Immediately after the start of hostilities in 1937, the Japanese protested to France (q.v.) over the use of the French-built railway in Vietnam (q.v.) from the port of Haiphong to Kunming, capital of Yunnan province (q.v.), for the transport of war materials. The French complied by banning the shipment of arms and ammunition. France fell to the Germans in June 1940, and that same month the Japanese demanded the closing of the border to the shipment of all war materials. The French again complied, leaving the Burma Road (q.v.) as China's only lifeline. The Japanese invaded Burma in January 1942, and closed the Burma Road. Only the supply of materiel by air over the "Hump" permitted the continuance of the Chinese war effort in what had become, by that time, World War II (q.v.).

Japan's defeat in World War II was the result of an American, not a Chinese, victory, and the Nationalist government had relatively little influence in the final settlement. It was, in any case, locked in a desperate struggle with the Communists for control of China. The People's Republic of China (q.v.) was established on October 1, 1949, by which time the Republic of China had removed to Taiwan. The allies signed a peace treaty with Japan in San Francisco in 1951, but neither Chinese government was invited to participate. Japan signed a separate peace treaty with the Republic of China on April 28, 1952, and maintained diplomatic relations until 1972, when it recognized the People's Republic.

Hall, John W. *Japan from Prehistory to Modern Times*. New York: Delacorte Press, 1970.

Jehol (Juohe). Former name of both a city and a province. The city, now known as Chengteh (Chengde), lies 145 miles northeast of Peking. It was the summer residence of the emperors of the Ch'ing dynasty (1644-1911, q.v.) from 1703 to 1820, when the emperor Chia Ch'ing (r. 1796-1820, q.v.) died there. For that reason it was shunned until 1860, when the emperor Hsien Feng (r. 1851-1861, q.v.) fled there as Anglo-French troops occupied Peking in the *Arrow War* (1857-1860, q.v.). He died there the following year and no emperor visited the city again.

In 1928, at the completion of the Northern Expedition (q.v.), the Nationalist government changed many place names in North China (q.v.). Chihli province (q.v.), in which Jehol was located, was changed to Hopeh (q.v.) and reduced in size. Jehol city became Chengteh, but a new province surrounding it, with an area of 180,000 sq. km. (69,500 sq. mi.) was named Jehol. After the establishment of the People's Republic of China (q.v.) in 1949, Jehol province was divided among Hopeh, the Inner Mongolia Autonomous Region, and Liaoning province (qq.v.). Chengteh is once again in Hopeh.

Jenghiz Khan. See under **Chinghis Khan**.

Jesuits. Unlike most religious orders, the Society of Jesus, founded in 1540, did not prescribe a distinctive habit, but did require that its members learn the language of the country where they lived. However, until 1578 the Jesuits in Macao (q.v.) made little or no effort to study the language and civilization of China, though they made converts within Macao itself.

The first Jesuit to be told to learn to read, write and speak Chinese was Father Michele Ruggieri (see under **Ricci, Father Matteo**). In 1582 he was invited by local Chinese officials to establish himself in Kwangtung province (q.v.) and was provided with a pagoda for his use. He was soon asked to leave, owing to Chinese political developments, but was then invited back. He returned with Father Matteo Ricci (q.v.), and established the first Christian presence in the interior of China since the YUAN dynasty (1279-1368, q.v.). Ruggieri returned to Italy in 1588, but Ricci stayed on. Recognizing the necessity for imperial acceptance of missionary activity, he was determined to reach Peking. He did so in 1601 and died there in 1610.

Persecution of Christianity broke out in China in 1616, based on traditional Confucian reasoning: Christianity is not mentioned in the Confucian classics; it is novel; it is subversive because it does not recognize the emperor's supreme spiritual authority; and it propounds a moral system which differs from the five Confucian relationships (see under **Confucius**). Although the Jesuits had some influential Chinese friends, an imperial edict in 1617 named two of the Jesuits resident in Peking for deportation. In all, four priests were deported, but eight European priests and six Chinese lay brothers remained in China.

In numerical terms, the Jesuits were moderately successful in conversions. Fr. Ricci wrote in 1608 of "more than 2,000 Christian converts." Far more important to the Chinese than their religious message was their skill in mathematics and astronomy. The successful prediction of a solar eclipse on June 21, 1629, led to an imperial edict in the following September authorizing employment of the Jesuits in the newly established Calendrical Bureau.

The arrival of Dominican and Franciscan missionaries in China in 1633 presented a new problem. The Jesuits were convinced that a process of adaptation—use of Chinese language, dress and etiquette—would be productive in the long run. The mendicant orders believed in public preaching and wearing their distinguishing habits (and sandals.). Since none of the first arrivals spoke any Chinese, the results were generally negative.

Jesuit efforts in Peking led to conversion of some members of the Ming imperial family, but when the Ch'ing dynasty (1644-1911, q.v.), was established in Peking, the new authorities retained the services of Fr. John Adam Schall von Bell, S.J. (q.v.) in the Board of Astronomy. He produced the new calendar for the new dynasty, and retained his position there until 1664. For several years he was a favorite of the emperor Shun Chih (r. 1644-1661, q.v.).

In 1664 a Chinese named YANG Kuang-hsien, a bitter opponent of Christianity, succeeded in getting the Jesuits dismissed from the Board of Astronomy and imprisoned on several charges. Father Schall and seven Christian Chinese were sentenced to death, and all the other missionaries in China were sentenced to deportation. The Chinese were executed, but Schall was spared. Most of the missionaries were sent to Canton, and all churches were closed.

The Manchu regents had named YANG to the Board of Astronomy in 1665, but in 1668 the emperor K'ang Hsi (r. 1662-1722, q.v.) dissolved the regency and sent YANG's calendar to Fr. Ferdinand Verbiest for critical appraisal. The Jesuit found a number of mistakes, and as a result was appointed associate director, while YANG was cashiered. The Jesuits retained control of the board until the suppression of the order by Pope Clement XIV in 1773, at which point it was given to the French Society of Foreign Missions.

By 1627 the Jesuits had received some 13,000 Chinese into the church, and by 1651 the number had reached 150,000. A major setback occurred in 1724, when the emperor Yung Cheng (r. 1723-1735, q.v.) banned all missionary activity in the empire, though the Jesuits at the Board of Astronomy were not disturbed.

A major issue for the Jesuits, the so-called rites controversy (q.v.), was whether a Chinese Christian could perform the rites commonly known as ancestor worship (q.v.). The Jesuit position, based on study of Chinese language and civilization, was that the rites were Confucian, and that the lack of theological content in Confucianism (q.v.) precluded it from being a religion. Since the rites were therefore not religious they were licit for Christians. The Dominican and Franciscan view was that the rites were religious, heathen and impermissible. The controversy was eventually decided against the Jesuits by the Congregation of Rites in Rome in 1704.

In addition to their religious and mathematical activities, the Jesuits performed notable services for several emperors. K'ang Hsi used them as interpreters in negotiating with Russia the Treaty of Nerchinsk (1689, q.v.). Ch'ien Lung (r. 1736-1796, q.v.) called on their architectural skills for the construction of buildings in the European Baroque style for the Summer Palace (q.v.) outside Peking.

The Jesuits' position as authorized residents of Peking made their periodic reports of interest not only to their religious superiors, but to many other Europeans as well.

Dunne, George H., S.J. *Generation of Giants*. Notre Dame: University of Notre Dame Press, 1962.

Gernet, Jacques, and Janet Lloyd, trans. *China and the Christian Impact: A Conflict of Cultures*. Cambridge: Cambridge University Press, 1986.

Lach, Donald F. *The Preface to Leibniz'*

'*Novissima Sinica*'. Honolulu: University of Hawaii Press, 1957.

Jews. Marco Polo mentions encountering Jews in China, but the survival of a Jewish community was unsuspected. In 1605 a district magistrate named AI T'ien called on Father Matteo Ricci, S.J. (q.v.), in Peking. He had read a report that Ricci was a foreigner preaching a monotheistic religion, and assumed that Ricci was a Jew. He introduced himself as a member of a small Jewish community in Kaifeng (q.v.). Neither AI himself, nor other members of the community were aware of the existence of Christianity.

Community tradition held that the Jews had reached China during the Han dynasty (206 B.C.-221 A.D., q.v.), and had moved to Kaifeng when it was the capital of the Sung (960-1127 A.D., q.v.). There was a synagogue, newly rebuilt after a flood, a number of Torah scrolls, and a community estimated at about 1,000.

The Jesuits established a mission in Kaifeng (q.v.) in 1628, and occasional reports were transmitted to Europe until 1724, when an edict of the Emperor Yung Cheng (q.v.) banned all missionaries except for a handful in Peking. Contact with outsiders was reestablished in the 1850s, but by the time the Protestant missionary W.A.P. Martin reached Kaifeng in the 1860s, the synagogue had been destroyed. There was no rabbi, and no member of the community could read or speak Hebrew.

The (non-Chinese) Jewish community in Shanghai made several efforts in the early part of the 20th century to assist their coreligionists in Kaifeng, but without success. Descendants of the Kaifeng Jews as recently as 1983 identified themselves as of Jewish descent to Western visitors, but they do not observe traditional Jewish practices.

Pollak, Michael. *Mandarins, Jews and Missionaries*. Philadelphia: The Jewish Publication Society of America, 1980.

Leslie, Donald D. *The Survival of the Chinese Jews*. Leiden: E.J. Brill, 1972.

Kublin, Hyman, ed. *Jews in Old China: Some Western Views*. New York: Paragon Book Reprint, 1971.

Shapiro, Sidney. *Jews in Old China*. New York: Hippocrene Books, 1984.

Jiangsu. See **Kiangsu**.

Jiangxi. See **Kiangsi**.

Jilin. See **Kirin**.

Joffe, Adolf. See under **Chinese Communist party; Kuomintang**.

John of Monte Corvino (1247-1328). Franciscan monk and founder of the earliest Roman Catholic missions in India and China. He was also the first Roman Catholic bishop of Peking (then called Khanbalick or Cambaluc). He left Europe in 1291 on a mission from Pope Nicholas IV to Khubilai Khan (r. 1260-1294, q.v.), arriving in Peking shortly before the latter's death in 1294. He traveled by way of Hormuz and the Persian Gulf to India. After a year on the Coromandel Coast he proceeded through the Indonesian archipelago to Canton, then overland to the capital.

The reign of Khubilai Khan, when Father John arrived in Peking, was the high point of the Yuan dynasty (1279-1368, q.v.). Several later missionaries arrived over the next half century, but by the end of that time the dynasty was in serious disarray and travel became impossible. John's letters to Rome dated 1305 and 1306 tell of the progress of the mission, claiming 3,000 converts, and of the opposition of the Nestorian Christians (q.v.) to the presence and activities of the Catholics. He died in Peking in 1328.

Juchen. Also, Jurchen and Nü-chih. A Manchurian people speaking a Tungusic language. They were subjects of the Khitans during the Liao dynasty (907-1125 A.D.) but overthrew them and established the Chin dynasty (1115-1234), to be conquered in turn by the Mongols who established the Yuan dynasty (1279-1368, qq.v.).

The Juchen did not disappear, however. Nurhaci, founder of the Ch'ing dynasty (1644-1911, qq.v.), was a Juchen. In 1635 his son Abahai (q.v.) changed the name to Manchu. One of the purposes of the emperor Ch'ien Lung (r. 1736-1796, q.v.) in implementing his literary inquisition was to expunge from Chinese historical records any unfavorable references to the Juchen.

Juohe. See under **Jehol**.

K

Kaifeng. City in Honan province (q.v.). Population: 300,000 (1980). Kaifeng, built on the site of several previous capitals, has served as such for the kingdom of Wei (q.v., also see under **Three Kingdoms**) and, more important, as that of the Sung dynasty from 960 to 1127 A.D. (q.v.).

A community of Jews (q.v.) has lived in Kaifeng since the Sung period. Their descendants, though nonpracticing, continue to inhabit the city. Some architectural remains of the community may still be seen.

K'ang Hsi (Kang Xi, 1654-1722). Reign title of the second emperor (r. 1662-1722) of the Ch'ing dynasty (1644-1911, q.v.). His personal name was Hsuan Yeh. K'ang Hsi, fourth son of the emperor Shun Chih (q.v.), like his father before him, came to the throne as a small child. K'ang Hsi's recovery from smallpox, a disease which eventually claimed the life of his father, influenced Shun Chih's choice of successor. It was assumed K'ang Hsi would have a long life. His reign, one of the longest in Chinese history, was distinguished and successful.

K'ang Hsi took control from his regents in 1667 and proceeded to consolidate Manchu rule by abolishing the Three Feudatories (see under **WU San-kuei**) and taking control of Taiwan from the descendants of CHENG Ch'eng-kung (q.v.) in 1683.

In external affairs, K'ang Hsi was faced with Russian expansion in Siberia, much of which had been conquered by mid-century. The Ch'ing authorities decided to clear the Russians from the border areas by force, and after two sieges at Fort Albazin in 1685 and 1686, a treaty was negotiated at Nerchinsk (q.v.), the first treaty signed between China and a Western power.

Galdan, king of the Eleuth (Kalmuk) tribe of Western Mongols, based in what is now Sinkiang, in 1688 invaded the territory of the Eastern Mongols, the Khalkhas, in Outer Mongolia. Many of the Khalkhas took refuge in Inner Mongolia, whose tribes had accepted Ch'ing suzerainty during the reign of Shun Chih, and begged K'ang Hsi for protection. In 1690 Galdan invaded Inner Mongolia, but was defeated by Ch'ing forces some 200 miles northwest of Peking. This led to Khalkha acceptance of Ch'ing suzerainty in 1691. Galdan invaded again in 1696, and K'ang Hsi went in person to lead the armies against him. Galdan was soundly defeated and committed suicide. The great gain for the Ch'ing was the allegiance of Outer Mongolia, which lasted until the end of the dynasty.

K'ang Hsi was a man of wide interests and made use of the Jesuits (q.v.) at his court. One of the government's principle concerns was the accurate computation of the calendar, including the accurate prediction of eclipses. The Jesuit mathematicians showed that their expertise considerably surpassed that of their Chinese competitors. They were also used as interpreters, as at Nerchinsk.

K'ang Hsi had twenty sons and eight daughters who lived to maturity. He designated his second son heir apparent, possibly because his mother, an empress of noble lineage, had died in childbirth. The heir was badly spoiled, and as he matured showed signs of ill temper, bad habits and mental instability. He was eventually confined. No other heir was named, which resulted in maneuvering and intrigue on the part of K'ang Hsi's other sons and their supporters.

K'ang Hsi died suddenly in December 1722, and was succeeded by his fourth son, who assumed the reign title Yung Cheng (q.v.). The new emperor imprisoned seven of the other sons and five of them died in prison.

Most historians consider K'ang Hsi one of the two greatest Ch'ing emperors, the other being Ch'ien Lung (q.v.). He was physically vigorous and made a number of inspection tours of the empire. He also enjoyed hunting in Mongolia and Manchuria (qq.v.) and took thousands of troops with him for training in the field. The experience proved valuable in the fighting with the Russians, Galdan and various Chinese opponents. At the time of his death the empire was strong, united and not under threat from any credible enemy.

Spence, Jonathan. *Emperor of China.* New York: Alfred A. Knopf, 1974.

Hummel, Arthur W., ed. *Eminent Chinese of the Ch'ing Period.* Washington: Government Printing Office, 1943.

K'ANG Yu-wei (1858-1927). Philosopher and leader of the reform movement of the late Ch'ing dynasty (1644-1911, q.v.). K'ANG was born near Canton of a prosperous and literary family which gave him a good education in the Confucian classics. He also spent several months in the study of Buddhism and Taoism. He then turned to the more modern topics of government, history, geography and Western civilization. He visited Hong Kong and Shanghai and bought translations of Western books.

China's defeat in the war with France (q.v.), 1884-1885, convinced him that the national weakness must be overcome. In 1888 he visited Peking and sent a memorial to the emperor Kuang Hsu (r. 1875-1908, q.v.), warning of the danger of foreign invasion, criticizing official corruption and urging reform.

In 1893 he passed the provincial examinations and became a chü-jen, and in 1895 became a chin-shih (see under **Examination system**). While in Peking for the examinations, he composed a memorial to the throne, also signed by several hundred other candidates, protesting the Treaty of Shimonoseki, which ended the Sino-Japanese War (1894-1895, q.v.), ceding Taiwan to Japan. He then started an association to promote reform, and a newspaper to promulgate his views. Both were suppressed, but K'ANG had prudently left Peking. However, reform associations, based on his model, were organized in many provinces in 1896 and 1897.

The German seizure of Tsingtao in 1897, the Russian occupation of Port Arthur and Dairen (qq.v.), and territorial claims by other powers in 1898 led to a belief that the partition of China might by imminent. The emperor was interested in reform, and on June 11, 1898, issued an edict which formally inaugurated the program known as the Hundred Days Reform (q.v.). K'ANG was appointed a senior adviser, and in the next three months wrote many recommendations which were incorporated in the reform decrees issued by the emperor.

Opposition to the reforms on the part of conservative officials was very deep, and on September 21, the empress dowager, Tzu Hsi (q.v.), resumed the regency which she had relinquished in 1889, rescinded the reforms and imprisoned the emperor and several of the reform officials. One week later six of the latter were executed, but K'ANG had left Peking on September 20. He barely escaped arrest in Shanghai, and was taken to Hong Kong on a British gunboat. He spent the next 15 years in exile.

K'ANG's efforts to interest the British and Japanese governments in supporting the emperor were unsuccessful. In 1899 he formed a monarchist society to protect the emperor, and branches were established in Chinese communities overseas, which brought him in conflict with SUN Yat-sen (q.v.), whose organization was working for the overthrow of the dynasty.

On the outbreak of the revolution in 1911, K'ANG opposed the republic and argued for a constitutional monarchy. He opposed the attempt of YUAN Shih-k'ai (q.v.) to establish a new dynasty in 1916, but supported CHANG Hsun in his abortive attempt to restore the Ch'ing. By that time he was regarded by most Chinese as out of date and irrelevant. His later years were spent studying and teaching cosmology.

K'ANG's most important philosophic work is the *Ta T'ung Shu*, or Book of Great Unity, a utopian outline of the future of mankind in an age of universal peace. The original ideas seem to have come to him in 1884. The book was written in 1902, and while parts were published in 1913, the whole did not appear until 1935. The utopian future he foresaw was one in which race, class and gender distinctions disappeared as well as the institution of the family. Children would be reared in state-operated nurseries and schools. There would be no private ownership of property and people would eat in communal dining halls seating thousands. Hygiene would be stressed, thus extending life expectancy to several hundred years. Those with incurable illnesses would be released from suffering by mercy killings.

While K'ANG was regarded in his later years as a hopeless reactionary, MAO Tse-tung referred to him as an early progressive who had written a book on world Communism.

Boorman, Howard L., ed. *Biographical Dictionary of Republican China*. New York: Columbia University Press, 1968.

Hsiao, Kung-chuan. *A Modern China and a New World*. Seattle: University of Washington Press, 1975.

K'ang, Yu-wei, and Lawrence G. Thompson, trans. *Ta T'ung Shu: The One World Philosophy of K'ang Yu-wei*. London: Allen & Unwin, 1958.

Kansu (Gansu) **province**. Area: 450,000 sq. km. (174,000 sq. mi.). Population: 18,940,000 (1980). Capital: Lanchow (Lanzhou). Kansu is bounded on the east by Shensi province, on the south by Szechwan, on the southwest by Tsinghai, on the west by Sinkiang, and on the north by the Mongolian People's Republic, the Inner Mongolia Autonomous Region, and Ningsia province (qq.v.).

The southeastern part of this long and narrow province is composed of loess soil, much of it heavily eroded.

Winter wheat is the main crop. Cotton, hemp, kaoliang (sorghum), millet, oats, soybeans and tobacco are also grown. To the northwest some crops are grown with irrigation.

Most of the population is Han Chinese, with a large minority of Chinese-speaking Muslims (Hui) and lesser numbers of Tibetans, Mongols and Kazaks.

KAO Ch'i (1336-1374). Considered by many critics to be the finest poet of the early Ming dynasty (1368-1643, q.v.), KAO was born of a gentry family in Soochow in the declining years of the Yuan dynasty (1279-1368, q.v.). The weakening of Mongol control and a succession of natural disasters led to a period of division and warfare and the eventual establishment of the new dynasty under the emperor Ming Hung Wu (q.v.).

KAO received a traditional education in the Confucian classics, and in peaceful times he might have looked forward to a civil-service career. However, Soochow was taken by the rebel forces of CHANG Shih-ch'eng in 1356. The conqueror wished to recruit scholars for his administration, but KAO, like most of the Soochow gentry, managed to remain aloof. He spent a few years traveling, possibly to maintain his distance better. However, such travel was traditional for Chinese poets, as in the cases of LI Po and TU Fu (qq.v.). After his return to Soochow in 1360, he did become involved with government figures. He moved to a farm for the years 1362-1365, where he spent most of his time writing poetry. He returned to Soochow in 1365, and the Ming forces invaded it late in 1366. Soochow surrendered in August 1367 and was under Ming control from that time on.

In 1369 KAO was invited to the newly established imperial capital in Nanking to participate in the writing of the Yuan history. The history was hastily done, and KAO was less happy as an official than he had hoped. Soon after the draft was presented to the emperor, KAO managed to extricate himself and returned to Soochow. Soochow's new governor was a capable man named WEI Kuan, who attracted KAO Ch'i by his ability and concern for the people. WEI got in trouble with the emperor by building a new prefectural hall on the ruined site of the palace of the rebel CHANG Shih-ch'eng. KAO wrote a congratulatory poem on the subject. Both men were executed by order of the emperor, whose reign saw thousands of people so treated.

Goodrich, L.C., and Chaoying Fang, eds. *Dictionary of Ming Biography.* New York: Columbia University Press, 1976.

Mote, F.W. *The Poet Kao Ch'i.* Princeton: Princeton University Press, 1962.

KAO Kang. See under **Long March**.

Kara Khitai. See under **Western Liao dynasty**.

Karakhan Declaration. Named after Lev M. Karakhan, Soviet deputy commissar for foreign affairs, who on July 25, 1919, addressed a declaration to Chinese authorities which renounced the Russian share of the Boxer indemnity (q.v.) as well as all extraterritorial rights which Russia had gained under earlier treaties. Russia was the first foreign country to take such a step, which was widely welcomed in China at the time.

Clubb, O. Edmund. *China and Russia.* New York: Columbia University Press, 1971.

Khitai. See under **Cathay**.

Khitan. Also Ch'i-tan and Khitai. A Manchurian people who spoke a tongue which scholars believe to have been a mixture of Mongol and Turkic. They first appear in Chinese history during the Wei dynasty (386-557 A.D., q.v.). They became dominant in northeast China in the late T'ang and established their own Liao dynasty (907-1125 A.D., qq.v.), with its capital at Peking, after the fall of the T'ang.

The word "Cathay" (q.v.) is derived from Khitai.

Khubilai Khan (1214-1294). Known in Chinese histories as Yuan Shih Tsu, he was the grandson of Chingis Khan (1167-1227, q.v.), and the fifth ruler in the line known from his time on as the Yuan dynasty (1279-1368, q.v.). He was the son of Tului, Chingis's youngest son, and a Kerait princess who was a Nestorian Christian. He was also the conqueror of the Southern Sung (1127-1279, see under **Sung**), and the first non-Chinese to rule all of China.

Khubilai was engaged in a campaign against the Sung when he heard of the death of his predecessor, Mangu (Mongka) in 1259. He hastened to North China (q.v.) where he was declared Great Khan. Khubilai reigned from 1260 until his death in 1294. The dynastic name Yuan was adopted in 1271, and he was enthroned as emperor of China in 1280, after the last Sung opposition had been crushed.

Khubilai's reign was the height of Mongol power. He suppressed revolts in Korea, but failed in joint Mongol-Korean invasions of Japan. He sent punitive expeditions to Vietnam, Champa and Java, and invaded Burma several times. None of these military adventures were more than temporarily successful. The tropical climate and Mongol unfamiliarity with maritime matters took their toll.

Khubilai was eclectic in religious outlook. He sent the father and uncle of Marco Polo (1254-1324, q.v.) back to Europe with a letter to the Pope. He honored Buddhism (q.v.), and supported Lamaism in Tibet. Yet he also ordered that all Taoist books, with the exception of the *Tao Te Ching* (q.v.), and texts on medicine and pharmacy, be burned.

Like his predecessors, Khubilai utilized non-Chinese as officials, though they needed Chinese subordinates for the necessary clerical work. Among other works, he reconstructed the Grand Canal (q.v.) connecting the Yangtze valley and China's northern cities.

Khubilai was succeeded by his grandson Timur, and there were eight more rulers before the fall of the Yuan dynasty in 1367, none of whom were comparable to Khubilai.

Kiakhta, Treaty of. Signed October 31, 1727, by the Manchu Tulisen and the Mongol Tsereng for the Ch'ing emperor Yung Cheng (r. 1723-1735) and by Savva Lukich-Vladislavich for Peter II of Russia. The Treaty of Nerchinsk (1689, q.v.) had delimited the boundary between Siberia and Manchuria (q.v.), but not that between Siberia and Mongolia, since the princes of Outer Mongolia did not recognize Ch'ing authority until 1692. The Russians had sent a number of embassies to have the matter clarified, and most of the negotiating was done in Peking by Vladislavich, though the final signing was done at Kiakhta on the border.

The treaty provided for trade, the establishment of a Russian hostel, with a church on the premises, in Peking, and for four Russian students and two tutors to reside at the hostel at Chinese expense, to study Chinese, Manchu and Mongol languages. The treaty was revised in 1768 and 1792, and remained in effect until superseded by the treaties of Aigun, 1858, and Peking, 1860 (qq.v.).

Clubb, O. Edmund. *China and Russia.* New York: Columbia University Press, 1971.

Kiangsi (Jiangxi) **province**. Area: 160,000 sq. km. (61,800 sq. mi.). Population: 32,290,000 (1980). Capital: Nanchang. Kiangsi is bounded on the east by Chekiang and Fukien provinces, on the south by Kwangtung, on the west by Hunan, and on the north by Hupeh and Anhwei (qq.v.).

Kiangsi is largely an alluvial plain surrounded on three sides by mountains and bounded on the north by the Yangtze river. One prominent feature is Poyang lake, which acts as a reservoir when the Yangtze is in flood in the summer months. The water flows back in the dry season, and thus the level of the lake fluctuates during the year, as does its size.

Rice is the main crop, and is double cropped in the plain. It is also grown in upland areas, as are wheat, tea, ramie and cotton. The coal mines at Pingxiang are the most important south of the Yangtze river, with an annual production of 10 million metric tons.

Kiangsu (Jiangsu) **province**. Area: 100,000 sq. km. (38,600 sq. mi.). Population: 58,930,000 (1980). Capital: Nanking (Nanjing) (q.v.). Kiangsu is bounded on the east by the Yellow Sea, on the south by Shanghai municipality and Chekiang province, on the west by Anhwei, and on the north by Shantung (qq.v.).

Kiangsu is a flat alluvial plain with the Huai river in the north and the Yangtze (q.v.) in the south. At one time the Huang Ho (Yellow river) (q.v.) also flowed through northern Kiangsu, but it changed course in 1851. The major crop is rice, planted

twice yearly south of the Yangtze. Silk and cotton textiles are also produced there.

Kirin (Jilin) **province**. Area: 180,000 sq. km. (69,500 sq. mi.). Population: 21,846,000 (1980). Capital: Changchun. Kirin is bounded on the east by the USSR, on the southeast by the Democratic People's Republic of Korea, on the southwest by Liaoning province, on the west by the Inner Mongolia Autonomous Region, and on the north by Heilungkiang (qq.v.).

The southeast region of Kirin is forested uplands, while the rest is part of the central Manchurian plateau. Lumbering is the principal activity in the uplands, while on the plateau the main crops are soybeans, corn and kaoliang (sorghum). Mineral resources include coal, iron, copper, lead, zinc and silver.

Kirin, also the name of the city which was formerly the capital of the province, is one of the three provinces which make up Manchuria (q.v.).

KOO, V.K. Wellington (KU Weichün, 1887-1985). Diplomat and international jurist. Born in Shanghai of a prosperous family, KOO earned B.A. and M.A. degrees from St. John's University, and then went to the United States, where he earned B.A., M.A., and Ph.D. degrees from Columbia University, as well as several prizes. He returned to China in 1912 and held various positions in the government of the Republic of China (q.v.). In 1915 he was appointed minister to Mexico, and within a few months became Minister to the United States. In 1919 he was a member of the Chinese delegation to the Paris Peace Conference and was influential in the Chinese decision not to sign the Treaty of Versailles (q.v.).

During his forty-year diplomatic career, KOO served as ambassador to

Britain, France and the United States, as foreign minister, and in several other posts. He became indentified with CHANG Tso-lin (1873-1928, q.v.), the Manchurian warlord who controlled Peking from 1926 until June 1928. CHIANG Kai-shek's Northern Expedition (q.v.) forced CHANG out of Peking in that month, and the Nationalists issued an order for KOO's arrest. This was later rescinded, and KOO served as an adviser to CHANG Hsueh-liang (q.v.), son of CHANG Tso-lin and the new warlord of Manchuria. The Japanese invasion of Manchuria in September 1931 brought KOO back to international diplomacy and he served several years as China's ambassador to France and, concurrently, chief delegate to the League of Nations.

He became ambassador to Britain in 1941, and negotiated several treaties, including the abolition of extraterritoriality (q.v.) in 1943. He represented China in signing the United Nations Charter on June 26, 1945. He became ambassador to the United States in May 1946, and played a major part in obtaining United States aid for the Nationalists in the Civil War (q.v.) against the Communists, and also in the unsuccessful effort to achieve a peace settlement in early 1949. He resigned as ambassador in 1956 and served 1957-1967 on the International Court of Justice at The Hague. He spent his later years in the United States.

Boorman, Howard L., ed. *Biographical Dictionary of Republican China*. New York: Columbia University Press, 1967-1971.

Korea. Ancestors of the present-day inhabitants have lived in the Korean peninsula for several thousand years. They were in communication with the Chinese at least as far back as the Warring States Period (484-221 B.C., q.v.),

and the emperor Han Wu Ti (r. 140-87 B.C., q.v.) incorporated Korea into the Chinese empire in 108 B.C. Chinese control was soon limited to the northern part of the country, and was thrown off completely in 313 A.D. Later Chinese attempts to regain control, in the Sui (589-618) and T'ang (618-906) dynasties (qq.v.) were not successful. However, the Koreans maintained diplomatic relations with the Sung dynasty (960-1279, q.v.) and acknowledged the suzerainty of the later dynasties.

The rise of Mongol power under Chingis Khan (1167-1227, q.v.) and his successors led to Mongol control of Korea from the mid-13th to the mid-14th centuries, including the use of Koreans in two attempted invasions of Japan, in 1274 and 1281 A.D. The Koreans welcomed the Mongol decline after 1350, and relations with the Ming dynasty (1368-1644, q.v.) were generally good. The Ming period also coincided with the rise of Japanese piracy, and their incursions continued until the end of the 16th century.

The most serious threat to Korean independence in several centuries occurred in 1592, when the Japanese warlord TOYOTOMI Hideyoshi (1537-1598, q.v.) invaded Korea in an attempt to conquer China. The Japanese troops swept all before them, and the Koreans called on the Ming for assistance. Chinese troops managed to push the Japanese to a toehold in the south, but Hideyoshi invaded again in 1597. With his death the following year, the threat disappeared.

The Koreans were grateful for Chinese assistance, but were too weakened by the vast destruction caused by the Japanese invasion to offer any help to the Ming in resisting Manchu encroachments. In 1639 the Manchu ruler Abahai (1592-1643, q.v.), conquered Korea and forced it to accept Manchu suzerainty, which lasted until the end of the 19th century. During this period Korea had no diplomatic relations with any nation except China, although there were commercial dealings with the Japanese.

Korea's position as a dependency of China was not clearly understood by the Western powers, and several unsuccessful attempts were made to establish relations in the 1860s. The Japanese, aware of the relationship but determined to break it, on February 26, 1876, forced a treaty of amity and commerce on a reluctant Korean king which stated that Korea was an independent state enjoying the same sovereign rights as Japan. It is not clear whether the handful of Koreans who had access to the text were aware of its implications, but tribute to Peking continued.

The Chinese, however, understood the Japanese policy and, lacking the strength to oppose it directly, encouraged the Koreans to conclude treaties with the Western powers to dilute Japanese influence. Treaties were signed with the United States (1882), Germany and Great Britain (1883), Italy and Russia (1884), and France (1886).

From the first, signing of the treaties stirred anti-foreign rumors and mob action. Both China and Japan sent troops to restore order, and in 1883 China sent YUAN Shih-k'ai (1859-1916, q.v.) as Resident to Seoul. His mission was to confirm Chinese suzerainty over Korea, and he remained until the outbreak of the Sino-Japanese War (1894-1895, q.v.). During this period Korea was wracked by dissension between conservatives, who wished to retain the China tie and reject all Westernization, and radicals, who believed that Korea's only safety lay in following the Japanese precedent and modernizing as rapidly as possibly.

The conservative position was held by a grass-roots organization know as *Tonghak*, meaning "Society of Eastern Learning," espousing Confucianism and opposing Christianity and Western learning. The movement became an antigovernment revolt in May 1894, and the Korean government appealed for Chinese help in its suppression. Both China and Japan sent troops. On June 25 the Japanese opened fire on the *Kowshing*, a chartered ship carrying Chinese troops, in the first action of the Sino-Japanese war. Korea declared its neutrality, which Japan ignored, and much of the fighting took place in Korea.

The Treaty of Shimonoseki (q.v.), which ended the war, confirmed Korea's independence of China, but Japan soon made it clear that this was a transitional stage to Korea's incorporation in the Japanese empire, which was finalized in 1910. Korea so remained until August 1945, when the defeat of Japan in World War II led to occupation by American forces below the 38th parallel and Soviet forces above it.

When the occupying powers proved unable to reach agreement on terms for a unified government, elections for a national assembly were held under United Nations auspices in south Korea on May 10, 1948. The Republic of Korea was proclaimed on August 15, and was immediately recognized by the Republic of China (q.v.). The Democratic People's Republic of Korea was established in north Korea in September, 1948.

On June 25, 1950, the Democratic People's Republic invaded the Republic of Korea. The United Nations came to the aid of the Republic and in a matter of months had cleared invaders from the south and advanced in the north as far as the Yalu river, the border with the People's Republic of China. On October 14, Chinese troops calling themselves volunteers entered north Korea and engaged the UN forces, which were forced back. On July 26, 1953, a truce agreement was signed by the Democratic People's Republic of Korea and the United Nations Command, and Chinese troops were withdrawn.

In 1985 the Democratic People's Republic of Korea maintained diplomatic relations with the People's Republic of China, and the Republic of Korea with the Republic of China.

Chinese cultural influence on Korea dates back to the first millennium B.C. Since the early Koreans were preliterate, their respect and admiration for the Chinese script and those skilled in its use was very great. It was adopted as the basis of the culture of the ruling classes and is still in use, now combined with the Korean alphabet, *Hangul*, which was introduced in 1443 A.D. Chinese influence is also visible in the arts and in the Korean adoption of Confucianism and Buddhism from Chinese sources.

Lee, Ki-baik, and Edward Wagner, trans. *A New History of Korea*. Cambridge: Harvard University Press, 1983.

Kotow. Pronounced *K'o t'ou* (*ketou*) in kuo yü (putonghua). It means "knocking the head (on the ground)" and refers to the ceremony of three kneelings and nine prostrations which Chinese ritual in the Ch'ing period (1644-1911, q.v.) required a foreign envoy to perform when received by the emperor. Representatives of vassal states performed the rite when presenting tribute. While the kotow was performed by Dutch embassies in 1655 and 1665, and by at least one Russian embassy, other Russian embassies refused to perform it and were denied reception as a result.

The British also refused to comply. Lord George Macartney, the first envoy, in 1793 proposed that a Chinese official of a rank equal to his own perform the kotow to a portrait of King George III. This caused such consternation that at his audience with the emperor Ch'ien Lung (r. 1736-1796, q.v.), he was permitted to bend one knee, as he would do for his own sovereign. The second British embassy under Lord Amherst in 1816 was not received by the emperor Chia Ch'ing (r. 1796-1820, q.v.), largely because Amherst refused to perform the rite, and the court was determined to allow no more exceptions.

In 1873, after the emperor T'ung Chih (r. 1862-1874, q.v.) had come of age, he received the envoys then resident in Peking in a general audience. By this time the issue of the kotow had become a dead letter, and the envoys were not asked to perform it.

Kowtow. See under **Kotow**.

Koxinga. See **CHENG Ch'eng-kung**.

KU K'ai-chih (c. 345-c. 406). KU is the first Chinese painter of whom we have any detailed knowledge. He was an official of the Eastern Chin dynasty (317-420, q.v.), as his father had been before him. His biography in the Chin history describes him as "a wit, a painter and a fool." KU was probably a follower of a superstitious cult of religious Taoism, and professed a belief in magic.

Three paintings attributed to KU are known to exist, though probably all are later copies. The best known, and the most likely to be at least an early copy, is *The Admonitions of the Imperial Instructress* at the British Museum.

Chen, Shih-hsiang. *Biography of Ku K'ai-chih*. Berkeley: University of California Press, 1953.

KUAN Yü (d. 219 A.D.). The Chinese god of war. Also known as KUAN Kung and KUAN Ti. He was a real man of the Three Kingdoms (221-265 A.D., q.v.), and his transformation into a popular god is the result of his reputation in the *Romance of the Three Kingdoms* (q.v.) and the many operas derived from it.

According to the novel, KUAN Yü swore blood brotherhood with LIU Pei and CHANG Fei (qq.v.) in a peach garden in the declining years of the Later Han dynasty (23-221 A.D., q.v.). The three swore to devote themselves to the restoration of the power and dignity of the dynasty. LIU went on to become ruler of the state of Shu (q.v.). KUAN Yü fought mainly on his side, but at one period fought on behalf of TS'AO Ts'ao, the ruler of Wei (qq.v.).

Although revered as the god of war, KUAN Yü was not the most successful of the strategists of his era. That was CHU-KO Liang (q.v.).

Kuang Hsu (1871-1908). Reign title of the ninth emperor of the Ch'ing dynasty (r. 1875-1908). Kuang Hsu's predecessor, T'ung Chih (q.v.), left no male heir and had no brother. Kuang Hsu was his cousin of the same generation and, under Ch'ing rules of dynastic succession, should not have been eligible to become emperor. However, he was also the nephew of the empress dowager (q.v.), who selected him for this honor and adopted him not as T'ung Chih's heir, but as the heir of the seventh emperor, Hsien Feng (q.v.), and herself. She promised that Kuang Hsu's first son would be named heir to T'ung Chih. This was a matter of some importance in dynastic terms,

since only the heir could properly perform imperial sacrifices (q.v.) at a deceased emperor's tomb.

Kuang Hsu was brought up under the domination of the empress dowager, and learned to fear her. He came of age officially in 1887, but the empress continued to withhold power until 1889. Even then, after she had retired to the Summer Palace (q.v.), she continued to appoint officials and to read all important documents.

The ferment of new ideas introduced by Westerners in the 19th century reached Kuang Hsu. He was the first emperor to study English, and after China's defeat in the Sino-Japanese War (1894-1895, q.v.), he received the Ten Thousand Word Memorial composed by K'ANG Yu-wei (q.v.) and signed by more than 1,200 successful candidates in the imperial examinations. The memorial protested the terms of the treaty of Shimonoseki (1895, q.v.), and proposed specific government reforms.

This bore fruit when the emperor issued a decree on June 11, 1898, the first official act of the Hundred Days' Reform (q.v.), which lasted only until September 20, 1898. On that day the dowager empress returned to Peking, imprisoned the emperor and resumed the regency. She was frustrated in her plan either to dethrone the emperor or have him assassinated by internal opposition and by veiled warnings from foreign diplomats.

Blaming her failure to remove the emperor on foreigners, the empress encouraged the Boxer Rebellion, 1900 (q.v.), which Kuang Hsu opposed. In the face of allied intervention in the rebellion, the empress took Kuang Hsu with her on her flight to Sian. Kuang Hsu's favorite concubine proposed that the emperor should remain in Peking to negotiate with the foreigners, and for this temerity was thrown down a well on the empress's orders.

Kuang Hsu had little more power after the return to Peking than he had had before. His death was announced as occurring one day before that of the empress. He was probably murdered, though that cannot be proved. He was succeeded by his nephew, known to the West as Henry P'u Yi (q.v.).

Hummel, Arthur W., ed. *Eminent Chinese of the Ch'ing Period*. Washington: Government Printing Office, 1943.

Kuldja, Convention of. Signed in 1851 by I-shan for China and Major E.P. Kovalevsky for Russia. The Russians had requested an increase in the number of towns through which trade with China might be conducted. Previously restricted by the Treaty of Kiakhta (q.v.) to that town, they requested facilities in Ili, Kashgar and Tarbagatai. The Chinese agreed to Ili and Tarbagatai, but refused permission to trade in Kashgar.

Morse, H.B. *The International Relations of the Chinese Empire*. London and New York: Longmans, 1910-1918.

Kumarajiva (343/344-413 A.D.). Born in Kucha in what is now Sinkiang province, Kumarajiva's father was Indian and his mother a member of the Kucha ruling house. At age seven he began Buddhist studies. Taken prisoner by invading Chinese in 384, he spent the rest of his life in China.

Kumarajiva was the most famous of the early Indian expounders of Buddhism (q.v.) to the Chinese. He was also an important translator of Buddhist texts, including the Lotus Sutra (q.v.) in 406. He established a translation institute with a large editorial staff. His long residence in China enabled him to acquire fluency in Chinese, and with the help of his Chinese staff, he went far in disentan-gling Buddhist concepts from those of Taoism (q.v.) which had been used by analogy to explain Buddhism. This huge undertaking was subsidized by the ruler of Ch'in, one of the Sixteen Kingdoms (302-439, q.v.).

KUO Sung-t'ao (1818-1891). Statesman and diplomat. KUO was born in Hunan province (q.v.) and passed the chin-shih examination in 1847 (see under **Examination System**). He participated in the fighting against the Taiping Rebellion (q.v.) in the 1850s. He also filled a number of posts, becoming acting governor of Kwangtung province (q.v.) in 1863. In 1875 he was judicial commissioner of Fukien province (q.v.).

The murder of the British interpreter, Augustus Raymond Margary, occurred in February in Yunnan province, giving rise to what became known as the Margary Affair (q.v.). KUO submitted a memorial to the throne suggesting that the governor of Yunnan be sent to Peking for questioning, thus raising a storm of criticism from officials who supported a stronger Chinese policy. However, as a result of the Chefoo Convention (q.v.), KUO was selected to be the minister to Britain, the first Chinese diplomat to reside in a foreign country in modern times. He arrived in London in January 1877. In 1878 he was appointed concurrently minister to France, and he took up residence in Paris. He was ordered back to China the same year.

KUO made many enemies among conservative officials by his policy of conciliation toward foreign powers and his recommentaions to introduce railways, machinery and other Western innovations. When he returned to China, he feared his life might be in danger and did not go to Peking, but went back to Hunan, pleading ill health. He continued writing, including memorials to the throne, until his death in 1891.

Hummel, Arthur W., ed. *Eminent Chinese of the Ch'ing Period*. Washington: Government Printing Office, 1943.

Frodsham, J.D., comp. *The First Chinese Embassy to the West*. Oxford: Clarendon Press, 1974.

Kuomintang (KMT). Political party founded by SUN Yat-sen (q.v.) in August 1912, as the successor to the earlier T'ung Meng Hui (q.v.), which merged with several other parties. The T'ung Meng Hui was a revolutionary party, but after its success in declaring a republic on January 1, 1912, and forcing the abdication of the Ch'ing emperor, many members felt it should adopt more openly republican institutions. The merger with smaller parties was effected to give the KMT the largest number of seats obtainable in the new national assembly. The members hoped in this way to achieve parliamentary control of YUAN Shih-k'ai (q.v.), the president of the Republic of China.

National elections were held in February 1913, and the KMT won a stunning victory. Relations between YUAN and the KMT worsened steadily, but the party also split into parliamentary factions. YUAN dismissed three KMT governors in June 1913, and this led to the Second Revolution (q.v.). YUAN died in June 1916, after an abortive attempt to found a new dynasty, but representative government was not introduced. The government in Peking became a shifting series of administrations as one or another warlord achieved dominance. (See under **Peking government**.) These men had no allegiance to, nor interest in, the KMT or its Three People's Principles (q.v.), namely nationalism, democracy and the people's livelihood.

SUN formed a new party, the Chung-hua Ko-ming-tang in June 1914, with the requirement that party members take a personal oath of loyalty to him. The confusion caused by the new name was widespread, and in October 1919, SUN renamed it the Chung-kuo Kuomintang.

Party matters, however, took a back seat to military activity as SUN tried to develop a base from which to attack the rulers in Peking. After two inconclusive military efforts in 1921 and 1922, he turned again to politics. On January 1, 1923, a manifesto was issued stating that the Three People's Principles were the platform of the party.

SUN was concerned with the search for military support and accepted the idea of cooperating with the USSR and the Chinese Communist party (CCP, q.v.), and to accept individual members of the CCP as members of the Kuomintang. On January 26, 1923, an agreement was reached between SUN and Adolf Joffe, a Soviet official.

SUN returned to Canton in the spring and Michael Borodin (q.v.), a Soviet adviser, arrived in the fall to assist in the organization of the KMT. He drew up the party's constitution, which was adopted by the First National Congress in Canton, in January 1924, basing it on the centralized system used by the Communist party of the Soviet Union (CPSU). However, while the party was centralized, there was a visible split between the left and right wings. In November 1924, SUN went to Peking to negotiate with TUAN Ch'i-jui (q.v.), the provisional president of the Republic, over the proposed national convention. TUAN had no intention of working with the KMT, but before this issue could be resolved, SUN died, on March 12, 1925.

SUN's death raised the problem of succession. In January 1926, the second KMT National Congress was held in Canton, and CHIANG Kai-shek and WANG Ching-wei (qq.v.) were clearly in control, with the support of Borodin and the CCP members. CHIANG was elected to the Central Executive Committee, and continued to work closely with the CCP until March 20, when he moved suddenly against them, acting on reports of a plot. A meeting of the Executive Committee on May 15 confirmed his power.

In August CHIANG launched the Northern Expedition (q.v.) to unite the nation under the KMT. Enjoying early success, CHIANG moved his headquarters to Nanchang, capital of Kiangsi province (q.v.) in December 1926, prior to establishing the capital in Nanking. In January 1927, the left wing of the KMT established alternative headquarters in Wuhan. The existence of two centers of power pointed up the possibilities of a split, and the Wuhan faction invited WANG Ching-wei, then traveling in Europe, to return. On his arrival at Shanghai, he issued a joint statement with CH'EN Tu-hsiu (q.v.), secretary general of the CCP, reaffirming the policy of cooperation. The statement was issued on April 5, 1927, and was followed later that month by CHIANG's purge of Communists in Nanking and Shanghai. At the same time CHIANG established a new seat of government in Nanking.

In July, WANG Ching-wei, convinced that the CCP would not abandon its radical policies, began a purge of Communists at Wuhan. Several of the CCP leaders escaped and participated in the Nanchang Uprising of August 1 (q.v.). August also saw a military setback for CHIANG which harmed his reputation. At the same time, the left-wing Wuhan faction opened negotiations with the right-wing Nanking faction aimed at integration of the two. In the interests of party harmony, CHIANG announced his retirement as commander-in-chief of the National Revolutionary Army and made a trip to Japan.

In early 1928, CHIANG resumed his position and made preparations for the last stage of the Northern Expedition, aiming to capture Peking, then under the control of CHANG Tso-lin (q.v.), warlord of Manchuria (q.v.). In their move north, the Nationalists captured Tsinan, capital of Shantung province (q.v.), in late April. The Japanese maintained a large garrison force in Shantung to protect the special interests they had taken over from Germany (q.v.) in World War I. On May 3, 1928, Chinese and Japanese troops clashed in Tsinan, resulting in many casualties and great indignation throughout China. CHIANG, unwilling to force a confrontation with Japan, ordered his troops to withdraw and detour around the area.

CHANG Tso-lin left Peking for Mukden on June 3, 1928, and was assassinated by the Japanese the following morning. Nationalist troops entered Peking later that month, and the name was changed to Peiping, meaning "Northern Peace." Nominally, at least, the Nationalists were in control of all of China south of the Great Wall. In December, CHANG Hsueh-liang (q.v.), son and heir of CHANG Tso-lin, declared his allegiance to Nanking and raised the Nationalist flag in Mukden.

The National Government was formally established at Nanking on October 10, 1928, with CHIANG as its chairman. But while the outside world may have thought of him as the leader of a united party and a united China, he was faced with a series of defections and shifting alliances, as different leaders and factions within the party jockeyed for position. The

Third National Congress of the KMT was held in Nanking in March 1929, and was dominated by supporters of CHIANG. Three days before it opened it was denounced by a dozen left-wing KMT leaders, including WANG Ching-wei, as being illegal. The Congress dismissed some of the dissidents from the party and threatened dismissal of others.

The dissidents organized an "enlarged Congress of the KMT" in Peiping in August 1930, and an alternative national government was established under YEN Hsi-shan (q.v.) with WANG as head of the new KMT. By November, this effort had collapsed. In February 1931, CHIANG placed the veteran KMT leader HU Han-min under house arrest in Nanking. Other senior KMT leaders called for CHIANG's impeachment, and in May an opposition government was formed in Canton. The Japanese invasion of Manchuria in September, at the time of the Mukden Incident (q.v.), caused a national emergency, which was solved by CHIANG's temporary retirement, and reconciliation between the Nanking and Canton factions.

While CHIANG had successfully overcome most of his internal opposition, he had failed to destroy the military forces of the CCP. He nearly did so in 1927, and again in 1935, during the Long March (q.v.). But the remnant of the CCP, under the leadership of MAO Tse-tung (q.v.), had successfully found refuge in a remote area of Shensi province (q.v.). In preparation for another campaign against the CCP, CHIANG sent Manchurian troops ousted from their homeland by the Japanese. They did not wish to fight other Chinese while the Japanese enemy occupied Manchuria, and a tacit cease-fire developed. In the Sian Incident (q.v.) of December 1936, CHIANG was forced to agree to a united front with the CCP against the Japanese.

This agreement is sometimes credited with precipitating the war with Japan, which started with the Marco Polo Bridge Incident (q.v.) on July 7, 1937. The Japanese moved rapidly to take over the major coastal cities and communications, and by December had forced the national government to flee Nanking (see under **World War II**).

CHIANG maintained control over the KMT throughout the war. While there was technically an agreement under which the CCP's forces were to be integrated with those of the national government, in practice that did not occur. Relations between the CCP and the KMT remained touchy, and after the surrender of Japan in 1945, it was only a matter of months before the Civil War (1946-1949, q.v.) began.

As a result of U.S. efforts to keep China in the war against Japan, the Americans agreed to supply and train some Chinese troops. Some Americans proposed doing the same for the CCP forces, but this was rejected by CHIANG.

One of the main theoretical issues which occupied the KMT after 1928 was the lack of a national constitution. KMT theory held that the country needed to experience a period of political tutelage before a constitution would be useful. Recognizing that the KMT's long monopoly of political power had become a drawback rather than an advantage, the party convened a constituent national assembly in Nanking on November 15, 1946. Boycotted by the CCP and the China Democratic League, it nevertheless adopted a new constitution on December 25, 1946, which included the essential political concepts of SUN Yat-sen.

At several points in the history of the party, CHIANG Kai-shek retired from office to permit the achievement of party unity. For a variety of reasons, such unity did not seem to result, and he was called back for further service. His last retirement was on January 21, 1949. By this time the military superiority of the Communist forces was beyond doubt, and the economic disaster of inflation had disillusioned many Chinese. His successor as president of the Republic of China was LI Tsung-jen (q.v.), though CHIANG maintained his party position. This situation continued until autumn. On October 1, 1949, the People's Republic of China was officially established in Peking. That same month what was left of the national government left Canton for Chungking. LI Tsung-jen left China in late November. CHIANG left Chungking the day it fell to the Communist forces and left Chengtu for Taiwan on December 10, 1949 (qq.v.). He remained chairman of the KMT until his death in 1975, and the KMT continues to exist as the ruling party of the Republic of China in Taiwan.

Kwangsi Chuang (Guangxi Zhuang) **Autonomous Region**. See **Kwangsi province**.

Kwangsi Clique. The term refers to a group of successful military men from the province of Kwangsi. The most prominent of these were LI Tsung-jen (q.v.), PAI Ch'ung-hsi and HUANG Shao-hung. They were an important element in the early years of the Republic of China (q.v.), and the only group in South China comparable to the Anhwei and Chihli cliques (qq.v.) in North China.

Kwangsi province (Kwangsi Chuang [Guangxi Zhuang] Autonomous Region). Area: 230,000 sq. km. (89,000 sq. mi.). Population: 34,700,000

(1980). Capital: Nanning. Kwangsi is bounded on the northeast by Hunan province, on the east by Kwangtung, on the south by the Gulf of Tonkin, on the southwest by Vietnam, on the west by Yunnan, and on the north by Kweichow (qq.v.).

It is largely hilly, with a subtropical to tropical climate. Rice, sugarcane, peanuts and fruit are important agricultural crops.

As indicated by its status as an autonomous region, Kwangsi's population is largely unassimilated non-Chinese. The Zhuang are the largest group, numbering 12,000,000 (1980), and are related to the Thai of Thailand.

Kwangtung (Guangdong) **province**. Area: 210,000 sq. km. (81,000 sq. mi.). Population: 56,810,000 (1980). Capital: Canton (Guangzhou) (q.v.). Kwangtung is bounded on the east by Fukien province, on the south by the South China Sea, on the west by Kwangsi, and on the north by Hunan and Kiangsi (qq.v.).

Much of Kwangtung is mountainous and drained by several rivers which join to form the Pearl river. The delta of the Pearl river is the only extensive area of level land. Difficulties of internal communication have led to the development of several dialects, of which Cantonese is the most widely spoken.

Rice is the main crop, and double, and sometimes triple, cropping is common in the delta.

Population pressures in Kwangtung have led to internal as well as external migration. (See under **Overseas Chinese**.)

Kwantung. (Distinguish from Kwangtung, q.v.) *Kwantung* means "east of the pass," in this case meaning Shanhaikwan, the point at which the Great Wall meets the sea. It refers to the southern area of Manchuria (q.v.), including the Liaotung peninsula (q.v.). The Kwantung Army was a Japanese Army, based in the Liaotung Leased Territory, which instigated and executed the Japanese takeover of Manchuria and the establishment of Manchukuo (qq.v.) in the period between World Wars I and II.

Kweichow (Guizhou) **province**. Area: 170,000 sq. km. (65,600 sq. mi.). Population: 27,310,000 (1980). Capital: Kweiyang (Guiyang). Kweichow is bounded on the east by Hunan province, on the south by Kwangsi, on the west by Yunnan and on the north by Szechwan (qq.v.).

Much of Kweichow consists of hills and mountains. Han Chinese form the majority population and grow rice in the lowlands and valleys. Many different minorities (q.v.) live in the uplands.

Kweichow became a separate province in 1413, in the reign of Ming Yung Lo (q.v.).

Kweilin (Guilin). Population: 430,000 (1982). Kweilin is the former capital of Kwangsi province (q.v.). It is famous for the unique and curiously formed steep hills (karst formations) which so intrigued Chinese painters that they have come to be a cliché in Chinese landscapes.

Kweiyang. Capital of Kweichow province (q.v.).

Language, spoken. The most widely-spoken version of Chinese is Mandarin, also known as *kuo-yü* or *p'u-t'ung-hua*. It is, in effect, the dialect spoken in Peking. There are many other dialects, some of which are mutually incomprehensible. Mandarin is limited to the use of about 400 syllables, with four tones, for a theoretical total of about 1,600 variations. Mandarin syllables end either with a vowel, or the sounds represented in English by "n" or "ng." Cantonese dialect has more syllables available, since syllables may be ended with a final "p," "t," or "k" and more tones are used. English, in contrast, makes use of some 8,000 different syllables.

Linguistic evidence shows that the Chinese spoken in past centuries had more syllables available than modern Mandarin, and that more final consonants were used. Each spoken syllable is represented in writing by one character. For this reason, some observers refer to Chinese as monosyllabic. Others point to the fact that many formulations are unintelligible unless spoken in a form which would be perceived as two or three syllables.

Chinese is a tonal language, that is, each word has one of several tones which is retained whether the sentence is a statement or a question, giving it a tonal quality quite unlike most Western languages.

Because Chinese word forms do not change (that is, neither declension nor conjugation is used), word order is an important element. In general, word order is as follows: subject + verb + object.

The question of how many dialects of Chinese there are is unanswerable, since it would require a strict definition of what makes a dialect and what would be merely a regional accent. But it should be borne in mind that Cantonese and Mandarin differ from each other even more than Italian does from Spanish. They are mutually unintelligible, though literate Chinese from one group can communicate with the other through the written language.

More non-standard dialects exist in the south than in other parts of the country, due to the physical difficulties of communication in mountainous areas. Cantonese and related dialects are spoken not only in Kwangtung province (q.v.) but also in Hong Kong, nearby. Cantonese is also the major Chinese dialect spoken in Saigon and San Francisco. The Amoy (q.v.) dialect is widely spoken in Taiwan, where it is also known as Taiwanese. It is the main dialect spoken by Overseas Chinese (q.v.) in Jakarta, Manila and Singapore.

Learning to speak Chinese is a time-consuming task for most Westerners for several reasons. One is the rarity of cognate words, which requires the student to commit his vocabulary to memory with little assistance in the way of clues.

Language, written.

ANALYSIS

It may assist a non-Chinese speaker to understand the nature of a Chinese character by comparing it to an Arabic numeral. "5" means the same thing to a speaker of English as it does to a speaker of French, Italian or German. In the same way, the character meaning "east" means that to a Japanese, Korean or Chinese (if literate) no matter what dialect he may speak.

The Chinese themselves have divided their characters into six categories. The first is pictograms, of which the characters for "mountain" and "tree" may serve as examples. Once shown the character, most people, Chinese speakers or not, will have no difficulty recognizing it later. A second category may be exemplified by the characters for the numbers "1, 2, 3" which are respectively one horizontal line, two such lines and three such lines. Unfortunately, the number of characters which can be so easily learned is limited.

A third category is made up of those where an association of ideas is easy to remember. The characters for "sun" and "moon" when combined mean "brightness," a concept which once explained is easily remembered.

Another group is those characters which combine an element indicating the pronunciation, and another giving a clue to the meaning. The Chinese spoken words for "sheep" and "ocean" are identical. In speech the meaning is clear from the context. In writing, the character for "sheep" is an easily learned pictogram. The character for "ocean" combines the symbol for "water" with the symbol for "sheep."

It should be clear that a Chinese character is not simply a random collection of brush-strokes. Except for that handful of characters containing only a few strokes, all are made up of elements which may be described, e.g., as a "mouth" (a small square), or a "man" (two legs), etc. A Chinese speaking on the telephone, for instance, might use a description of this kind to convey to his hearer the character he had in mind.

There are many thousands of characters in existence and new examples are created for new scientific words. Many old characters are no longer in common use, sometimes because they were created specifically as a name for an emperor, and in other cases because they describe articles, such as ritual bronzes, no longer current.

It is generally assumed that recognition of about 3,000 characters is necessary to read a newspaper. But a far larger vocabulary is necessary for any technical reading.

HISTORY

The oldest Chinese characters which have come to light date from the Shang dynasty (1766-1122 B.C., traditional dates, q.v.). This is some 1,600-1,800 years later than the earliest Sumerian writing. The distinguished archaeologist LI Chi (see below) suggests that the concept of writing may have been borrowed from a West Asian source, but notes that there is no similarity in either form or structure, so the system itself is not borrowed.

The Shang inscriptions appear on ritual bronzes and on "oracle bones," which are scapulae (shoulder bones) of cattle, and plastrons (ventral parts) of tortoise shells. The bronze inscriptions tend to be statements of ownership or dedication. The oracle-bone inscriptions are requests addressed to the spirits for predictions of success in hunting or fighting. Shang inscriptions were unknown before the 20th century, though their existence was assumed in traditional history. There are about 2,000 characters known from the Shang vocabulary.

The Chou dynasty (1122-256 B.C., q.v.) developed what is known as the Great Seal style, and the Han developed the Smaller Seal and the official style. The first emperor, Ch'in Shih Huang Ti, ordered the Burning of the Books in 213 B.C., and as a result it was possible in the Han dynasty (206 B.C.-221 A.D.) to standardize the forms of the characters (qq.v.). The Han also standardized literary style, which remained nearly unchanged for 2,000 years. There are many Chinese who are trained in this style and who find reading a Han dynasty text no more difficult than one written in the last century.

The writing system was developed for the purposes of the ruling classes and literacy (q.v.) was very much the preserve of specialists. The Han dynasty introduced the concept of an examination system (q.v.) for the recruitment of civil officials. With the invention of paper in the first century A.D., the cost of books decreased, and their convenience increased. (Earlier writing was incised on slips of wood or bamboo, and later texts were written with a brush on silk.)

The invention of printing some time in the T'ang dynasty (618-906, q.v.), and its widespread use in the Sung (960-1279, q.v.), permitted the spread of literacy far beyond its earlier narrow circles. The literary idiom, however, changed very little. The Confucian classics (q.v.), and the commentaries on them, remained the subject matter of the examination system, which was the traditional road to success.

The written language was never a transcription of the spoken language, but with the passage of time the separation between the two increased. It is not surprising to find a more popular literature developing, not to replace the classical literature, but to augment it. The earliest examples so far known are the texts of Yuan dynasty (1279-1368) dramas and Ming (1368-1644) popular novels (qq.v.). The first named are in many cases merely prompt books, but the latter are full-fledged novels.

Criticism of the classical language became vocal in the declining years of the Ch'ing dynasty (1644-1911, q.v.) and culminated in the pai hua movement and the May Fourth movement (qq.v.). It was the intent of the reformers to make the written language a transcript of spoken Chinese, and thus more accessible to those without classical education. To some extent this has been accomplished at the present time, but not completely. To understand a Chinese newspaper editorial being read as a radio commentary requires more literacy on the part of a Chinese listener than his English-speaking counterpart.

Efforts to simplify written Chinese in pursuit of wider literacy date back at least as far as the 19th century. Some missionary groups taught their illiterate converts a phonetic system and produced religious materials for them to read. But since the newly literate could not communicate with anyone except their fellow Christians, the technique was perceived to have limited potential.

Both the Nationalist and the Communist authorities have at various times attempted to promote universal literacy on the basis of either an alphabetic or a phonetic system. None have proved successful.

Complaints of the complexity of many Chinese characters have prompted efforts at simplification. Some of these date back several centuries and have their origin in the "running hand" or "grassy" styles of calligraphy. Others are more recent. The People's Republic has made the most sustained effort, and Chinese trained in traditional fashion must learn many simplified characters to read material printed in the new way.

The possession of a written language indicated immense cultural superiority to China's neighboring countries. Chinese characters were adopted by the Koreans, Japanese and Vietnamese for their own use. They persist in a limited way in the first two to the present day, and their use in Vietnam for such traditional purposes as New Year's greetings has also persisted.

The arrival of Buddhism (q.v.) in China in the Han dynasty may have been the first inkling that the Chinese had of an alternative (alphabetic) system, based on the Sanskrit. In any case, no nation which was exposed to an alphabet first ever adopted the complex Chinese writing system.

Chiang, Yee. *Chinese Calligraphy*. rev. ed. Cambridge: Harvard University Press, 1973.

Chan, Shau Wing. *Elementary Chinese*. 2d ed. Stanford: Stanford University Press, 1959.

Li, Chi. *The Beginnings of Chinese Civilization*. Seattle: University of Washington Press, 1957.

Lao Tzu. The author of the *Tao Te Ching* (q.v.), and father of Taoism (q.v.). The traditional account of his life tells us that he was born in 604 B.C. His mother had admired a falling star and he was carried in the womb for 62 years. He was born as an old man with white hair, and could speak at birth. He pointed to a plum tree and took the name LI (meaning plum) as his surname. He was an official of the Chou dynasty at Loyang (qq.v.), and had a son who was a soldier, from whom the T'ang emperors traced their descent.

At the age of 160, he left Loyang, in disgust at the decay of the dynasty. On his way west, to Central Asia, the Keeper of the Han-Ku Pass requested him to compose a book. Lao Tzu complied and the result was the *Tao Te Ching*. Upon its completion he resumed his journey and was never seen in China again.

In fact, little or nothing is known of the author (or authors) of the *Tao Te Ching*. Lao Tzu appears in later writings as a debater against Confucius and other wandering philosophers.

Welch, Holmes. *Taoism: The Parting of the Way*. Boston: Beacon Press, 1957.

Waley, Arthur. *The Way and its Power*. London: Allen & Unwin, 1934.

Lay, Horatio Nelson (1832-1898). First inspector general of the Imperial Maritime Customs (IMC). Born in London, the son of the first British consul at Canton, he went to Hong Kong in 1847 to study Chinese, and two years later entered the British Consular Service as an apprentice interpreter. In 1854 he was sent to Shanghai as acting interpreter, and in a short time was made acting vice consul. When Lay reached Shanghai, he found the Taiping Rebellion (1851-1864, q.v.) had disrupted life there. The Chinese customs house had been destroyed and the official in charge had moved his activities to the British-controlled section of the city. The British consul proposed that a temporary foreign inspectorate of customs be established to collect the duties payable to the Ch'ing government under the terms of the Treaty of Nanking (1842, q.v.). The foreign inspectorate, by eliminating bribery and other malfeasance, remitted far more money to Peking than its predecessor had ever done. Lay became inspector in 1855, and spent the next three years establishing a model customs house in Shanghai.

In 1858 he was invited by Lord Elgin to assist in negotiating the Treaty of Tientsin (q.v.). While he did not hold an official postion with the British delegation, he and Thomas Wade (q.v.) acted as interpreters and negotiators.

That same year, the Shanghai system of foreign inspectors of customs was established in the other treaty ports (q.v.), and in 1859 Lay was appointed inspector general of the IMC. In 1861 Lay was invited to Peking to consult with the Tsungli Yamen (q.v.), the predecessor to the Ministry of Foreign Affairs. Instead, he went to England on leave, and his deputy, Robert Hart (q.v.), substituted for him.

In England, Lay made arrangements for the purchase of a naval fleet for the Ch'ing authorities, for use against the Taiping rebels. In so doing he drew up an agreement with an English naval officer, Captain Sherard Osborn, without clearing the details with his superiors in China. When the so-called Lay-Osborn flotilla arrived in China in 1863, and the agreement was revealed to the Tsungli Yamen, it was disowned and Lay was dismissed. He was succeeded as inspector general of the IMC by Robert Hart.

Spence, Jonathan. *To Change China*. Boston: Little, Brown & Co., 1969.

Legalism. One of the major schools of philosophy of the Warring States Period (q.v.), Legalism espouses the belief that what the ruler wants is right, and what he doesn't is wrong. It has been compared to the views of Machiavelli, but it is more outspoken and straightforward than that. The Legalists were of importance because their philosophy was adopted by the state of Ch'in, which eventually overcame all the other states and established the Ch'in dynasty. (See under **Ch'in Shih Huang Ti**.)

The most important philosophers of this school were HAN Fei Tzu and Shang Yang (qq.v.). They were specifically opposed to the Confucian doctrine of filial piety, substituting loyalty to the prince as the supreme value. In enforcing this principle, they introduced the practice of mutual espionage, or mutual responsibility, which has lived on into the 20th century as the pao chia system (q.v.).

The Legalists proposed that laws should be lengthy and specific and that severe punishments be spelled out for transgressions. Their purpose was to sacrifice everything to the production of food and to military activity. This would result in a state strong enough to overcome all opposition, leading eventually to total peace, when the weapons of war could be stored away.

This totalitarian philosophy was anathema to the Confucianists. The Legalists reciprocated by regarding the Confucians and such others as the dialecticians as parasites. The high point of legalist victory probably occurred at the Burning of the Books by Ch'in Shih Huang Ti in 213 B.C. (qq.v.). This was a largely successful attempt to destroy all works outside the Legalist canon. One notable exception was the *I Ching*.

The Legalist victory was short-lived. Confucianism was the accepted philosophy of the Han dynasty (206 B.C.-221 A.D., q.v.) and was dominant through most of the imperial period until the early 20th century. With Confucianists writing the histories, legalism did not get a good press.

Yet many scholars have suggested that while the various dynasties paid lip service to Confucianism, the actual principles upon which they were run bore striking similarities to those of legalism. Opposition to imperial policies was usually treated as tantamount to rebellion. Mutual responsibility for one's neighbor remained a feature of Chinese government for centuries. Punishments for confessed criminals were usually severe. It is questionable whether either Confucius or Mencius would recognize such practices as congruent with the policies they preached.

Waley, Arthur. *Three Ways of Thought in Ancient China*. London: George Allen & Unwin, 1953.

Fung, Yu-lan, and Derk Bodde, trans. *A History of Chinese Philosophy*. Princeton: Princeton University Press, 1952.

Legendary Period. There are a great many Chinese legends about prehistoric figures, but the majority of these are Taoist (see under **Taoism**) inventions of the Han dynasty (206 B.C.-221 A.D., q.v.), or even later. The most important are the following: *P'an Ku*. He is described as being born from the Egg of Chaos, and as separating heaven from earth, and forming the sun, the moon, plants and animals.

The Three Emperors. 1) *Fu Hsi*, credited with teaching his people to fish with nets, to domesticate animals, to make musical instruments, and with having devised the pictograms which developed into the Chinese written language (q.v.); his consort, Nü Kua,

is credited with the regulation of marriage. 2) *Shen Nung*, the "divine husbandman," is credited with developing agriculture. 3) *Huang Ti*, the Yellow Emperor, is credited with inventing bricks for construction, with correcting the calendar and with introducing the 60-year cycle.

The Three Sages. After several other emperors with somewhat vaguer attributes, we come to the first who might be identifiably human, rather than simply culture heroes: 1) *Yao*, supposedly reigned 2357-2256 B.C., regarded by Confucians as an ideal emperor who passed over his son as incompetent and abdicated in favor of Shun. 2) *Shun*, supposedly reigned 2255-2206 B.C., a model of filial piety who managed to live peacefully with a stupid father and a malicious stepmother. 3) *Yü*, who is credited with draining the land of a great flood, and who passed the empire to his son, thereby founding the Hsia dynasty (2205-1766 B.C., q.v.).

Both Shun and Yao are the subject of passages in the *Shu Ching* (q.v.) or Classic of History. Yü is mentioned in the *Shih Ching* (q.v.), or Book of Songs, which is certainly older.

Legge, James (1815-1897). Translator of the Chinese classics, the Four Books (q.v.). Born in Aberdeenshire, Scotland, and a graduate of King's College, Aberdeen, Legge went to work for the London Missionary Society and was sent to Malacca in 1839, where he became principal of the Anglo-Chinese College. The college moved to Hong Kong in 1843; the year after the territory was ceded to Britain by the Treaty of Nanking (1842, q.v.). The first of his planned translations appeared in 1861.

He returned to England in 1873, and in 1876 was appointed to the Chair of Chinese Language and

Literature at Oxford, a position which was created for him, and which he held until his death.

Many of his translations are still in print, though the romanization he used makes it difficult for modern students to read them.

Li Ching. See under **Five Classics**.

Li Fan Yuan. Variously translated as the Mongolian Superintendency, the Court of Colonial Affairs and the Barbarian Control Office, this agency was formally established in 1638 by Abahai (1592-1643, q.v.), two years after he officially changed the name of his dynasty from Later Chin to Ch'ing (qq.v.). Its purpose was to handle relations between Manchus and Mongols (qq.v.), and when the Ch'ing dynasty was established in Peking in 1644, the Li Fan Yuan continued in this function. As Ch'ing power was extended over Tibet and Sinkiang (qq.v.) relations with these territories also became the responsibility of the Li Fan Yuan, as did relations with Russia (q.v.) when those began.

Under the preceding Ming dynasty (1368-1644, q.v.), all relations with foreign and tributary states were handled by the Board of Rites (q.v.), and this policy continued, with the exceptions noted above. With the establishment in 1860 of the Tsungli Yamen (q.v.), the first office established specifically to handle foreign relations in Chinese history, the importance of the Li Fan Yuan and the Board of Rites (q.v.) in foreign affairs declined.

LI Hung-chang (1823-1901). Statesman and diplomat. A native of Anhwei province (q.v.), LI was a protégé of TSENG Kuo-fan (1811-1872, q.v.). He became a chin-shih in the examinations (see under **Examination system**) of 1847, and a compiler in the Hanlin Academy (q.v.). His professional career was launched with his participation in the suppression of the Taiping Rebellion (1851-1864, q.v.). In 1862 he was named acting governor of Kiangsu province (q.v.), which was mostly in Taiping hands, though Western forces were defending Shanghai (q.v.).

LI's military success brought him high honors from the court and a series of increasingly important assignments. After the defeat of the Taiping, he was named acting governor general of Nanking, and also took part in the suppression of the Nien rebels (1851-1868, q.v.).

From 1870 to 1895, LI held the positions of grand secretary and superintendent of trade for the North, which involved him in every phase of relations with foreign countries, from diplomacy to the introduction of Western technology. His first diplomatic task was to complete the negotiations with France (q.v.) settling the compensation for the Tientsin Massacre (q.v.) of June 21, 1870. Next he was called upon to negotiate a treaty with Japan, signed July 21, 1871, and then to negotiate the cession of the Liu-ch'iu Islands (q.v.) to Japan.

LI's diplomatic skill was tested again in negotiating the Chefoo Convention (q.v.), which he signed with the British Minister, Sir Thomas Wade, on September 13, 1876. This brought to a conclusion the Margary Affair (q.v.), named after an interpreter of the British Consular Service, Augustus Raymond Margary, who was murdered while on official business. LI's concessions to the British did not damage his reputation as much as his later dealings with the French and the Japanese.

From 1860 to 1885, the French were

engaged in taking over the kingdom of Annam (see under **Vietnam**), a state tributary to China. French occupation of Saigon and three provinces of Cochin-China was confirmed by a treaty between France and Annam in 1862. Another treaty, in 1874, confirmed Annam's independence of any foreign power, and granted it French protection. A third treaty, in 1883, put Annam under a French protectorate and gave France control over all Annam's foreign relations, including those with China.

China had protested the second treaty, and on the signing of the third, the court called on LI to negotiate. On May 11, 1884, he signed a convention which recognized treaties between France and Annam, opened the borders of adjacent provinces for trade, and provided for the withdrawal of Chinese troops from northern Annam.

Unfortunately, fighting broke out along the Sino-Vietnamese border, and the French carried the war to Fukien (q.v.), where they destroyed fortifications and Chinese ships at Foochow, and Taiwan, where they captured the port of Keelung and blockaded the other ports. After several months of negotiation, the convention of May 11, 1884, was confirmed by the Treaty of Tientsin (q.v.), June 9, 1885.

The Korean issue was somewhat similar, as Korea had acknowledged the suzerainty of the Ch'ing dynasty (q.v.) in 1639, even before the Ch'ing had established their rule in Peking. The decline of Ch'ing power in the 19th century made Korea vulnerable to a change in status. The Treaty of Peking (q.v.) in 1860, between China and Russia, brought the latter as a contiguous neighbor to Korea for the first time. The Meiji Restoration in Japan (1868-1870) launched that nation into an active foreign affairs role

after centuries of self-imposed isolation. In 1876 Japan forced a treaty on the king of Korea which declared that Korea enjoyed the same rights of independence as Japan. The Korea-China relationship was weakened further by treaties between Korea and the United States, Great Britain, Germany, Italy, Russia and France in the 1880s. (See also under **Korea**.)

LI was aware of the erosion of China's position in Korea, and attempted to stem it by sending YUAN Shih-k'ai (1859-1916, q.v.) as Resident in Seoul. A riot occurred on December 4, 1884, and the following day Chinese forces opened fire on Japanese troops at the Royal palace, and forced them to withdraw from Korea. This incident was settled by an agreement signed on April 18, 1885, by LI and ITO Hirobumi for Japan, which put the two nations on an equal footing in Korea.

This did not dispose of the problem, however, and struggle between conservative and radical factions in Korea continued. In early 1894, Korea called on China for military aid in suppressing such disturbances. Japan also sent troops and proposed a joint effort to reform the Korean government. China declined and sent reinforcements. Japan fired the first shot in the Sino-Japanese War (1894-1895, q.v.), sinking a chartered troopship on July 24, 1894. While LI recognized that the Chinese were in no position to fight Japan, the court at Peking was in favor of resistance. The result was a disastrous defeat for which LI was blamed.

The Japanese soon had control of all of Korea and invaded Manchuria (q.v.). By the end of the year several efforts to make peace had been rebuffed by the Japanese, who would accept only LI as negotiator, and only if his credentials allowed him to cede territory. LI went to Japan in March

1895, and after an unsuccessful meeting on the terms of an armistice, was shot and wounded by a terrorist. This resulted in a change in public opinion and the terms were eased. The final terms of the Treaty of Shimonoseki (q.v.) were severe. They included the independence of Korea, and the cession of the Liaotung peninsula and Taiwan (qq.v.). A joint note from France, Germany and Russia advising Japan to retrocede Liaotung accomplished that, but the other conditions were permitted to stand.

In 1896 LI was China's representative at the coronation of Tsar Nicholas II of Russia, and while in Moscow signed a secret treaty which provided for the construction of the Chinese Eastern Railway (q.v.) across Manchuria. From Russia he made a triumphal tour calling on heads of state in Germany, the Netherlands, Belgium, France, Great Britain and the United States.

In 1898, at the time of the Hundred Days Reform (q.v.), LI was out of favor and had been sent off to other tasks, but the outbreak of the Boxer Rebellion (q.v.) in 1900 necessitated his recall to Peking, where he negotiated with the powers and signed the final treaty on September 7, 1901. He died two months later.

During his later years, LI Hungchang was certainly the Chinese official best known to the outside world. While he was involved in negotiations which resulted in the loss of Chinese territory and influence, the decline in Chinese power made that inevitable. In the late 19th century many observers believed that China would be split "like a melon" among several imperialist powers. That did not happen, and LI probably deserves some of the credit.

Hummel Arthur W., ed. *Eminent Chinese of the Ch'ing Period.* Washington: Government Printing Office, 1943.

LI Li-san (c.1900-1967). Chinese Communist leader, proponent of the orthodox Marxist theory that revolution must be based on the urban workers. LI came from a poor family in Hunan province (q.v.). He went to France in 1919 on the work-study program and while there was one of the orgainzers of the Chinese Communist Youth party, which soon merged into the Chinese Communist party (CCP). He was expelled from France in 1922 and went to Shanghai to work for CHANG Kuo-t'ao (q.v.) in the China Trade Union Secretariat.

LI was an effective organizer and was involved with many strikes in the 1920s. He helped organize the Nanchang Uprising (q.v.) of August 1, 1927. In 1928 he attended the Sixth National Congress of the CCP in Moscow, and on his return to Shanghai became the dominant figure in the party. In 1929 he proposed organizing the urban workers to participate in military uprisings. He was also critical of MAO's emphasis on peasant revolution.

On July 27, 1930, responding to LI's call for the conquest of industrial cities in China, the Red Army took Changsha and held it for 10 days. They established a soviet government and declared LI its chairman, but were driven out by the Nationalists. A second attempt in September failed, and as a result LI was sent to Moscow to answer charges of deviating from the Comintern's policies. He spent the next 15 years in exile in the Soviet Union and returned to China in 1945. He was then given a series of middle-level positions, and upon the establishment of the People's Republic (q.v.) on October 1, 1949, was made minister of labor.

He continued as a second-level official of the PRC until he was denounced in 1967 during the Cultural Revolution (q.v.). He died the same year under circumstances which are unclear.

LI's significance lies in his identification with the "LI Li-san line" which based social revolution on the urban proletariat. This is contrasted with MAO's theory which based revolution on the peasantry, and was ultimately successful.

Boorman, Howard L., ed. *Biographical Dictionary of Republican China.* New York: Columbia University Press, 1968.

North, Robert C. *Moscow and the Chinese Communists.* Stanford: Stanford University Press, 1953.

LI Po (LI Pai, LI T'ai-pai; 701-762). LI Po may well be China's most famous poet, both in the Chinese world and among non-Chinese. Some 26 of his poems are included in the collection *Three Hundred Poems of the T'ang Dynasty.* He is closely identified in the popular mind with wine-bibbing, and he was a notorious tippler. Wine shops in traditional China frequently carried a shop-sign with the characters "T'ai-pai yi-feng," meaning "the customs and habits of T'ai-pai." Since anyone who could read knew what the poet's habits were, the conclusion that the proprietor sold wine was obvious.

Most of his life was spent in wandering, though he did spend a short time (742-744) in Changan (see **Sian**) as a court favorite. He was called upon to write various official papers, which he was apparently able to do even when inebriated, but the officials were aware of his weakness and he never was given a position of responsibility.

LI was a Taoist (see **Taoism**), and referred to himself as a "banished immortal." This refers to a Taoist belief that an immortal who misbehaves in heaven was punished by banishment to the earth, where he passed a lifetime as an eccentric and unusual human.

LI was on friendly terms with a number of contemporary poets of great note, including MENG Hao-jan, TU Fu and WANG Wei (qq.v.). Tradition assigns him membership in a somewhat mythical group of scholars and poets known as the "eight immortals of the wine cup."

While LI's source of income is unclear, and he apparently never set up a home of his own, there is no indication of great poverty in his extant work, as there is in the writings of several other poets. LI's poems have been described as mystical and expressive of Taoist ecstasies. They have also been characterized as less than sympathetic to the sufferings of others, and indicative of irresponsibility. Nevertheless, he is still one of China's favorite poets and a major figure in literary history.

Waley, Arthur. *The Poetry and Career of Li Po.* London: Allen & Unwin, 1950.

LI Ssu. See under **Ch'in.**

LI Tsung-jen (1890-1969). Nationalist general, leader of the Kwangsi military clique (q.v.), and acting president of the Republic of China (q.v.), January 1949-February 1950. A native of Kwangsi province (q.v.), LI was educated in military schools there, together with PAI Ch'ung-hsi (1893-1966) and HUANG Shao-hung (1895-), later known as the leaders of the Kwangsi clique. LI proved adept at military and political fighting and by late 1924 was in control of Kwangsi. He was invited by Kuomintang (KMT, q.v.) authorities in Canton to discuss the unification of Kwangsi and Kwangtung provinces (qq.v.). When this was agreed, LI joined the Kuomintang in December 1924.

LI's forces were in the forefront of the Northern Expedition (q.v.)

launched by CHIANG Kai-shek (q.v.) in July 1926. LI's support was also important to CHIANG in his decision to purge the Communists in Shanghai in April 1927, and also to establish a national government in Nanking. CHIANG announced his retirement as commander in chief of the National Revolutionary Army, in the interests of party unity, in August 1927, and resumed command in January 1928. In the interim, LI was an important figure in the KMT, and joined in the invitation to CHIANG to return. With the establishment of the Nationalist government in Nanking in October 1928, LI became a member of the state council.

By January 1929, LI's military power and influence as head of the Kwangsi clique were at their peak, since his troops controlled an area stretching from Kwangsi to Peking. This did not last, however, as his colleague PAI Ch'ung-hsi lost his troops in a coup in March. A few days later LI and PAI were accused of plotting against the government, relieved of their posts and expelled from the KMT.

The Japanese invasion of Manchuria (q.v.) in September 1931 brought about a general truce among the Chinese. Kwangsi, however, remained practically independent under LI's rule until mid-1936, when he accepted the authority of the national government. In August 1937, one month after the war with Japan started with the Marco Polo Bridge incident (q.v.), LI was appointed commanding officer of the Fifth War Area, comprising parts of Anhwei, Kiangsu and Shantung (qq.v.), where he successfully fought the Japanese in 1938 and 1939.

After the Japanese surrender in 1945, he was appointed director of presidential headquarters in Peiping (see **Peking**), a position he held until 1948, in spite of requests by CHIANG to take command of the civil war (q.v.) against the Communists in Manchuria. In April 1948, LI was elected vice president of the Republic of China in spite of CHIANG's opposition. When CHIANG retired from the presidency on January 21, 1949, LI succeeded as acting president. He soon found that CHIANG retained control of much of the government through his position as chairman of the KMT. With CHIANG's approval, LI made a final attempt to negotiate peace with the Communists in the spring of 1949. It failed, and after the establishment of the People's Republic of China (q.v.) in October, LI flew to the United States for medical treatment.

In early 1954, as a result of an open letter he wrote to CHIANG in Taiwan protesting the latter's plan to be reelected by the national assembly, LI was impeached. CHIANG was reelected president, and CH'EN Ch'eng (1897-1965) was elected to succeed LI.

In July 1965, LI and his wife, who was in poor health, returned to China. In September he held a press conference in which he praised Chinese accomplishments under the leadership of MAO Tse-tung, and urging his former colleagues to return to the People's Republic. He lived quietly until his death.

Boorman, Howard L., ed. *Biographical Dictionary of Republican China.* New York: Columbia University Press, 1967-1971.

Tong, Te-kong, and Li Tsung-jen. *The Memoirs of Li Tsung-jen.* Boulder: Westview Press, 1979.

LI Tzu-ch'eng (1605-1645). Freebooter who captured Peking in 1644, bringing the Ming dynasty (1368-1644, q.v.) to a close. LI was born in Shensi province (q.v.), where he was a messenger at a post station. A skillful rider and good at archery, he had a quarrelsome disposition. Corruption in the central government in the late Ming period led to ecomonic depression and popular disaffection. A famine in 1628 led to widespread banditry, in which LI participated.

LI's career as a bandit, while it had some reversals, was generally successful. He called himself the "Dashing King," a title previously held by his uncle, who had been executed by Ming forces. By 1643 LI controlled large areas, including Honan and Shansi, and designated Sian, in Shensi, as his western capital (qq.v.).

Early in 1644 he adopted a new name for his kingdom and a reign title for himself, turned north, and captured Peking on April 25th. Peking then suffered the horrors of extortion, murder and rapine. The Chinese general WU San-kuei (q.v.), commander of the Ming troops facing the Manchus (q.v.) at Shanhaikuan, had been summoned to the defense of Peking by the last Ming emperor. He failed to arrive in time and was ordered to surrender by LI. WU refused, preferring to surrender to Dorgon (q.v.), the Manchu commander. LI marched against WU, but was defeated by the combined forces and hastened back to Peking. He declared himself emperor in early June, burned part of the imperial palace on June 3, and evacuated the city early the following morning. The combined forces of WU and Dorgon, entered Peking on June 6 and established the Ch'ing (Manchu) dynasty (q.v) in China. Over the next year Ch'ing forces pursued LI and his diminishing armies. He is said to have been killed by villagers in Hupeh (q.v.) while foraging.

Spence, Jonathan D., and John W. Wills, Jr., eds. *From Ming to Ch'ing*. New Haven: Yale University Press, 1979.

Hummel, Arthur W., ed. *Eminent Chinese of the Ch'ing Period*. Washington: Government Printing Office, 1943.

LI Yuan-hung (1864-1928). LI served twice as president of the Republic of China (q.v.), but proved to be powerless and ineffective. LI was in command of a brigade at Wuchang when the revolution broke out on October 10, 1911. A reluctant revolutionary, he was co-opted by the republicans and was elected provisional vice president a few days after SUN Yat-sen (1866-1925, q.v.) was named president on January 1, 1912. SUN resigned in favor of YUAN Shih-k'ai (1859-1916, q.v.), one of the conditions being that YUAN would transfer the capital from Peking to Nanking. YUAN evaded this obligation and forced LI to go to Peking, which he did in 1913. LI found that he had no power, and even when he succeeded to the presidency on YUAN's death in 1916, the situation did not change. He had no troops at his command, and therefore no influence.

The premier, TUAN Ch'i-jui (1865-1936, q.v.), wanted to declare war on Germany (q.v.), which LI refused to do without the consent of the national assembly. He dismissed TUAN in May 1917, and most of the military governors of the northern provinces then declared their independence. An exception was CHANG Hsün (1854-1923) who seized Peking and tried to restore the fallen Ch'ing dynasty (q.v.). LI then recalled TUAN, who induced him to resign in favor of FENG Kuo-chang (1859-1919, q.v.).

LI was recalled to the presidency in 1922, but soon discovered that his conditions (e.g., reduction in the various armies and abolition of the system of military governors) were not being met. He was hounded from office in 1923 and fled to Tientsin, where he lived in retirement.

Boorman, Howard L., ed. *Biographical Dictionary of Republican China*. New York: Columbia University Press, 1967.

Liang. The name of at least eight separate dynasties or states, none of major importance in Chinese history. Five of them were located in northern China in the 4th-5th centuries A.D. They were not connected with the Southern Liang dynasty which ruled at Nanking from 502 to 557 A.D. That dynasty was replaced by the Ch'en which fell to the Sui dynasty (589-618, qq.v.).

There was also a Liang dynasty which succeeded the T'ang on its fall in 906 A.D. (q.v.). It is the first of a group called the Five Dynasties (q.v.) covering the period between the T'ang and the Sung dynasties (q.v.).

LIANG Ch'i-ch'ao (1873-1929). Intellectual leader and government official. LIANG was born in Kwangtung province (q.v.) and showed signs of precocity. At the age of 16 he passed the examinations at Canton and became a chü-jen in 1889 (see **Examination system**). He took the metropolitan examinations at Peking in 1890, 1892, and 1894, but failed to pass them. On his return to Canton after the first exam, he bought translations of Western books, which profoundly affected his outlook.

Upon his return to Canton he came under the influence of K'ANG Yu-wei (q.v.). In 1895 K'ANG and LIANG went to Peking to take the exams again. K'ANG succeeded, but LIANG did not. Nevertheless, he helped in drafting K'ANG's memorial to the throne protesting the terms of the Treaty of Shimonoseki which ended the Sino-Japanese War (qq.v.). He also participated in the Hundred Days Reform under the emperor Kuang Hsü (qq.v.), and when that was brought to an end by the actions of the empress dowager (q.v.) on September 21, 1898, and an order was issued for his arrest, he was given refuge in the Japanese legation.

He spent the next several years living in Japan and traveling, with a brief visit to China to assist in an uprising against the empress dowager that had already been suppressed. His travels took him to America, where he lectured and called on President Theodore Roosevelt. He was also writing and editing a stream of articles on a variety of topics relevant to his proposals for change. LIANG was a proponent of constitutional monarchy, which put him at odds with the supporters of SUN Yat-sen (q.v.) who were in favor of a republic.

With the establishment of the Republic of China (q.v.) in 1912, LIANG took an active part, though primarily as a member of several parties in opposition to the Kuomintang (q.v.). LIANG became minister of justice in 1913, but resigned early in 1914, along with all the rest of the cabinet, when YUAN Shih-k'ai dissolved the Kuomintang and the assembly. However, in a matter of weeks he had accepted appointment as head of YUAN's monetary bureau.

Since his proposals were not accepted, LIANG distanced himself from the YUAN government and wrote extensively to encourage public opposition to Japan's Twenty-one Demands (q.v.). YUAN's decision to become emperor in 1915 drove LIANG to great activity in opposition, and when YUAN reverted to the presidency in March 1916, LIANG demanded the restoration of the assembly of 1913.

After YUAN's death in June 1916, LIANG again became active in party politics and assisted in getting China to join the Allies in declaring war on Germany (August 14, 1917). He then became minister of finance and tried again to effect currency reform, but without success. He resigned in November 1917, but traveled to Europe in 1919 as an unofficial delegate to the Paris Peace Conference.

In 1920 he returned to China and took up teaching Chinese history at Nankai University in Tientsin, while remaining active in several cultural and educational projects. He also produced a number of scholarly works. He continued his teaching and writing until shortly before his death.

Boorman, Howard L., ed. *Biographical Dictionary of Republican China*. New York: Columbia University Press, 1968.

Levenson, Joseph R. *Liang Ch'i-ch'ao and the Mind of Modern China*. Berkeley: University of California Press, 1970.

Liao. 1. The Ch'i-tan Tartars (see under **Cathay**) adopted the Chinese name Liao for their dynasty (907-1125). They were also known as Khitan or Khitay and it is from this word that Cathay derives. The Liao spoke an Altaic language and established their empire at the time of the collapse of the T'ang dynasty (618-906, q.v.), including much T'ang territory in the northeast and northwest. While many Chinese resided in Liao areas, political and military power were in the hands of the Ch'i-tan, who maintained their own ways as hunters and herdsmen, and avoided being assimilated to the agricultural Chinese.

The Liao were in military contact with the Sung dynasty (q.v.), which controlled the southern parts of China. Periodically the Liao forced the Sung to cede territory and pay tribute. At least once they threatened the Sung capital at Kaifeng (q.v.).

The Liao were overthrown by the Juchen of Manchuria, who established the Chin dynasty (qq.v.). But the Liao example of barbarian rule over a Chinese population was one which was closely studied by other invaders who ruled Chinese: the Chin, the Yuan (Mongols) and the Ch'ing (Manchus). A descendant of the Liao royal family, Yeh-lü Ch'u-ts'ai (q.v.), was a chief adviser to Chingis Khan (q.v.) and his son Ogotai at the time of the Mongol conquest.

2. Western Liao Dynasty (1125-1168). The fall of the Liao dynasty prompted some of the Ch'itan (Khitai) who were its dominant element to move west to the steppes of Central Asia. Under the leadership of Yeh-lü Ta-shih, a member of the royal family, they established the Western Liao, also known as the Kara Khitai. Its historical records have been accepted as part of the canon of dynastic histories (q.v.).

Wittfogel, Karl A., and Feng Chia-sheng. *History of Chinese Society, Liao*. Philadelphia: American Philosophical Society, 1949.

Liaoning province. Area: 140,000 sq. km. (54,000 sq. mi.). Population: 34,426,000 (1980). Capital: Shenyang, population 4,000,000 (1978); formerly known as Mukden (q.v.). Liaoning is bounded on the northeast by Kirin province (q.v.), on the southeast by the Democratic People's Republic of Korea, on the south by the Pei Hai Gulf (formerly the Gulf of Chihli), on the west by Hopeh province (q.v.), and on the northwest by the Inner Mongolia Autonomous Region (q.v.).

Manchuria (q.v.) was divided into three provinces in 1903: Heilungkiang, Kirin and Liaoning, of which the last is the southernmost. It was originally known as Fengtien, then as Shengking, and became Liaoning in 1928.

The most productive agricultural area is the plain of the Liao river, where corn, millet, kaoliang (sorghum), tobacco and cotton are grown. Liaoning is heavily industrialized, with coal and iron mines and many factories.

Dairen (Lüda), the main seaport for northeast China, and Port Arthur (Lüshun) (qq.v.), an important naval base, are within the province.

Liaotung peninsula. *Liaotung* means "east of the Liao river." The name, used since Ming times, is applied to the southeastern portion of Liaoning province (q.v.). The peninsula separates the Pei Hai Gulf, formerly the Gulf of Chihli, from Korea Bay, and is the site of Dairen and Port Arthur (qq.v.). It was ceded to Japan by China in the Treaty of Shimonoseki in the aftermath of the Sino-Japanese War (1894-1895, qq.v.). Fearing excessive Japanese influence in North China, France, Germany and Russia (qq.v.) asked Japan to return the peninsula to China, which was done.

In 1898, China leased the peninsula to Russia, and the Russians built Port Arthur as a naval base. On February 9, 1904, Japan attacked Port Arthur, thereby opening the Russo-Japanese War (1904-1905, q.v.). In the aftermath Japan occupied the peninsula and used it as a springboard in the effort to take over the rest of Manchuria (q.v.) in the 1920s and 1930s. The peninsula reverted to Chinese control in 1945, though Russian troops, entering Manchuria in the closing days of World War II, occupied Port Arthur until 1955.

Lieh Tzu. See under **Taoism**.

Likin. The likin was an internal customs tax, introduced during the Taiping Rebellion (q.v.), levied on any commodity which moved from one area to another. Since it was levied on a local basis, the complexities of the system were very great, and with the internal difficulties of the Ch'ing dynasty (1644-1911, q.v.) in the 19th century, the extent to which the tax would be levied was not always certain. One result was that it was frequently cheaper to import many goods from overseas into the treaty ports (q.v.), rather than to transport them from nearby provinces, even though the original price where they were produced was below the international level. Imposition of the likin made the difference.

Many Chinese recognized the negative effect of the likin on the national economy and there were a number of efforts to eliminate it, particularly after the fall of the Ch'ing. The Nationalist government finally abolished it in 1931. One reason for the difficulty in getting rid of it was the dependence of local authorities on the likin as a source of funds.

Beal, Edward G. *The Origin of Likin, 1853-1864*. Cambridge: East Asian Research Center, Harvard University, 1958.

LIN Piao (LIN Biao). 1907-1971. Chinese Communist military leader. Born in Hupeh province (q.v.) and influenced toward socialism by older cousins, in 1925 he joined the Socialist Youth League (q.v.) in Shanghai and then went to Canton where he enrolled in the Whampoa Military Academy (q.v.), and soon came to the attention of CHOU En-lai (q.v.), deputy director of the political department. In 1926 he participated in the Northern Expedition (q.v.) and in 1927 joined the Chinese Communist party (CCP, q.v.). He participated in the Nanchang Uprising (q.v.) on August 1, 1927, an event usually regarded as the birth of the Red Army. He then joined the Communist forces under MAO Tse-tung (q.v.) on the Hunan-Kiangsi (q.v.) border.

LIN rose steadily in the military, and accompanied MAO on the Long

March (q.v.) in 1935. He headed the military academy in Yenan and fought successful engagements against the Japanese in North China (q.v.) after the war started in July 1937. He was elected to the Central Committee at the Seventh National Congress of the CCP in Yenan in 1945.

LIN was sent to Manchuria (q.v.) in October 1945 to accept the surrender of Japanese troops and to work with the Soviet troops that had entered in August. The Soviets refused to permit the Nationalist troops to enter Manchuria through the port cities, and by the time they moved up the railway, LIN's troops had consolidated their positions. The Nationalists occupied several cities, but LIN's troops, armed with surrendered Japanese weapons provided by the Soviets, controlled the countryside. LIN's capture of Mukden (see **Shenyang**) on November 1, 1948, was the beginning of the Nationalist collapse.

LIN captured Tientsin and Peiping (Peking) in January 1949, and on the establishment of the People's Republic of China (q.v.) on October 1, 1949, he became a member of the Government Council. In the autumn of 1950, units of LIN's Fourth Field Army formed the vanguard of the "Chinese People's Volunteers," which crossed the Yalu river to participate in the Korean War, and LIN may have been with them at times.

LIN continued to rise both in the party and in the military, and in 1959 became minister of defense. The influence of the military grew steadily in the early 1960s, and with MAO's call for the Cultural Revolution (q.v.) in May 1966, LIN replaced LIU Shao-ch'i (q.v.) as number two man in the party.

LIN reportedly died in a plane crash in 1971 under mysterious circum-

stances. He was accused of having tried to overthrow MAO and, when the plot failed, of having tried to escape to the Soviet Union. Since the very fact of his death was not admitted until July 1972, the true circumstances may never be known.

Boorman, Howard L., ed. *Biographical Dictionary of Republican China*. New York: Columbia University Press, 1971.

Yao, Ming-le. *The Conspiracy and Death of Lin Biao*. New York: Knopf, 1893.

LIN Sen (1868-1943). Revolutionary and chairman of the Nationalist government (1932-1943). A native of Fukien province (q.v.), LIN was educated in the Chinese classics and then in Christian missionary schools. He spent several years employed by the Taipei Telegraph Office in Taiwan, until its cession to Japan in the aftermath of the Sino-Japanese War (1894-1895, q.v.). Opposed to the Ch'ing dynasty (1644-1911, q.v.), he became a revolutionary. He spent several years working for the Imperial Maritime Customs (q.v.) and at the same time disseminated anti-Ch'ing literature. When the revolution started on October 10, 1911, LIN was instrumental in getting the support of the imperial naval forces, as many of the officers were fellow Fukienese.

LIN was a delegate to the assembly that elected SUN Yat-sen (1866-1925, q.v.), provisional president of the new republic. In 1912 he was elected to the Senate at Peking, and soon became its chairman. He left Peking in 1913 when it became obvious that YUAN Shih-k'ai (1859-1916, q.v.), the second president, planned to suppress the Kuomintang (q.v.). He spent the next few years soliciting financial support for SUN among the Chinese communities in Hawaii, the United States and Cuba, returning after YUAN's death. He then held a number of party and government psoitions, usually as a supporter of SUN.

When the Nationalist government was organized in Nanking in October 1928, he became vice president of the Legislative Yuan. In 1931, while he was on an official trip abroad, CHIANG Kai-shek (1887-1975, q.v.), chairman of the national government, placed the president of the Legislative Yuan, HU Han-min (1879-1936), under arrest. LIN returned to China and joined in proposing CHIANG's impeachment.

A government crisis was averted by the Japanese invasion of Manchuria (q.v.) in September 1931, which served to unite the dissident factions. In the reorganization which followed, CHIANG resigned as chairman, and was succeeded by LIN, under whom the post became largely ceremonial. He held it until his death in Chungking in August 1943.

Boorman, Howard L., ed. *Biographical Dictionary of Republican China*. New York: Columbia University Press, 1967-1971.

LIN Tse-Hsü (1785-1850). Government official and key figure in the Opium War (1839-1842, q.v.). By 1838 opium smuggling had become a major problem and the subject of a number of memorials to the throne. LIN submitted one recommending drastic laws to prohibit the drug, and proposing a systematic program to implement them. He was governor of Hupei and Hunan (qq.v.) at the time, and enforced the measures he proposed within his jurisdiction. He was called to Peking, and after a long series of audiences with the emperor, he was appointed Imperial Commissioner at Canton to deal with the problem.

LIN arrived in Canton in March 1839, and immediately issued a warning to the Chinese merchants of the Cohong (q.v.), the official syndicate which monopolized all foreign trade, threatening serious consequences if the opium trade were not suppressed. He also demanded the surrender of all opium in possession of the foreign traders. After a blockade of the "factories" outside Canton where the foreigners lived during the trading season, some 20,000 chests of opium were surrendered. LIN destroyed it all by mixing it with salt water and lime.

Another source of friction with the British arose with the death of a Chinese after a brawl with British and American sailors. LIN demanded the surrender of the murderer. The British were unable to identify the man responsible, but after a trial of those accused, sentenced the most likely to imprisonment in England. Following a tradition of many years, they refused to turn over anyone to the Chinese authorities.

LIN ordered the expulsion of all British residents from Macao (q.v.), which led to a series of incidents between Chinese and British. Finally, an imperial edict of December 13, 1839, banned British trade altogether. The British carried the war to the north in 1840, capturing several cities and arriving in August at Tientsin, where they negotiated with Ch'i-shan (q.v.), whose diplomatic stance was the opposite of LIN's.

The British success led to accusation that LIN's policy had been too harsh and provocative, and in September 1840, he was dismissed from office and banished to Sinkiang (q.v.). After three years there he returned to tackle other assignments, all of which he carried out with success. He was appointed imperial commissioner for suppression of the Taiping Rebellion (q.v.) in 1850, but died before assuming his duties.

Chang, Hsin-pao. *Commissioner Lin and*

the Opium War. New York: W.W. Norton, 1970.

Hummel, Arthur W., ed. *Eminent Chinese of the Ch'ing Period*. Washington: Government Printing Office, 1943.

Literacy. Because of the complexity of the Chinese written language (q.v.), it is not only more difficult to achieve literacy than it would be with an alphabetic system, it is also more difficult even to define the term. From the beginning of the Shang dynasty (q.v.) in the second millennium B.C. until the T'ang dynasty (618-906, q.v.), it is unlikely that more than a few outside the ruling classes were literate. With few exceptions, such literature as existed was concerned with governmental affairs and the subject matter of the examinations (see **Examination system**).

Just as in the western world, prior to the invention of printing, which made ownership of a book a possibility for others than a small minority, literacy was not widespread in China until after the development of paper in the 1st century A.D. and the invention of printing in the T'ang. In the Sung dynasty (960-1279, q.v.) printed books were common enough for many families to own them. Their possession made the education of young boys far easier to achieve, and greatly increased the number of those sitting for examinations.

The expansion of trade in the Sung also brought about the development of a secondary level of literacy. This was the province of merchants who could read and write materials pertinent to their business affairs, even if they were unable to read the Confucian classics (q.v.), or write the stylized essays required in the examinations.

This presumably laid the groundwork for the development of vernacular literature. The Yuan dynasty (1279-1368, q.v.) was the period when drama (q.v.) achieved its golden age, at least partially because the suspension of the examination system during most of the period, and the Mongols' practice of utilizing non-Chinese for many official posts, left many Chinese scholars without their traditional government careers.

In the Ming dynasty (1368-1644, q.v.) the development of the novel (q.v.), written in the vernacular, provided reading matter for many who had little or no interest in the classics. By the time of the Ch'ing dynasty (1644-1911, q.v.), literacy at some level was fairly widespread. Nearly every family counted a literate member, and nearly every village had a school of some sort.

Estimates of literacy at the present time vary considerably. Literacy is practically universal in Taiwan, but is acknowledged to be much lower in the People's Republic, which has a much larger population and many intractable problems. In 1950, some 54 percent of the population of Shanghai was literate, far higher than the 20-30 percent range estimate for China as a whole.

The 1982 census reported that 23.5 percent of China's population was illiterate.

Rawski, Evelyn Sakakida. *Education and Popular Literacy in Ch'ing China*. Ann Arbor: University of Michigan Press, 1979.

Literature. Chinese literature begins with the Confucian Five Classics: the *Shu Ching* (Book of History), *Shih Ching* (Book of Songs), *I Ching* (Book of Changes), *Li Ching* (actually three Books of Rites), and the *Ch'un Ch'iu* (Spring and Autumn Annals of the state of Lu) (qq.v.). All of these have been provided with extensive commentaries, since, with the exception of the Book of Songs, all are close to incomprehensible without them. The commentators on the Songs have provided them with political interpretations, although modern scholars generally consider them simply transcripts of songs of an earlier era. All these works are products of the Chou dynasty (1122-256 B.C., q.v.), though much of the material in the History purports to describe events of an even earlier period.

These five books formed the course of study of Confucius' disciples and became the backbone of later Confucian literary activity. They also provided the categories of respectable literature until modern times.

The next important group is known as the Four Books: the *Lun Yü* (Analects of Confucius), *Ta Hsüeh* (Great Learning), *Chung Yung* (Doctrine of the Mean), and *Meng Tzu* (Book of Mencius). This set forms the introduction to Confucian learning, and in later dynasties study of it preceded study of the earlier Five Classics. For most of the last 800 years every educated Chinese was expected to be able to quote passages from these four and to recognize literary references.

Some other texts from the Chou dynasty have also survived, notably the *Tao Te Ching* (q.v.), and a number of forgeries have been ascribed to the period in later years. Many more works existed but were destroyed in the wars that marked the end of the Chou. Many books were also purposely destroyed by the first emperor of the Ch'in dynasty in the celebrated Burning of the Books (q.v.). The Confucian classics were proscribed by the emperor, but a number of them had been inscribed on stone and were preserved in this way. Since this was before the invention of paper, all the books destroyed were either written with a brush on

silk, or inscribed on wood or bamboo with a stylus. Literacy was restricted largely to members of the ruling class or their immediate retainers, and concealment of a library was unlikely. In the circumstances, the existence of as much early literature as we now have is remarkable.

Because of the inclusion of the Book of Songs in the Confucian canon, the writing of poetry was considered an acceptable avocation for a literary man. And since the achievement of literacy was done through study of the canon and passing the civil examinations, Chinese history is filled with examples of high officials who were also poets. Not until centuries later do we find stories, novels and plays written by literary men, though some may have been written and lost.

For this reason, the branch of Chinese literature most accessible to Chinese and non-Chinese alike is poetry, and much Chinese poetry now appears in translation.

Probably the greatest literary achievement of the Han dynasty (206 B.C.-221 A.D., q.v.) was the *Shih Chi* (Historical Record) of SSU-MA Ch'ien (qq.v.). This was a comprehensive history of China (which to its author represented the entire known world) from mythical times to the second century B.C. Its format has been followed by all the dynastic histories (q.v.) which followed. (There are now 25 of them in the accepted canon.) One of the most important innovations of the *Shih Chi* was a section devoted to the biographies of important men. This was continued in succeeding histories and provides a rich source of historical material.

Another achievement of the Han period was the earliest known Chinese dictionary, the *Shuo Wen*, compiled by HSÜ Shen. This dictionary contains about 10,000 characters, which are arranged under 540 "radicals." (Present-day dictionaries use only 214.)

The Period of Disunity (q.v.), which lasted from the fall of the Han in 221 A.D. until the successful reunification of China under the Sui (589-618, q.v.), saw the introduction of Buddhism and the appearance of translations of Buddhist texts. This is also the period in which the Chinese Buddhist monk Fa-hsien (q.v.) made a pilgrimage to India and returned to write an account of his travels.

Perhaps the most famous poet of the period is T'AO Ch'ien (q.v.), who wrote a long allegorical poem about a man who is traveling in a small boat and finds a peach garden by the side of the river. He lands and finds the entrance to a cave which leads him to a village whose residents have been cut off from the rest of humanity for centuries, but who live in prosperity and happiness. When he tries to find it again, the place is gone.

The T'ang dynasty (618-906 A.D., q.v.) is considered the golden age of Chinese poetry. It boasts such poets as HAN Yü, LI Po, MENG Hao-jan, PO Chü-yi and TU Fu (qq.v.), and many others less well known outside of China. A selection of poems from the best-known poets, called *300 Poems from the T'ang Dynasty* has been used as a school literary text for centuries, and has been translated into English several times. An educated Chinese would be expected to recognize and be able to quote from this collection. It was this school of lyric poetry which inspired the Imagist School of English poetry, because most of the poems in the collection are composed as a series of images evoking a mood. This is quite different from a story, though the existence of a story may be inferred from the images or from literary allusions.

The T'ang also saw a tremendous increase in the number of Buddhist translations, texts and treatises. Some of this was due to the activity of the Buddhist priest Hsüan-tsang (q.v.), who made an extensive trip to India and wrote an account of it. (This was later used as the basis for one of China's most famous novels, the *Hsi Yu Chi* [q.v.], or "Record of Western Wanderings.") It was also the occasion of a bitter protest against Buddhism (q.v.) by the official (and poet) HAN Yü, who wrote a memorial to the throne objecting to preparations being made to receive Buddhist relics at the capital. HAN was not alone in his antipathy to Buddhism, and some years after his death in 823, there occurred a massive repression of Buddhism (see under **Ennin**).

The Sung dynasty (960-1279, q.v.) benefited from a technological breakthrough of extraordinary proportions. Just as the invention of paper in the Han dynasty had lowered the cost of materials for copying books, so the invention of printing (q.v.) in the T'ang made it possible for books to be made cheaply in multiple copies for wide distribution. Because of the availability of books, literacy became more widespread than ever before, and education received a major stimulus.

Sung poetry is generally regarded as being more conventional than that of the T'ang. Among the most famous of the Sung poet-officials was SU Tung-p'o (q.v.), but there were many others. The Historian SSU-MA Kuang (q.v.) wrote a history of China from the 5th century B.C. to the beginning of the Sung dynasty, thus departing from the pattern of dynastic histories which had been established. He is regarded as the equal of his predecessor SSU-MA Ch'ien of a millennium earlier.

The Yuan dynasty (1279-1368, q.v.) marked a radical departure. It was the first time that all of China had come under the rule of a non-Chinese people, though parts of North China (q.v.) had been under such rule in the Liao and Chin dynasties (qq.v.). The Mongol rulers distrusted the Chinese literati who had provided the Sung administraion with competent and literate bureaucrats. They suspended the examinations and utilized non-Chinese in administrative positions. Marco Polo (q.v.) is the example best known to Westerners, but he was one among thousands.

Since the examinations no longer led to official preferment, many of the literary men took up other activities. It was during the Yuan dynasty that we can mark the beginnings of Chinese drama and the novel (qq.v.). Actually, the Chinese had been enjoying dramatic performances of various kinds for centuries. In the T'ang dynasty the emperor Ming Huang established a school for court performers which he called the Pear Garden. "Children of the Pear Garden" has been a literary term for actors and performers ever since.

The dramatic form which is known as Peking Opera (see under **Drama**) has its roots in the Yuan drama. Traditional Chinese tend to divide the operas into two types—literary, which tend to be love stories and ghost stories, and military, which usually involve symbolic battles and spectacular acrobatic feats. The division follows that of government officials: the literary officers are those who are recruited, theoretically, through the literary examinations, and the military are those who have achieved success in that field.

There are a number of Yuan dramas extant, though perhaps few are in their original form. Students of Western drama usually describe them as not well constructed, in Western terms. However, the dramas should be viewed from a Chinese perspective. Many are based on historical events, and their presentation to a largely illiterate populace was an effective means of presenting certain aspects of Chinese history in an intelligible form to the people. Many characters in Chinese history are widely known, if not entirely accurately, from their appearances in popular operas. For example, TS'AO Ts'ao and Kuan Yü (qq.v.), two characters from the *Romance of the Three Kingdoms* (q.v.), are based on historical personalities of the third century A.D.

The *Romance of the Three Kingdoms*, just mentioned, is one of the earliest of Chinese novels to survive. It may be the most widely read novel in world history, or at least familiar to the most people. It is a historical narrative, rather than a novel as known in the present day, based on events which occurred during the period of the Three Kingdoms (q.v.), which followed the downfall of the Han dynasty in 221 A.D. As noted, these events have been used in numerous operas, but the novel itself has been read by hundreds of millions of Chinese, Japanese, Koreans and Vietnamese. Many Chinese scholars of centuries past have admitted that when bored with Confucian moral strictures, they have amused themselves by reading the *Romance*, enjoying the tales of derring-do and clever military strategems. It has even been suggested that an understanding of the traditional Chinese mind requries an acquaintance with this novel.

The Ming dynasty (1368-1643, q.v.) saw an even greater increase in literacy and in the number of books published. Three of China's most famous novels—*Chin P'ing Mei, Hsi Yu Chi* and *Shui Hu Chuan* (qq.v.)—date from this era. The Ming restored the examination system as the accepted avenue to an official career, and literary production of the standard sort (poems and essays) was considerable. Literary efforts, however, could be dangerous. The poet KAO Ch'i (q.v.) was executed in 1374 by the first Ming emperor because of a poem he had written.

The Ch'ing dynasty (1644-1911, q.v.) was the final period of literary production in the classic style, though many Chinese living today can not only read classic Chinese literature but are perfectly capable of producing poems and essays in the classic style. The Ch'ing also saw the production of *The Dream of the Red Chamber* (q.v.), which has been described as the greatest Chinese novel.

The Ch'ing also witnessed the greatest literary inquisition since the Burning of the Books more than 2,000 years earlier. This was conducted under the emperor Ch'ien Lung, presumably for the purpose of rooting out any opposition to the dynasty, whether direct or expressed in terms of impolite references to the Manchus or their non-Chinese dynastic predecessors, such as the Liao and Chin dynasties (qq.v.).

The first European influence on China came at the end of the Ming and the beginning of the Ch'ing dynasties, and was expressed in the form of Jesuit translations of mathematical texts and explanations of Christian doctrine. Since mathematics (q.v.) had practically disappeared as a subject of scholarly interest during the Yuan dynasty, and civil service examinations during the Ming and Ch'ing were restricted to the subject matter of the Confucian canon, the Jesuit works had no impact on the world of letters. The second invasion of European ideas occurred in the 19th century, and, like the first, was not immediately perceived in literary terms.

Conflict between the Ch'ing and the European powers came to a head first in the Opium and *Arrow* wars (qq.v.), and only the establishment of the Tsungli Yamen and the T'ung-wen Kuan in the aftermath of the Treaties of Tientsin (qq.v.) made the necessity of Chinese acquaintance with western civilization apparent to the educated classes. Awareness of the widespread literacy in Europe and America and the widespread illiteracy of the Chinese population raised questions about the appropriateness of the Chinese literary language in which all official documents and literature were written. Novels and plays, being "unofficial," had been written more or less in the vernacular since the Yuan dynasty, and to that extent were easier to read. Concern over this issue led to the movement to adopt *pai hua* ("clear language," q.v.), or vernacular expression, for written communication.

Adoption of pai hua was one of the issues of the May Fourth movement (q.v.), and one of its key proponents was HU Shih (q.v.). While in the view of some observers it would be an exaggeration to suggest that written Chinese today is as close to a transcription of the spoken language as is true in European languages, there is no question that it is far closer than was true a century ago. However, it is true that a newspaper editorial read over the radio might still be incomprehensible to listeners without a transcript of the characters used.

The 20th century has seen a flowering of literature based on such Western forms as the short story. Surviving tales from earlier centuries tend to be involved with ghosts and magic transformations, while those of the modern era are more concerned with psychology, a set of beliefs more acceptable to the contemporary mind. Relatively little of this has appeared in translation. Without such translations, it is difficult for a Western observer to make any judgment on the quality of modern Chinese literature.

Birch, Cyril, ed. *Anthology of Chinese Literature*. New York: Grove Press, 1972.

Giles, H.A. *A History of Chinese Literature*. pbk ed. Rutland: Charles E. Tuttle Co., 1973.

Liu-ch'iu Islands. Better known as the Ryukyu Islands, the largest of which is Okinawa. Although the archipelago currently belongs to Japan, the king of Liu-ch'iu was for centuries tributary both to the emperor of China and to the Japanese feudal lord of Satsuma. Tribute was first sent to China in 1372, shortly after the establishment of the Ming dynasty (1368-1644, q.v.), and the last Liu-ch'iu ambassador to China paid tribute in 1875. The lord of Satsuma conquered the islands in 1609, and Japanese claims to suzerainty were based on that event.

In 1871, some sailors from Liu-ch'iu were shipwrecked on Taiwan, where they were killed and eaten by Taiwanese aborigines. Japan demanded redress, but the Chinese declared it to be an entirely internal Chinese affair. Under threat of military action, China paid an indemnity, and in the papers drawn up, the Liu-ch'iu islanders were referred to as "people belonging to Japan." On this basis, Japan took over the islands directly in 1875, and in 1879 made them a Japanese prefecture.

China's willingness to pay an indemnity, and Japan's success in absorbing the Liu-ch'iu, set the pattern for the alienation of other Chinese dependencies, such as Annam (Vietnam), Burma and Korea (qq.v.).

LIU Ming-ch'uan (1836-1896). Ch'ing dynasty soldier and official; first governor of Taiwan. LIU was born to a farm family in Anhwei province (q.v.), and started his military career with a group of freebooters. When the area was threatened by the Taiping Rebellion (1850-1864, q.v.), he organized a volunteer defense corps, and became a commander in the imperial forces. After the suppression of the Taipings in 1864, LIU went on to greater success in the final suppression of the Nien rebels (q.v.) in 1868. This was followed by several years of retirement, though he was called to court several times for advice.

When the Franco-Chinese War (see under **France**) broke out in 1884, LIU was appointed governor of Fukien province (q.v.), of which Taiwan (q.v.) was a part, and was instructed to organize the defense of the island. While French forces were able to seize the ports of Keelung and Tamsui after heavy fighting, LIU held Taipei against attack. The French blockaded the other ports, thus cutting off LIU from reinforcements and supplies. However, the war ended with the Treaty of Tientsin (q.v.) signed on June 9, 1885, and LIU went back to Fukien to take up his governorship.

In November 1885, the post of governor of Taiwan was created, though it remained a part of Fukien province. LIU was made the first governor, and in 1887 Taiwan was upgraded to the status of an independent province. LIU remained governor until 1891, when he was recalled.

LIU's actions as governor were regarded as radical by conservative Chinese. They included administrative reform, improved military defense, railway construction and the establishment of schools. Most of these policies suffered benign neglect under his successors.

When the Sino-Japanese War (q.v.) broke out in 1894, the emperor summoned him, but he pleaded ill health and was excused. He died several months after the cession of Taiwan to Japan in the Treaty of Shimonoseki, concluded April 17, 1895 (q.v.).

Hummel, Arthur W., ed. *Eminent Chinese of the Ch'ing Period*. Washington: Government Printing Office, 1943.

LIU Pei (160-223 A.D.). Founder of the state of Shu, or Shu Han, one of the Three Kingdoms (qq.v.). He was a minor member of the imperial family of the Han dynasty (206 B.C.-221 A.D., q.v.). The dynasty was in decline as a succession of weak emperors reigned under the corrupting influence of eunuchs. The countryside was troubled by drought and pestilence, as well as by local warlords. LIU's ambition to save the empire and restore peace ended in failure, as the Han dynasty was followed by the Period of Disunity (221-589 A.D., q.v.). LIU Pei's name is known to all Chinese who have been exposed to traditional culture, as he figures prominently in the novel *Romance of the Three Kingdoms* (q.v.) and the many operas whose plots are derived from it.

LIU Shao-ch'i (1900-1969). Communist leader and politician. LIU was born in Hunan province (q.v.) and studied at Changsha's First Normal School where MAO Tse-tung and LI Li-san (qq.v.) were also students. He was in Shanghai in the summer of 1920 and joined the Socialist Youth League (q.v.) founded by the Comintern representative Gregory Voitinsky. In the winter of

that year he was sent with a group of students to the USSR, where he attended the Communist University for the Toilers of the East.

The First National Congress of the Chinese Communist party (CCP, q.v.) was held in Shanghai in July, 1921, and shortly after that LIU joined the Moscow branch of the party. He returned to China in 1922 and spent the next few years in labor organization, including a successful coal-mine strike at Anyuan. In the winter of 1923 he went to Canton where preparations for the alliance between the CCP and the Kuomintang (KMT, q.v.) were being made. In 1925 he was elected vice chairman of the All-China Federation of Labor.

1927 saw LIU elected to the Central Committee of the CCP, and general secretary of the All-China Federation of Labor. It also saw the Communist labor apparatus shattered by the efforts of CHIANG Kai-shek, FENG Yü-hsiang and WANG Ching-wei (qq.v.) after the CCP-KMT split. LIU went underground but surfaced in Shanghai in 1930 where he worked with CHOU En-lai (q.v.) in organizing Communist labor unions once again. In 1932 he moved to the rural Communist base in Kiangsi (see under MAO Tse-tung).

While he started on the Long March (q.v.) he soon dropped out to go underground again. Between 1936 and 1942 he was active in north and central China and served as head of the regions' bureaus of the Central Committee. He also spent time in Yenan during that period. He continued his rise within the party and in 1945 was made third-ranking member of the Central Committee, after MAO and CHU Teh (q.v.). With the establishment of the People's Republic of China (PRC, q.v.) at Peking on October 1, 1949, LIU became the second chairman of the government, again following MAO and CHU.

When MAO announced in December 1958 that he was stepping down as head of government, LIU was elected chairman of the PRC in April 1959. In 1966 he became a target of the Cultural Revolution (q.v.) and was replaced as number two man in the CCP by LIN Piao (q.v.). LIU was not restored to favor before his death in 1969. He was rehabilitated posthumously in 1980, and memorial services were held for him throughout the People's Republic.

Boorman, Howard, ed. *Biographical Dictionary of Republican China*. New York, Columbia University Press, 1971.

Livadia, Treaty of. Signed October 2, 1879, by the Manchu official Ch'ung-hou (1826-1893) for China, and Nicholas de Giers for Russia. The treaty was signed in Livadia, a vacation resort, because the Tsar and his high officials were in residence there at the time. The decline in the power of the Ch'ing dynasty (1644-1911, q.v.) in the mid-19th century coincided with the rise of Russian power in Central Asia. In 1864 a Muslim rebellion in Sinkiang (Turkestan, q.v.) led by Yakoob Beg (1820[?]-1887), q.v.), provided Russia with an opportunity to occupy Ili, which it did in 1871, announcing its intention of returning Ili when China could maintain authority. By 1878 the Chinese general TSO Tsung-t'ang (1812-1885, q.v.) had suppressed the rebellion, and the Chinese sent Ch'ung-hou to Russia to negotiate the return of Ili.

Ch'ung-hou agreed to an indemnity and conceded the larger part of the Ili region to Russia. The treaty was denounced in Peking and Ch'ung-hou was sentenced to death, though the sentence was not carried out. The treaty was superseded by the Treaty of St. Petersburg (1881, q.v.).

Clubb, O. Edmund. *China and Russia.* New York: Columbia University Press, 1971.

Long March. This refers to the Communist retreat from the base at Juichin, Kiangsi province (q.v.), to its final destination at Yenan, Shensi (q.v.), covering a distance of about 6,000 mi. (9,650 km.) on foot. It was a military feat which not only preserved the Chinese Communist party (CCP) and the Red Army, but enabled MAO Tse-tung (q.v.) to eliminate his internal opposition.

MAO and CHU Teh (q.v.) had been forced out of their location on the Hunan-Kiangsi border by Nationalist military pressure in early 1929, and established their new base at Juichin in southeastern Kiangsi. The Nationalists made a series of attacks on Juichen and finally encircled it in 1934. In October the Chinese soviet government at Juichin was dissolved and the Long March began. There were approximately 100,000 troops at the beginning, although only 7,000 or so reached Yenan.

This force, known as the First Front Army, was not the only Communist military force in China. The Fourth Front Army, under CHANG Kuo-t'ao (q.v.), was in Szechwan province; the Second Front Army, under HO Lung, was in the Hunan-Kweichow border area; and a secure base had been established in northern Shensi (q.v.) by troops under KAO Kang and LIU Chih-tan. The First Front Army headed northwest, proposing to join the Second Front Army. To do so required crossing the Hsiang river in northern Kwangsi. Nearly two-thirds of the original troops were lost in the attempt. They then turned west into Kweichow (q.v.), and in January, 1935, captured the city of Tsunyi.

A conference of the political bureau of the CCP was held at Tsunyi, and it was at this conference that MAO became the leader of the CCP. The conference specifically rejected the policy of the leadership in Shanghai of depending on the urban workers and adopted a military policy of mobility and guerrilla warfare. They also decided to join CHANG Kuo-t'ao and the Fourth Front Army in Szechwan (q.v.). This involved crossing two major rivers, the Yangtze, known as the Chinsha in its upper reaches, and the Tatu.

Both crossings were the stuff of legend. In the first case, the Communist advance guard, traveling by forced march, surprised the commander of the Nationalist detachment, who was supposed to be on the other side of the river with all available boats. In the second, a band of soldiers captured a small suspension bridge (the only one) at a crossing called Luting. According to Snow's account (see below) half the planking on the iron bridge had been removed and the first wave had to go hand-over-hand while being covered by the guns of their colleagues.

MAO's forces, the First Front Army, joined CHANG's Fourth Front Army in mid-July 1935. The two men soon found themselves in conflict, with CHANG proposing a move westward into Sikang (q.v.), and MAO preferring to move north to Shensi. The Communist forces split, with CHU Teh and others accompanying CHANG into Sikang, and MAO proceeding to Shensi. MAO's forces had even greater difficulty in the last stage of the march, since the area known as the Grasslands was a treacherous bog and close to impassable. They also had to face hostile non-Chinese tribes and cross several mountain ranges.

MAO's forces reached Shensi province in October 1935, though remnants of the Long March forces continued trickling in until the spring of 1937.

Salisbury, Harrison. *The Long March: The Untold Story*. New York: Harper & Row, 1985.

Snow, Edgar. *Red Star over China*. New York: Random House, 1938.

Wilson, Dick. *The Long March, 1935*. New York, Viking Press, 1971.

Longmen. See under **Lungmen**.

Lotus Sutra. This sutra is regarded by many Buddhists as an important exposition of the thought and doctrine of Shakyamuni, the historical Buddha (see under **Buddhism**). It is a key text for the T'ien T'ai (Japanese Tendai) sect (q.v.), and is mentioned frequently by the Japanese monk Ennin (793-864, q.v.), an adherent of the sect. Recitation of the Lotus Sutra was frequently undertaken to avert calamity, whether natural or man-made, and courses of lectures on the text were scheduled at many temples and monasteries during the T'ang dynasty (618-906, q.v.).

The Sanskrit original was translated into Chinese several times, notably by Kumarajiva (q.v.) in 406 A.D. For many years the Sanskrit original was presumed lost, but recent discoveries in Central Asia and Nepal may have turned up Sanskrit versions, though whether they are identical to the Chinese texts has not been determined.

The Lotus Sutra was the first Buddhist text to be translated, though in somewhat abbreviated form, from Chinese to English, other Buddhist translations being largely from Pali.

Soothill, William E. *The Lotus of the Wonderful Law*. Oxford, Oxford University Press, 1930.

Davidson, J. LeRoy. *The Lotus Sutra in Chinese Art*. New Haven: Yale University Press, 1954.

Loyang (Luoyang). Population: 500,000 (1979). Located in Honan province (q.v.), it was the capital of the Later Chou dynasty (771-255 B.C.), the Eastern Han (25-221 A.D.), the Western Chin (266-316), the Northern Wei (494-534), and was the secondary capital of the T'ang (618-906). Nearby is Lungmen (Longmen) (q.v.), a major Buddhist site, with hundreds of caves filled with religious sculptures.

Lu, State of. A minor state of the Warring States Period (q.v.). Located in present-day Shantung (q.v.), its importance in history lies primarily in the fact that Confucius (q.v.) was born there.

Lungmen (Longmen). Site of hundreds of caves cut into the cliffs and filled with Buddhist sculpture dating from the fifth to the tenth century A.D. There are said to be 100,000 carved figures. The earliest works date from the Northern Wei dynasty (386-534), and thousands more were added during the Sui (589-618) and T'ang (618-906) dynasties (qq.v.). It is located a few miles south of Loyang in Honan province (qq.v.).

Luoyang. See under **Loyang**.

M

Macao. Portuguese colony on the coast of Kwangtung province (q.v.), about 50 miles west of Hong Kong and 6 miles south of Canton (qq.v.). In 1984 its population numbered 400,000, of whom 95 percent are ethnic Chinese. The first Portuguese trading ship arrived in Chinese waters in 1517, but the accepted date of the founding of Macao is 1557. Sovereignty over the land was exercized by China, as indicated by the rent the Portuguese paid until 1849. In 1887 China signed a treaty ceding Macao to Portugal. This is regarded by the Chinese as one of the "unequal treaties" (q.v.) forced upon a weakened Ch'ing dynasty (1644-1911, q.v.).

Because of trouble with European traders, all ports except Canton were closed to them in 1550, a situation which lasted until British victory in the Opium War (1839-1842, q.v.) succeeded in opening four other treaty ports (q.v.). Since the traders were not permitted to reside in Canton, many took up temporary residence in Macao.

The British victory in 1842 led to the cession of Hong Kong (q.v.), whose immediate prosperity cut deeply into Macao's economy. In March 1849, the Portuguese governor, Joao M.F. do Amaral, expelled the Chinese customs officers and declared Macao a free port. In August he was assassinated while riding by several Chinese. His head and right hand were severed and not returned by Chinese authorities until January 1850, with apologies.

Macao continued to fall behind Hong Kong as a trading center, but achieved some importance in World War II (q.v.) when Portuguese neutrality made it a small island of peace. In 1977 it was the sole surviving remnant of Portugal's overseas empire, and the Portuguese offered to retrocede it to the People's Republic of China. The offer was declined, but many observers expect that Macao will lose its anomalous status immediately after Hong Kong becomes part of China in 1997.

Boxer, C.R. *Fidalgos in the Far East: 1550-1770.* London: Oxford University Press, 1968.

Mahayana Buddhism. Mahayana means "greater vehicle" and is used to distinguish the form of Buddhism (q.v.) common to China, Japan, Korea, Mongolia, Nepal, Tibet, Vietnam etc., from the Hinayana Buddhism (q.v.) common in Burma, Cambodia, Ceylon, Laos and Thailand.

While in Hinayana Buddhism salvation is an individual concern, Mahayana Buddhism stresses the concept of the bodhisattva (q.v.). A bodhisattva is a being who has achieved the point of Buddhahood, or enlightenment, but postpones it to assist all other sentient beings reach the same point.

Mahayana Buddhism also acknowledges the existence of many thousands of gods of varying kinds. The majority of the Mahayana canon texts were originally written in Sanskrit, and thousands have been translated into Chinese and other languages, thus preserving them when the Sanskrit originals were lost with the disappearance of Buddhism in India. Some of the Sanskrit versions have been recovered in recent years, in Nepal and Central Asia.

One aspect of Mahayana Buddhism that has no counterpart in its southern relative is sudden enlightenment, a tenet of Ch'an Buddhism (q.v.). Mahayana is also the home of the Pure Land sect (q.v.), which achieved massive popularity in China and Japan through the teaching that the mere pronunciation of the name of Amitabha (*O-mi-t'o-fo* in Chinese) would earn the believer entrance into the Western Paradise.

Wright, Arthur F. *Buddhism in Chinese History*. New York: Atheneum, 1965. (paper, reprint)

Fung, Yu-lan, and Derk Bodde, trans. *History of Chinese Philosophy, Vol. II.* Princeton, Princeton University Press, 1953.

Manchu. The term refers to the Manchu people, the language they speak and the dynasty they established, the Ch'ing (1644-1911 A.D., q.v.). The people are related to the dominant group of the Chin dynasty (1115-1234 A.D., q.v.) usually known as Juchen (q.v.). Nurhaci (1559-1626, q.v.), founded the Later Chin dynasty in 1616 in Manchuria (q.v.), and adopted that dynastic name to indicate the connection. Nurhaci's son and successor, Abahai (1592-1643, q.v.), in 1635 adopted the name "Manchu" for his people and

banned the use of the name Juchen to conceal the fact that they had been under Chinese rule at various times. In 1636 he changed the name of the dynasty to Ch'ing.

Spoken Manchu belongs to the Tungusic branch of the Ural-Altaic family, related to Mongol but not to spoken Chinese. Under the Chin dynasty, Juchen officials wrote official documents in a script borrowed from the Khitan (q.v.). By the 16th century, they were using Mongol language and script for documents. In 1599 Nurhaci ordered the creation of a Manchu script based on Mongol script.

After the establishment of the Ch'ing dynasty in China, many Manchus left Manchuria to participate in the administration of the empire. Hereditary Manchu military units (see **Banners**) were stationed in many Chinese cities throughout the dynasty and were targets of Chinese animosity in insurrections such as the Taiping Rebellion (q.v.), and in the revolution of 1911.

The Manchus have always been a relatively small ethnic group. In his book, *China and Russia*, (New York, Columbia University Press, 1971), author O. Edmund Clubb estimates their number in the early 17th century at around 400,000.

At the time of the establishment of the Republic of China (q.v.) in 1912, the Manchu were designated as one of the five constituent races of the republic. They are still officially regarded as a minority by the People's Republic of China (q.v.), whose statistics (1980) show 2,600,000 Manchus living primarily in Manchuria, Inner Mongolia, Peking and Hopei province (qq.v.). However, the processes of acculturation and assimilation have made many Manchus nearly indistinguishable from other Chinese. While most of them presumably are aware of their Manchu descent, many can no longer read or speak Manchu.

Manchukuo. The name means "country of the Manchu" in Chinese, and is sometimes written Manchoukuo. The Japanese set up the puppet state of Manchukuo in Manchuria in 1932, having completed the occupation of the area in about six months. They also set up P'u-yi (q.v.), the last of the Manchu emperors, as titular ruler, but all power was in the hands of Japanese advisers. In doing this the Japanese apparently accomplished the permanent subjugation of Manchuria, an objective they had sought against both Chinese and Russian competition for nearly half a century. However, the state lasted only until August 1945, when it was swept away in the aftermath of the Japanese surrender at the end of World War II. Recognizing that it was only a Japanese puppet, no more than a handful of other states ever extended diplomatic recognition to Manchukuo.

Manchuria. Homeland of the Manchu (q.v.), Manchuria is now divided into three provinces: Heilungkiang, Kirin and Liaoning (qq.v.). It is known to the Chinese as the Three Eastern Provinces, or simply the Northeast. Archaeological evidence of both Chinese and Korean cultural influence in the first millennium B.C. has been found. Parts of southern Manchuria were included in the state of Yen (q.v.) of the Warring States Period (484-221 B.C., q.v.), and were also under the control of the Han dynasty (206 B.C.-221 A.D., q.v.) and the T'ang (618-906 A.D., q.v.). It was the base for the Liao (907-1125) and Chin (1115-1235) dynasties (qq.v.), and it was con-trolled by the Yuan (Mongol) dynasty (1206-1368, q.v.). Parts of it were controlled by the Ming dynasty (1368-1644, q.v.), and it was the homeland from which the Ch'ing (Manchu) dynasty (1644-1911, q.v.) arose.

For most of its history, Manchuria was sparsely populated by nomadic hunters and herdsmen of several related ethnic strains. The relatively few Chinese residents, mostly settled farmers and traders, were located in the south, near the Chinese border. The Manchus, who achieved dominance in the area in the 16th century, were proud of their non-Chinese culture, and the ruling class made great efforts to retain certain aspects of it, specifically riding horses, hunting and fishing. While many of the Manchus who lived in China after the establishment of the Ch'ing dynasty there became culturally assimilated, the imperial family resisted the Sinicization of Manchuria, and banned Chinese immigration, not always successfully.

While the border between China and Manchuria had been fought over for centuries, very little thought was given to the northern borders until the middle of the 17th century when adventurers from Russia (q.v.) appeared. The Treaty of Nerchinsk (1689, q.v.), which delimited the border well north of the Amur river as far as the line of the Yablonovy and Stanovoi mountains, east to the Sea of Okhotsk, was the first attempt at settling the borders. It confirmed the Ch'ing in possession of the entire drainage basin of the Amur river, and reflected China's strength under the emperor K'ang Hsi (r. 1662-1722, q.v.).

By the middle of the 19th century, the Ch'ing dynasty was no longer strong. In 1857 the Russians offered to assist in the suppression of the Taiping Rebellion (q.v.) in exchange for the cession of the three northernmost of the nine provinces into which Manchuria was then divided. This was refused, but in 1858 under the Treaty of Aigun, and in 1860 under the Treaty of Peking (qq.v.), the Ch'ing authorities were forced to cede to Russia an immense stretch of territory including all the land north of the Amur and east of the Ussuri rivers, including the mouth of the Amur. The Soviet cities of Khabarovsk, at the junction of the two rivers, and Vladivostok, at the southern end of the Maritime Province, are in the area ceded at that time.

Japanese aspirations on the Asian mainland led to the Sino-Japanese War (1894-1895, q.v.). Under the Treaty of Shimonoseki (q.v.) which resulted, Japan was given a free hand in Korea and received the Liaotung peninsula (qq.v.) in southeastern Manchuria. Pressure from Russia, France and Germany forced the retrocession of Liaotung. In gratitude, China in 1896 agreed to the construction of the Chinese Eastern Railway (q.v.) across Manchuria. By avoiding the route of the Amur river, it drastically shortened the traveling time between Irkutsk and Vladivostok.

In 1898 Russia leased the Liaotung peninsula, built a naval base at Port Arthur (q.v.) and won the right to build the South Manchurian Railway, linking Harbin (q.v.) on the Chinese Eastern Railway with Port Arthur and Dairen (q.v.). At the outbreak of the Boxer Rebellion (q.v.) in 1900, Russia increased its military presence in Manchuria and after peace was restored, delayed in removing it.

In 1903, the Ch'ing court recognized that permitting unlimited Chinese immigration into what had previously been the imperial preserve would impede either a Russian or Japanese takeover of a relatively empty territory. Consequently, Manchuria was made a part of China and divided into three provinces, Heilungkiang, Kirin and Fengtien (qq.v.). (The name of the latter province was later changed to Shengking, and then to Liaoning, by which it is now known.)

Japan retaliated for perceived slights with the Russo-Japanese War (1904-1905, q.v.), which deprived Russia of Port Arthur and the Liaotung peninsula. While China did not participate, the war was fought in Manchuria, and dominance over the area was the objective on both sides. While Japan replaced Russia in Liaotung, Russian influence in the north, and Russian control of the Chinese Eastern Railway remained. Japan had some Chinese support in the war, specifically from CHANG Tso-lin (q.v.), the warlord who ruled a quasi-independent Manchuria from 1912-1928.

The fall of the Ch'ing dynasty and the establishment of the Republic of China (q.v.) in 1912 led to a period of disunity and civil war dominated by various warlords (q.v.). The articles of abdication on behalf of the infant emperor, drafted by YUAN Shih-k'ai (q.v.), handed over to the new republic all the territories then held by the Ch'ing dynasty. These included Manchuria, but republican sovereignty over CHANG Tso-lin was theoretical only.

On July 25, 1919, by the Karakhan Declaration (q.v.), the USSR renounced all extraterritorial rights and privileges in China, an edict which affected Manchuria more than other areas. On May 31, 1924, the Peking government (q.v.) signed an agreement with the USSR defining the status of the Chinese Eastern Railway, but CHANG Tso-lin declared that it did not apply in Manchuria. The Soviets signed a separate agreement with him on September 20,

1924, over the protests of the Peking government. But the precedent for treating Manchuria as autonomous was set.

CHANG Tso-lin was assassinated by the Japanese in 1928, and was succeeded by his son CHANG Hsueh-liang (q.v.). The younger Chang acceded to the Nationalist government on December 29, 1928, theoretically completing the unification of China.

In 1929 CHANG's police raided Soviet consulates in Manchuria and seized compromising documents. They followed up by taking over the Chinese Eastern Railway and deporting several hundred Russians. A Soviet ultimatum was refused, and Soviet forces invaded in November, forcing CHANG to capitulate and restoring the *status quo ante bellum*.

In September 1931, the Japanese seized Mukden and several other Manchurian cities, and CHANG's government collapsed. China appealed to the League of Nations, without success. In 1932 Japan created the puppet state of Manchukuo (q.v.) and consolidated its control over Manchuria. The USSR sold its interest in the Chinese Eastern Railway to Manchukuo for about one-eighth of the investment made. From 1932 until the end of World War II in August 1945, Japan established a major industrial area in Manchuria, the source of much of Japan's military strength and far surpassing the Chinese industrial center at Wuhan (q.v.) on the Yangtze river.

Though China did not participate in the Yalta Conference (q.v.) of February 1945, major concessions to the USSR at China's expense were made there. In exchange for Soviet agreement to enter the war against Japan after the German surrender, the USSR was given joint control of the Chinese Eastern Railway, and restoration of Czarist Russian rights in Manchuria, including Port Arthur and Dairen.

The USSR declared war on Japan on August 8, 1945, the day the second atomic bomb was dropped, on Nagasaki, and the following day Soviet troops entered Manchuria. Encountering little resistance from the Japanese, by the end of the month they had occupied the whole of Manchuria. Although originally promising to evacuate within 90 days, the date was postponed until the end of April 1946. The Soviet troops used the time to strip the Japanese industrial establishment of plant and equipment, even stripping coal mines of their pumps, and thus denying heating fuel to the local population during the winter. Contemporary estimates of plant and equipment lost run to $2 billion.

The Soviets also turned over Japanese arms to Chinese Communist military forces who came over the border from nearby North China, and prevented Nationalist troops from using either Dairen or Port Arthur to enter Manchuria until the former were well-entrenched. The first significant battles of the Civil War (1945-1949, q.v.), were fought in Manchuria, and its loss was a major blow to the Nationalists.

From the establishment of the People's Republic of China (q.v.) on October 1, 1949, relations with the USSR were excellent until 1956. It was during this period that the USSR returned its interests in Manchurian railways, and evacuated Port Arthur and Dairen. Relations worsened in the years that followed, and in addition to ideological differences there were border disputes. During the Cultural Revolution (qq.v.) in 1967, some 2 million Chinese were said to have demonstrated along the Soviet border, and in 1969 skirmishes on a disputed island in the Ussuri river between Heilungkiang and the Soviet Maritime Province resulted in the deaths of several soldiers on both sides.

Relations at present are more formal and correct, but there are still thousands of troops within a few miles of the border on both sides.

At the end of World War II, there were hundreds of thousands of Japanese residents in Manchuria, and at its peak, the city of Harbin (q.v.) had more than 100,000 Russian residents. Within a very few years, both populations had been expelled, with negligible exceptions. The majority population is Han Chinese, with the Manchus a minority. Other minorities, such as Mongols and Koreans, are also resident.

Mandate of Heaven. A concept attributed to the Confucian philosopher Mencius (371-289 B.C., q.v.) holding that an emperor lacking in virtue has forfeited his right to the throne. The mandate is then awarded (by heaven) to the conqueror who establishes the next dynasty. This solves the philosophical problem of transferring loyalty from a declining dynasty to its successor. Mencius specifically referred to the last emperor of the Shang dynasty (1766-1122 B.C., q.v.) who was put to death by the founder of the Chou (1122-255 B.C., q.v.). Mencius denied that this amounted to regicide. The concept has been cited in every dynastic change since then.

Manicheism. A religion founded by the Persian Mani (216-276 A.D.). It is based on two opposing principles, good, or light, and evil, or darkness. The material world and the human body pertain to the second principle. Time is regarded as belonging to three phases, in the first of which good and evil are separated, in the second mingled, and in the third separated again. Man exists as both body and spirit only in the second phase. It is man's duty to cleanse himself of evil to the greatest extent possible. When the third phase of time arrives (mankind now being in the second), those who have succeeded will dwell in the light, those who have failed in the darkness.

The Manichean clergy were required to observe celibacy and fasting, while the laity were permitted to marry and eat normally, though luxury was frowned upon and generosity and almsgiving encouraged.

Manicheism was widespread in many parts of Asia, and was known in T'ang China. The Uighurs (q.v.) were converted to the religion in 763, and it persisted as a cult into the early years of the Ming dynasty (1368-1644, q.v.). As an apocalyptic religion it was believed to have had some influence on the White Lotus Society (q.v.). There is no indication that the religion has survived into the 20th century.

MAO Tse-tung (MAO Zedong; 1893-1976). Born in Hunan province (q.v.), the eldest of four children of a moderately well-off peasant family, MAO did not get along well with his authoritarian and grasping father. He attended primary school, then spent several years on the family farm, but left in 1909 to further his education. While he studied in several schools, he also spent considerable time reading such works as traditional Chinese novels and translations of Western books on politics, economics and philosophy.

In 1918 MAO graduated from the First Normal School in Changsha and went to Peking where he worked in the library at Peking University. He spent the next few years in Peking, Shanghai and back in Hunan, where he came to the attention of the authorities for his organizational work on behalf of students. He also taught in Changsha, though he spent most of his time promoting Marxism. He represented Hunan in the formal establishment of the Chinese Communist party (CCP, q.v.) in Shanghai in July 1921. He fled Hunan for Canton in April 1923, to escape a warrant for his arrest issued because of his involvement in a series of strikes.

During this period, the Comintern followed Lenin's policy of promoting the revolution in Asia through cooperation with Asian nationalists. The joint statement of SUN Yat-sen (q.v.) and Adolf Joffe affirming cooperation between the USSR and the Kuomintang (KMT, q.v.) was made in January 1923. This provided for the admission of CCP members to the KMT as individuals. The Third National Congress of the CCP was held in Canton in June 1923, and conceded that the KMT must assume the leadership of the revolution in China. When the KMT held its first National Congress in Canton in January 1924, MAO was elected an alternate member of the Central Executive Committee.

MAO spent much of 1925 in Hunan organizing peasant associations. He also helped organize a strike, which forced him to flee again to Canton. There he became secretary of the KMT's propaganda department. By early 1927, back in Hunan, he wrote "A Report of an Investigation into the Peasant Movement in Hunan," in which he credited the peasantry with 70 percent of the achievements of the revolution, as against 30 percent for the urban inhabitants and the military. In this, he was clearly drawing away from the Leninist analysis which described the urban proletariat as the leaders of the revolution.

MAO participated in the KMT's Central Executive Committee meeting in Wuhan in March 1927, and in the CCP's Fifth National Congress in April-May. There his ideas on the role of the peasantry were not accepted. Far more important, to most of the participants, was the purge of Communists in Shanghai and Nanking which CHIANG Kai-shek (q.v.) started in April. At the Congress, CHANG Kuo-t'ao (q.v.) proposed an end to the alliance with the KMT, but this, too, was rejected as being opposed to Comintern policy.

In July, WANG Ching-wei (q.v.), leader of the left faction of the KMT, started a purge of Communists in Wuhan. MAO was ordered by the CCP to return to Hunan, where he directed a peasant uprising in the autumn. It was crushed, but MAO later claimed that one of the purposes was to establish rural soviets, which was directly contrary to Comintern policy.

MAO spent the winter with the remnants of his forces in the Chingkang mountain area along the Hunan-Kiangsi border. CHU Teh (q.v.) arrived in April 1928, with reinforcements, and they combined the forces into the Fourth Red Army, with CHU as commander and MAO as political commissar. In January 1929, KMT military pressure forced them to retreat to Juichin in Kiangsi, which they made their base until 1934.

MAO spent part of 1929-1930 in campaigns in Kiangsi and Fukien. In 1930, LI Li-san (q.v.), then the leading figure in the CCP and a supporter of Comintern policy toward urban workers, called for military attacks on several Chinese cities. After several failures, MAO refused further participation. In November 1931, the CCP convened the first All-China Congress of Soviets at Juichin, but although this was the most important Communist base, MAO was clearly not in charge of the CCP.

The Nationalist government launched five successive campaigns against the Juichin base and finally, in October 1934, succeeded in forcing the Communists out. At that point they began the Long March (q.v.), during which MAO finally achieved the unquestioned leadership of the CCP. This occurred in January 1935, at the city of Tsunyi (Zunyi), Kweichow province, at an enlarged conference of the Political Bureau. MAO was the first leader of the CCP who had not been selected by the Comintern, and the first such leader of any major Communist party anywhere.

MAO started out with about 100,000 troops, but only about 7,000 reached Yenan, Shensi province. The Long March was not only the opportunity for MAO to achieve the leadership he sought, it was also a legendary feat. It proved to be a unifying experience for the CCP leadership, and it was decades before any party member who had not participated in the Long March reached any senior position in the party.

MAO took advantage of Japanese military activity in North China to call for an end to the KMT-CCP war. On December 25, 1935, the Political Bureau called for an "Anti-Japanese National United Front." One result was the Sian Incident (q.v.) of December 1936, in which CHIANG Kai-shek was forced to agree to joint action against the Japanese.

On July 7, 1937, the Marco Polo Bridge Incident (q.v.) occurred, marking the beginning of war between China and Japan, which eventually became a part of World War II (q.v.). The Japanese seized the major cities and the communications network. Nationalist troops were faced with a superior enemy and employed a strategy which depended on set-piece battles. The Communist forces, following MAO's strategy, avoided open battle and used guerrilla tactics. Over a period of years, this Communist guerrilla force effectively replaced Nationalist administration in much of North China.

In spite of differences, the two parties consented to cooperation against the Japanese. An agreement on integrating the two military forces was reached in September 1937, and was in partial effect until the New Fourth Army Incident (q.v.) of January 1941, in which Communist troops were decisively defeated and retreated north of the Yangtze river.

MAO utilized the early 1940s to consolidate his hold on the party leadership. In 1943 and 1944 he was elected chairman of the Central Committee and of the Political Bureau. The CCP held its Seventh National Congress (the first since 1928) in Yenan in early 1945. The preamble to the newly adopted constitution noted that "the thought of MAO Tse-tung" was essential to guiding the work of the party.

The end of World War II in August 1945 found the CCP in a vastly different position from 10 years earlier. Instead of an exhausted remnant of a few thousand veterans of the Long March, party membership was estimated at 1.2 million, with another 900,000 in the armed forces, controlling an area with a population of 90 million Chinese. And while MAO was one of several CCP leaders in the earlier period, by 1945 he was in complete control. American efforts to encourage cooperation between the CCP and the KMT government in Chungking failed. The eventual result was the Civil War (1946-1949, q.v.), which led to the establishment of the People's Republic of China (PRC, q.v.) in Peking on October 1, 1949, with MAO as Chairman.

His first move was to suppress opposition and confiscate landholdings. An estimated 1 to 3 million people were killed in this program. In January 1952, the "Three Anti Movement" (q.v.) against corruption, decay and bureaucracy was launched against officials who had served under the Nationalist government. In March the "Five Anti Movement" (q.v.) against bribery, tax evasion, theft of state assets, theft of state economic secrets and fraud was launched against private businessmen.

On May 1, 1957, MAO proclaimed the "Hundred Flowers Movement" (q.v.), which encouraged intellectuals to express their criticisms. Those who went beyond limits acceptable to the CCP were subsequently punished. In January 1958, the Great Leap Forward (q.v.) was launched, communes were established, as were "backyard furnaces" for producing pig iron. Unreachable targets of production were set, reflecting MAO's ambition to achieve communism within a few years. The USSR withdrew its technical assistance and aid, and an estimated 20 million people died of starvation because of the disruption of agriculture.

In April 1959, LIU Shao-ch'i (q.v.) was elected chairman of the PRC, succeeding MAO, who retained the chairmanship of the CCP. Until the launching of the Cultural Revolution (GPCR, q.v.) in 1966, MAO lived somewhat in retirement, though his influence and his presence continued to be felt.

The GPCR turned the tables and LIU was replaced as number two man to MAO by LIN Piao (q.v.), who lasted in this position only until his mysterious death in 1971. The three most important figures in the early years of the GPCR were MAO, LIN and CHIANG Ch'ing (q.v.), MAO's wife. After LIN's death, CHIANG and her Gang of Four (q.v.) were at the forefront of the "continuing revolution." It was only brought to a halt by MAO's death on September 9, 1976.

MAO was married at least three times, possibly more. His first wife remained in Hunan when MAO retired to the Ching-Kang mountains in 1927, and was executed in 1930. Another wife accompanied him on the Long March, which she was one of the few women to survive. They separated in Yenan and he packed her off to Moscow, presumably for medical treatment. In 1939 he married CHIANG Ch'ing, a former film actress from Shanghai.

MAO's experience of the world outside China was minimal. He made only two trips abroad, both times to Moscow.

Boorman, Howard, ed. *Biographical Dictionary of Republican China.* New York: Columbia University Press, 1971.

Chou, Eric. *Mao Tse-tung: The Man and the Myth.* London: Cassell, 1984.

Schwartz, Benjamin I. *Chinese Communism and the Rise of Mao.* Cambridge: Harvard University Press, 1951.

Snow, Edgar. *Red Star Over China.* New York: Random House, 1938.

Klein, Donald W., and Anne B. Clark. *Biographic Dictionary of Chinese Communism, 1921-1965.* Cambridge, Harvard University Press, 1971.

Terrill, Ross. *Mao: A Biography.* New York, Harper and Row, 1980.

Marco Polo Bridge Incident (July 7, 1937). This is generally regarded as the opening shot of the war between China and Japan which merged into World War II. Japanese intentions in northeast China were clear to the

Nationalist government. They were to establish a Japanese-sponsored autonomous area including the provinces of Chahar, Hopeh, Shansi, Shantung and Suiyuan. This area covered the northeastern part of China proper and the eastern part of Inner Mongolia, in other words the areas adjacent to the puppet state of Manchukuo (q.v.). The Chinese response was to execute a delaying action which would not involve the cession of territory but would provide more time to prepare for the impending conflict.

The Japanese apparently provoked the clash with Chinese troops intentionally. The Chinese attempted to negotiate, but it became clear that the Japanese would settle for nothing less than an autonomous area independent of the Nanking government. By the end of the month the Japanese held Peking and Tientsin, and the Chinese forces were forced to pull back to the south.

Margary Affair. Augustus R. Margary, a Chinese interpreter in the British Consular Service, was murdered in Yunnan province (q.v.) on February 21, 1875, while accompanying a British expedition exploring a possible trade route between Burma and China. The expedition had been provided with special passports by the Chinese government, but was attacked and forced to return to Burma.

Sir Thomas Wade (q.v.), the British Minister at Peking, learned of the incident on March 11 by cable from the India Office in London. He framed a set of six demands which he presented to the Chinese government. The first three were directly connected with the incident, but the next two were not. The final demand was for immediate satisfaction of all claims.

The Chinese did not object to the first three demands, but objected to the introduction of extraneous matters. They also could not agree to immediate satisfaction prior to receipt of a full report from the governor of Yunnan, TS'EN Yü-ying (1829-1889). Because of the primitive nature of travel and communications, it had taken Margary five months to travel from Shanghai to Yunnan, and TS'EN's report did not arrive until July.

In accordance with Wade's first demand, a commission of inquiry was held with British officers present. It found the murder to be the work of hill tribesmen. Wade demanded that TS'EN be tried for the crime, but the Chinese refused. The issues were resolved with the signing on September 13, 1876, of the Chefoo Convention (q.v.).

Margary, Augustus Raymond. See under **Margary Affair**.

Marshall Mission. 1946. The failure of Chinese Communist and Nationalist troops to cooperate in the war against Japan proved frustrating to the Allied Powers in World War II (q.v.), particularly the United States, which found itself bearing the brunt of the war in the Pacific. American attempts to mediate began as early as 1943, but were not successful, owing to the longstanding distrust between the Chinese Communist party (CCP) and the Kuomintang (KMT, qq.v.).

The American perception that avoidance of civil war between the two factions was crucial for postwar peace in Asia led U.S. President Harry Truman to nominate General George C. Marshall, the U.S. Chief of Staff during the war, to lead a mission to achieve this end. He arrived in China in December 1945, and met with representatives of the two antagonists early in January. Within three days an agreement to cease hostilities had been reached, but the proposed policies of the two sides proved impossible to reconcile. The Civil War (q.v.) was resumed in the summer of 1946, Marshall acknowledged failure in the autumn, and returned to the United States at the end of the year. In an official statement he laid the blame equally on both parties to the quarrel.

Feis, Herbert. *The China Tangle*. pbk. ed. Princeton: Princeton University Press, 1972.

Martin, William Alexander Parsons (1827-1916). American missionary and educator. Born of a religious family in Indiana, and a graduate of Indiana University, he went to China as a missionary in 1850. After a brief stay in Canton, he moved to Ningpo, where he stayed for several years, learning both Mandarin and the Ningpo dialect, and developing his own romanization system (q.v.) for the latter. In 1854 he met and befriended Robert Hart (1835-1911, q.v.), later the inspector general of the Imperial Maritime Customs (q.v.).

Meeting with the same disappointment in making converts that other missionaries experienced, and aware of the precedent set by the Jesuits (q.v.), Martin turned to translation and to writing Chinese texts on mathematics, geography, and Greek and Roman history. With the help of Chinese scholars, he translated Henry Wheaton's *Elements of International Law*, and presented it to the Tsungli Yamen (q.v.), the newly established office for foreign affairs. Initially skeptical, the Yamen officials soon found that citing Wheaton precedents was effective in dealing with foreign powers.

In 1866 Martin visited Kaifeng, the first foreigner to do so in more than a century. He found descendants of an ancient community of Jews (q.v.), but

the synagogue had been destroyed. In 1869 he was appointed president of the T'ung-wen Kuan (q.v.), the school for interpreters of the Tsungli Yamen, which was supported by a subsidy from the Imperial Maritime Customs. In the aftermath of the Boxer Rebellion (1900, q.v.), the T'ung-wen Kuan became part of the Imperial University, of which Martin was dean for several years. He died in Peking.

Martin, W.A.P. *A Cycle of Cathay*. New York: Fleming H. Revell Co., 1896.

Mathematics. The traditional method of writing numbers in Chinese produces the following for, say, 624: "six hundred two ten four." Since traditional Chinese is written vertically, though it can also be written horizontally and in either direction, the problem of performing calculations on paper was not easily solved. Nevertheless, by the end of the Sung dynasty (960-1279, q.v.) the Chinese had made considerable progress in mathematics, using a system of calculation by rods called *ch'ou-suan*, which could be used to solve algebraic equations with as many as four unknowns. A knowledge of mathematics was required of candidates in the examinations for government appointments, and was prevalent in the official class.

The Yuan dynasty (1279-1368, q.v.), established by Mongol conquest, introduced the abacus (q.v.), which uses the positional system to express numbers, and makes simple calculations much easier than writing the traditional Chinese numbers on paper. For more complex calculations, such as the preparation of the official calendar, the Yuan rulers depended on non-Chinese who were familiar with Arabic numerals and Muslim astronomy. Since the traditional examinations were only offered a few times during the dynasty, Chinese scholars had little motivation to study the traditional mathematics, and very little interest in the work of the foreign astronomers.

The restoration of Chinese rule under the Ming dynasty (1368-1644, q.v.) restored the examination system (q.v.), but limited the subject matter to the Confucian canon. The Ming also entrusted the preparation of the calendar to Chinese Muslims. The emperor Ming Hung Wu (r. 1368-1398, q.v.) moved the capital from Peking to Nanking, and ordered the imperial Yuan astronomical instruments transferred. Father Matteo Ricci (1552-1610, q.v.) saw them in Nanking and recognized that they had been built for a more northerly latitude. Whether the official astronomers were aware of the problem is unclear, but the Jesuits (q.v.) soon demonstrated their superior skills in both mathematics and astronomy.

The Ch'ing dynasty (1644-1911, q.v.) retained the subject matter for the examinations used by the Ming, and while some effort was made to reprint Sung works on mathematics, the subject did not receive much attention. The Ch'ing also retained the Jesuits for astronomical work, but the number of Chinese interested in this was very small. In the late 19th century, after the establishment of the T'ung-wen Kuan (q.v.), where Western mathematics formed part of the curriculum, mathematics was given an optional position in the examinations.

The use of Arabic numerals and modern methods of calculation are now universal in Chinese schools, but the use of the abacus continues to be widespread.

Libbrecht, Ulrich. *Chinese Mathematics in the Thirteenth Century: The Shu-shu Chiu-chang of Ch'in Chiu-shao.* Cambridge: MIT Press, 1973.

May Fourth Incident. On May 4, 1919, some 3000 students in Peking protested against the decision of the Paris Peace Conference to award Japan (q.v.) the former concessions of Germany (q.v.) in Shantung province. The protest had been planned for May 7, the fourth anniversary of China's acceptance of Japan's Twenty-one Demands (q.v.), seen to be a serious infringement of China's sovereignty.

The students marched to the legation quarter to present their objections to the British, French, Italian and U.S. ministers, none of whom were present. They then turned to the home of TS'AO Ju-lin (q.v.), minister of communications and former vice minister of foreign affairs, in which capacity he had negotiated China's acceptance of the Twenty-one Demands. The students broke into the house, beat up some of the occupants (TS'AO escaped through the back) and set fire to it. Some were then arrested.

The arrests raised a storm of protest throughout China, and the students were released on bail on May 7, which was being observed by millions of Chinese as "National Humiliation Day." The incident was soon over, but it sparked the May Fourth Movement (q.v.), which had a major impact on Chinese culture.

Chow, Tse-tsung. *The May Fourth Movement.* Cambridge, Harvard University Press, 1960.

May Fourth Movement. This was a widespread popular reformist movement triggered by the student-led May Fourth Incident (q.v.) of 1919. The incident was soon over, but the student actions in protest against decision of the Paris Peace Conference to award German properties in China to Japan sparked a nationwide response. This took the form of strikes, anti-Japanese boycotts and expressions of support from a wide variety of organizations. The high point came on June 28, 1919, when public pressure on Chinese delegates at the conference dissuaded them from signing the Treaty of Versailles (q.v.).

The movement continued to generate excitement among students and the general populace, and broader objectives were adopted. These included a program to promote literacy (q.v.); the use of the vernacular, pai hua (q.v.), for written Chinese; anti-imperialism, particularly against the Japanese; and an effort to replace the traditional ethics of Confucianism (q.v.) by more modern concepts. concepts.

Several student leaders obtained nationwide publicity, and went on to become important figures in both the Nationalist and Communist governments. Two such were CH'EN Tu-hsiu (1879-1942) and HU Shih (1891-1962, qq.v.).

Chow, Tse-tsung. *The May Fourth Movement.* Cambridge: Harvard University Press, 1960.

May Third Incident. On this date in 1928, Nationalist forces participating in the second stage of the Northern Expedition (q.v.) clashed with Japanese troops at Tsinan, Shantung. The Nationalists were proceeding toward Peking to crush the northern warlords and unify China. The Japanese had been in occupation of Shantung province since taking over the former German concessions in 1914, early in World War I (q.v.). Japan perceived a strong and unified China as a threat to its interests in East Asia, and acted to protect those interests.

The clash outraged Chinese opinion, but CHIANG Kai-shek (q.v.), the commander in chief, unwilling to be deflected, ordered the Chinese troops to detour around the city and continue toward Peking. It was the first major clash between Chinese and Japanese troops in many years. The next occurred in September 1931 when Japan invaded Manchuria.

Medicine. The traditional Chinese approach to medicine was influenced by two different schools of thought, Confucianism and Taoism (qq.v.). The main Confucian contribution is the concept of the human body as a sacred legacy from one's ancestors, one which should never be harmed. This effectively inhibited medical practitioners from dissecting cadavers and resulted in serious misperceptions of the body's internal organs.

The secondary Confucian contribution was the general ban on any contact between men and women except for married couples. This meant that a doctor could not even take the pulse of a female patient. For this reason, it was customary for a doctor to have a figure of a woman, sometimes carved in ivory, so the patient could point to the area where pain was felt.

The first Taoist contribution was the concept whereby attuning himself to nature man could achieve longevity and possibly immortality. Taoist legends refer to sages who lived in the wilds for hundreds of years subsisting on a diet of berries, nuts and roots. From this idea arose the practice of concocting elixirs which were said to be capable of conferring extreme sexual potency, immortality or some other attribute on those who took them. Some historians have speculated that the death of Ch'in Shih Huang Ti (q.v.) in 210 B.C. may have been the result of some such activity.

At the same time, on a more practical level, the Chinese developed an empirical pharmacology, as happened in other areas of the world. It contains hundreds of herbs and drugs, some whose uses are unknown in the West. There is no doubt that many are effective, but a complete study remains to be made.

More exotic, to Western eyes, is the Chinese art of acupuncture (q.v.) in which needles are inserted in different parts of the body to relieve pain or to rectify a specific disorder. Nineteenth-century Western medical missionaries showed great skepticism toward the art, not only because the philosophical explanations were at variance with their own medical theories, but also because they were occasionally called upon to treat a patient who had been previously, and ineffectively, subjected to acupuncture.

Since, in the traditional system, there were no medical schools, and medical knowledge was considered proprietary information, it was passed on by masters of the art only to a handful of selected disciples, in many cases from father to son. Because of these circumstances, much of such lore is now believed to have been lost.

The arrival of medical missionaries under the aegis of Christianity (q.v.) in the 19th century provided a challenge to traditional Chinese medicine, particularly in the treaty ports (q.v.), and over a period of years it was accepted as superior to its rival. However, the scarcity of foreign doctors restricted its practice to a very small number of patients. Most Chinese continued to be treated with traditional medicine.

It soon became clear that the extension of modern medical practice to the general population would require the training of Chinese doctors in significant numbers. To this end a number of teaching hospitals were established, the best-known being the Peking Union Medical Center, built with Rockefeller money in the 1920s. The outbreak of war with Japan in 1937 caused many of its staff to make the long trek to West China.

The establishment of the People's Republic of China (q.v.) in 1949, and the subsequent departure of nearly all Westerners, together with many Western-trained Chinese doctors, left a vacuum. Chinese efforts to replace this loss is reflected in the metaphorically named "barefoot doctors," who are paramedicals at various levels of competence. No reliable figures exist on their numbers.

During the Cultural Revolution (1966-1976, q.v.), all education, including medical education was brought to a halt, and many Chinese doctors were banished to the countryside for reeducation. While efforts are now being made to restore the system, it may be worth noting that to provide as many doctors per capita for China as are now in practice in the United States, China will need 1.3 million. This will take a long time.

Mencius (371-289 B.C.). Mencius is the Latin form of MENG Tzu, meaning Master MENG. His real name was MENG K'o, and he is said to have been a pupil of the grandson of Confucius, whose philosophy he followed. Warfare among the feudal states of the Warring States Period (q.v.), in which he lived, was even more prevalent than in Confucius' time. Mencius offered his services to a number of the feudal lords, but although he was well received, none followed his advice. Consequently he retired and devoted himself to teaching. The *Book of Mencius* is the work by which he is known to later Confucians.

Mencius espoused two principles as being the most important: *jen*, or goodness, and *hsiao*, or filial piety, which may be extended to family feeling in general. He urged the feudal lords to practice benevolence, pointing out that the common people would then fight to retain a good ruler.

As a Confucian, Mencius was opposed to Taoists, Legalists, followers of MO Tzu, and other members of the Hundred Schools (qq.v.), but he was not regarded at the time as the preeminent Confucian. He shared that position with HSUN Tzu (q.v.) and others. Mencius's posthumous rise to preeminence is due to the attention given him by HAN Yü (q.v.) of the T'ang dynasty (618-906, q.v.) one of the founders of Neo-Confucianism (q.v.). As a result of that movement, the Book of Mencius became part of the syllabus for the imperial examinations for a thousand years.

Waley, Arthur. *Three Ways of Thought in Ancient China*. London: George Allen & Unwin Ltd., 1953.

MENG Hao-jan (689-740). Poet of the T'ang dynasty (618-906, q.v.). A brief biography appears in each of the *Old T'ang History* and the *New T'ang History*, but very little is known about his life. He failed the *chin-shih* examination at the age of 40, and later was given a very minor post. His failure, however, did not preclude his becoming good friends with other notable poets of the time, such as WANG Wei and LI Po (qq.v.). MENG is known as a recluse, largely because of his failure to achieve a government career. But the large body of his extant work clearly shows his interest in nature and implies that much of his time was spent in travel and writing.

Frankel, Hans H., trans. *Biographies of Meng Hao-jan*. Chinese Dynastic History Translations. Berkeley: University of California Press, 1952.

Kroll, Paul. *Meng Hao-jan*. Boston: Twayne Publishers, 1981.

Min. Literary name for Fukien province (q.v.), derived from an independent kingdom which existed from 909 to 945 A.D., with its capital at Foochow (q.v.). In the breakup of the T'ang dynasty (618-906 A.D., q.v.), several states contested for power, one of which was Min.

Schafer, Edward H. *The Empire of Min*. Rutland: Charles E. Tuttle Co., 1954.

Ming Cheng Te (1491-1521). Reign title (q.v.) of the tenth emperor of the Ming dynasty (q.v.); personal name CHU Hou-chao (r. 1506-1521). He was the son of Ming Hung Chih (q.v.). Cheng Te was 14 when he ascended the throne, and it soon became apparent that he had no interest in matters of state, preferring such pastimes as riding, archery and hunting. He was also fond of music and entertainment. He made his residence in a newly constructed building in the palace enclosure, and called it the Leopard House.

Cheng Te was immortalized in folklore, and has been referred to as a "merry monarch." He was reportedly strongly sexed and looked constantly for new sexual partners, occasionally finding them in the concubines of his commanders. This shocked his Confucian officials, but he shocked them still further by taking a personal interest in the suppression of bandits in Szechwan, Hukuang (i.e., what is now Hunan and Hupeh) and the Yangtze valley. This developed into an interest in military affairs, which he demonstrated by drilling his eunuchs and dressing in military uniform, which became a fashion of the day.

He toured the northern frontier in 1517-1519 and decided to build a residence there. He took part in one battle against the Mongols and claimed to have killed one himself. In 1518 he gave himself the title of Supreme Commander of Military Affairs and also that of Duke of Chen Kuo, thus further confusing the Confucians.

In 1519 one of the imperial princes rose in rebellion, but was soon put down and captured by WANG Yangming (q.v.), better known to history as a philosopher than a government official. The emperor made a trip south arriving in Nanking in 1520. On his return to the capital, a boat from which he was fishing capsized. He became ill and died without issue in Peking in 1521.

Chen Te's activities so scandalized the Confucian officials that none of his successors was permitted to behave so independently. (Compare with Ming Wan Li, q.v.) Also, his death without issue created a succession crisis. His successor was Ming Chia Ching (q.v.). This in turn led to a policy of providing more opportunities for his successors to have access to palace women.

Cheng Te was almost certainly unaware of it, but it was in the last years of his reign that Tomé Pires (q.v.) arrived as an envoy from the Portuguese in Goa, the first European so accredited to arrive after the opening of the sea route around Africa.

Goodrich, L.C., and Chaoying Fang, eds. *Dictionary of Ming Biography*. New York: Columbia University Press, 1976.

Huang, Ray. *1587, A Year of No Importance*. New Haven: Yale University Press, 1981.

Ming Cheng T'ung (1427-1464). Reign title (q.v.) of the first reign of the sixth emperor of the Ming dynasty (q.v.); personal name CHU Ch'i-chen (r. 1436-1449), and again under the reign title T'ien Shun (1457-1464). He was the elder son of Ming Hsuan Te (q.v.) and came to the throne at the age of eight. Since the dynasty had no provision for a formal regency, he was technically the emperor from the start, though he was deeply influenced by his grandmother, the empress Chang, widow of Hung Hsi (See **Ming Hung Hsi**) and mother of Hsuan Te. The empress died in 1442, and Cheng T'ung married that same year.

Cheng T'ung's reign was relatively uneventful until 1449. In that year the Ming forces had celebrated their second victorious campaign in Yunnan. In July reports of Mongol border raids were reported from the Northwest and the emperor resolved to lead an army against them. An army reported at half a million men was gathered, and the foray began. Unfortunately, the emperor was not the warrior he thought himself, and the army was soon in disarray. After a minor battle, the Chinese retreated on August 30 to T'u Mu, which turned out to have no water. On September 1 the Mongols, under their leader Esen, attacked and killed thousands of Chinese troops. They also captured the emperor and led him off to Mongolia.

The reaction in Peking was swift, though not aggressive. The city was fortified and Cheng T'ung's younger brother ascended the throne on September 17, 1449, declaring his brother "superior emperor," a term usually used for an emperor who has been forced to abdicate. Esen hesitated for two months before attacking Peking. He besieged it for four days, October 27-31, and then gave up. The Chinese refused to ransom Cheng T'ung, and Esen found he had an exemperor on his hands. He treated Cheng T'ung well, and in September 1450 he released him without conditions.

The new emperor reigned as Ming

Ching T'ai, 1450-1456 (q.v.). There is no indication that he had imperial ambitions before his brother's capture, but he was obviously reluctant to give up the throne when his brother returned. He sent out a retinue to receive him which consisted of two officials on horseback and a sedan chair. When Cheng T'ung arrived in Peking he was assigned living quarters where he remained under house arrest.

Ching T'ai replaced Cheng T'ung's son as heir apparent by designating his own infant son to that office in 1452. The child died some 18 months later, leaving the situation unsettled. Ching T'ai fell ill early in January 1457, and a coup d'état freed Cheng T'ung on February 11. Ching T'ai died in March, and may well have been murdered.

Cheng T'ung adopted a new reign title, T'ien Shun, and proceeded to expunge all record of Ching T'ai, to the extent possible, following in this the pattern set by his great-grandfather Yung Lo (q.v.). Ching T'ai did not receive a temple name until after the fall of the dynasty, when the Southern Ming court was in Nanking.

Goodrich, L.C., and Chaoying Fang, eds. *Dictionary of Ming Biography.* New York: Columbia University Press, 1976.

Ming Ch'eng Hua (1447-1487). Reign title (q.v.) of the eighth emperor of the Ming dynasty (q.v.); personal name CHU Chien-shen (r. 1465-1487). He was the eldest son of Cheng T'ung (q.v.), the sixth Ming emperor. He was designated as heir apparent until displaced by the seventh emperor, Ching T'ai (q.v.). Before he ascended the throne a twelve-man council of advisers was appointed to assist him. Ch'eng Hua seems to have been a passive and easily dominated man. There were disputes involving his mother and his father's other consorts and between his wife and his own consorts. One of the latter was Lady Wan, some 17 years older than the emperor. She was the mother of the emperor's first son, who died in infancy. A second son was born to another consort, and his death was popularly attributed to Lady Wan. A third son was born in secrecy and hidden until the age of five. He survived to become the next emperor, Ming Hung Chih (q.v.).

The first part of Ch'eng Hua's reign was regarded as one of the most enlightened periods of Ming history, probably because power was in the hands of the council of twelve. Later the reign was marked by corruption, much of which seemed to be dominated by the Lady Wan. This involved the selling of offices, and the emperor was almost certainly involved.

The period also saw a revival of Ming military power with conquests in Kwangtung and Szechwan provinces (qq.v.) and the extension of Ming power into southern Manchuria (q.v.), which remained under Ming domination until the rise of Nurhaci (q.v.), the founder of the Ch'ing dynasty (1644-1911, q.v.).

Goodrich, L.C., and Chaoying Fang, eds. *Dictionary of Ming Biography.* New York: Columbia University Press, 1976.

Ming Chia Ching (1507-1567). Reign title (q.v.) of the 11th emperor of the Ming dynasty (q.v.); personal name CHU Hou-ts'ung (r. 1522-1566). He was the nephew of his predecessor, Ming Cheng Te (q.v.), who died without issue. He had the second longest reign of the dynasty, and for the first half of it he attended scrupulously to affairs as his Confucian officials wished him to. However, after 20 years the audience rituals bored him and he spent the last half of his life engaged largely in study of esoteric Taoist doctrines and pursuit of medicines for longevity.

Mindful of the unsettling behavior of his predecessor, the officials were determined to keep Chia Ching away from contact with military affairs and other distractions from the Confucian concept of imperial rectitude. After a trip to his birthplace in Hukuang province, he spent the last 27 years of his life without leaving Peking, thus setting the precedent for his grandson, Ming Wan Li (q.v.).

Chia Ching thought of himself as an able ruler, and for that reason was outraged by the memorial submitted by the official HAI Jui (q.v.) which suggested that the emperor was morally responsible for all the ills of the empire. After several months of delay, he ordered HAI imprisoned. The emperor died about a year after the memorial, and it is likely that the stress occasioned by it was a contributory factor.

Goodrich, L.C., and Chaoying Fang, eds. *Dictionary of Ming Biography*. New York: Columbia University Press, 1976.

Ming Chien Wen (1377-1402[?]). Reign title (q.v.) of the second emperor of the Ming dynasty (q.v.); personal name CHU Yun-wen (r. 1399-1402). He was the grandson of Ming Hung Wu (q.v.) and inherited the throne because his father, the crown prince, died in 1392. Chien Wen had been educated by Confucianists and came to the throne determined to put the Confucian values of civil control into effect. This led to conflict with his uncle, the Prince of Yen, who was a competent soldier and whose power base was on the northern frontier, facing the Mongols.

Chien Wen's basic problem on assuming the throne was his uncles' control of military power in different parts of the empire. They had been placed there by Hung Wu, who only at the end of his life realized what a challenge their military power would present to his successor. The Prince of Yen, the fourth son of Hung Wu and the oldest of those surviving, was the strongest of all, and was supported by his troops. Chien Wen started to remove his other uncles from the scene, and had removed five of them by summer 1399. He then moved to arrest the Prince of Yen, who rebelled.

The rebellion lasted until July 13, 1402, when the Prince entered the capital, Nanking, and in the ensuing confusion the imperial palace was burned. Several days later a charred corpse said to be that of Chien Wen was buried with official honors, but rumors that the emperor had escaped persisted until the end of the dynasty.

For his part, the Prince of Yen ascended the throne and adopted the reign title Yung Lo (see under **Ming Yung Lo**) and changed the designation of 1402 to the 35th of Hung Wu, and 1403 the first of Yung Lo. In this way he eliminated Chien Wen as an emperor, an action which was not reversed until much later in the dynasty. Yung Lo also tampered with the official records of the last years of Hung Wu and with those of Chien Wen. For this reason all records pertaining to that period are suspect.

Dreyer, Edward L. *Early Ming China*. Stanford: Stanford University Press, 1982.

Goodrich, L.C., and Chaoying Fang, eds. *Dictionary of Ming Biography*. New York: Columbia University Press, 1976.

Ming Ching T'ai (1428-1457). Reign title (q.v.) of the seventh emperor of the Ming dynasty (q.v.); personal name CHU Ch'i-yü (r. 1450-1456). He was a younger son of Ming Hsuan Te (q.v.) and the younger brother of Ming Cheng T'ung (q.v.). His short and unhappy reign came about only because of the capture of Cheng T'ung by the Mongols. Cheng T'ung was released after one year and Ching T'ai kept him under house arrest for the next six years. Cheng T'ung was restored by a coup d'état in February 1457, and Ching T'ai died of illness the following month or he may have been murdered.

Goodrich, L.C., and Chaoying Fang, eds. *Dictionary of Ming Biography*. New York: Columbia University Press, 1976.

Ming Ch'ung Chen (1611-1644). Reign title (q.v.) of the 16th and last emperor of the Ming dynasty (q.v.); personal name CHU Yu-chien (r.1628-1644). He was the brother of his predecessor, Ming T'ien Ch'i (q.v.). Ch'ung Chen inherited an empire which was in an advanced state of collapse, and while he made some efforts to stem the tide they were ineffective. Recognizing that the eunuchs were a serious part of his internal problems, Ch'ung Chen sent the most notorious of them, WEI Chung-hsien (q.v.), into retirement, but WEI committed suicide en route.

During Ch'ung Chen's reign, the major external problem was the encroachment of the Manchus (q.v.). Capable generals had been the targets of WEI Chung-hsien's animosity in the previous reign, and even after his removal the atmosphere was one of partisanship and cliques. In addition, the country had been so impoverished by decades of misrule that frequently the armies went unpaid, and deserted to the enemy. Since the Manchu policy was to treat such newcomers well, the result was continuing attrition of Ming military power.

In 1629 the emperor abolished the courier-post system, which was dependent on conscription and acted as a transport system for various forms of freight. Presumably this was an attempt at economy, but the result was further unrest. Throughout the 1630s, because of deteriorating economic conditions, there were local uprisings all over China.

In 1644 one of these bandit groups, led by LI Tzu-ch'eng (q.v.), himself a former employee of the courier post, seized Peking, which he occupied from April 25 until June 5, when it was taken by the Manchus. The emperor hanged himself on the Coal Hill on April 25.

Hummel, Arthur W., ed. *Eminent Chinese of the Ch'ing Period*. Washington: Government Printing Office, 1943.

Ming Dynasty (1368-1644). The Ming dynasty, following the Mongol Yuan dynasty (1279-1368, q.v.) and preceding the Manchu Ch'ing (1644-1911, qq.v.), was the last imperial dynasty whose ruling family was of Chinese origin. It was also the ruling dynasty in the period when Europeans first arrived in East Asia by ship around Africa, in the early 16th century. While a handful of Europeans, such as Marco Polo (1254-1324, q.v.), left some accounts of their contacts with the Yuan dynasty, the records of European contact with the Ming are far more extensive.

The Ming dynasty was a conscious effort to restore Chinese control to South China, which had been under Mongol rule for about a century, and to North China (q.v.), which had been under the rule of the Tartar dynasties (q.v.), and then under the Mongols for nearly 500 years. The dynasty was founded by CHU Yuan-chang (1328-1398), who reigned as Ming Hung Wu (1368-1398, q.v.). Like the founder of the Han dynasty (206 B.C.-221 A.D.), CHU was not a member of the ruling class.

By the middle of the 14th century, the Yuan hold on China was slipping badly. A series of natural disasters had caused flooding of the Huang Ho (Yellow river, q.v.) in 1344, with destruction of the Grand Canal (q.v.) through silting, and much damage to irrigation. CHU Yuan-chang saw most of his family die in the resulting famine. Peasant unrest was expressed in an apocalyptic Buddhist sect called the White Lotus Society, whose military arm was the Red Turbans (qq.v.). Rebellions resulted in fragmented control of China under various warlords, some of whom professed loyalty to the Yuan while others did not.

CHU Yuan-chang had spent several years as a Buddhist monk before he joined an armed rebel band in 1352, where he soon rose to a position of command. Under CHU's leadership the forces that later became the Ming army first achieved control of an area with Nanking as its capital. This was followed by wars against other regional warlords, and in 1367 direct war against the remnants of the retreating Mongols in the north. On January 23, 1368, CHU went through the rites of accession to the imperial throne, established the Ming dynasty and adopted the reign title of Hung Wu.

While the new dynasty was expressly designed to be a restoration of Chinese sovereignty and rule, there was a continuation of the Mongol tradition of military activity and dominance by military commanders throughout the first reign, and that of the emperor's son, who reigned as Ming Yung Lo (1403-1424, q.v.). This was quite out of keeping with the Confucian tradition of civilian control. The emperor was not particularly sympathetic with the Confucian scholars and did not reestablish the examination system (q.v.) on a regular basis. However, he recognized that the empire could not be administered without the Confucians.

The major problems facing the early Ming rulers were consolidation of control in China, acceptance of Ming suzerainty by such tributary states as Korea and Vietnam (qq.v.), and the military security of the northern border. Ming Hung Wu was interested in the political aspects of the tribute system (q.v.), but wanted to restrict trade to a very low level. This was a reversal not only of the Yuan policy, but also of policies of the T''ang dynasty (618-906) and of the Sung (960-1279, qq.v.), of an earlier period. It struck at the economic livelihood of both Chinese and foreign traders, and led to smuggling and piracy.

Military security on the northern border was essential, because it was here that the only significant threat to the dynasty existed. The Mongols were not reconciled to the loss of China. Battles were fought over the years, but the Mongols were not united, and those nearby were forced to acknowledge the Ming.

In most previous Chinese dynasties, the emperor had utilized the services of one or more officials who held the rank of prime minister or chancellor. In 1380 Ming Hung Wu had his prime minister executed on the grounds of sedition, abolished the office entirely and stipulated the death penalty for any official who proposed reviving the institution. The result was a sea of paper work with which the first emperor proceeded to cope, but none of his successors did. Instead, as somewhat ambiguous position of grand secretary was established, and succeeding emperors worked through this secretariat and through their eunuchs (q.v.).
their eunuchs (q.v.).

The Yuan dynasty had followed the Mongol rules of succession, which required the election of the khan from among the eligible male relatives. In a positive decision to revert to Chinese practice, Ming Hung Wu named his eldest son crown prince and heir apparent. Unfortunately, the young man died before his father, and on the emperor's death the throne went to his grandson, who reigned as Ming Chien Wen (1399-1402, q.v.).

The second emperor was not a military man, and proved no match for his uncle, the Prince of Yen, who rebelled and seized the throne, reigning as Ming Yung Lo (1403-1424, q.v.). A successful soldier, somewhat like his father, he transferred the capital from Nanking to the former Yuan capital in the north, which he renamed Peking, meaning "northern capital."

Since the Confucian administrators recruited through the revived examination system opposed military conquests of nearby areas as well as foreign trade and contacts, Ming Yung Lo depended on his military officers and the eunuch establishment to further these projects. He sent the eunuch CHENG Ho (1371-1433, qq.v.), as captain of a series of naval expeditions, to Southeast Asia, India, the principalities of the Persian Gulf and the coast of Africa from Somaliland to Zanzibar. CHENG's fleet carried embassies to China to pay tribute, and carried them back with what the Chinese referred to as gifts, though it looked like trade to other eyes.

Ming Yung Lo died in 1424, and was succeeded by his eldest son, who reigned as Ming Hung Hsi (q.v.), but died within a year. None of the later emperors (for a complete list see next entry) are regarded by traditional Chinese historians as outstanding rulers. The sixth emperor overestimated his military skills, was captured by the Mongols in 1449 and held hostage for a year. His return to the throne required the use of a new reign title for his second reign. The next two emperors, Ming Ch'eng Hua (1447-1487, q.v.) and Ming Hung Chih (1488-1505, q.v.), were not remarkable, although the first half of Ming Ch'eng Hua's reign was regarded as one of the most enlightened periods in Ming history. The next emperor, who reigned as Ming Cheng Te, 1506-1521 (q.v.), was a sore trial to his Confucian officials, since he developed an interest in military affairs and absented himself from the capital for long periods of time. He was famous for wine-bibbing and for his promiscuous sexual activity, and died without an heir.

The Confucians were determined that Ming Cheng Te's example not be repeated, and the next three reigns, covering nearly a century, saw three sovereigns who had comparatively little power, and laid the groundwork for the fall of the dynasty. All three of these emperors soon wearied of the official audiences and eventually refused to continue them. While there was some contact with the highest level officials, most of the business of the empire was conducted through the eunuchs. One result was increased corruption at court, and weakening of the economic strength of the empire to keep the court in luxury.

It is an open question whether Manchu strength or Ming weakness brought about the end of the dynasty, but Chinese rebels under the leadership of LI Tzu-ch'eng (q.v.) captured Peking in April 1644, and held it until June, when it passed to the Manchus. The last emperor hanged himself on the Coal Hill in Peking on April 25, 1644. While this brought the dynasty to an end in the official histories, various princes of the imperial family continued their struggle against the Manchus for several decades. Chinese loyalty to the Ming continued for many years, presenting problems to the Manchus throughout most of their rule.

European ships appeared for the first time along the China coast in the early 16th century, not long after the Portuguese Vasco da Gama had rounded Africa in 1498. The Portuguese traders' behavior led to their restriction to the port at Macao by the middle of the 16th century, but European power was never a threat to the Ming. For most of its rule, outside threats to the Ming dynasty were kept in check fairly easily. There was trouble with Burma and Vietnam, but neither country threatened the empire. The Mongols presented a more dangerous challenge, but their own disunity diminished it. Japanese piracy flourished in the mid-16th century, partially because Ming defenses had been neglected. In the 1590s the Japanese warlord TOYOTOMI Hideyoshi (1537-1598, q.v.), having conquered all of Japan, sought to keep his warriors occupied by invading Korea. His eventual aim was the overthrow of the Ming and its replacement by a Japanese dynasty. His death brought an end to that threat, but Ming military incompetence may well have inspired the Manchu leader Nurhaci (1559-1626, q.v.) to think of replacing the Ming with his own dynasty.

The Ming dynasty saw a vast expansion in the availability of printed books, and an expansion of the education system as a result. Another development was the growth of vernacular literature, particularly novels (q.v.). It was not otherwise a period of great innovation, and art historians regard it as a time of consolidation and refinement, but not, generally, of vigor.

The Manchu conquest of China after 1644 resulted in much less destruction than most previous dynastic changes. As a result, the number of Ming structures extant is many times greater than the number of those dating from previous eras. Ming printed books, while extremely rare, exist in significantly greater numbers than those of Sung or Yuan times. Ming historical records are also voluminous, but only in the last few decades have significant numbers of historical studies appeared in Western languages.

Dreyer, Edward L. *Early Ming China.* Stanford: Stanford University Press, 1982.

Goodrich, L.C., and Chaoying Fang, eds. *Dictionary of Ming Biography.* New York: Columbia University Press, 1976.

Huang, Ray. *1587, a Year of No Importance.* New Haven: Yale University Press, 1981.

Hucker, Charles O. *The Traditional Chinese State in Ming Times.* Tucson: University of Arizona Press, 1961.

Spence, Jonathan D., and John E. Wills, Jr., eds. *From Ming to Ch'ing.* New Haven: Yale University Press, 1979.

Struve, Lynn A. *The Southern Ming: 1644-1662.* New Haven: Yale University Press, 1984.

MING DYNASTY EMPERORS

Reign title	Temple Name	Personal name	Reign dates
1 Hung Wu	T'ai Tsu	CHU Yuan-chang *	1368-1398
(Hong Wu	Tai Zu	ZHU Yuan-zhang)	
2 Chien Wen	Hui Ti	CHU Yun-wen *	1399-1402
(Jian Wen	Hui Di	ZHU Yun-wen)	

Reign title	Temple Name	Personal name	Reign dates
3 Yung Lo	Ch'eng Tsu	CHU Ti *	1403-1424
(Yong Le	Cheng Zu	ZHU Di)	
4 Hung Hsi	Jen Tsung	CHU Kao-chih *	1425
(Hong Xi	Ren Zong	ZHU Gao-zhi)	
5 Hsuan Te	Hsuan Tsung	CHU Chan-chi *	1426-1435
(Xuan De	Xuan Zong	ZHU Zhanji)	
6 Cheng T'ung	Ying Tsung	CHU Ch'i-chen *	1436-1449
(Zheng Tong	Ying Zong	ZHU Qizhen)	
7 Ching T'ai	Tai Tsung	CHU Ch'i-yü *	1450-1456
(Jing Tai	Dai Zong	ZHU Qi-yu)	
*** T'ien Shun	Ying Tsung	CHU Ch'i-chen *	1457-1464
(Tian Shun	Ying Zong	ZHU Qi-zhen)	
8 Ch'eng Hua	Hsien Tsung	CHU Chien-shen *	1465-1487
(Cheng Hua	Xian Zong	ZHU Jian-shen)	
9 Hung Chih	Hsiao Tsung	CHU Yu-t'ang *	1488-1505
(Hong Zhi	Xiao Zong	ZHU You-tang)	
10 Cheng Te	Wu Tsung	CHU Hou-chao *	1506-1521
(Zheng De	Wu Zong	ZHU Hou-zhao)	
11 Chia Ching	Shih Tsung	CHU Hou-ts'ung *	1522-1566
(Jia Jing	Shi Zong	ZHU Hou-cong)	
12 Lung Ch'ing	Mu Tsung	CHU Tsai-hou *	1567-1572
(Long Qing	Mu Zong	ZHU Zai-hou)	
13 Wan Li	Shen Tsung	CHU I-chün *	1573-1619
(Wan Li	Shen Zong	ZHU Yi-jun)	
14 T'ai Ch'ang	Kuang Tsung	CHU Ch'ang-lo **	1620
(Tai Chang	Guang Zong	ZHU Chang-luo)	
15 T'ien Ch'i	Hsi Tsung	CHU Yu-chiao **	1621-1627
(Tian Qi	Xi Zong	ZHU You-jiao)	
16 Ch'ung Chen	Szu Tsung	CHU Yu-chien **	1628-1644
(Chong Zhen	Si Zong	ZHU You-jian)	

Note: Ming dynasty emperors can be found in this book listed under the dynasty plus the reign title, e.g., Ming Hung Wu.

 * Biographies of these emperors are listed under their personal names in Goodrich, L.C., and Chaoying Fang, eds. *Dictionary of Ming Biography: 1368-1644*. New York, Columbia University Press, 1976.

 ** Biographies of these emperors are listed under their personal names in Hummel, Arthur W., ed. *Eminent Chinese of the Ch'ing Period*. Washington, Government Printing Office, 1943.

*** The 6th emperor, Ming Cheng T'ung, was captured by the Mongols in 1449 and held prisoner for one year. When he resumed the throne he adopted a new reign title.

Ming Hsuan Te (1399-1435). Reign title (q.v.) of the fifth emperor of the Ming dynasty (q.v.); personal name CHU Chan-chi (r. 1426-1435). He was the eldest son of Ming Hung Hsi (q.v.) and followed most of his father's policies. While not as strong an emperor as either Ming Hung Wu or Ming Yung Lo (qq.v.), he is regarded as a good ruler. He permitted the eunuch CHENG Ho (q.v.) to make one last voyage to Southeast Asia, the Persian Gulf and the coast of Africa in 1431-1433. In 1432 he succeeded in reopening trade with the Japanese Ashikaga shogun (military leader) Yoshinori, which lasted until 1549, through the port of Ningpo.

The Vietnamese leader Le Loi defeated the Chinese several times, thus presenting Hsuan Te with the choice of raising major military forces for a reconquest of Vietnam, or of accepting Le Loi's rule. The emperor opted for acceptance, and while Le Loi, who had usurped the throne from the Tran dynasty, was not immediately granted the title of king of Annam, it was granted to his son in 1436.

Hsuan Te was faced with the rebellion of an uncle, just as his earlier predecessor Ming Chien Wen (r. 1399-1402, q.v.) had been, but he put it down easily, since his uncle had no troops at his disposal.

Hsuan Te occasionally led Chinese armies in patrolling the frontier with Mongolia, and his death on January 31, 1435, occurred shortly after his return from one such expedition. He was succeeded by a minor son who reigned as Ming Cheng T'ung (q.v.).

Goodrich, L.C., and Chaoying Fang, eds. *Dictionary of Ming Biography*. New York: Columbia University Press, 1976.

Ming Hung Chih (1470-1505). Reign title (q.v.) of the ninth emperor of the Ming dynasty (q.v.); personal name CHU Yu-t'ang (r. 1488-1505). Hung Chih was the third, but the eldest surviving, son of Ming Ch'eng Hua (q.v.). His mother was a serving girl in the palace, and came from an aboriginal tribe of the southwest, possibly the Yao (q.v.). When she became pregnant, she was taken under the protection of one of the empresses, in fear that her child might share the fate of others who aroused the jealousy of Lady Wan, Ch'eng Hua's consort. Hung Chih's existence was not revealed to the emperor until he was five years old. He was then named heir apparent, and his mother was dead under suspicious circumstances one month later.

Soon after his accession, Hung Chih tried to find his mother's family, but those who came forward with family trees were soon seen to be forgers. It isn't even certain what his mother's name was. Hung Chih felt the lack of relatives very keenly and when he married a lady from a Chang family near Peking, he favored her family, causing criticism.

The reign did not see any military conquests.

Goodrich, L.C., and Chaoying Fang, eds. *Dictionary of Ming Biography*. New York: Columbia University Press, 1976.

Ming Hung Hsi (1378-1425). Reign title (q.v.) of the fourth emperor of the Ming dynasty (q.v.); personal name CHU Kao-chih, who reigned less than one year, in 1425. Hung Hsi was the eldest son of Yung Lo (q.v.), but had become estranged from his father. He was influenced by the Confucian officials and with them deplored many of his father's policies, specifically leading military expeditions against the Mongols and encouraging international trade and diplomacy. In the Confucian tradition he felt that agriculture was China's most important activity and that other things, such as trade, might be tolerated but not encouraged.

Yung Lo died in August 1424, and Hung Hsi immediately issued decrees reversing his father's policies. He banned the naval expeditions of CHENG Ho (q.v.), and banned the trade in which tea was exchanged for horses on the northwestern frontier. He also issued a general amnesty and went so far as to remove legal disabilities from the families of officials who had been executed for their support of the second emperor, Ming Chien Wen (r. 1399-1402, q.v.). He also planned to return the capital to Nanking, but died at the end of May 1425 before this project could be carried out. He was succeeded by his eldest son who reigned as Ming Hsuan Te (q.v.).

Hung Hsi established Confucian policies which were continued by his son and by his grandson, as long as the latter was a minor under the regency of Hung Hsi's widow, the grand dowager empress Chang. Thus some of Hung Hsi's policies continued until the empress's death in 1442. No further effort was made to move the capital back to Nanking.

Goodrich, L.C., and Chaoying Fang, eds. *Dictionary of Ming Biography*. New York: Columbia University Press, 1976.

Ming Hung Wu (1328-1398). Reign title (q.v.) of the founder and first emperor of the Ming dynasty (1368-1644, q.v.), personal name CHU Yuan-chang (r. 1368-1398). His temple name (q.v.), by which he is also known, is Ming T'ai Tsu. The youngest of six children, he was born to a poor family in what is now Anwhei province (q.v.). Most of his family died in an epidemic in 1344. CHU was sent to a Buddhist monastery, but because of famine conditions was soon sent out to beg. He spent several years wandering but returned to the monastery for several more. He then learned to read and write.

Much of China was in turmoil. The Yuan dynasty (1279-1368, q.v.) was in decline. The Huang Ho (Yellow river, q.v.) flooded, requiring work to restore the levees. The Red Turbans (q.v.) were everywhere, sowing anti-Mongol beliefs and causing uprisings. CHU decided to leave the monastery and joined a local strongman, KUO Tzu-hsing, and soon married KUO's foster daughter, who later became his empress. KUO died in 1355, and CHU succeeded him as military leader. He distinguished himself from some of his competitors by not permitting his men to kill and plunder, thus earning the gratitude of the population. He also sought educated men to join and advise him. It may well be that one of these encouraged him to emulate a predecessor, the commoner LIU Pang who established the Han dynasty (q.v.) in 206 B.C. (See under **Han Kao Tsu**.)

CHU established his capital at Nanking and soon captured other cities in the Yangtze valley. In 1368 his armies captured Peking and the last of the Mongol emperors fled. CHU announced his new dynasty, with Nanking as his capital.

CHU's objective was the restoration of a Chinese imperial system on the lines of the preceding T'ang (618-906) and Sung (960-1279) dynasties (qq.v.). This meant the elimination of as many of the foreign influences brought in by the Mongols as possible. The examination system (q.v.) which had largely fallen into disuse in the former dynasty, was restored as a key element in recruiting officials.

CHU's most important task throughout his reign was reasserting Chinese power, not only within China but also in many border areas. He secured the coast against Japanese piracy, conquered southern

Manchuria, twice chased the Mongols out of Karakorum, their ancient capital, and forced many rulers in Sinkiang and Central Asia to acknowledge Chinese suzerainty.

He seems to have suffered from self-consciousness and an inferiority complex, presumably because of his famed ugliness (he was pock-marked and had a protruding chin) and his lowly background. As his reign progressed he became more brutal in his suppression of those whom he suspected of criticism of any kind. He had many of his former comrades-in-arms executed, as well as many scholar-officials. In many cases, not only were the suspects themselves executed, but also their families, friends, neighbors and acquaintances, often running into the thousands, as was traditional for some serious crimes.

CHU adopted the name Hung Wu as his reign title and set the pattern of retaining the title throughout his reign, a practice that continued, with one exception, until the fall of the Ch'ing dynasty (q.v.) in 1911. He had 36 sons and 16 daughters, and named a number of the sons princes of various areas, particularly in areas on the northern and northwestern frontiers, to guard against military invasions. Previous dynasties had given such titles to imperial princes, but rarely the military power of a real command.

Hung Wu named his eldest son as heir apparent. He has been described as more kind-hearted than his father. Unfortunately he died in 1392, and at the death of Hung Wu in 1398, the young son of the heir, at the age of 21, ascended the throne with the reign title of Ming Chien Wen (q.v.). He proved no match for his uncle, whose title was prince of Yen, and whose military fief was based at Peking (Yenching). His uncle overthrew him

in 1402 and reigned as Ming Yung Lo (q.v.).

Because of Yung Lo's efforts to justify his usurpation in the eyes of future generations, he altered the records of the end of Hung Wu's reign, as well as those of Chien Wen's.

Dreyer, Edward L. *Early Ming China.* Stanford: Stanford University Press, 1982.

Goodrich, L.C., and Chaoying Fang, eds. *Dictionary of Ming Biography.* New York: Columbia University Press, 1976.

Ming Lung Ch'ing (1537-1572). Reign title (q.v.) of the 12th emperor of the Ming dynasty (q.v.); personal name CHU Tsai-hou (r. 1567-1572). He was the son of his predecessor, Ming Chia Ching (q.v.), and probably the most colorless ruler of the dynasty. His reign lasted only six years, and he held regular morning audiences for his Confucian officials only for the first year or two. After that he remained secluded in the palace. The reigns of his father and his son were the longest of the dynasty, so that these three emperors together reigned for nearly a century, 1522-1619.

Goodrich, L.C., and Chaoying Fang, eds. *Dictionary of Ming Biography.* New York: Columbia University Press, 1976.

Ming T'ai Ch'ang. 1582-1620. Reign title (q.v.) of the 14th emperor of the Ming dynasty (q.v.); personal name CHU Ch'ang-lo. He reigned for only one month, August 28 to September 26, 1620. T'ai Ch'ang was the eldest son of his predecessor, Ming Wan Li (q.v.). His mother was a palace attendant, and his father preferred his third son, born of his favorite consort, Lady Cheng. Under Ming dynastic rules, imperial princes were given empty titles and forced to live away from the capital. Lady Cheng was unwilling to see her son sent away to a distant fief and conspired for years to have him named heir apparent. The Confucian officials were just as firmly convinced that the eldest son should be named the heir, and the resulting conflict embittered Wan Li's later years.

Wan Li died on August 18, and T'ai Ch'ang ascended the throne some 10 days later. He fell ill on September 6, and was given medicine by a eunuch of the Lady Cheng. It made him worse, and further medication by an official probably killed him.

The controversy over the course of T'ai Ch'ang's life did not cease with his death, and continued to be a bone of contention between the Confucian scholars who made up the Tung-lin party and the eunuchs (qq.v.). It was a significant factor in the dissension which so weakened the dynasty during the next reign. T'ai Ch'ang was succeeded by his son, who reigned as T'ien Ch'i (q.v.).

Hummel, Arthur W., ed. *Eminent Chinese of the Ch'ing Period.* Washington: Government Printing Office, 1943.

Ming T'ien Ch'i (1605-1627). Reign title (q.v.) of the 15th emperor of the Ming dynasty; personal name CHU Yu-chiao (r. 1621-1627). T'ien Ch'i was the eldest son of his predecessor Ming T'ai Ch'ang (q.v.). Of his 15 brothers and sisters only four reached maturity. One brother succeeded him, and three sisters married. His own five childred died in infancy. He has been described as "not having enough leisure to learn to write," though he is said to have been an excellent carpenter and cabinetmaker.

As a result of policies followed by his grandfather, Ming Wan Li (q.v.), contact between the court and the Confucian officials was conducted almost entirely through the eunuchs (q.v.), the most notorious of whom was WEI Chung-hsien (q.v.). Soon after ascending the throne, T'ien Ch'i

conferred high rank on WEI and turned over the reins of government to him.

Eunuch rule taxed the country heavily to provide luxuries for the court, thus engendering unrest among the people. The eunuchs also prevented the military from effective action against external enemies, i.e., the Manchus. In this way, the collapse of the empire was speeded up long before LI Tzu-ch'eng (q.v.) led his bandits to capture Peking, or WU San-kuei (q.v.) let the Manchu troops through Shanhaikuan ("where the Great Wall meets the sea") to oust LI, in 1644.

Hummel, Arthur W., ed. *Eminent Chinese of the Ch'ing Period.* Washington: Government Printing Office, 1943.

Ming T'ien Shun. Reign title (q.v.) adopted for his second reign by Ming Cheng T'ung (1427-1464, q.v.). This second reign lasted from 1457-1464.

Ming Wan Li (1563-1620). Reign title (q.v.) of the 13th emperor of the Ming dynasty (q.v.); personal name CHU I-chün (r. 1573-1619, the longest reign in the dynasty). Wan Li was the son of Lung Ch'ing, the 12th emperor (r. 1567-1572, q.v.). Wan Li ascended the throne at the age of nine, and since the Ming dynastic regulations made no provision for regency, he was immediately introduced to the complexities of imperial rule, under the supervision of his grand secretary, the highest literary official in the palace.

Wan Li was precocious (he learned to read at the age of four), well-favored and active. He was unhappy with the imperial traditions which kept him cooped up in the Forbidden City (q.v.), but it was in the interests of his officials to continue the custom.

The grand secretary, CHANG Chü-cheng, died in 1582, and his successor started to undo many of the programs and policies he had initiated. This in turn led to a series of revelations and accusations which discredited the deceased and which eventually disillusioned Wan Li with the entire administrative and bureaucratic apparatus.

Wan Li's eldest son was born of a palace attendant who was raised to the level of imperial consort. But his favorite was his third son, born of his favorite consort, Lady Cheng. This was another source of conflict with his court and the bureaucracy. Following tradition, they wanted the eldest son named heir apparent and eventually Wan Li was forced to do this, but it merely added to his embitterment toward the court bureaucracy.

But the question continued to bedevil his reign until the end, when the eldest son eventually did succeed to the throne as Ming T'ai Ch'ang (q.v.).

In 1587 Wan Li suspended his morning audiences and study sessions, in effect cutting himself off from the court, with the exception of his grand secretaries who were occasionally summoned to his presence. For the rest, he was kept company only by his eunuchs and the court women. In 1588 he made his last trip outside Peking, when he went to visit his mausoleum, some 50 miles away. In 1590 he proposed making another trip, but his officials pointed out that since he had suspended the morning audiences on the grounds of health, he should remain in the palace until he was better. Wan Li did not leave the palace again before his death in 1620.

Wan Li's reclusive and introspective reign set the seal on the decline of the dynasty, which lasted less than 25 years after his death. While some historians have assigned the blame for this to the emperor himself, others have recognized that the inflexibility of Ming institutions made resolution of certain issues impossible.

Goodrich, L.C., and Chaoying Fang, eds. *Dictionary of Ming Biography*. New York: Columbia University Press, 1976.

Huang, Ray. *1587, A Year of No Importance*. New Haven: Yale University Press, 1981.

Ming Yung Lo (1360-1424). Reign title (q.v.) of the third emperor of the Ming dynasty (q.v.); personal name CHU Ti (r. 1403-1424). CHU Ti was the fourth son of Ming Hung Wu (r. 1368-1398, q.v.), the founder of the dynasty. Ming Hung Wu's policy was to settle his sons as princes in various parts of the empire, where they were, in effect, local rulers. CHU Ti's fiefdom was based in present-day Peking, the capital of the previous Mongol Yuan dynasty (1279-1368, q.v.). Ming Hung Wu had changed its name from Tatu to Peip'ing, meaning "the pacified north." CHU Ti's title was Prince of Yen, an earlier name for the area.

CHU Ti was a competent soldier and proved it during his father's reign. The Mongols were by no means acquiescent over the establishment of the Ming dynasty, and the military threat was quite real. At Ming Hung Wu's death in 1398, the throne went to his grandson, Ming Chien Wen (r. 1399-1402, q.v.). The latter's father, Ming Hung Wu's oldest son, had been designated crown prince, but died in 1392. Ming Chien Wen was faced with the problem of imperial princes with military force at their command. He attempted to deal with this by removing the princes from their commands, starting with those whose power was least, and leaving the Prince of Yen until last. He succeeded in removing five of the princes, and sent officials to arrest the Prince of Yen in July 1399. The prince rebelled and three years later had captured Nanking.

After his father, Ming Yung Lo was certainly the strongest ruler of the dynasty. He moved his capital from Nanking to Peip'ing and changed the name to Peking, meaning "northern capital," and decreed that after 1421 it would be the primary capital, a position it held for some 500 years.

While Ming Yung Lo accepted the Confucian idea of a Chinese emperor, he also continued some of the Yuan traditions. He continued the Confucian examination system (q.v.), but also maintained a military establishment, and a group of eunuchs (q.v.) who were quite separate from the Confucian bureaucracy and happy to do his bidding without protest. The Confucian officials objected to military adventures and wished to isolate China from foreign trade and influences. The emperor carried on a number of military campaigns, including an invasion and annexation of Vietnam (q.v.) which ultimately failed. He reversed Ming Hung Wu's policy on trade and tribute (which were intermingled) and not only encouraged overland trade through Central Asia, but also sent a fleet of ships under the eunuch CHENG Ho (q.v.) to show the flag in Southeast Asia, India and the coast of Africa.

Ming Yung Lo had ascended the throne by rebelling against his predecessor, who presumably died in the burning of the imperial palace in Nanking in 1402. He tried to expunge or alter all the records pertaining to Ming Chien Wen, and for that reason many of the records of that period are highly suspect. Ming Yung Lo was also bothered by the persistent rumor that his predecessor had not died in the fire but had escaped to Southeast Asia. That may have been one of the reasons for sending the expeditions under CHENG Ho.

There were official diplomatic exchanges between Ming Yung Lo and the Ashikaga shogun (military ruler) Yoshimitsu of Japan, who was anxious for trade with China. These ended at the shogun's death in 1408. (Yoshimitsu had abdicated in 1395 but continued to rule until his death.) A later effort to revive trade was unsuccessful. Ming Yung Lo's motivation was in large part an effort to have the shogun suppress Japanese pirates.

Ming Yung Lo was successful in holding off the Mongols, though his expeditions were far less successful than his father's. This was partly because his general officers were either elderly men who had served his father or younger men who were inexperienced. But he was also using more infantry and fewer cavalry, a mix that was unsuitable for the Mongolian terrain. Fortunately for the Chinese, the Mongols themselves were split. In fact the only major threat from the Mongols came from the aging Tamerlane (1336-1405), a military genius unreconciled to the loss of China and determined to avenge it. He died while his expedition was still on its way through Central Asia, and the project died with him.

Ming Yung Lo's death occurred in August 1424, while returning from an expedition to chastise the Mongols. It was the last of a series, none of which had been very successful, and the emperor's death was concealed until the expedition returned to Peking. He was succeeded by his eldest son, who reigned less than a year as Ming Hung Hsi (q.v.).

Dreyer, Edward L. *Early Ming China*. Stanford: Stanford University Press, 1982.

Goodrich, L.C., and Chaoying Fang, eds. *Dictionary of Ming Biography*. New York: Columbia University Press, 1976.

MO Tzu (468-376[?] B.C.). MO Ti, to give his actual name, was a philosopher of the Warring States Period (q.v.). His school has been called "utilitarian," since he was deeply concerned with economy, and deplored waste and show. He opposed the extravagant funeral practices advocated by the Confucians.

He also advocated "universal love," by which he meant love of people in other kingdoms, which would preclude the recurrent wars of the time in which he lived. However, he did not rule out righteous wars.

He formed his followers into a tightly-knit group of obedient warriors, and after his death this leadership was passed on to several others.

The Mohists were mentioned disparagingly by CHUANG Tzu and Mencius (qq.v.) and are given only a brief mention in the *Shih Chi* (q.v.), by which time the movement seems to have faded into oblivion.

Interest in Mohism was revived at the end of the 19th century by a group studying the New Text School of the Earlier Han dynasty (206 B.C.-8 A.D.). These scholars were critical of the school of Neo-Confucianism (q.v.) and were investigating alternative sources of Chinese philosophy.

Fung, Yu-lan, and Derk Bodde, trans. *A History of Chinese Philosophy*. Princeton: Princeton University Press, 1952.

Waley, Arthur. *Three Ways of Thought in Ancient China*. London: George Allen & Unwin, 1953.

Money. Money in the form of coins and bullion was in circulation in the later years of the Chou dynasty (1122-256 B.C., q.v.). The coins were made of bronze in the shapes of knives and spades. In the Han dynasty (206 B.C.-221 A.D., q.v.) gold bullion was used in large transactions, and in the following years bolts of silk of standard size were used as a medium of exchange. The Han dynasty also saw the development of the round coin with a square hole in the middle for routine transactions. (This is the familiar "cash.") The hole is used for stringing the coins together, and at various periods prices were quoted in "strings of cash" with each string supposedly containing one hundred cash, though in practice the number might be considerably lower. Such coins remained in use until the early part of the 20th century, a period of more than 2,000 years.

Coins were made of copper and iron as well as bronze, and in later periods, brass. They might be issued by a central government or a provincial authority, and in some cases by individuals with special government approval. The standard cash was largely copper, with additions of tin or zinc. The increase in the value of copper over time led to a decrease in the proportion of copper in the coins. During the Sung dynasty (960-1126 A.D., q.v.) the adoption of Chinese coinage for use in international trade led to a shortage of coins in China itself.

The first use of silver in coinage is attributed to the emperor Han Wu-ti (r. 140-87 B.C., q.v.), though no examples have come down to us. Silver bars from the T'ang dynasty (618-906 A.D., q.v.) and the Sung have been preserved, and indicate that the use of precious metals for monetary purposes was widespread. However, there is only one other known example of silver used in coins prior to modern times. That occurred in 1197 A.D. and was soon discontinued.

The origin of paper money was in the use of drafts in the T'ang dynasty. Tea merchants shipped large quantities of tea to the capital Changan (Sian, q.v.) and found that carrying the cash back to the south (where the tea was grown) was both awkward and dangerous. At the same time provincial authorities found it necessary to ship tribute to the capital. By exchanging drafts, the provincial representatives in the capital could obtain the money needed to pay the central government, and the merchants found money awaiting them at home.

The development of printing (q.v.) in the Sung dynasty permitted the use of paper money. The earliest known example appeared early in the 11th century. The notes were printed from blocks and indicated that the possessor had deposited a certain sum with an "exchange medium shop." The Sung dynasty, hard pressed as it was, soon used the easily printed currency in inflationary ways. The earliest paper money bore expiration dates and was theoretically exchangeable for new money. This was changed in 1189 A.D. by the Sung emperor Chang-tsung. Henceforward the paper money did not expire.

As the Sung military difficulties increased, so did the issuance of new currency notes. The older notes did not disappear, they were simply devalued.

The Mongols adopted paper money even before their conquest of China and the establishment of the Yuan dynasty (1279-1368, q.v.). William of Rubruck (q.v.), one of the earliest European travelers to Asia to leave a written record of his experience, reports the existence of printed money in the 1250s. Later, it was government policy to redeem old Sung dynasty notes for current Yuan money. The notes were backed by gold and silver and circulated throughout the empire. The early years of the dynasty, until 1350, saw persistent but relatively mild inflation. A new issue of currency, with little or no reserve behind it, added

fuel to the flames of revolt. The paper money became worthless and soon ceased to circulate at all. The last 20 years of the dynasty (1348-1368) saw commercial activity return to barter or the use of metal coins.

The Ming dynasty (1368-1643, q.v.) tried to utilize paper currency, but without success. Instead, silver became the medium of exchange and eventually was the medium in which salaries of officials were computed. The Ch'ing dynasty (1644-1911, q.v.) did not make much use of paper money, having before it the example of Ming failure. One exception was the issuance of notes in 1853, when the suppression of the Taiping Rebellion (q.v.) was a major problem. Less than a decade later the notes had devalued to the point of worthlessness.

However, various Chinese banks issued their own bank notes, and in 1866 the Hongkong & Shanghai Banking Corporation started issuing bank notes, to be followed by other foreign banks. Much of China's foreign trade was conducted in such foreign currencies as the Mexican dollar and the Austrian (silver) thaler. Some of the various Chinese currencies were accepted only in limited areas. All major trading centers had money-changing shops which dealt both in paper money and the various regional coinages.

The use of foreign silver dollars in China led to the minting of silver dollars there. Shanghai dollars dated 1856 are known, but they may not be the earliest. After the establishment of the Republic of China (q.v.) in 1912, silver dollars were issued by the government.

In 1933, T.V. SOONG (q.v.), then Minister of Finance, managed a currency reform which established the silver dollar as standard legal tender, and notes were issued which were

Khutuktu as monarch
ath. The MPR was
on after. A secret
reaty was signed
The independence
provisionally
public of China
aty of 1945

USSR, the
icies in
1940s
llic
al

as
.ent was
by printing
backing, and the
.nation of 1937-1949 was
.ult. The inflation was a con-
.ributory cause to the decline in popular support for the republic in the period of the Civil War (1946-1949, q.v.).

During World War II (q.v.) several Japanese-sponsored currencies existed, as well as those issued by the republic and the Communist authorities in the areas they controlled. Postwar efforts to replace these with one national currency did not succeed, and the authorities concluded that by maintaining separate currencies, inflation in one area might be prevented from spreading to others. The New Taiwan Dollar, issued by the Bank of Taiwan and currently in use in the Republic of China, has remained stable in relation to the U.S. dollar for many years.

After its establishment in 1949, the People's Republic of China (q.v.) issued the Jen Min Pi (renminbi) which was for many years not convertible to foreign currencies, nor to silver or gold.

Chou, Shun-hsin. *The Chinese Inflation: 1937-1949*. New York: Columbia University Press, 1963.

Tamagna, Frank M. *Banking and Finance in China*. New York: Institute of Pacific Relations, 1942.

Yang, Lien-sheng. *Mon. China*. Cambridge: Harva. Press, 1952.

Mongolia. Land of the M. .v.). The term usually re. .ter Mongolia, now the Mong .le's Republic (MPR), witl .al at Ulan Bator, formerly Ur. .d to the Inner Mongolia Autonc. .nous Region of the People's Republic of China (PRC, qq.v.), which are contiguous. The Mongols reached the peak of their power in the time of Chingis Khan (1167-1227, q.v.), and his immediate descendants. For a period of several decades immediately before and after the establishment of the Yuan dynasty (1279-1368, q.v.), Mongolia was the central area of the largest empire in history. At the time of the Ming dynasty (1368-1644, (q.v.), Inner and Outer Mongolia were still under Mongol control, but disunity prevented any effective projection of Mongol power in China. By the time of the rise of the Ch'ing dynasty (1644-1911, q.v.), the Mongols of Inner Mongolia had become vassals of the Manchu (q.v.) rulers. An effort by Galdan, 1644-1697, ruler of the Western Mongols (Oirat, Eleuth or Dzungars), to conquer the Khalkhas of Outer Mongolia resulted in their acceptance of Ch'ing rule in 1691. Galdan was defeated by the emperor K'ang Hsi (r. 1662-1722, q.v.) in 1696. His successors were defeated by the emperor Ch'ien Lung (r. 1736-1796, q.v.) in 1759, and their people scattered. At that point no independent Mongol state existed.

Ch'ing policy toward Mongolia was to encourage intermarriage between Manchu and Mongol noble families, to preserve the Mongol culture as free of Chinese influence as possible, and to use the Mongols in military service. The Ch'ing decline in the 19th century

the Mongols, but with
of unity, they were only
repared for the train of
owing the Chinese revolu-
ctober, 1911.

February 12, 1912, the infant
g emperor P'u-yi abdicated. The
les of abdication, drawn up by
AN Shih-k'ai, (1859-1916, q.v.), in
s capacity as prime minister to the
Ch'ing court, transferred title to all
territories acknowledging Ch'ing
suzerainty to the Republic of China
(q.v.). On February 15, YUAN acceded to the presidency of the new
republic, which claimed to include
five "races": Han Chinese, Manchu,
Mongol, Tibetan and Hui (Muslim,
largely in Sinkiang). Neither the Dalai
Lama of Tibet (qq.v.) nor the Mongols
accepted this claim, and both Tibet
and Mongolia declared their independence of China. The Khalkhas of
Outer Mongolia proclaimed a monarchy under the 8th Jebtsundamba
Khutuktu, sometimes known as the
"Living Buddha." The Khutuktu
retained this position as a symbol of
Mongol unity until his death in 1924.

Although Tibet and Mongolia
signed a treaty in January 1913, in
which each recognized the independence of the other, Mongolia obtained
little international recognition.
Surrounded as it was by Russia and
China, Mongolia was forced to sign a
tripartite agreement with the two larger powers at Kiakhta in 1915 under
which it was reduced to autonomy
under Chinese suzerainty.

The Russian revolution in 1917 gave
China the opportunity to intervene in
Mongolia, and in 1919 it was incorporated in the Republic of China. In
early 1921 the monarchy was restored
by a White Russian leader, Baron Un-
gern-Sternberg. In April 1921, a
revolutionary provisional government was established, though it

accepted th
until his d
proclaimed s
Soviet-Mongol
November 5, 1921.
of the MPR was
recognized by the Re
in the Sino-Soviet T
(q.v.).

While not a part of the
MPR has followed Soviet p
every significant respect. In th
the MPR adopted a modified C
alphabet in place of the traditi
Mongol script. The MPR maintai
diplomatic relations with the People'
Republic of China (q.v.), but their
tone tends to reflect the tone of
relations between the two larger
nations.

Clubb, O. Edmund. *China and Russia.*
New York: Columbia University Press,
1971.

Lattimore, Owen. *Nationalism and
Revolution in Mongolia.* New York: Oxford
University Press, 1955.

Mongols. An ethnic and linguistic
group most of whom (2.6 million;
1981) live in China's Inner Mongolia
Autonomous Region (q.v.), the
Mongolian People's Republic (1.7
million; 1980) and the Buryat Autonomous Republic of the USSR (estimated at fewer than 1 million). Unlike the
Chinese, the Mongols were traditionally nomadic herdsmen and skilled
horsemen. Social structure was limited to a few noble families, from which
hereditary chiefs were selected, and
ordinary people who acknowledged
loyalty to them. In addition there was
an organized Buddhist church, related to that of Tibet (q.v.), with
monasteries and attached land for
their support. This arrangement
proved more conducive to inter-tribal
fighting than to national unity, as
Mongol history shows.

While sometimes identified with

the Hsiung Nu (q.v.), they appear under their own and related names as early as the T'ang dynasty (618-906 A.D. q.v.) and achieved their greatest power in the 13th century, under the leadership of Chingis Khan (1167-1267, q.v.) and his immediate descendants. He laid the basis for the most extensive, if short-lived, empire in world history. After uniting the Mongols in 1206, he turned his attention to the conquest of North China (q.v.). In 1215 he took Peking from the Chin dynasty (1115-1234, q.v.) and died in the final conquest of the Hsi Hsia (882-1227, q.v.). His son and successor, Ogodai, finished off the Chin and began the war against the Sung (960-1278, q.v.). Chingis's grandson, Khubilai Khan (1214-1294, q.v.), succeeded to the khanate in 1260, adopted the dynastic name Yuan in 1271, and was the first non-Chinese to rule all of China, as first emperor of the Yuan dynasty (1279-1368, q.v.).

The Mongols also exacted tribute from Korea (q.v.), and forced the Koreans to assist in two abortive attempts to invade Japan in 1274 and 1281. Invasions of Burma, Champa, Java and Vietnam were brief and not successful, as the Mongols were unaccustomed to the tropical climate and unfamiliar with naval warfare. They were more successful in Yunnan, where they extinguished the Nan Chao kingdom (q.v.) in 1252, and incorporated the area directly into their empire. In Tibet they established as their viceroys the Sakya dynasty, which lasted from 1244 to 1358.

Chingis's son Batu Khan conquered Russia in 1240, and got as far west as Hungary, but returned to Karakoram, the Mongol capital, on hearing of Ogodai's death in 1241. The Mongols, known in Russian history as the Golden Horde, did not rule Russia directly, but continued to exact tribute until 1480. (See Vernadsky, George. *The Mongols and Russia*. New Haven, Yale University Press, 1953.)

Chingis's grandson Hulegu conquered Iran, Iraq and Transcaucasia, and established in Iran the Ilkhan dynasty, which lasted from 1256 to 1353. Chingis's son Chaghatai established his own dynasty in Transoxania and Turkestan. It lasted from 1227 to 1363. In the same area Tamerlane (1336[?]-1405), a Mongol, but not of Chingis's family, established the Timurid dynasty, which lasted from 1370 to about 1500. Tamerlane died while on his way to invade China, then ruled by the emperor Ming Yung Lo (r. 1403-1424, q.v.). One of Tamerlane's descendants, Babur (Babar) (1483-1530), established the Mughal dynasty in India. The last of the Mughals, Bahadur Shah II (1777[?]-1862), died a prisoner of the British in Rangoon, exiled after the suppression of the Indian Mutiny (1857).

Chingis Khan had united the divided Mongol tribes, but his successors were unable to maintain this unity. Khubilai was acknowledged as Grand Khan, but distance alone kept him from ruling all the territories under Mongol control. His successors were even less able to do so, and this is one reason why the Silk Road (q.v.), which was open to European travelers in the 13th century, was all but closed by the mid-14th century. When the last of the Yuan emperors was dislodged by forces of the Ming dynasty (1368-1644, q.v.), he had theoretical control over all Mongols, and some power over the tribes of Inner Mongolia and the Khalkhas of Outer Mongolia, but none over the Western Mongols. The Mongols continued fighting the Ming forces, and in 1449 captured the sixth emperor, Ming Cheng T'ung (q.v.), and held him prisoner for a year.

They also fought each other. The greatest promise of unity came under Dayan Khan, who reigned from 1479 until some time early in the 16th century. The empire was divided among his nine surviving sons, and while the prince of Chahar was nominally emperor, Dayan's great-grandson, Daraisun Kudang Khan (r. 1547-1557), found it advisable to distance himself from a more powerful prince by moving his tribe to pastures in southern Manchuria (q.v.). A final effort to unite the Mongols was made by their last emperor, Ligdan Khan (r. 1605-1634), who brought pressure on other Mongol princes to swear allegiance.

By the late 16th century there was a new factor. This was the rise of the Juchen (q.v.), whose Chin dynasty had been destroyed by Ogodai in 1234. Their leader was Nurhaci (1559-1626, q.v.), who in 1616 founded the Later Chin dynasty, forerunner of the Ch'ing dynasty (1644-1911, q.v.). Nurhaci's military successes led several Mongol princes to confer a title, Kundulun Khan, on him in 1606. His son and successor, Abahai (1592-1643, q.v.), was even more successful, and conquered most of the nearby Mongol tribes, incorporating them into his own forces and assigning them their own "banners" (q.v.).

Ligdan Khan's campaign for unity brought him into direct conflict with Abahai, who defeated him in 1632. Ligdan fled to the Ordos desert with 100,000 of his people, most of whom died. Ligdan died in 1634, probably of smallpox, and the next year his son returned to Manchuria and submitted to Abahai, reportedly surrendering the imperial gold seal of the Yuan emperors. In 1636 Abahai announced the establishment of the Ch'ing dynasty, and all the Inner Mongol princes became vassals. To cement ties, the Ch'ing arranged marriages between Manchu and Mongol princely families.

The Khalkha princes of Outer Mongolia did not accept Manchu suzerainty even after the Ch'ing conquest of China. But in 1691, they were hard pressed by the Western Mongols, under their king, Galdan (1644[?]-1697), and in consequence many of them fled to Inner Mongolia and swore allegiance to emperor K'ang Hsi (r. 1662-1722, q.v.). K'ang Hsi defeated Galdan in 1696, and the latter died the next year, possibly a suicide. The Khalkha princes, while not as close to the Ch'ing ruling class as their Inner Mongolian counterparts, intermarried as well and remained loyal to the dynasty till its end, except for a minor rebellion in 1756 which the Manchus easily suppressed.

The Ch'ing dynasty valued the Mongols as a buffer against the advancing Russians, and also as a source of skilled cavalry, a function which they continued to perform until the mid-19th century. The last successful Mongol general, Seng-ko-lin-ch'in (d. 1865, q.v.), defeated the northern army of the Taiping Rebellion (1851-1864, q.v.) and fought the British and French in the *Arrow* War (1857-1860, q.v.). Mongol troops were involved in the Sino-Japanese War (1894-1895, q.v.), but were ineffective against modernized Japanese arms and tactics.

The decline of the Ch'ing dynasty in the 19th century was apparent to the Mongols, but since each tribal prince was an individual vassal of the emperor and each tribe was loyal to its prince, Mongol unity did not exist. At the time of the revolution of 1911, the Mongols in Inner Mongolia were outnumbered by the Chinese. The Khalkhas of Outer Mongolia proclaimed an independent Mongol state, but the Chinese revolutionaries declared that the Republic of China (q.v.) was constituted of five nationalities, one of which was Mongol.

In spite of centuries of contact with China, Mongol culture shows comparatively little Chinese influence. This is due not only to the great disparity between a nomadic, pastoral way of life and that of settled farmers, but also to the fact that the Mongols never adopted the Chinese script. Traditional Mongol script was based on that of the Uighurs (q.v.), their neighbors to the west. Until 1599 the Manchus used Mongol in their diplomatic correspondence. In that year a Manchu script based on the Mongol script was developed.

Mongolian culture was deeply influenced by that of Tibet, however, particularly after the mid-16th century. In 1573, Altan Khan, chief of the Tumet tribe, and the powerful prince from whom Daraisun had found it discreet to distance himself, was converted to the Yellow sect of Buddhism. In 1578 he was persuaded to invite the Tibetan lama Sonam Gyantso to Mongolia, where he conferred on him the title of Dalai Lama (q.v.), meaning "Ocean of Wisdom" in Mongolian, not Tibetan. Since he was the third in his line, he became the third Dalai Lama. The 4th and 5th were Mongols, but their successors were Tibetans.

The influence of the Buddhist church on Mongolia was strengthened by the line of eight Jebtsundama Khutuktus, regarded as reincarnations of a boddhisattva (q.v.), and sometimes referred to as "living Buddhas." The first of these, 1635-1723, was the younger son of the Tushetu Khan. The second Khutuktu, 1723-1759, was of the same family, and caused great concern to the Ch'ing authorities because of his attitude toward a Mongol rebellion in 1756. In the event, he stayed neutral, but the emperor Ch'ien Lung (q.v.) decreed in 1761 that all future Khutuktus would be found in Tibet. The continuity of the Khutuktus provided a focus of unity for the Mongols, and when Outer Mongolia declared its independence in 1911, the eighth Jebtsundama Khutuktu was named king, a title he held until his death in 1924.

Bawden, C.R. *The Modern History of Mongolia.* New York: Frederick A. Praeger, 1968.

Phillips, E.D. *The Mongols.* New York: Praeger, 1969.

Morrison, Dr. Robert. See under **Christianity**.

Most-favored-nation clause. This refers to a stipulation which may be made in a treaty under which if one of the signatories grants a privilege to a third nation, the other signatory may claim the same privilege as the "most-favored nation." The clause was first used with China when it was included in the Treaty of the Bogue, concluded October 8, 1843, which was supplemental to the Treaty of Nanking, signed August 29, 1842, ending the Opium War (1839-1842, qq.v.). Both treaties were signed by Ch'i-ying (q.v.) for China and Sir Henry Pottinger for Great Britain. Pottinger was an experienced diplomat, but Ch'i-ying was not, and there is reason to doubt that he had any understanding of the implications of this and other clauses in the treaty.

The "most-favored-nation" clause can be reciprocal, but in these treaties, and in those China later signed with other powers, it wasn't. It was included in most of the treaties China signed in the 19th and early 20th centuries, and led to a progressive weakening of China's position in relation to other countries. It was an important element in Chinese characterization of such agreements as "unequal treaties" (q.v.).

Mukden. See **Shenyang.**

Mukden Incident. On September 18, 1931, Japan's Kwantung Army occupied Mukden as the start of their takeover of Manchuria (q.v.). Mukden was the seat of the Manchurian government under CHANG Hsueh-liang (q.v.), but large numbers of his troops were stationed in North China (q.v.). On instructions from the Nationalist government in Nanking, CHANG withdrew before the Japanese forces, with the result that by the end of the year the Japanese had completely occupied Manchuria. They established the puppet state of Manchukuo under P'u- yi (qq.v.), the last Manchu (q.v.) emperor.

Music. While a few musical instruments of an even earlier period have recently been unearthed, it is the musical culture of the Shang dynasty (1766-1122 B.C., q.v.), that shows us the most about the origins of Chinese music. Many examples of four types of instruments have been recovered: *ch'ing* (stone chimes), bells, ocarinas and drums. There is also indirect evidence in the form of inscriptions on oracle bones (q.v.) of wind instruments such as flutes and panpipes.

More information is available on the musical culture of the Chou dynasty (1122-256 B.C., q.v.), since many instruments have been recovered from Chou tombs. A new type is the *sheng*, a hand-held instrument of several vertical bamboo pipes of different lengths set in a wind-chest frequently made of a gourd. The musician blows through a mouthpiece, utilizing the same principle as the present-day pipe organ. Variations of the *sheng* are still in use in China, Japan, Korea and Southeast Asia. It is also likely that stringed instruments, like zithers, existed.

There are also references to musical performances in Chou texts, and it is clear that these were largely ceremonial in nature, involving sacrifices to gods and ancestors. While Confucius (q.v.) extolled music, MO Tzu (q.v.) condemned it. Several of the rulers at whose courts the ritual concerts were held complained of boredom, though they apparently enjoyed more exotic imported music.

Tombs of the Han dynasty (206 B.C.-221 A.D., q.v.) show scenes of musicians using some or all of the instruments mentioned. Since the Han period saw the extension of Chinese influence into Central Asia, it is probable that musical influences were brought back. In the T'ang dynasty (618-906 A.D., q.v.), which also saw Chinese power exercised in Central Asia, there are references to types of music and dancing derived from nomadic peoples in that area. There is also mention of ensembles called "Kucha orchestras" named after the city in Sinkiang (q.v.). Some lists of tune titles have survived from the T'ang era, and several instruments of the period, or later reproductions, have survived in the collection of the *Shosoin* in Japan.

The division of China into north and south after the fall of the T'ang in 906 resulted in the growth of two different musical traditions. The north was ruled by the Tartar dynasties (q.v.) of Liao (907-1125 A.D.) and Chin (1115-1234, qq.v.), until conquered by the Mongols at that time. The south was ruled by the Sung dynasty (960-1279, q.v.), at which time Khubilai Khan united all China under the Yuan dynasty (1279-1368, qq.v.). It seems likely that by the end of the T'ang period imported music had replaced traditional per-' formances completely, because under the Sung efforts were made to recreate the old styles, using only those instruments known to have existed in the Chou dynasty. The performance of vocal music accompanied by ensembles seems to have been a Sung development also, and this led to the music-dramas of the Yuan period (see under **Drama**).

In the Sung and Yuan eras, professional musicians performed for the public in such formats as drum-songs and similar story-telling activities, and also as accompanists to the music-drama. They were not highly regarded in the social context, but other musical traditions engaged the upper classes. These involved private study of genteel instruments, such as the *cheng* (zither) and *ch'in* (lute), as a scholar's hobby. Many pictures exist showing a scholar regaling himself with such music with no audience but an attendant who prepares tea, or perhaps another scholarly friend listening attentively. This tradition has persisted to the present day, and until the 20th century there were no practitioners of this type of art who could legitimately be called professional. Equally, there was no Chinese equivalent of the sort of musical performances which marked post-Renaissance Europe.

The arrival of Europeans by sea in the 16th century brought the introduction of several European instruments, such as the dulcimer, known to Chinese as the yang-ch'in (*yang* = foreign). However, there was no real Chinese interest in Western music until the 20th century. The presence of thousands of Russians in Shanghai and other cities in the wake of the Russian revolution of 1917 resulted in the development of musi-cal life on the Western pattern, and Shanghai had a symphony orchestra prior to World War II.

The vast difference between the Chinese and European musical traditions was noted by Western observers over the centuries. The oldest extant Western transcription was prepared by the Jesuit Father Jean Joseph Marie Amiot (1718-1793) in 1779, in a manuscript held by the Bibliothèque Nationale in Paris.

Liang, Tsai-ping. *Chinese Musical Instruments and Pictures.* Taipei: Chinese Classical Music Association, 1970.

Lieberman, Fredric. *Chinese Music: An Annotated Bibliography.* 2nd ed. New York: Garland Publishing, Inc. 1979.

Picken, Laurence E.R. "Chinese Music," in *Encyclopedia Brittanica*, 14th ed., 1966, Vol II.

"Asian Music," *Journal of the Society for Asian Music*, New York. (Semiannual) Vol. V, No. 1, 1973; Vol. VI, Nos. 1 and 2, 1975; Vol. X, No. 1, 1978; Vol. IV, No. 2, 1983; Vol. XV, No. 2, 1984.

Mustard Seed Garden Manual of Painting. This is a famous manual showing how to paint landscapes and much else in the Chinese traditional fashion. It is divided into books according to subject: trees, rocks, people and things, orchids, bamboo etc. The first volume was published in 1679, and it was expanded later. It has gone through many Chinese editions, and the manual is known to every traditional-style painter.

An English-language version, profusely illustrated and provided with explanations of the material, is listed below.

Sze, Mai-mai. *The Way of Chinese Painting*. New York: Vintage Books, 1959.

N

Name taboos. The most important name taboo is that the personal name of an emperor may not be used during his reign, nor during the rest of the dynasty. This requires that all literate people know the name, in order to avoid using it. Sometimes a text may be datable by noting the name avoidance within it. This inconvenience was avoided in the Ming (1368-1644) and Ch'ing (1644-1912) dynasties (qq.v.) by giving the emperors personal names using characters so abstruse as never to be needed in literary or administrative work.

Other taboos also existed. The given name of Confucius was a character, now pronounced *ch'iu*, which was avoided by Confucianists for centuries.

Names. In Chinese usage the surname comes first, followed by the given name. Most surnames consist of one syllable, and most given names of two, but there are exceptions. Some Chinese (e.g., CHU Hsi) have a given name of only one syllable. Some Chinese surnames consist of two syllables, and for this reason are referred to as "double surnames." A Chinese with a double surname will usually, but not always, have a given name of a single syllable (e.g., OU-YANG Hsiu).

The Chinese use a limited number of surnames, as indicated by the phrase "the hundred names," meaning the Chinese people. There are over 400 in current use, though the *Chung-kuo jen-ming ta-tz'u-tien* (Chinese Biographic Dictionary) shows a total of 1458 in use at one time or another. Some observers claim that nearly half of all Chinese use one of four names: Chang, Ch'en, Li or Wang.

In contrast, nearly any favorable combination of characters may be used for a given name. Some families use the same character for one of the two given-name characters for all brothers, though this may be extended to all males of the same generation. Thus two sons of LIANG Ch'i-ch'ao were named LIANG Ssu-ch'eng and LIANG Ssu-yung. The generation-identifying characters are sometimes taken from a literary text, so that family members will know the characters used in preceding and following generations. When this is done, it is possible to classify members of an extended family by generational status, even if the individual is not personally known to the observer.

Nanchang Uprising (August 1, 1927). In the wake of the expulsion of Communist members of the Kuomintang (q.v.) in July, the Communist soldiers of the garrison in the Kiangsi provincial capital of Nanchang attempted to seize the city. They were led by CHU Teh (q.v.), and the incident is celebrated as the birth of the Chinese Communist army. While initially successful, the Communist troops were able to hold the city only for a few days, and were then forced to move south and then west, arriving eventually at the Ching-kang mountains on the Hunan-Kiangsi border, where they joined the remnants of the peasant army of MAO Tse-tung (q.v.), from central Hunan province.

Nan Chao (Nan Zhao). Name of a kingdom located in Yunnan province (q.v.) which usually acknowledged Chinese suzerainty. Chinese records indicate a series of 42 kings between 629 and 1252 A.D., when it was destroyed by the Mongols under Khubilai Khan (qq.v.). The people were related to the present-day Thai and accepted Chinese suzerainty under the T'ang dynasty (618-906 A.D., q.v.), but took advantage of T'ang disarray at the time of the rebellion of AN Lu-shan (q.v.) in 757 to war against China with the support of Tibet (q.v.). Relations with the Sung dynasty (q.v.) were at arms length. The Mongol conquest extinguished the kingdom and encouraged migration of its people to what are now Laos and Thailand.

Nanking (Nanjing). Capital of Kiangsu province (q.v.), it has a population of 3 million (1980). The name means "southern capital." It served as the capital of the Kingdom of Wu (222-280 A.D., q.v.) and of several other minor states. It was the first capital of the Ming dynasty (1368-1644, q.v.), until the third emperor, Ming Yung Lo (r. 1403-1424, q.v.), moved the capital to Peking.

Nanking became the national capital again on October 10, 1928, when CHIANG Kai-shek (1887-1975, q.v.) established the Nationalist govern-

ment there. The Rape of Nanking (q.v.) in December 1937 marked the city's fall to the invading Japanese. After the defeat of Japan in 1945, the Chinese government returned to Nanking from the wartime capital at Chungking. It fell to victorious Chinese Communist forces in April 1949.

Nanking has been destroyed several times over the centuries, and comparatively few early structures have survived. It is the site of the mausoleum of SUN Yat-sen (1866-1925, q.v.), father of the revolution of 1911.

Nanking, Rape of. The Japanese armies entered Nanking on December 11, 1937, and proceeded to engage in an orgy of violence, rape and massacre of the civilian population, an occurrence which caused world-wide revulsion at the time. Estimates of the number who lost their lives range from 100,000 to 250,000.

Wilson, Dick. *When Tigers Fight: The Story of the Sino-Japanese War, 1937-1945.* New York: Viking Press, 1982.

Nanking, Treaty of. Signed August 29, 1842, by Ch'i-ying (q.v.) for the Chinese and Sir Henry Pottinger for the British, it concluded the Opium War (1839-1842, q.v.). The most significant provisions were cession of the island of Hong Kong to the British, the opening of five "treaty ports" (q.v.) to foreign trade (Canton, Amoy, Foochow, Ningpo and Shanghai), an indemnity of $21 million, and acceptance of diplomatic equality between Chinese and British high officials.

On October 8, 1843, a supplementary Treaty of the Bogue (q.v.) was signed by the same representatives. This granted consular jurisdiction and other extraterritorial rights to the British, and also contained the "most-favored nation" clause, which provided that if China granted privileges to any other nation, the British could claim treatment equal to that given the "most-favored nation." This clause was included in many later treaties.

The Treaty of Nanking is regarded as the first of the "unequal treaties" (q.v.) because of the lack of reciprocity.

Beeching, Jack. *The Chinese Opium Wars*. New York: Harcourt Brace Jovanovich, 1976.

Nanning. Capital of Kwangsi province (q.v.).

Neo-Confucianism. The term is applied to a synthesis of Confucian and Buddhist concepts that became the dominant philosophy in the Sung dynasty (960-1279 A.D.) and remained so through the Ming (1368-1644, q.v.) and most of the Ch'ing (1644-1911, q.v.). Its first protagonist was the Confucian scholar HAN Yü (768-824 A.D., q.v.), a critic of Buddhism (q.v.) in the T'ang dynasty (618-906, q.v.). HAN's writings condemn Buddhism and defend Confucianism (q.v.), but show a deep awareness and even adoption of many Buddhist concepts. This approach was taken farther by the Sung scholar CHU Hsi (1130-1200, q.v.) and the Ming scholar WANG Yang-ming (1472-1528, q.v.). Neo-Confucianism remained dominant until the close of the 19th century, when a number of Chinese scholars felt that Chinese weakness in the face of European strength indicated basic difficulties in the major school of Chinese philosophy. The critics were known as the New Text School, since they based their studies on criticism of certain philosophic works identified as "new texts" of the Han dynasty (206 B.C.-221 A.D., q.v.).

De Bary, William Theodore. *The Unfolding of Neo-Confucianism*. New York & London: Columbia University Press, 1975.

Fung Yu-lan, and Derk Bodde, trans. *A History of Chinese Philosophy*. Princeton, Princeton University Press, 1953.

Nepal. Nepal shares a border with Tibet (q.v.), but had no relations with China until the late 18th century. In 1768 Nepal's Buddhist rulers, who had marriage ties with the Tibetan aristocracy, were supplanted by the Gurkhas, who were Hindus. The Gurkhas invaded Tibet in 1788 and again in 1792. The second time they were repelled by Chinese forces under the command of the Manchu (q.v.) general Fu-k'ang-an (see Hummel, *Eminent Chinese of the Ming Period*). Pursued by the Chinese, the Gurkhas retreated to Khatmandu, where they acknowledged the suzerainty of the emperors of the Ch'ing dynasty (1644-1911, q.v.). Tribute was sent regularly every five years until 1908. The last known payment was sent to the Republic of China (q.v.) in Nanking in 1948.

Nepal asked the East India Company in Bengal for military assistance in 1792, but this was refused out of British concern for trade at Canton (q.v.). The British victory in the Anglo-Nepalese War of 1814-1816 gave Britain some control over Nepal's foreign affairs, and provided for a British Resident at Khatmandu. However, because of the Sino-Nepalese relationship, Britain did not interfere in Nepal's internal affairs, nor with its relations with China and Tibet. Nor did it permit British travelers to enter Nepal, until after India's independence in 1947.

In the 1950s, Nepal used China to counterbalance Indian influence and to maintain its independence. In October 1961, King Mahendra signed a treaty with the People's Republic of China (PRC, q.v.) which defined the boundary between Nepal and Tibet. Chinese claims to suzerainty over Nepal seem to have been abandoned, as the PRC accepted Nepal as a sovereign state.

Hummel, Arthur W., ed. *Eminent Chinese of the Ch'ing Period.* Washington: U.S. Government Printing Office, 1943-1944.

Lamb, Alastair. *Asian Frontiers: Studies in a Continuing Problem.* New York: Praeger, 1968.

Nerchinsk, Treaty of. Signed September 7, 1689 (August 27, O.S.), by the Manchu Songgutu for the emperor K'ang Hsi (r. 1662-1722, q.v.) and Fedor Alekseivitch Golovin representing the Russian emperor, Peter the Great. It was the first treaty signed by China and a Western power, and its six articles were written in five languages: Chinese, Latin, Manchu, Mongol and Russian. Two Jesuit priests, Jean-François Gerbillon and Thomas Pereira, accompanied the Ch'ing delegation as interpreters.

The Russians had been moving into Northeast Asia for decades and had encountered no effective resistance from the pre-literate tribes in Siberia. The Manchus were accepted as overlords by all the Tungusic tribes with whom they had contact and had probably given little thought to just how far their northern borders might go. The arrival of the Russians resulted in conflicts, and K'ang Hsi decided to settle the issue. Songgotu arrived with a military escort far in excess of anything the Russians were able to field.

Manchu power was sufficient to persuade the Russians to accept a line on the crest of the mountains, following the watershed separating the valleys of the Lena and the Amur rivers, to the Sea of Okhotsk. The outpost at Albazin was surrendered, and except for its headwaters, the Amur river was entirely within the Ch'ing empire. Since the princes of Outer Mongolia did not acknowledge Ch'ing authority until 1692, that area was not mentioned.

The treaty also provided for limited commerce and established the basis for extraterritoriality by stipulating that if Russian or Chinese subjects committed crimes in the territory of the other signatory, they were to be turned over to their own officials for punishment. The treaty, modified by the Treaty of Kiakhta (1727, q.v.), remained in effect until superseded by the Treaties of Aigun (1858) and Peking (1860, qq.v.). By that time the Ch'ing empire was no longer strong, and the Russians were able to win major territorial concessions.

Lamb, Alastair. *Asian Frontiers: Studies in a Continuing Problem.* New York: Praeger, 1968.

Mancall, Mark. *Russia and China.* Cambridge: Harvard University Press, 1971.

Nestorian Christians. A sect condemned as heretical by the Council of Ephesus, 431 A.D. It is the first Christian group whose presence in China has been verified. Flourishing for several centuries in Persia and Central Asia, a community also existed in Sian during the T'ang dynasty (618-906 A.D., qq.v.) Evidence of this in the form of a stele inscribed in Chinese and Syriac, with a date equivalent to February 4, 781 A.D., turned up in Sian in the 1620s. It was important to Jesuit missionaries of the time since a Confucianist argument against Christianity was that it had never before been known in China.

Nestorians are also mentioned in the Yuan dynasty (1279-1368 A.D.) by European travelers such as John of

Monte Corvino (1247-1328) and Marco Polo (1254-1324, qq.v.). John was the first Roman Catholic bishop of Khanbalick (Cambaluc), now Peking, and his letters to Rome report Nestorian opposition to Catholic activities within China.

The Keraits, a Central Asian tribe, were Nestorians, and Khubilai Khan's mother was a princess of the tribe, and a Nestorian.

Netherlands. The first Dutch ship arrived at Canton (q.v.) in 1604, but was refused permission to trade through the influence of the Portuguese in Macao (q.v.). A second ship in 1607 fared no better. In 1622 a Dutch fleet attacked Macao, but was repulsed by the Portuguese. In 1624, the same fleet established a settlement on Taiwan (q.v.). In 1662, the Dutch were driven from Taiwan by CHENG Ch'eng-kung (1624-1662, q.v.), known to Westerners as Koxinga.

The Dutch sent two embassies to Peking, in 1655 and 1665, to obtain trading privileges, which were refused. They traded clandestinely at ports on the coast of Fukien province (q.v.) from 1662 to 1762, at which time they were able to establish a factory (trading post) at Canton. Dutch trade was not a major factor during the period of the monopoly of the Cohong (1760-1842, q.v.), nor after the opening of the treaty ports by the Treaty of Nanking, in 1842 (qq.v.).

New Fourth Army Incident. January 6-14, 1941. The Sian Incident (q.v.) of December 1936 laid the basis for cooperation between the Chinese Communist party (CCP) and the Kuomintang (KMT, qq.v.), in the war against Japan which followed only half a year later. In September 1937, two months after the outbreak of the war, the two parties published the terms of their agreement, which included provisions for the integration of CCP military forces into the KMT military establishment.

Friction began to build between the two military establishments and finally led to a pitched battle between the CCP's New Fourth Army and KMT troops of the Third War Area in Anhwei and Kiangsu provinces (qq.v.), which covered the coastal area south of the Yangtze. The Communists were badly defeated and were never again able to exert military influence south of the Yangtze until after the war.

Nien Rebels (1851-1868). *Nien Fei* in Chinese. Bandits who ravaged parts of Anhwei, Chihli (Hopei), Honan, Hupei and Shantung (qq.v.). Their activities were contemporanious with the Taiping Rebellion (1850-1864, q.v.), and the two groups sometimes worked together. The Taipings' pseudo-Christian orientation and contact with Westerners made them well-known to the outside world. In contrast, the Nien had no particular ideology and received little attention outside of China. They were a major problem to the Ch'ing authorities, and the Mongol general Seng-ko-lin-ch'in (q.v.) lost his life fighting them. They were finally suppressed by LIU Ming-ch'uan (q.v.).

Perry, Elizabeth J., ed. *Chinese Perspectives on the Nien Rebellion*. Armonk, NY: M.E. Sharpe, Inc., 1981.

Ningpo (Ningbo). Population 900,000 (1980). Seaport in Chekiang (Zhejiang) province (q.v.), and one of the first five treaty ports (q.v.) opened to foreign trade by the Treaty of Nanking, 1842 (q.v.). Trade with Japan started in the 12th century, and the Portuguese traded there in the 16th. Ningpo capitalists were prominent in Shanghai (q.v.) from its founding.

The Ningpo dialect is related to other Wu dialects, e.g., Shanghai, but is quite distinct.

Ningsia (Ningxia) **Hui Autonomous Region**. Area: 60,000 sq. km. (23,000 sq. mi.). Population: 3,640,000 (1980). Capital: Yinchuan. Ningsia is bounded on the east by Shensi, on the southeast and southwest by Kansu, and on the northwest and northeast by the Inner Mongolia Autonomous Region (qq.v.). The Hui (Chinese-speaking Muslims) make up about a third of the population, with Mongols representing another minority. The Huang Ho (Yellow river, q.v.) goes through the province, and most agriculture is conducted in its valley. The climate is dry, requiring irrigation, and the winters are too cold for winter wheat. Spring wheat, millet and kaoliang (sorghum) are the principal crops.

Ningsia was a much larger province under the Republic of China (q.v.), but the People's Republic has incorporated much of the former province into the Inner Mongolia Autonomous Region.

North China. Until the establishment of the People's Republic of China (q.v.) on October 1, 1949, North China was taken to mean the provinces of Hopei, Honan, Shansi and Shantung (qq.v.), all of which lie south of the Great Wall. In current use the term frequently refers to the provinces of Heilungkiang, Kirin and Liaoning (qq.v.), which make up what was formerly known as Manchuria (q.v.). Readers consulting older texts should be aware of the difference.

Northern Expedition. The term refers to the military effort led by CHIANG Kai-shek (q.v.) to unify China from 1926 to 1928. As early as 1917, SUN Yat-sen (q.v.) had decided that military force would be necessary to crush the warlords (q.v.) in North China (q.v.) and unite the nation under Kuomintang (KMT, q.v.) rule. In 1921 he launched a military expedition to crush the Kwangsi warlords from his base at Canton. This succeeded, but a second expedition to crush opposition in Hunan and Kiangsi failed.

After SUN's death in 1925, CHIANG proposed another military attempt to unify the country. It was launched in the summer of 1926 and moved rapidly. Changsha, capital of Hunan province, was taken in August, Hankow and Hanyang in early September, and Wuchang in October. Nanchang, capital of Kiangsi, fell in November, Hangchow in January, 1927, Nanking and Shanghai in March. While the KMT was occupied with the establishment of a government in Nanking and the suppression of the Chinese Communist party (q.v.), the expedition marked time.

It was resumed in January 1928, and the Nationalist forces captured Peking in June. That was the symbolic end of the expedition, and by the end of the year the remaining warlords, such as YEN Hsi-shan in Shansi and CHANG Hsueh-liang in Manchuria (qq.v.), had accepted the Nationalist government, at least in name.

Jordan, Donald A. *The Northern Expedition.* Honolulu: The University Press of Hawaii, 1976.

Novels. The Chinese name for a novel is *hsiao-shuo,* which may be translated "small talk." The oldest novels extant date from the Yuan dynasty, 1279-1368, when the suspension of the examination system and the use of non-Chinese in administrative positions by the Mongol rulers reduced the traditional opportunities open to educated Chinese. In consequence, many of them turned to the writing of novels and plays.

Nevertheless, the novel was not highly regarded and the early examples are anonymous, or attributed to an author, but not necessarily claimed by him. Five of these are discussed in this book: *Romance of the Three Kingdoms, Shui Hu Chuan, Chin P'ing Mei, Hsi Yu Chi* and *The Dream of the Red Chamber* (qq.v.).

In spite of the official disrepute in which they were held, novels were widely read as entertainment. Many Chinese have admitted in their memoirs that they sometimes neglected their studies of the Confucian classics to indulge in such "dissipation." (This was disapproved of by their mentors since the examination system (q.v.) was based on the classics, and success in the examinations was the key to a government career.)

Chinese attitudes towards the novel were changing slowly during the Ming (1368-1643) and Ch'ing (1644-1911) dynasties (qq.v.), and the introduction of knowledge of Western literature at the end of the 19th century speeded up the process. The early novels, unlike official essays and historical writings, were composed in the vernacular (see under **Language, written**), and for this reason were relatively more accessible to students. With the success of the pai-hua movement, and the May Fourth movement (qq.v.) to encourage vernacular literature, thousands of novels have been published in the 20th century.

For the Western observer the Chinese novel presents certain difficulties, among them the large number of unfamiliar names and the fact that some characters have more than one name (which was quite customary in traditional China). Those novels mentioned above are also extremely long. They do, however, provide a detailed picture of Chinese society at certain points in history.

Hsia, C.T. *The Classic Chinese Novel.* New York: Columbia University Press, 1968.

Nurhaci (1559-1626). The founder of the Later Chin dynasty (q.v.) in 1616. In 1636 his son and successor Abahai (q.v.) changed the name to the Ch'ing (Manchu) dynasty (q.v.) which ruled China from 1644-1911.

Nurhaci was a member of the Aisin Gioro clan of the Juchen (q.v.) tribe. They were subjugated by the Khitan (q.v.) of the Liao dynasty (907-1125 A.D., q.v.) but turned the tables and established the Chin dynasty (1115-1234, q.v.). They were then conquered by the Mongols, who established the Yuan dynasty (1279-1368, q.v.). During the Ming dynasty (1368-1643, q.v.) the Juchen controlled much of present-day Manchuria (q.v.). Nurhaci's selection of the name for his dynasty was based on this sequence of events.

Nurhaci's father was killed in intertribal fighting, and at the age of 25 he was given the right to his father's title. He waged successful war against various enemies to avenge the deaths of his father and other relatives. He paid tribute to the Ming court in Peking in 1590, and in 1595 was granted a high title as a reward for proposing to lead an army against the Japanese under TOYOTOMI Hideyoshi (q.v.), who were then ravaging Korea. In 1608 he signed a boundary treaty with Ming officials, and in 1616 declared his independence of the Ming by proclaiming his Later Chin dynasty. He invaded Ming territory in 1618, seizing several Chinese cities. He failed to take Ning-yuan in 1626 and died that same year.

In 1601, Nurhaci introduced a military system under which his fighting forces were divided into four groups of 300 men each, identified by a different colored banner (see **Banners**). As his military successes mounted, more men rallied to his rule and other companies were attached to the four banners. In 1615, the four banners became eight, and everyone under the Later Chin empire belonged to one of the banners.

The banners included the fighting men and their families, and membership was hereditary. Since they were used as military units, the entire population became part of Nurhaci's war machine. The system proved effective until well past the middle of the 17th century, and included Mongols and Chinese as well as Manchus.

At his death in 1626, Nurhaci was succeeded by his eighth son Abahai, who held the title of khan but who ruled at first with three other princes.

Hummel, Arthur W., ed. *Eminent Chinese of the Ch'ing Period*. Washington: Government Printing Office, 1943.

O

Odoric of Pordenone (c. 1286-1331). Franciscan monk and early traveler to China. Odoric was born near Friuli in northern Italy. He left Europe in 1316 on a mission to the reigning emperor of the Yuan dynasty (1279-1368, q.v.). He traveled via India, Sumatra, Java, Borneo and Champa to Canton, an itinerary much like that of his predecessor, John of Monte Corvino (q.v.). He traveled extensively in China and spent some three years in Peking, possibly in charge of one of the churches founded by John. He returned to Europe by way of Central Asia, and may have visited Lhasa. Upon his return he wrote *Description of the East* which is regarded as one of the most useful travel books of the period. (Also see **Marco Polo**.)

One hundred eight. A mystical number for followers of Buddhism (q.v.). Traditionally it is the number of evil passions which man is subject to, as taught by the historical Buddha. In consequence, there are 108 beads on a Buddhist rosary and in many cases a temple bell is struck 108 times both morning and evening. Mathematically, 108 is the product of $1^1 \times 2^2 \times 3^3$. It may have been selected for its magical properties.

Open Door Policy. The weakness of the Ch'ing dynasty in the 19th century led to a number of inroads by foreign powers. China lost Hong Kong to Britain in 1842, the land beyond the Amur river to Russia in 1860, the Liuch'iu Islands to Japan in 1875, Vietnam to France in 1885, Burma to Britain in 1886, and Taiwan to Japan in 1895 (qq.v.). Some of these areas were indisputably parts of China, while others were states recognizing China as a suzerain power.

The effect was to close such areas to foreign trade of other nations, and this was opposed by Great Britain and the United States. Britain was the dominant trading power in the Yangtze basin but did not want to annex Chinese territory there, preferring trade without the responsibility of governing.

In consequence, with British encouragement, on September 6, 1899, John Hay, the American Secretary of State, sent notes to the American Ambassadors in Germany, Great Britain and Russia outlining American opposition to further Chinese concessions of territory or special privilege to other nations, and requesting reactions from the foreign governments. The replies received were vague and did not, in fact, prevent further incursions on Chinese sovereignty. However, the Open Door remained the basis of American policy toward China for several decades.

Griswold, A. Whitney. *The Far Eastern Policy of the United States*. New York: Harcourt Brace, 1939.

Opium Trade. Opium is not an indigenous Chinese product, and was probably introduced sometime in the 16th century. In 1678 a duty was levied on the small amount imported as medicine. Imports did not exceed 200 chests a year until late in the 18th century, but in 1799 they totaled 4,000 chests. That same year an imperial decree noted that the opium-smoking habit was moving inland from the Kwangtung and Fukien coasts, and banned both opium's import and use.

Most of the opium shipped into China in the late 18th and 19th centuries was grown in British India and shipped in British ships, though some American firms also participated. The British interest in the sale of opium was based on trade imbalance. British demand for Chinese silk and tea was tremendous, but Chinese interests in British exports was minor, until the development of the Chinese market for opium. This reversed a previous flow of silver into China into an outflow, to pay for opium.

Some Chinese officials were aware of the economic problems connected with the reversal of the terms of trade, but most of the Chinese objection to opium was based on moral grounds. Though import of the drug was banned, smuggling continued. It is estimated that by the late 1830s annual imports exceeded 30,000 chests.

In 1838 the issue of opium smuggling and consumption came to a head with a series of memorials to the throne from concerned officials, and further imperial decrees banning it. Steps taken to enforce the ban in 1839 by LIN Tse-hsü (q.v.), imperial commissioner at Canton, led to hostilities with the British and the Opium War (1839-1842, q.v.).

Beeching, Jack. *The Chinese Opium Wars*. New York: Harcourt Brace Jovanovich, 1976.

Opium War (1839-1842). Fought between China and Great Britain, to the Chinese the issue was suppression of the opium trade (q.v.), while the British were concerned with free trade and diplomatic access. Although banned by imperial decree, the amount of opium smuggled reached an estimated 30,000 chests annually by the late 1830s. In 1839 LIN Tse-hsü (q.v.), the new imperial commissioner for Canton, threatened the Chinese merchants of the Cohong (q.v.), the syndicate which held a monopoly on foreign trade, with serious consequences if the trade were not suppressed. He also demanded that the foreign traders surrender all the opium in their possession and, after a blockade of the "factories" where the foreigners lived outside Canton, collected 20,000 chests and destroyed them.

Another issue arose with the death of a Chinese following a brawl with British and American sailors. LIN called for the surrender of the murderer. The British were unable to identify the man responsible, but held a trial and sentenced several men to prison in England. The British refused to turn over anyone to the Chinese authorities. Angered, LIN ordered the expulsion of all British residents from Macao. Finally, in December 1839, all British trade was banned.

The British, finding LIN intransigent, sailed up the coast taking Amoy, Ningpo and Chu Shan Island with no effective opposition. They sailed on to Tientsin, where negotiations with Ch'i-shan (qq.v.) began in August 1840. Ch'i-shan was diplomatic and persuaded the British to return to Canton for further negotiations, and he himself was appointed to replace LIN Tse-hsü, with full powers to reach an agreement.

As negotiations dragged on the British became impatient, and in January 1841, seized the forts at Chuenpi, near Canton. Ch'i-shan, recognizing Chinese inability to withstand British force, signed an agreement with Sir Henry Pottinger, ceding Hong Kong to the British. For this, Ch'i-shan was denounced and sentenced to death, later commuted to banishment.

The British resumed the initiative and seized several cities in Chekiang province, and by July 1842, were threatening Nanking. Recognizing the futility of further resistance, the emperor authorized Ch'i-ying (q.v.) to agree to British demands. Ch'i-ying and Pottinger signed the Treaty of Nanking on August 29, 1842, and the supplementary Treaty of the Bogue (qq.v.) on October 8, 1843. Except for those with Russia, these were the first treaties China ever signed with a Western power.

The treaties ceded Hong Kong, opened five "treaty ports" (q.v.)—Canton, Amoy, Foochow, Ningpo and Shanghai—to foreign trade, established certain rights of extraterritoriality and included the "most-favored-nation" clause (qq.v.). The last provided that if China granted any privilege to a third nation, Britain would automatically be given the same privilege as the "most-favored" nation. These were the first "unequal treaties" (q.v.), so called because they were not reciprocal and were obtained under threat of force.

The signing of the two treaties with Great Britain led to the signing of the treaties of Wanghia, July 3, 1844, with the United States, and Whampoa, October 24, 1844 (qq.v.), with France.

Dissatisfaction with the implementation of the treaties led to the *Arrow* War (1857-1860, q.v.). The two wars are sometimes referred to as the Opium Wars, since they are closely linked.

Beeching, Jack. *The Chinese Opium Wars.*

New York: Harcourt Brace Jovanovich, 1976.

Oracle Bones. The rulers of the Shang dynasty (1766-1122 B.C., q.v.) practiced divination by applying heat to certain bones and "reading" the cracks which resulted. Interpretation was by methods still unknown. The outcome was inscribed on the bone, however, and sometimes other matters were added. The bones used were mainly scapulae of domestic cattle, including water buffalo, but plastrons and carapaces of turtles were also used.

These bones were first brought to the attention of scholars in 1899, though they had been known to peasants living near the site of the last Shang capital at Anyang (q.v.), and had been used for agricultural fertilizer and also ground into powder for medicinal purposes. The discovery was of major importance, because it provided documentary evidence of the existence of the Shang dynasty and confirmed the traditional list of kings which had come down through the Chou dynasty (q.v.) records and was recorded by SSU-MA Ch'ien in his *Shih Chi* (qq.v.).

At first glance the pictographs used in the inscriptions do not appear to resemble modern Chinese characters, but tracing the standard script (which was established in the third century B.C.) back through the Chou inscriptions shows that many modern characters are indeed descended from Shang originals. About 2,000 Shang characters are known, and about half of these have been identified with their modern counterparts. The others are mostly personal or place names which probably have no modern counterparts.

OU-YANG Hsiu (1007-1072). Scholar and official of the Northern Sung dynasty (960-1126, q.v.). He was considered the outstanding scholar of his time, and a great stylist. He was the chief examiner when SU Tung-p'o (q.v.) took his examinations and SU regarded him as his teacher. OU-YANG's prose style is one of clarity rather than high-flown prose. He was the author of the New History of the Five Dynasties, which covered the period 906-960, and was one of two editors in chief of the New T'ang History, covering the T'ang dynasty from 618 to 906.

OU-YANG Hsiu was an early patron of WANG An-shih (q.v.), but soon became disillusioned with WANG's theories of reform as well as his stubbornness. He became one of WANG's severest critics, in company with SSU-Ma Kuang (q.v.) and SU Tung-p'o.

Liu, James T.C. *Ou-yang Hsiu: An Eleventh Century Neo-Confucianist.* Stanford: Stanford University Press, 1967.

Overseas Chinese. The term refers to all Chinese living outside of China, but particularly those in Southeast Asia. Chinese traders were present in Southeast Asia in the T'ang dynasty (618-906 A.D., q.v.) and possibly earlier than that. Until fairly recent times, Chinese emigrants were largely male, and the resulting overseas communities were of mixed descent. There was also a certain amount of assimilation. Under traditional Chinese law, anyone whose parents were Chinese had a claim to Chinese nationality. The presence of a large and economically powerful minority suspected of divided loyalties lies at the root of problems between the Overseas Chinese and their host countries. In Indonesia and Malaysia problems are exacerbated by religious differences.

Emigration was banned by both the Ming (1368-1644) and Ch'ing (1644-1911) dynasties (qq.v.). Since emigrants had broken the law, the imperial governments in Peking were not committed to protecting their interests, though this attitude changed in the late 19th century.

Most of the Chinese residents in Southeast Asia are from Kwangtung and Fukien provinces (qq.v.), or are the descendents of emigrants from there. The greatest emigrations occurred in the 19th and early 20th centuries when population and economic pressures were very high in China, and relatively lower in Southeast Asia. The immigrants to Southeast Asia came of a hard-working tradition and had the reputation of working harder than the peoples among whom they settled. The Chinese traders also had the advantage of a network of relatives and friends in all the major ports of the area. As a consequence, much of the international trade, as well as internal businesses, tended toward being a Chinese monopoly, causing resentment.

In the Dutch East Indies, now Indonesia, the Dutch administration used the Chinese for retail business, keeping wholesale international trade in Dutch hands. The Indonesian perception of the Chinese as cooperating with the imperialists and prospering as a result was a further irritant.

Current estimates (1985) of the number of Chinese living outside of China run to 18 or 19 million, with some 95 percent of those living in Asia. These figures include the populations of Hong Kong and Macao (qq.v.), though residents of those two areas are referred to in Chinese as "compatriots," *t'ung pao* (*tong bao*), rather than "Overseas Chinese," *hua ch'iao* (*hua qiao*).

Huang, Tsen-ming. *The Legal Status of the Chinese Abroad*. Taipei: China Cultural Service, 1954 (reprint).

Purcell, Victor. *The Position of the Overseas Chinese in Southeast Asia*. New York: Institute of Pacific Relations, 1950.

Williams, Lea E. *The Future of the Overseas Chinese in Southeast Asia*. New York: McGraw Hill, 1966.

P Q

Pai Hua. Literally "white" or "clear speech." The term refers to Chinese written in the vernacular. The Chinese literary language is not a transcription of the spoken word (see under **Language, Written**). It was used for official purposes and in poetry, history and literary essays from the Chou dynasty (1122-255 B.C., q.v.) to the 20th century. One benefit was that a literate Chinese would have little or no difficulty in reading such materials no matter when they were written. A serious drawback was the length of time needed to achieve that level of literacy. It restricted that ability to a small minority of the population, particularly to those whose families could afford to subsidize such an education.

At the same time, some things were written in the vernacular. These certainly included communications on commercial matters, but the extant materials include the texts of plays (see under **Drama**) and novels (q.v.). We also have testimony from readers of earlier eras that they read such works in private as a relief from the required study of the Confucian canon.

The arrival of Western influence in the 19th century, and China's defeat in several wars by Britain, France and Japan (qq.v.) led many Chinese to deplore China's weakness. Some reached the conclusion that the con-tinued use of the literary language and the examination system (q.v.) were basic obstacles to modernization and strength. Proponents urged the abolition of the examinations (the last were held in 1905) and, after the revolution of 1911, the use of pai hua for written Chinese.

The May Fourth movement of 1919 (q.v.) stimulated its use, and a number of publications appeared in the vernacular. Some of these were ephemeral and many were imbued with democratic, socialist, anarchistic and other ideas imported from the West. The most prominent supporter of the movement was HU Shih (1891-1962, q.v.), some of whose essays on the subject are translated in Chapter XXVI of *China's Response to the West*.

Most material published in Chinese today is theoretically written in the vernacular. However, such things as newspaper editorials and even many news items would be incomprehensible to most listeners if read on a radio broadcast. Knowledge of the characters used is essential to understanding. Radio and film scripts, however, are truly in the vernacular, since they must be comprehensible to the listener.

Teng, Ssu-yu, and John K. Fairbank, eds. *China's Response to the West*. 2d pbk. ed. New York: Atheneum, 1967.

P'an Ku. Name given to a figure of the legendary period (q.v.), said to have been born of the Egg of Chaos, and to have been involved with the creation of heaven and earth. There are many legends in which he figures, but the earliest of them cannot be traced back farther than the third century B.C.

Panay Incident. The U.S. gunboat *Panay* was sunk in the Yangtze river at Nanking on December 12, 1937, while evacuating American embassy officials. The Japanese army had captured the city and were engaged in the incident known as the Rape of Nanking (q.v.). Japanese bombers sank the *Panay* and three ships belonging to the Standard Oil Co. Since the *Panay* had every right to be where she was under various treaties, this caused outrage in the United States.

Japan offered lame excuses and apologized even before receiving the official protests. It also paid an indemnity promptly.

Pao Chia. This is a system of social control whose origin is sometimes attributed to the Legalist official Shang Yang of the Warring States Period (484-255 B.C., qq.v.). Under the system each household belongs to a group of 10, called a *p'ai*; ten *p'ai* formed a *chia* of 100 families, and 10 *chia* formed a *pao* of 1,000 families. Each family in the unit of 10 was responsible for any crimes committed in any of the other families, unless they reported the infractions to the authorities. For this reason it was necessary to keep track of all visitors and to make note of any unusual activity. The system has persisted with varying degrees of intensity into the 20th century.

Hsiao, Kung-ch'uan. *Rural China*. Seattle: University of Washington Press, 1960.

Paper. The invention of paper in China is credited to an official of the Han dynasty (206 B.C.-221 A.D., q.v.) in 105 A.D. His name was TS'AI Lun, and he was rewarded with the title of marquis for his efforts. The first paper was made of silk refuse, and the technique was later adapted for the use of hemp, tree bark, or bamboo.

While silk was used for writing prior to this time, most early books were inscribed on wood or bamboo. The invention of paper was a significant step in the increase of literacy and the spread of books. It was also a necessary predecessor to the invention of printing (q.v.).

Laufer, Berthold. *Paper and Printing in Ancient China*. New York: B. Franklin, 1973 (reprint).

Pauley Mission (May 4-July 21, 1946). In early 1946 the U.S. government, disturbed by reports of Soviet removals of Japanese assets in Manchuria (q.v.) as "war booty," sent American businessman Edwin W. Pauley and a team of industrial engineers to Manchuria to investigate. The mission visited many places in Manchuria, but was refused entrance to Dairen (q.v.) by Soviet authorities, and to Antung by local Chinese Communist authorities.

The mission found the contrast between the condition of the Manchurian industrial plant at the time of the Japanese surrender and the time of the survey "appalling." Contemporary estimates of the replacement value of the removals and destruction ranged as high as $2 billion. They ascribed the majority of the damage to Soviet removals and failure to preserve order. It also noted that the small amount of benefit received by the Soviet government in its removals could readily have been supplied by reparations from Japan proper at much smaller cost.

The mission's report noted that contrary to Soviet claims, the Soviet military effort in Manchuria, which lasted only a few days and encountered no significant Japanese opposition, did not entitle the USSR to claim all Japanese property in Manchuria as reparations.

The report also noted the extreme contrast with Soviet policy in Korea, where there were "practically no capital removals or destruction of industry." While refraining from speculating on Soviet motives for stripping Manchuria of industrial plants, the report comments that "the damage which Manchurian industry has sustained since V-J Day has set back China's industrial progress for a generation."

United States Relations With China. Washington: Department of State, 1949.

Pear Garden. This is a literary term for the theater. The emperor T'ang Ming Huang (r. 713-755, q.v.), established the Li Yuan, meaning "pear garden," as an academy for the training of singers and dancers for court functions. The Chinese regard this as their first formal establishment for such a purpose, and it was continued for several centuries. Even today actors and actresses are sometimes referred to as "children of the Pear Garden."

Scott, A.C. *The Classical Theatre of China.* London: George Allen & Unwin, 1957.

Peiping (Beiping). See **Peking**.

Peiyang Group. The term refers to the group of military officers who were protégés of YUAN Shih-k'ai (1859-1916, q.v.), who held the title *Peiyang Tach'en*, meaning High Commissioner of Military and Foreign Affairs in North China, from 1901 until nearly the end of the Ch'ing dynasty (q.v.) in 1911. This group, and the armies they commanded, enabled YUAN to become president of the new Republic of China (q.v.) in February 1912, and to control North China (q.v.) by mili-

tary force. Even before YUAN's death in 1916, the group's unity was eroding. It eventually split to form the Anhwei Clique, led by TUAN Ch'i-jui (1865-1936), and the Chihli Clique, led by FENG Kuo-chang (1859-1919, qq.v.), both of whom later became presidents of the republic.

Peking (Beijing). Capital of the People's Republic of China (q.v.). Population 8,700,000 (1980). Peking means "northern capital" and the city has been the capital of China for most of the last 700 years. When the capital has been elsewhere, it has been called Peiping (Beiping), which means either "northern peace" or the "pacified north." The capital of the kingdom of Yen (q.v.) of the Warring States Period (484-255 B.C., q.v.) was nearby. Much later it was one of several capitals of the Liao dynasty (907-1125 A.D., q.v.). The Chin (1115-1234, q.v.) also used it, and both dynasties called it Yenching. The Mongols took it in 1215, and it was the capital of China during the Yuan dynasty (1279-1368, q.v.). It was then known as Tatu to the Chinese, and as Khanbalick (Cambaluc). This is the name Marco Polo (1254-1324, q.v.) gives it.

The founder of the Ming dynasty (1368-1644, q.v.), emperor Ming Hung Wu (q.v.), established his capital at Nanking (meaning "southern capital") and named the former Yuan capital Peiping. The third emperor, Ming Yung Lo (q.v.), established his capital there in 1403 and changed the name to Peking. It retained the name and remained the capital throughout the Ming and Ch'ing (1644-1911, q.v.) dynasties and through the early years of the Republic of China (q.v.). In 1928 the Nationalists under CHIANG Kai-shek (q.v.) established Nanking as the capital, and Peking became Peiping until 1949. In that year the People's

Republic of China was established and the name reverted to Peking.

Although Peking has such a long history, there is little in the way of architectural remains prior to the Ming dynasty. What remains is the most impressive collection of Chinese imperial palaces and ancillary structures still extant.

Lin, Yutang. *Imperial Peking*. New York: Crown Publishers, 1961.

Peking Government. The term is sometimes used to refer to the People's Republic of China (PRC, q.v.), but previously referred to the series of governments which ruled at Peking in the early years of the Republic of China (q.v.), from 1912 to 1926. (For a list of the heads of government, see under **Republic of China, Presidents**.) The Republic of China was formally established at Nanking on January 1, 1912, with SUN Yat-sen (q.v.) as provisional president. To achieve national unity he offered to resign in favor of YUAN Shih-k'ai (q.v.) on certain conditions, one of which was that YUAN would move the seat of government from Peking, seat of the Ch'ing dynasty (1644-1911, q.v.) to Nanking. YUAN agreed, but managed by a ruse to remain in Peking, and it was technically the seat of government until 1926.

At no time was all of China under Peking's control. Added to the natural problems of the size and diversity of the country were the underdevelopment of transportation and communications, and the economic problems caused by the lack of a unified monetary system and internal trade barriers such as the *likin* tax (q.v.). Conflicting ambitions on the part of various warlords (q.v.) and the differing political theories espoused by republicans and monarchists rendered unity unattainable.

By 1924 the succession of presidents in Peking had lost nearly all their power and for a period in 1926 there was no recognized government at all. The last ruler in Peking was the Manchurian warlord CHANG Tso-lin (1873-1928, q.v.), who evacuated the city in June 1928 in the face of the advancing armies of the Northern Expedition (q.v.). The Nationalists occupied Peking that month and changed the name to Peiping (see under **Peking**), to indicate that it was no longer the capital.

Houn, Franklin W. *Central Government of China: 1912-1928*. Madison: University of Wisconsin Press, 1957.

Peking Man. Known scientifically as *Sinanthropus Pekinensis*. Bones, including a skull, were found at the village of Chou-k'ou-tien, southwest of Peking in Hopei province (q.v.), in excavations carried out in 1929. These were dated to about 500,000 B.C. Evidence shows that Peking man used tools and that he had shovel-shaped incisors. That form of dentition exists in many ethnic strains, but it is particularly prevalent among members of the Mongoloid race, leading to the distinct possibility that Peking Man was an ancestor of present-day Chinese.

The fossils were lost during the Japanese invasion, but recent excavations have turned up more in the same area.

Cheng, Te K'un. *Prehistoric China*. Cambridge: W. Heffer & Sons, 1959.

Peking, Treaty of. Signed November 14, 1860 by I-hsin (q.v.) for China and Nikolai Pavlovich Ignatieff for Russia. The treaty was signed shortly after the destruction of the Summer Palace (q.v.) by the British (see under **Arrow War**) and the Chinese were in no position to resist. The new treaty ceded to Russia the land between the Ussuri river and the sea, now the Soviet Maritime Province. It also granted the right to the Russians to trade through the treaty ports (q.v.). Previously they had been permitted only overland access through Mongolia.

Beeching, Jack. *The Chinese Opium Wars*. New York and London: Harcourt Brace Jovanovich, 1976.

P'ENG Te-huai (PENG Dehuai) (1898-1974). Soldier and official of the People's Republic of China (PRC, q.v.). Born in Hunan province (q.v.) of a poor family, he had only a few years of schooling. He joined the Hunan provincial forces soon after the revolution of 1911, receiving a commission in 1918. By the time of the Northern Expedition (q.v.) in 1926, he was a major. Identified as a leftist, he was purged at the time of the split between the Kuomintang (KMT, q.v.) and the Chinese Communist party (CCP, q.v.) in 1927. After more than a year of guerrilla activity against KMT troops, he joined forces with CHU Teh (1886-1976) and MAO Tse-tung (1893-1976, qq.v.). KMT pressure forced the latter to retreat into Fukien province (q.v.), while P'ENG and his troops remained in the Hunan-Kiangsi border area.

In 1930, LI Li-san (1900-1967, q.v.), the dominant figure in the CCP, called for attacks on China's industrial centers, in line with orthodox Communist theory at the time. Responding to this, P'ENG took Changsha, the Hunan provincial capital, twice, but held it only a few days each time. He then became more closely connected with CHU and MAO, and participated in the Long March (q.v.) in 1934.

After the second Sino-Japanese War began in July 1937 (see **World War II**), CCP forces in Northwest China were reorganized with CHU as commander and P'ENG as deputy. Except for a brief period in 1937, CHU remained in Yenan and P'ENG served as field commander. He became a member of the Central Committee of the CCP in 1945. During the Civil War (q.v.) of 1946-1949 against the KMT, he commanded the First Field Army which controlled Ningsia, Kansu and Sinkiang (qq.v.).

After the establishment of the PRC on October 1, 1949, P'ENG held a number of important positions. In October, 1950, he led the Chinese People's Volunteers into North Korea to assist in the Korean War (see under **Korea**). He signed the armistice agreement at Panmunjom on July 27, 1953, and returned to a hero's welcome in Peking. In 1954 he was named minister of national defense, and was also de facto commander of the People's Liberation Army. In 1955 he was given the newly-created rank of marshal. He started a program to modernize and professionalize the army, and in 1956 introduced graduated salary scales, policies which ran counter to Maoist theory.

MAO's countermove came in 1958, during the Great Leap Forward (q.v.), in the creation of a nonprofessional militia. P'ENG's opposition to MAO was fueled by his perception of the economic chaos resulting from the failure of the Great Leap. The conflict came to a head at the CCP leadership meeting held at Lushan, a mountain resort in Kiangsi province (q.v.), in the summer of 1959. P'ENG took the lead in criticizing party policies and, by implication, MAO himself. In September, P'ENG was dismissed as minister of national defense, and spent the next seven years in obscurity. In December 1966 Red Guards (q.v.) took him into custody, and he was denounced during the Cultural Revolution (q.v.). In November 1974 P'ENG died in prison, denied medical attention on

MAO's orders. No word of his death reached his family or the public until four years later (after MAO's death), when he was posthumously rehabilitated by TENG Hsiao-p'ing (q.v.).

Boorman, Howard L., ed. *Biographical Dictionary of Republican China.* New York: Columbia University Press, 1967-1973.

Domes, Jurgen. *Peng Te-huai: The Man and the Image.* Stanford: Stanford University Press, 1985.

People's Republic of China (PRC). Proclaimed in Peking on October 1, 1949, as a result of the victory of the forces of the Chinese Communist party (CCP, q.v.) over those of the Kuomintang (KMT, q.v.), the dominant party of the Republic of China (ROC, q.v.), in the Civil War (q.v.), 1946-1949. It was established as a Communist state and was immediately recognized by the USSR (see under **Russia**). Recognition by several other states, including Great Britain, soon followed. The first head of state was MAO Tse-tung (1893-1976, q.v.), chairman of the CCP.

The first decade of the PRC saw a confident party suppressing all internal opposition under MAO's strong leadership. Buddhist monasteries were closed and their religious forcibly returned to lay life. Foreign Christian missionaries either departed voluntarily or were asked to leave. Those who remained, like the Chinese clergy, were targets of popular trials and many suffered imprisonment. In September 1951 all Catholic schools and colleges were taken over by the government. Protestant institutions met the same treatment. Privately published periodicals were also either seized or suppressed.

The destruction of the rural elites was accomplished by the abolition of land ownership. This was followed in 1952 by the Three Anti Movement (q.v.), against officials of the previous government, and the Five Anti Movement (q.v.), against private businessmen. Collective farms on the Soviet model were introduced in 1954. In 1957 the Hundred Flowers Campaign (q.v.) encouraged intellectuals to make constructive criticisms of government policy, and punished those whose comments were deemed too pointed.

In the field of external affairs, the PRC looked with approval at the North Korean invasion of South Korea in June 1950, and when the counterthrust of the United Nations forces approached the Yalu river, which forms part of the Sino-Korean border, sent in hundreds of thousands of troops, officially labeled Chinese People's Volunteers, under the command of the veteran general P'ENG Te-huai (1898-1974, q.v.). With this assistance, the North Koreans were able to push back the UN forces to a line approximating the earlier division along the 38th parallel. P'ENG remained in Korea until the armistice, which he signed on July 27, 1953, before returning to a hero's welcome in Peking.

The PRC also took steps to incorporate Tibet (q.v.) into the Chinese state. Chinese troops entered Tibet in October 1950, and the following month Tibet appealed unsuccessfully to the UN for assistance. In May, 1951, China announced the "peaceful liberation" of Tibet.

The PRC's international position was enhanced by participation in the 29-nation Afro-Asian Conference at Bandung, Indonesia, in April 1955. The USSR was denied participation, on the grounds that its Asian possessions did not make it an Asian nation. In consequence, the two dominant leaders at the meeting were Indian Prime Minister Jawaharlal

Nehru and Premier CHOU En-lai (1898-1976, q.v.).

The PRC received massive aid from the USSR in the first years of its existence. This has been estimated at $2 billion in loans (approximately the value of the Japanese-built industrial plant in Manchuria looted by the Soviets in 1945-1946), and the services of 10,000 Soviet technicians working on some 250 projects. In addition, 13,000 Chinese students and specialists received training in the USSR. The relationship cooled in 1956 after Nikita Khrushchev denounced the late Marshal Josef Stalin, but the PRC was not prepared to do so. Chinese criticism of the USSR was indirect, aimed at Yugoslav revisionists. The Soviets replied with barbs aimed at Albanian dogmatists, but it was soon clear to any observer that the intended targets were larger and nearer at hand.

The Great Leap Forward (q.v.) was introduced in February 1958. By the end of the year 26,500 communes covered all of China. The rural communes established backyard furnaces for the production of pig iron; communal mess halls replaced family kitchens; and farm hands were required to march to work in military formations. In December MAO announced his decision to retire from his government posts, while retaining his chairmanship of the party. In April 1959, LIU Shao-ch'i (1900-1969, q.v.) replaced him as chairman of the PRC and head of state. March 1959 also saw an anti-Chinese uprising in Tibet, which was soon crushed. The Tibetan Dalai Lama (q.v.) fled to India, where he still lived in 1986.

The Great Leap caused economic chaos, concealed at first by inaccurate reporting. Eventually, it became an issue at the highest levels. In the summer of 1959, the Central Committee of the PRC met for six weeks at the mountain resort of Lushan, Kiangsi province, to discuss national affairs. For the first time, criticism of MAO's policy was expressed, if somewhat indirectly. The leader was P'ENG Te-huai, minister of national defense, who had been dismayed by his observations in the countryside. He found that household utensils were sometimes seized to be melted down in the backyard furnaces, and wooden buildings had been torn down for fuel. Farmers resented marching in military formations, and communal mess halls were occasionally put to the torch. Resistance and low morale were widespread. MAO rejected P'ENG's views and threatened to lead the peasants to overthrow the government if the conference accepted them. Shortly afterward, in September, P'ENG was dismissed from his post.

The obvious failure of the Great Leap led to its abandonment in 1960. The economic problems were exacerbated by the sudden withdrawal of Soviet technicians that year. The USSR was expressing its disapproval of MAO's policies, and his proclaimed ambition to achieve communism within his own lifetime.

In October, 1962, China sent troops from Tibet into India's North East Frontier Area, so straining relations between the two nations that India asked for military assistance from Britain and the United States.

In 1964 China announced the successful detonation of an atomic device at Lop Nor, Sinkiang province.

In 1966, MAO emerged from his relative retirement to launch a new program, the Cultural Revolution (q.v.), to combat elitism, revisionism and bureaucracy. It destroyed most of the CCP's old-guard leadership, starting with LIU Shao-ch'i. He was replaced as number two man in the CCP by LIN Piao (1907-1971, q.v.). MAO's wife, CHIANG Ch'ing, 1914- , (q.v.), emerged as the leader of the Cultural Revolution, and with the support of extreme leftist supporters brought the country to a state of near anarchy. Xenophobia became a virtue, with emphasis on self-reliance in national development. In August, students and Red Guards (q.v.) demonstrated at the Soviet embassy, and in September all embassies were asked to withdraw their student nationals. In October, the USSR expelled all Chinese students in retaliation. In 1967, the Soviet embassy was attacked and the British legation burned. Most Chinese diplomats abroad were recalled to take part in the Cultural Revolution.

Education was brought to a standstill, as all schools were closed and millions of young people were sent from urban to rural areas. Competence and experience were disparaged, and the Chinese were urged to esteem those who were ideologically sound rather than those who were technically proficient, i.e., "red before expert." Red Guards occupied government offices and factories, bringing most activities to a halt, and clashes with military units occurred. Traditional Chinese culture and art became targets of destruction, and Red Guards rampaged through private homes destroying anything which offended them. Special camps were established to retrain government officials through physical labor, criticism and self-criticism.

Relations with the USSR declined in 1969, with two clashes involving several thousand troops along the Ussuri river border with the Soviet Maritime Province. In September 1971, LIN Piao died under mysterious circumstances, though his death was not revealed until the following July. Relations with the United States improved with the 1971 secret visit to China of National Security Council Chairman Henry Kissinger. In October, the UN voted to seat the PRC representatives and to expel those of the ROC. In February 1972, U.S. President Richard Nixon visited China, and the Shanghai Communiqué (q.v.) was issued on his departure. In 1973, the U.S. and the PRC established liaison offices in Peking and Washington.

1976 was a year of change. The death of CHOU En-lai in January resulted in massive demonstrations which were suppressed with force. CHOU was succeeded in his post as premier by HUA Kuo-feng (HUA Guofeng), a little-known vice premier. In July two major earthquakes devastated the mining and industrial center of Tangshan, Hopeh province, with casualties estimated at between 100,000 and 1 million, though no official figures were published. Many Chinese, mindful of the tradition that a change in the dynastic cycle is frequently accompanied by natural calamities, were prepared to see a cosmic link with the death of Chairman MAO in September. In October, Premier HUA succeeded MAO as chairman of the CCP. CHIANG Ch'ing and three close associates, collectively dubbed the Gang of Four (q.v.), were arrested and purged. They were tried in 1980 and convicted in 1981.

MAO's death cleared the way for the rehabilitation of many former leaders, some only posthumously. The most conspicuous of these was TENG Hsiao-p'ing (DENG Xiaoping; 1902- , q.v.), who regained in July 1977 the posts from which he had been purged after CHOU's death in 1976. While technically a vice premier, TENG soon showed himself the major force behind post-MAO reforms.

On January 1, 1979, the PRC and

the United States extended mutual diplomatic relations to each other. At the same time, the United States broke relations with the ROC. That same month TENG, as a major supporter of the policy to normalize relations with the United States, made a state visit to Washington.

The PRC had welcomed the surrender of South Vietnam to forces from North Vietnam on April 30, 1975, but by 1978 Vietnamese repression had resulted in the flight of hundreds of thousands of refugees, by land and sea. Many of these were ethnic Chinese, and some had fled to the PRC. In July 1978, all Chinese aid to Vietnam was halted, and in February 1979, more than 200,000 Chinese troops invaded Vietnam, six weeks after Vietnamese troops had invaded Cambodia. The Chinese retired in March.

Under TENG's leadership, the PRC has changed in many ways. He retired from his government positions in August 1980, while retaining his positions in the party structure. In 1982 a major reorganization of the government reduced 98 government ministries, boards and agencies to 52, and eliminated one-third of their personnel. In 1983 a new system of economic responsibility was introduced, encouraging local initiative and individual accountability. In 1984 many senior officials were encouraged to retire, and were replaced by younger people, known to be supporters of TENG's reforms. By 1985 thousands of Chinese were studying abroad, and increasing numbers of government officials were visiting foreign countries.

Boorman, Howard L., ed. *Biographical Dictionary of Republican China.* New York: Columbia University Press, 1967-1971.

Chou, Eric. *Mao Tse-tung: The Man and the Myth.* London: Cassell, 1984.

Klein, Donald W., and Anne B. Clark. *Biographic Dictionary of Chinese Communism, 1921-1965.* Cambridge: Harvard University Press, 1971.

Terrill, Ross. *Mao: A Biography.* New York: Harper & Row, 1980.

Yim, Kwan Ha. *China Since Mao.* New York: Facts On File, Inc., 1980.

Period of Disunity. The term refers to the period between the fall of the Later Han dynasty (25-221 A.D.) and the founding of the Sui dynasty (589-618, qq.v.). This covers the Three Kingdoms, the Western Chin, the Northern, Eastern and Western Wei, etc. (See the Dynastic Sequence chart for details.) Many Chinese of the period looked back to the Han dynasty (206 B.C.-221 A.D.) as a time of unity and classical civilization, and regarded later centuries as a time of decline, marked by warfare, hardship and unrest. The pessimism of the age is credited by some historians with the growth and acceptance of Buddhism (q.v.).

It should be noted that this was not the only time when China was not united. North China (q.v.) slipped from Chinese rule at the fall of the T'ang dynasty (618-906), and was ruled by the Liao dynasty (907-1125) and the Chin (1115-1234, qq.v.), while parts of the South were ruled by the Sung (960-1279, q.v.). China was united again in 1279 under the hated Mongol Yuan dynasty (1279-1368, q.v.) but North China did not come under Chinese rule again until the establishment of the Ming dynasty in 1368 (q.v.). From this perspective, it can be seen that China has been united under Chinese rule for about half the period since the fall of the Later Han in 221 A.D.

Philosophy. Chinese philosophy enjoyed its most creative and diverse era during the second half of the Chou dynasty (q.v.), historically known as the Warring States Period (484-221 B.C., q.v.). Although three philosophic schools—Confucianism, Legalism and Taoism (qq.v.) —survived the centuries, at one time there were so many divergent philosophies they were referred to as the Hundred Schools of Thought.

The Confucianists accepted the belief of their founder, Confucius (551-479 B.C., q.v.), that the Earlier (Western) Chou dynasty (1122-771 B.C., q.v.) was a golden age, and that a ruler's observance of certain rites and the practice of "benevolence" (*jen*) would restore that utopia. The Legalists, in contrast, preached that the interests of the ruler were preeminent, and that the state would best be served by a rule of harsh law and pervasive police control that present-day observers would recognize as totalitarian. The philosophical Taoists concentrated on rooting out ambition and achieving harmony with nature, frequently as recluses in unsettled areas. With the exception of the Taoists, the various schools were propounded to the feudal lords by itinerant scholars hoping to be appointed to high office. Some of the feudal lords maintained courts at which hundreds of scholars might be supported.

The eventual conquest of the other feudal states by Ch'in, and the establishment of the Ch'in dynasty by Ch'in Shih Huang Ti (qq.v.) in 221 B.C., seemed to mark a permanent victory for the Legalists, since theirs was the philosophy of the victors. The Burning of the Books (q.v.) in 213 B.C. which was the destruction of all Confucian and heterodox texts which could be found, might have resulted in the loss of all other philosophical and historical works. However, the fall of the Ch'in dynasty, and its replacement by the Han (206 B.C.-221 A.D., q.v.) changed the terms. Confucianism was the official philosophy of the Han, though many of its administrative practices were clearly derived from Legalist precedents. The restoration of Confucian texts was partly based on some which had been preserved and on others which were recreated by scholars who had memorized them. While this served to preserve Confucian teaching, many of the essential arguments of the other schools are preserved only in texts written to refute them. Moreover, the Confucians shared with the Legalists a predilection for orthodoxy and a distaste for heterodox dispute.

Because Confucianism was the official ideology of the Han dynasty and the content of the new civil service examinations (see **Examination system**) was based on familiarity with the Confucian canon, the other schools either disappeared or were subsumed into some aspect of Confucianism. The general requirement for conformity reduced speculation to examination and interpretation of existing texts. It also provided an opportunity for forgeries of many kinds, since no new doctrine could gain a hearing unless rooted in a preexisting classic, many of which were composed for that purpose.

Buddhism (q.v.) presented the first major external challenge to indigenous Chinese philosophy. It reached China some time in the Han dynasty, but its major impact was felt in the years of disunity which followed. The circumstances of the time were favorable to the spread of an otherworldly philosophy of this kind. It was adopted as an official ideology by some of the rulers of the Northern Wei (386-534, q.v.). Another element in its favor was that it was a universal religion, whereas non-Chinese (such as the rulers of the Northern Wei) had some difficulty in accepting the ethnocentricity of Confucianism. Stumbling blocks for the Chinese in accepting Buddhism were certain unfamiliar concepts, such as reincarnation and nirvana, and practices which were counter to Chinese tradition, such as celibacy and religious mendicancy.

Widespread Chinese understanding of Buddhism required translation of Buddhist texts. Many of the translations were done under imperial patronage in the T'ang dynasty (618-906, q.v.), and in spite of the official use of the Confucian canon as material for the civil service examinations, Buddhist speculation became the dominant philosophic activity of the time.

The major Chinese contribution to Buddhism was the Ch'an school (see **Ch'an Buddhism**), better known in the West as Zen, its Japanese name, which stresses sudden enlightenment, rather than the arduous path of formal logic characteristic of other schools.

Inevitably, reaction against Buddhism set in. HAN Yü (q.v.) wrote a memorial to the throne in 819 protesting the imperial reception given a Buddhist relic. By the late 840s a campaign of repression against the Buddhist church was under way. By the end of the dynasty Buddhism's tide had begun to ebb, but Chinese civilization had become so permeated by Buddhist ideas and concepts that they could not be rooted out.

This became evident in the Sung dynasty (960-1279, q.v.), whose most important philosophic school was Neo-Confucianism (q.v.), and whose most important thinker was CHU Hsi (q.v.). CHU codified Neo-Confucianism in the form in which it survived into the 20th century, combining the Confucian concepts of Mencius (q.v.) with a number of ideas which were basically Taoist or Buddhist. It was CHU's curriculum of the Four Books (q.v.) which formed the basis for Chinese education aimed at the civil service examinations and subsequent government service. For this reason all educated Chinese became familiar with the content of his philosophy, whether or not they supported it.

CHU Hsi's dominance was challenged in the Ming dynasty (1368-1643, q.v.) by WANG Yang-ming (1472-1528, q.v.), the founder of the Idealist school. The principal difference between the two schools is that while CHU believed that knowledge ("the investigation of things") was necessary as preparation for right conduct, WANG taught that self-knowledge was the highest kind of learning. Both philosophers are classified as Neo-Confucians.

The final development in traditional Chinese philosophy occurred in the latter half of the Ch'ing dynasty (1644-1911, q.v.) when the Chinese were being affected by a number of Western influences. Among these were the effect of Christian missionaries and the forced acceptance of Western trade. The Chinese became aware that China was not the center of all civilization, but one among many nations more powerful than it. Scholars who wished to challenge the prevailing orthodoxy recognized that in order to get a hearing they must phrase their speculations in orthodox terms. To do this they revived interest in the New Text school of the Han dynasty, which had lost out to the Old Text school some 2000 years earlier. Since they were not abandoning Confucianism their writings were acceptable for discussion. One of the most important thinkers in this group was

K'ANG Yu-wei (q.v.), who wrote of Confucius as a religious leader and political reformer and rejected much of the exegesis of Confucian texts in later ages on the basis that it did not go back to Confucius himself. K'ANG's book the *Ta T'ung Shu* or Book of Great Unity is a utopian outline of the future of mankind in an age of universal peace. While cast in a Chinese mold, it contains a number of non-Chinese ideas and predicts that nations and religions, including Christianity, Confucianism and Islam, will fade away and men's minds will turn to Taoist and Buddhist concepts. Marriage contracts will be limited to one year, the family and private property will vanish. While some of these concepts can be traced to antiquity, the influence of the West can be seen in others.

Fung, Yu-lan, and Derk Bodde, trans. *A History of Chinese Philosophy*. Princeton, Princeton University Press, 1953.

Brière, O., S.J. *Fifty Years of Chinese Philosophy: 1898-1950*. London: George Allen & Unwin, Ltd., 1956.

Pinyin. See under **Romanization**.

Pires, Tomé (c. 1468-1524). The first European envoy to China after the Middle Ages. (Earlier Catholic visitors to China, such as John of Monte Corvino or Odoric of Pordenone (qq.v.), might be classified as envoys from the Pope.) Pires was a Portuguese apothecary who traveled in India and Southeast Asia (1512-1516). In 1516 the Portuguese governor of Goa appointed him envoy to China. He sailed to Canton the following year. In 1520 he went to Peking, arriving in July. In January 1521 the emperor Ming Cheng Te (r. 1506-1521, q.v.), arrived in Peking from a long inspection trip. He was ill and died three months later. All foreign envoys, most of whom were merchants from Central Asia, were ordered to return home. Pires went back to Canton, arriving in the summer. He was imprisoned by the local governor and eventually died there.

Pires's book, the *Suma Oriental*, containing the earliest description of China by a European after Marco Polo (1254-1324, q.v.), is considered the most complete and important account of East Asia produced in the first half of the 16th century.

Goodrich, L.C. and Chaoying Fang, eds. *Dictionary of Ming Biography: 1368-1644*. New York: Columbia University Press, 1976.

PO Chü-yi (BAI Juyi, 772-846). T'ang dynasty (618-906, q.v.) poet and official. PO was born in Honan province (q.v.) and spent his early years living with relatives in that area. His father was a government official assigned to a series of provincial posts to which PO apparently did not accompany him. PO grew up in a period of unrest and at one point was sent to Soochow and Hangchow, south of the Yangtze and a safe distance from disturbances in North China.

He began writing poetry at an early age and passed the imperial examinations (see **Examination system**) in 800. His official career was one of some distinction as he served as governor of Hangchow from 822-824 and Soochow in 825. As an official, he was widely known at the time for the quality of his memorials to the throne, but it is his poetry which has ensured his place in Chinese history. Seven of his poems, including the most famous, the "Song of Unending Sorrow" are included in the collection *Three Hundred Poems of the T'ang Dynasty*.

The "Sorrow" is a poem about the emperor T'ang Ming Huang (q.v.) who lost his throne for the love of his favorite consort, YANG Kuei Fei (q.v.), whose name has become a byword for feminine beauty.

PO's poems are famous for their simplicity. According to tradition he recited them habitually for an illiterate peasant woman and changed the words she did not understand. Having only well-known literary and historical allusions, the poems are relatively easy to translate, with little need for explanatory footnotes. Several hundred of PO's poems have been translated into English, particularly by Arthur Waley.

PO's poetry was greatly appreciated by his contemporaries; it was widely quoted and was inscribed on the walls of village schools and Buddhist temples. (PO was a Buddhist.) PO's poetry also found an appreciative audience in Japan. But the simple quality of PO's poetry declined in popularity during the Ming dynasty (1368-1643, q.v.) when it was criticized as being somewhat common and prosaic.

Waley, Arthur. *The Life and Times of Po Chü-i.* London: Allen & Unwin, 1949.

Polo, Marco (1254-1324). Born in Venice, he was the son of Niccolo Polo and the nephew of Maffeo Polo, traders who in 1260 traveled from Constantinople to the Mongol empire of Khubilai Khan (q.v.). In 1265 the khan sent the two Polos back overland with letters to the pope. (Khubilai's mother was a Nestorian Christian, q.v.) The Polos reached Venice in 1269, and returned to Asia in 1271, taking young Marco with them and carrying letters from Pope Gregory X to the khan.

Marco apparently became a favorite of the khan, and occupied a number of positions in the Mongol administration. The highest was as an official of the city of Yangchow for a three-year period between 1282 and 1287. The Polos left China around 1290, accompanying a Mongol princess on her way to Persia to be married. Since Khubilai died in 1294 at the age of 80, the Polos may have felt that with a change of rulers imminent, it would be politic for them to return home. Traveling largely by sea, they embarked at Zayton (present-day Ch'uanchow, q.v.), reaching Venice in 1295.

Not long after their return, Marco was taken prisoner in a battle between Genoa and Venice. While Marco was in captivity, a fellow prisoner took down an account of his travels, which was circulated widely in manuscript copies before the introduction of printing in Europe.

Polo's book has been translated into many languages, but there is no authentic text because of errors in transcription and because many of the names used were entirely unfamiliar to the copyists. Though for many years Polo's book was regarded as fiction, modern scholarship has confirmed that it is quite accurate. The book includes a vivid account of the Silk Road (q.v.), yet critics have noted that it does not mention the Great Wall (q.v.), the use of tea, the Chinese ideographic script, nor the invention of printing. However, since printing may not have been used for anything but Chinese texts, which were inaccessible to the Polos, or money, the implications and possibilities of such an invention may have escaped them.

According to tradition, Marco Polo was asked on his deathbed to retract the "lies" he had told in his book. His comment was that he hadn't told of one-half the wonders he had seen.

Waugh, Teresa, trans. *The Travels of Marco Polo.* New York: Facts On File, 1985.

Population. Population figures for China were recorded as early as the Han dynasty (206 B.C.-221 A.D., q.v.)

and possibly earlier, but there is disagreement on their exact interpretation. One reason is that the figures were obtained in connection with tax registration, rather than by census. For tax purposes, either the number of adults of working age or the number of households was significant, and some reports give only one or the other figure. Since it is possible only to estimate the average number of persons per household, some margin for error is present. Comparability over time is also problematic since the boundaries of the empire changed from one period to another. In later periods, figures broken down by province (q.v.) exist, but provincial boundaries changed.

The 13th-century scholar MA Tuan-lin wrote that a census taken in the ninth century B.C. (Chou Dynasty, [q.v.], 1122-255 B.C.) gave the figure of 13.7 million persons between the ages of 15 and 65 living north of the Yangtze river, from which an estimated population of 21.7 million has been derived. MA goes on to provide figures from 10 censuses from 2 A.D. to 155 A.D. The range indicated is from 83.6 million in 2 A.D. down to 29.1 million, pointing to the devastation resulting from civil war and banditry in the declining years of the Han dynasty.

SSU-MA Kuang (1019-1086, q.v.) provides a series of figures for the T'ang dynasty (618-906, q.v.), including the following:

740 A.D.	48 million
742	48.9
754	52.9
764	16.9

The sharp drop reflects the terrible toll taken by the rebellion of AN Lu-shan (703-757, q.v.).

E.A. Kracke, Jr. (see end of entry), in commenting on figures given for the Sung dynasty (960-1279, q.v.), notes a fall in population from the figures given at the start of AN Lu-shan's (q.v.) rebellion in 755 to those given for the early years of the Sung. The earlier number of households was 9.6 million, while in 997 A.D. the number was only 4.5 million. He gives a figure of slightly less than 62 million for 1063 A.D.

Figures given for the Yuan dynasty (1279-1368, q.v.) range from 55 to 60 million, in spite of the vast loss of life incurred in the conquest of North China (q.v.). One explanation is that the area occupied by the Tartar Dynasties, Liao (907-1125) and Chin (1115-1234, qq.v.), were not included in the Sung figures.

The best discussions of population for the Ming dynasty (1368-1644, q.v.), the Ch'ing (1644-1911, q.v.) and the 20th century are in the books by HO Ping-ti and Dwight Perkins cited at end of entry. They offer ranges, rather than specific figures, for the reasons noted above. Some of these are 65-80 million for 1393 A.D., 120-200 million for 1600 A.D. and 100-150 million for 1650 A.D. The drop indicates the effect of the calamities which accompanied the fall of the Ming and the Ch'ing conquest. For 1850 the range is 385-534 million, and in 1873 it is 325-375, reflecting the devastation resulting from the Taiping Rebellion (1851-1864, q.v.).

In the 20th century, the figures start at 405-455 million in 1913 and rise to 622-672 million in 1957. Finally, *The Encyclopedic Yearbook of China*, Shanghai, 1980, gives a total of 970,796,400 for the nation, excluding Taiwan. The Foreign Demographic Analysis Division, U.S. Bureau of the Census, monitors a variety of sources, but must depend on Chinese figures. The 1980 total is regarded as credible.

Aird, John S. "Population Growth in Mainland China" in Eckstein, A., W.

Galenson, and T.C. Liu, eds. *Economic Trends in Communist China*. Chicago: Aldine Publishing Co., 1968.

Ho, Ping-ti. *Studies on the Population of China, 1368-1953*. Cambridge: Harvard University Press, 1959.

Kracke, E.A. Jr. *Civil Service in Early Sung China, 960-1067*. Cambridge: Harvard University Press, 1953.

Perkins, Dwight. *Agricultural Development in China*. Chicago: Aldine Publishing Co., 1969.

Port Arthur. This is the English name for the port of Lüshun, at the tip of the Liaotung peninsula in Manchuria (qq.v.). As part of the settlement of the Sino-Japanese War (1894-1895, q.v.), the peninsula was ceded to Japan. Russia, Germany and France forced Japan to return it, but Russia leased the area from China in 1898, and proceeded to turn Port Arthur into a naval base. The Russo-Japanese War (1904-1905, q.v.), left Japan in control of the area, which lasted until the end of World War II (q.v.). Under the terms agreed upon at the Yalta Conference (February 1945, q.v.), the lease of Port Arthur as a naval base was to be restored to the USSR, reversing the outcome of the Russo-Japanese War.

The Soviets declared war on Japan on August 8, 1945, and entered Manchuria the following day. They soon had control of most of the area, including Port Arthur, which they held until 1955, when it was turned over to the People's Republic of China.

Portsmouth, Treaty of. See under **Russo-Japanese War**.

Portugal. The Portuguese were the first Europeans to arrive on the China coast. In 1517 the first Portuguese sailing ship reached China and the Portuguese settlement of Macao (q.v.), the oldest European establishment in China, dates from 1557. Before that, however, the Portuguese had traded at Chuanchow and Foochow in Fukien province, and Ningpo in Chekiang. A Portuguese settlement at Ningpo was attacked in 1545 by the Chinese because of the riotous and objectionable behavior of the settlers. The Portuguese Tomé Pires (q.v.) was the first European envoy to reach Peking after the Middle Ages, in 1520, but he was not received by the emperor.

Portuguese dominance of Asian sea-lanes did not last into the 17th century. While possession of Macao provided Portugal with a unique advantage in that it was the only place in China where Western traders were permitted to live, Portugal's share of the China trade declined. Several Portuguese embassies were sent to Peking in the hope of gaining greater trading advantages, but nothing was achieved. Portugal negotiated two treaties with China in the 19th century, both of which the Chinese regarded as unequal treaties (q.v.).

Portugal was neutral in World War II, and Macao's neutrality was respected by both sides. In 1977 Portugal offered to retrocede Macao to the People's Republic of China (q.v.), but the offer was refused.

Prince Kung. See under **I-hsin**.

Printing. The Chinese used seals carved of wood, ivory or stone, or cast in bronze, to make inked impressions on silk sometime in the first millennium B.C. The invention of paper (q.v.) in the first century A.D. permitted the development of the technique of "rubbing" stone carvings and inscriptions. To do this, dampened paper is applied to the stone and pressed gently into the cavities. Ink is then applied to the raised portions and the result, when dried, is a faithful copy of the original. Since the seals had to be carved in reverse in any case, printing was an obvious next step.

Printing was invented as early as the T'ang dynasty (618-906, A.D., q.v.) and period examples have been found in Sinkiang and Kansu provinces (qq.v.), preserved in the dry climate. However, the earliest example known in 1986 is a printed Buddhist charm found in 1966 in a Korean pagoda. It antedates 751, the date of the structure's completion.

Printed books did not start to displace manuscript copies until sometime in the Sung dynasty (960-1279, q.v.) but by the end of the period they had had considerable impact on the spread of literacy (q.v.). Curiously enough, though Marco Polo (1254-1324, q.v.) spent several years in China at the end of the 13th century, he makes no mention of printing.

The traditional method is as follows: to prepare a printed page, a smooth wooden block would be covered by a page of manuscript, face down. A skilled woodcarver would then cut away all the wood except where ink showed a character should remain. The completed block could be used until worn away.

While this may seem less flexible than movable type, with which the Chinese also experimented, it should be noted that the earliest European printers needed two fonts, upper and lower case, for an alphabet of no more than 26 letters. The Chinese do not distinguish between upper and lower case, but a font of type requires a minimum of 3,000 characters for a modern newspaper.

Because the Chinese started printing some 700 years before Gutenberg produced his bible, some historians believe that it was only in the 18th century that the number of books printed in all the rest of the world exceeded those printed in China alone.

The Chinese adopted movable type in the late 19th century, and now all printing, with an occasional exception, is done that way.

Carter, Thomas F. *The Invention of Printing in China and its Spread Westward.* (Revised by L. Carrington Goodrich.) New York: Ronald Press, 1955.

Twitchett, Denis. *Printing and Publishing in Medieval China.* New York: Frederic C. Beil, 1983.

Provinces. The establishment of provinces as they exist today dates from the early Ming dynasty (1368-1644, q.v.), though they were based on the administration of the preceding Yuan dynasty (1279-1368, q.v.). Earlier dynasties had larger numbers of smaller administrative units reporting directly to the central authorities. This tradition dates from the Ch'in dynasty (221-206 B.C., q.v.) and was designed to prevent the growth of regional power.

Under the Ming, China was divided into 15 provinces, 12 of which have survived to the present, though some of the boundaries have been changed: Chekiang, Fukien, Honan, Kiangsi, Kwangsi, Kwangtung, Kweichow, Shansi, Shantung, Shensi, Szechwan and Yunnan. In the early Ch'ing dynasty (1644-1911, q.v.) three more were added by dividing the Ming province of Hukuang into Hunan and Hupeh, Nan Chihli into Anhwei and Kiangsu, and forming Kansu from part of Shensi plus additional land taken from Inner Mongolia. Pei Chihli simply became Chihli, which means the area around the capital. In 1884, Sinkiang was changed from a dependent territory to a province. In

1903, Manchuria was divided into three provinces, now known as Heilungkiang, Kirin and Liaoning.

The Republic of China (q.v.) added six more: Chahar, Ningsia and Suiyuan, comprising most of Inner Mongolia; Jehol, carved from parts of Chihli, Inner Mongolia and Liaoning; and Sikang and Tsinghai, carved from eastern Tibet and part of Szechwan. They also changed Chihli's name to Hopeh.

The People's Republic of China (q.v.) eliminated Jehol, restoring its parts to Hopei, the Inner Mongolia Autonomous Region and Liaoning. Chahar, Suiyuan and part of Ningsia were also returned to the Inner Mongolia Autonomous Region. Sikang was divided between Szechwan and the Tibetan Autonomous Region.

Taiwan was a prefecture of Fukien province from 1684, the date of undisputed Ch'ing control of the settlements on the west coast of the island, until 1887, when it was made a province. It was ceded to Japan in 1895 after the Sino-Japanese War (1894-1895, q.v.). It was retroceded to the Republic of China in October 1945, after World War II (q.v.). It has been under the control of the Republic of China since then.

Provincial Examinations. See under **Examination system**.

Pure Land sect. Originating in China, this Buddhist sect became the most popular sect in China, Japan and Korea, garnering hundreds of millions of adherents over time. Its philosophical basis was laid by Hui-yuan (334-416 A.D., q.v.), who started out as a Confucian scholar and later became interested in Taoism (q.v.). After his attention was drawn to Buddhism (q.v.) he became a convert.

Hui-yuan taught that salvation might be attained through the Buddha of the future, known as Amitabha, or Amida Buddha, as well as through the teachings of the historical Buddha, Gautama. Since Amitabha has not yet become a buddha, he is immanent as a bodhisattva (q.v.). Salvation would take the form of admission to Amitabha's Western Paradise, and may be achieved merely by pronouncing his name. In modern Mandarin Chinese this is *O-mi-t'o-fo*. Since this means of salvation is available even to the illiterate, which studying abstruse texts is not, the appeal was very great.

However, though salvation was available to all, the texts on which the Pure Land school was based were as complex as those of the other schools. These were the Prajna sutras which had proved so convincing to Hui-yuan in the first place.

The Japanese monk Ennin (793-864 A.D., q.v.) refers to devotees of the Pure Land sect, though he himself belonged to the T'ien T'ai sect (q.v.). Several centuries after his death the Pure Land sect became dominant in Japan.

Wright, Arthur F. *Buddhism in Chinese History*. pbk. ed. New York: Atheneum, 1965.

P'u-yi (1906-1967). Personal name of the last emperor of the Ch'ing dynasty (q.v.). His reign title (q.v.) was Hsüan-t'ung, but unlike his predecessors, he was widely known by his name, and also by the name of Henry P'u-yi. He was a nephew of his predecessor, the emperor Kuang-Hsu, and a grand-nephew of the empress dowager (qq.v.), who personally selected him for the succession shortly before her death. He was enthroned as a child of three, and his reign lasted a mere three years (1909-1911).

Under the abdication agreement of February 12, 1912, he retained his status by the terms of the "Articles of Favorable Treatment." The terms permitted the retention of his title, his residence in the Forbidden City (q.v.), and an annual allowance of 4 million taels (about $3 million) for the imperial establishment.

The Republic of China (q.v.) was proclaimed in 1912, but there was lack of agreement among the various politicians and military men (see under **SUN Yat-sen** and **YUAN Shih-k'ai**) of its administration. YUAN made an abortive attempt to become emperor in 1916, and CHANG Hsün, a warlord who had maintained his loyalty to the Ch'ing dynasty, attempted a restoration in 1917. It lasted less than two weeks.

On November 5, 1924, FENG Yü-hsiang (q.v.) surrounded the Forbidden City with his troops and forced P'u-yi to flee to the house of his father, Prince Ch'un. Some time later he took refuge with the Japanese legation and later still fled to the Japanese Concession in Tientsin, where he lived from February 1925 until November 1931. Much of this time was spent in various intrigues aimed at restoration of the dynasty, presumably with Japanese help. P'u-yi's relations with the Chinese Nationalists were not friendly, and became worse after the Nationalists captured Peking in 1928. Shortly after this the tombs of the emperor Ch'ien-lung (q.v.) and of the empress dowager were broken into and looted, in violation of the Articles of Favorable Treatment.

P'u-yi went to Port Arthur aboard a Japanese ship in November 1931, and the state of Manchukuo (q.v.) was established on March 1, 1932. P'u-yi was head of state, but remained a mere figurehead; all decisions were taken by the Japanese. With the outbreak of the war in the Pacific in 1941, Manchuria became increasingly important to the Japanese war effort, but P'u-yi had little or no role in this.

P'u-yi was captured by Soviet troops in Mukden (q.v.) while fleeing to Japan on August 18, 1945. He spent five years as a Soviet prisoner, though he appeared in Tokyo in August 1946 as a prosecution witness in the war crimes trial. On August 1, 1950, he was turned over to the authorities of the People's Republic of China (q.v.) in Peking as a war criminal. He was kept in prison until granted amnesty in 1959.

P'u-yi died in Peking on October 17, 1967. As in the case of several of his predecessors, there is no certainty of the circumstances surrounding his death.

P'u-yi was the first emperor of China ever to learn a Western language. He studied English under Reginald Johnston, a Scot from the Colonial Office who had spent 20 years in China and spoke fluent Chinese. This took place, however, after the abdication from the throne.

Brackman, Arnold C. *The Last Emperor.* New York: Charles Scribner's Sons, 1975.

Boorman, Howard, ed. *Biographical Dictionary of Republican China.* New York: Columbia University Press, 1967.

Pu Yi. *The Last Manchu.* New York: Putnam, 1967.

Pu Yi, and W.J.F. Jenner, trans. *From Emperor to Citizen: The Autobiography of Aisin-Gioro Pu Yi.* Peking: Foreign Languages Press, 1964-1965.

Qing. See under **Ch'ing**.

Qinghai. See **Tsinghai**.

R

Railroads. The first railway built in China connected Shanghai and Woosung, a distance of 10 miles. It was built by a syndicate of British merchants through some deception, and opened for business in June 1876, in spite of the objections of local Chinese officials. On August 3, 1876, a man walking along the line was killed under circumstances which suggested either suicide for political reasons (i.e., to discredit the foreign backers) or genuine misunderstanding of the threat to life and limb a moving train posed. Traffic was suspended and China bought the line from its owners, tore up the rails and shipped them to Taiwan, where they rusted on the beach.

Chinese objections to railroad construction had several rationales. Popular belief held that the construction of railways would disturb the spirits in the earth (see under **Feng-shui**). At the official level some Chinese felt that construction of railways would render the country more vulnerable to foreign invasion and domination. Others saw the need for railways but wanted them constructed under Chinese rather than foreign supervision and domination.

The next railway built was an extension of the Kaiping coal line down to Tientsin, with a projected extension to Peking. This was done with the support of LI Hung-chang (q.v.). Opposition to the Peking extension was led by CHANG Chih-tung, who proposed instead an inland line from Peking to Hankow.

The disastrous Sino-Japanese War (1894-95, q.v.) showed the dangers of China's lack of development and the extension of the line to a point near Peking was completed by 1896. That same year the construction of the Peking-Hankow railway was mandated, though completion was not until 1905.

Russia's assistance in forcing Japan to disgorge the Liaotung peninsula, ceded by the Treaty of Shimonoseki (q.v.), encouraged the Chinese to approve the construction of the Chinese Eastern Railway (q.v.) by Russia. This link would permit the Russians to reach Vladivostok by rail without following the northerly curve of the Amur river.

Efforts to build a railway south from Tientsin to the Yangtze valley ran into German obstruction as German concessions (q.v.) gave that country special rights in Shantung province. The issue became moot with the outbreak of the Boxer Rebellion (q.v.) in 1900. When the issue was raised again in 1906, the Ch'ing authorities had adopted a policy of constructing and operating railroads under Chinese supervision with the assistance of foreign loans. The line was eventually constructed from Tientsin to Pukow, opposite Nanking.

Construction of railroads in China

during the period before World War II was done with foreign capital and was usually connected with foreign ambitions in specific areas. The Russians were much concerned with the development of Manchuria (q.v.), the British with the Yangtze valley, and the French constructed a line connecting Haiphong in Vietnam (q.v., then French Indochina) with Kunming in Yunnan province, an area which the French hoped to add to their colonial empire. The Americans and the Belgians built the line which connects Canton and Peking, though there was then no bridge across the Yangtze at Hankow.

Most of the railways were constructed in the northeastern quadrant of China, though there have been efforts since then to increase the rail net in other areas.

The railways were severely damaged during the war against Japan and the civil war which followed. Prior to the war, there were about 28,000 kilometers of railway line, but by 1949 only 11,000 kilometers existed. In 1980, there were some 54,400 kilometers (33,800 mi.) of tracks in use.

Chang, Kia-ngau. *China's Struggle for Railroad Development*. New York: John Day & Co., 1943.

Red Chamber, The Dream of. See under **Dream of the Red Chamber**.

Red Eyebrows. This was a sect of religious Taoism (q.v.) which focused peasant dissatisfaction during the reign of WANG Mang (9-23 A.D., q.v.). It is generally considered the first of a long line of peasant rebellions in Chinese history. The Red Eyebrows' rebellion was successful in that WANG was overthrown and the Han dynasty (q.v.) restored in 25 A.D.

Red Guards. Term used to describe the young people who rallied to the call of Chairman MAO Tse-tung (q.v.) in May 1966 for a cultural revolution to combat elitism, revisionism and the "bourgeois mentality" of the bureaucracy. In the period of their activity they are estimated to have numbered as many as 11 million, though their number may have been even higher. They murdered an estimated 400,000 people, destroyed places of worship, vandalized private homes and brought the school system and much of the government to a halt in the late 1960s. After MAO's death in September 1976, the Cultural Revolution (q.v.) was halted and the Red Guards disbanded.

Red Turbans. This term applies to the soldiers who belonged to the White Lotus Society (q.v.), a heterodox Buddhist sect which flourished in the Yangtze valley in the middle of the 14th century. The Red Turbans rebelled against the Yuan dynasty (1279-1368, q.v.) and assisted in the establishment of the Ming (1368-1644, q.v.). The success of the Red Turbans in the early 1350s resulted in the growth of local warlords in the area, sometimes to protect themselves against the Red Turbans, and at other times in order to rebel directly against the Mongol authorities in Peking. In 1358 the Yuan forces were so weakened that the Red Turbans were able to conduct successful campaigns through much of North China (q.v.). They captured Kaifeng (q.v.) in midsummer and the pretender to the earlier Sung dynasty (960-1279), HAN Lin-erh, was installed as Sung emperor in the former capital. He reigned there for about a year.

Other Red Turban forces campaigned successfully in Shantung, Shansi and Shensi. One army swept around the Yuan capital in Peking, invaded Manchuria and got as far as the border with Korea. In 1359 the Red Turbans suffered a severe reversal, partially because none of the Confucian literati would consent to serve them in administrative capacities, and partly because their depredations called opposition forces into being to resist them. The Red Turban forces are described in the official Ming history as pillaging and burning like bandits, in direct contrast with the soldiers under the founder of the dynasty, Ming Hung Wu (r. 1368-1398, q.v.).

After the establishment of the dynasty, and the death in 1366 of Han Lin-erh, the Red Turbans were absorbed into the Ming armies or returned to the general population and their organization ceased to exist. The emperor suppressed the White Lotus Society, and finding his earlier connections with the Red Turbans an embarrassment, tried to eliminate all record of them.

Reign title. Starting early in the Han dynasty (206 B.C.-221 A.D., q.v.) each Chinese emperor on accession to the throne adopted a title by which his reign would be known. Many emperors changed reign titles more than once, in response to some auspicious or inauspicious event. Thus one emperor might have several reign titles, each referring to a specific time period during his overall reign. In the Ming dynasty (1368-1644, q.v.), with one exception, and in the Ch'ing (1644-1911, q.v.), each emperor retained the same reign title throughout his reign. These titles are frequently found in the markings of porcelains of the last two dynasties (though they are no guarantee of authenticity) and are, therefore, familiar to collectors and connoisseurs.

On accession to the throne, use of an emperor's personal name became taboo, and its characters could not be used. (See under **Name taboos**.) After his death, an emperor was given a temple name (q.v.) and a posthumous name by his successor, and these names are usually used by traditional Chinese scholars. Biographic entries on individual emperors in the *Dictionary of Ming Biography: 1368-1644* as well as in *Eminent Chinese of the Ch'ing Period* appear under the personal name of the emperor, with cross-references from the posthumous name, reign title and temple name, but most English-language works use the more familiar reign title.

Republic of China. Less than three months after the outbreak of revolution at Wuchang on October 10, 1911, the Republic of China was proclaimed in Nanking on January 1, 1912, with SUN Yat-sen (1866-1925, q.v.) as its provisional president. Since the military power available to the republican forces was inadequate to control the country, SUN agreed to turn the presidency over to YUAN Shih-k'ai (1859-1916, q.v.), then the most powerful official of the Ch'ing dynasty (1644-1911, q.v.). A key condition was that YUAN would move the seat of government from Peking to Nanking, to escape lingering Ch'ing influence. Since his power base was in the north, YUAN evaded this through a ruse.

YUAN drafted the abdication document for the infant emperor P'u-yi (q.v.), last of the dynasty. The republic was promulgated on February 12, 1912, and included the cession of those areas which had previously acknowledged Ch'ing suzerainty for incorporation into the territory of the republic. Since Manchuria and Sinkiang (qq.v.) had already been incorporated as Chinese provinces, and other territories had been detached by Britain, France, Japan and Russia (qq.v.), what was left were Mongolia and Tibet (qq.v.). This is the legal basis for later claims by the republic and later the People's Republic of China (PRC, q.v.) to sovereignty over these two areas.

The United States was the first major nation to extend recognition, on May 2, 1913. Britain, France, Japan and Russia jointly followed suit on October 10, 1913, the second anniversary of the revolution. The major external problem faced by the republic was encroachment by Japan. World War I (q.v.) started on July 28, 1914, and on August 23 Japan declared war on Germany, attacked the German concessions in Shantung province, and by December had occupied the entire province. On January 28, 1915, Japan presented the Twenty-one Demands (q.v.), which, if accepted, would have given Japan preeminent rights and privileges and would have reduced China to dependent status. With moral support for China from Britain and the United States, Japan was forced to soften the demands, but the treaty signed on May 25, was still a deep infringement on China's sovereignty.

The Republic of China declared war on Germany on August 14, 1917, largely for the purpose of denying Japan permanent title to the German concessions in Shantung. When the Paris Peace Conference awarded the German properties to Japan on April 30, 1919, China refused to sign the Treaty of Versailles (q.v.). Anti-Japanese feelings in China led to the May Fourth Incident (q.v.).

Japan's pursuit of imperialist aims in China was possible because of Chinese disunity. The conflict between YUAN Shih-k'ai with his northern supporters and the southern-based Kuomintang (KMT,

q.v.) surfaced immediately after the establishment of the republic and continued after YUAN's death in 1916. He was followed by a series of presidents (see next entry) some of whom were figureheads and others powerful warlords (q.v.). The period from 1916 to 1928 is frequently called the warlord period because of this. SUN Yat-sen spent part of this period in exile, and part in Canton trying to weld his supporters into a national government.

Not long after the Russian revolutions of March and October 1917, the USSR unilaterally renounced all extraterritorial rights formerly held by the Russian empire, by means of the Karakhan Declaration (q.v.) of July 25, 1919. It was welcomed by the Chinese, who noted that none of the other powers seemed inclined to follow suit. Soviet efforts to influence the Chinese revolution led to the agreement between SUN and a Soviet official, Adolf Joffe, in January 1923, under which the KMT would accept individual members of the Chinese Communist party (CCP, q.v.) as members, and the KMT would cooperate with the CCP and the USSR. Soviet advisors were sent to Canton to work with SUN and to organize the KMT.

Diplomatic recognition between the USSR and the Republic of China was marked by the Sino-Soviet Treaty of May 31, 1924 (q.v.). China protested the September signing of a separate treaty between the USSR and CHANG Tso-lin (1873-1928, q.v.), the warlord of Manchuria (q.v.), who did not recognize the authority of the Peking government.

SUN died in March 1925, and in January 1926 the second KMT National Congress found CHIANG Kai-shek (1887-1975) and WANG Ching-wei (1883-1944, qq.v.) as the new leaders, with CCP and Soviet support. In

August 1926, CHIANG launched the Northern Expedition (q.v.), an effort to unify the country by force of arms. The last provisional president of the republic at Peking, TUAN Ch'i-jui (1865-1936, q.v.) withdrew from his office in March 1926, and until the establishment of the new government at Nanking in October 1928, China had no head of state.

The Northern Expedition was an initial success, and by early 1927 the Nationalists had occupied the major centers of the Yangtze valley. Reflecting the internal split in the KMT, there were two seats of government, CHIANG's in Nanking, and WANG Ching-wei's in Wuhan. In April 1927, CHIANG purged the CCP members in his area, and WANG followed suit in July. The CCP members regrouped and organized the Nanchang Uprising (q.v.) of August 1, 1927, opening the warfare between the two parties which lasted, with some interruptions, for more than 20 years.

The summer of 1927 also saw an attempt at unifying the Nanking and Wuhan factions of the KMT. CHIANG suffered a military reversal in August, and in the interests of party harmony retired as commander of the National Revolutionary Army. However, he returned to his post in early 1928 and resumed the Northern Expedition. Nationalist troops set out to capture Peking, which they did in June, renaming it Peiping. On the way, they clashed with Japanese troops in Tsinan, capital of Shantung province, causing many casualties on both sides. CHIANG, who had received a military education in Japan and was conscious of Chinese military inferiority, was unwilling to risk a major confrontation. In spite of Chinese indignation at the incident, he ordered the troops to detour and continue their campaign.

On October 10, 1928, the National Government was formally established in Nanking, with CHIANG as its chairman. It was organized in five branches, called yuan, following SUN's theories: Executive, Judicial, Legislative, Examination (recruitment of officials) and Control (investigation and review of other branches). In December, CHANG Hsueh-liang (1898- , q.v.), son and heir of CHANG Tso-lin and the new ruler of Manchuria, declared his allegiance to Nanking. On paper, at least, the Republic of China was unified.

The national government explicitly announced its intention to carry out the programs outlined by SUN Yat-sen in his "Three Principles of the People" (q.v.), which have been translated as nationalism, democracy and the people's livelihood. A new constitution, the "Organic Law of the National Government," was adopted and an agenda of social and economic policies was prepared. In the economic field, land reform, designed to ameliorate the poverty of the peasants, was planned. A new monetary system was introduced to replace the confusing use of different currencies in different areas (see under **Money**). The likin (q.v.), an internal customs tax introduced as a temporary expedient during the Taiping Rebellion (1851-1864, q.v.) was eliminated in 1931. Afforestation of areas which had been barren of trees for centuries was begun, and a start was made in systematic flood control. In the social field, the most important step was the provision of free primary education in the first six grades.

Disunity within the KMT continued, however, and in August 1930, an alternative government was established in Peiping. It soon collapsed, but another was set up in Canton in May 1931. The Japanese invasion of Manchuria in September 1931, caused a national emergency.

Reconciliation between the two factions was accomplished by CHIANG's temporary retirement. He was succeeded as head of state by LIN Sen (1868-1943, q.v.), who held the post until his death, although he wielded little power. CHIANG retained his position as head of the KMT and commander of Nationalist troops.

CHIANG made Chinese unification his main priority. The Japanese invasion of Manchuria averted civil war among KMT factions and various warlords, but the CCP enclaves were a constant reminder that the objective had not been achieved. CHIANG pressed hard against them and finally, in October 1934, overran the base in Kiangsi province from which MAO Tse-tung (q.v.) led the Long March (q.v.) to a remote refuge at Yenan, Shensi province.

CHANG Hsueh-liang and his Manchurian troops had been ousted from their homeland by the Japanese and were ordered to attack the CCP forces at Yenan. Unwilling to fight other Chinese while the Japanese continued their occupation, CHANG and the CCP arranged a de facto ceasefire, and in December 1936, kidnapped CHIANG Kai-shek, who was on an inspection trip, in the Sian Incident (q.v.), forcing him to agree to a united front against the Japanese.

On July 7, 1937, the Japanese attacked Chinese troops in the Marco Polo Bridge Incident (q.v.), which quickly escalated into full-scale war. Peiping and Tientsin fell within the month, but CHIANG's crack German-trained troops defended Shanghai from August until November, suffering heavy casualties. The Rape of Nanking (q.v.) marked the capital's fall in December. The Chinese government moved to Hankow, and in October 1938 to Chungking. By early 1939 Japan controlled all major Chinese cities on or near the coast, and banned all imports of war material. Limited supplies could reach China only through the Burma Road (q.v.) and the railway through French Indochina, now Vietnam (q.v.).

The Japanese invasion brought most of the Nationalist's social and economic programs to a halt. All efforts were turned to resistance and survival. Many Chinese left the Japanese-occupied areas and traveled long distances to the remote areas still under Chinese control. Faculty and students from many institutions went together. China's plight generated considerable international sympathy, but little more. The USSR signed a nonaggression pact with China in August 1937, and agreed to sell some planes and munitions.

World War II (q.v.) started in Europe in September 1939, and France fell in June 1940. Japan forced the closure of the Burma Road that summer, and the Indochina railway in September, thus isolating China completely. In October 1940, Britain reopened the Burma Road. On December 7 (December 8 in Asia), 1941, Japan attacked the United States at Pearl Harbor and Britain at Hong Kong. At once, China had allies, but the fall of Rangoon, Burma, in March 1942, closed the Burma Road again, leaving China dependent on the U.S. airlift from Assam, India, over the southern spur of the Himalayas to Kunming and Chunking. By May, the Japanese had occupied most of Burma and threatened to cut the airlift either by invading India or moving up the Burma Road to capture Kunming.

Japan's surrender in August 1945, found the Republic of China seriously weakened. The U.S. airlift had managed to increase tonnage, and the first truck convoy on the reopened Burma Road reached Kunming in February

1945. But the economy suffered from a high inflation rate and serious dislocations. Allied perceptions of China's inability to make a major contribution to the defeat of Japan led to major concessions to the USSR at China's expense at the Yalta Conference (1945, q.v.). Under its terms, Soviet troops entered Manchuria on August 9 to accept the surrender of Japanese troops. They then looted or destroyed the Japanese industrial plant, and turned surrendered Japanese weapons over to CCP troops moving in from nearby North China.

Efforts to mediate in the rivalry between the CCP and the KMT by U.S. Ambassador Patrick J. Hurley (q.v.) in 1945, and by the Marshall Mission (q.v.) in 1946, were unsuccessful. By mid-1946 the Civil War (q.v.) had started. It ended in 1949 with the establishment of the PRC on October 1, and the flight of the Republic of China to Taiwan.

Relations between the Republic of China and the United States, its major ally, deteriorated significantly after World War II. CCP successes in the Civil War led to U.S. doubts that KMT forces could hold Taiwan. The start of the Korean War on June 25, 1950, caused a drastic reversal in U.S.

policy, and relations improved. In 1954 a mutual defense treaty was signed. Economic aid was provided in significant quantities until 1964, when it was deemed to have accomplished its objectives.

With the gradual improvement of relations between the United States and the PRC, the international position of the republic declined. In 1969 the United States lifted restrictions on trade and travel with the PRC. In 1971 the republic was ousted from the United Nations, of which it had been a founding member. In 1972 President Richard Nixon visited China and the Shanghai Communiqué (q.v.) was issued on his departure. In 1973 liaison offices were established in Peking and Washington. In December 1978 President Jimmy Carter announced that diplomatic relations with the PRC would be established on January 1, 1979.

The U.S. embassy in Taiwan was closed and diplomatic relations with the republic ended. The U.S. action was followed by many other nations, and as of 1986 the republic has diplomatic relations with 23 nations, though it has trade relations with 100 more.

REPUBLIC OF CHINA PRESIDENTS

PEKING GOVERNMENT

SUN Yat-sen (provisional)	January-February 1912
YUAN Shih-k'ai (provisional)	February 1912-October 1913
YUAN Shih-k'ai	October 1913-June 1916
LI Yuan-hung	June 1916-July 1917
FENG Kuo-chang	July 1917-October 1918
HSÜ Shih-ch'ang	October 1918-June 1922
LI Yuan-hung	June 1922-June 1923
TS'AO K'un	October 1923-November 1924
TUAN Ch'i-jui (provisional)	November 1924-April 1926

CHIANG Kai-shek	October 1928-December 1931
LIN Sen	December 1931-August 1943
CHIANG Kai-shek	October 1943-January 1949
LI Tsung-jen	January 1949-February 1950
CHIANG Kai-shek	March 1950-April 1975
YEN Chia-kan	April 1975-May 1978
CHIANG Ching-kuo	May 1978-

Rhubarb. The root of the rhubarb (*Rheum officinale*, etc.) is a purgative and was a major Chinese export to the West from the 16th to 19th centuries.

Ricci, Father Matteo (1552-1610). Born in Macerata, Italy, Ricci entered the Society of Jesus (see **Jesuits**) in 1571. He volunteered for the Far Eastern Mission and sailed from Lisbon in 1578 on the six-month trip which took him to Goa. He was ordained to the priesthood there in 1580, and was ordered to Macao in 1582. He immediately started his study of the Chinese language and over a period of several years achieved a very high level of proficiency in both the spoken and written languages, almost certainly the first Western European to accomplish this.

In 1583 Ricci accompanied Father Michele Ruggieri to establish the first Christian presence inside China since the Yuan dynasty (1279-1368, q.v.). At first Ricci dressed like a Buddhist monk, but deciding that acceptance by the Confucian literati was essential to his mission, he obtained permission from his superiors to adopt the latter style. He worked out a standardized romanization (q.v.) system for the spelling of Chinese words in the Roman alphabet, and devised suitable Chinese terms for the expression of Christian ideas.

In 1595 he moved to Nanking, the secondary capital, hoping that by so doing he could broaden his contacts with the educated class and would be one step closer to getting imperial approval for missionary work. Such approval, he felt, would reduce or eliminate occasional difficulties caused by anti-foreign sentiment or the backlash of Chinese politics. Because of the invasion of Korea by the Japanese TOYOTOMI Hideyoshi (q.v.), whose aim was the conquest of China, Ricci left Nanking and settled in Nanchang, the capital of Kiangsi province. Three years later he was invited to travel with a high Chinese official to Peking.

China of the Ming dynasty (1368-1644, q.v.) was very different from the Cathay (q.v.) described by Marco Polo (1254-1324, q.v.), and there was some question whether it was the same country. Ricci's first visit to Peking was brief, but it permitted him to make astronomical observations and to gather information about the city which convinced him that Peking was Marco Polo's Khanbalic (Cambaluc) and that China and Cathay were one and the same. In 1599 Ricci moved again to Nanking and it was there he made the acquaintance of HSÜ Kuang-ch'i, the most influential Christian convert of the period. Ricci also revised an earlier map of the world, the first published in China giving a reasonably accurate idea of foreign countries and their geographic locations. It was well received by the literati.

In May 1600, Ricci started again for Peking, convinced that imperial approval for missionary activity could be obtained only by personal application. Unfortunately, he was delayed for several months by a powerful eunuch named MA T'ang, who prevented him from proceeding. In January 1601, an imperial edict ordering the foreigners and their gifts to Peking released them from the eunuch's power. The gifts pleased the emperor, particularly some religious paintings, a spinet and two clocks. The paintings made use of perspective, which was handled in a totally different fashion by Chinese painters. The result was considered almost frighteningly realistic. The clocks amused the emperor by striking the hours. Several palace eunuchs were put to work learning to play the spinet.

Ricci lived the last nine years of his life in Peking, dying in 1610. His presence there was accepted as tacit approval by the emperor, and his circle of friends expanded. In 1608, in a letter to his brother in Italy, he put the number of Christians in China at "more than 2,000." Ricci's knowledge of astronomy, geography and mathematics were far more important to most of the Chinese he met than the religion he professed. His long residence in China and his fluency in both spoken and written Chinese enabled him to deal with members of the ruling class who would otherwise have been inaccessible.

Cronin, Vincent. *The Wise Man From the West*. New York: E.P. Dutton, 1955.

Dunne, George H., S.J. *Generation of Giants*. Notre Dame: University of Notre Dame Press, 1962.

Rites, Board of. (See under **Board of Rites.**)

Rites Controversy. This term refers to the question of whether it is permissible for a Chinese Christian to perform the Confucian rites known as "ancestor worship" (q.v.). Matteo Ricci and other Jesuits (q.v.) held that Confucianism (q.v.) was not a religion, and that performance of the rites was devoid of theological content and was not to be equated with worship in a Buddhist or Taoist temple. The Dominicans and Franciscans, on the other hand, held that a Christian could not in good conscience perform the rites. The issue was hotly debated by Catholic theologians during the 17th century and resulted in a decision by the Congregation of Rites in Rome in 1704 which proscribed any such activity.

Cronin, Vincent. *The Wise Man From the West*. New York: Dutton, 1955.

Dunne, George H., S.J. *Generation of Giants*. Notre Dame: Indiana, University of Notre Dame Press, 1962.

Gernet, Jacques, and Janet Lloyd, trans. *China and the Christian Impact: A Conflict of Cultures*. Cambridge: Cambridge University Press, 1986.

Roman Empire. While there was no direct contact between the Roman Empire and the contemporary Han dynasty (206 B.C.-221 A.D., q.v.), the two powers were aware of each other. Trade was conducted through Parthia, and from the Chinese side consisted largely of silk (q.v.).

The Romans referred to the Chinese as *Seres*, identified only as the people located somewhere in eastern Asia, who produced silk. The Chinese referred to the Roman Empire as *Ta Ch'in* (sometimes romanized as *Ta Ts'in*). Chinese records show at least two instances of foreigners who claimed to come from *Ta Ch'in* reaching Han China.

The Chinese method of dealing

with embassies (see under Foreign Relations) was to accept the gifts they brought and return even greater largesse. This continued even up to the 18th century. As a result, many groups of foreign merchants represented themselves as emissaries from distant lands. It seems unlikely that Roman Emperor Marcus Aurelius knew that anyone was representing him in Han China.

In 73 A.D. PAN Ch'ao started on an expedition to the west which led him to the shores of the Caspian Sea. He was aware of the empire of Ta Ch'in further to the west, but no contact was made.

Ta Ch'in is sometimes equated with Syria, or the Middle East, rather than Rome. The Nestorian Christian (q.v.) monument of the T'ang dynasty (q.v.) refers to that creed as the "luminous religion of Ta Ch'in."

In 643, T'ang T'ai Tsung (q.v.) received envoys from "the king of Rome," according to the T'ang historical records, who complained of Arab incursions into their territory.

Franck, Irene M., and Brownstone, David M. *The Silk Road.* New York: Facts On File, Inc., 1986.

The Romance of Three Kingdoms. In Chinese *San Kuo Chih Yen Yi.* This is the oldest extant Chinese novel, compiled by LO Kuan-chung (c. 1330-1400) in the late Yuan dynasty (1279-1368) or early Ming (1368-1644, qq.v.). LO utilized stories of the period of the Three Kingdoms (221-265 A.D., q.v.) at the fall of the Han dynasty in 221. The Three Kingdoms were trying to unify the empire, each under its own sway. In fact, unity was not achieved until 589, under the Sui dynasty (q.v.).

The period of the Three Kindgoms bears some resemblance to that of the Warring States Period (q.v.) of the late Chou dynasty, and also a slight similarity to the period of Arthurian legend in English history. The events chronicled in the *Romance* are fictionalized, and the heroes wear mantles of nobility not always confirmed by historical sources.

The novel itself has possibly been read by more people than any other in world history. It was a favorite of hundreds of millions of Chinese, to say nothing of Japanese, Koreans and Vietnamese. It is reported that Thailand's King Bhumibol recommended it to American President Richard Nixon as an indispensable aid in learning to understand the traditional Chinese mind. Its attraction lies not in its narrative, for it is more a historical review than a well-plotted novel, but in its stirring account of chivalrous actions and devious military stratagems.

Many of the incidents in the novel have been used as plots in Chinese opera, thus expanding its influence far beyond the millions who have read it. The key figures in the novel have become a part of traditional culture. They include TS'AO Ts'ao, a gifted general who founded the kingdom of Wei; LIU Pei, who ruled in Shu; CHU-KO Liang, an official in Shu, not a soldier but the greatest strategist of the time; CHANG Fei, sworn blood brother of LIU Pei; and KUAN Yü, a wily general who fought for both Wei and Shu and became apotheosized as the God of War (qq.v.).

A complete English translation of the *Romance* was produced early in the 20th century by C.H. Brewitt-Taylor.

Hsia, C.T. *The Classic Chinese Novel.* New York: Columbia University Press, 1968.

Romanization. Because of the nature of the Chinese written language (q.v.), it is necessary for certain purposes to use a phonetic system to indicate the pronunciation. When such a system uses the Roman alphabet, as English does, it is called romanization, and many such systems exist. The system used in this book is called Wade-Giles, and was developed in the 19th century by Sir Thomas Wade (q.v.) and modified by H.A. Giles. In common with all other systems, Wade-Giles has shortcomings. Its greatest strength is that it is the most widely used; most of the scholarly apparatus (i.e., books, articles, dictionaries, library indexes, etc.) is keyed according to it.

In the Wade-Giles system, all "a"s are pronounced like the "a" in "father." If "ch", "k", "p" and "t" are followed by an apostrophe, pronounce them as you would in English. If there is no apostrophe, pronounce them as "j", "g", "b" and "d".

In this book geographic entries are spelled in the former Post Office system, since that was used on maps, and in gazetteers, etc. This system tries to approximate the local pronunciation in many cases, e.g., Amoy, Hong Kong. It also introduced the spelling *Shensi* for one of China's provinces. The problem is that there is an adjacent province called *Shansi*. The difference in pronunciation is in the tone of the first syllable, a distinction which the Chinese speaker can hear easily enough, and since the characters used are quite different, no problem arises in writing. In romanization confusion arises. The former Post Office system handles it as indicated above. The new pinyin system spells Shensi as *Shaanxi* to differentiate it from *Shanxi*.

The pinyin romanization was developed in the mid-1950s in the People's Republic of China (q.v.) and has been adopted as the standard romanization there. It neatly solves the problem of some initial consonants by adding "b", "d" and "g"

and eliminating apostrophes to indicate voiceless initials. However, for an English speaker these advantages are mitigated by the introduction of other initial sounds which may be phonetically distinct, but which have no phonemic function. Thus, the initial sound in *ch'in* is spelled "q" and that in *ch'an* is spelled "ch".

The chart below shows the equivalence of the two systems.

CONVERSION TABLE FOR ROMANIZATION SYSTEMS

Wade-Giles	pinyin
a	a
ai	ai
an	an
ang	ang
ao	ao
cha	zha
ch'a	cha
chai	zhai
ch'ai	chai
chan	zhan
ch'an	chan
chang	zhang
ch'ang	chang
chao	zhao
ch'ao	chao
che	zhe
ch'e	che
chei	zhei
chen	zhen
ch'en	chen
cheng	zheng
ch'eng	cheng
chi	ji
ch'i	qi
chia	jia
ch'ia	qia
chiang	jiang
ch'iang	qiang
chiao	jiao
ch'iao	qiao

Wade-Giles	pinyin	Wade-Giles	pinyin
chieh	jie	fa	fa
ch'ieh	qie	fan	fan
chien	jian	fang	fang
ch'ien	qian	fei	fei
chih	zhi	fen	fen
ch'ih	chi	feng	feng
chin	jin	fo	fo
ch'in	qin	fou	fou
ching	jing	fu	fu
ch'ing	qing		
chiu	jiu	ha	ha
ch'iu	qiu	hai	hai
chiung	jiong	han	han
ch'iung	qiong	hang	hang
cho	zhuo	hao	hao
ch'o	chuo	hei	hei
chou	zhou	hen	hen
ch'ou	chou	heng	heng
chu	zhu	ho	he
ch'u	chu	hou	hou
chua	zhua	hsi	xi
ch'ua	chua	hsia	xia
chuai	zhuai	hsiang	xiang
ch'uai	chuai	hsiao	xiao
chuan	zhuan	hsieh	xie
ch'uan	chuan	hsien	xian
chuang	zhuang	hsin	xin
ch'uang	chuang	hsing	xing
chui	zhui	hsiu	xiu
ch'ui	chui	hsiung	xiong
chun	zhun	hsü	xu
ch'un	chun	hsüan	xuan
chung	zhong	hsüeh	xue
ch'ung	chong	hsün	xun
chü	ju	hu	hu
ch'ü	qu	hua	hua
chüan	juan	huai	huai
ch'üan	quan	huan	huan
chüeh	jue	huang	huang
ch'üeh	que	hui	hui
chün	jun	hun	hun
ch'ün	qun	hung	hong
		huo	huo
e, o	e		
en	en	i, yi	yi
eng	eng		
erh	er	jan	ran

Wade-Giles	pinyin	Wade-Giles	pinyin
jang	rang	kun	gun
jao	rao	k'un	kun
je	re	kung	gong
jen	ren	k'ung	kong
jeng	reng	kuo	guo
jih	ri	k'uo	kuo
jo	ruo		
jou	rou	la	la
ju	ru	lai	lai
juan	ruan	lan	lan
jui	rui	lang	lang
		lao	lao
jun	run	le	le
jung	rong	lei	lei
		leng	leng
ka	ga	li	li
k'a	ka		
kai	gai	lia	lia
k'ai	kai	liang	liang
kan	gan	liao	liao
k'an	kan	lie	lieh
kang	gang	lian	lien
k'ang	kang	lin	lin
kao	gao	ling	ling
k'ao	kao	liu	liu
ke,ko	ge	luo	lo
k'e,k'o	ke	lou	lou
kei	gei	lu	lu
ken	gen	luan	luan
k'en	ken	lun	lun,lün
keng	geng	long	lung
k'eng	keng	lü	lü
ko,ke	ge	lüan	lüan
k'o,k'e	ke	lüe	lüeh
kou	gou		
k'ou	kou	ma	ma
ku	gu	mai	mai
k'u	ku	man	man
kua	gua	mang	mang
k'ua	kua	mao	mao
kuai	guai	mei	mei
k'uai	kuai	men	men
kuan	guan	meng	meng
k'uan	kuan	mi	mi
kuang	guang	miao	miao
k'uang	kuang	mie	mieh
kuei	gui	mian	mien
k'uei	kui	min	min

Wade-Giles	pinyin	Wade-Giles	pinyin
ming	ming	p'en	pen
miu	miu	peng	beng
mo	mo	p'eng	peng
mou	mou	pi	bi
mu	mu	p'i	pi
		piao	biao
na	na	p'iao	piao
nai	nai	pieh	bie
nan	nan	p'ieh	pie
nang	nang	pien	bian
nao	nao	p'ien	pian
nei	nei	pin	bin
nen	nen	p'in	pin
neng	neng	ping	bing
ni	ni	p'ing	ping
niang	niang	po	bo
niao	niao	p'o	po
nie	nieh	pou	bou
nian	nien	p'ou	pou
nin	nin	pu	bu
ning	ning	p'u	pu
niu	niu		
no	nuo	sa	sa
nou	nou	sai	sai
nu	nu	san	san
nuan	nuan	sang	sang
nun	nun	sao	sao
nung	nong	se	se
nü	nü	sen	sen
nüeh	nüe	seng	seng
		sha	sha
o, e	e	shai	shai
ou	ou	shan	shan
		shang	shang
pa	ba	shao	shao
p'a	pa	she	she
pai	bai	shei	shei
p'ai	pai	shen	shen
pan	ban	sheng	sheng
p'an	pan	shih	shi
pang	bang	shou	shou
p'ang	pang	shu	shu
pao	bao	shua	shua
p'ao	pao	shuai	shuai
pei	bei	shuan	shuan
p'ei	pei	shuang	shuang
pen	ben	shui	shui

Wade-Giles	pinyin	Wade-Giles	pinyin
shun	shun	tsang	zang
shuo	shuo	ts'ang	cang
so	suo	tsao	zao
sou	sou	ts'ao	cao
ssu,szu	si	tse	ze
su	su	ts'e	ce
suan	suan	tsei	zei
sui	sui	tsen	zen
sun	sun	ts'en	cen
sung	song	tseng	zeng
szu,ssu	si	ts'eng	ceng
		tso	zuo
ta	da	ts'o	cuo
t'a	ta	tsou	zou
tai	dai	ts'ou	cou
t'ai	tai	tsu	zu
tan	dan	ts'u	cu
t'an	tan	tsuan	zuan
tang	dang	ts'uan	cuan
t'ang	tang	tsui	zui
tao	dao	ts'ui	cui
t'ao	tao	tsun	zun
te	de	ts'un	cun
t'e	te	tsung	zong
tei	dei	ts'ung	cong
teng	deng	tu	du
t'eng	teng	t'u	tu
ti	di	tuan	duan
t'i	ti	t'uan	tuan
tiao	diao	tui	dui
t'iao	tiao	t'ui	tui
tieh	die	tun	dun
t'ieh	tie	t'un	tun
tien	dian	tung	dong
t'ien	tian	t'ung	tong
ting	ding	tzu	zi
t'ing	ting	tz'u	ci
tiu	diu		
to	duo	wa	wa
t'o	tuo	wai	wai
tou	dou	wan	wan
t'ou	tou	wang	wang
tsa	za	wei	wei
ts'a	ca	wen	wen
tsai	zai	weng	weng
ts'ai	cai	wo	wo
tsan	zan	wu	wu
ts'an	can		

Wade-Giles	pinyin	Wade-Giles	pinyin
ya	ya	ying	ying
yai	yai	yu	you
yang	yang	yung	yong
yao	yao	yü	yu
yeh	ye	yüan	yuan
yen	yan	yüeh	yue
yi,i	yi	yün	yun
yin	yin		

pinyin	Wade-Giles	pinyin	Wade-Giles
a	a	chao	ch'ao
ai	ai	che	ch'e
an	an	chen	ch'en
ang	ang	cheng	ch'eng
ao	ao	chi	ch'ih
		chong	ch'ung
ba	pa	chou	ch'ou
bai	pai	chu	ch'u
ban	pan	chua	ch'ua
bang	pang	chuai	ch'uai
bao	pao	chuan	ch'uan
bei	pei	chuang	ch'uang
ben	pen	chui	ch'ui
beng	peng	chun	ch'un
bi	pi	chuo	ch'o
bian	pien	ci	tz'u
biao	piao	cong	ts'ung
bie	pieh	cou	ts'ou
bin	pin	cu	ts'u
bing	ping	cuan	ts'uan
bo	po	cui	ts'ui
bou	pou	cun	ts'un
bu	pu	cuo	ts'o
ca	ts'a	da	ta
cai	ts'ai	dai	tai
can	ts'an	dan	tan
cang	ts'ang	dang	tang
cao	ts'ao	dao	tao
ce	ts'e	de	te
cen	ts'en	dei	tei
ceng	ts'eng	deng	teng
cha	ch'a	di	ti
chai	ch'ai	dian	tien
chan	ch'an	diao	tiao
chang	ch'ang	die	tieh

pinyin	Wade-Giles	pinyin	Wade-Giles
ding	ting	han	han
diu	tiu	hang	hang
dong	tung	hao	hao
dou	tou	he	ho
du	tu	hei	hei
duan	tuan	hen	hen
dui	tui	heng	heng
dun	tun	hong	hung
duo	to	hou	hou
		hu	hu
e	e,o	hua	hua
en	en	huai	huai
eng	eng	huan	huan
er	erh	huang	huang
		hui	hui
fa	fa	hun	hun
fan	fan	huo	huo
fang	fang		
fei	fei	ji	chi
fen	fen	jia	chia
feng	feng	jian	chien
fo	fo	jiang	chiang
fou	fou	jiao	chiao
fu	fu	jie	chieh
		jin	chin
ga	ka	jing	ching
gai	kai	jiong	chiung
gan	kan	jiu	chiu
gang	kang	ju	chü
gao	kao	juan	chüan
ge	ke,ko	jue	chüeh
gei	kei	jun	chün
gen	ken		
geng	keng	ka	k'a
gong	kung	kai	k'ai
gou	kou	kan	k'an
gu	ku	kang	k'ang
gua	kua	kao	k'ao
guai	kuai	ke	k'e,k'o
guan	kuan	ken	k'en
guang	kuang	keng	k'eng
gui	kuei	kong	k'ung
gun	kun	kou	k'ou
guo	kuo	ku	k'u
		kua	k'ua
ha	ha	kuai	k'uai
hai	hai	kuan	k'uan

pinyin	Wade-Giles	pinyin	Wade-Giles
kuang	k'uang	mo	mo
kui	k'uei	mou	mou
kun	k'un	mu	mu
kuo	k'uo		
		na	na
la	la	nai	nai
lai	lai	nan	nan
lan	lan	nang	nang
lang	lang	nao	nao
lao	lao	nei	nei
le	le	nen	nen
lei	lei	neng	neng
leng	leng	ni	ni
li	li	nian	nien
lia	lia	niang	niang
lian	lien	niao	niao
liang	liang	nie	nieh
liao	liao	nin	nin
lie	lieh	ning	ning
lin	lin	niu	niu
ling	ling	nong	nung
liu	liu	nou	nou
long	lung	nu	nu
lou	lou	nuan	nuan
lu	lu	nun	nun
luan	luan	nuo	no
lun	lun, lün	nü	nü
luo	lo	nüe	nüeh
lü	lü		
lüan	lüan	ou	ou
lüe	lüeh		
		pa	p'a
		pai	p'ai
ma	ma	pan	p'an
mai	mai	pang	p'ang
man	man	pao	p'ao
mang	mang	pei	p'ei
mao	mao	pen	p'en
mei	mei	peng	p'eng
men	men	pi	p'i
meng	meng	pian	p'ien
mi	mi	piao	p'iao
mian	mien	pie	p'ieh
miao	miao	pin	p'in
mie	mieh	ping	p'ing
min	min	po	p'o
ming	ming	pou	p'ou
miu	miu	pu	p'u

pinyin	Wade-Giles	pinyin	Wade-Giles
qi	ch'i	shou	shou
qia	ch'ia	shu	shu
qian	ch'ien	shua	shua
qiang	ch'iang	shuai	shuai
qiao	ch'iao	shuan	shuan
qie	ch'ieh	shuang	shuang
qin	ch'in	shui	shui
qing	ch'ing	shun	shun
qiong	ch'iung	shuo	shuo
qiu	ch'iu	si	ssu,szu
qu	ch'ü	song	sung
quan	ch'üan	sou	sou
que	ch'üeh	su	su
qun	ch'ün	suan	suan
		sui	sui
ran	jan	sun	sun
rang	jang	suo	so
rao	jao		
re	je	ta	t'a
ren	jen	tai	t'ai
reng	jeng	tan	t'an
ri	jih	tang	t'ang
rong	jung	tao	t'ao
rou	jou	te	t'e
ru	ju	teng	t'eng
ruan	juan	ti	t'i
rui	jui	tian	t'ien
run	jun	tiao	t'iao
ruo	jo	tie	t'ieh
		ting	t'ing
sa	sa	tong	t'ung
sai	sai	tou	t'ou
san	san	tu	t'u
sang	sang	tuan	t'uan
sao	sao	tui	t'ui
se	se	tun	t'un
sen	sen	tuo	t'o
seng	seng		
sha	sha	wa	wa
shai	shai	wai	wai
shan	shan	wan	wan
shang	shang	wang	wang
shao	shao	wei	wei
she	she	wen	wen
shei	shei	weng	weng
shen	shen	wo	wo
sheng	sheng	wu	wu
shi	shih		

pinyin	Wade-Giles	pinyin	Wade-Giles
xi	hsi	zang	tsang
xia	hsia	zao	tsao
xian	hsien	ze	tse
xiang	hsiang	zei	tsei
xiao	hsiao	zen	tsen
xie	hsieh	zeng	tseng
xin	hsin	zha	cha
xing	hsing	zhai	chai
xiong	hsiung	zhan	chan
xiu	hsiu	zhang	chang
xu	hsü	zhao	chao
xuan	hsüan	zhe	che
xue	hsüeh	zhei	chei
xun	hsün	zhen	chen
		zheng	cheng
ya	ya	zhi	chih
yai	yai	zhong	chung
yan	yen	zhou	chou
yang	yang	zhu	chu
yao	yao	zhua	chua
ye	yeh	zhuai	chuai
yi	yi, i	zhuan	chuan
yin	yin	zhuang	chuang
ying	ying	zhui	chui
yong	yung	zhun	chun
you	yu	zhuo	cho
yu	yü	zi	tzu
yuan	yüan	zong	tsung
yue	yüeh	zou	tsou
yun	yün	zu	tsu
		zuan	tsuan
za	tsa	zui	tsui
zai	tsai	zun	tsun
zan	tsan	zuo	tso

Russia. Individual Russians served in China under the Yuan dynasty (1279-1368, q.v.), but the first contact between the two countries occurred in the Ming dynasty (1368-1644, q.v.). Russian explorers and traders appeared in Siberia in the 16th century, and by 1639 had reached the Sea of Okhotsk, an arm of the Pacific Ocean. Russian embassies reached Peking in 1567 and 1619, but failed to gain access to the emperor. In 1655 a third Russian embassy reached Peking, by then under the rule of the Ch'ing dynasty (1644-1911, q.v.). The ambassador refused to perform the kotow (q.v.) and was refused an audience.

The Ch'ing dynasty was Manchu (q.v.), not Chinese. It controlled Manchuria (q.v.) and claimed suzerainty over many ethnic groups living in adjacent areas, from Korea to Mongolia (qq.v.). Whatever the northern limits of their domain, they regarded the Russians as unwelcome interlopers.

Border skirmishes convinced the emperor K'ang Hsi (r. 1662-1722, q.v.) that the matter must be settled. The result was the Treaty of Nerchinsk (1689, q.v.), which called for the removal of the Russian outpost at Albazin on the Amur river, and defined the boundary as following the watershed between the valleys of the Lena and the Amur rivers, leaving the entire basin of the Amur to the Ch'ing. The treaty was the first between China and a Western power, and was noteworthy for being negotiated between two putative equals (a drastic departure from Chinese custom), and for laying the basis for extraterritoriality (q.v.). It also permitted trade between Russia and China.

While the treaty delimited the boundary between the two empires in the Manchurian area, it did not mention the boundary farther west in Outer Mongolia, since the Khalkhas of the area had not accepted Ch'ing suzerainty. They did so in 1691, the Russians then suggesting delimiting the boundary in the west. This was done by the Treaty of Kiakhta (1727, q.v.), which also restricted the Russian caravans to Kiakhta, instead of Peking, and provided for the establishment of a Russian hostel in Peking for four Russian students of languages (Chinese, Manchu and Mongol) and for two Russian Orthodox priests, as well as a chapel, all at the expense of the Ch'ing state. Emperor Yung Cheng (r. 1723-1735, q.v.) also sent two embassies to Moscow, which arrived there in 1731 and 1732. They were the first to be sent to a Western country, and no more were sent until the reign of the emperor T'ung Chih (1862-1874, q.v.).

By the beginning of the 19th century, the Ch'ing dynasty was in decline, while Russia was still strong. In 1806, two Russian ships put in at Canton, at the time the only port in China open to Western trade. The Russians completed their transactions just before the arrival from Peking of instructions forbidding it, on the grounds that Russia had access through Kiakhta on the land frontier, and could not also claim access by sea. In 1850 Russia asked for authorization of trade at Ili (Kuldja), Tarbagatai (Chuguchak) and Kashgar in Turkestan (Sinkiang). By the Treaty of Kuldja (1851) China agreed to the first two, but refused Kashgar.

In the second half of the 19th century four issues dominated relations between China and Russia. The first was the trade issue just mentioned. Russia had not participated in the Opium War (1839-1842, q.v.), but was aware of the great increase in trade at the treaty ports (q.v.) opened under the terms of the Treaty of Nanking (1842, q.v.). In 1857 Russia sent Admiral Count Euphemius Putiatin to Peking by sea to present Russia's case. He was not permitted to go beyond Tientsin, and so went to Hong Kong, where he joined the American, British and French envoys, then concerned with the *Arrow* War (1857-1860, q.v.). Like his American counterpart, he was under instructions to avoid belligerency, but both signed the Treaties of Tientsin (1858, q.v.). The importance for Russia was the inclusion of the "most-favored-nation" clause (q.v.) which automatically granted access to the treaty ports.

The second issue was Manchuria. Russia offered arms and assistance in suppressing the Taiping Rebellion (1851-1864, q.v.) in exchange for the northern reaches of Manchuria, which was refused. However, the

Ch'ing authorities, pressed by internal rebellion and the external *Arrow* War with Britain and France, agreed to negotiate with Russia. In the Treaty of Aigun (1858, q.v.) which resulted, the Russian negotiator, Nikolai Muraviev, governor of Siberia, obtained agreement to the Amur river, as far as its junction with the Ussuri, as the northern boundary and the Ussuri river as the eastern boundary. The land between the Ussuri and the sea was to be jointly administered.

The treaty was not ratified by Ch'ing authorities, but was overtaken by the events of 1860, in which the French and British fought their way to Peking and burned the Summer Palace (q.v.). There was no Russian participation in these events, but Putiatin was able to negotiate the Treaty of Peking (1860, q.v.), which superseded the Treaty of Aigun. The new treaty confirmed the Amur and Ussuri boundaries, but gave Russia the land between the Ussuri and the sea, now the Maritime Province of the USSR. Muraviev lost no time in founding the city of Vladivostok at the southern end of the territory, and in making the Russian presence felt. But Russian ambitions in Manchuria were not satisfied, as later events were to show.

The third issue was the status of Turkestan (Sinkiang, q.v.). The decline of Ch'ing power coincided with the rise of Russian power in Central Asia, and Russia was absorbing semi-independent khanates. A Muslim rebellion in Turkestan in 1864 aimed at resisting both Chinese and Russian influence. In 1871, Russia occupied Ili, announcing publicly it would be returned when the Chinese could reassert their authority. By 1873 the Muslim leader Yakoob Beg (q.v.) was in control of most of Turkestan, but by 1878 the Chinese general TSO Tsung-

t'ang (q.v.) had reconquered the area. The matter was settled by the treaties of Livadia (1879) and St. Petersburg (1881, qq.v.).

The fourth issue was Korea (q.v.). The acquisition of the Maritime Province gave the Russians a common border with Korea, and they immediately requested diplomatic relations. Korea acknowledged Chinese suzerainty and had no relations with any other powers. This isolation was broken by Japan (q.v.), which forced a treaty of amity and commerce on Korea in 1876. It was followed by treaties with several other powers, and in 1886 a treaty with Russia. Russian attempts to exert influence in Korea were dwarfed by the struggle between China and Japan, which led to the Sino-Japanese War (1894-1895, q.v.), and the Treaty of Shimonoseki (1895, q.v.), which effectively established Japan's dominance.

The terms of the treaty included, among other things, Chinese recognition of Korean independence and the cession of the Liaotung peninsula (q.v.) in southeast Manchuria. Since Russia considered all of Manchuria as within its own sphere of influence, it offered its good offices to prevent any alienation of Manchurian territory. With the support of France and Germany, Russia pressured Japan to retrocede Liaotung.

In 1896 a secret treaty with the Chinese statesman LI Hung-chang (q.v.) gave Russia the right to build the Chinese Eastern Railway (q.v.) across Manchuria. By avoiding the route of the Amur river, it drastically shortened the distance between Irkutsk and Vladivostok. In 1898, Russia leased the Liaotung peninsula, built a naval base at Port Arthur (q.v.) and won the right to build the South Manchurian Railway, linking the Chinese Eastern Railway with Port

Arthur and Dairen (q.v.). At the outbreak of the Boxer Rebellion (1900, q.v.), Russia strengthened its military presence in Manchuria, and after peace was restored, delayed in removing it.

Japan retaliated for perceived slights with the Russo-Japanese War (1904-1905, q.v.), which deprived Russia of Port Arthur and the Liaotung peninsula. While China did not participate, the war was fought on Chinese soil, and the objective was Chinese territory and privileges. Russian influence in Manchuria did not disappear. Russia continued to run the Chinese Eastern Railway with Harbin as its administrative center.

The Republic of China (q.v.) was established in 1912, but was not recognized by Russia until October 10, 1913, in concert with Britain, France and Japan. The articles of abdication by the last emperor had been drafted by YUAN Shih-k'ai (q.v.) and gave title to all Ch'ing territory to the new republic. This included Manchuria, Mongolia, Sinkiang and Tibet (qq.v.). There were independence movements in Mongolia and Tibet (qq.v.). There were independence movements in Mongolia and Tibet, and the Mongols asked for Russian support.

Bolshevik revolution of November, proved welcome to the Peking government (q.v.), properly described as a warlord regime at this point. Recognition by the Chinese government was not the Soviets' main concern in the years immediately following the revolution. Anti-Bolshevik activity throughout the former Russian empire had resulted in several European possessions gaining or regaining their independence. Similar activity in Asia, aided most importantly by Japan, but also including China and other countries, threatened to deprive the Soviets of Russia's Asiatic territories. The main Soviet objective was to prevent this, and the secondary objective was to support movements in Manchuria, Mongolia and Sinkiang which might detach those areas from China. On July 25, 1919, through the Karakhan Declaration (q.v.), the USSR became the first of the foreign powers to renounce all extraterritorial rights, as well as its share of the Boxer Indemnity (q.v.). By early 1920, the Soviets had the situation in Asia under control, and shortly thereafter Peking ordered the Tsarist representatives to leave. Final recognition came with the signing of a treaty on May 31, 1924.

Negotiation of the treaty was protracted because of two main issues: Outer Mongolia and the Chinese Eastern Railway. The Soviets had signed a secret treaty with the People's Revolutionary Government of Mongolia on November 4, 1921, and Soviet support for the Mongols was evident. In the treaty with China, the Soviet government recognized that Outer Mongolia was an integral part of the Republic of China. The treaty confirmed Soviet ownership of the railway, but allotted to China control of political, military and police matters in the railway zone. Manchuria, however, the location of the railway, was not under the control of the Peking government, but instead under the warlord CHANG Tso-lin (q.v.). He declared that the treaty did not apply in Manchuria, but signed a separate agreement on September 20, 1924, at Mukden (q.v.), thus setting a precedent for Soviet recognition of Manchurian autonomy. The Peking government protested.

Even before the establishment of diplomatic relations, Russian and other foreign Communists were active in China, working to influence the political situation and to establish the

Chinese Communist party (CCP, q.v.). Soviet advisers were accepted by SUN Yat-sen (q.v.) and the Kuomintang (KMT, q.v.) and were ejected only in March 1926 by CHIANG Kai-shek (q.v.) in a purge of the "right" faction of the KMT. On April 6, 1927, CHANG Tso-lin, the Manchurian warlord and by then the de facto ruler in Peking, raided the Soviet embassy there and seized several truckloads of documents in both Chinese and Russian, which spelled out in detail the Communist plans for China. In July, M.N. Roy, the Comintern representative at Wuhan, the base of the "left" faction of the KMT, revealed the Comintern's plans for China, which led to the expulsion of all Soviet advisers and a purge of all Communists.

On May 27, 1929, Chinese police raided Soviet consulates in four Manchurian cities and seized documents indicating that the USSR was disseminating Communist propaganda in violation of the agreement of 1924. On July 10, the Chinese seized the telephone and telegraph system of the Chinese Eastern Railway, and replaced its Russian officials with Chinese. They also arrested or deported several hundred Russian employees. On July 13, the USSR presented an ultimatum demanding a return to the *status quo ante*. This was refused and led to a break in diplomatic relations. After several months of border skirmishes, the Soviets invaded in force in November 1929, and captured several Manchurian cities, thus forcing the local authorities to return to the status quo. The national government in Nanking was also forced to come to terms, though diplomatic relations were not restored until December 12, 1932, after Japan had established the puppet state of Manchukuo (q.v.) and had made a naval attack on Shanghai.

In March 1935, the Soviets turned over control of the Chinese Eastern Railway to Manchukuo at a price representing a small fraction of the total investment.

The Marco Polo Bridge Incident, July 7, 1937 (q.v.), opened the war between China and Japan. Though divided by ideological differences, common fear of Japan led the antagonists to sign the Sino-Soviet Non-Aggression Treaty in Nanking on August 21. By 1939 Japan had occupied most of China's coastal cities, and the Nationalist government was beleaguered in Chungking. Seeking to assure a free hand in China and the rest of Asia, Japan signed a neutrality pact with the USSR on April 13, 1941. The trickle of Soviet aid to China through Sinkiang came to a halt.

In any case, the outbreak of World War II (q.v.) in Europe on September 1, 1939, overshadowed developments in China. France fell in June 1940, and the German invasion of the USSR started on June 22, 1941. Japan attacked the U.S. fleet at Pearl Harbor on December 7, and in 1942 occupied most of Southeast Asia. These military actions led the Atlantic powers to ally themselves with China in Asia, and with the USSR in Europe, but since the USSR was not at war with Japan, it was not a four-power alliance.

China did not participate in either the Tehran Conference of November-December 1943, nor the Yalta Conference of February 1945 (qq.v.), but Chinese interests were at stake. At Tehran, President Roosevelt suggested that a warm-water port at Dairen (q.v.) might be justified recompense to the USSR for participating in the war against Japan. At Yalta, several concessions at China's expense were agreed upon: restoration of rights which Russia had lost in the Russo-

Japanese War, and those renounced by the treaty of 1924; a Soviet "preeminent" interest in an internationalized port at Dairen; the lease of Port Arthur, as a naval base, to the USSR; and a joint Soviet-Chinese company to operate the Chinese Eastern and South Manchurian Railways.

At Yalta, the USSR agreed to go to war against Japan within two or three months after the end of the war in Europe. The USSR gave notice of the termination of the Soviet-Japanese neutrality pact on April 5, 1945, two days before the German surrender. The USSR was pledged not to go to war until a year after such notice, but two things urged quicker action: Japanese requests to mediate with the United States, and the dropping of the first atomic bomb on August 6. On August 8 the second bomb was dropped, and the USSR declared war on Japan. On August 9 Soviet troops entered Manchuria, and by the end of the month had occupied the whole area. In November they announced the postponement of their withdrawal until 1946.

To clarify the terms of the Yalta agreement, the national government negotiated the Sino-Soviet Treaty of Friendship and Alliance, signed in Moscow on August 14, 1945. It confirmed the Yalta terms, but went beyond them in giving the Soviets the lease of half the facilities at Dairen, free of charge. It also noted China's agreement to recognize the independence of Outer Mongolia "should a plebiscite . . . confirm this desire."

In the exchange of notes accompanying the treaty, the USSR recognized Chinese sovereignty in Manchuria and promised to give moral support and military aid solely to the "National Government as the central government of China." However, when the Soviets took over Manchuria in August 1945, they turned surrendered Japanese arms over to Chinese Communist troops and impeded Nationalist troops in their efforts to reach Manchuria. They also stripped the Japanese industrial plant in the area, contending it was war booty. Soviet actions in Manchuria were in striking contrast to their policy in northern Korea, where no such stripping took place.

The Chinese Communists, having won the Civil War (1945-1949, q.v.), established the People's Republic of China (PRC, q.v.) on October 1, 1949, in Peking. The USSR recognized the PRC on October 2. The Republic of China severed relations with the USSR on October 3.

Relations between the USSR and the PRC were unlike anything that had gone before. The CCP had been the recipient of Soviet guidance since its founding in 1921, though the advice was frequently ignored. Many observers, both inside and outside the two nations, assumed that friendly cooperation would characterize the relationship, and that was the case until 1956. During that period the USSR provided the arms and material for the North Korean invasion of South Korea, and then for the Chinese "volunteers" who entered the war in late 1950. They also agreed to the turnover of Soviet interests in Manchurian railways, evacuated Port Arthur and Dairen, and signed an agreement on nuclear cooperation. Soviet aid to China in the period up to 1959, when it was withdrawn, has been estimated at some 250 projects: factories, dams, laboratories etc. More than 10,000 Soviet technicians assisted, and some 13,000 Chinese students and specialists were trained in the USSR. Soviet loans to China totaled more than $2 billion.

The relationship cooled in 1956, after the 20th Party Congress of the CPSU, at which Nikita Khrushchev denounced Stalin, who had died in 1953. The first Chinese reaction was positive, but was followed by attacks on Yugoslav "revisionists." The Soviets countered with attacks on Albanian "dogmatists," but it soon became clear that the targets were the USSR and the PRC, with the smaller nations acting as surrogates. The USSR was abandoning the cult of Stalin, but China was not prepared to do so. The USSR also attacked Chinese policies such as the introduction of communes, and the Great Leap Forward (q.v.).

Ideological differences also intensified border disputes. China considered the treaties of Aigun and Peking, which determined the present-day borders of Manchuria, to be unequal, since they had been forced upon a weakened Ch'ing empire. During the 1960s there was a massing of troops on both sides of the border, and in October 1966, during the Cultural Revolution (q.v.), as many as 2 million Chinese were reported to have demonstrated on the Soviet frontier. In February 1967 the Soviet embassy in Peking was under siege, and all Chinese frontier troops were put on the alert. In 1969 fighting broke out on a disputed island in the Ussuri river, which separates Heilungkiang from the Soviet Maritime Province, and several soldiers were killed.

The death of MAO Tse-tung (q.v.) in 1976, and the gradual liberalization of the Chinese economy have provided fresh fuel for mutual animosity. The 30-year Sino-Soviet Treaty of Friendship was not renewed when it expired in April 1980. Other sources of friction included Soviet support for Vietnam in its border conflict with China (1978-1979) and in the Vietnamese invasion of Cambodia. In December 1979 the Soviet invasion of Afghanistan caused more Chinese criticism.

The death of Soviet leader Leonid Brezhnev in November 1982 has led to a slight improvement in relations, but three issues remain intractable: Afghanistan, Vietnam, and the large numbers of Soviet troops on China's borders. As of 1985, relations are correct but cool.

Clubb, O. Edmund. *China and Russia.* New York: Columbia University Press, 1971.

United States Relations with China. Washington: Department of State, 1949.

Mancall, Mark. *Russia and China: Their Diplomatic Relations to 1728.* Cambridge: Harvard University Press, 1971.

Jones, Peter, and Siân Kevill. *China and the Soviet Union: 1949-1984.* New York: Facts On File, Inc., 1985.

Russo-Japanese War (1904-1905). China was not an official participant in the war, but it was fought on Chinese soil, as well as at sea, and the prizes sought were Chinese territory and/or privileges on such territory. In the Sino-Japanese War (1894-1895, q.v.), Japan had detached Korea from Chinese suzerainty, and had obtained the cession of the Liaotung peninsula (q.v.) and Taiwan. Pressure from France, Germany and Russia forced Japan to return Liaotung, but in 1898 Russia obtained the area on lease. Japan was determined to avenge that slight and did so.

Japan broke off diplomatic relations with Russia on February 5, 1904, and launched an attack on Port Arthur (q.v.) on February 9. Port Arthur surrendered on January 1, 1905. The Russian Baltic fleet sailed in October 1904 for the Far East. It proceeded around Africa, put in at Camranh Bay, then a French naval base in Indochina, and steamed north to the Straits of Tsushima, where it was defeated by Admiral Togo on May 27-28, 1905. This was the first major military battle in which an Asian power defeated a European power, ending a series dating back to the Battle of Lepanto in 1571.

The war was settled by the Treaty of Portsmouth (q.v.), signed September 5, 1905. It required the Russians to surrender the Liaotung peninsula to the Japanese, and to evacuate Manchuria. It also ceded the southern half of Sakhalin to Japan. Japan's special position in Korea was recognized, and it was agreed that the sovereignty of Korea should not be mentioned in any international treaty. Japan annexed Korea in 1910, but lost all the gains mentioned in World War II.

Ryukyu Islands. See **Liu-ch'iu Islands**.

St. Petersburg, Treaty of. February 24, 1881. Signed by TSENG Chi-tse (1839-1890), son of TSENG Kuo-fan (1811-1872, q.v.), for China and Nicholas de Giers for Russia. It superseded the Treaty of Livadia (1879, q.v.), and provided for the return of more land to the Ch'ing empire than its predecessor. It also provided a larger indemnity to Russia and authorized the opening of additional Russian consulates in China.

Clubb, O. Edmund. *China and Russia*. New York: Columbia University Press, 1971.

Schall von Bell, Father John Adam, S.J. (1591-1666). One of the most prominent of the Jesuits (q.v.) in the China mission, Father Schall was born in Cologne, Germany, and reached China in 1622. He spent most of the rest of his life in Peking. A trained mathematician and astronomer, as well as a priest, Father Schall accurately predicted a lunar eclipse in Peking on October 8, 1623, and another in September of the following year. In 1630 he was appointed to the Imperial Board of Astronomy, one of whose most important functions was the publication of the official calendar.

The presence of Christian missionaries in the Board of Astronomy aroused opposition from the other astronomers, but the accuracy of their calculations carried the day with the imperial court. After the transfer of power to the Ch'ing dynasty (q.v.) in 1644, Schall continued with the Board and became a favorite of the emperor Shun Chih (r. 1644-1661, q.v.). He was eventually made a mandarin of the first class, the highest rank that any European ever achieved under the Ch'ing. Schall hoped to convert the young emperor to Christianity, and his failure to do so was at least partially due to Shun Chih's unwillingness to practice monogamy.

Shun Chih died in 1661, and soon after Schall was accused of having selected an inauspicious burial day for the deceased infant son of the late emperor. In fact, Schall had had nothing to do with the selection of the date, but the charge, if true, would have been treasonable in the eyes of the court, since it might have contributed to the emperor's death.

All Christians were removed from the Board of Astronomy, and several Chinese converts among them were executed. In November 1664 Schall and the three other Jesuits in Peking were imprisoned. Schall was sentenced to death, and the others to deportation. The sentences were canceled because of a bad omen—an earthquake which caused a fire in the imperial palace. The Jesuits were released in May 1665, and Schall died in August 1666.

Dunne, George H., S.J. *Generation of Giants*. Notre Dame: University of Notre Dame Press, 1962.

Second Revolution. The term refers to the events of 1913. The newly formed Kuomintang (KMT, q.v.) won a majority of the seats in the national assembly in the elections of February 1913, and hoped to impose parliamentary control on President YUAN Shih-k'ai (1859-1916, q.v.). KMT leader SUNG Chiao-jen was assassinated on March 20, probably by agents of YUAN. SUN Yat-sen (1866-1925, q.v.) was in Japan but returned to Shanghai and called for a complete investigation. In June YUAN dismissed three provincial governors who were KMT members, and sent his army south from Peking to the Yangtze valley. The KMT governor in Kiangsi province declared his independence and organized the Kiangsi Anti-YUAN Army, but the northern forces had little trouble routing the KMT troops and in September captured Nanking.

YUAN formally dissolved the KMT in November and the assembly in January 1914. The Second Revolution had failed, leaving YUAN free to rule as an autocrat, though opposition continued until his death in 1916.

Secret History of the Mongols. This text, written in Mongolian using Uighur (q.v.) script, was completed sometime in the 13th century. An account of Mongol history prior to the establishment of the Yuan dynasty (1279-1368, q.v.), it was found by officials of the Ming dynasty (1368-1644, q.v.) when Peking was captured in 1367. It was incorporated in the encyclopedia prepared for the emperor Ming Yung Lo (r. 1403-1424, q.v.) in a transliteration in Chinese characters with an accompanying translation into Chinese, and is known as the *Yuan Ch'ao Pi Shih*. The term "secret history" refers to the fact that it was for the exclusive use of the ruling family. The dynastic history (q.v.) of the Yuan was compiled and published under the Ming dynasty, according to Chinese custom, and covers a later period.

Cleaves, Francis W., ed. and trans. *The Secret History of the Mongols*. Cambridge: Harvard University Press, 1982.

Kahn, Paul. *Secret History of the Mongols*. San Francisco: North Star, 1984.

Seng-ko-lin-ch'in (Senggerinchin). A hereditary Mongol prince (d. 1865), descended from the first of the Inner Mongolians to pledge loyalty to the Manchus. This gave the family preeminence throughout the Ch'ing dynasty (1644-1911, q.v.). Seng-ko-lin-ch'in's first great military achievement occurred during the Taiping Rebellion (1850-1864, q.v.), when he defeated the Taiping army sent to conquer Peking in 1853. This was shortly after the establishment of the Taiping government in Nanking. He defeated them again in 1854, and in 1855 his forces annihilated the remnant Taiping army in Shantung, earning him great honors from the court.

In 1858, during the *Arrow* War (q.v.), British and French forces occupied the forts at Taku, near Tientsin, and negotiated the Treaties of Tientsin (q.v.). Seng-ko-lin-ch'in was sent to direct defense in the region. When the allied forces returned south for the winter, he reinforced the defenses and blockaded the river. Upon their return in 1859 to exchange ratifications of the treaties, they found their passage blocked. The following year the allies landed August 1, and on September 21 defeated Seng-ko-lin-ch'in in battle. The following day the emperor fled the Summer Palace for Jehol (qq.v.). Three weeks later allied troops entered Peking and then destroyed the Summer Palace.

Seng-ko-lin-ch'in was stripped of his rank, but was sent to fight against the Nien rebels (q.v.), mostly in

Shantung province, where he was successful. His titles were restored and he continued his successful campaign against the Nien. He was killed in ambush in 1865 after a month-long pursuit of rebel troops.

The high esteem in which Seng-ko-lin-ch'in was held by the court is indicated by the fact that his name was placed in the imperial family temple, one of only two non-Manchus to be so honored in the entire dynasty. (The other was Tsereng [d. 1750], also a Mongol.)

Hummel, Arthur W., ed. *Eminent Chinese of the Ch'ing Period*. Washington: Government Printing Office, 1943.

Shaanxi. See **Shensi**.

Shandong. See **Shantung**.

Shang dynasty (1766-1122 B.C.). The dates are traditional and were regarded with skepticism by modern historians, but archaeological evidence tends to confirm them. The Shang followed the Hsia (q.v.) and ushered in the Bronze Age. Much that is known about Shang culture is a result of the excavations at Anyang (q.v.), Honan, which was the Shang capital.

The Shang ruling class indulged in warfare and hunting. At the time of death a ruler would be buried with his favorite hunting dogs and his retainers, in later centuries replaced with effigies.

In the view of many scholars, the two most significant aspects of the Shang culture were the introduction of metalworking (i.e., bronze) and the creation of a written language (q.v.). Shang bronzes are widely regarded as among the most impressive ever made. Many are ritual objects such as wine beakers, though whether they were ever used for such a purpose is open to question. Others are weapons, such as knives and halberds. Shang possession of the requisite skill in casting bronze undoubtedly led to its dominance of the Hsia and other neighbors.

The development of the written language may have been even more important, though the discovery of Shang inscriptions is almost entirely a 20th-century development. Many of the bronzes from Anyang have brief inscriptions, and most of these have now been deciphered. Characters were also inscribed on bones and turtle shells. These were then subjected to fire and the resulting cracks in the bone and shell would indicate good or bad luck. (See **Oracle bones**.)

The development of a written language made the Shang the first literate group in Asia east of the Urals. The fact that there were some 2,000 characters in use in the period suggests a great number of years in the evolution of Shang language.

The Shang also had developed silk to a degree indicating that its use started even earlier.

The name of the first Shang king was T'ang and the last was Chou. In accordance with traditional belief, the first was a paragon and the last was execrable, a dissolute ruler whose crimes caused the downfall of the dynasty. There are 28 Shang kings on the traditional list. The 17th changed the dynastic title from Shang to Yin. The traditional history was transmitted by SSU-MA Ch'ien in his *Shih Chi* (qq.v.).

Chang, Kwang-chih. *The Archaeology of Ancient China*. New Haven: Yale University Press, 1968.

Li, Chi. *The Beginnings of Chinese Civilization*. Seattle: University of Washington Press, 1957.

Shanghai. China's largest city, its population is over 11 million (1980). It is also China's largest port, located near the mouth of the Yangtze river, and is a municipality directly administered by the central government. Settlements in the area date back to the T'ang dynasty (618-906 A.D., q.v.), but Shanghai's rise to prominence occurred in the 19th century. Its garrison was defeated by the British in the Opium War (1839-1842, q.v.), and it was one of the first treaty ports opened by the Treaty of Nanking (1842, qq.v.).

Shanghai's growth as a port was phenomenal, and by 1936 an estimated 60,000 Westerners were resident in the city, making it second only to Harbin as a Western enclave in China. The city's growth also attracted Chinese from many provinces, particularly those with a taste for entrepreneurial activities.

Natives of Shanghai speak one of the Wu dialects, which pose problems for the speaker of Mandarin, though less so than the Fukien and Kwangtung dialects. English was widely spoken in Shanghai at one time, and many residents still speak it.

The literary name for Shanghai is *Hu*. When the Nanking-Shanghai railway was opened it was called the *Ching-hu* railway, *ching* (*jing*) for Nanking and *hu* for Shanghai.

Shanghai is also the home of one of China's best-known cuisines.

Shanghai Communiqué (February 27, 1972). Issued at the conclusion of meetings between U.S. President Richard Nixon and Premier CHOU En-lai (q.v.) of the People's Republic of China (PRC), the communiqué sets forth policy positions on Japan, Korea, South and Southeast Asia. However, the key statements refer to Taiwan. The PRC statement says, in part: "The liberation of Taiwan is China's internal affair in which no other country has the right to interfere . . . ." The U.S. statement says, in part:

"The United States acknowledges that all Chinese on either side of the Taiwan Strait maintain there is but one China and that Taiwan is a part of China. The U.S. Government does not challenge that position. It reaffirms its interest in a peaceful settlement of the Taiwan question by the Chinese themselves."

Shang Yang (d. 338 B.C.). Original name: KUNG-SUN Yang. Shang Yang is also known as Lord Shang. A contemporary of Mencius (q.v.), he was a Legalist (see under **Legalism**). As a chief administrator of the state of Ch'in (q.v.) he was responsible for many of the totalitarian practices with which that state is identified. The laws he introduced were extremely strict and punishments were many and drastic. Lord Shang himself incurred the displeasure of the heir apparent, and when the latter succeeded to the throne, Lord Shang was executed.

The *Book of Lord Shang*, attributed to him, is almost certainly a later compilation. However, it gives an accurate representation of his views.

Duyvendak, J.J.L. *The Book of Lord Shang*. London: Probsthain, 1928.

Shansi (Shanxi) **province**. Area: 150,000 sq. km. (58,000 sq. mi.). Population: 24,472,000 (1980). Capital: Taiyuan. Shansi is bounded on the east by Hopeh province, on the southeast by Honan, on the west by Shensi, and on the north by Inner Mongolia (qq.v.).

Shansi lies on a high plateau (1,000 meters) of loess soil. It produces wheat, kaoliang (sorghum) and millet. In the present day its minerals, bituminous and anthracite coal, are more important than its agriculture.

Shantung (Shandong) **province**. Area: 150,000 sq. km. (58,000 sq. mi.).

Population: 72,310,000 (1980). Its capital is Chi-nan (Tsinan). The eastern region of Shantung is a peninsula with the Pohai Gulf on the north and the Yellow Sea on the southeast. It is bounded on the south by Kiangsu and Anhwei provinces, on the west by Honan and on the northwest by Hopeh.

Shantung was the site of the state of Lu, where Confucius was born, and also the home of Mencius (qq.v.). For this reason, the German concessions of 1898 and the Japanese assumption of them after World War I were particularly offensive to classical scholars and those Chinese of the Confucian persuasion.

Shanxi. See **Shansi**.

Shen Nung. The second of three emperors of the legendary period (q.v.), he reigned from 2737 to 2697 B.C. One translation of the name is "divine husbandman," and Shen Nung is credited with the introduction of agriculture to the world.

SHENG Shih-ts'ai (1895-   ). Warlord and ruler (1933-1944) of Sinkiang province (q.v.), SHENG was born in Manchuria and studied political economy in Japan, returning to China in time to participate in the May Fourth movement (q.v.) of 1919. He studied in military academies in Kwangtung province, Manchuria and Japan. He participated in the Northern Expedition (1926-1928, q.v.) and then went to Sinkiang, arriving in 1930. As aide to the governor, he established an officer-training program, but his work was disrupted by a local rebellion. Efforts to crush this were unsuccessful until the arrival of Chinese troops from Manchuria in 1933. (They had been forced out by the Japanese invasion of 1931.) The rebels continued fighting, however,

with the support of Muslim coreligionists from Kansu province, and in January 1934, SHENG obtained the support of Soviet troops, forcing the rebels to retreat.

SHENG continued his amicable relations with the Soviets and on May 16, 1935, signed an agreement by which he obtained a loan and technical assistance. After the outbreak of the war between China and Japan—the Marco Polo Bridge Incident (q.v.), July 7, 1937—Soviet troops were stationed at Hami, in eastern Sinkiang, about 100 miles from the border of Kansu province. In 1938 SHENG made a trip to Moscow and joined the Communist party of the Soviet Union. He signed another pact on November 24, 1940, which granted the Soviets economic rights in Sinkiang for 50 years.

1941 brought a change of heart. Soviet reverses in the war against Germany provided an opportunity for China's Nationalist government to bid for SHENG's support, if not loyalty. In April the Nationalists appointed SHENG governor of Sinkiang, and in October 1942 SHENG ordered the Soviets out. They left in 1943 and SHENG joined the Kuomintang (q.v.). The Nationalists then proceeded to bring Sinkiang under more direct control and finally brought SHENG to Chungking (q.v.) in September 1944.

SHENG's record in Sinkiang had been one of bloodshed, and he was not popular in China. He was given the post of Minister of Agriculture and Forestry, but was later moved to a less prominent position. He went to Taiwan before the Communist victory on the mainland in 1949.

Boorman, Howard L., ed. *Biographical Dictionary of Republican China*. New York: Columbia University Press, 1967.

Whiting, Allen S., and Sheng Shih-ts'ai. *Sinkiang: Pawn or Pivot?* East Lansing: Michigan State University Press, 1958.

Shengking. Former name of Liaoning province (q.v.).

Shensi (Shaanxi) **province**. Area: 190,000 sq. km. (73,500 sq. mi.). Population: 28,070,000 (1980). Capital: Sian (Xi'an, q.v.). Shensi is bounded on the east by Shansi and Honan provinces, on the southeast by Hupeh, on the south by Szechwan, on the west by Kansu and Ningsia, and on the north by Inner Mongolia (qq.v.).

Shensi is one of the earliest areas of Chinese civilization and dominance. The capital, Sian, is the site of former capitals of the Chou dynasty (1122-256 B.C.), the Ch'in (256-206 B.C.), the Han (206 B.C.-221 A.D.) and the T'ang (618-906, qq.v.).

Yenan (Yanan), the Communist capital in World War II, is situated in Shensi.

Shenyang (Mukden). Capital of Liaoning province (q.v.), it has a population of 4 million (1978). Shenyang was selected in 1616 as the capital of the Later Chin empire by its founder Nurhaci (1559-1626, qq.v.). His son Abahai (1592-1643, q.v.), also had his capital there. Since Abahai changed the dynastic name to Ch'ing in 1636, Shenyang is known as the Ch'ing capital before the dynasty was established in Peking in 1644. It contains palaces which were used as summer retreats by later emperors of the Ch'ing dynasty (1644-1911, q.v.). Shenyang is now one of China's major industrial centers.

Shih Chi. The first history of China, written by SSU-MA T'an and his son, SSU-MA Ch'ien (qq.v.) during the reign of emperor Han Wu Ti (r. 140-86 B.C., q.v.), it covers the period from the earliest mythical times up to the early years of the Han dynasty. The writers had access to the annals of the state of Ch'in and those of the state of Lu, of the Warring States Period (qq.v.), but the other annals had been destroyed by the Ch'in rulers at the time of the establishment of the Ch'in dynasty (q.v.).

The earlier annals had been simply a chronological listing of events, but the *Shih Chi* is organized in five sections: Basic Annals, Chronological Tables, Treatises, Hereditary Families and Biographies. The annals are highly compressed accounts of the principal events in Chinese history. The chronological tables are a schematic attempt to coordinate the events which happened in the various states of the late Chou period. Treatises cover such matters as the calendar, control of rivers and canals, and the economy. The hereditary familes are those of the rulers of the states of the Chou period, plus the family of Confucius. The biographies are those of important persons, plus essays on non-Chinese groups with which China had contacts, such as aboriginal tribes, Central Asians and Koreans.

The form of the *Shih Chi* was used later by Pan Ku when he wrote the history of the Former Han dynasty, and was the pattern for later dynastic histories as well. It should be noted that the *Shih Chi* was more than a dynastic history, it was a world history, as the world was known to the Chinese. Not until the Sung historian SSU-MA Kuang (q.v.) wrote another comprehensive history did anyone try to emulate the scope of the *Shih Chi*.

Ssu-ma Ch'ien, and Burton Watson, trans. *Records of the Historian: Chapters from the Shih Chi*. New York: Columbia University Press, 1969.

Shih Ching, or Book of Songs. One of the Five Classics (q.v.) of the Confucian canon, and quite probably the oldest extant Chinese text of any significance. The songs date from the early Chou dynasty (1122-255 B.C., q.v.) and seem to be folk songs or religious works. However, later commentators professed to see political implications in nearly all of them, and students preparing for the civil-service examinations (see **Examination system**) learned to discuss them in those terms.

Pound, Ezra. *The Confucian Odes*. pbk. ed. New York: New Directions, 1959.

Waley, Authur. *The Book of Songs*. pbk. ed. New York: Grove Press, 1960.

Shimonoseki, Treaty of. Signed April 17, 1895, it settled the Sino-Japanese War (1894-1895, q.v.). The Japanese had won an unqualified military victory over the Chinese, who sued for peace in November 1894. Japan refused to accept the first negotiators or to make known its terms except to an acceptable plenipotentiary who was authorized to cede territory. They indicated that LI Hung-chang (1823-1901, q.v.) was the only possible nominee. The first meeting took place on March 20, when Japan presented very harsh terms. LI was shot by a fanatic on March 24, and the resulting publicity generated profuse apologies and more lenient terms. LI's nephew and adopted son took his place as plenipotentiary.

The terms of the peace included independence for Korea (q.v.), cession of the Liaotung peninsula (q.v.), Taiwan and the Pescadores, a huge indemnity, the opening of seven new treaty ports (q.v.) in China and concessions to Japanese merchants. Russia persuaded France and Germany to join in exerting pressure on Japan to retrocede Liaotung, which was done, at the cost of great resentment in Japan.

Shu. Name of a minor state of the Warring States Period (484-221 B.C., q.v.) and, more famously, one of the Three Kingdoms (q.v.), also known as Shu Han. Located in Szechwan, Shu is still used as a literary name for the province. Emperor T'ang Ming Huang (r. 713-755, q.v.), fled to Shu at the time of the AN Lu-shan rebellion (q.v.) in 757 A.D.

Shu Ching. The Book of History, one of the Five Classics (q.v.) of the Confucian Canon. In the view of James Legge (q.v.), the first Western translator of this book, parts of it at least date back to the 22nd century B.C. It was one of the classics destroyed by the first emperor, Ch'in Shih Huang Ti, in the Burning of the Books (qq.v.), but it was restored in the Han dynasty (206 B.C.-221 A.D., q.v.) by scholars who had memorized the text. (Since paper had not yet been invented, books were rare and memorization of texts was standard practice.) It has been regarded as an important historical source ever since.

The text describes the reigns of the (mythical ?) emperors Yao and Shun, then the Hsia, Shang and the early years of the Chou dynasties (qq.v.). It was used as a source by the Han historian SSU-MA Ch'ien in writing his *Shih Chi* (qq.v.).

The accounts of the Shang dynasty (1766-1122 B.C.) were regarded with skepticism by Westerners when the translation of the text first appeared, but much of the material has since been confirmed by archaeological discoveries.

Waltham, Clae. *Shu Ching, Book of History*. Chicago: Henry Regnery Co., 1971.

Shui Hu Chuan. This is the name of a famous Ming dynasty (1368-1644, q.v.) novel which has been translated as *All Men Are Brothers*, by Pearl S. Buck, and as *Water Margin* by J.H. Jackson. The author may have been SHIH Nai-an, but that is disputed. The story is set in the final years of the Northern Sung (c. 1120 A.D.) and describes the activities of a group of outlaws led by SUNG Chiang. Other sources indicate that such a band actually existed, but the details of the novel are mostly fiction.

The novel describes the members of the band and the circumstances which induce them to become outlaws, usually injustice at the hands of some official. It also describes the activities of the band and its eventual return to allegiance to the Sung emperor. Unlike *The Romance of the Three Kingdoms* (q.v.), its characters are not historic persons, nor are the events based on historic happenings. In this sense it is probably more a work of fiction than the other.

It has many scenes of physical brutality and acrobatic agility. It also provides a picture of life in the Sung dynasty, at least as imagined by the author several centuries later.

Buck, Pearl S, trans. *All Men Are Brothers*. New York: Grove Press, 1957 (reprint).

Shih, Nai-an. J.H. Jackson, trans. *Shui Hu Chuan: Water Margin*. New York: Paragon, 1968 (reprint).

Shun. Name of an emperor (r. 2255-2206 B.C.) of the legendary period (q.v.). His predecessor, Yao, abdicated in Shun's favor, passing over his own unworthy son. Shun, in turn, passed the empire to Yü the Great (q.v.), founder of the Hsia dynasty (2205-1766 B.C., q.v.). Shun is regarded as a model emperor by traditional Confucians. He set an example of filial piety by living amicably with his father, described as stupid, his mali-cious stepmother and his arrogant half brother.

Shun Chih. (Shun Zhi, 1638-1661). Reign title (q.v.) of the first emperor of the Ch'ing (Manchu) dynasty to rule over China, though he was the third of his line. He reigned from 1644 to 1661. Shun Chih was the ninth son of his predecessor, Abahai (q.v.), at whose death he was selected by a council of state to succeed to the throne. He reigned under the regency of two uncles, Dorgon (q.v.) and Jirgalang, until the former's death in 1651.

Dorgon laid a solid military foundation for Ch'ing control of China. Within China, the leader of the Ming opposition had been confined to the southwest, while on the borders the Tibetans and the tribes of Inner Mongolia accepted Ch'ing suzerainty. However, Dorgon had made a number of enemies, and after his death Shun Chih disgraced him posthumously and executed a number of his followers.

Shun Chih realized when he came to power that his command of literary Chinese was inadequate and he improved it. His mother had been influenced by the Jesuit Adam Schall (q.v.), and he called on the priest for advice on statecraft as well as matters of morality until 1657. At that time he turned to the study of Ch'an (Zen) Buddhism (q.v.) and favored Buddhist monks.

Shun Chih came under the influence of eunuchs (q.v.) after Dorgon's death, possibly because of the assistance of several eunuchs in eliminating Dorgon's supporters. He also suffered from ill health, possibly tuberculosis. Before his death from smallpox he dictated a will, but historians believe it was replaced by a forgery, since in it he blamed himself for various misdeeds, such as restoring the eunuchs to the position they held under the preceding Ming dynasty and favoring Chinese officials over Manchus. He was succeeded by his third son, Hsuan Yeh, whose reign title was K'ang Hsi (q.v.).

Hummel Arthur W., ed. *Eminent Chinese of the Ch'ing Period*. Washington: Government Printing Office, 1943.

Sian (Xi'an). Also known as Ch'angan (Changan). Capital of Shensi (Shaanxi) province (q.v.), population 2 million (1980). Sian means "Western Peace" and Changan means "Eternal Peace." The city has been the site of China's capital repeatedly over the centuries. It reached its zenith as the capital of the T'ang dynasty (618-906 A.D.) when it was probably the world's greatest and most cosmopolitan city. In 742 A.D., during the reign of T'ang Ming Huang (q.v.), the population of the Ch'angan metropolitan district was 1.96 million, with 1 million in the city itself. Descriptions of its wonders exist in many Chinese sources, and also in the diary of the Japanese Buddhist monk Ennin (793-864, q.v.), who visited it in the mid-ninth century.

Sian is the site of one of the oldest Chinese structures extant, the Big Wild Goose Pagoda. It is also the site of the tomb of the first emperor, Ch'in Shih Huang Ti (r. 221-206 B.C., q.v.), now a major tourist attraction.

Sian Incident. In 1936 the Manchurian troops of CHANG Hsueh-liang (q.v.), ousted from their Manchurian base by the Japanese, were in Northwest China facing Communist troops. Morale was low because the Manchurians were unwilling to fight other Chinese while Japanese occupied their homeland.

CHIANG Kai-shek (q.v.) was planning a major offensive to destroy the Communists in the northwest and went to Sian on December 4 to announce the campaign would commence on the 12th. CHANG and his officers argued for a united anti-Japanese front, and on December 12 arrested CHIANG and presented eight demands.

Some of the officers proposed executing CHIANG, but a Communist delegation including CHOU En-lai (q.v.) arrived on December 15 with word that the Soviets wanted CHIANG to continue as China's leader. T.V. SOONG (q.v.) and his sister, Mme. CHIANG (see **SOONG Mei-ling**), arrived a few days later, and on December 25 CHIANG accepted the demands and flew back to Nanking.

CHANG Hsueh-liang accompanied CHIANG and this marked the end of his active career. He was tried by a military court and kept under surveillance for the rest of his life, in the interior during World War II and later in Taiwan.

Sichuan. See **Szechwan**.

Sikang. Former province, in the Republican period (1911-1949). It has been absorbed by Szechwan and Tibet.

Silk. Like tea (q.v.), silk is one of China's major contributions to the world, and was for several centuries a major commodity in international trade. Archaeological evidence indicates that silk was produced in the Shang dynasty (1766-1122 B.C., q.v.). It is mentioned in texts of the Chou dynasty (1122-255 B.C., q.v.), and was exported in the Han dynasty (206 B.C.-221 A.D., q.v.), being sent as far as Rome, where an ounce of silk was worth an ounce of gold. To slow the export of gold, the Roman emperor Tiberius (r. 14-37 A.D.) forbade men to wear silk. Silk was shipped to the West over the Silk Road (q.v.) and also through the port of Haiphong in Vietnam (q.v.), then under Chinese control. It was carried by ship to the Red Sea and then overland to Alexandria.

Bolts of silk of standard length and width were used as money for large transactions in China from the Han dynasty until well into the T'ang (618-906) and sometimes in later periods.

The secret of making silk was a Chinese monopoly until about the sixth century A.D., when silkworms were smuggled to Western Asia. Silk was the major Chinese export to the West in the 16th century, as tea was unknown in Europe at that time. China remained the most important source for silk until the late 19th century, when it was overtaken by Japan.

Leggett, William F. *The Story of Silk.* New York: Lifetime Editions, 1949.

Silk Road. The term refers to the routes used since ancient times for trade between China and the Mediterranean world. Tunhuang (Dunhuang) in Kansu province is usually cited as the eastern end of the Silk Road, but there are a number of trails through Central Asia which were utilized at different times, depending on considerations of security. Since transport was on the backs of animals, and hence expensive, only the most valuable of commodities would be worth transporting. One of these was silk (q.v.) which China had developed at a very early period. During the Han dynasty (206 B.C.-221 A.D.), the Chinese controlled much of Central Asia and could offer security to traders for a great distance beyond

China proper. Early Chinese traders exchanged their silk for gold with the Parthians, and the Parthians in turn sold it to the Romans at a price which is estimated to have been set at one ounce of gold for one ounce of silk. (The drain on the Roman economy was a serious matter and sumptuary laws were called for.)

As Chinese power waxed and waned over the centuries, as did the power of more temporary kingdoms in Central Asia, the trade over the route also rose and fell. Probably the period when the Silk Road was most open to trade between China and the West was during the period of Mongol dominance from about 1200 to 1360. One of the best accounts available is that of Marco Polo (q.v.) who wrote an account of his trip in the late 13th century. Much of this was regarded as fictional by his contemporaries and succeeding generations. Political changes in Asia in the years which followed made retracing his route an impossibility, which added to the skepticism.

It should be borne in mind that except for the early centuries, the Silk Road was not the only trade route to the West. In the Tang dynasty (618-906), there were Arab ships trading at Canton and other Chinese ports, and this continued until the Portuguese seizure of Malacca in 1511, which gave them a dominant position in the sea trade of Southeast Asia.

The trade along the Silk Road was severely limited by the reclusive nature of the Ming dynasty (1368-1643). Nor did it thrive in the succeeding Ch'ing dynasty (1644-1911). By the early 19th century Russian advances against the khanates of Central Asia closed off all possibility of the routes being used for anything except local trade and travel. In the 20th century occasional travelers have received permission from the various governments involved to travel over various sections of the Silk Road and have written entertaining accounts of their experiences.

Collins, Robert J. *East to Cathay: The Silk Road*. New York: McGraw Hill, 1968.

Franck, Irene M., and Brownstone, David M. *The Silk Road*. New York: Facts On File, 1986.

Sining. Capital of Tsinghai province (q.v.).

Sinkiang province (Xinjiang Uygur Autonomous Region). Area: 1,600,000 sq. km. (617,700 sq. mi.). Population: 12,560,000 (1980). Capital: Urumchi (Ürümqi). Sinkiang is bounded on the northeast by the Mongolian People's Republic, on the southeast by Kansu and Tsinghai provinces (qq.v.), on the south and west by Tibet, India and a narrow finger of Afghanistan, and on the northwest by the USSR. It was formerly known as Chinese Turkestan.

Chinese records of the area go back to the Han dynasty (206 B.C.-221 A.D., q.v.) when Han armies conquered and occupied parts of it. The decline of the Han led to the withdrawal of the occupation forces, but the rise of the T'ang dynasty (618-907 A.D., q.v.) saw new Chinese occupiers. The Silk Road (q.v.) crosses Sinkiang and was the route by which exotic imports reached the T'ang court.

Sinkiang was conquered by the Mongols before they established the Yuan dynasty (1279-1368, q.v.) and it was through Sinkiang that such Western visitors as Marco Polo (q.v.) reached China. After the fall of the Yuan dynasty, Sinkiang had little or no contact with China until it was conquered in 1758-1759 by the emperor Ch'ien Lung (r. 1736-1796) of the Ch'ing dynasty (1644-1911, qq.v.). By the mid-19th century, Russian subjugation of previously independent khanates to the west brought Russian soldiers and traders to Sinkiang's borders.

The Treaty of Kuldja (1851, q.v.), authorized the use of two towns in Sinkiang through which the Russians might trade with China. The Treaty of Livadia (1879, q.v.), returned to China areas where Muslim rebellions had permitted the Russians to step in and restore order (see under **TSO Tsung-t'ang**). The present borders are largely the result of the Treaty of St. Petersburg (1881, q.v.).

Sinkiang became a province of the Ch'ing empire, as distinct from a tributary region, in 1884. At that time the Han Chinese represented less than 10 percent of the population, with the balance being an ethnic mix consisting mainly of Uighur, Kazakhs and Kirghiz, with smaller numbers of Mongols, Tajiks, Tatars, Uzbeks and other groups. The vast majority were Muslim and ethnically related to the population on the other side of the border in Russia.

The Chinese maintained strict border controls, and in 1918 closed the border in the face of war and revolution in Russia, while providing refuge for anti-Communists and to White Russian military in 1920-1921. In 1920 local authorities signed an agreement with Soviet representatives providing for the establishment of consulates in two cities on each side. A new agreement in 1924 expanded the number of consulates and paved the way for a vast increase in Soviet influence and activity in Sinkiang.

Developments in China proper, such as the success of the Northern Expedition (1926-1928, q.v.) and the expulsion of Soviet advisers and consular officials from China, had only a faint echo in Sinkiang. Soviet officials remained, though the new flag of the

Nanking government was raised in 1928.

In 1933 a Muslim rebellion in Hami assumed threatening proportions when the rebels were joined by coreligionists from nearby Kansu province. The rebels were outside the walls of Urumchi when the defenders were strengthened by the arrival of Chinese reinforcements. SHENG Shih-ts'ai (q.v.) took over the government in April 1933. The fighting continued and in January 1934, Soviet military units came to SHENG's assistance and helped defeat the rebels. In May 1935, SHENG signed an agreement with the Soviets for a major loan and technical assistance.

After the outbreak of the Sino-Japanese War in 1937 (see **World War II**), the Soviets increased aid and stationed troops at Hami. SHENG signed another agreement in 1940 granting the Soviets extensive rights in Sinkiang for a 50-year period. He left Sinkiang in 1944, and Nationalist efforts to consolidate their rule were ineffective.

According to current sources, the Han Chinese now make up a bare majority of the population, the result of massive government-sponsored immigration since 1949. The second largest group is the Uighur, who number about five million. Chinese efforts to Sinicize Sinkiang face major problems because of ethnic, linguistic and religious differences.

Whiting, Allen S. *Soviet Policies in China, 1917-24.* New York: Columbia University Press, 1954.

Whiting, Allen S., and Sheng Shih-ts'ai. *Sinkiang: Pawn or Pivot?* East Lansing: Michigan State University Press, 1958.

Sino-Japanese War (1894-1895). The proximate cause of the war was the relationship of Korea (q.v.) to China. The real cause was the continuing decline of the Ch'ing dynasty (1644-1911, q.v.) and the rise of a militaristic and expansionist Japan.

Korea had acknowledged the suzerainty of the Ming (1368-1644) and Ch'ing dynasties, and Ming troops had responded to Korean appeals for assistance in resisting Japanese invasions led by TOYOTOMI Hideyoshi (1537-1598, q.v.) in 1592 and 1597. Hideyoshi's death ended the threat, but Korean animosity lingered because of the destruction caused by Japanese troops.

The opening of China after the Treaties of Tientsin (1858, q.v.), and the opening of Japan to international trade at the time of the Meiji Restoration (1868) prompted several Western nations to try to establish relations with Korea. These were rebuffed on the grounds that, as a state tributary to China, Korea could not maintain direct international contacts. While the Western powers were uncertain about Korea's ties to the Ch'ing dynasty, Japan was thoroughly informed and determined to break them. In 1876, Japan forced Korea to sign a treaty of amity and commerce which declared both countries to be independent states. In the 1880s, treaties were signed with France, Germany, Great Britain, Italy, Russia and the United States.

From the first, signing of the treaties stirred unrest and mob action in Korea. Both China and Japan sent troops to restore order, but the antiforeign mobs soon turned to antigovernment actions, and in 1894, the king of Korea appealed to China for assistance in putting down the riots.

China was not ready for war with Japan (see under LI Hung-chang), but sent ships in a show of support. Japan attacked the fleet on July 24, 1894, and sank one of the troop transports. Fighting on land followed, with a series of quick Japanese victories. With the Chinese troops in retreat, the Korean government had no choice but to accept all Japanese terms. The antigovernment rebels rose again in October, but were no match for the modern and disciplined Japanese.

The Japanese then expelled the Chinese from Korea, and occupied Lushun (Port Arthur) on the Liaotung peninsula (qq.v.) and Weihaiwei in Shantung province. The Chinese sued for peace in November, and the Treaty of Shimonoseki (q.v.) was signed on April 17, 1895. The most important provisions were Chinese acknowledgement of the independence of Korea, cession of the Liaotung peninsula and Taiwan to Japan, and the opening of several new treaty ports in China.

The effects of the defeat by Japan were far-reaching. The incompetence of the Ch'ing administration was visible for all to see, and the efforts of such reformers as K'ANG Yu-wei (1858-1927, q.v.), received new impetus. Japan's success in annexing Chinese territory also led to increased speculation by the Western powers that China might be ripe for dismemberment.

Sino-Soviet Treaty of 1924. The treaty was signed May 31, 1924, and marked diplomatic recognition between the USSR and the Republic of China (q.v.). The treaty terms recognized Outer Mongolia as an integral part of the Republic of China, although the Soviets had a secret treaty with the People's Revolutionary Government of Mongolia, and Soviet support of Mongol independence was apparent. The terms also confirmed Soviet ownership of the Chinese Eastern Railway in Manchuria (q.v.), but assigned control of military, police and political matters in the railway zone to China.

However, Manchuria was not at that time under the control of the Peking government, but was ruled by CHANG Tso-lin (1873-1928, q.v.), who announced that the treaty did not apply in Manchuria. On September 20, 1924, he signed a separate agreement with Soviet representatives in Mukden (Shenyang), thus setting a precedent for Soviet recognition of Manchurian autonomy. Protests from Peking were ignored.

Clubb, O. Edmund. *China and Russia.* New York: Columbia University Press, 1971.

Sino-Soviet Treaty of 1945. This treaty was signed in Moscow on August 14. It was necessitated by the agreement reached at the Yalta Conference (q.v.) held in February 1945 and attended by the heads of government of Great Britain, the United States and the USSR. China was not represented, but the three allies agreed that in return for Soviet participation in the war against Japan, the USSR would be granted joint control (with China) of the Chinese Eastern Railway, access to the warmwater port of Dairen and the use of Port Arthur as a naval base (q.v.). Stalin pressed for the restoration of the rights which Russia had had in Manchuria prior to the Russo-Japanese War in 1904-1905 (q.v.).

When the Chinese were informed of the terms of the agreement, they pointed out that the Soviets had renounced special concessions in Manchuria by the Treaty of May 31, 1924. To clarify the situation a new treaty was drawn up. The most important points were as follows: the USSR promised to give moral support and military aid solely to the national government as the central government of China; the USSR recognized Chinese sovereignty in Manchuria;

China agreed to recognize the independence of Outer Mongolia if a plebiscite confirmed that that was the desire of the people; China agreed to declare Dairen a free port open to all nations. However, the treaty went beyond the Yalta agreement in providing the USSR a lease of half the port facilities at Dairen at no charge.

Sixteen Kingdoms (302-439 A.D.). The term refers to a group of autonomous non-Chinese states of North China after the downfall of the Western Chin (265-316, q.v.). They were not all contemporaneous, and records exist of at least 17, but the traditional term has persisted. The ruling classes were of Central Asian stock, i.e. Hsiung Nu (or Mongol), Tibetan or Turkic.

Socialist Youth League. This organization was the forerunner of the Chinese Communist party (q.v.). It was organized in Shanghai in August 1920 by CH'EN Tu-hsiu (q.v.) and branches were soon established in other centers. MAO Tse-tung (q.v.) established the branch in Changsha, Hunan. In July 1921, it was replaced by the establishment of the Chinese Communist party.

Soochow (Suzhou). City in Kiangsu province. Population: 540,000 (1975). Because of its many canals, it is sometimes called the Venice of China. Together with Hangchow it is the subject of an old saying: "Heaven above, Soochow and Hangchow below."

Soochow was the seat of the kingdom of Wu during the period of the Warring States (484-255 B.C., q.v.). With the development of the Yangtze valley area in the years after the fall of the Han dynasty (206 B.C.-221 A.D.), Soochow became a regional center of an area of immense wealth. The area produces rice in quantity, and the Grand Canal (q.v.) built in the Sui dynasty (589-618) goes past the city.

It also has a reputation for literary activity and a long record of successful participants in the imperial examinations (see **Examination system**). Perhaps its most famous native son was the Ming poet KAO Ch'i (q.v.), said by some to be the most gifted poet of the 14th century. He was executed by the first Ming emperor, Ming Hung Wu (q.v.), because of suspicion that KAO had supported an opposing contender for the throne of China. In fact, the only connection seems to be that the unsuccessful contender, CHANG Shih-ch'eng, had used Soochow as his capital.

The city suffered considerable damage during the Taiping Rebellion (q.v.), but because of the great concentration of wealth, most of this was rapidly repaired.

The Soochow dialect, one of the Wu family of dialects, is said to fall more pleasantly on the ear than any other.

SOONG, Charles Jones (1866-1918). Original name: HAN Chiao-shun. Father of SOONG Ch'ing-ling (Mme. SUN Yat-sen), SOONG Mei-ling (Mme. CHIANG Kai-shek), T.V. SOONG (qq..v.) and SOONG Ai-ling (Mme. H.H. K'UNG). Charles Jones SOONG was born on Hainan Island. He was adopted by a childless uncle and taken to the United States in 1878. He worked in his uncle's shop in Boston, then joined the U.S. Coast Guard as a cabin boy. His mentor was a devout Methodist and in 1880 SOONG was baptized and added the names Charles and Jones to his surname. He graduated from the theological seminary of Vanderbilt University in 1885 and was sent back to China as a missionary.

He arrived in Shanghai in January 1886, and set about learning the local language. He resigned as a missionary in 1892, and set up the Sino-American Press, which published Chinese editions of the Bible, and engaged in other successful commercial activities. He taught Sunday school, helped found the YMCA, and was a generous supporter of the Methodist church.

SOONG married a descendant of HSÜ Kuang-ch'i, one of the first Christian converts in China. His eldest daughter, Ai-ling, became SUN Yat-sen's English secretary in 1912. In 1914 she married H.H. K'UNG, a direct descendant of Confucius and a prominent banker. SOONG later served in several capacities in the national government in Nanking and Chungking. In addition to the children named, SOONG had two younger sons.

Boorman, Howard L., ed. *Biographical Dictionary of Republican China*. New York, Columbia University Press, 1967.

SOONG Ch'ing-ling (1892-1981). Wife of SUN Yat-sen (q.v.) and daughter of Charles Jones SOONG (q.v.). In 1908 she went to the United States, taking her younger sister Mei-ling (q.v.) with her, and entered Wesleyan College for Women in Macon, Georgia, where her older sister, Ai-ling, was already enrolled. After graduating, she returned to China in 1913. Because the revolutionary movement was suffering reverses at the hands of YUAN Shih-k'ai (q.v.), SUN Yat-sen felt it politic to retreat to Japan in August 1913, and the SOONG family went with him. Ai-ling was SUN's English secretary, but she resigned the following year to marry H.H. K'UNG (see under **SOONG, Charles Jones**), and Ch'ing-ling took her place. Ch'ing-ling married SUN that same year, and was at his side until his death in 1925.

While SUN was alive, Ch'ing-ling did not take an active part in Kuomintang (KMT, q.v.) politics, but after his death she became the symbol of the founder of the republic, and found herself in a more conspicuous position. With the rise of factionalism in the party, most importantly because of the question of Communist participation in party affairs, she found herself more and more in opposition to the positions taken by CHIANG Kai-shek (q.v.). She was identified with the left-wing Wuhan faction, while CHIANG was the leader of the right-wing Nanking faction. In July 1927, she announced that she would no longer participate in the KMT because of her opposition to new policies.

In August she made a trip to the Soviet Union, where she remained for nearly two years. In her absence, her sister Mei-ling married CHIANG, a union to which Ch'ing-ling was bitterly opposed. She returned to China in 1929 for the state burial of her late husband in Nanking. She spent most of the next decade living in Shanghai, and moved to Hong Kong in 1937, after the start of the war with Japan. She flew to Chungking in 1940, where she was honored by CHIANG with a lawn party, which gave the appearance, at least, of restored family unity.

In 1945, she returned to Shanghai, where she lived most of the rest of her life in the house willed to her by SUN in 1925. She organized the China Welfare Fund which directed funds mostly to Communist-related organizations. In September 1949 she participated in the Chinese People's Political Consultative Conference in Peking. This organization led to the founding of the People's Republic of China (q.v.), and Madame SUN became one of three non-Communist vice chairmen. She held a series of official positions in the People's Republic until her death.

Boorman, Howard L., ed. *Biographical Dictionary of Republican China*. New York: Columbia University Press, 1967.

SOONG Mei-ling (1897?-   ). Wife of CHIANG Kai-shek and daughter of Charles Jones SOONG (qq.v.). In 1908 SOONG Mei-ling went with her sister Ch'ing-ling (q.v.) to the United States. She was too young to enter college as her sister did, and spent several years studying privately. In 1913 she entered Wellesley College, to be near her brother, T.V. SOONG (q.v.), who was studying at Harvard.

After graduation she returned to Shanghai. Both her sisters, Ai-ling and Ch'ing-ling, were married, the latter to SUN Yat-sen (q.v.), and it was at the latter's home that she met CHIANG. He was a determined suitor, but in the eyes of her family there were impediments. He was 10 years older, not a Christian and already married. He overcame the objections of her mother by promising to study Christianity, but Mme. SUN remained opposed. The marriage took place in December 1927, and Mei-ling became her husband's English secretary and interpreter.

Mme. CHIANG played a key role in the Sian Incident (q.v.) and made a significant contribution to China's war effort through her effectiveness in dealing with America and Americans. In February 1943, while on a visit to the United States, she became the first Chinese and the second woman to address a joint session of Congress. Her speeches and magazine articles were well received. For nearly 25 years her name appeared on American lists of the 10 most admired women in the world.

As CHIANG's interpreter in World War II, she accompanied him to the Cairo Conference in November 1943. She also acted as a buffer between CHIANG and General Joseph W. Stilwell (q.v.), earning praise from that somewhat peppery soldier.

In 1948 she made another trip to the United States to generate support for the Nationalist fight against the Communist forces. In the wake of the failure of the Marshall Mission (q.v.) she was unsuccessful. President Truman was polite, but unwilling to alter the policy of non-involvement in Chinese affairs. She remained in the United States until 1950, by which time the Nationalist government had moved to Taiwan.

Boorman, Howard L., ed. *Biographical Dictionary of Republican China*. New York: Columbia University Press, 1967.

Hahn, Emily. *The Soong Sisters*. Garden City, NY: Doubleday, Doran & Co., 1941.

SOONG, T.V. (1894-1971). Diplomat and financier, his initials come from the Shanghai pronunciation of his name, which in standard romanization is SUNG Tzu-wen. Son of Charles Jones SOONG, brother of Mme. SUN Yat-sen (SOONG Ch'ing-ling) and Mme. CHIANG Kai-shek (SOONG Mei-ling) (qq.v.), T.V. SOONG was born in Shanghai and educated at St. John's University and Harvard, from which he graduated in 1915. SUN Yat-sen enlisted his aid in 1923 in bringing order to the finances of Kwangtung province. SOONG held a series of high positions in the national government, and served as an important link between the political leaders in Nanking and the bankers and businessmen of Shanghai. Financial support from this group was an essential element in the success of the Nanking government in the 1930s.

Two of SOONG's major financial accomplishments were the abolition of the *likin*—an internal customs tax which greatly impeded internal trade—and the abolition of the *tael*—a unit weight used for measuring silver—and the establishment of the silver dollar *yuan* as China's national currency.

In 1940 SOONG was appointed CHIANG Kai-shek's personal representative in Washington, where he successfully negotiated for American credit. Because of his success he was named minister of foreign affairs, a post which he took up on his return to Chungking in late 1942. In January 1943 Great Britain and the United States signed treaties which surrendered the right of extraterritoriality (q.v.) and various other rights associated with the "unequal treaties" (q.v.).

SOONG headed the Chinese delegation to the conference which organized the United Nations in San Francisco in 1945 and was elected one of its chairmen. He made two trips to Moscow that summer to negotiate the Sino-Soviet Treaty of Friendship and Alliance (q.v.) which was signed on August 14, 1945. This treaty acknowledged the independence of Outer Mongolia.

After the war, SOONG was deeply involved with the unsuccessful Marshall Mission (q.v.), and eventually moved to the United States.

Boorman, Howard L., ed. *Biographical Dictionary of Republican China*. New York: Columbia University Press, 1967.

Tamagna, Frank M. *Banking and Finance in China*. New York: International Secretariat, Institute of Pacific Relations, 1942.

South Seas. This phrase is a translation of the Chinese *nan-yang*. It refers to Southeast Asia, which was generally approached by sea from such seaports as Canton and Amoy. Chinese trade with the area goes back at least as far as the T'ang dynasty (618-906 A.D.). Some of the kingdoms of the area were in diplomatic contact with China (i.e., they acknowledged

tributary status) and accepted Chinese confirmation of their legitimacy. Chinese settlement there dates back centuries, though the largest number of settlers went in the 19th and 20th centuries. (See **Overseas Chinese**.)

Spring and Autumn Period (771-484 B.C.). Historians divide the Chou dynasty (q.v.) into three periods, of which this is the second. The name is derived from the *Spring and Autumn Annals*, the official records of the state of Lu. The book was supposedly edited by Confucius (qq.v.), and followed the style of other annals of states of the period, none of which has survived.

The Chou capital had been moved from Sian to Loyang in 771 B.C. (qq.v.), and Chou power and prestige continued its slow decline. This period was typified by diplomatic and military relations between the great feudal lords. A protracted series of changing alliances makes the political history extremely complicated, but provided an opportunity for philosophers and statesmen of the period to offer their services to different rulers. Warfare tended to be characterized more by diplomatic maneuvers than by full-scale bloodshed.

The period saw the beginnings of the three indigenous Chinese schools of philosophy: Confucianism, Legalism and Taoism (qq.v.).

The Spring and Autumn Period was followed by the Warring States Period (q.v.), which saw the end of the Chou dynasty.

SSU-MA Ch'ien (145-90 B.C.). SSU-MA Ch'ien has been likened to Herodotus in that he was a professional historian who set the pattern for others for 2,000 years. He was the only child of SSU-MA T'an (q.v.), a Grand Historian of the Han dynasty, and a descendant of a family of feudal courtiers of the Chou period.

SSU-MA Ch'ien was a retainer at the court of the emperor Han Wu Ti (q.v.), and traveled widely with the emperor. He inherited his father's post as Grand Historian at the death of the latter. He was punished with castration for attempting to defend a Chinese general who had been defeated and captured by the Hsiung-nu (q.v.). (The general apparently surrendered when no reinforcements reached him.) This disgrace weighed heavily on Ch'ien, but he determined to complete his history in order to leave a memorial to the credit of his father as well as himself.

His work, the Shih Chi (q.v.), was the first history of China, and set the pattern for later works, particularly the dynastic histories (q.v.).

Watson, Burton. *Ssu-ma Ch'ien, Grand Historian of China*. New York: Columbia University Press, 1958.

SSU-MA Kuang (1019-1086). Historian and government official of the Northern Sung dynasty (960-1126; see **Sung**). He was a Confucian scholar whose major literary work was a general history of China from 403 B.C. to 959 A.D., that is, from the period of the Warring States through the Five Dynasties, ending just before the establishment of the Sung dynasty (qq.v.) in 960. This was unlike the traditional dynastic histories and more similar to SSU-MA Ch'ien's *Shih Chi* (qq.v.), completed about 100 B.C. SSU-MA Kuang's work may be regarded as a Neo-Confucian defense of the importance of history in the face of the intellectual challenge of other-worldliness posed by Buddhism and Taoism (qq.v.).

SSU-MA Kuang spent about 25 years writing his history, many of them years out of office during the period when WANG An-shih (1021-1086, q.v.) was in power and carrying out his reforms. SSU-MA Kuang was a conservative and opposed the form of centralized economic control proposed by WANG. He succeeded WANG when the latter resigned from office in 1076, and spent the next few years undoing the reforms.

SSU-MA T'an (170[?]-110 B.C.). Grand Historian at the court of Han Wu Ti (q.v.). He held this position from 140 until his death in 110 B.C., when it passed to his son, SSU-MA Ch'ien (q.v.). What little we know of SSU-MA T'an is derived from his son's autobiography in the *Shih Chi* (q.v.). We are told that the family had been historians to the Chou dynasty, and held other positions at court over a period of centuries. SSU-MA T'an wrote parts of the *Shih Chi* and his son finished it. It is impossible to quantify the amount which each was responsible for, but internal evidence confirms that the elder man was responsible for some of the work.

Stilwell, Joseph W. (1883-1946). American general who commanded the U.S. China-Burma-India Theater in World War II (q.v.), acting concurrently as Chief of Staff for Allied forces of Generalissimo CHIANG Kai-shek (1887-1975, q.v.). A West Point graduate, Stilwell served in World War I, and later had three tours of duty in China as a language student, a military attaché, a construction engineer on a road built for famine relief, and as an observer with Chinese armies engaged in civil war.

Japan had been at war with China since 1937, but the simultaneous attacks on Pearl Harbor and Hong Kong December 7 (8), 1941, made the United States and Britain China's allies. American military strategy was to keep China active in the war against Japan, and to keep open the Burma lifeline to China. Stilwell received his dual appointment on January 23, 1942, reached India in February, and Chungking, China's wartime capital, March 4. Japanese troops captured Rangoon March 6, effectively closing the Burma Road (q.v.) and by May had occupied most of Burma, isolating China.

One of Stilwell's first responsibilities was to organize a military airlift from India to China over the southern spur of the Himalayas, which extends into northern Burma and separates the two countries. The airlift, covering a route known colloquially as "The Hump," was the sole logistical support for the American Volunteer Group (q.v.) until the reopening of the Burma Road at the end of 1944. It also carried some military supplies for the Chinese.

With the Japanese in a position to close the airlift either by seizing Kunming, capital of Yunnan province, and the China terminus, or the air bases in Assam, India, at the other end, Stilwell proposed a Chinese offensive from Kunming towards Burma and an Anglo-American offensive to clear them from northern Burma entirely. Although some Chinese troops were assigned to Stilwell's command for this purpose, he soon found that they were also receiving orders directly from CHIANG. Stilwell objected, perhaps not diplomatically, and his recall was eventually requested by the Chinese government. He left for the United States in October 1944, and was replaced by Lt. Gen. Albert C. Wedemeyer.

Romanus, Charles F., and Riley Sunderland. *Stilwell's Mission to China* and *Stilwell's Command Problems*. Washington: Dept. of the Army, 1953 and 1956.

Stilwell, Joseph W. *The Stilwell Papers.* New York: William Sloane Associates, 1948.

Tuchman, Barbara. *Stilwell and the American Experience in China, 1911-1945.* New York: MacMillan, 1971.

Stilwell Road. See under **Burma Road.**

SU Tung-p'o (1036-1101). Sung dynasty (q.v.) poet, calligrapher and official, also known as SU Shih. His father and brother were also great stylists and the three are listed among the "eight great prose masters of the T'ang and Sung dynasties." SU was born in Szechwan province and educated there. He passed his *chin-shih* examination (see **Examination system**) with brilliance in April 1057. Before he could be appointed to a government office, his mother died. According to Confucian practice, he retired to his home to spend 27 months in mourning. At the end of that period he moved to the capital (present-day Kaifeng) and in 1061 was appointed an assistant magistrate in Shensi province.

SU's career was a distinguished one, notable for his sympathy for the people and for his opposition to the state capitalism policies of WANG An-shih (q.v.), which involved centralized government ownership and control of foodstocks. His assignments included two tours of duty in Hangchow, first as deputy magistrate and later as commander and governor of Chekiang. He was also secretary to the emperor from 1086 to 1089.

SU's political enemies banished him three times, sending him finally to Hainan Island—the first Chinese official to be so exiled. (Hainan was theoretically a part of China, but very few Chinese lived there. The population consisted mostly of minority tribes.)

SU's continuing reputation is based on the clarity and simplicity of his style. He was fortunate when he took his *chin-shih* examination that the chief examiner was the famous scholar OU-YANG Hsiu (q.v.), who prized clarity and disdained pretentious writing. SU's success in the examination immediately made him a well-known figure and his writings were copied and passed from hand to hand. During his periods of banishment his writings were also banned, but they continued to circulate despite that. His work was so highly prized that much of it is still extant.

LIN, Yutang. *The Gay Genius*. New York: The John Day Co., 1947.

Sui dynasty (581-617 A.D.). The Sui dynasty reunited China for the first time since the downfall of the Han (q.v.) and laid the basis for the succeeding T'ang. The significance of this reunification was enormous, because the preceding four centuries of disunity had created the possibility that China might develop as Europe did, a collection of separate political entities sharing a certain cultural and historical background, but with different experience and linguistic traits.

The Sui rulers came from the northwest and built their capital at Sian, then called Changan. They, like most of the inhabitants of that area, were of mixed Tartar-Chinese blood. The dynasty was founded by the emperor Sui Wen Ti, and came to an end after the reign of his son Sui Yang Ti (qq.v.).

The preceding period of disunion had seen a significant migration of Chinese from the north to the Yangtze river area, where they mingled with the southern Chinese and various aboriginal groups then being Sinicized. The area became the richest and most heavily populated in China. One of the great Sui accomplishments was the building of the Grand Canal, actually a series of connected waterways which linked Hangchow, near the coast, to Sian, far away to the north and west. Yang Ti later extended the waterway to the vicinity of Peking.

The emperor Wen Ti showed himself a wise ruler by moving to achieve support from Confucians by establishing governmental forms which were in accordance with Han precedents, and from Buddhists and Taoists by endowing temples. His conquest of the south was accomplished with comparatively little bloodshed and destruction.

The emperor Yang Ti has a totally different reputation. He is suspected of having poisoned his father. He was energetic and sent armies south to Vietnam, and also to the north making three attempts in three years to conquer the Korean kingdom of Koguryo. He also raised levies to reconstruct the Great Wall. After a disastrous military setback in 617 at the hands of the Turks, he fled to Nanking, where he was murdered the next year by one of his retainers.

Wright, Arthur F. *The Sui Dynasty*. New York: Alfred A. Knopf, 1978.

Sui Wen Ti (541-604 A.D.). Reign title (q.v.) of the first emperor (r. 589-604) of the Sui dynasty (589-618, q.v.). YANG Chien, his original name, came of an aristocratic Chinese family which had intermarried with the dominant Turko-Mongol elite in Northwest China. His father served the Western Wei dynasty (534-557) and had the title Duke of Sui. YANG Chien was married at 16 to a well-educated and strong-willed daughter of a Chinese mother and a non-Chinese father, both of noble families.

YANG was a successful military commander for the dynasty, which had become the Northern Chou in

557, and his infant daughter was betrothed to the crown prince. The latter succeeded to the throne in 578, but soon proved himself a tyrant. His relations with his father-in-law deteriorated, and YANG started laying plans to usurp the throne. Before this could happen the ruler died of a stroke, leaving his young son, YANG's grandson, as his heir.

YANG assumed full powers as regent, and there followed a period of fighting between supporters of the Chou and supporters of YANG Chien. YANG prevailed, but at some cost. He arranged for the murder of some 59 members of the royal family, including his own grandson.

The Northern Chou was replaced by the Sui in 581 in North China, but conquest of the south did not come about until 589. For that reason the official beginning of the imperial dynasty is placed at 589. Sui Wen Ti and his advisers were thoroughly aware of the brief history of the Ch'in dynasty (221-206 B.C., q.v.), which had unified China some 800 years earlier. For this reason, a conscious effort was made to make clear that the Sui dynasty was planned as a revival of the customs of the Han dynasty (206 B.C.-221 A.D.). Sui Wen Ti was an ardent Buddhist, but he made efforts to placate Confucians and Taoists as well.

One of the great achievements of his reign was the construction of the Grand Canal (q.v.), a series of linked rivers and canals connecting Hangchow to Sian. His successor later extended it to Peking.

Sui Wen Ti's greatest achievement was the reunification of China after several centuries of disunity. While his dynasty lasted less than 15 years after his death, it laid the groundwork for the succeeding T'ang dynasty (618-906), and a firm basis which sustained later dynasties until the early 20th century. He was succeeded by his son, Sui Yang Ti (q.v.).

Wright, Arthur F. *The Sui Dynasty.* New York: Alfred A. Knopf, 1978.

Sui Yang Ti (569-617 A.D.). Second emperor of the Sui dynasty, he reigned from 605 to 617 A.D. Yang Ti was the second son of Wen Ti (q.v.). His parents married him to a princess of the Liang dynasty (q.v.) which had ruled at Nanking, an intelligent and literate woman. He was nominal commander-in-chief of the expedition which eliminated the Ch'en dynasty (q.v.), the last holdout against Sui reunification. He then ruled as a viceroy in Yangchow, and is credited with reconciling the southerners of the area to Sui rule.

The histories accuse him of plotting to remove his older brother from his position as crown prince, and with poisoning his father, and both may be true. In the tradition of a corrupt last emperor, so familiar to Chinese historians, the picture may be overdrawn. Yang Ti's very active style included constant tours of inspection of the country, expansion of the Grand Canal from Hangchow to Peking, repairs on the Great Wall, fighting in Vietnam and against the Turks and three attempts to conquer the Korean Kingdom of Koguryo, in 612, 613 and 614, none of which was successful.

Yang Ti's forces were defeated by the Turks in 615, and he himself was nearly captured in 617. He fled to Nanking, where he was assassinated that same year.

The downfall of the Sui is attributed to Yang Ti by traditional (Confucian) historians. He is accused of profligacy and tyranny. Certainly he was not as puritanical as his parents, but his record of tyranny, as exemplified by execution of subordinates, is no worse than his father's. His downfall may well have been hastened by the continued exactions upon the populace to support his construction projects and the unpopular wars in Korea.

Wright, Arthur F. *The Sui Dynasty*. New York: Alfred A. Knopf, 1978.

Suiyuan. Former province of the Republican period (1911-1949). Now part of the Inner Mongolia Autonomous Region (q.v.).

Summer Palace. There have been two Summer Palaces. The first, the Yuan Ming Yuan, about five miles northwest of Peking, dates back to the Chin dynasty (1115-1234, q.v.) and was taken over by succeeding dynasties. It was given by the Ch'ing emperor K'ang Hsi (r. 1662-1722, q.v.), to his son and heir as a summer residence. After his accession, Yung Cheng (r. 1723-1735, q.v.), spent several months there each year. His successor, Ch'ien Lung (r. 1736-1796, q.v.) expanded it to cover 80 square miles, and enriched it by constructing, with Jesuit aid, several buildings in baroque European style, as well as many Chinese-style palaces and pavilions. He made it his third main residence, together with palaces in Peking and Jehol. Later emperors also used it until it was destroyed on October 18, 1860, on the orders of Lord Elgin at the end of the *Arrow* War (1857-1860, q.v.). This act was in reprisal for Chinese execution of several British and French personnel taken prisoner while negotiating under a flag of truce.

The second Summer Palace, the Yi Ho Yuan, was constructed nearby in the 1880s by the empress dowager (q.v.). To build it she diverted money which had been appropriated for the Chinese navy. Partly as a result of this, the navy was quite unprepared for the Sino-Japanese War (1894-1895, q.v.). It is this palace, somewhat more than a square mile in area, which is now accessible to tourists.

Sun Tzu. Author of *The Art of War*. The book is presumed to have been written during the period of the Warring States (484-221 B.C., q.v.), but little is known about its author. However, the version which has come down to us includes passages describing military actions from the Period of Disunity (221-589 A.D., q.v.) and even later. Sun Tzu's biography appears in the *Shih Chi* of SSU-MA Ch'ien (qq.v.), which tells us his surname was WU, and cites an incident in which he instilled military discipline in a group of palace ladies by executing two of their number for failing to exercise discipline on their subordinates. The book was translated into French in 1782, and is said to have been admired by Napoleon Bonaparte.

Sun Tzu. James Clavell, ed. *The Art of War*. New York: Delacorte Press, 1983.

Sun Tzu. Samuel B. Griffith, trans. *The Art of War*. New York: Oxford University Press, 1963.

SUN Yat-sen (1866-1925). This is the romanized spelling of the Cantonese pronunciation of SUN I-hsien. Also known as SUN Chung-shan and SUN Wen. Leader of the republican revolution and known as the father of his country, he was born in Kwangtung province, near Macao. At the age of 13 he was sent to live with his elder brother in Hawaii, where he studied at Iolani College, an Episcopal boarding school. Upon graduation in 1882 he returned home, and soon showed that his education had made him skeptical of his neighbors' religious beliefs. He broke off the finger of an image of the local god and was expelled from the village, a portent of his later life.

SUN studied medicine in Canton and Hong Kong, and tried to set up practice in Macao. The Portuguese did not recognize his qualifications, would not permit him to practice, and forced him to leave. In 1893 he opened a practice in Hong Kong. SUN's interest in political reform had already started, probably stirred by accounts of the Taiping Rebellion (q.v.), whose leader, HUNG Hsiu-ch'uan (q.v.), was a fellow Cantonese. The general inefficiency of the Ch'ing dynasty (1644-1911, q.v.) in its declining years, added to southern dislike of the Manchus (q.v.), was also an element.

1894 found him in Honolulu where he founded the Hsing Chung Hui (q.v.), whose stated purpose was the revitalization of China. Japanese victories in the Sino-Japanese War (1894-95, q.v.) which threatened Peking seemed to offer opportunities for revolutionary activity. SUN hurried back to Hong Kong and in 1895 was in Canton seeking recruits among the soldiers who had been demobilized by the provisions of the Treaty of Shimonoseki (q.v.). The revolutionary plot was discovered by Ch'ing authorities, and several participants were executed. SUN escaped to Hong Kong, but was ordered to leave by the British, at the request of Chinese authorities. For the next 16 years he carried out his revolutionary activities outside of China, a fugitive with a price on his head.

SUN was catapulted into the international limelight by a kidnapping incident in England. He was seized on the street on October 11, 1896, while walking past the Chinese legation. Dragged inside and held captive, SUN managed to alert English friends and the British government effected his release.

SUN went to Japan in 1897 to seek support in the Chinese communities there. In 1900 he was involved in an abortive revolt in Kwangtung. In 1903 he went to Southeast Asia to establish branches of the Hsing Chung Hui in communities of overseas Chinese (q.v.). In 1904 he went to England and in 1905 set up branches of the organization in Europe. He then returned to Japan where a new organization, the T'ung-meng-hui (q.v.), was born. 1906 found him again in Southeast Asia, establishing new branches of the T'ung-meng-hui. When he returned to Japan he gave a dramatic speech to several thousand Chinese students. Japanese authorities, concerned at the growing radicalization of Chinese students, acceded to a request from Peking for SUN's expulsion from Japan.

He went to Hanoi, and in 1907 launched a campaign in support of local uprisings in adjacent Kwangsi province. This succeeded only in generating Chinese pressure on the French authorities to expel him, which they did. By 1909 he had become unwelcome in nearly every part of East Asia, and as a consequence he departed for the West. He continued to travel and succeeded in raising funds, particularly in the United States. He first learned of the outbreak of the revolution (on October 10, 1911, at Wuchang) while he was traveling by train from Denver to Kansas City in the United States. Recognizing the importance of Western support he proceeded to Europe to ask for diplomatic recognition and economic aid. He persuaded the British to lift all restrictions on his activities in their East Asian possessions. He then returned to China.

When he arrived in Shanghai on December 25, 1911, the Ch'ing government had turned over its authority to YUAN Shih-k'ai (q.v.) and parts of southern China had declared their independence. SUN was elected provisional president of the Republic of China on December 29. On January 1, 1912, he proclaimed the establishment of the republic in Nanking.

Many problems remained, and in an effort to resolve some of them SUN offered to resign on January 22, 1912, in favor of YUAN, with certain conditions. These included the end of the Ch'ing dynasty and the formal abdication by the emperor, P'u-yi (q.v.); YUAN's open declaration of support of the republic; transfer of the capital from Peking to Nanking; and YUAN's agreement to the new constitution. However, YUAN did not transfer the capital from Peking, which remained the capital for the next 15 years (see under **Peking government**).

The T'ung-meng-hui was superseded by the Kuomintang, which was established in Peking in August, 1912, with SUN as its director. The Kuomintang obtained control of the National Assembly in elections held in February, 1913. YUAN set out to destroy the party. He was denounced by SUN, but YUAN's troops captured Nanking. YUAN issued orders for SUN's arrest, and the latter fled to Japan, where he determined to destroy YUAN at all costs.

YUAN's decision to establish a new dynasty provided SUN and his followers with an opportunity to stage revolts in several provinces. YUAN's death in June 1916 brought these to an end. SUN telegraphed to the new president, LI Yuan-hung, and the premier, TUAN Ch'i-jui (qq.v.), asking them to restore the constitution of 1912 and the national assembly which had been dismissed in 1914.

Developments in Peking did not suit SUN, and he went to Canton, where he established a military government on August 31, 1917. Maneuvers by various military leaders resulted in SUN's position

being reduced, and he withdrew from the government in May 1918, and moved to Shanghai. In April 1921 the rump parliament in Canton abolished the military government and elected SUN president of a new government. Two months later he announced a northern expedition to unite China by military force.

Early in 1922 he was in Hunan province, and had forged an alliance with TUAN and CHANG Tso-lin (q.v.) against TS'AO K'un and WU P'ei-fu (qq.v.). In so doing, SUN aligned himself with the Anhwei military clique against the Chihli Clique (qq.v.). SUN's efforts were complicated by the rebellious activities of a former subordinate who occupied Canton and demanded that SUN resign from the presidency.

SUN went to Canton to settle the matter, though warned of an attempted coup. He escaped to a gunboat, where he was joined by CHIANG Kai-shek (q.v.). He then went to Shanghai where he devoted his time to a reorganization of the Kuomintang (q.v.). It was at this point that he decided to work with the Communists, both Russian and Chinese, and agreed to permit individual Chinese Communists to join the Kuomintang. It seems likely that he was more influenced by the need to obtain military assistance than in Communist ideology, which was not in accord with his Three Principles of the People (qq.v.).

In October 1923 Soviet adviser Michael Borodin (q.v.) arrived in Canton, to which SUN had returned, and played a major part in the reorganization of the Kuomintang. In its final session the First National Congress of the Kuomintang in January 1924 elected three members of the Chinese Communist party to membership on the Central Executive Committee. This was opposed by conservative members, but without success.

The need for military support led to the establishment near Canton of the Whampoa Military Academy (q.v.) with CHIANG Kai-shek as its first commandant. SUN made plans for another northern expedition, but the defeat of the Chihli Clique and TS'AO K'un's resignation from the presidency seemed to make that unnecessary.

TUAN Ch'i-jui, leader of the Anhwei Clique, and CHANG Tso-lin invited SUN to come to Peking to discuss governmental affairs. Before SUN reached Peking, TUAN had already announced several key decisions with which SUN was not in agreement. TUAN had no intention of having formal Kuomintang participation in the national convention he was preparing.

SUN was critically ill by the time he reached Tientsin, and he died in Peking of inoperable cancer on March 12, 1925. He was 59, and was given a private Christian funeral service as well as a state funeral. After lying in state for several days, his body was moved to a temple in the Western Hills outside Peking. Later it was buried in a magnificent mausoleum in Nanking.

SUN was married twice. His first wife, whom he married while still in his teens, was the mother of his three children. His second wife was SOONG Ch'ing-ling (q.v.).

After his death, the county where he was born was renamed Chungshan in his honor. There are also many parks, roads etc., which are called Chung-shan. To his followers in the Kuomintang SUN remains the "father of his country."

Boorman, Howard L., ed. *Biographical Dictionary of Republican China*. New York: Columbia University Press, 1967.

Isaacs, Harold R. *The Tragedy of the Chinese Revolution*. Stanford: Stanford University Press, 1961.

Sharman, Lyon. *Sun Yat-sen: His Life and Its Meaning*. Stanford: Stanford University Press, 1968 (reprint).

Sung. 1. Name of one of the Warring States (q.v.); conquered by Ch'i in 286 B.C.

2. Earlier Sung (420-479 A.D). One of the southern dynasties of the Period of Disunity (q.v.), contemporaneous with the Northern Wei (see under **Wei**).

3. Sung dynasty (960-1279 A.D.). The Sung is divided between the Northern Sung (960-1126), which had its capital at Kaifeng, and the Southern Sung (1127-1278), which ruled from Hangchow. Unlike the T'ang dynasty (618-906, q.v.), which was the cultural model for the Sung, the latter was never militarily powerful. It was constantly faced with the depredations of the Hsi Hsia (882-1227, q.v.) on the northwestern frontier and the Liao (907-1125) and the Chin (1115-1234, qq.v.) to the northeast.

The Sung genius was expressed in such accomplishments as art, poetry and the development of printing, which caused education and literacy to spread dramatically. The Sung introduced the use of paper money, which contributed to an explosion of commercial activity, leading in turn to growth in the size and wealth of the merchant class.

The dynasty was founded by CHAO K'uang-yin (927-976), better known by his temple name (q.v.) Sung T'ai Tsu (r. 960-976, q.v.). He was the military commander of the Later Chou dynasty, last of the Five Dynasties (906-960, q.v.) which preceded the Sung. He conquered much of China that had been under the T'ang, though not in the northwest nor north of the Huang Ho (Yellow river, q.v.). He was succeeded by his brother, temple name Sung T'ai Tsung (r. 976-997). He, too, was an effective ruler, but was defeated by the Liao in 986 in his bid to extend Sung control as far as the Great Wall. This northern area, which includes Peking, did not come under Chinese control again until the establishment of the Ming dynasty in 1368.

Later Sung emperors have been described as mediocrities or weaklings, patrons of literature and art, but incapable of providing the political and military leadership needed when faced with vigorous enemies. Relations with the Liao and the Hsi Hsia alternated between hostilities, in which the Sung usually lost territory, and humiliating periods in which the Sung sent tribute (q.v.), though it was never referred to as such.

Early in the 12th century the Liao began to feel pressure from a Tungusic group based in Manchuria, called Juchen (q.v.), or Nü-chih, ancestors of the Manchus who conquered China in the 17th century and established the Ch'ing dynasty (1644-1911, q.v.). At first the Sung welcomed the Juchen as distant allies, and coordinated attacks against the Liao. By 1115, the Juchen had taken Peking from the Liao and established the Chin dynasty (q.v.). By 1125 the Liao had been overthrown, and by 1127 the Chin had captured Kaifeng, and with it the eighth emperor, Sung Hui Tsung (r. 1101-1126, q.v.), one of the most famous calligraphers in Chinese history.

A son of Sung Hui Tsung, temple name Sung Kao Tsung (r. 1127-1162), escaped capture and acceded to the throne. The capital was relocated to present-day Hangchow, where the Southern Sung continued until the Mongol conquest of 1278. The Venetian traveler Marco Polo (1254-1324,

q.v.) spent several years in Hangchow after the Mongol conquest, and provided the first description of the city by a Westerner. What he described was essentially the Sung capital under Mongol occupation.

Key figures of the Sung period include SU Tung-po, famous poet, essayist and official; WANG An-shih, his adversary in politics; CHU Hsi, Neo-Confucian philosopher; and YÜEH Fei, the most famous general of the era (qq.v.).

Sung artistic achievements are notable, and the wealth of the new merchant class provided patronage for painters and calligraphers. The important ceramic center of Chingtechen (q.v.) was founded in the Sung dynasty and has been producing ceramics nearly continuously ever since.

Gernet, Jacques. Daily Life in China. pbk. ed. Stanford: Stanford University Press, 1970.

SUNG Chiao-jen. See under **YUAN Shih-k'ai** and **Second Revolution.**

Sung Hui Tsung (1082-1135 A.D.). Temple name (q.v.) of the eighth emperor of the Sung dynasty (960-1279 A.D.) who reigned from 1101 to 1126. Hui Tsung followed his brother on the throne, and soon proved himself something less than a strong ruler, though he was a famous painter, calligrapher and patron of the arts. At the time of his accession, the Juchen (q.v.) were exerting pressure on the Liao dynasty (q.v.), based at Peking. Since the Liao were perceived as a threat, the Sung welcomed the Juchen pressure, and cooperated with them. The Juchen overthrew the Liao, replacing their rule with their own Chin dynasty (1115-1234 A.D., q.v.), and proceeded to capture Kaifeng, the Sung capital, in 1126.

Hui Tsung abdicated in favor of his son, but the two were soon captured by the Juchen, and Hui Tsung lived out his life in exile. The Sung did not disappear, but moved their capital to Hangchow, where the dynasty known to history as the Southern Sung continued to rule until defeated by the Mongols in 1279.

Hui Tsung is famous for his artistic gifts. Both paintings and calligraphy attributed to him are extant. He is credited with creating the academy style of painting and his calligraphic style, "Slender Gold," is widely admired. An example of it may be seen in Chiang Yee's *Chinese Calligraphy*, Cambridge, Harvard University Press, 1973 (revised edition).

The first emperor of the Southern Sung was another son of Hui Tsung, and it is possible that his reluctance to restore the throne to his brother in captivity led to unwillingness to permit the able general YUEH Fei (q.v.) to invade the Chin.

Sung T'ai Tsu (927-976 A.D.). Temple name (q.v.) of CHAO K'uang-yin, founder of the Sung dynasty (960-1279, q.v.), who reigned from 960 to 976. He was commander of military forces of the Later Chou dynasty (951-960), the last of the Five Dynasties (906-960, q.v.), which are accepted by traditional Chinese scholars as legitimate successors to the T'ang dynasty (618-906, q.v.). A skilled strategist, he overthrew the Later Chou ruler, conquered several semi-independent states in South China and managed to reunite under the Sung dynasty all the T'ang lands south of the Huang Ho (Yellow river). He was unable to conquer the part of North China between the river and the Great Wall, which was held by the Liao dynasty (907-1125, q.v.), or the northwest, which was held by the Hsi Hsia (882-1227, q.v.).

Szechwan (Sichuan) **province**. Area: 570,000 sq. km. (220,000 sq. mi.). Population: 97,740,000 (1980). Capital: Chengtu (Chengdu, q.v.). Szechwan is bounded on the east by Hupeh and Hunan, on the south by Kweichow and Yunnan, on the west by Tibet, and on the north by Tsinghai, Kansu and Shensi (qq.v.).

Szechwan consists of a large and fertile central plain surrounded by mountains. While the Han Chinese predominate, there are significant minority populations, particularly Tibetans in the western mountains. Large harvests of rice and wheat are important in agriculture, as well as peanuts, soybeans and fruit.

The old name for Szechwan was Shu (q.v.), for the kingdom of that name. Because of the mountains, Szechwan is not easy to conquer militarily. The emperor T'ang Ming-huang (r. 713-755, q.v.) retreated to Szechwan during the rebellion of AN Lu-shan (q.v.). It is also the site of Chungking (Chongqing), the Nationalist capital during World War II.

Szechwan (the name means "four rivers") has a distinctive spicy cuisine, similar to that of Hunan province. One of the province's most famous tourist attractions is the ride down the Yangtze river from Chungking to Ichang (Yichang). The river drops 500 feet in a distance of 400 miles through a series of spectacular gorges.

Tael. A word of Malay derivation referring to a unit of account equivalent to one ounce of silver. China did not have a national currency until 1933 (see under **Money**) and international trade was conducted in terms of foreign currencies, while internal trade was calculated in ounces of silver. Since different localities used different scales, taels could vary considerably. Some banknotes denominated in taels were issued, but its primary use was as a unit of account.

Taiping Rebellion (1850-1864). The major internal military challenge to the Ch'ing dynasty (1644-1911, q.v.) in the 19th century, it has also been described as the most destructive war in the entire century, with casualties of at least 20 million, though some estimates run much higher. The leader of the Taiping movement, HUNG Hsiu-ch'uan (1813-1864, q.v.), was a Hakka (q.v.) from Kwangtung province. He was influenced by Protestant Christianity and adopted some elements of Christian belief in establishing his ideology. After a series of visions some years earlier, in 1843 he declared himself the son of God and younger brother of Jesus Christ, thus completing a new trinity.

The first adherents of HUNG's new movement were largely his relatives and friends. Forced out of Kwangtung by local opposition, they moved to Kwangsi, where they converted fellow Hakka and members of the Miao tribal minority. They were joined by local outlaws and by July 1850 were strong enough to come into open rebellion. Efforts by the local governor to suppress the rebels were unsuccessful, even when augmented by additional troops sent by the central government.

In September 1851 HUNG was named "Celestial King of the Celestial Kingdom of Peace," and 1851 was declared the first year of the new dynasty. In 1852 Taiping troops began to move northward towards Hunan, though constantly under attack from Ch'ing forces. Their success in Hunan, although they failed to take Changsha, attracted thousands of recruits to the cause. In December they reached the Yangtze valley. In January 1853 they occupied Wuchang for a month, then moved on to take Kiukiang, Anking and, finally, Nanking in March. Nanking remained the Taiping capital until its fall in July 1864. Shortly after this success, an expedition was sent north to capture Peking and overthrow the Ch'ing dynasty. It was unsuccessful in dealing with cavalry, and was finally defeated in 1855 by the Mongol general Seng-ko-lin-ch'in (q.v.). Although defeated in the north, the rebellion continued in the Yangtze valley for nearly another decade.

The Taiping movement was

fortunate in attracting in its early years several men who rose to high military position and demonstrated great capability. It was unfortunate in that HUNG's decision to lead a life of ease in his palace led to thoughts of usurpation, rivalry and dissension among these leaders. Several were assassinated, along with thousands of their followers. HUNG's relatives, who replaced them, proved incompetent.

While the rebels enjoyed some sympathy from Western observers in the beginning, toward the end the attacks on Shanghai were successfully resisted chiefly by Western troops. The two Westerners best known in this connection were the American Frederick Townsend Ward (1831-1862) and the British soldier Charles George ("Chinese") Gordon (1833-1885, qq.v.), who were successive commanders of a Western-trained and Western-officered Chinese force known as the Ever-Victorious Army.

Final defeat of the Taiping was due mainly to the efforts of the Chinese, particularly LI Hung-chang (1823-1901), TSENG Kuo-fan (1811-1872) and TSO Tsung-t'ang (1812-1885, qq.v). The final siege of Nanking lasted from May 31, 1862 until July 19, 1864. HUNG Hsiu-ch'uan committed suicide some time in June, and his body, wrapped in yellow satin embroidered with imperial dragons (a color and decoration reserved expressly for members of the imperial family), was found in a sewer beneath his palace.

The Taiping introduced a number of reforms, some based on ancient Chinese ideals and others on Christian concepts. A new calendar was introduced, including, for the first time in Chinese history, Sunday as a day of rest. While there were periods when strict celibacy was enforced, marriage was compulsory for women, and monogamy was the rule. Prostitution, adultery, slavery, witchcraft, gambling, and the use of opium, tobacco or alcohol were all banned. Footbinding (q.v.) was also banned, probably a reflection of the strong Hakka influence on the movement.

The roots of the rebellion probably include such factors as the decline in the prestige of the Ch'ing dynasty after the defeat in the Opium War (1839-1842, q.v.), the long-rankling southern antipathy to the Manchu (q.v.) rulers, economic difficulties connected with population increase, the decline of country handicrafts in the face of foreign imports and dissatisfaction with official corruption.

The Taiping Rebellion was ultimately unsuccessful, but it has remained a topic of intense interest to historians. The Cantonese SUN Yat-sen, 1866-1925 (q.v.), father of the Republic of China (q.v.), grew up in an area where the Taiping traditions survived and was clearly influenced by them.

Jen, Yu-wen. *The Taiping Revolutionary Movement.* New Haven: Yale University Press, 1973.

Meadows, T.T. *The Chinese and Their Rebellions.* Stanford: Academic Reprints, no date. (Original, 1856.)

Taiwan province. Area: 35,800 sq. km. (13,850 sq. mi.). Population: 18,500,000 (1983). Taiwan is an island, separated from Fukien province on the mainland by the Taiwan Strait (also known as the Formosa Strait), which is some 80 miles wide at its narrowest. Taiwan is also known as Formosa, meaning "beautiful," a name given to it by Portuguese sailors, though there is no indication that there was ever a Portuguese settlement there.

The earliest residents of Taiwan were not Chinese. Their descendants, known as Taiwan Aborigines, still live in the mountainous areas on the eastern side of the island. They are believed to be ethnically related to several minority groups found elsewhere in China, notably the Miao. Linguistically, these people are classified as Deutero-Malay, and the languages they speak are related to some of those in use in the Philippines and other parts of Southeast Asia. The languages are unrelated to Chinese.

The first Western settlements on the island were made by the Dutch in 1624 near the southern city of Tainan. The Spanish arrived a few years later and settled near Keelung in the north. They were driven out by the Dutch in 1641. The Dutch dealt directly with the indigenous population, brought in Protestant clergy and converted many aborigines to Christianity. When the island was seized by CHENG Ch'eng-kung (1624-1662, q.v.) in 1662, five of these ministers were put to the sword. (CHENG Ch'eng-kung, also known as Koxinga, was a supporter of the fallen Ming dynasty and his heirs held out against the Manchus until 1683.)

In 1884 France invaded Taiwan in connection with its war with China over what is now Vietnam (q.v.). The Chinese government sent LIU Ming-ch'uan (q.v.) as military commander, a position he filled with ability and relative success. The French left in 1885. In 1886 Taiwan was declared a separate province and LIU was named the first provincial governor. He built Taipei, the capital, in Western style, with paved streets. He also constructed one of the first railroads on Chinese soil, connecting Taipei with Keelung. Under suspicion by the court at Peking for his radical reforms in Taiwan, he was removed in 1891.

As a result of the Sino-Japanese War (q.v.), Taiwan was ceded to Japan in 1895. Prior to the arrival of the Japanese troops, however, Taiwanese leaders had declared their independence, establishing the "Republic of Formosa" (Taiwan Min Chu Kuo) on May 23, 1895. They appealed for support to foreign powers, but none was forthcoming, since the declaration had come after the signing of the Treaty of Shimonoseki (q.v.) and had been made with the known support of the Ch'ing government.

The Japanese occupied Taiwan from 1895 until their surrender in 1945 after World War II. While they were no more free from civil unrest than their predecessors, on the whole the strict controls they used seem to have been effective. The Japanese modernized Taiwan by extending the railway network, providing electricity nearly island-wide, and by introducing such amenities as municipal garbage collection.

In November 1943, following the Cairo Conference (q.v.), which was attended by U.S. President Franklin Roosevelt, British Prime Minister Winston Churchill and Generalissimo Chiang Kai-shek (q.v.), the Cairo Declaration was issued announcing Allied aims against Japan and pledging the return of Manchuria, the Pescadores and Taiwan to China. Japan surrendered on August 14, 1945, and Taiwan was officially returned to China on October 25.

On December 7, 1949, the Nationalist government moved its seat to Taipei, where it has remained ever since.

Less than 2 percent of Taiwan's population may be counted as aboriginal tribesmen. This group lives in the mountainous area of eastern Taiwan and is referred to in Chinese as *kao shan tzu*, or "high mountain people." Their lowland cousins have long since been Sinicized or assimilated. The vast majority of the residents of Taiwan are of Chinese descent, whether they themselves emigrated from China or whether their ancestors did so many centuries ago. Prior to the Japanese takeover in 1895, the overwhelming preponderance of these Taiwanese came from Fukien province, principally Amoy, with some from Kwangtung. The Taiwanese dialect is nearly indistinguishable from that of Amoy.

Some of Taiwan's native inhabitants are Hakka (q.v.) and that dialect is also spoken in Taiwan. Those inhabitants who arrived in Taiwan after 1945 have more disparate origins. One thing they tend to have in common is an ability to speak Mandarin (*kuo yü*; see under **Language, spoken**). However, since Mandarin has been the medium of instruction in all schools in Taiwan since 1945, most Taiwanese who have been educated since that time also speak it. Older Taiwanese may have been educated in Japanese and are frequently still at home in that language.

Taiyuan. Capital of Shansi province (q.v.).

Talas, Battle of (751 A.D.). The battle was fought near the river Talas in Central Asia, hence its name. Chinese troops were roundly defeated by Muslim Arabs. It was a dramatic setback for the T'ang dynasty (q.v.) which lost command of the Kashgar area. For this reason it may have been a contributory factor in the AN Lu-shan Rebellion (q.v.) which began in 755.

A secondary result of the defeat was the Arab capture of significant numbers of Chinese acquainted with the technique of making paper (q.v.). By the end of the century the technique was known in Bagdad and more than three centuries later was used in Europe.

T'ang 1. T'ang Dynasty (618-906 A.D.). The T'ang dynasty was one of the glorious periods of Chinese history. The list of rulers includes 20 emperors and one empress—the only woman in Chinese imperial history who reigned in her own right. The dynasty was founded by LI Yuan and his son LI Shih-min, who are known to history by their temple names (q.v.) as T'ang Kao Tsu and T'ang T'ai Tsung, respectively (qq.v.).

The LI family was one of aristocratic origin in North China, and had intermarried with non-Chinese (Tartar) families. Both LIs were accomplished military figures. T'ang China was strong enough to reestablish a Chinese military presence in Central Asia, which had been absent since the end of the Han dynasty (206 B.C.-221 A.D., q.v.).

T'ang rule was also extended to Kwangtung province, whose people to this day identify themselves as "men of T'ang" rather than "men of Han," which is more customary among other Chinese. Chinese influence also extended to Korea, and cultural influence to Japan. The Japanese sent a series of embassies, first to the preceding Sui dynasty (589-618, q.v.) and then to the T'ang. The last of these, which reached China in 838, was accompanied by the Japanese Buddhist monk Ennin (q.v.) whose diary is the oldest extant firsthand account of China written by a non-Chinese.

T'ang poetry (q.v.) is held by many scholars to be the finest flowering of that literary art. Some 50,000 poems from the period are known, and several hundred of these have been translated into English. Several of China's best-known literary figures (e.g., LI Po, PO Chü-yi and TU Fu [qq.v.]) are remembered chiefly for their poetry.

Among the most famous painters of

the period are WANG Wei (q.v.), WU Tao-tzu and YEN Li-pen. While it is unlikely that any paintings of the period have survived, with the exception of some in Japan, copies made in later periods can give us some idea of the masterworks. Religious paintings done by anonymous artists do exist, particularly frescoes.

Foreign trade flourished during the T'ang and many foreigners were to be found in China. Foreigners brought in religions other than Buddhism, and there is evidence of Nestorian Christians (q.v.) in Changan, as well as other religions, including Islam (q.v.). Trade came not only over the well-traveled Silk Road (q.v.), but also by ship to Canton. Persian and Arab traders are known to have conducted trade at that port, and special administrative offices existed to control it.

Buddhism (q.v.) which had been introduced some time in the later Han dynasty, and which had flourished in the following years, reached its zenith under the T'ang. Indian monks, and those from Central Asia, had brought the foreign religion, and during the T'ang such Chinese pilgrims as Hsuan-tsang (q.v.) traveled to India and brought back sacred texts for translation. Temples and monasteries were erected throughout China and men and women repaired to these institutions as monks and nuns.

A great reaction occurred in the 840s, under the emperor Wu Tsung, who was an ardent believer in Taoism (q.v.). There was a tradition that held that the imperial family, whose surname was LI, was descended from Lao Tzu, the founder of Taoism and the author of the Tao Te Ching (qq.v.), and that may have influenced the emperor. The next emperor lifted the ban on Buddhism which was carried out under Wu Tsung, but Buddhism never again attained such levels of prosperity.

The influence of Buddhism on Chinese thought, however, was undeniable, and even those who developed Neo-Confucianism in the Sung dynasty (960-1279, qq.v.) were affected by Buddhist concepts.

Two unsuccessful efforts to overthrow the dynasty were made. The first was by Empress WU (q.v.) who ruled first through her husband, the emperor Kao Tsung, from 660-683, and then usurped the throne in 684. She changed the name of the dynasty to Chou in 690 and ruled until 705, when the T'ang dynasty was restored.

The second effort was made by AN Lu-shan (q.v.) in 755. He was a general of Tartar ancestry whose area of control was centered near Peking. His rebellion was suppressed after a few years, but it resulted in the flight and abdication of the emperor T'ang Ming Huang, and succeeding emperors never had the power of the earlier rulers of the dynasty.

The rebellion had another result, in that the northeastern part of China remained somewhat independent of central rule in Changan. When the dynasty fell in 906, this area was held by the Liao, Chin and Yuan dynasties (qq.v.) until the establishment of the Ming in 1368.

The T'ang dynasty collapsed in 906 after a generation or more of disunity and unrest. Later Chinese historians regard a series of short-lived states known as the Five Dynasties (q.v.) as the legitimate heirs of the Mandate of Heaven (q.v.), although the Tartar dynasties of Liao and Chin are also accepted in the canon of imperial dynasties. Parts of the empire remained under the control of local rulers. These states are referred to as the Ten Kingdoms (q.v.).

2. Later T'ang (923-936). The second of the Five Dynasties.

3. Southern T'ang (937-975). One of the Ten Kingdoms.

T'ang Hsuan Tsung. There are two emperors of the T'ang dynasty (618-906 A.D., q.v.) whose temple names (q.v.) are romanized with this spelling, though the characters used for "Hsuan" are different. The distinction is apparent to a reader of Chinese.

1. The first, Hsuan Tsung (685-762, r. 713-755), better known as T'ang Ming Huang (q.v.), was the seventh ruler of the dynasty. He was forced to abdicate as a result of the rebellion of AN Lu-shan (q.v.). His love affair with his favorite consort, YANG Kui Fei (q.v.) is known to all students of T'ang history, and was the inspiration for one of the most famous of Chinese poems, the *Song of Unending Sorrow*, by PO Chü-yi (772-846, q.v.).

2. The second, Hsuan Tsung (r. 847-859), was the 17th ruler of the dynasty. His predecessor, T'ang Wu Tsung, is remembered primarily as the man responsible for the suppression of Buddhism (see under **Ennin**). Hsuan Tsung reversed that policy, though the Buddhist church never regained its former preeminent position.

T'ang Kao Tsu (566-635 A.D.). Temple name (q.v.) of the first emperor of the T'ang dynasty, 618-906 A.D., who reigned 618-625. His original name was LI Yuan, and he came from an aristocratic North China (q.v.) family much intermarried with ruling Turkic families. He and the emperor Sui Yang Ti (r. 605-617 A.D., q.v.) married sisters who were non-Chinese.

The last years of the Sui dynasty (589-618, q.v.) found the empire in disarray. This was at least partly due to the heavy exactions in men and money required to support the emperor Yang Ti's unsuccessful campaigns against the Turks and the Koreans, as well as his grandiose public works, such as the Grand Canal (q.v.). Hundreds of thousands of men were conscripted for these purposes, and many died.

LI Yuan was military commander of North China and, after emperor Yang Ti's murder at Yangchow, set up the emperor's grandson as a puppet. Within a year he had eliminated the child and established a new dynasty. In 626 his son LI Shih-min killed his oldest brother, the heir apparent, seized the capital and forced his father's abdication. T'ang Kao Tsu spent the next 10 years in retirement with the title "retired emperor."

Traditional Chinese history has pictured Kao Tsu as a luxury-loving and rather unworthy emperor, and has credited the establishment of the dynasty to his son, LI Shih-min, who reigned as T'ang T'ai Tsung (q.v.). Present-day historians regard this as a misleading interpretation fostered during T'ai Tsung's reign to please that emperor. Kao Tsu's record of military activity both before his ascent of the throne and during the early years when he was assuring the success of his dynasty by defeating competitors is proof of his capability.

T'ang Kao Tsung (?-683). Temple name of the third emperor of the T'ang dynasty (618-906, q.v.) who reigned from 650 to 683. Kao Tsung was the son of T'ang T'ai Tsung (q.v.), the second T'ang emperor, but quite unlike his predecessor. Far from being an astute warrior, he was compliant and was soon under the influence of his consort, known to later history as Empress Wu (q.v.).

Taking advantage of Kao Tsung's illness in 660, Empress Wu started to accompany him to imperial audiences, hiding at first behind a screen, but soon dispensing with that subterfuge. At Kao Tsung's death in 683, he was succeeded first by one son and then by another. Both were also sons of the empress. She ruled through them until 690, then abolished the dynasty and established her own.

While Kao Tsung's reign ended inauspiciously, it witnessed some solid accomplishments. The military power of the preceding reign continued to grow, enhancing Chinese presence in Central Asia and down to the borders of India. The Koreans were defeated, and the Japanese, who had established a foothold in southern Korea, were ousted.

However, toward the end of Kao Tsung's reign, the Tibetans gained possession of some of the cities of the Tarim basin, and the Turks in Ili and Mongolia took advantage of the situation to throw off Chinese control. Similarly, the Koreans rebelled and regained much of their former independence.

T'ang Ming Huang (685-762 A.D., r. 713-755). Customary name for the sixth emperor and seventh ruler of the T'ang dynasty (618-906 A.D., q.v.). The sixth ruler was Empress Wu (q.v.). T'ang Ming Huang, whose temple name (q.v.) was T'ang Hsuan Tsung (q.v.), was the grandson of T'ang Kao Tsung (q.v.) and Empress Wu. His father T'ang Jui Tsung, reigned briefly both before and after the notorious empress, but was not a strong figure and abdicated in 712 in favor of his third son.

Ming Huang's reign covered the period when T'ang culture was at its peak. The poets LI Po and TU Fu (qq.v.) lived and wrote at that time,

and the poet-painter WANG Wei (q.v.) was active in the capital at Changan. Ming Huang established both the Hanlin Academy and the Pear Garden (qq.v.); the first was made up of those scholars who had distinguished themselves in the imperial examinations (see **Examination system**), and the second, a training school, of actors, dancers and musicians.

Changan was perhaps the most brilliant city of its time. The population of the metropolitan district in 742 A.D. was reported at 1,960,188, and we may assume that 1 million of those were living in the city itself. The Chinese empire was at its apogee, as Ming Huang's troops extended Chinese influence in Central Asia even farther than before. The capital sheltered a wide range of foreigners, both residents and transients. In addition to the flourishing Buddhist church, adherents of Nestorian Christianity (q.v.), Manicheans and Zoroastrians, and refugees from Muslim victories in Persia and nearby areas are known to have been present.

Three embassies from Japan reached Changan during Ming Huang's reign, in 717, 733 and 752. Changan was the model for the capital of Heian Japan, present day Kyoto. (For a later Japanese visitor to T'ang China, see **Ennin**.)

Ming Huang is famous not only for his luxurious style of life, which was conducted in vast palaces similar to those that survive in Peking, but also for his infatuation with his famous consort YANG Kuei Fei (q.v.), and for his ultimate fall from power.

Under the concept of the Mandate of Heaven (q.v.), the emperor was held responsible for the well-being of the state and civil polity. A series of disasters—droughts, earthquakes, floods, fires and invasions—in the early 750s were attributed to a lack of imperial virtue, and led in 755 to the rebellion of AN Lu-shan (q.v.). Ming Huang fled to Szechwan, former seat of the kingdom of Shu (q.v.), taking YANG with him. (Paintings purporting to show the flight of Ming Huang to Shu are a staple of Chinese art.) His army forced YANG's execution, an event which has been immortalized by one of the most famous of all Chinese poems, the *Song of Unending Sorrow*, by PO Chü-yi (q.v.).

Ming Huang abdicated in favor of one of his sons in 756 and lived until 762. T'ang forces eventually retook Changan, and the dynasty survived for another century and a half. But the glory days were over, and no succeeding emperor ever achieved the position of T'ang Ming Huang.

Pulleyblank, E.G. *The Background of the Rebellion of An Lu-shan*. London: Oxford University Press, 1955.

T'ang T'ai Tsung (600-649). Temple name (q.v.) of the second emperor of the T'ang dynasty (618-906, q.v.). His original name was LI Shih-min, and he reigned from 627 to 649. Handsome, vigorous and personable, he is the most admired emperor in Chinese history. The LI family, like other aristocratic families of North China (q.v.), was of mixed ancestry; both his mother and his paternal grandmother were non-Chinese.

LI Shih-min was a dashing young officer who rescued the second emperor of the Sui dynasty, Yang Ti (qq.v.) from the Turks in 617, and later encouraged his father to establish the new dynasty. His father did so, and became T'ang Kao Tsu (q.v.) in 618.

LI Shih-min was the second son, and not the heir apparent. By a stratagem, T'ang Kao Tsu arranged to have his eldest son assassinated. (It should be noted that the eldest son seems to have been caught trying to murder his younger brother.) In 627,

T'ang Kao Tsu abdicated in favor of T'ang T'ai Tsung, whose successful reign became legendary.

T'ai Tsung administered such a military defeat to the Turks that peace on the northwest frontier lasted for half a century. He extended Chinese rule as far as Samarkand and Bokhara. While the empire reached an even greater extent after his death, T'ai Tsung extended it farther than at any time since the Han dynasty (206 B.C.-221 A.D., q.v.).

The non-Chinese parts of the empire were administered by their own princes, many of whose sons were sent to the T'ang capital at Changan as hostages. The Chinese parts were administered by a centralized bureaucracy, many of whose members were selected through the examination system (q.v.).

T'ai Tsung's greatest military setback was his failure to subdue the Koreans, but this did not lead to disaster as it had in the Sui dynasty. He beat off an attack by the recently unified Tibetans and sent an imperial princess to marry their king, thus cementing an alliance.

The LI family claimed descent from Lao Tze (q.v.), whose surname was also LI, and thus was predisposed towards Taoism. T'ai Tsung was eclectic, however, and strengthened the Confucian cult. He also showed favor to Buddhism, and received the Buddhist pilgrim Hsuan-tsang (qq.v.) on the latter's return from India.

T'ai Tsung was succeeded by his son, whose temple name was Kao Tsung (q.v.), and who was a much less dominant personality than his father. One inadvertent legacy was the Lady Wu, who had been a concubine in T'ai Tsung's court. At his death she, along with all the other court ladies, was sent to a Buddhist convent. She had taken the precaution of attracting the attention of the heir apparent prior to the emperor's death, and he visited her in the convent. She soon left to become the new emperor's consort and bore him a son. She later was known as the Empress Wu (q.v.), the only woman to rule imperial China in her own right.

Fitzgerald, C.P. *Son of Heaven: A Biography of Li Shih-min, Founder of the T'ang Dynasty.* New York: AMS Press, 1971 (reprint).

Tangshan earthquake. On July 28, 1976, two earthquakes occurred, 16 hours apart, centered near Tangshan, an industrial and mining center in Hopeh province, 100 miles southeast of Peking. The first shock registered 8.2 on the Richter scale, and the second 7.9. Although no official figures were released, it is estimated that about 650,000 people may have died in the disaster, making it the most lethal natural calamity in several centuries.

Conventional Chinese belief holds that a change of dynasty is portended by natural disasters. Since CHOU Enlai (1898-1976) had died in January and CHU Teh (1886-1976) in July, the death of MAO Tse-tung (1893-1976, qq.v.) in September came as no surprise to traditionalists.

Tao Te Ching. This book, written by Lao Tzu (q.v.), is credited with being the philosophical basis of Taoism (q.v.). It was written some time between the sixth and third centuries B.C. It is a short book, about 5,000 characters, but it is obscure and vague enough to be interpreted in almost any way its devotees may choose. It has been translated into English at least 35 times, and many of these translations differ greatly from one another. One reason is that it does not mention specific persons, places or events. If anything, it is a discussion of metaphysics.

The *Tao Te Ching* has fascinated generations of Chinese scholars and many of them have become "philosophical " Taoists, pursuing the doctrine of inaction and attempting to attune their lives to the concept of the "Tao." The word means way, or road, literally, but can be taken as a metaphor for nature in the cosmic sense.

The book has inspired many commentaries, in Chinese, similar to the commentaries which are attached to the Confucian classics (q.v.). At one time this set of Taoist classics was accepted as the material for the imperial examination system (q.v.) but that did not last. One T'ang emperor decreed that every noble family have a copy of the book.

Waley, Arthur. *The Way and Its Power.* London: Allen & Unwin, 1934.

Welch, Holmes. *Taoism: The Parting of the Way.* Boston: Beacon Press, 1957.

Tao Kuang (1782-1850). Reign title (q.v.) of the sixth emperor (r. 1821-1850) of the Ch'ing dynasty (q.v.). He was the second son of Chia Ch'ing (r. 1796-1820, q.v.). Inheriting an empire with a depleted treasury, he faced repeated calls for expenditure on a war in Central Asia and frequent flooding of the Huang Ho (q.v.) (Yellow river). Tao Kuang was frugal and reduced palace expenses to the extent he could. He also ended the war, but was less successful in dealing with the floods.

He was also faced with the problem of the opium trade (q.v.), conducted largely by the British. By the 1830s the increase in the import of opium led to the export and shortage of silver. The result was economic dislocation. In addition, the Board of Revenue reported a population of 400 million for the first time in 1835. A combination of moral and economic reasons led the emperor to ban the import of opium and to send LIN Tse-hsü (1785-1850, q.v.) to Canton to stop the trade. The measures LIN took outraged the foreign traders and led to the Opium War (1839-1842, q.v.). Only foreign victories persuaded the emperor to negotiate peace through Ch'i-shan (d. 1854, q.v.). The Treaty of Nanking (1842, q.v.) which resulted called for an indemnity, which, because the emperor refused to pay it from central government funds, was taken from provincial levies.

The military defeat revealed to many Chinese the weakness of their Manchu (q.v.) rulers, and in this way led to the later outbreak of the Taiping Rebellion (1851-1864, q.v.), which Tao Kuang did not live to see. He was succeeded by his fourth son, who reigned as Hsien Feng (1851-1861, q.v.).

Hummel, Arthur W., ed. *Eminent Chinese of the Ch'ing Period*. Washington: Government Printing Office, 1943.

T'AO Ch'ien (365-427 A.D.). Also known as T'AO Yuan-ming, and generally regarded as the outstanding poet of the Period of Disunity (q.v.) between the fall of the Han dynasty (q.v.) in 221 A.D. and the rise of the Sui (q.v.) in 589. He was known as a recluse, and spent only a short time as a government official.

T'AO is most famous not for a poem but for a story in prose whose title is sometimes translated as "The Peach-Tree Spring." It concerns a solitary fisherman who finds an orchard of blooming peach trees on a riverbank. He stops to admire them and follows a small stream flowing from a cave-like opening. He enters the cave and finds it opens onto a small valley, whose inhabitants welcome him. He learns that they have been living in isolation for 500 years, having fled the disorders of the previous dynasty. He

stays for several days, then returns to report the marvelous finding to the local magistrate. The ensuing expedition fails to find any trace of the valley or its mysterious entrance.

This story held immense attraction for later scholars, such as WANG Wei (701-761, q.v.), who wrote a poem on the subject. Many others have used the theme in one way or another. T'AO's poems in praise of the simple life and expressing appreciation of nature drew a large following for centuries, and his work is still available both in Chinese and in translation.

Hightower, James Robert, trans. *The Poetry of T'ao Ch'ien*. Oxford: Clarendon Press, 1970.

Taoism. Taoism is one of the three major indigenous Chinese philosophies (the other two being Confucianism and Legalism, qq.v.), though in one aspect it became a popular religion. The origin of Taoism is Lao Tzu's *Tao Te Ching* (qq.v.), a short text which has been in existence since the late Chou dynasty (q.v.). Two other early texts are the *Chuang Tzu* and the *Lieh Tzu*.

In Chou times, particularly during the Warring States Period (q.v.), different philosophic schools arose proposing solutions for the problem of chronic warfare. The Taoist solution might be described as getting in tune with nature, rooting out ambition and returning to a simpler (and possibly imaginary) past. In chapter 80 of the *Tao Te Ching* the ideal is described as a land of villagers content to be able to hear the dogs bark and roosters crow in a nearby village without ever paying it a visit.

At the same time, what might be described as the religious, as contrasted with the philosophic, brand of Taoism developed into a search for immortality and/or longevity. This involved a search for the "Isles of the Blest," believed to be in the sea off Shantung, as well as elixirs and pills with marvelous properties. According to their promoters they could confer invisibility and the gift of levitation, among other qualities. The religious branch of Taoism also produced the Eight Immortals (q.v.), each with an identifying emblem. These are frequently found as decorations.

Taoism was influenced by Buddhism (q.v.) in several ways—the burning of incense and the establishment of monasteries are two obvious examples. Taoism also saw Buddhism as an opponent, and at various times debates were held at which Buddhists, Taoists and Confucians were required to uphold their positions in the presence of the emperor. Though the Taoists sometimes won these debates, the lack of a systematic theology was a drawback. Nevertheless, the Taoists managed to engineer two drastic suppressions of Buddhism in 446 and 845 A.D., having secured imperial support for their position. The struggle with Buddhism continued intermittently, and the Taoists were suppressed from time to time. In 1281 Khubilai Khan (q.v.) ordered the burning of all Taoist texts except the *Tao Te Ching*. The destruction was not complete, but it did reduce the Taoist canon from 4565 volumes to 1120 in the subsequent Ming dynasty (q.v.) edition.

Waley, Arthur. *Three Ways of Thought in Ancient China*. London: George Allen & Unwin, 1953.

Welch, Holmes. *Taoism: The Parting of the Way*. Boston: Beacon Press, 1957.

Tartar Dynasties. The term refers to the Liao (907-1125), the Western Liao (1125-1168) and the Chin (1115-1234, qq.v.). The Liao dynasty was based in Manchuria (q.v.) and was established at the time of the fall of the T'ang dynasty (618-906, q.v.). It never controlled all of China since it was contemporaneous with the Sung dynasty, 960-1279 (q.v.), which controlled Central and South China, but at its greatest extent it covered an area from Korea in the east to Central Asia in the west. The Liao were known to Chinese historians as Ch'itan and in Central Asia as Khitai (see under **Cathay**). They spoke an Altaic language and were stock breeders, as well as hunters and fishers, leaving agriculture to their Chinese subjects.

The Liao were overthrown by the Chin, also based in Manchuria and related ethnically and linguistically. The Chin extended their rule farther south than the Liao had been able to do, taking Kaifeng, the Sung capital, and forcing the Sung to flee south to the Yangtze valley.

At the time of the Chin victory not all the Liao were content to submit to the conquerors, and some of the royal family, under the leadership of Yeh-lü Ta-shih, fled to the steppes of Central Asia and there established what is known in Chinese history as the Western Liao, and to those farther west as the Kara Khitai, or Black Khitai. Both the Western Liao and the Chin were conquered by the Mongols who established the Yuan dynasty (1279-1368, q.v.).

The dynastic histories of the Liao, Western Liao and Chin are accepted by Chinese scholars as part of the canon of dynastic histories (q.v.).

Wittfogel, Karl A. and Feng Chia-sheng. *History of Chinese Society, Liao*. Philadelphia: American Philosophical Society, 1949.

Tea. Like silk (q.v.), tea is one of China's major contributions to the world. The shrub is believed to grow wild in some parts of the Himalayas and was introduced to China by Buddhist monks some time before the

T'ang dynasty (618-906 A.D., q.v.). It was widely used at that time, and is mentioned by the Japanese Buddhist monk Ennin, (q.v.) whose account of his travels in China in the ninth century provides a contemporary view.

Tea was exported overland to Russia, but the greatest export was by sea in the 19th century. In 1867 tea contributed 59 percent of China's exports, but by 1905 it had fallen to 11 percent. This reflected an increase in other exports but, more importantly, an absolute loss in the market. The British succeeded in establishing tea plantations in India and Ceylon, and the opening of Japan provided competition from a new direction. China now produces about 15 percent of the world's tea.

Tehran Conference (November-December 1943). After the completion of the Cairo Conference with CHIANG Kai-shek (qq.v.), British Prime Minister Winston Churchill and U.S. President Franklin Roosevelt flew on to Tehran for a conference with Soviet Marshal Joseph Stalin. While China was not a participant at Tehran, decisions taken there affected it. In return for the definite promise of a second front in Europe in 1944, Stalin agreed to enter the war against Japan when Germany had been defeated. Roosevelt proposed that the port of Dairen (q.v.) would be appropriate compensation for Russian participation. This offer was later expanded at the Yalta Conference (February 1945, q.v.).

Telegraph lines. Conservative Chinese in the late Ch'ing dynasty (1644-1911, q.v.), as well as the authorities themselves, were not anxious for the introduction of telegraph lines, which they lumped with railroads and mining concessions as threats to China's integrity. (See under **Feng Shui**.) There were efforts to construct lines in the 1860s and 1870s.

Telegraphic communication from Shanghai to London was opened on June 3, 1871. LI Hung-chang (q.v.) recommended a line from Shanghai to Tientsin and this was completed on December 24, 1881. It was extended to Peking three years later. The system was rapidly expanded and by the end of the dynasty the Imperial Chinese Telegraph Administration had 560 offices in operation.

The use of telegrams in political communication was a widespread feature of the period of the Republic of China (q.v.), prior to World War II.

Telegraphic code. The introduction of the telegraph to China in the late 19th century posed a new problem. Western languages written with an alphabet could make use of the Morse code, but the Chinese written language (q.v.) is far more complex. The solution was to assign a four-digit number to each of nearly 10,000 characters, and also assign to each one a three-letter combination ranging from AAA, which corresponds to 0000, to ZZY, which corresponds to 9931. Thus a text written in Chinese could be encoded either in numbers or in the Roman alphabet. There are a number of blanks in the system to accommodate special characters which do not appear in the commercial code but which may be important to certain communicators. The code is not secret, and code books may be purchased at Chinese stationary stores.

Temple name. The temple name was assigned to an emperor after his death, and is the name by which he is generally known to posterity. Use of his personal name was taboo during his reign, and for as long as the dynasty lasted. While the emperor lived, the period was referred to by his reign title (q.v.), but this could be changed in consideration of a good omen or a misfortune. The emperor Han Wu Ti (r. 140-87 B.C., q.v.) used 11 reign titles in 54 years, and the emperor T'ang Kao Tsung (r. 650-683 A.D., q.v.) used 14 in 34 years.

With the exception of the last emperor of the Ch'ing, P'u-yi (q.v.), all the Ming dynasty (1368-1644) and Ch'ing dynasty (1644-1911) emperors have temple names, but sources in Western languages rarely refer to them in this way. Instead, the emperors are referred to by their reign titles. With the exception of one Ming emperor who used two reign titles, all the Ming and Ch'ing rulers used only one. At first Westerners assumed the reign title was the emperor's name, and referred to him that way. Chinese emperors of earlier periods are referred to by their temple names, but emperors of the last two dynasties are referred to by their reign titles, particularly by Western historians.

Ten Kingdoms. This term applies to 10 independent states which existed in the period after the fall of the T'ang dynasty and the rise of the Sung, i.e., the Five Dynasties Period (906-960, q.v.). Later historians regard the latter as legitimate, and these states as less so, despite the fact that some of the rulers styled themselves emperor. One of the states, Min (q.v.), is the subject of a study in English, but very little has appeared in Western languages on the others.

TENG Hsiao-p'ing (DENG Xiaoping) 1902-). Born in Szechwan, TENG's political consciousness was apparently awakened by the May Fourth movement (q.v.) of 1919. He joined the work-study movement, spent 1920-1925 in France where he learned French and joined the Chinese Communist party (CCP, q.v.). He returned to China via the USSR. From 1926 to 1932 he was engaged in CCP activities in Shensi and later Kwangsi provinces. In 1932 he moved to the Kiangsi base area controlled by MAO Tse-tung (q.v.), whose faction he joined. He made the Long March (q.v.) with MAO, and held several important posts in North China during the war against Japan (1937-1945).

He was elected to the Central Committee of the CCP in 1945, and after the establishment of the People's Republic of China (PRC, q.v.) in 1949, he held a regional post in Chungking. In 1952 he was transferred to Peking and became a vice premier. After serving a year as minister of finance, he was identified as secretary general of the Central Committee of the CCP in May 1954. His position as chief executive officer of the CCP was enhanced by his prominence in dealing with the international Communist movement. He traveled to Moscow several times as relations between the two powers declined in the early 1960s.

In the aftermath of the Great Leap Forward (q.v.) of 1958, TENG worked closely with LIU Shao-ch'i (q.v.) in an effort to restore the national economy. His pragmatic views were expressed in his famous statement: "I do not care whether a cat is black or white, the important thing is whether it catches mice."

TENG's pragmatism and his identification with LIU made him a prime target of the Cultural Revolution (q.v.). He was purged as the "second capitalist roader" after LIU. In 1973 CHOU En-lai (q.v.) reinstated him as deputy premier. At the time of CHOU's death in January 1976, it was expected that TENG would be named to succeed him as premier. Instead, HUA Kuo-feng, relatively unknown outside party circles, was named acting premier, and TENG was deposed in April, stripped of all his party and government posts, though not of his party membership.

The death of MAO Tse-tung on September 9, 1976, was followed a month later by the elevation of HUA to the chairmanship of the CCP and the purge of CHIANG Ch'ing (q.v.), MAO's widow, and the Gang of Four (q.v.). Posters calling for TENG's reinstatement appeared in Peking in January 1977, and in July he reassumed the deputy premiership, as well as his other party and government posts.

Although officially outranked by other CCP leaders, TENG has clearly been the dominant force in PRC affairs since 1977. Mutual diplomatic recognition between the United States and the PRC was announced on December 15, 1978, and TENG arrived in Washington on an official visit on January 28, 1979.

TENG resigned from his government posts in August 1980 in an action intended to bring younger leaders into the government. However, he retained his party posts and is still, in 1986, the dominant force in China.

Boorman, Howard L., ed. *Biographical Dictionary of Republican China*. New York: Columbia University Press, 1971.

Klein, Donald W. and Anne B. Clark. *Biographic Dictionary of Chinese Communism, 1921-1965*. Cambridge: Harvard University Press, 1971.

Yim, Kwan Ha, ed. *China Since Mao*. New York: Facts On File, 1980.

Thailand. Known as Siam until 1939. The Thai majority of Thailand is related to the Tai (Dai) ethnic minority in China. Ancestors of the Thai were at one time residents of Yunnan province, where their country was known to the Chinese as Nan Chao (q.v.). It was based at Tali and lasted until the Mongols destroyed it in 1253. The defeat caused a flow of refugees to the south, where they joined Thai kingdoms already in existence.

The second king of Sukhothai, Rama Khamheng, sent tribute to the Yuan dynasty (1279-1368, q.v.), and may have visited Peking himself. The decline of the Yuan and the rise of the Ming dynasty (1368-1644, q.v.) coincided with the decline of the Sukhothai kingdom and the rise of Ayudhya in Thailand. Tribute missions went from Ayudhya to the Ming emperors on a frequent and regular basis. Records of the Ch'ing dynasty (1644-1911, q.v.) list Siam as a tributary state with envoys due in Peking every three years. The tributary relationship was denounced by King Chulalongkorn in 1882, a time when Ch'ing weakness precluded any sort of retaliation. While the Ch'ing invaded Burma (q.v.) twice, there was no invasion of Siam. (China and Thailand do not share a common border.)

Thailand opened diplomatic relations with the Republic of China (q.v.) for the first time in 1946, accepting an ambassador and consular personnel. Diplomatic recognition was switched to the People's Republic of China (q.v.) in 1975.

Hall, D.G.E. *A History of South-East Asia*. 4th ed. New York, St. Martin's Press, 1981.

Three Anti movement. An internal-struggle campaign launched by the People's Republic of China (PRC, q.v.) on January 10, 1952. The three targets were corruption, decay and bureaucracy. The human targets were largely government officials who had previously worked for the Republic of China (q.v.), including those who had welcomed the victory of the PRC. Two months later the Five Anti movement (q.v.) was launched against private enterprise.

Three Kingdoms. The term is applied to the successor states to the Han dynasty (206 B.C.-221 A.D., q.v.). They were Wei (220-266 A.D.), Wu (222-280) and Shu (221-263, qq.v.), the latter sometimes known as Shu Han. Wei was located in the north, with its capital at Loyang; Wu was located in the Yangtze valley, with its capital at Wuchang and Nanking successively; and Shu in Szechwan (Shu is the literary name for Szechwan), with Chengtu as its capital.

The period was marked by warfare and diplomacy reminiscent of the period of the Warring States (484-221 B.C., q.v.), as the three kingdoms strove for control of the empire. The kingdom of Wei conquered Shu in 263 and Wu in 280. But it was taken over in 266 by SSU-MA Yen, the chief minister, who changed the name to Chin. His briefly-united empire is known as the Western Chin (266-316, q.v.). The history of the period is the basis for China's oldest extant novel, the *Romance of the Three Kingdoms* (q.v.), which in turn is the source for many Chinese operas.

Three Principles of the People. Known in Chinese as the San Min Chu I, the principles are the basic philosophy of SUN Yat-sen (q.v.). They are nationalism, democracy and the people's livelihood, and are said to derive from Abraham Lincoln's phrase "government of the people, by the people and for the people." The first known reference to them comes in 1905, but a complete elaboration did not appear until 1917, and the final exposition was made in 1924, not long before SUN's death (March, 1925).

The San Min Chu I is also the name of the national anthem of the Republic of China (q.v.), and the text is designed to remind the listener of SUN's position as the "father of his country."

Linebarger, Paul M. *The Political Doctrines of Sun Yat-sen*. Baltimore: The Johns Hopkins Press, 1937.

Three Sages. See under **Legendary Period**.

Tianjin. See **Tientsin**.

Tibet (Xizang Autonomous Region). Area: 1,200,000 sq. km. (463,300 sq. mi.). Population: 1,830,000 (1980). Capital: Lhasa. Tibet is bounded on the east by Szechwan and Yunnan, on the south by Burma, Bhutan, India and Nepal, on the north by Sinkiang and Tsinghai (qq.v.). The boundaries correspond to what was at one time known as Outer Tibet, Inner Tibet having been absorbed in Szechwan and Tsinghai.

The Tibetan people are ethnically, culturally and linquistically distinct from the Chinese, and have been in contact with them since the T'ang dynasty (618-906 A.D., q.v.) according to Chinese records. Tibetan records also exist, but many of them, particularly from later centuries, are more concerned with religious matters than with historical events.

Tibetan records indicate the existence of two dynasties, the second of which ended in 842 A.D. Their contacts with the Chinese were of a warlike nature, and the Tibetans even sacked Changan, the T'ang capital, in 763 A.D. After the fall of the second dynasty in 842, Tibet disintegrated into petty states, with the exception of the large and successful state known as the Hsi Hsia (882-1227, q.v.), which was conquered by the Mongols (q.v.) under Chingis Khan (1167-1227, q.v.).

The Mongols absorbed the Hsi Hsia territory under their direct rule, but ruled Tibet under lamas of the Sakya sect, who acted as viceroys (1224-1358). The Sakyas acknowledged the suzerainty of the Yuan dynasty (1279-1368, q.v.), but were overthrown even before the fall of the Yuan to the Ming dynasty (1368-1644, q.v.).

Relations between Tibet and the Ming dynasty were formal and intermittent. From time to time delegations of lamas went to Peking on journeys which the Ming professed to view as acts of homage. Ming emperors conferred titles on several of the lamas and in this way attempted to influence Tibetan affairs. Tibetan kingship was reestablished in 1358 and lasted until 1750, although the rulers' power and authority were in serious decline after 1550. The decline in the power of the kings coincided with the rise in the power and authority of the Buddhist church, particularly the reformist Yellow Sect, named for the color of their robes. At the same time, the Yellow Sect was gaining adherents among the Mongols. In 1578, Sonam Gyatso (1543-1588), abbot of Drepung monastery and the most eminent lama of his time, was invited to visit Mongolia (q.v.) by the Mongol Altan Khan, prince of the Tumet tribe. When he did so, the khan conferred on him the title of Dalai Lama (q.v.), meaning "Ocean of Wisdom" in Mongol.

Reincarnation is an essential element of Buddhist belief, and in the Tibetan view Sonam Gyatso, as a high lama, was the reincarnation of his two predecessors, and all of them were successive reincarnations of the bodhisattva (q.v.) Avalokitesvara, known in Tibetan as Chen-re-zi. For this reason, he is referred to as the third Dalai Lama. After his death his followers searched for a child born about the same time, and found an acceptable candidate in Mongolia. The 4th and 5th Dalai Lamas were both Mongols, but later incarnations were all Tibetans. The fifth Dalai Lama, Ngawang Lobsang Gyatso (1617-1682), institutionalized the position of the Panchen Lama, the first of whom was one of his tutors. Panchen Lamas are considered to be reincarnations of the bodhisattva Amitabha, and assist in locating new reincarnations of the Dalai Lama.

The fifth Dalai Lama ushered in a period of Mongol dominance of Tibet when he assumed both spiritual and temporal power in 1642. He did this with the support and assistance of Gushi Khan, prince of the Khoshote tribe of the Western Mongols. In return, one of the khan's sons was made king of Tibet, but subordinate to the Dalai Lama. Having solidified his control of Tibet, the fifth Dalai Lama made a trip to Peking in 1652, where his rule over Tibet was recognized by the emperor Shun Chih (r. 1644-1661) of the newly established Ch'ing dynasty (1644-1911, q.v.).

The death of a Dalai Lama should be publicly announced, according to Tibetan law, and a commission appointed to search for his successor. The death of the fifth Dalai Lama in 1682 was kept secret by the Depa, his temporal administrator, who was a strong supporter of Galdan (1644-1697), khan of the Western Mongols. Only after the emperor K'ang Hsi (r. 1662-1722, q.v.) had defeated Galdan in 1696 did it become clear that the fifth Dalai Lama was dead. The Depa then announced that the sixth Dalai Lama, Tsang Yang Gyatso (1683-1706) had indeed been found and that he would commence his reign on December 8, 1697. The young man proved to be dissolute, and as a pawn in political intrigue was sent by the king, Latsan Khan, a descendant of

Gushi Khan, to Peking, and was murdered on the way.

Latsan Khan appointed another lama to the post, but he was not accepted by the Tibetans. Many of the lamas of the Yellow Sect secretly appealed to Tsewang Arapten (1643-1727), nephew of Galdan and khan of the Western Mongols, who sent an army which entered Lhasa in 1717. Within three years the Mongols had alienated the Tibetans by looting homes and temples, and in 1720 a Ch'ing army arrived in Tibet and routed the Mongols. They brought with them the seventh Dalai Lama, Kezang Gyatso (1708-1757). When the Ch'ing forces departed in 1723, they left behind two *ambans*, a Manchu word meaning resident commissioner. The arrangement was the beginning of the Ch'ing presence in Tibet and continued until the end of the dynasty. The ambans were always Manchu, never ethnic Chinese. Relations with Tibet, like those with Russia, Sinkiang and Mongolia were handled by the Li Fan Yuan (q.v.), originally established to handle relations between Manchus and Mongols.

In 1792 the Ch'ing authorities responded to an invasion of Tibet by Nepal (q.v.) by sending the Manchu general Fu-k'ang-an with an expeditionary force. The Ch'ing were successful in forcing Nepal to acknowledge Ch'ing suzerainty, and thus reinforced their control over Tibet.

Ch'ing unwillingness to permit any inroads into the seclusion of Tibet was confirmed in 1846. Two French priests, Abbés Huc and Gabet, taking advantage of their new-found privilege of traveling and residing in China, granted by the Treaty of Whampoa (1844, q.v.), made a journey to Tibet. They were told to leave by the Manchu amban Ch'i-shan (q.v.) on the grounds that

permission to travel and reside in China did not include Tibet.

Ch'ing policy toward Tibet was similar to policy toward other outer dependencies: Korea, Manchuria, Mongolia, Turkestan (Sinkiang) and Vietnam. Of these the first and last were the most Sinicized, since both used the Chinese written script. (Tibetan script is based on the Indian Devanagari alphabet.) Ch'ing authorities did not encourage Chinese emigration to any of these areas, preferring to retain them as buffers against more distant centers of power. France detached Vietnam in 1885, and Japan detached Korea in 1895. Russia's interest in absorbing Manchuria and Mongolia was evident, as was British interest in Tibet.

The reign of the 13th Dalai Lama, Thupten Gyatso (1876-1933) coincided with the declining years of the Ch'ing dynasty. He reached maturity in 1895, the first Dalai Lama in the 19th century to reach that point, as his predecessors had died young, leaving power in the hands of regents. He made serious efforts to throw off Ch'ing dominance and to assert Tibetan independence. Toward this end he refused to recognize Sino-British agreements involving Tibet. The first positive action of this nature was a refusal to permit the opening of trade with India.

Ch'ing weakness had been manifest in the Sino-Japanese War (1894-1895) and the Boxer Rebellion (1900, qq.v.), and Tibetan contacts with Russia had disturbed the British in India. In consequence, the British expedition to Tibet led by Colonel Francis Younghusband forced the Dalai Lama to flee to Mongolia, and resulted in an agreement signed by the Tibetan Grand Council in September 1904. While in Mongolia the Dalai Lama continued to negotiate with Russia, but the latter's defeat in the Russo-Japanese War (1904-1905, q.v.), eliminated the possibility of support from that quarter.

The treaty which Younghusband signed was not acceptable to either London or to Peking, and was superseded by a convention signed in Peking in April 1906 by the British Minister Ernest Satow and by T'ANG Shao-i for the Ch'ing government. No Tibetans participated in the negotiations preceding that agreement.

After a visit to Peking in 1908, the Dalai Lama returned to Tibet in 1909 just before the arrival of a Chinese army. He fled to India seeking British support, but the British were unwilling to alter their China policy. After the revolution in 1911, the Chinese garrison in Tibet was repatriated through India and the Dalai Lama returned to Lhasa.

On February 12, 1912, the infant Ch'ing emperor P'u-yi (q.v.) abdicated. The articles of abdication, drawn up by YUAN Shih-k'ai (1859-1916, q.v.) in his capacity as prime minister at the Ch'ing court, transferred title to all territories acknowledging Ch'ing suzerainty to the Republic of China (q.v.). On February 15, YUAN acceded to the presidency of the new republic, which claimed to include five "races": Han Chinese, Manchu, Mongol, Tibetan and Hui (Muslim, largely in Sinkiang). Neither the Dalai Lama nor the religious leader of Mongolia, the eighth Jebtsundama Khutuktu, accepted the claim, and both declared independence of China. They signed a treaty in January 1913, each recognizing the independence of the other. The new Chinese commissioner to Tibet was appointed in 1913, but was unable to reach Lhasa and remained in India.

Britain, concerned with the status of Tibet and with its own interests there, convened the Simla Confer-ence in 1913, attended by British, Chinese and Tibetan representatives. The agreement reached was initialed by all three and recognized Tibet's de facto independence and the restoration of its original boundaries. It was to be divided into Inner (Eastern) and Outer Tibet, with the latter to have full autonomy. China had made Inner Tibet two provinces, Sikang and Tsinghai, and refused to accept either the boundaries or the pledge of autonomy. It disowned its plenipotentiary and refused to acknowledge the validity of the convention.

Because of internal warfare in China in the early years of the republic, the Dalai Lama had a relatively free hand in Tibet. The Chinese attacked in Inner Tibet in 1917 and were routed by Tibetan troops. The Chinese sent missions to Lhasa in 1919 and 1920, but were unable to regain their previous position. The British sent a diplomatic mission in 1920, the first ever from a Western nation. British influence soon declined, however, and by 1925 the Dalai Lama had reoriented his policy toward China. In 1930 he sent a representative to Nanking, the new Chinese capital, but the Chinese envoy sent in return died on the way. The Dalai Lama died in December 1933, before the question of relations was agreed upon. In January 1934, the new regent asked Nanking for confirmation of his position, which was immediately granted.

Developments within China in the 1930s—the establishment of Manchukuo in 1932 (q.v.), the start of the war with Japan in 1937 and the removal of the national government from Nanking to Chungking—diverted Chinese attention from Tibet. World War II and the postwar struggle between the Nationalists and Communists postponed any further serious attention by the Chinese until the establishment of the People's Republic in 1949. In 1950 the government in Peking announced the forthcoming liberation of Tibet and in October attacked the Tibetan frontier. In spite of an appeal to the United Nations, no assistance for Tibet came from any quarter.

In November 1950, though only 15, the 14th Dalai Lama, Tenzin Gyatso (1935-), assumed full political power. In May 1951 a Tibetan delegation to Peking signed a 17-point "Agreement on Measures for the Peaceful Liberation of Tibet." The Chinese guaranteed the internal autonomy of the Tibetan government, freedom of religion and the preservation of the status of the Dalai Lama. In September thousands of Chinese troops invaded Tibet and established a new administration which emptied the monasteries and forced the monks to return to lay life; established communal farms; forced the change from the cultivation of barley to wheat; and introduced the use of the Chinese language, threatening all aspects of Tibetan culture.

On March 10, 1959, an anti-Chinese uprising occurred, which resulted in the flight of the Dalai Lama to India and a period of severe repression. This involved great loss of life and the destruction of the majority of Tibetan temples and monasteries, together with their artifacts and collections of manuscripts in Sanskrit and Tibetan. A 1985 statement by the Dalai Lama from his place of exile in India cites the deaths from unnatural causes of 1.2 million Tibetans, perhaps 25 percent of the population, between 1951 and 1985. Since 1979 a number of Tibetans living outside Tibet have been permitted by Chinese authorities to visit their homeland, though always under severe restrictions. They have report-ed that the population of Lhasa is now 70 percent Chinese and that there are also many Chinese in other parts of Tibet.

Boorman, Howard L., ed. *Biographical Dictionary of Republican China*. New York: Columbia University Press, 1968.

Li, Tieh-tseng. *The Historical Status of Tibet*. New York: King's Crown Press, 1956.

Snellgrove, David, and Hugh Richardson. *A Cultural History of Tibet*. Boulder: Prajna Press, 1980.

Shakabpa, Tsepon W.D. *Tibet: A Political History*. New Haven: Yale University Press, 1967.

T'ien T'ai sect. The T'ien Tai sect of Buddhism (q.v.), known as Tendai in Japan, was one of the most important sects of the T'ang dynasty (618-906 A.D., q.v.) and later. Its founder, the Chinese monk Chih-k'ai (Chih-i, 538-597), lived and taught in the T'ien-t'ai mountains of Chekiang province, hence the name. The sect, while based on Indian Buddhist ritual and iconography, is essentially Chinese in its attempt to harmonize different Buddhist beliefs and principles into one syncretic whole. According to T'ien T'ai views, the universe consists of a single absolute mind, of which all phenomena partake.

The Japanese monk Ennin (793-864, q.v.), was an adherent of the T'ien T'ai sect, and his main purpose in joining the Japanese embassy to the T'ang court in 838 was to obtain texts and icons, and to resolve points of doctrine. He was not permitted to visit T'ien T'ai, which was a disappointment, though he spent time at other temples and monasteries which belonged to the sect.

The sect put particular emphasis on the reading and discussion of the Lotus Sutra (q.v.), one of the major texts of Mahayana Buddhism (q.v.).

This concentration on literary material, so different from the emphasis of the Pure Land sect (q.v.), made T'ien T'ai a school which appealed largely to the literary class.

Fung, Yu-lan, and Derk Bodde, trans. *A History of Chinese Philosophy, Vol. II.* Princeton, Princeton University Press, 1953.

T'ien T'sung. See under **Abahai**.

Tientsin (Tianjin). China's third largest city (Population: 7,449,000 [1980]) and the seaport for Peking, formerly the capital of Hopeh province, but now an independent municipality, it is a major transport hub, located on the Grand Canal and served by several railways.

Tientsin has a history of several centuries as a major port for North China. It played a major part in the *Arrow* War (1858-1860, q.v.), and was opened to foreign trade as a treaty port (q.v.) as a result of the Treaty of Tientsin (1860, q.v.).

The British and French had "concessions" in Tientsin from 1860. The Japanese were granted one in 1895, after the Sino-Japanese War (q.v.), and in 1900 concessions were granted to Austria-Hungary, Belgium, Germany, Italy and Russia in the aftermath of the Boxer Rebellion (q.v.). In the period between the two world wars, Tientsin had the third largest European population in China, many of the residents being refugees from Russia. Because of the extent of the foreign influence in Tientsin, the city still seems more Westernized than most inland cities.

Tientsin Convention. See under **Yuan Shih-k'ai**.

Tientsin Massacre. Long-simmering Chinese resentment of Christian missionary activity exploded on June 21,
1870. Tolerance of Christianity had been a provision of the various Tientsin treaties (q.v.), although there was widespread opposition to it by the Chinese gentry. Anti-Christian sentiment in Tientsin was more acute than elsewhere since the French constructed a Catholic cathedral on the site of a former Chinese temple, which had been razed, and French nuns accepted Chinese novices, who were thereafter unable to receive their families. The nuns also established orphanages and were so incautious as to offer a small sum of money for each child brought to them. This gave rise to accusations of kidnapping.

The local magistrate demanded an inspection of the mission premises, and the French consul, Henri Fontanier, accused him of fomenting trouble. The superintendent of trade, who was the ranking Chinese official in the area, attempted to intervene and calm the situation. On the morning of the 21st, word reached the consul that the magistrate and other officials were outside the cathedral demanding entrance. The consul rushed to the superintendent's office, fired at him, but missed, and as office attendants tried to seize him, rushed outside.

A crowd of local officials and gentry was outside, and the consul and his chancellor plunged in, the latter clearing a path with his sword. Fontanier fired at the magistrate and killed one of his attendants. The two Frenchmen were killed on the spot. The crowd set the French premises afire (the consulate, the cathedral, the orphanage, etc.) and massacred 10 French nuns, two French priests, seven other foreigners and several Chinese converts.

Word of the incident did not reach Europe until July 25 because the nearest telegraph lines were in Ceylon and in Kiakhta, a town on the border between Russia and Outer Mongolia, 100 miles south of Lake Baikal. The fact that the Franco-Prussian War had started 10 days earlier may have prevented French military reprisals.

An official Chinese investigation led to the execution of 16 Chinese. A Manchu official, Ch'ung-hou (1826-1893), who was superintendent of trade and thus ultimately responsible, was sent on a mission of apology to France. He was the first Chinese envoy to a Western nation, excluding those who had accompanied Anson Burlingame (q.v.) in 1868.

In an effort to prevent a repetition of the incident, China tried to persuade the treaty powers to agree to a set of regulations to control missionary activity, but this was not successful.

Wright, Mary C. *The Last Stand of Chinese Conservatism*. Stanford: Stanford University Press, 1957.

Tientsin, Treaties of. The Chinese signed four treaties in Tientsin in 1858. The Manchu Kuei-liang and the Mongol Hua-sha-na signed for China. Admiral Count Euphemius Putiatin signed for Russia on June 13, William Bradford Reed signed for the United States on June 18, Lord Elgin signed for Great Britain on June 26, and Baron Jean Baptiste Louis Gros signed for France on June 27.

The treaties were of different lengths, but since the "most-favored-nation" clause (q.v.) had been previously accepted, the differences meant little. (The Chinese may not have been completely aware of this.) Key provisions were the opening of Tientsin as a treaty port, the right of Christian missions to own real property, the right of foreign envoys to reside in Peking, and the opening of the Yangtze river to foreign trade. The treaties were presumed to end the *Arrow* War (q.v.), but were not ratified until after the allied victory at Peking in 1860.

On June 9, 1885, China signed another Treaty of Tientsin with France, which brought the Franco-Chinese war to an end. In this treaty China accepted France's annexation of Vietnam (q.v.).

TOYOTOMI Hideyoshi (1537-1598). Warlord who led Japan's first serious attempt to conquer China. Sixteenth-century Japan (q.v.) was racked by feudal warfare, but by 1590 Hideyoshi had conquered his rivals and brought peace to the islands for the first time in a century. He then turned his attention to conquering China, for which he demanded free passage through Korea (q.v.). This was refused, on the grounds that Korea acknowledged Chinese suzerainty.

In 1592, Hideyoshi transported an invasion force of 200,000 men across the Straits of Tsushima, and fought his way through Korea as far north as present-day Pyongyang. The first Chinese counterforce of 5,000 men was wiped out, but the Japanese withdrew in face of a much larger force. They evacuated most of their troops in 1593. In 1597, Hideyoshi sent a second army to Korea which caused immense destruction and the deaths of many thousands of Koreans and Chinese. His own death brought the Korean adventure to a conclusion. Hideyoshi was succeeded in Japan by TOKUGAWA Ieyasu (1543-1616), who became *shogun* (military governor) of Japan in 1603. His descendants held the shogunate until 1868, and during this period expelled nearly all foreigners and kept Japan's contacts with the outside world, including China, to a minimum.

Treaty ports. For much of the Ch'ing dynasty (1644-1911, q.v.) foreign trade was restricted to the port of Canton, and to a guild of merchants called the cohong (q.v.). Dissatisfaction with the restriction on the part of Western traders was one of the causes of the Opium War, which ended with the signing of the Treaty of Nanking (qq.v.). One of the provisions of that treaty was the opening of the first five "treaty ports": Canton, Amoy, Foochow, Ningpo and Shanghai. The foreign powers were not satisfied with these, however, and forced the Chinese to open still more ports, a process which continued to the end of the dynasty, at which point there were 48 of them.

Under the Ch'ing, foreigners were not allowed to hold property, reside or do business in China, though missionaries were excepted from this. The foreigners were allowed these privileges in the treaty ports. They also enjoyed the benefits of extraterritoriality (q.v.), the principle under which a foreigner could be tried only in a foreign court, and not under the Chinese system of justice.

Tribute system. The concept of tribute is inherent in the traditional Chinese system of foreign relations (q.v.). According to the official view, the emperor of China was the mediary between heaven and mankind; one of his titles was Son of Heaven. In consequence, all other rulers were inferior to him and had to acknowledge his suzerainty by periodic submission of tribute. Those who failed to abide by this system were regarded either as rebellious or barbarian, or both.

In consideration of the tribute rendered, the imperial court presented gifts to the envoys, but the terms used to describe the two transactions were quite different and made the difference in status explicit. For long periods the imperial court's gifts were of much greater value than the tribute received, and in consequence many traders, from Central Asia particularly, claimed to represent distant sovereigns who were quite unaware of their existence. The court was also aware of the imposture, since efforts to control these foreigners were made. The expense of the gifts also led the court to discourage many purported embassies from coming at all.

As late as the 18th century, the official list of tributaries to the Ch'ing empire included the following: Korea, Liu Ch'iu, Annam (Vietnam), Laos, Siam, Sulu, the Netherlands, Burma, Portugal, Italy (Papal States) and England. (Morse, H.B. *International Relations of the Chinese Empire*. Longman, London and New York, 1910-1918. Vol. I, p. 50.)

The last tribute-bearing embassies arrived in Peking in the closing years of the Ch'ing dynasty (1644-1911) and tribute has not been a part of Chinese diplomacy since then.

Tripitaka. A Sanskrit word meaning "three baskets," the Tripitaka refers to the Buddhist canon. Originally it meant baskets for palm-leaf manuscripts covering (1) rules of discipline for monks and nuns, (2) collected discourses and anecdotes of the Buddha, and (3) abstruse scriptures dealing with philosophy and metaphysics. The Chinese version of the Tripitaka is the largest extant, and contains many texts whose Sanskrit originals have been lost.

Tripitaka is also the name applied to the hero of the Chinese novel *Hsi Yu Chi* (q.v.) based on the book written by the monk Hsuan-tsang (602-664 A.D., q.v.) about his quite genuine travels to Central Asia and India in search of Buddhist texts.

Waley, Arthur. *The Real Tripitaka*. London: George Allen & Unwin, 1952.

TS'AI Lun. See under **Paper**.

TS'AI O (1882-1916). Military governor of Yunnan after the revolution of 1911 (see **Republic of China**). TS'AI was a Hunanese from a well-to-do peasant family. In 1895 he passed the provincial examinations (see **Examination system**), and after failing the second level entered a modern school in Changsha where he came under the progressive influence of LIANG Ch'i-ch'ao (q.v.). In 1899 he went to Japan at LIANG's invitation and in 1900 returned to China to help in preparations for an uprising at Hankow. TS'AI was absent when the Manchu (q.v.) authorities discovered the plot and executed his colleagues. He returned to Japan where he graduated from the Seijo Military Preparatory School and from the Shikan Gakko Military Academy.

He spent much of the next few years in Kwangsi province, and in 1911 became an instructor in the Yunnan Military Academy and commander of the 37th Brigade in Yunnan. Hearing of the October 10 revolution at Wuchang, TS'AI organized a successful rebellion against the Manchus, and on October 31 was elected military governor of the province, an office he filled with conspicuous success. He resigned in the summer of 1913, expecting to be appointed governor of his native Hunan, but YUAN Shih-k'ai (q.v.), then president of the republic, called him to Peking and gave him a series of positions in which he exercised no power at all.

TS'AI soon learned of YUAN's plan to become emperor, and set about to overthrow him. To do this he utilized a strategy that might have come out of the Chinese *Romance of the Three Kingdoms* (q.v.) or the Japanese tale *Chushingura: The Forty-seven Ronin*. He divorced his wife and sent her back to Hunan, and took up with a prominent demimondaine, leading a luxurious and seemingly depraved life.

The ruse succeeded. YUAN relaxed his surveillance and TS'AI escaped from Peking in December 1915. He returned to Yunnan and with several colleagues sent a cabled ultimatum to YUAN giving him 24 hours to declare his loyalty to the republic. YUAN did not respond and on December 25 the group declared Yunnan's independence.

The military forces were organized into First, Second and Third National Protection Armies. At the start of 1916 TS'AI led the First Army into Szechwan, while the others moved into Kwangsi and Kweichow. YUAN had proclaimed himself emperor on January 1, 1916, but abandoned the monarchy on March 22, in response to the violent reaction in China and the lack of support from foreign countries. TS'AI's military activities were a significant contribution to this reaction.

TS'AI took part in a military council which was established as the legitimate government of China until YUAN stepped down. It was dissolved after YUAN's death on June 6, 1916. LI Yuan-hung (q.v.) succeeded YUAN and appointed TS'AI governor of Szechwan. TS'AI took office in July but resigned two weeks later when it was discovered he had throat cancer. He went to Japan for treatment and died there in November.

Boorman, Howard L. ed. *Biographical Dictionary of Republic of China*. New York: Columbia University Press, 1968.

TS'AI Yüan-p'ei (1868-1940). He was the leading liberal educator of China during the early years of the republic. TS'AI was educated in the Chinese classics (see **Five Classics**) and was successful in his examinations, achieving the chin-shih degree in 1890 (see **Examination system**). In 1892 he was named a scholar of the Hanlin Academy (q.v.). China's defeat by Japan in 1895 convinced TS'AI that traditional education had failed to serve China's needs, and he returned to his native Chekiang province to promote education. In 1902 he went to Shanghai, where he became the president of an anti-Manchu (see **Manchu**) education society.

In 1907 he went to Germany and from 1908 to 1911 he studied at Leipzig University. He returned to China shortly after the revolt of 1911, and early the next year SUN Yat-sen appointed him minister of education. This did not last, however, and TS'AI returned twice to Germany. He spent several years in France during World War I.

In 1916 he was appointed chancellor of Peking University, China's most prestigious. He held the post until 1926. While he was chancellor the university was a center of the May Fourth movement (q.v.). He also made several trips abroad. During the period of the Northern Expedition (q.v.), he supported CHIANG Kai-shek's (q.v.) Nanking government against a rival group in Wuhan.

In 1928 TS'AI helped to found the Academia Sinica (q.v.) and became its first president. In 1935, following the assassination of one of his subordinates, he issued a public statement criticizing the Nanking government for repressive policies and resigned all official positions.

He did not accompany the Republican leaders to Chungking as the war with Japan worsened, but went to Hong Kong, where he died.

Boorman, Howard L. ed. *Biographical Dictionary of Republican China*. New York: Columbia University Press, 1967.

TS'AO Hsueh Ch'in. See under **The Dream of The Red Chamber**.

TS'AO Ju-lin (1876-1966). TS'AO was a pro-Japanese official in the late Ch'ing (q.v.) and early Republican periods (see **Republic of China**). He studied in Japan from 1899 to 1904, and served in the Ch'ing Board of Foreign Affairs. He was an attaché to the Chinese delegation which signed the agreement with Japan under which China accepted the conditions agreed to between Japan and Russia in the Treaty of Portsmouth (q.v.). These included the Japanese right to hold concessions in several Manchurian cities.

After the revolution, TS'AO became a personal adviser to YUAN Shih-k'ai (q.v.), and in that capacity negotiated the Twenty-one Demands (q.v.) which Japan presented in January 1915. After YUAN's death, TS'AO worked with TUAN Ch'i-jui (q.v.) and negotiated massive loans from the Japanese, in return for which the Peking government (q.v.) made valuable concessions.

In February 1919 the Paris Peace Conference, convened to negotiate an end to World War I, upheld China's concessions to Japan in Shantung (where Japan had taken over the German concessions earlier in the war) and elsewhere. Public fury was aroused against TS'AO and in the May Fourth Incident (q.v.) his house was burned by a crowd of students.

TS'AO was dismissed from his post as minister of communications a few days later, and except for a brief stint as a special commissioner in 1922, he spent the rest of his active life as a banker and businessman.

He remained in Peking throughout World War II and fled to Taiwan at the time of the Communist takeover. He eventually died at the home of a daughter in Detroit.

Boorman, Howard L. ed. *Biographical Dictionary of Republican China*. New York: Columbia University Press, 1967.

TS'AO K'un (1862-1938). Military commander and sixth president of the Republic of China (q.v.), October 1923-November 1924. TS'AO came of a poor family but made friends with YUAN Shih-k'ai (1859-1916, q.v.) as a young man. He served as a soldier in Korea and Manchuria during the Sino-Japanese War (1894-1895, q.v.) and rose to be a division commander in 1906. When revolution broke out in October 1911, YUAN transferred TS'AO's division to Peking to maintain order and to strengthen his own hand in dealing with the imperial court and the revolutionaries.

In February 1912, YUAN became the provisional president of the republic, and was expected to proceed to Nanking for his investiture. TS'AO's disciplined troops staged a "mutiny," which persuaded the southerners that YUAN's presence was needed in Peking.

After YUAN's death in 1916, the politico-military machine he had created, known as the Peiyang Group (q.v.), began to split. One faction, the Anhwei Clique (q.v.), was headed by TUAN Ch'i-jui (1865-1936, q.v.), and TS'AO eventually found himself in the opposing Chihli Clique (q.v.), headed by FENG Kuo-chang (1859-1919, q.v.). After FENG's death, TS'AO headed the Chihli Clique, and defeated TUAN's troops in battle in July 1920. Two years later he defeated CHANG Tso-lin (1873-1928, q.v.), the Manchurian warlord, forcing him back to Manchuria. TS'AO then tried to achieve the unification of China, and served as president from 1923 to 1924, when he was forced to resign by the warlord FENG Yü-hsiang (1882-1948, q.v.). TS'AO lived in Tientsin from 1927 until his death. During that period the Japanese approached him with an invitation to participate in a puppet regime in North China, which he refused.

Boorman, Howard L. ed. *Biographical Dictionary of Republican China*. New York: Columbia University Press, 1967.

TS'AO Ts'ao (154-220 A.D.). TS'AO Ts'ao (the names are expressed in different Chinese characters) was from a rich and aristocratic family of the later Han dynasty (23-221 A.D.). His father was the adopted son of a chief eunuch (q.v.). TS'AO Ts'ao himself became a highly successful general who was eventually credited with suppressing the Yellow Turban rebellion (q.v.), a peasant uprising with Taoist overtones which started in 184 A.D. and contributed to the downfall of the Han.

In 192 TS'AO Ts'ao "persuaded" the weak Han emperor to leave the capital at Loyang and accompany him to Yenchou in the northeast. He then made himself chief minister and, in effect, ruler of the empire. The empire, however, was far from united, and TS'AO Ts'ao soon found himself at war with another scion of the dynasty, LIU Pei (q.v.), who set himself up in the kingdom of Shu (Szechwan), as well as with the kingdom of Wu (qq.v.). After TS'AO Ts'ao's death in 220, his son deposed the last Han emperor and founded the kingdom of Wei. Shu, Wei and Wu were the Three Kingdoms (q.v.) of the period from 221 to 265 A.D., and the source of the *Romance of the Three Kingdoms* (q.v.).

Although TS'AO Ts'ao died before the establishment of the kingdom of Wei, or at least before the elimination of the last Han emperor, he is an important figure in the history of the period and appears in the novel and in many of the plays based on it. He was an extremely successful soldier.

While he did not hesitate to kill, he recognized the importance of goodwill and avoided massacres as a matter of policy.

His legendary skill in appearing suddenly where he was least expected gave rise to the saying "Speak of TS'AO Ts'ao, and TS'AO Ts'ao is here," the Chinese equivalent of "speak of the devil."

TSENG Kuo-fan (1811-1872). General, statesman and scholar. Born of a poor family in Hunan province, he became a chin shih in the examination of 1838 (see **Examination system**) and was appointed to the Hanlin Academy (q.v.). He held a series of government positions which provided him with a wide range of administrative experience.

In January 1853 he accepted the assignment of recruiting and training the Hunan militia, also known as the "Hunan Braves," to resist the Taiping Rebellion (1851-1864, q.v.). TSENG's insistence on methodical training of his troops before sending them into battle was criticized by generals already fighting the rebels and in need of assistance. In the long run, TSENG's policy paid off, and he is given the major credit for the ultimate defeat of the rebels. The Taiping capital at Nanking, under siege by the "Hunan Braves" led by TSENG's younger brother, TSENG Kuo-ch'uan (1824-1890), eventually fell.

In 1865, as governor of Kiangnan and Kiangsi TSENG established official printing offices in Nanking, his headquarters, and four other cities to reprint classics and histories, and restored the examination system, which had been suspended during the Taiping years. He also approved the establishment of an ironworks at Shanghai, later known as the Kiangnan Arsenal, from which the first China-built steamship was launched in 1868.

TSENG was called away from this work later in 1865 to replace the Mongol general Seng-ko-lin-ch'in (q.v.) who had been killed fighting the Nien rebels (q.v.). After a year of fighting without a clear victory, he recommended LI Hung-chang (1823-1901, q.v.) as his replacement.

In 1868 TSENG was made governor-general of Chihli (Hopei) province and greatly improved administrative efficiency there. In 1870 he was ordered to investigate and settle the problem of the Tientsin Massacre (q.v.), which he did with skill and tact until he fell ill. The final settlement was signed by LI Hung-chang.

TSENG is known as a man of great honesty and integrity in a period when corruption was common. He was also an excellent judge of men, and was able to retain their loyalty. Several of his protégés, such as LI Hung-chang and TSO Tsung-t'ang (1812-1885, q.v.), achieved great success.

Hummel, Arthur W., ed. *Eminent Chinese of the Ch'ing Period*. Washington, Government Printing Office, 1943.

Tsinghai (Qinghai) **province**. (Also known as Chinghai.) Area: 720,000 sq. km. (278,000 sq. mi.). Population: 3,720,000 (1980). Capital: Sining (Xining). Tsinghai is bounded on the northeast by Kansu province, on the southeast by Szechwan, on the southwest by Tibet, and on the northwest by Sinkiang (qq.v.). The population includes Han Chinese, Tibetans, Mongols, Kazaks and Chinese-speaking Muslims (Hui).

The Huang Ho (Yellow river, q.v.) rises here, as does the Yangtze (q.v.) in the Kun Lun mountains in the southern region. The northwestern plateau is desert, with the occasional rivers draining into salt marshes and shallow lakes. Barley and spring wheat are the main crops around Sining, and to the south, millet, oats and buckwheat also are grown. Much of the province is pastureland, and many of its residents are nomads.

TSO Tsung-t'ang (1812-1885). TSO was born in Hunan of an educated family and was classically educated himself. In addition to the Confucian classics, he gave serious attention to geographic works and agriculture. He became a chü-jen in 1832 but failed three times to achieve the chin-shih degree (see under **Examination system**). While he took no part in the Opium War (q.v.) of 1842, he came to the attention of higher officials and was a vigorous and successful soldier in the Taiping Rebellion (q.v.). It was during this period that he met TSENG Kuo-fan (q.v.).

TSO made a major contribution to the quelling of the rebellion and was rewarded by the throne with an earldom. He also made a name for himself as an administrator in rehabilitating Chekiang and Fukien provinces. Troubles in the north called him away from his administrative duties, and in 1866 he was appointed governor-general of Shensi and Kansu to suppress a Muslim uprising. On the way he was instructed to suppress the Nien (q.v.), a group of bandits-on-horseback who were ravaging several northern provinces. This was accomplished in 1868.

TSO then turned his attention to the Muslim rebellion, and by the end of 1873 Shensi and Kansu had been pacified. One Muslim leader had escaped from Shensi to Sinkiang (Turkestan), which was also tending toward rebellion from the Ch'ing dynasty (q.v.) yoke. In spite of opposition in Peking, TSO pleaded the necessity of retaining Sinkiang in order to hold Mongolia and protect Peking. The semiautonomous Muslim leaders in Central Asia were already coming under both British and Russian influence, and several khanates had been absorbed into the Russian empire.

The key figure in Sinkiang was Yakoob Beg (q.v.), a Muslim who controlled the entire Tarim Basin in 1873. For this reason he attracted diplomatic courtesies from Britain, Russia and Turkey. TSO moved to reconquer the area, and by 1878 had accomplished his mission, with Yakoob Beg a suicide.

The Russians had occupied Ili in 1871, announcing publicly that it would be returned to China when the Chinese could assert their authority. TSO's effective military campaigns were a major factor in forcing the Russians to live up to their commitment, which they did under the Treaty of St. Petersburg (1881, q.v.).

TSO, though rewarded by the court, begged permission to retire in 1881. Instead, he was given three months sick leave and then several more assignments. In June 1884 he was given complete command of military affairs, as the war with France (q.v.) over the annexation of Vietnam (q.v.) was brewing. In August the French attacked Foochow, Fukien and Keelung, Taiwan. TSO was appointed governor of Fukien, which he reached in December. By this time hostilities had given way to diplomacy, and the war was ended by the Treaty of Tientsin, June 9, 1885 (see under **Tientsin, Treaties of**). TSO died at Foochow in September.

Bales, W.L. *Tso Tsung-t'ang: Soldier and Statesman of Old China.* Shanghai: Kelly & Walsh, 1937.

Hummel, Arthur W., ed. *Eminent Chinese of the Ch'ing Period.* Washington: Government Printing Office, 1943.

Tsungli Yamen. The term may be translated "Office of the Prime Minister," but it was in fact the forerunner of the ministry of foreign affairs. Established in 1861 as a result of the *Arrow* War (1857-1860, q.v.), it retained the name until 1901, when in the settlement of the Boxer Rebellion (q.v.), it became a ministry.

Foreign relations (q.v.) had been handled by the Board of Rites (q.v.) since the T'ang dynasty (618-906 A.D., q.v.). Since these were mostly dealings with tributary states, the Board arranged details of the periodic tribute missions. This continued into the Ch'ing dynasty (1644-1911, q.v.), though the Ch'ing also established the Li Fan Yuan (q.v.) for dealings with Mongolia, Russia, Sinkiang and Tibet. The Ch'ing defeat in the *Arrow* War persuaded the court that dealing with the Western powers required a more consistent approach than was possible under the previous system.

Banno, Masataka. *China and the West 1858-1861: The Origins of the Tsungli Yamen*. Cambridge: Harvard University Press, 1964.

Wright, Mary C. *The Last Stand of Chinese Conservatism*. Stanford: Stanford University Press, 1957.

TU Fu (712-770). Poet of the T'ang dynasty (618-906). TU is frequently grouped with LI Po and WANG Wei (qq.v.), both of whom he knew, as the three greatest poets of the era. There are some 1500 examples of his poetry extant, as well as some prose pieces. There is a brief account of his life in the T'ang historical records but the details are meager because of the relative obscurity in which he lived. It is the quality of his poetry, rather than his career, which has earned him his place in history.

The eldest son of a prosperous and distinguished family, he spent several years traveling before taking the imperial examinations (see under **Examination system**). His failure to obtain a degree in 736 was a great disappointment, since it precluded, or at least delayed, an official career. He resumed traveling for eight more years. It was during this period that he met LI Po, and the two became good friends.

When TU returned to Changan, he spent several years mingling with the scholarly society of the time, writing poems addressed to various people. He also attracted the attention of the emperor T'ang Ming Huang (r. 713-755, q.v.) by submitting three long poems, which resulted in his being allowed to take a special examination in 752, which he passed.

He was given a job in late 755, and went off to visit his wife and children, who were staying some 80 miles northeast of the capital. The outbreak of the rebellion of AN Lu-shan (q.v.) in late December prevented his return to the capital until the summer of 756. He was on his way to join the court of the new emperor, T'ang Su Tsung (r. 756-762), when he was captured by rebels. He escaped the following year, and reached the court, where he was appointed "reminder" to the emperor. A memorial he wrote in defense of another official so incensed the emperor that he had TU arrested and tried. He was pardoned, however, and in September went to visit his wife and family again.

In November 757 the imperial forces recaptured Changan, and TU hurried to join the emperor for his triumphal return on December 8. In the summer of 758, TU was appointed education commissioner at Huachou, some 60 miles from the capital. This involved preparing and administering the provincial examinations for those aiming at the higher examinations and a government career. Unhappy in this post, in 759 he resigned and moved his family to Chengtu, Szechwan. He never returned to Changan again.

The AN Lu-shan (q.v.) rebellion was finally put down in February, 763, with a toll of death, destruction and dislocation affecting millions of people. The Tibetans took advantage of the unsettled conditions to capture Changan and hold it from November 763 to February 764. In that year TU was appointed military adviser to the governor of Sezchwan. The governor died in 765 and TU spent the few remaining years of his life along the Yangtze river and near Tung Ting Lake in East China.

TU's official career was not a success, but his literary talents were appreciated by his contemporaries, and TU was able to make himself useful to various officials by drafting memorials to the throne. His success in attracting the attention of the emperor by his three poems also added to his reputation.

TU's poetry is greatly admired for its apt historical and literary allusions bearing on many subjects, but much is descriptive of nature and devoid of such references. This makes them relatively easy to translate. The first book cited below contains translations of 374 poems, about a quarter of those extant, as well as provides an account of the poet's life and the necessary historical background on the era in which he lived.

Hung, William. *Tu Fu: China's Greatest Poet*. Cambridge: Harvard University Press, 1952.

Hung, William. *Notes for Tu Fu: China's Greatest Poet*. Cambridge: Harvard University Press, 1952.

TUAN Ch'i-jui (1865-1936). Military leader, head of the Anhwei Clique (q.v.), and provisional president (November 1924-April 1926) of the Peking government (q.v.), TUAN graduated at the top of the first class at the Peiyang Military Academy in 1887, and in 1888 was one of five graduates selected for study abroad. He spent a year in Germany. He met YUAN Shih-k'ai (q.v.) after his return to China and spent several years in a variety of assignments under YUAN's patronage. When YUAN became president of the new republic, TUAN became minister of war and eventually the most important figure in the government outside YUAN himself. He opposed YUAN's plan to establish a new dynasty and resigned in May 1915. He was called back, and a struggle for power with YUAN ensued, ended only by YUAN's death in June 1916.

The next president, LI Yuan-hung (1864-1928, q.v.), held office from June 1916 to July 1917, but largely as a figurehead. De facto power was wielded by TUAN, who acted as premier. In a dispute over whether to declare war on Germany at the start of World War I, LI dismissed TUAN, who then made it possible for CHANG Hsün (1854-1923), another military leader, to attempt a restoration of the Ch'ing dynasty. This occurred in June 1917, but by July TUAN had denounced the move, entered Peking at the head of his army, and forced LI from the presidency. Under TUAN's influence, China declared war on Germany in August.

Disaffection with the Peking government on the part of southern leaders caused them to declare a military government in Canton in August, headed by SUN Yat-sen (1866-1925, q.v.). TUAN suggested the use of military force to suppress the Canton government and unify China. Widespread opposition caused TUAN to resign in the autumn.

FENG Kuo-chang (1859-1919, q.v.),

then president, tried a policy of conciliation towards the dissident factions, but his hand was soon forced by TUAN, who resumed office as premier in March 1918. TUAN conducted a pro-Japanese policy, accepting huge loans (see under **TS'AO Ju-lin**), in exchange for which Japan was granted wide-ranging concessions. Reports that TUAN's government had agreed to hand over the German concessions in Shantung province to the Japanese set off the May Fourth Incident (1919, q.v.). TUAN's military opponents, including CHANG Tso-lin (1873-1928, q.v.), warlord of Manchuria, and TS'AO K'un (1862-1938, q.v.), leader of the Chihli military clique (qq.v.), defeated his forces south of Peking in July 1920. TUAN retired to Tientsin.

In 1924 CHANG Tso-lin and FENG Yü-hsiang (1882-1948, q.v.), having outmaneuvered TS'AO K'un and WU P'ei-fu, asked TUAN to head a provisional government, which he did. As a gesture of conciliation to the Kuomintang (q.v.), TUAN invited SUN Yat-sen to Peking to discuss governmental organization. However, he promulgated the articles of government without SUN's acquiescence and held a preliminary conference on governmental organization without the formal participation of the Kuomintang.

By late 1925 CHANG and FENG were struggling for power, and TUAN, who had no troops at his disposal, resigned in April 1926 and fled to the Japanese concession in Tientsin. The Japanese tried to obtain his support for their puppet state of Manchukuo (q.v.), but TUAN refused and moved to Shanghai, where he died in 1936.

Boorman, Howard L., ed. *Biographical Dictionary of Republican China*. New York: Columbia University Press, 1967.

T'ung Chih (Tong-zhi, 1856-1875). Reign title (q.v.) of the eighth emperor of the Ch'ing dynasty (r. 1862-1875). He was the only surviving son of the emperor Hsien Feng (q.v.) and Tzu Hsi, the dowager empress (q.v.). He ascended the throne at the age of five, but China was governed by a regency in which his domineering mother played an increasingly important part.

T'ung Chih reached his majority early in 1873 and took nominal charge of the empire, though he was still under the thumb of his regent-mother. He had married a few months earlier, but not the candidate his mother favored. He died in January 1875, supposedly of smallpox. His widow committed suicide less than three months later. She was reportedly pregnant, and if she had borne a son she would have become empress dowager in place of her mother-in-law.

T'ung Chih's successor should have been selected from the next generation. Instead, in violation of the Ch'ing rules of succession, the Empress Dowager selected his cousin, her own nephew, who reigned under the title Kuang Hsu (q.v.).

The importance of T'ung Chih's reign, however, lies in what is known as the T'ung Chih "restoration," alluding to a return to the strength and power of the earlier years of the dynasty. In fact, China made considerable progress during this period. The Taiping Rebellion (q.v.) was finally suppressed, and China's foreign relations (q.v.) were put on a more realistic plane with the establishment of the Tsungli Yamen (q.v.). T'ung Chih was also the first Chinese emperor to receive foreign ambassadors without the requirement of the kotow (q.v.).

Hummel, Arthur W., ed. *Eminent Chinese of the Ch'ing Period*. Washington, Government Printing Office, 1943.

Wright, Mary C. *The Last Stand of Chinese Conservatism*. Stanford: Stanford University Press, 1957.

T'ung Meng Hui. The T'ung Meng Hui was the second revolutionary party founded by SUN Yat-sen (q.v.). It was formed in Tokyo in July 1905 from the merger of SUN's Hsing Chung Hui and several other revolutionary organizations. At its first formal meeting on August 20, 1905, SUN was elected director.

SUN's Three Principles of the people (San Min Chu I, q.v.) were incorporated into the party's constitution, and became a part of the revolutionary ideology. Unlike its predecessor, the T'ung Meng Hui had a great many intellectual members, mainly drawn from the revolutionary Chinese students in Japan. The party coordinated a series of unsuccessful revolutionary attempts in South China, which resulted largely in the revolutionaries becoming unwelcome not only in China but in Southeast Asia as well.

The outbreak of revolution on October 10, 1911, at Wuchang reversed the situation. SUN was in the United States when it occurred, and went on to Europe to negotiate for recognition and loans. He arrived in Shanghai on December 25, 1911, and on January 1, 1912, assumed office as president of the republic in Nanking.

However, the Ch'ing dynasty was still in existence and recognized by foreign powers. Negotiations for a transfer of power were at an impasse until SUN offered to resign in favor of YUAN Shih-k'ai (q.v.). The Ch'ing emperor abdicated on February 12, SUN resigned on February 13 and the government moved to Peking.

With the convening of the National Assembly in Peking, many members of the T'ung Meng Hui felt that it should change from its previous revolutionary and conspiratorial character to an open political party. SUN had remained in the south, but the party leaders in the Assembly arranged a merger with several smaller parties and formed a new party called the Kuomintang (q.v.). SUN was invited to Peking and at the inaugural meeting on August 25, 1912, was elected director of the new party.

Tung-lin party. The term refers to a group of Confucian officials of the late 16th and early 17th centuries who organized a movement to restore Confucian morality and eliminate corruption. While they achieved popular renown and admiration, they failed in their ultimate objectives. A major difficulty was the political structure of the civil administration which had been established at the beginning of the Ming dynasty (1368-1644, q.v.). This provided for civil servants to be paid at a level which was sometimes below subsistence. The officials usually indulged in corrupt practices to make up for their lack of salary.

A second problem was the power of the eunuchs (q.v.) in the declining years of the Ming period. To some extent this was personified in WEI Chung-hsien (1568-1627, q.v.), who effectively ruled the empire during the reign of emperor Ming T'ien Ch'i (r. 1621-1627, q.v.). WEI consigned several members of the Tung-lin party to prison. The next reign, that of emperor Ming Ch'ung Chen (r. 1628-1644, q.v.), saw the dismissal and suicide of WEI, but the Tung-lin party did not gain power.

T'ung-wen Kuan. Also known as the Interpreters School or the College of

Foreign Languages. The aftermath of the *Arrow* War and the resulting Treaties of Tientsin, 1860 (qq.v.), made it clear that Chinese officials of the Tsung-li Yamen (q.v.) dealing with foreign affairs needed some familiarity with foreign languages. Hence the T'ung-wen Kuan was established in 1862 under the Yamen and with the assistance of Thomas Hart, Inspector General of the Chinese Maritime Customs (qq.v.).

At first the curriculum consisted only of classes in English, French, German and Russian. In 1866 astronomy and mathematics were added. In November 1869, W.A.P. Martin (q.v.), a missionary and Sinologist, was appointed president and a new eight-year curriculum was established, including instruction in sciences as well as Western languages.

A printing press with movable Chinese type was attached to the college, and a number of works on disparate subjects such as international law, the sciences, geography, history, the French and English codes of law, etc., were translated at the college and printed for distribution to government officials.

Entrance to the T'ung-wen Kuan was limited to members of the Manchu and Mongol banners (q.v.) and holders of civil service degrees, and never exceeded 120. Several successful graduates went on to careers in China's diplomatic service and others to internal administrative posts.

In 1902, in the aftermath of the Boxer Rebellion (q.v.), the T'ung-wen Kuan was merged with the Imperial University, which had been established in 1898 during the "Hundred Days Reform" (q.v.).

Tunhuang (Dunhuang). Tunhuang, located in Kansu province (q.v.), is the eastern end of the Silk Road (q.v.) and the location of an important series of Buddhist shrines carved out of the natural rock between the fourth and 14th centuries A.D.

Turkestan. Nineteenth century name for the Central Asian area now mostly included in Sinkiang province (q.v.).

Twenty-one Demands. World War I presented Japan with an opportunity to advance its interests in Asia at the expense not only of China, but of several of its European rivals. The opening shots of the war were fired on July 28, 1914. Japan declared war on Germany on August 23, and by December had occupied all of Germany's leased territory in Shantung, as well as the rest of the province.

In order to consolidate the gains already made, and to preempt the interests of Great Britain and Russia, both too deeply involved in the war with Germany to intervene in China, on January 18, 1915, the Japanese presented to the Chinese government in Peking, headed by YUAN Shih-k'ai (q.v.), what came to be known as the Twenty-one Demands.

In five groups, the demands included (1) China's "full assent" to whatever disposition Japan might see fit to make of German rights in Shantung after the war; China's promise not to cede or lease any part of Shantung to a third power; and the grant to Japan of widespread commercial and railway privileges in that province; (2) China's confirmation of Japan's special position in Manchuria and Eastern Inner Mongolia; (3) exclusive mining and industrial privileges in the Yangtze valley, including joint ownership of the mines and industrial facilities around Hankow, China's largest industrial center; (4) a pledge not to cede or lease any harbor, bay or island on the China coast to any power; (5) widespread political rights for Japan throughout China proper.

The first group confirmed Japan's takeover of German positions in Shantung. The second group aimed at the elimination of any Russian presence in Manchuria and Inner Mongolia. The third group was a direct threat to Great Britain's preeminent position in the Yangtze basin. The fourth group was intended to secure Japan's sphere of interest in Fukien province, opposite Taiwan, which had been ceded to Japan after the Sino-Japanese War (q.v.) in 1895. The fifth group would have given Japan supervision over nearly all Chinese institutions, from schools to the government itself.

Japan presented the demands secretly, but the Chinese leaked them to the American minister in Peking, and the matter was soon known internationally. With the moral support of London and Washington, but not much more, China was able to make significant modifications. The conditions of group five were withdrawn almost completely. The final treaty was signed on May 25, 1915, after a Japanese ultimatum of May 7.

Perhaps the most significant result of the demands was the galvanizing effect it had on Chinese public opinion, and the impetus it gave to the movement for national unification. Chinese anger against Japan remained high for years, and the decision of the Paris Peace Conference (see **Versailles, Treaty of**) to award the German concessions in Shantung to Japan resulted in the May Fourth movement of 1919 (q.v.).

Tz'u Hsi. See **Empress Dowager.**

U

Uighur (Uygur). Name of the third largest (5.4 million) recognized minority group in China, mostly resident in Sinkiang (q.v.). The Uighur are of Turkic stock, unrelated to the Chinese culturally, ethnically or linguistically. They first appear in history in the T'ang dynasty (618-906 A.D., q.v.), as the dominant nomadic group controlling what is now Mongolia. A strong Uighur empire existed from 744 to 840 A.D. and for most of this time was allied with the T'ang, probably because of Chinese assistance in overthrowing their previous overlords.

The Uighur reciprocated by assisting the T'ang in suppressing the rebellion of AN Lu-shan (q.v.) in 755 A.D., and as a reward were permitted to plunder the eastern capital of Loyang in 763. Thousands of Chinese died and it is thought the carnage affected the Uighur ruler, who converted to Manicheism (q.v.), bringing some of his subjects with him. Others later became Buddhists and Nestorian Christians (q.v.).

In 840 the Uighur state was conquered by the Kirghiz, another Central Asian group. They survived as a people and provided many officials to the Mongol state under Chingis Khan (1167-1227), q.v.) and his successors throughout the Yuan dynasty (1279-1368, q.v.). The Mongol script, developed during this period, was based on a Uighur model.

With the decline of Mongol power, the Uighur were converted to Islam and eventually abandoned their old script for one based on Arabic.

The Ming dynasty (1368-1644, q.v.) did not control Central Asia and had no dealings with the Uighur, but the emperor Ch'ien Lung (r. 1736-1796) of the Ch'ing dynasty (1644-1911, qq.v.) listed his pacification of the Muslims of the Ili region in 1762 as among his 10 greatest military achievements, and the Uighur were among those so pacified. They remained vassals of the Ch'ing until 1864, when a Muslim rebellion occurred, leading to Russian occupation of the region in 1871. The area was reconquered in 1878 by the Chinese general TSO Tsung-t'ang (q.v.) and became part of the province of Sinkiang in 1884. It has been under direct Chinese control most of the time since.

The Uighur form the largest minority group in Sinkiang, though their number has now been exceeded by Chinese immigrants, the result of conscious policy of the People's Republic of China.

Mackerras, Colin, ed. and trans. *The Uighur Empire According to the T'ang Dynastic Histories*. Columbia: University of South Carolina Press, 1973.

Unequal treaties. The term refers to those signed by China in the 19th and early 20th centuries under pressure or the threat of force from foreign powers. The Treaty of Nanking (August 29, 1842, q.v.) was the first of these, and resulted in the cession of land (Hong Kong island) to Great Britain and the opening of five "treaty ports" (q.v.). In Chinese eyes the lack of reciprocity in the terms of the treaties made them unequal, and the threat of force made them subject to repudiation.

In July 1919 the Soviet government repudiated the czarist treaties in the Karakhan Declaration (q.v.), which had a great impact on Chinese opinion. The Nationalist government announced in 1928 its determination to revise or abolish all unequal treaties, but after several years of unsuccessful negotiation, decided to take matters into its own hands and abolish such treaties unilaterally by law on January 1, 1932. Implementation was prevented by the Japanese invasion of Manchuria. On January 11, 1943, Britain and the United States signed new treaties with China which abolished extraterritoriality (q.v.) and other rights.

Chiu, Hungdah. *The People's Republic of China and the Law of Treaties*. Cambridge: Harvard University Press, 1972.

United States of America. Like other Western traders, the Americans at first conducted their business in China through the port of Canton (Guangzhou) without diplomatic relations with the Chinese empire. The first American ship to sail for Canton, the *Empress of China*, left New York in 1784. The first diplomatic contact was the signing of the Treaty of Wanghia, 1844 (q.v.). It gave the United States the rights and privileges obtained by Great Britain in the Treaty of Nanking (1842, q.v.). The Treaty of Tientsin (1858, q.v.) granted foreign envoys the right to reside in Peking. The first American to do so was Anson Burlingame (1820-1870, q.v.),

who impressed the Ch'ing authorities with his sympathetic attitude. When he resigned his post in 1867, he was asked to accept an appointment as ambassador from the emperor of China to foreign governments. He accepted, and in this capacity negotiated the third Sino-U.S. treaty in Washington in 1868.

The first two treaties deal with American commercial and diplomatic access to China. The third opened a new chapter by calling for the encouragement of immigration by Chinese laborers. The earliest Chinese immigrants, arriving at the time of the Gold Rush in 1848, were welcomed, but within a few years they were subject to a series of local laws and regulations which singled them out for repression. Most of these laws were declared unconstitutional, but the increasing power and influence of America's western states led to another treaty, signed in Peking on November 17, 1880, which in effect reversed the immigration clause of the Burlingame treaty. This was followed by the Chinese Exclusion Acts of 1882 and 1884. On March 17, 1894, another treaty was signed in Washington prohibiting Chinese immigration for 10 years.

Before the expiry of the treaty of 1894, the U.S. Congress passed an extension of the Chinese Exclusion Law in 1902, extending the exclusion to U.S. possessions, including the Philippines and Hawaii. China protested that neither had been a U.S. possession in 1894, and China would not have signed the treaty if they had been covered by it. On the expiry of the treaty in 1904, Congress reenacted all the Chinese immigration laws. The popular reaction was a boycott of American goods, the first in China's history. The official reaction was the omission of all mention of the treaties of 1880, 1888 and 1894 in the official volume of treaties then being published.

Under American law, Chinese who were legally resident in the United States could not qualify for naturalization because of their race, though children born in the United States of Chinese parents were acknowledged as American citizens. This provision became more important under the immigration act of 1924, which barred immigration to those not eligible for citizenship. Not until the passage of the Immigration and Naturalization Act of 1952 were ethnic and racial barriers eliminated.

In the late 19th century, it appeared possible that China might be dismembered by France, Germany, Japan and Russia (qq.v.), with each country taking over a specific area as a colonial domain. Both Britain and the United States perceived their national interests better served by a China in which equal trade access would be available to all. In consequence, the United States adopted the Open Door Policy (q.v.) in 1899. For the next 40 years, American policy toward China was based on the principle of maintaining China's territorial integrity, without military participation in China's defense. The policy continued when the Ch'ing dynasty (1644-1911, q.v.) was replaced by the Republic of China (q.v.) in 1912. The United States was the first major power to extend diplomatic recognition to the republic, which it did in May 1913.

At the outbreak of World War I (q.v.) in August 1914, China requested U.S. assistance in obtaining declarations by all belligerents not to engage in hostilities in Chinese territory, leased territories or adjacent waters. China's main concern was the likelihood of Japanese encroachments. On August 23, Japan declared war on Germany, starting military actions against German concessions on August 27. By December it held all of Shantung province. On January 18, 1915, Japan presented China with the Twenty-one Demands (q.v.), which, if accepted, would have reduced China to vassal status. The United States warned that it could not recognize any agreement between China and Japan which would impair the political or territorial integrity of China, citing the Open Door Policy. A milder version of the Twenty-one Demands was accepted by China on May 25.

On February 3, 1917, the United States broke diplomatic relations with Germany and suggested similar action be taken by all neutral countries. China broke relations on March 14, and declared war on August 14, thus earning the right to participate in the postwar peace conference. The Chinese delegation which went to Paris in January 1919 was determined to regain the German concessions in Shantung, and in this it had U.S. support. The Japanese were equally determined to retain them, and had support from Britain, France and Italy, which had similar policies with regard to former German possessions. Eventually, the Chinese delegation refused to sign the Treaty of Versailles (q.v.). The United States signed, but never ratified it.

For most of the 1920s, U.S. policy remained that of supporting China's territorial integrity. However, civil wars, both a cause and effect of China's weakness, tempted both Japan and the USSR to contemplate further demands with respect to Manchuria (q.v.). In 1926 CHIANG Kai-shek (1887-1975, q.v.) launched the Northern Expedition (q.v.), and in June 1928 his troops captured Peking, thus theoretically uniting China. The Chinese Nationalist flag was raised in Manchuria in December. Chinese efforts to reduce Soviet and Japanese influence in Manchuria backfired, and in September 1931 forces of Japan's Kwantung Army moved to seize the major cities of southern Manchuria. China appealed to the League of Nations and to the United States. Both supported the Chinese position, but did little more. The United States protested to Japan citing the treaty rights of its citizens and the Open Door Policy. Japan established the puppet state of Manchukuo (q.v.) in March 1932. The United States announced its policy of nonrecognition of the Japanese conquest, but this had no effect.

On July 7, 1937, war broke out between China and Japan, precipitated by the Marco Polo Bridge Incident (q.v.). American policy was concerned largely with the safety of its citizens, and by November nearly half the estimated 10,000 Americans in China had been evacuated. The Japanese advance in China left them in command of all major ports and many other cities, cutting off supplies and communications between Chungking, the wartime Chinese capital, and the outside world. The U.S. ambassador moved to Chungking with most of his embassy, leaving a small group of caretakers in the embassy in Nanking.

World War II (q.v.) commenced in Europe on September 1, 1939. While Japanese successes in China were disturbing to the United States, greater concern was felt toward Europe. However, the United States did provide credits to China and indicated that military aid would be forthcoming. In August 1941, the American Volunteer Group (AVG, q.v.) was established to provide air support to China. On December 7, 1941, Japan attacked American forces at Pearl Harbor, making China and the United States allies.

Chinese and American interests coincided, in that both nations wanted to defeat Japan, and to keep open the Burma lifeline to China. In January 1942, General Joseph W. Stilwell (1883-1946, q.v.) was appointed commander of the U.S. China-Burma-India Theater and concurrently chief of staff for Allied forces to CHIANG Kai-shek. Stilwell arrived in Chungking in March, but the Japanese seizure of Rangoon within days of his arrival closed the Burma Road (q.v.).

Disagreements between CHIANG and Stilwell over priorities and strategy led to the latter's recall in October 1944 and his replacement by the more diplomatic Lt. Gen. Albert C. Wedemeyer. U.S. concern over the fact that more of the Kuomintang (KMT) and Chinese Communist party (CCP, qq.v.) troops were facing each other than were fighting the Japanese, and fear that civil war might break out, led to the appointment of Ambassador Patrick J. Hurley (1883-1963, q.v.), who tried unsuccessfully to mediate between the two factions throughout 1945.

China's inability to make what Britain and the United States regarded as a significant contribution to the defeat of Japan led to Allied efforts to induce the USSR to join the war against Japan. The Soviets agreed to do so at the Yalta Conference (February 1945, q.v.) in exchange for concessions at China's expense, though China did not participate in the conference.

Japan's defeat in August 1945 ended World War II, but did not bring peace to China. American mediation efforts continued under the Marshall Mission (1946, q.v.), with no success. The Civil War (1946-1949, q.v.), led to Nationalist defeat and evacuation to Taiwan, and the establishment of the People's Republic of China (PRC, q.v.) on October 1, 1949. The U.S.

Ambassador, John Leighton Stuart, remained in Nanking when it was overrun by CCP troops in April 1949 in the hope of making contact with CCP authorities, but was forced to leave. In 1950 the U.S. embassy and all consular offices were withdrawn.

Soviet actions in Europe after World War II led to confrontation between the USSR and the Western powers. Communist successes in Asia were a source of concern to many Americans, and China policy became a major internal political issue in the United States. The success of the CCP in China raised accusations that U.S. policy had aided them. At least partially as a result of such accusations, in August 1949 the U.S. State Department published *United States Relations With China*, the so-called "White Paper."

The United States maintained a consulate in Taipei, Taiwan (q.v.), prior to World War II, when it was occupied by Japan. Taiwan was retroceded to China in October 1945, and the consulate was raised to consulate general status. U.S. officials were not confident that the Nationalists could hold Taiwan, but the outbreak of war in Korea on June 25, 1950, caused a reversal in U.S. policy. It was announced that Taiwan would be defended from invasion, and in August Karl Rankin arrived, at first designated as chargé d'affaires, but later as ambassador. Relations with the Republic of China became friendly again, but there was no diplomatic contact with the PRC. However, in an effort to keep informed of developments in the PRC, the U.S. consulate general in Hong Kong established a press monitoring unit, which translated and distributed articles of significance from the Chinese press. These were made available to U.S. authorities in Washington, to American universities with programs of Chinese studies and to the embassies of friendly nations in Peking. For several of these, it was the single most important source of information on trends and events in China.

In 1954 the United States and the Republic of China signed a mutual defense treaty. In 1955 U.S. and PRC ambassadors held talks in Geneva, the first of a series of ambassadorial level meetings which continued intermittently in Warsaw for 15 years. In 1969 the United States eased travel and trade restrictions with the PRC, and in 1971 Henry Kissinger, then National Security Council chairman, made a secret trip to Peking. That same year the United Nations expelled representatives of the Republic of China and seated those of the PRC. In 1972 U.S. President Richard Nixon visited the PRC and on his departure the joint Shanghai Communiqué (q.v.) acknowledged that all Chinese maintain that there is only one China and that Taiwan is part of China. In 1973, liaison offices were established in Peking and Washington.

In December 1978, U.S. President Jimmy Carter announced recognition of the PRC as the government of China. The U.S. embassy in Taiwan was closed. As of 1986, the United States maintains an embassy in Peking, and the PRC maintains an embassy in Washington. Relations with the Republic of China are maintained through the American Institute in Taiwan and the Coordination Council for North American Affairs in Washington.

Fairbank, John K. *The United States and China*. rev. ed. Cambridge: Harvard University Press, 1965.

Griswold, A. Whitney. *The Far Eastern Policy of the United States*. New York: Harcourt Brace, 1938.

United States Relations With China. Washington: Department of State, 1949.

Versailles, Treaty of (June 28, 1919).
China's participation in World War I
(q.v.) was marginal, and intended
primarily to deny Japan permanent
possession of the concessions seized
from Germany (q.v.) in Shantung
province in 1914. A Chinese delegation including V.K. Wellington Koo
(1887-1985, q.v.), attended the Paris
Peace Conference (q.v.) in early 1919,
but was unsuccessful in getting the
German properties returned to
China. The United States supported
the Chinese position, but the other
Allies, intent on annexing German
colonial territories, sided with Japan.
Public opinion in China radically
opposed the decision, and this was
expressed in the May Fourth Incident
(q.v.). The Chinese delegation
refused to sign the treaty, though instructions not to sign arrived after the
decision was made.

Vietnam. The earliest kingdom of the
Viets (*Yueh* in modern Chinese) was in
South China. It was conquered by the
emperor Han Wu Ti (r. 140-87 B.C.,
q.v.) and incorporated into the
Chinese empire as Chiao-chih
province (*Giao Chi* in Vietnamese)
from 111 B.C. to 935 A.D. The
Vietnamese were able to regain their
independence after the fall of the
T'ang dynasty (618-906 A.D., q.v.),
and in 968 reached agreement on
terms of suzerainty with China. Except for brief periods, these terms las-

ted until annexation by France (q.v.)
in 1883. They were: (1) Vietnam
acknowledges it is a vassal of China,
provided that its territory be free of
Chinese troops and administration;
(2) China accepts Vietnamese
dynasties ruling independently,
provided they acknowledge their
vassal status; (3) vassal status is
demonstrated by triennial tribute sent
to China, by acceptance of Chinese
laws and the Chinese calendar, and
by adherence to China's external
policy.

While Vietnam is the name used by
its inhabitants, it was known to the
Chinese as Annam, meaning "The
Pacified South." Sixteenth-century
Portuguese traders used the term
Cochin China for the area of the
Mekong delta. In the 19th century,
Tongking (Tonkin) was used to refer
to the Red river delta in the north. The
narrow coastal strip between the two
was called Annam, with its capital at
Hué. (French Indochina included
Cambodia and Laos, as well.)
Vietnamese have lived along the Red
river delta for at least two millennia.
Their slow movement south began
more than a thousand years ago, and
they reached the Mekong delta in the
16th century.

During the Yuan dynasty (1279-
1368 A.D., q.v.) the Mongol rulers
tried to impose harsher terms on the
Vietnamese than their predecessors.
They invaded in 1280, 1285 and 1287,

but were defeated each time. The emperor Ming Yung Lo (r. 1403-1424, q.v.) conquered Vietnam in 1408 and restored direct Chinese rule, but this lasted only until 1427.

The first Europeans to reach Vietnam by sea were Portuguese traders who arrived in 1536. They were followed in the 17th century by the Dutch, English and French traders. The trade was not profitable, and by 1700 had virtually ceased. The only Europeans left were Portuguese and French missionaries. An anti-Catholic policy set by the Vietnamese emperor Minh Mang (r. 1820-1841) stirred the missionaries to seek French government support.

The French invaded Saigon in 1859 and established a garrison, reinforced in 1861 after the end of the *Arrow* War (1857-1860, q.v.). On June 6, 1862, a treaty was signed ceding Saigon and three provinces of Cochin China to France. In 1867 the French seized the rest of Cochin China. In 1873 they invaded Tongking and briefly held much of the Red river delta. They withdrew, but forced another treaty on the Vietnamese, the terms of which declared Vietnam independent of any power, while accepting French protection. China protested, citing the historical record. Vietnam continued sending tribute to China.

In August 1883, the French invaded Tongking again, and on August 25 signed a Treaty of Protectorate, which enlarged the area of Cochin China under direct French rule, put Tongking under a French resident, and put an end to Vietnam's independence. While this brought government contact between China and Vietnam to an end, trade was opened and revolutionaries from both countries were in contact with each other.

In July 1937 the Japanese opened the war on China and immediately protested the use of the French-built railroad for the transport of war materials from the port of Haiphong to Kunming, the capital of Yunnan province (q.v.). The French limited the use of the line to the shipment of trucks, gasoline and textiles. In June 1940 France fell to the Germans, and in that same month the Japanese demanded the closure of the Vietnamese border with China to all war materials. The French complied, leaving the Burma Road (q.v.) as China's only lifeline.

Japanese troops entered French Indochina in September 1940, and on December 8, 1941 (Pearl Harbor Day), surrounded the French garrisons and threatened to disarm them. The French capitulated and Vietnam was incorporated into the Japanese Co-Prosperity Sphere. On March 9, 1945, the Japanese disarmed the French forces, and on March 10 declared an independent Vietnam under the emperor Bao Dai. On August 25, after the Japanese surrender, Bao Dai resigned in favor of the Viet Minh (a coalition of nationalist and Communist groups) leader, Ho Chi Minh. On September 2, Ho announced the establishment of the Democratic Republic of Vietnam in Hanoi.

The participants at the Potsdam Conference, held in July 1945, agreed that Chinese Nationalist troops would accept the Japanese surrender in Vietnam north of the 16th parallel, and British troops south of it. The British paved the way for the French return, but the Chinese would not permit the French to enter until the signing of a Franco-Chinese treaty on February 28, 1946.

French troops arrived in Saigon in September 1945 and immediately ousted the Vietnamese administration there. They arrived in the north in March 1946, after a treaty had been signed by representatives of the Democratic Republic of Vietnam which recognized Vietnam as a free state, although within the Indochinese Federation and the French Union. In November fighting broke out in the north, and in December 1946 Ho Chi Minh and his government fled from Hanoi to spend the next eight years directing the war against the French from jungle hideouts.

The People's Republic of China (q.v.) was established on October 1, 1949, and was immediately recognized by the Democratic Republic of Vietnam. The first known Chinese aid to the Viet Minh was sent in early 1950. In October, the French lost control of the border areas, and Chinese aid increased. The Geneva Conference, at which the People's Republic was represented, convened in April 1954 to negotiate an armistice. The fall of the bitterly contested French outpost at Dien Bien Phu on May 7 forced the French to accept an agreement which sealed the fate of French colonialism in the north and led to the division of the country at the 17th parallel.

In June 1954 the emperor Bao Dai, who had been reinstalled by the French in 1949 as nominal ruler of Vietnam, appointed Ngo Dinh Diem to form a new government in the south. Diem spent more than a year consolidating his control and then announced a referendum. On October 26, 1955, having won the referendum with over 98 percent of the vote, he proclaimed the Republic of Vietnam. It was immediately recognized by the Republic of China, based in Taiwan, and diplomatic relations were maintained until the fall of Saigon on April 30, 1975.

The establishment of the Republic of Vietnam marked the end of the French colonial administration, and the last French soldier left Vietnam on April 28, 1956. In Diem's nine years of rule before his murder in a coup d'état on November 2, 1963, he was unable to solve his major problem—Communist control of much of the countryside. His successors saw the transformation of what had been basically a counterinsurgency effort against local Communists strengthened by support from North Vietnam into a massive American effort to crush the insurgency and interdict the supply of men and war materials from the north. Both the People's Republic of China and the USSR made significant contributions to the Communist victory, providing trucks, tanks and munitions on a massive scale.

Relations between the People's Republic and the Democratic Government of Vietnam were excellent until 1978. Relations cooled when the Vietnamese invaded Cambodia. Since then there have been occasional border incidents and considerable animosity. Vietnam's most important ally in 1986 is the USSR.

Buttinger, Joseph. *The Smaller Dragon.* New York: Praeger, 1958.

Hammer, Ellen. *Vietnam: Yesterday and Today*. New York: Holt Rinehart & Winston, Inc., 1966.

W X

Wade, Sir Thomas Francis (1818-1895). British diplomat and Sinologue. Born of a military family, Wade attended Harrow and Cambridge. His father purchased him a commission in the British army in 1838, which he held until 1846, when his father died. Wade was more scholar than soldier, however, and showed a flair for languages. He arranged to be sent out with troops going to China at the time of the Opium War (1839-1842, q.v.), and studied Chinese en route. In 1845 he became a student interpreter and became proficient in Chinese.

Wade's scholarly contribution was his 1859 standardization of the romanization (q.v.) which bears his name and that of Herbert A. Giles (1845-1935), who modified it in 1892. Prior to Wade's system there was no accepted standard, and each scholar tended to develop his own.

Wade's diplomatic career was marked first by his service as an interpreter for the British in negotiating the Treaty of Tientsin (1858, see **Tientsin, Treaties of**), which was intended to mark the end of the *Arrow* War (1857-1860, q.v.), and the Conventions of Peking (1860, q.v.), which actually did so. He was appointed British minister to Peking in 1871, and served until September 1882, when he was recalled to London to report. His most significant achievement was the Chefoo Convention (1876, q.v.). He was not well enough to return to China and retired from the diplomatic service in 1883. In 1888 Cambridge University created a chair in Chinese studies for him, and he occupied it until his death. His successor at Cambridge was Herbert A. Giles.

WANG An-shih (1021-1086). Sung dynasty (q.v.) official, scholar and poet, and architect of the fourth attempt to enforce centralized control on the Chinese economy. WANG An-shih combined a brilliant mind with a carelessness about his personal cleanliness and appearance so notable that it was commented upon by his contemporaries. He was also stubborn and persistent.

WANG passed his examinations (see under **Examination system**) at the age of 21 and spent the next years in minor posts in the provinces, declining court appointments. When the emperor Sung Shen Tsung came to the throne in 1067, at the age of 20, he had already heard of WANG and brought him to the capital. WANG was appointed premier in 1069 and held the post until 1076. He introduced a series of economic reforms which ended in disaster.

The Sung dynasty had established government granaries to stabilize prices by buying when crops were in surplus and selling when they were in shortage. WANG's new measure was intended to continue this program, but it tended to replace it. It was a system of loans from government funds to farmers in planting time and repayment at harvest time. Interest was at the rate of 30 percent, not unusual for the period, and the loans soon became compulsory, with severe punishments for failure to repay.

WANG also took over all wholesale and retail trade, throwing the merchants and traders out of work. He revived the pao chia system (q.v.), a method of ensuring social control through mutual responsibility. He abolished conscription and replaced it with a tax, which was then extended to those, such as widows and families without children, who had previously been exempt.

WANG's reforms caused controversy on two levels. His philosophic and political opponents accused him of subscribing more to Legalism than to Confucianism (qq.v.). These opponents included some of the most prominent Chinese of the age: OU-YANG Hsiu, SSU-MA Kuang and SU Tung-p'o (qq.v.). Opposition on the popular level was expressed in terms of unrest as farmers were dispossessed. Economic dislocation was widespread and gave rise to the conditions described in fictional form in the famous novel *Shui Hu Chuan* (q.v.).

WANG was able to conceal the state of affairs in the country from the emperor through his control of official appointments, but eventually even the emperor became aware of the extent of the problem. WANG resigned in 1076, and the job of undoing the reforms fell to SSU-MA Kuang (q.v.). WANG died a decade later and was buried with honors, but his reputation among traditional scholars has been one of infamy. His reforms are blamed for seriously weakening the fabric of the economy of the Northern Sung, which fell in 1126.

Liu, James T.C. *Reform in Sung China: Wang An-shih (1021-1086) and His New Policies*. Cambridge: Harvard University Press, 1959.

WANG Chao-chun. WANG was a beautiful young lady who was selected to be a concubine for the emperor Han Yuan Ti (r. 48-33 B.C.). Because her family was poor and unable to bribe officials, her portrait was made less flattering than that of other concubines. As a result the emperor never sent for her.

When it became necessary to send a palace lady to wed a Hsiung Nu (q.v.) prince, WANG was selected, and only then did the emperor discover how beautiful she was. She bore two sons to her Hsiung Nu husband, but the story of her regret for her exile in Mongolia became legendary. It is the subject of many poems and one drama of the Yuan dynasty (q.v.). In the latter, called *Autumn in Han Palace*, the lady commits suicide on her way to her "barbarian" husband to show her love and devotion to the emperor.

Because of its popularity as a theme in poetry and drama, the story of WANG Chao-chun is familiar to most Chinese. Her fate, whether suicide (fiction) or marriage to a non-Chinese and life beyond the Great Wall (fact), is regarded as pitiable.

WANG Ching-wei (1883-1944). Kuomintang (q.v.) leader and opponent of CHIANG Kai-shek (q.v.), and leader of the pro-Japanese puppet government in Nanking during World War II (q.v.). WANG went to Japan on a government scholarship in 1904, and earned a degree at Tokyo Law College in 1906. By this time he was already an officer of the anti-Manchu T'ung-meng-hui (q.v.), a republican group founded in Japan by SUN Yat-sen (q.v.). At the time, another group, anti-Manchu but in favor of constitutional monarchy, led by K'ANG Yu-wei and LIANG Ch'i-ch'ao (qq.v.), was also prominent in Chinese circles in Japan. WANG distinguished himself in his editorial debates against the monarchists.

WANG left Japan in 1907 with SUN, delivering eloquent speeches in support of the T'ung-meng-hui in Singapore and other cities of Southeast Asia. WANG achieved national fame by participating in a plot to assassinate the Manchu prince regent, father of the emperor P'u-yi (q.v.). The plot was discovered but WANG was imprisoned, not executed, and was released after the outbreak of the revolution at Wuchang on October 10, 1911. He became something of a national hero.

WANG spent the next few years in France, returning to China in 1917, and spent the next seven years as a member of SUN's personal entourage. It was he who drafted SUN's political testament, which SUN signed just before his death in March 1925. In the following years, WANG was regarded as the leader of the left wing of the Kuomintang, which advocated cooperation with the Communists, while CHIANG Kai-shck headed the right wing. The year 1927 found WANG heading up the coalition government at Wuhan which was opposed to CHIANG's government at Nanking. WANG broke with his Communist collaborators on learning of their plans for China, but conflicts with CHIANG's group continued.

The next few years saw WANG in a variety of efforts aimed at reducing CHIANG's power, and it was only the Japanese occupation of Manchuria in 1931 that forced the various elements of the Kuomintang to make peace. From 1932 to 1935 WANG headed the government in Nanking in uneasy alliance with CHIANG, who was occupied with the military attempt to eliminate the Communists. In his position as acting foreign minister, WANG had to deal with Japanese authorities over restoration of railway and mail communications between China and Manchukuo (q.v.), and in this way he became identified in Chinese eyes with all efforts to placate the Japanese. On November 1, 1935, he was wounded by a would-be assassin, and went abroad for medical care. He returned at the time of the Sian incident (q.v.).

With the outbreak of the war with Japan in 1937, WANG found himself playing second fiddle to CHIANG, and became increasingly convinced of the futility of war with Japan. In December 1938 he flew to Hanoi and from there sent a telegram to Chungking, where the government had retreated, urging CHIANG to stop military resistance and make peace. In March an apparent effort to murder WANG failed, but a long-time protégé, was killed. He then proceeded to Japanese-occupied Shanghai to work with other Chinese who were collaborating with the Japanese.

In March 1940 a new national government, so-called, was established at Nanking with WANG at its head. A treaty with Japan was signed at the end of the year, but the Nanking government was granted little autonomy. WANG's pessimistic view of China's ability to resist Japan was strengthened by his perception of the fall of France and Germany's commanding position in Europe. WANG's government declared war on the United States and Great Britain on January 9, 1943, and signed a new treaty of alliance with Japan on October 30, 1943. Japan consistently tried to use the Nanking government to persuade Chungking to abandon the war and concentrate on eliminating the Communists.

WANG went to Japan for medical treatment in 1944, and died in Nagoya on November 10. By this time it was clear that the Japanese war effort was in serious difficulty.

Boorman, Howard L., ed. *Biographical Dictionary of Republican China*. New York: Columbia University Press, 1967.

Mote, Frederick W. *Japanese-Sponsored Governments in China, 1937-1945*. Stanford: Stanford University Press, 1954.

WANG Hung-wen. See under **Gang of Four**.

WANG Mang (d. 23 A.D.). A usurper who overthrew the Earlier Han dynasty (q.v.) in 9 A.D., he established his own Hsin dynasty, and was overthrown and killed in 23 A.D. The Han was restored as the Later Han in 25 A.D.

WANG Mang was the nephew of an empress dowager, and became a powerful figure at court. He was known for his scholarship, his frugal lifestyle, his filial piety and his patronage of learning, all of which were in marked contrast to the luxury and dissipation which characterized other members of the family.

The death of emperor Han Ch'eng Ti in 6 B.C. brought to power the family of another empress, lessening the position of the WANG family. The next emperor, Han Ai Ti, died in 1 A.D. WANG arranged to become regent for Ai Ti's successor, and in 9 A.D. swept the Han away entirely, taking the imperial throne for himself.

WANG Mang's rule was activist. He brought all land under imperial control, dispossessing the great families, and ordered it to be given to its cultivators. He abolished slavery (about 1 percent of the male population was enslaved) and forbade the purchase and sale of either land or retainers. He continued the imperial monopolies of salt and iron, and added wine and mines. He reformed the currency, replacing the relatively simple Han system with one of such complexity that the people could not understand it. WANG was an antiquarian, and claimed that many of his monetary reforms were a return to the methods of the Chou dynasty (1122-255 B.C., q.v.). One such was an effort to reintroduce cowrie shells as a medium of exchange. It failed.

WANG also tried to help the farmers in their dealings with merchants by equalizing prices. The state bought up surplus stocks in times of plenty, and sold them in times of shortage.

He patronized Confucian education and built dormitories for thousands of students.

Many of his reforms did not work and had to be repealed—the law against the sale of land and slaves, for example. Opposition came not only from supporters of the Han and those landowners most affected, but also from bands of brigands, or peasant rebels, calling themselves Red Eyebrows (q.v.). The internal disorder encouraged many of the frontier peoples to reject Chinese rule, and Chinese outposts in Central Asia had to be abandoned.

One of WANG's most spectacular achievements was in calling for all gold to be turned in and exchanged for bronze. The repercussions were felt as far away as the Roman empire, where the emperor Tiberius banned the wearing of silk, since it was paid for with Roman gold. At the time of WANG's death, the central government had some 600,000 catties of gold in its possession, an amount which has been variously estimated at 5 to 11 million ounces.

WANG's statist experiments were the third in Chinese history, their predecessors being the Legalist rule of the Ch'in dynasty (221-206 B.C., q.v.)

and the measures taken by Han Wu Ti (r. 140-87 B.C., q.v.) to pay for his military expeditions in Central Asia. The next after WANG Mang to experiment with a centralized economy was WANG An-shih (1021-1086 A.D., q.v.).

Loewe, Michael. *Crisis and Conflict in Han China*. London: George Allen & Unwin Ltd., 1974.

WANG Wei (701-761). Official, poet and painter of the T'ang dynasty (618-906, q.v.). WANG was born to an aristocratic family and showed his precocity by passing his first examinations at 19 and becoming a chin-shih (see **Examination system**) at 20.

In 723 he was sent away from the court at Changan for reasons that are not entirely clear. He was assigned to a minor post in distant Shantung province and spent the next 10 years there. He expressed some bitterness in the poems he wrote during this period, perhaps the result of his wife's death in 730—he never remarried—and his absorption of Taoist and Buddhist philosophy. WANG Wei was a friend of many of the other poets of the period, such as MENG Hao-jan and TU Fu (qq.v.), and many of the poems were addressed to such friends.

On his return to the court in 733 he was given the first of a series of appointments which kept him as a member of the bureaucracy through several administrations, indicating some degree of political ability. WANG's positions were apparently lucrative and not overly time-consuming. He was able to buy a country estate some 30 miles from Changan and to spend considerable time there, as his poems attest.

A crisis occurred in 756 when he was captured by the rebels under the command of AN Lu-shan (q.v.). He was coerced into serving the rebel administration in the same capacity as he had the emperor T'ang Ming Huang (q.v.), who had fled to Szechwan. While imprisoned in a monastery WANG wrote two poems which were instrumental in his obtaining a pardon from the emperor Su Tsung (r. 756-762). He went on to hold a series of positions of increasing importance until his death.

WANG's behavior during the An Lu-shan rebellion has been criticized by later Confucians, including the Sung dynasty (q.v.) philosopher CHU Hsi (q.v.), on the grounds that WANG should have committed suicide rather than serve the rebels. However, WANG's action was not unique, and many other officials were also pardoned.

Several years after WANG's death, the emperor Tai Tsung (r. 763-779, q.v.), grandson of Ming Huang who had been WANG's patron, asked his brother, a high official, to collect WANG Wei's poems.

Unlike his poems, none of WANG's paintings survives, though there are copies enough to give some idea of his style. His importance as a painter lies in the fact that he was a true amateur, recognized by later generations as the first member of the scholarly official class to become famous for his paintings, unlike his contemporary WU Tao-tzu (q.v.) who was a professional and therefore considered an artisan. Since the materials used in Chinese painting (brush and paper) are the same as those used in writing, and since calligraphy was important in the pursuit of an official career, many successful scholars found no difficulty in taking up painting.

Wagner, Marsha L. *Wang Wei*. Boston: Twayne Publishers, 1981.

WANG Yang-ming (1472-1529). Ming dynasty (q.v.) philosopher and official also known as WANG Shou-jen and WANG Po-an. Not only was WANG the foremost philosopher of the period, he also had a remarkable career as an official. He came of a scholarly family and in 1499 passed his chin-shih examinations (see **Examination system**) second on the list. In 1506 he memorialized the emperor criticizing the imprisonment of censors who had accused one of the emperor's eunuchs (q.v.) of corruption. For his pains he was punished with 40 strokes of the bamboo and exiled to Kweichow. In 1510 he was recalled to the capital and went on to a successful career, which included suppressing banditry and quelling rebellion. These activities took place in Fukien, Kwangsi and Kwangtung, largely, as these areas were becoming more integrated with other parts of China at the time. Many of the areas were still under the control of their minority chieftains.

WANG's fame, however, rests on his philosophic writings in the Neo-Confucian tradition. In this he was a successor to CHU Hsi (q.v.) of the Sung dynasty (q.v.). Like CHU he studied both Buddhism and Taoism (qq.v.), but eventually rejected both. WANG stressed intuitive knowledge, and where CHU recommended the investigation of things, WANG was devoted to the study of the human heart. His school of Neo-Confucianism is usually referred to as the school of "idealism."

CHU and his followers believed that knowledge was necessary as preparation for right conduct, and therefore called for "the investigation of things." WANG and his followers believed that self-knowledge was the highest kind of learning and that self-culture was man's highest duty. While not opposed to learning, they believed in the rule of conscience and attached great importance to introspection.

WANG's philosophy had great impact in Japan, where he is known as O Yo-mei. The Tokugawa Shogunate (1603-1867) espoused the Neo-Confucianism of CHU Hsi as its official ideology, but WANG's more individual system proved the intellectual basis for the critics who eventually toppled it and paved the way for the Meiji Restoration in 1867.

WANG was also the favorite philosopher of CHIANG Kai-shek (q.v.), and the mountain north of Taipei is named Yang Ming Shan in his honor.

Fung, Yu-lan, and Derk Bodde, trans. *A History of Chinese Philosophy*. Princeton, Princeton University Press, 1953.

Wanghia, Treaty of. Signed July 3, 1844, by Ch'i-ying (q.v.) for China and Caleb Cushing for the United States, it was the first treaty between the two nations. The Treaty of the Bogue (q.v.), which China signed with Great Britain on October 8, 1843, included the "most-favored nation" clause (q.v.). Cushing included that clause and also introduced a provision for renegotiation of the treaty after 12 years. This meant that all treaties with Western powers were open for renegotiation in 1854, 12 years after the Sino-British Treaty of Nanking (August 29, 1842, q.v.).

Ward, Frederick Townsend (1831-1862). American military adventurer. Born in Salem, Massachusetts, he shipped out to China as a second mate in 1846. He returned to the United States the following year and attended a military school, but did not graduate. From 1849 to 1858 he wandered the world and, by his own account, fought in Central America as well as with the French in the Crimean War (1853-1856). In 1859 he reentered China at Shanghai.

The Taiping Rebellion (1851-1864,

q.v.) was at its height and the rebels threatened Shanghai. The foreign community was neutral in the conflict. However, when Ward approached the Chinese merchants and offered to recruit European mercenaries at their expense, they agreed. Ward's first attack on Sungkiang, about 30 miles from Shanghai, was a failure. He replaced his Europeans, mostly sailors and British navy deserters, with Filipinos, and in July 1860 captured Sungkiang.

In May 1861, he was seized by the British navy on charges of enticing sailors to desert, but escaped. The Treaties of Tientsin (1858, q.v.) had been ratified, and in hopes of trade in the Yangtze valley, the foreign community no longer remained neutral. Ward proposed training Chinese troops and providing European officers to fight the rebels. With the assistance of the Chinese merchants again, he recruited and trained an army. His success led to his becoming a Chinese citizen with an official rank in the Chinese hierarchy, and the bestowal by imperial decree of the title "Ever-Victorious Army" on his troops.

Ward was killed in battle on September 21, 1862, near Ningpo, and was succeeded by another American, Henry A. Burgevine, and then by a Britisher, Charles George Gordon (q.v.). Ward is credited with being the first Westerner in the 19th century to show that properly trained and led, Chinese troops would be as competent as any.

Spence, Jonathan. *To Change China.* Boston: Little Brown & Co., 1969.

Warlords. As the term is generally used today, it refers to Chinese military leaders who based their power on the control of a specific area whose population could be counted on to provide troops for their support. The pattern can be traced back more than 2,000 years, and several founders of dynasties may be said to fit it.

YUAN Shih-k'ai (q.v.) attempted to establish his own dynasty, after being named president of the Republic of China (q.v.) following the fall of the Ch'ing dynasty (q.v.), whose last emperor, the child P'u-yi (q.v.), abdicated in January 1912. His death in 1916 was followed by some 10 years of maneuvering by various warlords for possession of Peking and North China. These rivals included the Manchurian warlord CHANG Tso-lin and his son CHANG Hsueh-liang, FENG Yü-hsiang, TUAN Ch'i-jui and YEN Hsi-shan (qq.v.), as well as others.

One of the chief objectives of the Northern Expedition (q.v.) in 1926 was to bring these local authorities under the control of the central government. To some extent it succeeded, and the transfer of the capital to Nanking in 1928 provided a change of focus of national attention.

The Japanese seizure of Manchuria in 1931 was a key factor in the eventual elimination of CHANG Hsueh-liang as a major player in the game, and the onset of war with Japan in 1937 changed the rules. Throughout the war, parts of China were occupied by Japan, and other parts by the Nationalists and Communists. But large areas nominally under Nationalist control were actually under the control of resident warlords. (There were warlords in the south as well as in the north.) The defeat of Japan led to a final effort by CHIANG Kai-shek (q.v.) to eliminate opposition, both Communist and warlord. Several of those he was able to reduce to subservience were transported to Taiwan where they spent the rest of their lives under surveillance comparable to house arrest. Others remained on the continent when the Communists took over in 1949 and some appeared as figurehead officials in various Communist government organs.

It should be noted that neither CHIANG Kai-shek nor MAO Tsetung (q.v.) should be considered a warlord, since they derived power not from regional geographic bases, but from ideologically committed supporters. Both regarded the warlords as impediments to their own plans for national unity.

Ch'i, Hsi-sheng. *Warlord Politics in China, 1916-1928*. Stanford: Stanford University Press, 1976.

Pye, Lucian W. *Warlord Politics*. New York: Praeger, 1971.

Warring States Period (484-221 B.C.). Historians divide the Chou dynasty (q.v.) into three periods, of which this was the last. The preceding Spring and Autumn Period (q.v.) had seen the growth of the power of the feudal lords and the decline in the prestige of the Chou kings. The Warring States Period saw the extinction of the dynasty.

During the fifth century, the character of contention between the feudal states changed from one of diplomatic maneuver to more serious fighting. The theoretical justification for the warfare was the necessity for a unified China. This made it impossible for any single state, or even an alliance, to maintain a neutral and peaceful stance toward all others. It also resulted in the progressive decrease in the number of states participating in the struggle for hegemony. The final victor was the state of Ch'in whose ruler established the short-lived Ch'in dynasty (q.v.), and from which the word "China" is derived.

The period provided an opportunity for philosophers of opposing schools to practice the art of persuasion on their feudal masters. There were so many different schools that the term "100 schools of thought" has been applied to them. (See under **Philosophy**.) A number of examples of this type of intellectual exercise have come down to us. The three most important schools identified with the period are Confucianism, Legalism and Taoism (qq.v.).

Walker, Richard L. *The Multistate System of Ancient China*. Westport: Greenwood Press, 1971 (reprint).

Crump, J.I., Jr. *Intrigues*. Ann Arbor: University of Michigan Press, 1964.

Wei. 1.   One of the Warring States (q.v.). It was formed in the breakup of the state of Chin (q.v.) in 424 B.C. and was conquered by the Ch'in (q.v.) in 225 B.C.

2.   One of the Three Kingdoms (q.v.). It was founded in 220 A.D. by the son of TS'AO Ts'ao (q.v.), who deposed the last Han emperor. In 266 SSU-MA Yen, the chief minister, deposed the last ruler of the TS'AO family and changed the name of the state to Chin, then proceeded to unite China.

3.   The state known as Northern Wei (386-534). It was founded by the T'o-Pa Tartars, and split into Eastern and Western Wei in 534. These two states lasted only a short time and were succeeded by the Northern Ch'i and Northern Chou dynasties (qq.v.).

Since the ruling Wei were not Chinese, they were not in a position to lay claim to the Confucian tradition. The result was that Buddhism enjoyed its first period of government patronage. As a universal religion, it served as a unifying factor between Chinese and Tartar. Many of the most noted examples of Buddhist art date from this period and show the favorable position the religion held in the state.

WEI Cheng (580-643). Confucian official and chief adviser to emperor T'ang T'ai Tsung (r. 627-649, q.v.). WEI was an adviser to a competitor of the founder of the T'ang Dynasty (q.v.), the emperor T'ang Kao Tsu (r. 618-626, q.v.). Thanks to the policy of the latter, WEI was accepted as a supporter and was assigned to advise the heir apparent, elder brother of T'ai Tsung. T'ai Tsung brought about the death of the heir and the abdication of Kao Tsu. He took WEI as his chief adviser, respecting him for his outspoken honesty and Confucian principles.

WEI's policies were in favor of frugality and in opposition to aggressive military action. Since T'ai Tsung was not particularly frugal and was one of the most successful Chinese emperors in history at expanding the empire, WEI's advice was not always followed. This became increasingly clear as the emperor consolidated his power and formalized his bureaucracy, thus permitting external adventures. Nevertheless, at his death, WEI was buried in the "tomb city" that T'ai Tsung had prepared for himself and for his immediate family.

After his death WEI became deified as a door-god (q.v.) in the popular religion. For this reason he is a familiar figure in traditional Chinese culture.

Wechsler, Howard J. *Mirror to the Son of Heaven*. New Haven: Yale University Press, 1974.

WEI, Chung-hsien (1568-1627). The most powerful and most hated eunuch (q.v.) of the late Ming dynasty (q.v.). His original name may have been LI. He became a eunuch to pay off his youthful gambling debts, and became an official in the household of the chief concubine of the prince who became the emperor Ming T'ai Ch'ang (q.v.). In this position WEI curried favor with T'ai Ch'ang's son, who reigned as Ming T'ien Ch'i (1621-1627, q.v.). Soon after T'ien Ch'i's accession to the throne, WEI and his mistress, who was the emperor's nurse, dominated palace affairs.

WEI's opposition crystallized as the Tung-lin party (q.v.), but for several years WEI's influence seemed unstoppable. He conducted a vendetta against several of the top military officials, and it was during this period that all of the territory east of the Liao river was lost to the Manchus (q.v.).

The death of the emperor T'ien Ch'i on September 30, 1627, led to WEI's downfall. The next emperor, who reigned as Ming Ch'ung Chen (1628-1644, q.v.), was not in the least sympathetic to WEI, and sent him into retirement. Several days after that blow, he was accused of crimes. He hanged himself in December 1627.

Hummel, Arthur W., ed. *Eminent Chinese of the Ch'ing Period*. Washington: Government Printing Office, 1943.

WEI Yuan (1794-1856). Government official and scholar. WEI was born of an official family from Hunan, the second of four sons. He obtained the chü-jen degree in 1822 and the chin-shih in 1844 (see under **Examination system**). His skill as an administrator was shown in 1849 when he took measures to save the peasants' crops which would have been flooded by water-conservancy actions proposed by his superiors.

His reputation as a scholar is based mainly on two major works: a new history of the Yuan dynasty (q.v.) and *Hai-kuo t'u-chih* (Illustrated Treatise on the Sea Kingdoms). As an official, WEI was deeply concerned with the visible decline of the dynasty he served and its growing inability to control its destiny. The opium trade was seen as a symptom of this, and China's defeat in the Opium War (q.v.) in 1842 seemed to him proof that the Chinese desperately needed to know more about the countries of Southeast Asia with which it traded by sea. Since the Western European countries also traded by sea, they were placed in this category. WEI included material from Chinese sources and also translations of Western sources provided by his friend LIN Tse-hsü (q.v.), the commissioner at Canton whose seizure of British-owned opium had provided the occasion for the war. WEI's treatise was the first formal work on the geography and history of foreign lands published in Chinese in centuries. It went through several editions and was republished in Japan.

Hummel, Arthur W., ed. *Eminent Chinese of the Ch'ing Period.* Washington: Government Printing Office, 1943.

Leonard, Jane K. *Wei Yuan and China's Rediscovery of the Maritime World.* Cambridge: Harvard University Press, 1984.

Weihaiwei. Port on the extreme tip of the Shantung peninsula. Britain obtained the lease of Weihaiwei for use as a naval port in March 1898 to counter the Russian lease of Port Arthur and the Liaotung peninsula (qq.v.). The British were at pains to reassure Germany, which had obtained concessions in Shantung province, that the purpose of the lease was not to interfere with German rights and privileges, and the port was never fortified. Britain gave up the lease on April 18, 1930. Weihaiwei was the site of a Japanese concentration camp for Allied nationals during World War II.

Western Liao dynasty (1125-1168). The fall of the Liao dynasty (907-1125, q.v.) prompted some of the Ch'itan (Khitai) who were its dominant el-

ement to move west to the steppes of Central Asia. Under the leadership of Yeh-lü Ta-shih (see under **Tartar Dynasties**), a member of the royal family, they established the Western Liao, also known as the Kara Khitai. Its historical records have been accepted as part of the canon of dynastic histories (q.v.).

Whampoa Military Academy. It was established by SUN Yat-sen (q.v.) at Whampoa, near Canton, in 1924, to train military officers to help in the unification of China. CHIANG Kai-shek (q.v.), its first commandant, personally supervised the training of the 2000 men in the first three classes. A policy of cooperation between the Kuomintang (KMT) and the Chinese Communist party (CCP, qq.v.) was agreed upon in January 1923 in a joint statement by SUN and Adolf Joffe, a Soviet official. Under this policy, several Russian advisers in Canton, e.g. Michael Borodin (q.v.) and Vasily Konstantinovich Bluecher (known as "Galen"), and Communist leaders such as CHOU En-lai (q.v.), were political instructors at the academy.

Many of the students went on to careers in the Nationalist military forces, where they became known as the Whampoa Clique. Others went on to military careers with the Communists after the split between the KMT and the CCP in 1926.

Whampoa, Treaty of. Signed October 24, 1844, by Ch'i-ying (q.v.) for China and Théodose de Lagrené for France. The French were less interested in trade than the British, but considered themselves the protectors of all Roman Catholics in China, of whom there were an estimated 200,000 at the time. The treaty granted religious toleration, rescinding the ban on Christianity imposed by the emperor

Yung Cheng (q.v.) in 1724. It also gave Christian missionaries the right to travel and reside in China.

Beeching, Jack. *The Chinese Opium Wars*. New York: Harcourt Brace Jovanovich, 1976.

White Lotus Society. The White Lotus Society was a heterodox Buddhist sect which flourished in the Yangtze valley in the 14th century. It was opposed to the reigning Yuan dynasty (1279-1368, q.v.), and contributed to the turmoil which led to the rise of the Ming dynasty (1368-1644, q.v.). The sect's followers believed in the imminent appearance of Maitreya, the Buddha of the future, and prayed that he would arrive within their own lifetimes to establish a "Pure Land" (see under **Pure Land sect**). Members of the sect also believed that it was their duty to establish this kingdom, and consequently felt justified in rebelling against the Yuan.

The military arm of the sect was known as the Red Turbans (q.v.), and it attempted a restoration of the Sung dynasty (960-1279, q.v.) in the person of a man called HAN Shan-t'ung, who claimed to be a descendant of the emperor Sung Hui-tsung (r. 1100-1126, q.v.). Many of the soldiers in the army of CHU Yuan-chang, the founder of the Ming dynasty who reigned 1368-1398 as Ming Hung Wu (q.v.), were members of the White Lotus Society, and for this reason CHU was careful not to oppose the Sung pretenders. However, the second pretender, HAN Lin-erh, son of HAN Shan-t'ung, drowned in 1366. This paved the way for CHU to cut his ties to the White Lotus Society, and after the establishment of the new dynasty in 1368, he suppressed it and destroyed its temples.

The organization persisted, however, and a White Lotus rebellion was suppressed in 1622, in the declining years of the Ming dynasty. The sect revived again in the late 18th century, and a full-scale rebellion occurred from 1795 to 1803. It was suppressed only after the death of the emperor Ch'ien Lung (r. 1736-1796, q.v.), in 1799, when his successor, the emperor Chia Ch'ing (r. 1796-1820, q.v.), removed the corrupt Manchu official Ho-shen (q.v.), his predecessor's favorite, from power.

William of Rubruck (1215[?]-1295 A.D.). French Franciscan monk and early traveler to the court of Mangu Khan, brother of Khubilai Khan (q.v.), the latter's predecessor as ruler of the Mongols. Friar William never reached China, since at the time of his visit to the Mongol khan, the conquest of China had not been completed.

William of Rubruck was an unofficial envoy of France's King Louis IX and traveled across Central Asia reaching the great khan's camp near Karakoram on December 27, 1253, where he found in residence priests of the Nestorian Christians (q.v.), who resented the presence of a Western Christian. Instructed to leave the following spring, he left in July, and reached Lebanon in August 1255. He wrote a report for the king on his experiences in Mongolia, which was used by the English Franciscan Roger Bacon in his *Opus Majus*.

Work-study Movement. This was an outgrowth of a program established in 1912 to permit Chinese students to study in France at low cost. By 1915 the labor shortage in France, because of World War I, permitted a change to a work-study plan, whose participants worked in factories and offices to support their studies. Among the 2,000 or so who participated were CHOU En-lai and LI Li-san (qq.v.). The work-study program came to an end when some of its members, organized and led by Communist students, forced their way into the new Institut Franco-Chinois at Lyons in September 1921. They were deported, and while Chinese students continued to study in France, the work-study program was disbanded.

World War I. The war was fought largely in Europe, but China felt its repercussions. The opening shots were fired on July 28, 1914, and China proposed to the United States that it try to obtain the consent of the belligerents to agree not to conduct hostilities on Chinese territory or waters, or in adjacent leased territories. China's prime concern was over the Kiaochow Leased Territory, in the possession of Germany (q.v.). An agreement was never reached.

Japan declared war on Germany on August 23rd, and by December it occupied all of Shantung province and most of the German islands in the Pacific north of the equator. On January 18, 1915, Japan presented China with the Twenty-one Demands (q.v.). The demands, if met, would have left Japan in permanent possession of Germany's former territories in Shantung, recognized Japan's special position in Manchuria (q.v.) and Inner Mongolia, and granted Japan exclusive rights in the Yangtze valley, as well as other rights and privileges.

The Chinese leaked the terms of the secret demands to the American minister in the hope of receiving some international support to rebuff them. American policy in China, known as the Open Door Policy (q.v.), supported equal access for all nations to the China market, and American interests would be damaged by recognizing Japan's special position in any area. British interests, centered on the Yangtze basin, would also be damaged by granting Japan exclusive privileges in the area. But while both nations were opposed to the demands, their attention was centered on Europe. In consequence, they offered China little but moral support.

China declared war on Germany on August 14, 1917, largely for the purpose of denying Japan permanent title to the Kiaochow Leased Territory and Shantung. When the Treaty of Versailles (q.v.) awarded the German properties to Japan, China refused to sign. Chinese popular outrage at Japan was expressed in the May Fourth Incident of 1919 (q.v.).

Japan emerged from World War I greatly strengthened vis-à-vis its Western competitors on the China scene. Germany had been completely eliminated in the Pacific, and both Great Britain and France had been weakened. Russia had undergone a revolution, which transformed the nature of its relationships with both China and Japan.

World War II. The Chinese usually refer to this conflict as "The War of Resistance to Japanese Aggression." Chinese perception of Japan's aggressive intentions was based on events, the most significant of which were the following: (1) Japanese assertion of jurisdiction over the Liu Ch'iu (Ryukyu) Islands (1875, q.v.); (2) the Sino-Japanese War (1894, q.v.), which resulted in Japanese seizure of Taiwan and the Liaotung peninsula, though Japan was forced to return the latter; (3) the Russo-Japanese War (1904-1905, q.v.), which was largely fought on Chinese soil and resulted in Japan taking over Russian concessions in Manchuria (q.v.); (4) Japan's seizure of German properties and concessions in Shantung province (1914, q.v.); (5) the Twenty-one Demands (1915, q.v.); (6) the Treaty of Versailles' (q.v.) award of German concessions in Shantung to Japan (1919); (7) the despatch of Japanese troops to Shantung (ostensibly to protect Japanese interests) in May 1927; (8) the clash between Chinese and Japanese troops at Tsinan, capital of Shantung (May 3, 1928); (9) Japanese occupation of Mukden (q.v.) and other Manchurian cities (September 18, 1931); (10) Japan's naval attack on Shanghai (January 28, 1932); and (11) Japanese establishment of Manchukuo (March 1, 1932, q.v.).

The Chinese national government was established in Nanking in October 1928 with CHIANG Kai-shek (1887-1975, q.v.) as chairman and also as head of the ruling Kuomintang (KMT, q.v.) party. The Northern Expedition of 1926-1928 (q.v.) had succeeded in neutralizing most of the warlords or gaining their adherence to the government. The main obstacle to unity, in the view of Nanking, was the continued existence of enclaves controlled by the Chinese Communist party (CCP, q.v.). While recognizing the danger of further Japanese aggression, CHIANG's policy was to achieve Chinese unity before resisting Japan.

The Japanese conquest of Manchuria in 1932 dispossessed CHANG Hsueh-liang (1898- , q.v.), the local warlord, who retreated to North China with his troops. In 1935 he was ordered to move to Northwest China to suppress the CCP survivors of the Long March (q.v.) in Shensi province. Unwilling to fight Chinese while the Japanese occupied their homeland, the Manchurians arranged a de facto cease-fire. In the Sian Incident (q.v.) of December 1936, CHIANG Kai-shek was kidnapped and forced to agree to a united front against Japan.

Six months later, on July 7, 1937, the Japanese attacked Chinese forces outside Peiping (Peking) in the Marco Polo Bridge Incident (q.v.), and by the end of July had occupied Peiping and Tientsin. In August the Japanese attacked Shanghai, but CHIANG's German-trained troops gave a good account of themselves in the lower Yangtze valley. In September, representatives of the KMT and CCP issued a joint statement spelling out the terms of their cooperation, which included the integration of CCP military forces into the government armies.

Shanghai fell in November, and the Rape of Nanking (q.v.) occurred in December when that city fell. The national government moved upriver to Wuhan. In 1938 the Japanese continued moving up the Yangtze valley, and in October they took Wuhan. At the same time they seized Canton on the southern coast. In December the government was established in Chungking, where it remained until 1945. The Nationalist-held center was surrounded by a buffer zone 50 to 100 miles deep in which rail lines had been torn up, bridges destroyed, roads trenched and mountain passes barricaded.

By the beginning of 1939, the Japanese occupied much of North China, the lower Yangtze valley, many of the southern ports and most of the lines of communication. The Nationalists controlled much of West China, and much of the countryside behind Japanese lines. The CCP forces occupied the northwest and also controlled much countryside behind Japanese lines, particularly in North China.

War in Europe started with the German invasion of Poland in September, 1939. The Germans turned west in 1940, and France fell in June. The Japanese took swift advantage of this to negotiate entry into northern

French Indochina (see under **Vietnam**), which they executed in September, forcing closure of the railway from Haiphong to Kunming, Yunnan province. At Japan's request, Britain closed the Burma Road (q.v.) from mid-July to mid-October 1940, thus isolating China completely for a period. The Japanese also set up a puppet government in Nanking, with WANG Ching-wei (1883-1944, q.v.) at the head. WANG had been the number-two man in the KMT, but his defection had little effect.

Internally, the integration of CCP units into the Nationalist armies made little progress, but there was no pitched battle between the two until January 6-14, 1941, when the New Fourth Army Incident (q.v.) took place. The CCP forces were badly defeated and withdrew north of the Yangtze river.

On April 13, 1941, the Japanese signed a neutrality treaty with the USSR. This was a blow to the Chinese, as the Soviets had been selling them a small quantity of arms, which would now cease. On April 17, the first U.S. military aid program to China, amounting to $45 million, was approved. Under it, the first shipment, bound for Rangoon, Burma, went out in May. In June, Germany invaded the USSR. In July, Japan occupied southern Indochina. On August 1, 1941, the American Volunteer Group (AVG, q.v.) of the Chinese air force was established under Col. (later Maj. Gen.) Claire L. Chennault. In keeping with U.S. policy, both the U.S. Army and Navy released pilots and aircrews who volunteered for this duty. The first group of AVG pilots and crewmen had arrived in Burma for training in late July.

By late summer the U.S. government had broken the Japanese diplomatic code and knew that Japan would not declare war on the USSR.

Instead, the Japanese planned to bring the war in China to a conclusion and to move into Southeast Asia to seize natural resources, principally oil and rubber, in British Malaya and the Netherlands East Indies. On December 7, 1941, Japan attacked the American fleet at Pearl Harbor, and the same day (December 8, locally, because of the International Date Line) attacked Hong Kong and served an ultimatum on Thailand demanding the right of military passage across Thai territory. The following day the first attack was made on Malaya, and on December 25, Hong Kong fell.

The Japanese attacks prompted the creation of an Allied China Theater, with Generalissimo CHIANG Kai-shek as supreme commander. U.S. General Joseph W. Stilwell (1883-1946, q.v.) was appointed CHIANG's Allied chief of staff, in command of all allied forces in the theater and of any Chinese forces CHIANG might assign to him. Stilwell was also commander of the U.S. China-Burma-India Theater.

The Japanese pressed their military activities in Southeast Asia; Singapore fell on February 15, 1942, and Rangoon on March 6, thus closing the Burma Road. One of Stilwell's first responsibilities was to organize a military airlift from India to China over the southern spur of the Himalayas, which extends into northern Burma and separates the two countries. As first established, the airlift went from several airfields in Assam (India) to Kunming, and was later extended to Chungking.

Japanese activity in Southeast Asia precluded intensive ground action in China in early 1942, but the air raid on Tokyo by Lt. Col. James H. Doolittle on April 18, with a force of 16 B-25s, stirred the Japanese to action. The bombers took off from a carrier, but could not return. They planned to fly to Chinese air bases, but a combination of bad weather, poor communications and a long flight resulted in the loss of all planes. The planes crashed in Chekiang province, where the crews were welcomed by the Chinese population. In retaliation, the Japanese moved through Chekiang in force and seized all the Chinese air bases there.

By the end of May 1942, Japan held most of Burma and was in a position to attack either India or China's Yunnan province. The Japanese proceeded to move up the Burma Road into Yunnan, reaching the banks of the Salween river, about 100 miles from the border. By continuing up to Kunming, or by moving into Assam and seizing American air bases there, they would eliminate the airlift. To counter this threat, Stilwell proposed a Chinese force to push the Japanese out of Yunnan and back into Burma, in coordination with an Anglo-American effort to push the Japanese out of upper Burma, permitting the construction of a road from Ledo, Assam, to a point on the Burma Road near the Chinese border.

There was no major military activity in China in 1943. In that year the British were bombing Germany, and in August Italy surrendered to the Allies. The German offensive in the USSR ground to a halt. The Japanese were concerned with American naval successes in the Pacific, and with American seizures of Japanese-held islands there. China, at the end of the longest supply line in military history, was a side issue.

In August 1943, the Quebec Conference, attended by British Prime Minister Winston Churchill and U.S. President Franklin Roosevelt, decided to undertake a campaign to drive the Japanese out of upper Burma. The campaign opened in October, using Chinese forces which had retreated to

India in the First Burma Campaign and had been retrained by the Americans. On October 30, they stumbled on a much larger Japanese force than anticipated, as the Japanese were building-up for an attack on India.

While the campaign was getting under way, Generalissimo CHIANG flew to Cairo to meet with Churchill and Roosevelt. The Cairo Conference (q.v.), held in late November, resulted in the Cairo Declaration of December 1, which announced that Japan would be stripped of its overseas possessions and restricted to the home islands; Manchuria and Taiwan would be returned to China; and Korea would regain its independence. This was the only time that CHIANG met Churchill and Roosevelt in person, and, unfortunately, his reversal of position on several key issues left the impression that Chinese commitments were not firm. There is no doubt that this affected Allied strategy in terms of using China for military action against Japan.

CHIANG returned to Chungking after the conference, but Churchill and Roosevelt went on to meet Soviet Marshal Joseph Stalin at the Tehran Conference (q.v.). In exchange for a definite promise of a second front in Europe in 1944, Stalin agreed to enter the war in Asia after Germany's defeat. At this, Roosevelt proposed that the port of Dairen (q.v.) would be appropriate compensation for Soviet participation. This offer was later expanded at the Yalta Conference (q.v.) in February 1945.

The North Burma Campaign was a stalemate for two months, but a successful Chinese attack was launched under Stilwell's command on Christmas Eve 1943. While the Chinese and American forces inched forward through difficult jungle terrain, the Japanese launched a drive against Imphal, just over the border in India. If successful, it would have cut the Bengal & Assam Railway, which transported supplies from Calcutta to the airfields in Assam. The Japanese attack began on March 4, 1944, and ended in failure in the monsoon rains of July. Some 65,000 of the 155,000 Japanese troops involved in the drive on Imphal died, and the battle was a major turning point in the ground war in Asia.

Stilwell had urged the Chinese to clear the China end of the Burma Road of Japanese troops west of the Salween river, and on May 11, 1944, Chinese troops started crossing the river. Stilwell wanted the Chinese to move quickly into Burma, but the Chinese opted to move more slowly and eliminate each Japanese position as they went along. As a result, the reopening of the Burma Road did not take place until the end of 1944.

Meanwhile, a serious crisis was building in East China, where Chennault's 14th Air Force (successor to the AVG) had several bases from which attacks were made on rail lines, bridges and Japanese shipping in the Yangtze river. The possibility of attacks against the homeland was also disturbing to the Japanese. In consequence, they launched an operation in early 1944 designed to capture the airfields and then open up the rail line between Hankow and Canton. This would permit the shipment of military supplies from Manchuria to Canton, close to Indochina, and avoid the long trip by sea which was threatened by American naval and air power. By the end of May the Japanese had complete control of the rail line north of the Yangtze river, and had seized the airfield at Hengyang some 300 miles to the south. The Japanese drive to the south also raised fears for the security of the bases

being built near Chengtu, Szechwan province, to accommodate B-29 bombers.

The lifting of the monsoon in the autumn of 1944 permitted the resumption of the North Burma Campaign. Bhamo fell on December 15, and at that point Chinese troops in Burma were only 50 miles from Chinese troops fighting the Japanese inside Yunnan. On February 4, 1945, the first official truck convoy arrived in Kunming, thus ending the road blockade of China.

General Stilwell's original orders in January 1942 had been "to increase the effectiveness of United States assist in improving the combat efficiency of the Chinese Army." Stilwell assist in improving the combat efficiency of the Chinese Army." Stilwell believed that Chinese soldiers, when properly trained, equipped, fed and led, could fight as well as any. This was borne out by the effectiveness of the American-trained troops in the North Burma Campaign. But by early 1945, Allied planning for the defeat of Japan did not include aggressive use of Chinese ground forces, in view of the failure of those forces to contain the Japanese in East China. Instead, Allied plans included the seizure of one or more ports on the China coast, with support for arriving Allied forces from Chinese troops. To that end, Stilwell's successor, General Albert C. Wedemeyer, concentrated on upgrading a force of 36 divisions. The program was long-range, but the defeat of Germany was still to come and the defeat of Japan was not anticipated before mid-1946.

The Yalta Conference (q.v.), attended by Churchill, Roosevelt and Stalin, but at which China was not represented, spelled out in detail the conditions under which the USSR would enter the war against Japan. The most important for China were the assignment to the USSR of the commercial port of Dairen and the naval base at Port Arthur, the creation of a joint Soviet-Chinese company to run the Chinese-Eastern Railroad and the South Manchurian Railroad, and the preservation of the status quo in Outer Mongolia (i.e., the Mongolian People's Republic). Also included was an acknowledgment that these conditions would require Chinese concurrence, which the United States would take measures to obtain.

By the end of January 1945, the Japanese had succeeded in capturing and opening the Hankow-Canton rail line, and on April 8 opened a campaign directed at Chennault's airfield at Chihchiang, Hunan province. The newly-armed and trained Chinese troops resisted, and by June 7 the Japanese had been defeated and pushed back to their earlier positions in an effective demonstration of Sino-American cooperation.

The final Chinese military operation planned against Japanese troops never actually took place. This was Plan Beta, designed to seize a port on the South China coast as a preliminary to the destruction of Japanese military power on the continent. It was to include the 36 American-trained and equipped divisions with their American advisers, which were to secure several cities on the way to Canton and Hong Kong, the eventual targets.

The Japanese, seeing a major threat from the USSR on land and the United States in amphibious assaults on North China, began the transfer of troops from south to north. This enabled the Chinese to move in as they retreated. By early August Chinese troops had retaken Kweilin, Kweiyang province, and were preparing to launch further attacks. On August 6 the United States dropped the first atomic bomb on Hiroshima, Japan, and on August 8 the second one on Nagasaki. That same day, the USSR announced it would enter the war against Japan, and on August 9 Soviet troops entered Manchuria. On August 14 Japan surrendered, and active hostilities in China, as elsewhere, came to an end. World War II was over.

THE PROBLEM OF NON-GOVERNMENT TROOPS

Throughout World War II, the lack of unity in China was a continuing problem for the Allied powers, as well as for China itself. The Japanese were able to play upon this disunity to some extent, and obtained the services of a number of Chinese for their puppet governments in North and East China. The most prominent of these was WANG Ching-wei, who headed the regime in Nanking. Japanese authorities were apparently in communication with Chinese leaders of all persuasions at one time or another, and it is known that communication between different areas was continuous, if not always convenient.

Since WANG Ching-wei had defected to the Japanese, CHIANG could not be certain that other leaders were totally dependable, unless they were personally loyal to him. Hence, he was unwilling to have any American aid provided to any troops other than those he designated. More than one military leader asked for such military aid directly. As a matter of policy, the United States decided not to provide any aid outside Chinese government channels.

The CCP forces were different in nature from the warlord troops, because they were imbued with an ideological set of beliefs, rather than simple loyalty to an individual warlord. They were also successful in conveying a favorable image to those few Americans who visited or were stationed in CCP-controlled areas, as well as to Americans and other Westerners who met their chief representative in Chungking, CHOU En-lai (1898-1976, q.v.). The political advisers to General Stilwell reported favorably on the lack of luxury and corruption in CCP-held areas.

The first suggestion that an American military mission be sent to the Communists was made in June 1943. This was based on the example of the contemporary British mission to Marshal Tito in Yugoslavia. CHIANG rejected the suggestion, but he reversed himself in June 1944, at the suggestion of visiting U.S. Vice President Henry Wallace, who made no effort to obtain the views of General Stilwell. The observer mission, code-named Dixie Mission, proceeded to Yenan in July 1944.

The purpose of the mission was to obtain military order-of-battle intelligence, but the first reports were not helpful. Untrained observers failed to ask the proper questions. In December 1944, without the knowledge of General Wedemeyer, Stilwell's successor, an OSS officer, visited Yenan and reached an agreement for cooperation with CCP forces. This action was perceived as U.S. government recognition of the Communists and led to a stalemate in negotiations between the CCP and the Nationalist government then being conducted by U.S. Ambassador Patrick J. Hurley (q.v.), and subsequently to a decline in the already unsatisfactory flow of intelligence from the CCP area.

Communist military activity against the Japanese, for theoretical as well as practical reasons, was in the nature of guerrilla warfare. The theory was propounded by MAO Tse-tung, who believed that the peasants could conquer the cities. The CCP force's only source of arms was very small-scale manufacture and whatever they might capture from the enemy. Some American sources suggested they might be better utilized if arms were provided. While CHIANG would not permit this, the question was largely academic, since government troops received very little in the way of American arms. Most of the airlift tonnage was provided to Chennault's 14th Air Force. It was not until the reopening of the Burma Road in early 1945 that American arms began to arrive in China in significant quantities.

While the CCP activities hampered the Japanese in their control of the countryside, their main contribution was in tying down vast numbers of occupation troops who might otherwise have been sent elsewhere. After the war, Marshal Shunroku Hata, supreme commander of Japan's China Expeditionary Army, made the following comment: "Chinese Communists merely resorted to guerrilla warfare and planned the expansion of the area under their influence, and the weakening and disintegration of the Nationalist forces through the war against Japan."

During the Japanese drive to take Chennault's East China air bases in early 1944, the 14th Air Force made increasingly effective efforts to impede Japanese progress by destroying railroad bridges and locomotives. After the war, a Japanese military historian noted that until the summer of 1945, the 14th Air Force had been the principal obstacle to Japanese operations and troop movements in China.

Ho-yungchi. *The Big Circle: China's Role in the Burma Campaigns.* New York: The Exposition Press, 1948.

Romanus, Charles F., and Riley Sunderland. *U.S. Army in World War II: The China-Burma-India Theater.* Washington: Department of the Army, 1959. 3 Vols.

Service, John S. *Lost Chance in China.* New York: Random House, 1974.

Wilson, Dick. *When Tigers Fight: The Story of the Sino-Japanese War, 1937-1945.* New York: The Viking Press, 1982.

Wu. 1. One of the Warring States (q.v.), lasting from 677-743 B.C. Wu was located in the Yangtze valley, and was considered insufficiently Sinicized and therefore barbarian.

2. The name was revived at the time of the Three Kingdoms (q.v.) by a state in the same geographic area. It lasted from 222 to 280 and was conquered by the Western Chin (q.v.).

The name survives in literary usage to denote the area around Shanghai, and also in the various related Wu dialects, which include those of Shanghai, Soochow and Ningpo.

WU San-kuei (1612-1678). WU was born in Liaotung, though his family originated in Kiangsu province. His father was a military officer guarding the frontiers against the Manchus (q.v.). By 1640 WU's own military career had made him a brigade general, and in 1644 he was commander of Ming (q.v.) troops facing the Manchus at Shanhaikuan, a city some 150 miles northeast of Peking, at the point where the Great Wall meets the sea. It is a strategic location on the border between what are now Hopei and Liaotung provinces. When the bandit LI Tzu-ch'eng (q.v.) was threatening Peking, WU was summoned to its defense by the last Ming emperor. The city fell to LI's troops before WU reached it, and he turned back to Shanhaikuan.

LI was holding WU's father as a hostage, and had taken his favorite concubine. WU determined to oppose LI, who personally led an army out to conquer him. WU appealed to the Manchu regent Dorgon (q.v.) for aid, promising him more territory, but Dorgon used the opportunity to prepare for the conquest of China. WU and Dorgon together defeated LI and went on to take Peking on June 6, 1644. Before evacuating the city, LI executed WU's father and all his family, but not, apparently, the favorite concubine.

WU continued his military career under the Ch'ing (q.v.) for nearly 30 years. He was offered a title by the Ming pretender in Nanking, but refused and went on to fight Ming supporters in a number of areas. He conquered the last of the Ming princes in Yünnan in 1659, bringing the prince back from Burma, where he had fled. The prince was strangled.

WU was appointed feudatory for Yunnan and Kweichow, but his power soon spread to Hunan, Szechwan, Shensi and Kansu. His army cost the national treasury some 9 million taels (q.v.) annually, and when it was proposed to reduce his forces and cut expenses, WU launched wars against the aboriginal tribes, or against Burma.

In 1673, the court abolished WU's fuedatory, as well as those of two other generals. WU raised the standard of revolt, proclaimed the kingdom of Chou, and called for the restoration of Ming customs and ceremonies. For several years he was moderately successful in what historians call the "War of the Three Feudatories," but the tide turned. He proclaimed himself emperor of the Chou dynasty on March 23, 1678, and died a few months later of dysentery.

Hummel, Arthur W., ed. *Eminent Chinese of the Ch'ing Period.* Washington: Government Printing Office, 1943.

Wuhan. Capital of Hupeh (Hubei) province (q.v.). It comprises the three cities of Hankow, Hanyang and Wuchang, which are separated by the Han and Yangtze rivers. Population: 3.8 million (1980).

Xiamen. See **Amoy**.

Xi'an. See **Sian**.

Xinjiang Uygur Autonomous Region. See **Sinkiang**.

Xizang Autonomous Region. See **Tibet**.

Yakoob Beg. 1820(?)-1877. Turkic Muslim military leader who at one time controlled the Tarim Basin in Sinkiang (Turkestan) and achieved international recognition for his state. The mid-19th century decline of the Ch'ing dynasty (1644-1911, q.v.) coincided with the rise of Russian power in Central Asia. In 1864 a Muslim rebellion in Turkestan called on the khan of Khokand for assistance in overthrowing the Chinese troops stationed there. Khokand was being swallowed by the Russians, but two outstanding leaders were sent, one of whom was Yakoob Beg.

By 1873 Yakoob Beg was in control of much of Sinkiang and had assumed the leadership of most of the Muslims. He was given the title of amir of Kashgaria by the Turkish sultan and signed treaties with the British and the Russians. He was defeated by the Chinese general TSO Tsung-t'ang (q.v.), who thereby restored the area to Chinese control. Yakoob Beg is reported to have committed suicide in 1877 after the fall of Turfan.

Yalta Conference. In February 1945, three Allied leaders, Prime Minister Winston Churchill of Great Britain, President Franklin Roosevelt of the United States and Marshal Joseph Stalin of the USSR, met in conference at the Crimean resort town of Yalta in the USSR. China was not represent-

ed. With victory over Germany in the European theater imminent, one major purpose was to discuss the postwar settlement there. A second purpose, on the part of the Western Allies, was to persuade the USSR to enter the war against Japan. The Soviets agreed to do so under conditions spelled out in the agreement, which included: (1) preservation of the status quo in the Mongolian People's Republic (i.e., independence); (2) restoration of rights lost by Russia in the Russo-Japanese War (1904-1905, q.v.), including (a) retrocession of the southern half of Sakhalin Island, (b) internationalization of the commercial port of Dairen (q.v.), and the lease of Port Arthur (q.v.) as a naval base, and (c) joint Sino-Soviet operation of railroads in Manchuria. It was also agreed that the United States would obtain Chinese concurrence. In return, the Soviets agreed to enter the war against Japan within two or three months after the end of the war in Europe.

The terms were conveyed by U.S. Ambassador Patrick J. Hurley (q.v.) in Chungking to Generalissimo CHIANG Kai-shek (q.v.), who expressed several reservations. They were also conveyed by U.S. President Harry Truman in Washington to Chinese Premier and Foreign Minister T.V. SOONG (q.v.), who pointed out that the terms were in conflict with the Sino-Soviet Treaty of May 31,

1924, and with the Soviet Agreement of September 20, 1924, with CHANG Tso-lin (1873-1928, q.v.), the Manchurian warlord. SOONG then proceeded to Moscow to negotiate a new Sino-Soviet Treaty (q.v.).

The USSR carried out the terms of the treaty by declaring war on Japan on August 8, 1945, the same day the second atomic bomb was dropped (on Nagasaki, Japan), and on August 9 Soviet troops entered Manchuria. By the end of the month they had occupied all of the area, including Dairen and Port Arthur. They disarmed Japanese troops, turned over the weapons to Chinese Communist troops and looted the Japanese industrial establishment in Manchuria of equipment estimated at the time to be worth $2 billion. In response to Chinese and U.S. protests, the Soviets claimed that it was "war booty." Soviet troops were withdrawn from Manchuria in 1946, except for those at Port Arthur, which continued as a Soviet base until 1955.

Department of State. *United States Relations with China*. Washington: Department of State, 1949.

YANG Chu. Also known as YANG Sheng, he probably lived in the fourth century B.C. Of an aristocratic family of the state of Chao, he was a hedonist philosopher, one of the Hundred Schools (q.v.). Nothing that can be attributed to him has survived, and he is largely known through the criticism of Mencius (q.v.) and a chapter in the book Lieh-tzu (see under **Taoism**).

YANG Chu is quoted to the effect that he would not sacrifice a hair from his body to benefit the whole world. He also believed that a life of denial was unreasonable, and that man should satisfy all desires possible.

YANG Chu's philosophy did not so much disappear as enter into the mainstream of Taoism (q.v.) along with that of Chuang-tze (q.v.).

Fung Yu-lan, and Derk Bodde, trans. *A History of Chinese Philosophy*, Princeton: Princeton University Press, 1953.

YANG Kuei Fei. (d. 755 A.D.). *Kuei Fei* means "honorable consort," and is a title, not a name. Lady YANG was a consort of a son of the T'ang emperor Ming Huang (q.v.) when she came to his attention in 745. He was already 60, and she was presumably in her early twenties, or even younger. He fell in love with her and forced his son to surrender her. She became the prime consort among the reported 3000 in Ming Huang's palace.

She is described as being a friend of AN Lu-shan (q.v.), a non-Chinese general in the T'ang army, and adopted him. She also obtained lucrative posts for various relatives, one of whom, YANG Kuo-chung, became the most important official in the government.

In 750 began a series of major disasters (see under **T'ang Ming Huang**). According to Chinese political theory, such disasters indicated divine dissatisfaction with the emperor, who was held responsible. In 755 AN Lu-shan led a rebellion against the T'ang. Ming Huang fled Ch'ang-an, the T'ang capital, for the relative safety of Szechwan, and abdicated in favor of his son. On the way, his troops forced the execution of YANG Kuo-chung and demanded Lady YANG's head as well. The emperor gave her a silken cord with which she hanged herself.

The two lovers have been poetically described as two one-winged birds, neither of which could fly alone. The incident was the inspiration for the poem known as "The Song of Unending Sorrow" by the poet PO Chü-yi (q.v.), one of the most famous of all T'ang poems.

Yangtze kiang (Yangzi jiang). The Yangtze river is China's longest (6,000 km., 3,500 mi.), and largest in volume going ships for 1,000 miles downriver meters per second. It is exceeded in length only by the Nile, the Amazon and the Mississippi-Missouri, and in volume by the Amazon, the Congo and the Indus. It drains a basin of 1 million sq. km. (390,000 sq. mi.) and is a major trade artery.

The Yangtze rises in Tsinghai province, passes through Tibet and Yunnan, Szechwan, Hupeh, Anwei and Kiangsu provinces before emptying into the East China Sea north of Shanghai. Known in its upper reaches as the River of Golden Sands, it is a mountain torrent for nearly half its length. In its first 1570 miles, it falls an average 9.5 feet per mile. In the 400-mile section from Chungking to Ichang, known as the Yangtze Gorges, it drops from 635 to 175 feet above sea level, 14 inches per mile.

The river is navigable for ocean-going ships for 1,000 miles downriver from Ichang. Specially built ships can navigate the Yangtze Gorges, and the river is partly navigable for another 230 miles to the border of Yunnan. For many centuries boats going upriver were pulled by men walking on towpaths.

The river floods annually during the summer, but the effects are moderated by the existence of two large lakes, Tung Ting (Dongting) and Po Yang (Boyang), which act as natural reservoirs and sediment basins.

The Yangtze first appears in Chinese history in the period of the Warring States (484-221 B.C., q.v.). The state of Ch'u (q.v.), largest and southernmost, and regarded by its northern neighbors as only partly Sinicized, controlled territory on both banks. Only two cities south of the Yangtze have served as national capitals: Hangchow, capital of the

Southern Sung dynasty (q.v.) from 1127-1279 A.D., and Nanking, most prominently from 1368-1403 in the early Ming dynasty (q.v.), and again after 1928 when it served as the capital of the Nationalist government.

Control of the river was a military objective at various times, and emperor Ming Hung Wu (r. 1368-1398, q.v.) achieved his supremacy over his competitors partially by his naval skills. Control of part of the river was also an issue in the Taiping Rebellion (1851-1864, q.v.). and enabled the rebels to maintain their occupation of Nanking from 1853 to 1864. The opening of the Yangtze to foreign trade was a British objective in the 19th century, achieved by the Treaty of Tientsin, 1858 (see under **Tientsin, Treaties of**).

Hsieh, Chiao-min. *Atlas of China*. New York: McGraw-Hill, 1973.

Yao. Name of an emperor (r. 2357-2256 B.C.) of the legendary period (q.v.). He is the subject of a passage in the *Shu Ching* (q.v.), or Book of History, and is regarded by traditional Confucians as one of the ideal rulers of antiquity. He handed the empire to Shun (q.v.) rather than to his son, whom he considered unworthy.

YAO Wen-yuan. See under **Gang of Four**.

YEH Ming-ch'en (1807-1859). Government official and key figure in the *Arrow* War (1857-1860, q.v.). He was appointed governor of Kwangtung province in 1848, a time when the Taiping Rebellion (q.v.) was beginning in nearby Kwangsi, when bandits and various warlike sects brought chaos to Kwangtung, and piracy was rampant along the coast. YEH treated all these disturbances with harsh but successful measures, accompanied by great loss of life.

At the same time, he was faced with

a number of problems with foreign powers. In 1854 representatives of France, Great Britain and the United States pressed for revision of their treaties of Whampoa, Nanking and the Bogue, and Wanghia (qq.v.), respectively. Although the terms of the treaties provided for this, YEH responded that his government saw no need for revision. The request was repeated in 1856 with a similar result.

A series of incidents led to the *Arrow* War (q.v.), named for the lorcha *Arrow*, registered in Hong Kong, which was seized by Chinese authorities on October 8, 1856, on suspicion of piracy by the crew. British protests proved ineffectual, and British gunboats shelled Canton later that month. Lacking support from London for the use of force, they withdrew.

In December a British sailor was killed and the village involved was burned as a warning. In retaliation the Chinese burned the "factories" outside Canton where the foreigners lived.

In July, 1857, Lord Elgin and Baron Gros, representing Great Britain and France, arrived as high commissioners authorized by their governments to present final demands to YEH. On December 12 they presented simultaneous notes demanding direct negotiations, occupation of some nearby territory and an indemnity. YEH refused. On December 24 an ultimatum was sent, and the reply being unsatisfactory, bombardment of Canton began December 28. The city fell the following day and YEH was taken prisoner on January 5, 1858. He was taken on board a British warship and in February was taken to Calcutta, where he remained a prisoner until his death in April 1859.

During the period 1848-1858 YEH was acting, to all intents and

purposes, as China's foreign minister, a role that he was not equipped, either by inclination or preparation, to fill. His success in suppressing internal unrest through drastic measures may have led him to believe that this would succeed with foreign representatives. But his refusal even to receive the envoys simply made matters worse. His failure may have been inevitable, but he was the last governor of Canton to have this responsibility. After the conclusion of the *Arrow* War, responsibility for dealing with foreign powers resided with the imperial court in Peking.

Hummel, Arthur W., ed. *Eminent Chinese of the Ch'ing Period*. Washington: Government Printing Office, 1943.

Yeh-lü Ch'u-ts'ai (1190-1244). Statesman, official and poet. A descendant of the ruling family of the Liao dynasty (907-1125 A.D., q.v.), and an official of the Chin dynasty (1115-1234, q.v.) which succeeded it, he was captured by the Mongols in the fall of Peking in 1215. Chingis Khan (1167-1227, q.v.) reportedly said to him: "The house of Liao and the house of Chin were always enemies; I have avenged you." Yeh-lü Ch'u-ts'ai replied: "My grandfather, my father and I were all subjects and servants of the Chin; I should be a despicable liar if I were to tell you I had hostile feelings for my lord and father." He was immediately taken into service and rose to be chief minister.

As a descendant of one of the Tartar Dynasties (q.v.) and the servant of another, he was thoroughly conversant with Tartar policy in controlling the Chinese economy. He persuaded the Mongols that they could obtain more wealth by taxing the Chinese than by turning their farmlands into pasturage for horses, thereby earning Chinese gratitude. He tried unsuccessfully to persuade the Mongols to recruit Chinese officials through the examination system (q.v.). After Chingis' death in 1227, Yeh-lü Ch'u-ts'ai continued as chief minister to his son and successor, Ogodai.

Yeh-lü Ta-shih. See under **Tartar Dynasties, Liao dynasty** and **Western Liao dynasty**.

Yellow river. See **Huang Ho**.

Yellow Turbans. The Yellow Turbans were members of a Taoist religious sect whose rebellion (184-205 A.D.) in the declining years of the Later Han dynasty (q.v.) contributed to its eventual collapse. The Han emperors were weak and under the influence of eunuchs (q.v.) who encouraged luxury. The financial demands of the government, combined with famines and epidemics, reduced large areas to poverty and despair. The Taoist church appealed to such people and formed them into a rebellious army, convinced that the Han had indeed lost the Mandate of Heaven (q.v.).

The defeat of the Yellow Turbans was an achievement of TS'AO Ts'ao (q.v.), who replaced the Han dynasty with his own kingdom of Wei, but the disunity of the Three Kingdoms and the Six Dynasties (qq.v.) periods which followed was partially the result of the long rebellion.

Yen. 1. The northeasternmost of the Warring States (q.v.), it lasted from 864 to 222 B.C., when it was conquered by Ch'in (q.v.). With its capital located near Peking, it controlled the southern part of Manchuria (q.v.) and was the conduit for the transmission of Chinese culture to the early Koreans.

2. The name of five separate and short-lived states of the Sixteen Kingdoms period (302-439 A.D., q.v.).

While the extent of area controlled varied, they were all located in the general vicinity of the earlier state.

Yen lives on as a literary term for the area around Peking. Yenching University, for example, means University of the Yen Capital. Also, emperor Ming Yung Lo (r. 1403-1424, q.v.) was known as the Prince of Yen before his accession to the throne. His base of power was in that area, and he transferred the capital from Nanking to Peking in 1421, where it remained until 1928.

YEN Hsi-shan (1883-1960). Warlord of Shansi province (q.v.). YEN was the son of the manager of a small bank in a village of Shansi. He studied the Confucian classics (see **Four Books**) at school and helped at the bank, which failed in a depression around 1900. He entered the provincial military school in 1901 and in 1904 went to Japan on a government scholarship. By 1910 he was back in Shansi in command of a regiment.

On learning of the revolution of 1911, YEN seized control of Taiyuan, the provincial capital, and declared the province independent. YUAN Shih-k'ai (q.v.) appointed him military governor of Shansi, but denied him any voice in the civil government. In July 1917, a year after YUAN's death, YEN seized power from the civil government and took control of the province. For the next 30 years he showed himself an astonishingly gifted politician with a dizzying series of alliances and changes of alignment as the situation warranted. He was at times allied with TUAN Ch'i-jui, FENG Yü-hsiang and the Chihli Military Clique (qq.v.), and at times against them. He was also usually in opposition to CHANG Tso-lin (q.v.), the Manchurian warlord.

When the Nationalists launched the Northern Expedition (q.v.) in

1926, YEN at first offered to assist in negotiations between the Nationalists and CHANG, but then accepted appointment as commander in chief of the northern armies from the Nationalists. In 1928 YEN's forces occupied Peking and he was given several high positions in the Nationalist heirarchy. In 1930 YEN joined the opposition to CHIANG Kai-shek (q.v.) and was soon involved in civil war in the north. Effective military action by CHIANG's forces undercut the opposition, and YEN announced his retirement and moved to Dairen (q.v.), then under Japanese control. In September 1931, the Japanese attacked Mukden (q.v.) and YEN returned to Shansi. From 1932 to 1937 he was the Nationalist's pacification commissioner of Shansi and Suiyuan, and started a 10-year economic development plan whose main purpose was to strengthen the area against Japanese encroachment and Communist subversion. This involved construction of roads and railways, development of light industry, and mining production, redistribution of landholdings, a curb on drug addiction, an increase in women's rights and the establishment of a public school system.

On the outbreak of war with Japan in 1937, YEN was made commander in chief of the Second War Area, which included Shansi. He was accused of collaboration with the Japanese because of clashes between his troops and those of the Communists, and after the surrender in 1945, he used Japanese troops to defend his provincial capital against Communist attack. By April 1949, he had been forced out of the province. In June he became minister of national defense of the Republic of China (q.v.) and president of the Executive Yuan. In December he went to Taiwan. In March 1950, he stepped down from his government posts and became a presidential adviser, which he remained until his death in 1960.

Boorman, Howard L., ed. *Biographical Dictionary of Republican China*. New York, Columbia University Press, 1968.

Gillin, Donald G. *Warlord: Yen Hsi-shan in Shansi Province, 1911-1949*. Princeton, Princeton University Press, 1967.

Yi Ho Yuan. See under **Summer Palace**.

Yin. See under **Shang dynasty**.

Yinchuan. Capital of Ningsia Hui Autonomous Region (q.v.).

Yin-Yang school of philosophy. *Yin* and *Yang* are two complementary principles. *Yang* represents masculinity, warmth, light, activity, hardness and dryness. *Yin* represents femininity, coolness, darkness, passivity, softness and dampness. Interaction between these two principles produces the phenomena of nature. The pictorial representation of this concept is a circle whose area is divided in half by a curved line. The result looks somewhat like two fish represented head-to-tail.

The Yin-Yang school was one of many which flourished in the period of the Warring States (484-255 B.C., q.v.). In the Han dynasty (206 B.C.-221 A.D.) it was amalgamated with the Five Elements school (q.v.) and the two were absorbed by the Confucianism of the period. The concept has also been absorbed in popular Taoism (q.v.), and the symbol is widely used.

Fung, Yu-lan, and Derk Bodde, trans. *A History of Chinese Philosophy*. Princeton: Princeton University Press, 1952.

Yü the Great. Name of the founder of the Hsia dynasty (2205-1766 B.C., q.v.). Yü is credited with having spent several years in taming a great flood which afflicted China, and for this service was given the empire by his predecessor, Shun (q.v.). Yü is mentioned in the *Shih Ching* (q.v.) or Book of Songs, and is probably a real man, while his predecessors Yao and Shun are more problematical.

Yuan dynasty (1279-1368). Chinese name for the Mongol dynasty. The dates given cover the years when Mongol emperors reigned over all of China from Peking. The dynastic line descended from Temuchin (1167-1227), who assumed the title Chingis Khan (q.v.) in 1206, after he had unified the Mongols, and that date is sometimes used to mark the beginning of the dynasty.

Chingis Khan began but did not complete the conquest of China. He took Peking, capital of the Chin dynasty (1115-1234, q.v.), in 1215, though the Chin held on for two more decades in Kaifeng. He died in 1227 while engaged in the final conquest of the Hsi Hsia (882-1227, q.v.). He was succeeded by his son Ogodai, who eliminated the Chin and began the war against the Sung dynasty (960-1279, q.v.). The fifth ruler of the line was Khubilai khan (1214-1294, q.v.), a grandson of Chingis, who succeeded to the khanate in 1260, adopted the dynastic name Yuan in 1271, and became emperor of China in 1280 after the final defeat of the Sung. He was the first non-Chinese to rule all of China.

China was only part of the Mongol empire, but in the eyes of the Mongol rulers the richest and most important part. Mongol rule extended over Korea, but attempts to invade Japan (qq.v.) in 1274 and 1281 ended in failure. Mongol troops conquered Tibet and Yunnan, and invaded Burma, Vietnam (qq.v.), Champa and Java, though the impact was transitory. The Mongols controlled all or most of Central Asia and conquered Russia in 1240. Mongol troops under Batu Khan, another grandson of Chingis, got as far west as Hungary, turning back to Karakorum, the Mongol capital, only because of the death of Ogodai in 1241.

The Mongols controlled the entire length of the Silk Road (q.v.) and permitted traders to use it freely. This enabled many non-Chinese to travel to and within China for several decades, and provided opportunities for the international trade which had been absent since the T'ang dynasty (618-906, q.v.) several centuries earlier.

Mongol rule in China was deeply hated. The Mongols distrusted their Chinese subjects and utilized foreign officials whenever possible, including the Venetian Marco Polo, 1254-1324 (q.v.), whose account of Cathay (q.v.) gave Europe the first detailed description of China ever to reach the West.

The traditional examination system (q.v.), which had provided China's civil officials, was suspended until 1313, and even then was little used. Since the educated classes were no longer motivated to devote so much time to the study of Confucian classics (see **Four Books**), which formed the basis for the examinations, many of them turned to writing plays and novels. Popular and vernacular literature (q.v.) received a major boost from this circumstance, and the origins of the Peking opera tradition are traced to this period.

Khubilai died in 1294, at the age of 80. His nine successors were not outstanding rulers, and the dynasty fell in 1367 after many years of rebellions and internal warfare, to be succeeded by the Ming dynasty (1368-1644, q.v.).

Unlike other dynasties, the Yuan did not fade away when it lost control of China. Instead, a line of 19 khans ruled Mongolia until 1634. This line is known to Chinese scholars as the Northern Yuan.

YUAN Mei (1716-1798). Ch'ing dynasty poet. YÜAN Mei is regarded by some critics as the best poet of his time, though his hedonism is highly criticized by others. He was born in Hangchow and began to compose verse at the age of nine. Since he was being prepared for the civil service examinations (see **Examination system**), whose subject matter was Confucian texts and their interpretation, time spent reading or writing verse was regarded by his tutor as time wasted. He received his hsiu-ts'ai degree in 1728, his chin-shih in 1739 and was appointed to the Hanlin Academy (q.v.). He held a succession of magisterial posts from 1742 until 1748, but never held office after that time.

YUAN was successful in supporting himself by his writings and teaching and lived the rest of his long life in his villa and garden called the Sui Garden, near Nanking. It is thought by some that this establishment was the model for the one described in *The Dream of the Red Chamber* (q.v.) a famous Ch'ing dynasty (q.v.) novel.

YUAN's writings show a light and witty touch, a broad knowledge of history and a keen interest in life. By encouraging many women to write poetry, he earned the harsh criticism of moralistic scholars. He also was accused of being a libertine because he did not hesitate to note the importance of sexual love to the full life.

YUAN wrote an essay on cooking which has been translated, in part, into both English and French, but his reputation in China rests on his thousands of poems.

Waley, Arthur. *Yuan Mei*. London: George Allen & Unwin Ltd., 1956.

Hummel, Arthur W., ed. *Eminent Chinese of the Ch'ing Period*. Washington: Government Printing Office, 1943.

Yuan Ming Yuan. See under **Summer Palace**.

YUAN Shih-k'ai (1859-1916). Ch'ing dynasty (q.v.) military official, second provisional president of the Republic of China (q.v.) and self-proclaimed monarch. He was born into a family several of whose members were officials. Although educated in the classics (see **Five Classics**), he failed the examinations (see under **Examination system**), and in 1880 purchased a military title.

He was called to active service in 1882, when a power struggle erupted in Korea. Increasing Japanese influence threatened Chinese suzerainty there, and YUAN was part of a detachment of 3000 men sent to maintain the Chinese position. The presence of both Chinese and Japanese troops in Korea led to tensions which were only partially eased by the signing of the Tientsin Convention in April 1885, under which both nations withdrew their troops and military instructors.

YUAN returned to Korea later in 1885 as Chinese resident and commissioner of commerce. He slipped away in July 1894, just before the outbreak of the Sino-Japanese War (q.v.), whose major cause was continuing friction in Korea. YUAN's service in the war won the approval of high Manchu officials, and with the defeat there was recognition of the need of a modernized military. YUAN was chosen to organize and train it.

During the period of the Hundred Days Reform (q.v.), YUAN was promoted by the emperor Kuang Hsü (q.v.), but he is suspected of having betrayed the reform to the empress dowager (q.v.). After her return to power, he was appointed acting governor of Shantung province. His policy of suppressing the supporters of the Boxer Rebellion (1900, q.v.) made him acceptable to the foreign powers, and he became the most powerful military figure in North China. In 1908, the death of the empress dowager, whose protégé he was, led to his forced retirement.

At the outbreak of revolution on October 10, 1911, YUAN was recalled by the Ch'ing court, but declined until several conditions had been met, including the establishment of a cabinet and a national assembly and his own appointment as commander of all military forces. The court assented and in November YUAN was named prime minister. He acted swiftly to remove all Manchus from positions of influence, and to exert military pressure on the rebels at Wuhan.

Neither the rebels nor YUAN's forces were capable of eliminating the other, and since no one wanted widespread civil war, a truce was effected. While the talks were under way, a provisional government was proclaimed in Nanking on December 29, 1911, with SUN Yat-sen (q.v.) elected provisional president.

YUAN saw SUN as a challenge to his own bid for power, and proposed that SUN resign in his favor. SUN agreed to this on several conditions, one of which was the abdication of the emperor, a child of five, and the establishment of a republican government in Nanking. YUAN agreed, and on February 12, 1912, the emperor P'u-yi (q.v.) abdicated. SUN resigned the following day, and two days later YUAN was unanimously elected his successor.

YUAN had no intention of leaving his power base in Peking, and by permitting his own well-disciplined troops to riot, he conveyed the impression that his presence in the north was necessary to maintain order. He was inaugurated provisional president on March 12, 1912, in Peking.

In the summer of 1912, SUN was invited to Peking, and while there participated in the inauguration of the Kuomintang (KMT, q.v.). In the elections held early in 1913, the KMT became the majority party in the national assembly, and its leader, SUNG Chiao-jen, was assassinated, apparently with YUAN's complicity. YUAN then banned the party, and sent troops to attack several provinces with KMT governors. The KMT resistance was scattered and ineffective.

In 1914 the outbreak of World War I preoccupied the European powers. Taking advantage of this, Japan seized the German concessions in Shantung province. In January 1915, Japan secretly presented YUAN with the Twenty-one Demands (q.v.), and in May he acceded to all but a few of them. By that time the demands were no longer secret, and YUAN's capitulation severely damaged his reputation in China.

Just when YUAN first thought of establishing a new imperial dynasty isn't clear, but the terminology used for government officials, his efforts to restore the examination system (q.v.) and his officiation at the imperial sacrifices (q.v.) at the Altar of Heaven at the winter solstice in December 1914 made his aim unmistakable. In 1915 a series of orders appeared, paving the way for the change from a republic to a monarchy. Opposition had long been building, and in December 1915 military leaders in Yunnan province sent an open telegram denouncing YUAN and proclaiming their independence from his rule. Other leaders followed suit, and YUAN's efforts to crush the opposition failed.

The new dynasty was declared on

January 1, 1916. Pressure from the foreign powers and the failure to achieve military success against his opposition persuaded YUAN to restore republican rule on March 22. He was unsuccessful in his efforts to regain his former preeminence, and died of uremia on June 6, 1916.

Chen, Jerome. *Yuan Shih-k'ai, 1859-1916*. Stanford: Stanford University Press, 1961.

Boorman, Howard, ed. *Biographical Dictionary of Republican China*. New York, Columbia University Press, 1967.

Yüeh, Kingdom of. A small state of the Warring States Period (q.v.) located in Chekiang and Fukien (qq.v.). It was regarded as barbarian (i.e., insufficiently Sinicized) by the more northerly states. It was absorbed by Ch'u (q.v.) in 334 B.C.

The same Chinese character meaning Yueh is used to apply to Vietnam, and sometimes to Kwangtung (qq.v.).

YUEH Fei. (d. 1141). Also known as Yo Fei, he was a Sung dynasty (960-1278 A.D., q.v.) general. He came of a peasant family but soon distinguished himself as an able soldier. After the capture of the Sung capital at Kaifeng by the Chin Tartars in 1126 (see under **Chin dynasty**, 1115-1234 A.D.), YUEH was anxious to recapture the capital, and all of North China. He launched successful raids into Chin territory, but was prevented from achieving success by the peace party of the new capital, located in what is now Hangchow.

One reason may have been that the emperor, whose temple name is Kao Tsung, was the younger brother of his predecessor, Ch'in Tsung, who was being held in captivity by the Chin. If General YUEH had succeeded in defeating the Chin, Kao Tsung would probably have had to surrender the throne. In retrospect, the likelihood of the Southern Sung forces defeating the Chin seems small.

In any case, General YUEH was recalled to Hangchow, imprisoned by the chief minister, and murdered. Before he died he is reported to have uttered the words, "Return to us our mountains and rivers." The chief minister, CH'IN Kuei, lives on in infamy. YUEH Fei has been honored with temples, and his name is revered. The cult of YUEH Fei was much in evidence in the 19th century, when many Chinese felt that the alien rule of the Ch'ing dynasty Manchus (qq.v.) should be destroyed.

Yueh-chih. A nomadic Turkic people who first appear in the historical records of the Han dynasty (206 B.C.-221 A.D., q.v.). They were western neighbors of the Hsiung-nu (q.v.), another nomadic people in Mongolia. To avoid the aggressive Hsiung-nu, the Yueh-chih moved to present-day Afghanistan, thus permitting the Hsiung-nu to put more pressure on the settled Chinese. The emperor Han Wu Ti (r. 140-87 B.C., q.v.), sent his minister CHANG Ch'ien (q.v.) to persuade the Yueh-chih to return to their former lands, to act as a counterbalance to the Hsiung-nu. They declined to do so. The Yueh-chih are usually identified with people known as Kushans, who dominated Afghanistan and Northwest India in the first century A.D.

Yung Cheng (1678-1735). Reign title of the third emperor (r. 1723-1735) of the Ch'ing dynasty (1644-1911). He came between K'ang Hsi (r. 1662-1722) and Ch'ien Lung (r. 1736-1796, qq.v.), the two greatest Ch'ing emperors with the longest reigns. Yung Cheng was K'ang Hsi's fourth son and probably not the designated heir. He may have seized the throne at his father's death.

Unlike his father, he was not

athletically inclined, and is described as being frugal, introverted and irascible. He was also hard-working and profoundly interested in philosophy, being thoroughly grounded in Confucianism, Legalism, Taoism and Ch'an Buddhism (qq.v.). His primary goals were peace and order rather than military glory.

In order to consolidate his power, and possibly to suppress criticism of his possibly illegitimate succession, he imprisoned several of his brothers and reduced the power of the Manchu aristocracy by changing the rules allowing certain princes control of their own Banners (q.v.) and Bannermen. In order to preclude the kind of struggle for succession which he himself had won, he named his heir not publicly but in a secret will to be opened only after his death. He also suppressed factionalism in the bureaucracy, and exercised control over the literati by instituting a literary inquisition in which several prominent scholars and their families were executed or exiled.

Yung Cheng's frugality brought prosperity to the empire, and he proved himself an able financial administrator. He encouraged continuous attention to hydraulic works to avoid the flooding of the Huang Ho (Yellow river, q.v.). His reign also saw the signing of the Treaty of Kiakhta (1727, q.v.) with Russia, and the despatch of two embassies to Moscow. No further Chinese embassies were sent to Western nations until the reign of T'ung Chih (r. 1862-1874). Yung Cheng also issued an edict in 1724 banning the activity of Christian missionaries. This seems to have been a political move, provoked by the Rites Controversy (q.v.), which involved a papal ban on Christian performance of certain Chinese rites, notably ancestor worship (q.v.).

Yung Cheng's reign, remembered as having been prosperous, probably laid the basis for the impressive reign of his fourth son and successor, Ch'ien Lung.

Huang, Pei. *Autocracy At Work: A Study of the Yung Cheng Period.* Bloomington: Indiana University Press, 1974.

Hummel, Arthur W., ed. *Eminent Chinese of the Ch'ing Period.* Washington: Government Printing Office, 1943.

Yunnan province. Area: 390,000 sq. km. (150,500 sq. mi.). Population: 31,350,000 (1980). Capital: Kunming. Yunnan is bounded on the east by Kweichow and Kwangsi, on the south by Vietnam and Laos, on the west by Burma, on the northwest by Tibet, and on the north by Szechwan (qq.v.).

Yunnan is high and mountainous, with the most varied minority population of any province in China. Because of its altitude, the climate is relatively mild in most areas. Rice is the main crop, though corn is important in the southeast and sugarcane in low-lying areas.

Yunnan was the site of the kingdom of Nan Chao (q.v.), a non-Chinese state related to the Thai. It usually recognized Chinese suzerainty and was destroyed by the Mongols in the 13th century. Chinese control over Yunnan was tenuous in the Ming dynasty (1368-1644) and in the Ch'ing (1644-1911, qq.v.). It was the site of a Muslim rebellion in 1855-1875 in which thousands died.

Yunnan was also subject to pressure from Britain and France, both of which contemplated using it as an access point to the Chinese market.

Zayton. Zayton is the name of a major trading port of the T'ang, Sung and Yuan dynasties (qq.v.), roughly from the seventh to 14th centuries. It is usually identified with the present-day port of Ch'uanchow in Fukien province. Marco Polo (q.v.) mentions it. It is from *Zayton* that the English word "satin" is derived.

Ecke, Gustav, and Paul Demiéville. *The Twin Pagodas of Zayton*. Cambridge: Harvard University Press, 1935.

Zhejiang. See **Chekiang**.

CHRONOLOGY

With the exception of a few decades in the Yuan dynasty (1279-1368 A.D., q.v.), when Mongol control of China and Central Asia made overland access possible for European travelers, such as Marco Polo (1254-1324) and John of Monte Corvino (1247-1328, qq.v.), Western contact with China may be considered to start shortly after 1500 A.D. In 1498, the Portuguese Vasco da Gama rounded Africa and arrived in India. Within two decades, the Portuguese had defeated Arab sea power in the Indian Ocean, conquered Malacca, where many Chinese merchants from the southern ports traded, and arrived on the coast of China. This chronology covers the period from the arrival of the Portuguese until the present day. Readers should also consult the **Dynastic Sequence** chart for a listing of dynasties from the earliest period. Separate charts provide lists of emperors of the Ming (1368-1644) and Ch'ing (1644-1911) dynasties, and for presidents of the Republic of China (qq.v.).

1506	The emperor Ming Cheng Te accedes to the throne
1520	Tomé Pires, Portuguese, first European ambassador to China in modern times arrives. No imperial audience granted
1522	The emperor Ming Chia Ching accedes to the throne
1557	Portuguese settlement at Macao established
1567	The emperor Ming Lung Ch'ing accedes to the throne. First recorded Russian embassy arrives in Peking
1573	The emperor Ming Wan Li accedes to the throne
1575	Spanish traders arrive at Canton
1592	TOYOTOMI Hideyoshi invades Korea; first Japanese attempt to conquer China
1604	Dutch traders arrive at Canton
1616	Nurhaci establishes Later Chin dynasty, forerunner of Ch'ing dynasty
1620	The emperor Ming T'ai Ch'ang accedes to the throne
1621	The emperor Ming T'ien Ch'i accedes to the throne
1628	The emperor Ming Ch'ung Chen accedes to the throne
1636	Abahai establishes Ch'ing dynasty in Manchuria. Princes of Inner Mongolia become his vassals
1637	English traders arrive at Canton
1644	LI Tzu-ch'eng sacks Peking; Ming dynasty falls
	The emperor Shun Chih of Ch'ing dynasty (1644-1911) accedes to the throne

1662	The emperor K'ang Hsi accedes to the throne
1685	Imperial edict permits foreign trade at all ports
1689	Treaty of Nerchinsk between China and Russia signed
1691	Khalka princes of Outer Mongolia swear allegiance to the emperor K'ang Hsi
1702	Exclusive broker for foreign trade appointed at Canton
1720	First Cohong (monopoly) organized at Canton. Ch'ing forces enter Tibet and expel invading Mongols
1723	The emperor Yung Cheng accedes to the throne. Ch'ing forces leave Tibet
1724	Imperial edict orders expulsion of Catholic missionaries
1736	The emperor Ch'ien Lung accedes to the throne
1757	Canton given monopoly of foreign trade
1757-1758	Ch'ing forces conquer Sinkiang
1760	Second Cohong organized at Canton, monopolizes foreign trade until 1842
1774-1782	Literary inquisition under the emperor Ch'ien Lung imposed
1784	First American ship, *Empress of China*, reaches Canton
1792	Ch'ing forces expel Nepalese forces (Gurkhas) from Tibet, invade Nepal, then withdraw
1793	First British embassy arrives at Peking
1796	The emperor Chia Ch'ing accedes to the throne
1800	Imperial edict prohibits import of opium
1821	The emperor Tao Kuang accedes to the throne
1838	Chinese authorities seize opium at Canton
1839	Opium War breaks out
1842	Treaty of Nanking ends Opium War. Five "treaty ports" opened. Hong Kong ceded to Britain
1844	Treaties of Wanghia (American) and Whampoa (French) signed
1851	The emperor Hsien Feng accedes to the throne. Taiping Rebellion starts
1853	Taiping rebels capture Nanking. Huang Ho (Yellow river) changes course
1856	*Arrow* War begins
1857	Allies capture Canton
1858	Treaty of Aigun with Russia, Treaties of Tientsin with Britain, France, Russia and the United States signed
1859	Russian and U.S. treaties ratified
1860	China rejects Anglo-French ultimatum. Allied forces destroy Summer Palace, occupy Peking. British and French treaties ratified. Russian Treaty of Peking signed
1861	Foreign envoys permitted to reside in Peking. The emperor Hsien Feng dies
1862	The emperor T'ung Chih, under regency of two empresses dowager, accedes to the throne
1864	Taiping Rebellion ends
1866	Rebellion in Central Asia (Sinkiang) breaks out
1870	Tientsin massacre occurs
1871	Russians occupy Ili and Kuldja in Central Asia. Telegraph line reaches Shanghai

1873	Regency ends, the emperor T'ung Chih assumes power
1875	The emperor T'ung Chih dies. Emperor Kuang Hsü, under regency of empress dowager, accedes to throne. Japan claims jurisdiction over Liu Ch'iu (Ryukyu) Islands
1876	First trains run on British-owned Shanghai-Woosung Railway
1878	Rebellion in Central Asia suppressed. Ili and Kuldja returned by Russia
1880	First telegraph line within China completed from Shanghai to Tientsin
1884	Central Asia becomes province of Sinkiang. War breaks out with France over Annam
1885	Treaty of Tientsin with France signed
1886	Anglo-Chinese Convention on Burma and Tibet signed
1889	The emperor Kuang Hsu marries; regency ends
1894	Sino-Japanese War begins
1895	Treaty of Shimonoseki signed. China cedes Taiwan to Japan, acknowledges Korea's independence
1897	Germany occupies Tsingtao, Shantung province
1898	Conventions signed with Britain (Weihaiwei and Hong Kong's New Territories ceded), France (Kwangchowan ceded), Germany (Kiaochow ceded) and Russia (Port Arthur and Dairen ceded). Emperor Kuang Hsu inaugurates 100 Days' Reform (June 11). Empress dowager resumes regency (September 22), ends reforms
1899	Boxer movement founded
1900	Boxer Rebellion begins and is suppressed
1902	Russo-Chinese convention on Manchuria signed
1904	Russo-Japanese War begins
1905	Japanese defeat Russians
1906	Anglo-Chinese convention on Tibet signed
1907	Imperial decree announces prospective National Assembly
1908	The emperor Kuang Hsu and Empress Dowager die
1909	The emperor P'u-yi accedes to throne
1910	National Assembly convenes (October)
1911	Revolution breaks out at Wuchang (October 10)
1912	Republic of China (ROC) established (January 1). The emperor P'u-yi abdicates (February 12). Kuomintang (KMT) inaugurated
1913	Mongolia and Tibet, denying Chinese sovereignty, recognize mutual independence by treaty
1914	China declares neutrality in World War I. Japan seizes German properties in Shantung province
1915	Japan presents Twenty-one Demands (January 18). President YUAN Shih-kai accepts a modified set of demands (May). President YUAN declares himself emperor (December 12)
1916	YUAN dies (June 6), republic restored
1917	China declares war on Germany (August 14). SUN Yat-sen forms a military government in Canton (August 25)
1918	World War I ends (November 11)
1919	Paris Peace Conference awards German concessions in Shantung province to Japan (April 30). Peking students protest against

	Japan and the treaty (May 4). China refuses to sign the Versailles Treaty (June 28)
1920	China joins the League of Nations
1921	Chinese Communist Party (CCP) inaugurated
1922	China and Japan settle dispute over Shantung province
1923	USSR and KMT agree to cooperate for Chinese unification
1924	Sino-Soviet Treaty signed
1925	SUN Yat-sen dies
1926	Northern Expedition launched
1927	CHIANG Kai-shek purges CCP members in Shanghai and Nanking. WANG Ching-wei starts purge in Wuhan. Nanchang Uprising of CCP occurs
1928	Northern Expedition resumes. Chinese troops clash with Japanese at Tsinan, Shantung (May 3). Peking falls (June). National Government established in Nanking (October). Manchuria accepts National Government, completing unification (December)
1929	National Government severs relations with USSR
1931	Japan invades Manchuria (September). League of Nations urges Japan to withdraw (October)
1932	Japanese navy attacks Shanghai (January). Manchukuo established (March). Relations with USSR resumed (December)
1933	League of Nations refusal to recognize Manchukuo (February). Japan withdraws from League of Nations (March)
1934	Long March by CCP, led by MAO Tse-tung, starts (October)
1936	CHIANG Kai-shek, forced to suspend anti-CCP policy, adopts anti-Japanese policy after Sian Incident (December)
1937	Open war between China and Japan starts at Marco Polo Bridge (July 7). CCP and KMT announce solidarity against Japan (September). Rape of Nanking occurs (December)
1938	Wuhan falls; Canton falls in October. Chinese government established in Chungking (December)
1939	First heavy Japanese bombing of Chungking commences (March). World War II begins in Europe (September)
1940	WANG Ching-wei establishes pro-Japanese government in Nanking (March). (Thai-Japanese Treaty of Friendship signed in June.) Britain closes Burma Road (July-October). Japan occupies northern Indochina, closes railway to Yunnan
1941	CCP-KMT troops clash in New Fourth Army Incident (January). First US military aid to China approved (April). American Volunteer Group founded (August). Japan attacks Pearl Harbor, Hong Kong, making Britain and US China's allies (December 7, December 8 in Asia)
1942	Japanese capture Rangoon, close Burma Road (March 6). Most of Burma occupied by June.
1943	North Burma campaign begins (October). Cairo Conference held (November)
1944	Allies capture Myitkyina permitting reopening of Burma Road (August)
1945	First convoy reaches Kunming (February) over Ledo and Burma

	Roads. (February, Yalta Conference.) Atomic bomb dropped on Hiroshima (August 6; August 8 on Nagasaki). Soviet troops entered Manchuria (August 9). Japan surrenders (August 14)
1946	CCP-KMT representatives meet with Marshall Mission (January). CCP-KMT civil war resumes (summer)
1947	Marshall Mission ends (January)
1948	CCP forces defeat KMT in many areas
1949	CCP forces seize major cities. People's Republic of China (PRC) established at Peking (October 1). Republic of China (ROC) establishes temporary seat at Taipei, Taiwan (December)
1950	North Korea invades South Korea (June 25). Chinese People's Volunteers enter North Korea (October). North Korean and Chinese forces push United Nations troops back into South Korea (November). Chinese troops enter Tibet (October). Tibet appeals to the UN (November)
1951	China announces "peaceful liberation" of Tibet (May)
1952	Land reform concludes. Three Anti and Five Anti movements begin
1953	Korean armistice signed (July 27)
1954	Soviet-style collective farms established (January)
1957	Hundred Flowers campaign launched
1958	Great Leap Forward campaign launched. Communes established. PRC forces shell ROC forces on Quemoy and Matsu
1959	Tibetan revolt against PRC rule crushed (March). Dalai Lama flees to India.
1960	Soviet technicians withdraw from China. Chinese and Soviet troops clash on Sinkiang border
1962	October-November, Sino-Indian border war occurs
1964	Chinese conduct first atomic test (October)
1965	Cultural Revolution begins (January). Aid Treaty with North Vietnam concluded (December)
1966	All education stopped by Cultural Revolution (June)
1967	First Chinese hydrogen bomb exploded (June)
1969	Chinese and Soviet troops clash on the Ussuri River border (March)
1971	UN seats PRC, expels ROC (October)
1972	U.S. President Nixon visits China (February)
1975	CHIANG Kai-shek dies (April)
1976	CHOU En-lai dies (January). Tangshan earthquakes (July). MAO Tse-tung dies (September). Gang of Four arrested (October)
1978	China ends all aid to Vietnam (July)
1979	United States recognizes PRC, breaks relations with ROC (January). Sino-Vietnamese border war breaks out (February)
1981	Gang of Four convicted (January)
1982	Teng Hsiao-ping becomes China's leader (September)
1983	China adopts economic responsibility system
1984	U.S. President Reagan visits China (August). Sino-British agreement on reversion of Hong Kong to China reached
1985	PRC President LI Hsien-nien visits US, signs nuclear power cooperation agreement (July)

China: During the Chou Dynasty 1027-256 B.C.

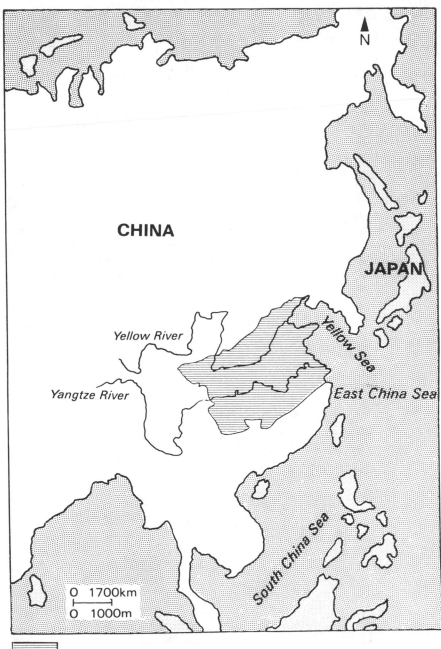

CHINA

JAPAN

Yellow River

Yangtze River

Yellow Sea

East China Sea

South China Sea

N

O   1700km
O   1000m

Area controlled by the Chou Dynasty

China Under the Warring States, (403-221 B.C.)

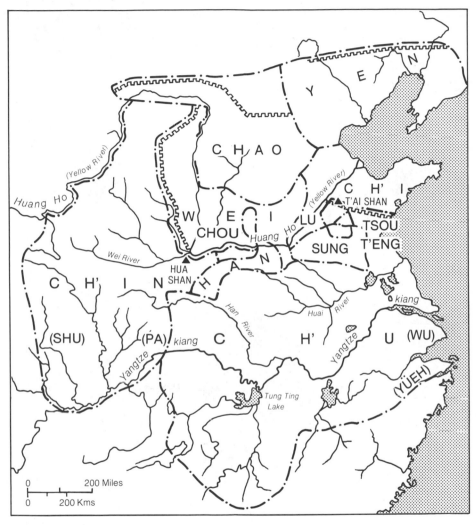

China during the Ch'in Dynasty, 221-207 B.C.

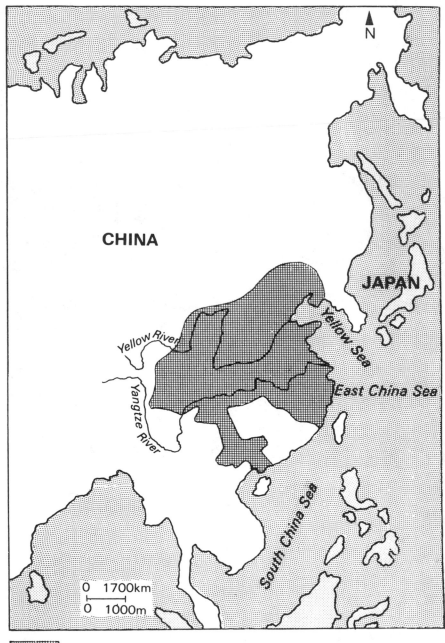

CHINA

JAPAN

Yellow River

Yangtze River

Yellow Sea

East China Sea

South China Sea

N

0 1700km
0 1000m

Area controlled by the Ch'in Dynastry

China During the Han Dynasty, 202 B.C.-220 A.D.

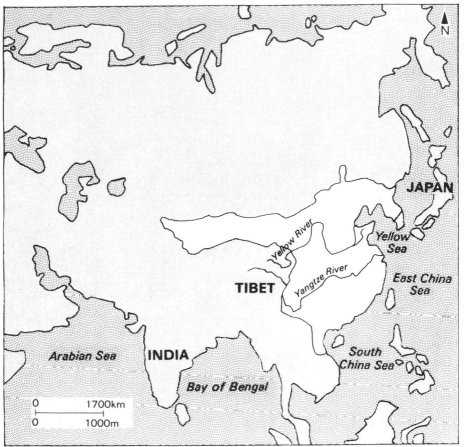

JAPAN

Yellow River

Yellow Sea

Yangtze River

East China Sea

TIBET

Arabian Sea

INDIA

South China Sea

Bay of Bengal

| 0 | 1700km |
| 0 | 1000m |

Area controlled by the Han Dynasty.

The Three Kingdoms
220 to 265-280

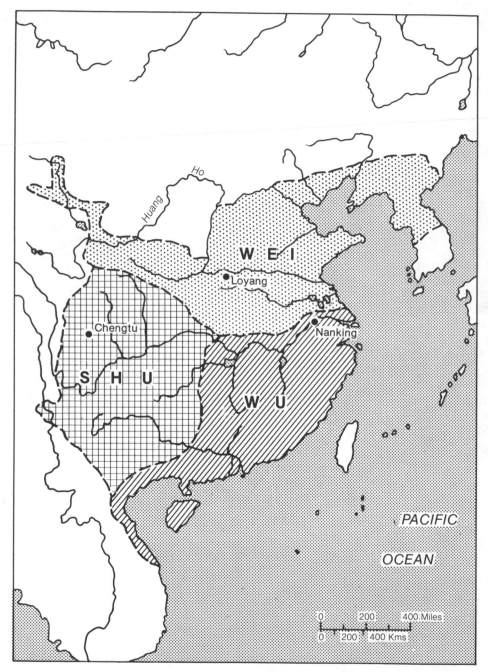

China During the T'ang Dynasty, 618-906 A.D.

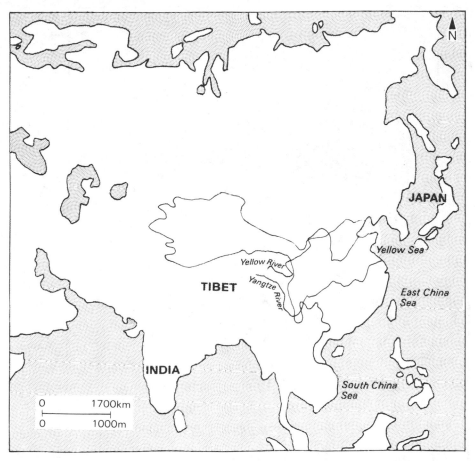

Area controlled by the T'ang Dynasty.

THE SILK ROAD IN CENTRAL ASIA IN THE 7TH CENTURY

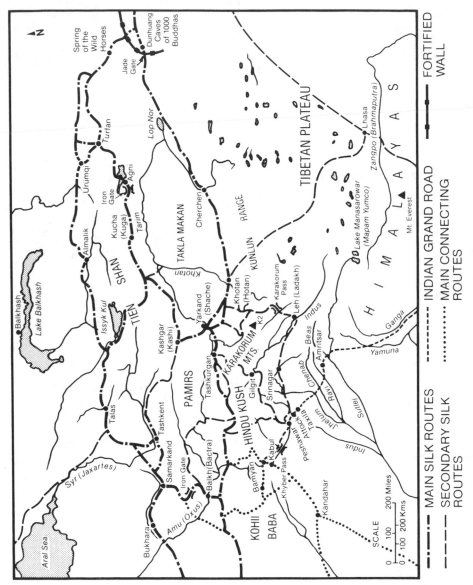

The Sung, Tangut and Liao Empires
Circa A.D. 1100

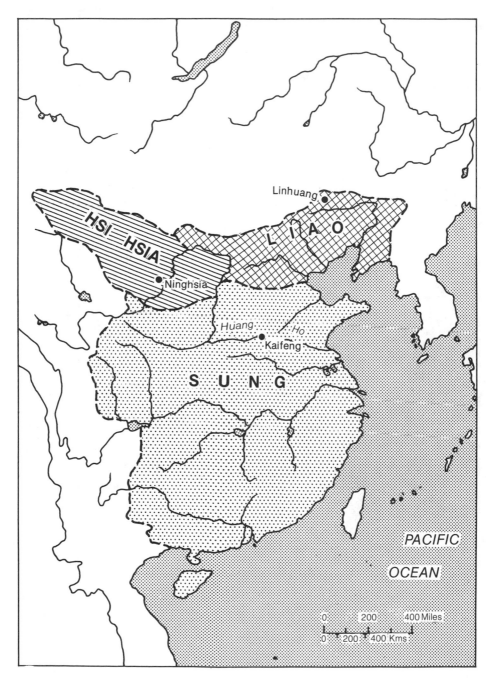

Mongol Empires of Eurasia, 1227-1405

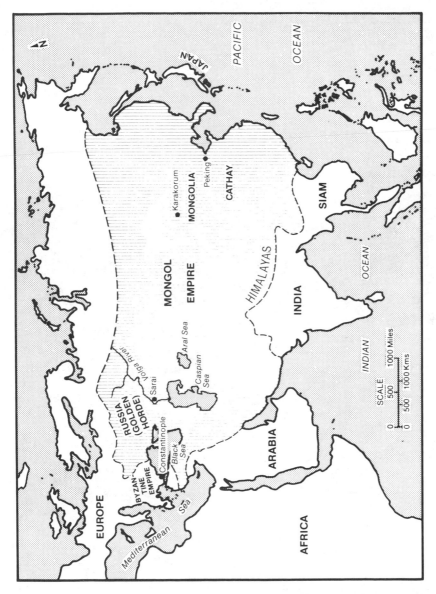

PACIFIC OCEAN

JAPAN

Karakorum

Peking

MONGOLIA

CATHAY

SIAM

MONGOL EMPIRE

HIMALAYAS

INDIA

OCEAN

INDIAN

Aral Sea

Volga River

Sarai

Caspian Sea

RUSSIA (GOLDEN HORDE)

ARABIA

SCALE
0   500   1000 Miles
0   500   1000 Kms

Constantinople

Black Sea

BYZAN-TINE EMPIRE

EUROPE

Sea

Mediterranean

AFRICA

• Capitals

MAIN EURASIAN ROUTES IN MONGOL TIMES (LATE 13TH AND EARLY 14TH CENTURIES)

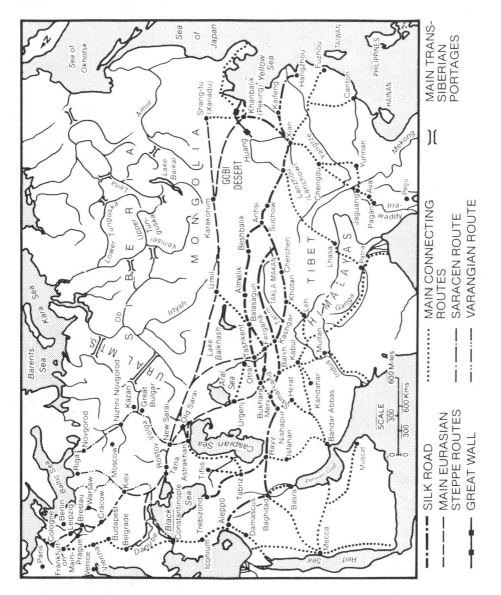

Republic of China, C.1935

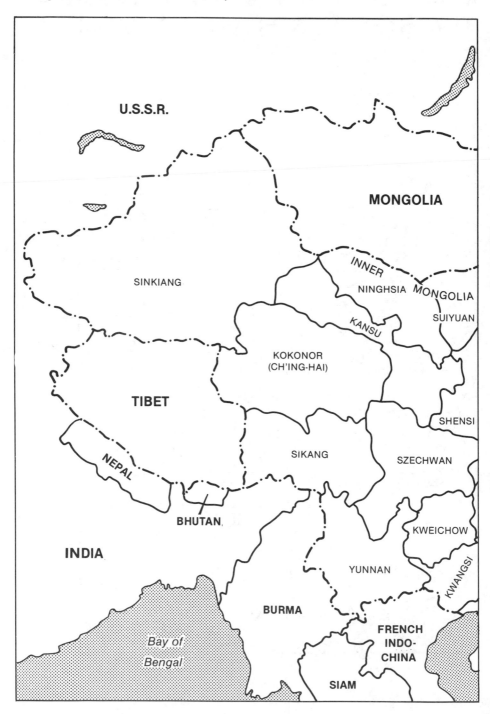

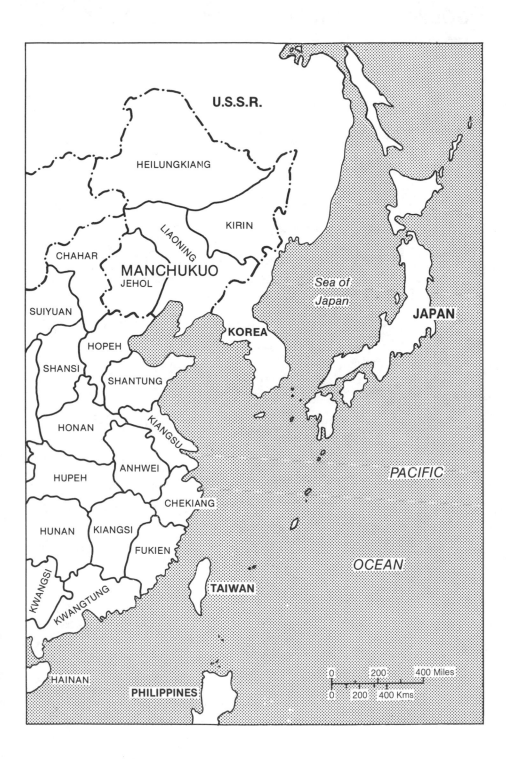

People's Republic of China, C. 1955

U.S.S.R.

MONGOLIA

XINJIANG

GANSU

NINGXIA

QINGHAI

XIZANG

SICHUAN

NEPAL

4

INDIA

BANGLADESH

YUNNAN

BURMA

LAOS

Bay of Bengal

THAILAND

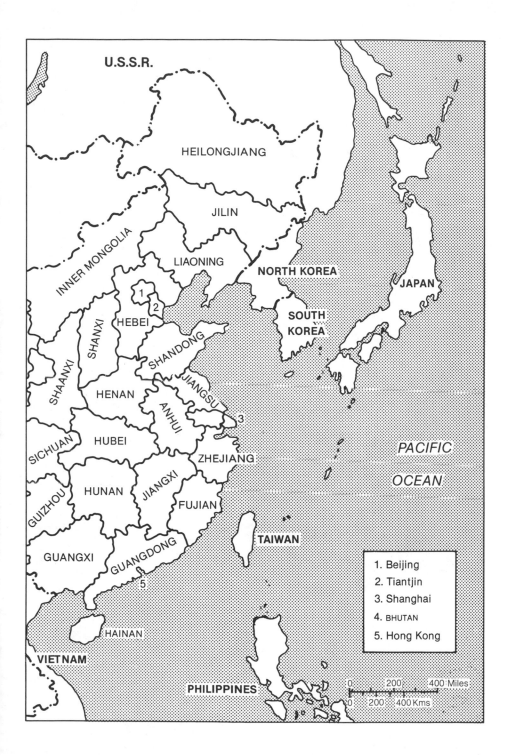

1.	Beijing
2.	Tiantjin
3.	Shanghai
4.	BHUTAN
5.	Hong Kong